# WILLIAM APPLEMAN WILLIAMS

AMERICAN RADICALS
A SERIES EDITED BY HARVEY J. KAYE
AND ELLIOTT J. GORN

*Also available in this Routledge series:*

MICHAEL HARRINGTON
SPEAKING AMERICAN

by Robert A. Gorman

# WILLIAM APPLEMAN WILLIAMS

## The Tragedy of Empire

PAUL M. BUHLE

and

EDWARD RICE-MAXIMIN

ROUTLEDGE

New York and London

Published in 1995 by

Routledge
29 West 35th Street
New York, NY 10001

Published in Great Britain in 1995 by

Routledge
11 New Fetter Lane
London EC4P 4EE

Copyright © 1995 by Routledge
Series design by Annie West
Printed in the United States of America on acid-free paper

Buhle, Paul, 1944–
    William Appleman Williams—the tragedy of empire / Paul M. Buhle,
Edward Rice-Maximin.
        p.    cm. —(American Radicals)
    Includes bibliographical references (p. 297) and index.
    ISBN 0-415-91130-3 (hb : acid-free paper). — ISBN 0-415-9113-1
(pb : acid-free paper)
    1. WIlliams, William Appleman. 2. Historians—United States—
Biography. I. Rice-Maximin, Edward Francis, 1941- II. Title.
III. Series
E175.5.w55b84 1995
973.92 092—dc20
[B]                                                    95-19420
                                                       CIP

# CONTENTS

To our days in Madison

# ACKNOWLEDGEMENTS

We gratefully acknowledge Harvey J. Kaye for his initiative in suggesting this project, and for seeing it through (with the collaboration of Elliott J. Gorn) a change of publishers in midstream. We wish to give our deepest thanks to those Williams family members who gave us their recollections and encouragement in interviews and family documents: Jeannie Williams, Corrinne Williams, Wendy Williams, and Kyenne Williams. Our critics and close readers, who gave us enormously helpful comments, include Alfred Young, Leonard Liggio, David Krikun, Michael Meeropol, Carl Marzani, Michael Sprinker, Jonathan Wiener, Harvey J. Kaye, Allen Ruff, George Mosse, Larry Gara, Elliott J. Gorn, Jim Lorence, Lloyd Gardner, and Bruce Cumings. Mari Jo Buhle's contributions significantly reshaped the manuscript. Interviewees especially eager to help us included, in addition to Williams family members, Merle Curti, the late Fred Harvey Harrington, Gerda Lerner, Alan Bogue, Lloyd Gardner, Theodore Hamerow, Thomas McCormick, Peggy Morley, and Peter Weiss. Hans Jakob Werlen supplied us with translations from German scholarly journals. The staff at the Pauling Papers, Kerr Library, Oregon State University, was helpful beyond the call of duty in many ways, but especially in making available all the Williams Papers most expeditiously. Likewise, the staffs at the State Historical Society of Wisconsin; Columbia University, Special Collections; the Nimitz Library; the history department at Oregon State University; and the Jeffries Archive of the U.S. Naval Academy extended every measure of assistance. We received extensive documents, otherwise unavailable, via Brian D. Fors, Mary Rose Catalfamo, Bea Susman, William Preston, Ed Crapol, Scott McLemee, Neil Basen, Henry W. Berger, Lloyd Gardner, Martin Sherwin, Walter LaFeber, William Preston, Karla Robbins, Gerald McCauley, and above all, William Robbins. (Many of these documents, with the permission of the holders, have been subsequently turned over to the OSU collection). Letters and phone calls exchanged with David Noble, John Higham, David Montgomery, Nando Fasce, Peter Wiley, James O'Connor, Howard Zinn, Staughton Lynd, Volker Berghahn, Paul Ringenbach, Martin Sherwin, James P. O'Brien, Mike Wallace, Paul Richards, Lee Baxandall, James B. Gilbert, James Weinstein, Paul Breines, and Charles Vevier, to name only a few, illuminated many dark reaches of Williams's past. And Christine Cipriani at Routledge polished off the production process. We are grateful to them all, and we hope that our book justifies their faith in our effort.

# INTRODUCTION

"I PREFER TO DIE AS A FREE MAN struggling to create a human community than as a pawn of Empire," wrote historian William Appleman Williams in 1976.[1] Annapolis graduate and decorated Naval officer, civil rights activist and president of the Organization of American Historians, Williams (1921-1990) is remembered as the preeminent historian and critic of Empire in the second half of the "American Century." More than any other scholar, he anticipated, encouraged, and explained the attack of conscience suffered by the nation during the 1960s. Radicals have hailed him as a supreme anti-imperialist, while libertarian conservatives have seen him as the "second Charles Beard," renewing the perspectives of the nation's foremost historian. Fellow historians consider him a great figure in American thought, one who looked for large patterns and asked the right questions. A physically small man with large hands and a wide smile, he seemed indifferent to the abuse heaped upon him from the political mainstream and to most of the praise he earned as well, choosing simply to walk alone.

His *Tragedy of American Diplomacy*, first published in 1959 and then expanded in subsequent paperback editions destined to reach tens of thousands of readers during the 1960s and 1970s, is probably the most important book ever to appear on the history of U.S. foreign policy. For more than thirty years, scholars have vigorously debated Williams's challenge to the prevailing assumptions. As a key source of dissenting wisdom cribbed by antiwar authors and orators, *Tragedy* helped frame the public discussion of the U.S. role in Southeast Asia. Williams explained this moral catastrophe as neither misguided idealism nor elite conspiracy but instead as the inevitable consequence of deeply rooted, bipartisan assumptions. Williams's *Contours of American History* (1961), one of the most influential scholarly books of the age, traced the roots of American expansionism to the nation's origins and attributed the rise of the security state with its planned deception of the public to the impossibility of managing a world empire. In these and other volumes, Williams also pleaded for a democratic renewal, a revived citizenship based upon the activities and decisions of local communities rather than upon the demands of a distant welfare-and-warfare state.

Williams's unique insights could be traced to his penetrating economic perspectives and to his long view of modern history. One of his best recent interpreters, Asia scholar Bruce Cumings, describes a twofold process of reading America "from the outside in," as those abroad have felt the effects of U.S. policy; and conversely, re-reading the historic documents of U.S. diplomacy for American leaders' understanding of the larger world developments at work.[2] Williams framed these insights with his own interpretation of the ways in which distinct social and economic systems evolved, from the rise of modern class society in the seventeenth and eighteenth centuries to the present. This dual or threefold approach is *sui generis,* and his development of it will shortly be seen through a close examination of his life. But its significance can be grasped preliminarily in several large ways.

Williams first of all inverted the dominant assumptions of American intellectuals by viewing conventional liberalism not as a great liberating force but as a suffocating ideology that has preempted both solid radicalism and thoughtful conservatism. In doing so, he drew upon long-neglected Anglo-American traditions of communitarianism and misunderstood traditions of what might be called a judicious paternalism. A Christian socialist and an undoubted patriot, he sympathized with writers as varied as John Ruskin, Brooks Adams, Lewis Mumford, and G. D. H. Cole, who all felt that too much had been lost with the collapse of the pre-modern order. He found in the politics of Tory radicals like Lord Shaftesbury and cautious statesmen like John Quincy Adams and Herbert Hoover the sense of equipoise and the pursuit of commonwealth missing in war leaders Abraham Lincoln, Woodrow Wilson, and Franklin Roosevelt.

For Williams the true antithesis of Empire was the heterogeneous tradition of community spiritedness, rather than the socialization of labor envisioned by Karl Marx and the Marxists. He therefore shared the dismay of those at various points across the political map who gauged the recklessness of modern government. Moderates and conservatives found in Williams what they could not find elsewhere in radical thought: the understanding that Empire had its roots not only in State Department and corporate aims but also in the expansionist assumptions of ordinary Americans that social problems could be successfully externalized and postponed through a constantly moving frontier. As he wrote a few years before his death, "America is the kind of culture that wakes you in the night. The kind of nightmare that may [yet] possibly lead us closer to the truth."[3] This was Greek tragedy in a modern setting, with the audience sharing the stage. Williams nevertheless stubbornly held to his own ideal vision of a *possible* America, running like a golden thread from the historic tragedy of self-deception toward a better future for America and the world.[4]

Seen from other quarters, Williams's message has had a profoundly international and cultural significance that might have surprised the confirmed Middle American. One of the most controversial critics of recent decades, Edward Said, has attributed to Williams the fundamental insight that Empire, more than an economic or political or cultural system, has organized modern thought and encompassed all else within it.[5] On the same note, the editors of the recent and perhaps definitive *Cultures of American Imperialism* suggest that their 672-page volume, with its many distinguished contributors, essentially "aims to explore more fully Williams's . . . understanding."[6] William Appleman Williams's contribution, by these related assessments, cannot be rendered obsolete by the passage of events. His value grows as we approach the twenty-first century.

Williams rarely wrote about culture as such. Yet in his final work, condensing the wisdom of a lifetime, he defined a myriad of words and phrases to explain how the empire operated at the level of internalized (or what theorist Sylvia Winter would call "auto-instituted"[7]) logic. Thus, for instance: dynamic=aggressive, enterprise=overtake, modernize=outstrip, order=regulate, discipline=surveillance, secure=patronize, and benevolent=lord-it-over, or in the most benign redefinitions, innocence=grant-a-favor and tolerance=reform. In each case, Americans took control of the land and its inhabitants. In the process, they transformed each term's meaning *for themselves*, often benefitting materially, but rarely understanding the full consequences. The various historic developments that Williams interpreted as a consequence of the "open" (or forcibly opened) space available to Americans, the almost unlimited resources and the commercial success they experienced in the colonial days and afterward, can also be seen as the shaping influence in the dominant cultural sensibility of the nation.

Amy Kaplan, co-editor of *Cultures of American Imperialism*, carries this dialogue between Williams and cultural studies a step further. She finds in his early work a "major challenge to what might be called the paradigm of denial," the absence of Empire from a scholarly or popular self-understanding of American history.[8] Privileging economics, Kaplan insists, the Williams of *Tragedy of American Diplomacy* insisted upon the strict economic rationality of Americans' expansionism. *Empire as a Way of Life* transcended these limitations, and in so doing, reached out to the future of international experience, Coke bottled in Russia and McDonald's opening shop in Beijing.[9] Williams, with his roots in the small-town America of the Depression, had managed to see these massive, world-changing developments from the inside.

William Appleman Williams passed from the scene just as the collapse of the Eastern Bloc had reached a crucial stage. Those who had vigorously opposed him in life quickly proclaimed their self-vindication: the cold war, with all its deleterious side effects from nuclear terror to environmental damage, had been a noble crusade or at least a necessary strategy after all. The long challenge to free enterprise was over, and the world's only surviving superpower could face the future relatively confident of its own status. Indeed, according to the frequently heard optimistic projections of the early 1990s, liberal democracy faced a golden future.

Not everyone was so optimistic, of course. George F. Kennan, who might rightly be called the father of cold-war strategy, wondered aloud whether the terrifying cost of the crusade had not long since outweighed its benefits.[10] Within a few years and a dozen or more continuing or impending disasters, from civil war and extreme economic uncertainty in Eastern Europe to the accelerating extermination of the planet's biological storehouse in its surviving rainforests, things did not look so good after all. Closer to home, regional issues such as the Haitian crisis recalled the ugly legacy of U.S. support (and CIA guidance) for almost incomprehensibly brutal, light-skinned elites. Doubts continued to plague Americans about many domestic issues as well, including their cities, their children, and their health.

Perhaps most revealing was an absence of any fresh solutions. Growth was finally, as it had always been before, seen as the key mechanism to create a happier society. "Liberal democracy" as a world plan or ideal for success and security outside the United States actually promoted a drastically sharpening division of social classes, growing petrochemical stress upon the environment through the explosion of automobile use, and a popular disillusionment that threatened ominously. No wonder personal detachment, mean-spiritedness, and cynicism remained the intellectual order of the day. The encompassing hate-love fascination of celebrity, from murder trials to the radio talk shows to Congress, seemingly filled the gap left by an exhausted political dialogue. The newer New Right rode to political triumph promising to finish off failed liberalism with the uncompromised rule of the market and the unabashed Pax Americana. Its leaders, as Williams would have predicted, claimed the legacy of Roosevelt and Truman for themselves.[11]

Williams had called the America of the later 1980s a "tired and nostalgic" society, at once weary of politicians' double-talk and terribly hungry in a spiritual sense for the reassurance that manipulated historical images offered to the gullible. He offered his readers, and Americans at large, a profoundly different possibility—but not a painless one. To dialogue seriously with their past, they had to wrestle with truths about themselves that politicians would never acknowledge, let alone face boldly. He never asked them to succumb to paralyzing guilt, or to repudiate their self-identity. Everyone, he believed, could learn from history. Decoding the empire, freeing its subjects at home and abroad from the tyrannical logic of the system, was for Williams the final, grand task of the citizen and the civilization.

# A Little Boy from Iowa

WILLIAM APPLEMAN WILLIAMS BEGAN HIS DAYS as he would end them, far from the centers of metropolitan culture. He often claimed that his origins explained his insight into U.S. history and had undergirded his moral strength to sustain himself through political hard times. Seen more objectively, the issues of his life look very different, far more contradictory and more pathos-ridden than he could admit. And yet something about his self-evaluation rings true. As he grappled to interpret his experiences through his historical studies but also in personal interviews, a private family memoir, and an unpublished novel, he could not possibly escape the stamp of the small-town Midwest, the Depression, and the fatherless family. But he had also spent his life literally discovering a wider world and trying to make sense of it in his own highly personal terms.

Attacked frequently as an America-hater, Williams cared about the nation passionately, even obsessively, as if from a sense of family responsibility. He believed that his family background and his life as a Naval officer reflected the economic development and the imperial mission that gave the modern nation its shape. But he also believed that the same resources and initiative could make possible a society organized along very different lines. His fondest political hopes were doomed to disappointment. But his capacity to marshall intense scholarship within a large philosophical framework permitted him a very unique insight into America as a civilization. Few others could have framed such insight in a sustained historical narrative, and Williams himself had enormous difficulty in doing so.

A Midwestern literary regionalist, some modern-day Hamlin Garland, might be able to capture through fiction the emotional toll exacted on the historian's life as he struggled to make sense of society and of himself. The novelist would have to contend, as well, with Williams's own fictionalizing. In attempting to explain or to interpret the sources of his immanent critique of American society, Williams created through screened memory a vividly nostalgic, heavily stylized childhood and native setting.[1] Decades after penning an appendix to his master's thesis, which described closely and without sentimentality the elite rule of his little hometown, he thus reinterpreted the same place in near-idyllic terms. It had become, quite remarkably, a site of approximate social equality and deep-felt community where citizens learned the importance of both public participation and individual restraint.

Here lay the source of the rending tension which might also be seen as the driving contradiction of Williams's life. The locale of community, for him the modern-day version of the Greek city-state, is likewise the source of Empire. Its ethos is successful in its own terms—and tragic as well. He projected this historical experience in all directions, from his idiosyncratic interpretation of agrarian history to his strained views of feminism and the family to his understanding of what a socialist movement might be and do. He also internalized the tension, as he sought to control the story of his life and give it a unified meaning.

Examined carefully and without his blinders, Williams's life and life's work express again and again the same contradictions of individualism and community, Empire and anti-Empire. Woven in and around the saga of boyhood, military academies, war, graduate school, scholarship and political engagement, the tensions reveal themselves.

Williams's own late-shifting version of the past reflected his growing disillusionment with the direction of the country and likewise his despair with the radical left. But he had another purpose, which he pursued through a last burst of non-history writing.[2] He had a large personal debt to acknowledge and, if possible, to repay. He later wrote repeatedly of various individuals and groups who had "honored" their "traditions" in one way or another.[3] They had done rightly, earning his praise and support, unlike those who fecklessly cast off the past without considering its consequences for the present and future. He blessed his childhood home, the mother and grandparents who raised the boy without a father.

Between the lines of the memoir, he asked himself why it had been William Appleman Williams, the most unlikely intellectual, who finally wrote controversial and influential books. He continued to set down his responses to the riddle even as his life drained away; he never finished. No wonder a high-school classmate, asked at the time of Williams's death about his classmate's notorious Marxism, answered matter-of-factly that no one could have anticipated anything like it. The sweetheart of his high-school years and wife of his youth agreed with this judgment.[4] The personally secretive Midwesterner and unabashed romantic eluded even his intimates' efforts to understand the sources of radicalism in his background.

Nor would they have been able to explain his rise into the nation's most important historian. To do so would be to unravel what Williams himself never could fully or candidly analyze: the complex chain of events leading him from childhood and adolescent years to Naval officership to civil rights activist and historian-in-training, or from Depression-era Iowa to wartime Annapolis to post–World War II Corpus Christi and late-1940s Madison, Wisconsin. Full understanding would require deep insight into a character fragmented by childhood tragedy, rebuilt through personal determination, challenged by world events, and settled as firmly as it could be settled through the self-identification of the citizen-scholar.

Some of his more perceptive friends found him looking perpetually for a community like the one he believed he had left behind. Others would say that the later Marxist internationalist, jazz buff, and intimate friend of gay intellectuals—during the days of hiding and persecution—had become a bohemian, if not necessarily an outsider, precisely in response to the claustrophobia of small-town life. Perhaps these two alternatives are not so contradictory after all.[5]

I

William Appleman Williams, during his days as a radical graduate student, carefully depicted his native Atlantic in commercial terms. Shipping center for crops, poultry, and livestock, this town of several thousand residents was also a commercial-retail locus of fertile southwestern Iowa in the later nineteenth century. Among the mostly German and Danish descendents, a small group of extended families dominated manufacturing, financing, merchandising, the judiciary, and political clout. If Atlantic nurtured one resident's radicalism and historical perspective, it most likely did so by fostering a boy's sense of contrast, perhaps the contrast between the small community's day-to-day social life on the one hand and the real power-wielding on the other. But this begins the story too late; Williams the memoirist insisted that his legacy be traced back several generations at least.

Williams's mother, Mildrede, who deserves to be called the most enduring influence on his life, traced her family back through the Appleman line to a Welsh-born Redcoat who deserted General Howe to join George Washington's forces. This Welshman's Philadelphia wife had ancestors in America long before the Revolutionary war. Williams's father, William Carlton Williams, could find still another revolutionary soldier in his family tree, a New Hampshire militiaman blinded in combat.[6] In short, Williams's family had been more than present at the primal act of national independence: he was self-conscious heir to the great tradition.

If Williams often felt "that American History is a pot of imperial porridge . . . of who fought where for what conquest," he could nevertheless find a family exception here and there. His mother's great-grandfather, Zopher Hammond, bought his son's way out of service in the Civil War and insisted that the North should have seceded first or simply let the South go its own way. Born in Patchogue, New York, in 1804, Zopher may have been the original "Little America" believer in the family, unwilling to pay the price for Empire. Zopher's son, Joseph, Williams's great-grandfather, attended Hillsdale College in Michigan and resettled in Marshall County, Iowa, in 1866. His Iowa-born wife, Amanda Louis Havens, was reputedly the first "strong-minded" woman of several generations of them to come. The couple moved by wagon to Iowa's southwest, claiming through the Homestead Act some of the richest farmland anywhere on earth.[7]

Williams neglected to mention the less rational, helter-skelter qualities of settlement and the troubled memories left behind. A naturally beautiful region of the Nishnabotna River Valley and the main drainage basin of southwestern Iowa, it had once been home to the Ioway, the Oto, the Omaha, and other tribes. Before its settling, James Audubon had praised the beauty of its trees, native wildflowers, and fabulously beautiful birds (a county was subsequently named after him), which were mostly destined like the Indians themselves to disappear for productive agriculture and commerce. The Mormons had crossed en route to the West in 1846, and a generation of later settlers debated the name of a nascent municipality. Thinking mistakenly that they were exactly halfway between the two oceans, they tossed a coin to decide whether to call their new place by one or the other. "Pacific" won, but another town had already been given that name, so they christened it "Atlantic."[8]

Williams's ancestors had made a shrewd economic choice. The farmer of the 1860s was no primitive pioneer but a modern agrarian. He needed mechanical mowers, hay rakes, reapers, corn planters, seeders, along with improved plows and decent weather, to realize a profit on his considerable investment. Still, corn, wheat, oats, rye, and other crops afforded abundant yields, while hogs, cattle, and (in southern Iowa particularly) even sheep production raced ahead. Decades later, the entire region would be known as the "Corn Belt," an oversimplified appellation that signified rich soil, adequate rain, and a summer heat which could make daily life extremely uncomfortable (not to speak of the bitter winters with their savage plains winds), but which also made possible a good living.

Iowa community life naturally reflected the intense self-consciousness of its businessmen-farmers. The local and regional newspapers described in detail the agricultural and market developments which made one line or another profitable or unprofitable. Farmers and their journalists put special emphasis on improvement of stock and a range of other innovations such as veterinary sciences (including rudimentary pesticides).[9] Williams took great pride in the solid business sense of his ancestors and their communities. A major investor in Atlantic had convinced the Rock Island Line to build its main trunk system for the region through the town and to stop every train there. As he wrote in the introduction to *Roots of the Modern American Empire*, the fathers of Atlantic then "plotted the town by plowing a furrow straight south from the spot they selected for the depot."[10]

Grids went up in the 1870s for the development of wide streets suited to civic affairs, while Joseph and Amanda Hammond established themselves outside town on a spread not far from the future golf course of the well-to-do. In Williams's imaginative recreation, they regularly joined perhaps five hundred neighbors on market days to sell surplus, take shaves or haircuts, buy calico, and gossip. Historians' accounts, indeed, describe this period as the "golden age" of the county fair, a market day writ large with exhibitions of machinery and seminars on scientific husbandry along with various competitions, including "female equestrianism."[11]

Williams's predecessors surely played their part in the rituals that he regarded with admiration. They raised churches with stained-glass windows, created schools, founded a public library, scheduled a lecture series and musical events. He viewed it as a "marvelous mix of town and country," much the way that Lewis Mumford had described the early nineteenth-century New England village. If considerably less picturesque than the rocky hills that many Yankee residents had left behind, Atlantic was at once human scale and connected by its visiting trains to New York, Chicago, Omaha, and San Francisco. Thus the great anti-imperialist Williams could write, without a hint of irony, that "Atlantic was part of the empire."[12] And not an insignificant part: according to his own account, Atlantic made itself the major agricultural-merchandizing center between Des Moines and Omaha. With less than six thousand residents, it reputedly maintained the nation's highest rate in turnover of retail goods for many years, off and on, until the Depression.

Atlantic and the surrounding region also entertained its share of dissidents and even radicals for at least an occasional moment in the nineteenth century. John Brown had briefly made his headquarters in Tabor—itself named for the legendary Czech city of communal resistance against king and clergy—during the 1840s. Never a major center of agrarian agitation like nearby Kansas or Nebraska, Iowa saw its Greenbackers and Populists mount third-party challenges during the 1870-80s. The major weekly of agrarian movement during the middle 1880s, *Industrial West* (later, the *Farmers' Tribune)* was published in Atlantic. One of its editors, Knights of Labor activist J. R. Sovereign, used the Atlantic base to project himself into Grand Master Workman of that fading organization a few years later.[13] After these unsettled days, modestly successful agrarian reforms and the rise of a world market for local commodities prompted Atlantic to become staunchly conservative, in politics and moral alike.

Given worldly success and social homogeneity, its citizens seemingly had no more pressing reason to doubt or to wonder. Less sympathetic observers might have described them as indifferent or hostile to the dramatic rise of the Socialist Party with its many small-town locals in Kansas or Oklahoma, likewise toward the Industrial Workers of the World headquartered in nearby Chicago. The great hopes and the savage repression of radicals made little impression on them because they evidently had other things on their minds. Indeed, during the war, a local manufacturer of folding stoves and Army cots produced nearly five million dollars of goods for the government. Afterwards, the large Atlantic Canning Company plant added sweet pumpkins to its profitable line of corn, converting the globes into pulp and sending the seeds as far away as China. From the perspective of the Atlantic Legion Memorial Building, which served as a community center, life was no doubt good.[14]

Writing about Atlantic during his graduate student days, Williams dissected the *mentalité* of the elite. Their way of seeing the world, he claimed, was based on parroting the ultraconservative *Chicago Tribune* positions on national and international issues. Local newspaper editorials—as Williams related from his own personal experiences—were hammered out at a breakfast club composed of the elite's second string. Their view of the world, notably of foreign affairs (and especially revolutions abroad, i.e., threats to continued U.S. economic expansion) lacked any element of enlightened conservatism let alone liberal acceptance. Perhaps this had been manipulation of small-town democracy from the metropolis, but it was not one that local elites resisted. They had chosen to respond to events in strictly business terms. It did not make them mediocre minds, or mediocre stylists. Indeed, the paper's savant Edwin Percy Chase won a Pulitzer Prize for the best editorial of 1934. But it limited their capacity to see other possibilities.[15]

But through the rose-colored glasses of the later Williams, the flourishing life of the county seat had been, if perhaps a "disorienting distortion of the reality of America," nevertheless "the best that *could* happen." He proved it with that most elusive evidence—memories of his childhood and the recollections of neighborliness which mattered to him most. Thus, for instance, he recalled Jewish and black families perfectly integrated into the community, when in reality so few existed that segregation would have been all but impossible.

Williams had his own version of the dark side of Atlantic social life. The town's proprietors sold medicinal whiskey and laudanum over the counter of the nominally dry town, and thousands of gallons of moonshine liquor mysteriously found their way into waiting hands. Railroad workers, farmhands, traveling businessmen, and prostitutes ("soiled doves" in the police blotter of the local press) drank and carried on beneath the averted eyes of the authorities. When law-breaking occasionally turned violent through the misdeeds of a frontier-style gang of criminals, citizens acted in concert to crush it. Williams's own great-grandmother died with a gun still under her pillow. She never used it, but presumably would not have hesitated had the need arisen.

The degraded and sometimes dangerous lower classes existed only at the margins of Atlantic life, certainly never becoming likely protagonists of social change. Hired agricultural workers were no more than "bummers," transients hired for harvest but expected to be gone soon. Railroad laborers, more stable but still fewer in number, kept to themselves.[16] To all this we might easily trace Williams's later aversion to class models of socialism, and his hopes for the "ordinary" middle class as the agency of redemption.

Williams's ancestors experienced troubles of their own, but rather than economic or social ones, these were more likely to be personal difficulties or perhaps a restlessness prompted by the psychological narrowness of small-town life. Great-grandfather Ed Hammond made a good living and belonged to the founding circles of local fraternal organizations like the Odd Fellows and the Masons. He emerged as an impressive local figure, probably too much so for his strong-willed mate, who sought more for her life than a comfortable home and an absentee husband. Their beloved first child had, as a teen, given birth to a baby out of wedlock, a grave embarrassment to a respectable family at that place and time. Their second child, Maude, always feeling ignored by the family, distanced herself from them through mental self-cultivation (eventually she would become a Christian Scientist). She also sought a marriage of acknowledged equals. Her choice, Porter Ikeler Appleman, would be the grandfather who played a central role in young Bill Williams's life. Four inches shorter than his wife, he was a man too playful to grow up entirely.

"Tossie," as the acrobatic figure was fondly called (Porter could, reputedly, leap over a handkerchief held out toward him), had attended a "normal" or teachers college in Shenadoah, Iowa, after his family moved west from Pennsylvania, and had opened a business office for loans, insurance, and real estate. An independent-minded Congregationalist and charter member of the local Elks, he was also a skilled shot and above all "magic with dogs." He won top prizes and trained the dogs for shipping across the U.S., Europe, and even Asia. Prone, however, to impractical investments and speculation, and self-indulgent about cars and clothes, Porter spent too much time with his friends in the bars and too little time at home. In doing so, he attained the negative virtue of removing himself from the business-minded Puritanism of his parents' generation. The community, of course, never took him seriously.[17]

For all his weaknesses, which would grow worse in time, he raised his one daughter as a sort of free soul. A young woman who could not only name birds and flowers but could shoot a gun accurately and became one of the first women in the county to drive a car, Mildrede (she added a final "e" to distinguish herself in grade school from two other Mildreds) was intelligent and musical, playing leading roles in school plays and opera. She was also, reputedly, part of a modest sexual revolution in early twentieth-century small-town life. She enjoyed being alluring on the dance floor with the Charleston or Black Bottom, yet she restrained herself from the increasingly common practice of "going into the bushes" with potential lovers.[18] In her son's retrospective view, she could be at once sexy and personally responsible: she had "pizzazz." Less sympathetic observers saw the same impulses as evidence of her fundamentally cold and domineering character.

She fell in love with only one man, the original "Billy" Williams. His parents and grandparents had made themselves prosperous around De Kalb, Illinois, with their prize cattle and hogs. They had also showed some interest in politics (as northern Democrats opposed to Republican support of railroads and banks). Billy's father, when they came west, was to become the first Democratic postmaster of Atlantic, and his mother became an amateur painter.

Billy went off to college and then joined the fledgling air force in World War I, while Mildrede attended the Indianapolis Conservatory of Music, with special work to qualify her to teach part-time in Iowa grade schools. Her beau, hopeful of becoming a flying ace and war hero, was so skilled with the experimental equipment that the service made him a demonstration pilot to prepare others. His marriage with Mildrede, although the result of a "Grand Passion" (in their son's eyes), began in physical separation and never achieved a long-run stability. When the war ended in 1919, Billy found himself unwilling to return to the mundane life of Iowa.

He had real adventures as a barnstormer. The best, no doubt, was running nitroglycerin across the border to Mexicans consolidating their revolution against the Church and against the U.S. State Department's wishes. Billy had little interest in the revolutionaries' politics as such. But he had the instincts of a small-town iconoclast mistrustful of contemporary America's business culture. From that standpoint, he appreciated his Mexican clients' romantic quest for freedom and their hostility toward the rich. Short on cash, the revolutionaries gave him classic Mexican pottery which remained the one art collection of the Williams household, redolent of faraway places and exotic history. When the work gave out, Billy turned to safer private jobs hauling wealthy clients. Still later he became a car salesman while Mildrede substitute-taught school, devoted his leisure to bridge and golf, and seemed to spend a lot of his time gazing into the sky.[19]

William Appleman Williams was born in 1921, after a labor so frightening that the parents determined to have no more children. Billy the father might have settled down for that reason alone, until the spectacular flight of Charles Lindbergh, Jr. (whom he knew slightly) across the Atlantic Ocean. Lindy's subsequent publicity tour through America led him near Atlantic, and at his fellow flyer's request he passed overhead, waggling his wings in recognition as the whole family sat in the front yard and waved. Most remarkably, the son later reinterpreted Lindbergh, Jr., as personifying the imaginary escape from corporate bureaucracy, a "last national hero from the past" preserving the "nineteenth century dream that the individual could become one with his tools and his work."[20] This observation hints at Williams casting his father as a man who also had one last chance to elude twentieth-century depersonalization and took it desperately, knowing the risks.

It would not be hard to imagine a more distant scientist–father figure for the boy: that favorite son of Iowa, Herbert Hoover. Solidly Republican, Atlantic shared a particular fondness for the engineer-president born in West Branch, whose political and intellectual reputation Williams the scholar would continually seek to rehabilitate. Until the Depression, Hoover represented the proud contribution of Iowan ways to Washington, the mixture of know-how, moralism, and resistance to centralization.

Within a year of Lindy's aerial visit, at any rate, Billy had joined the Army Air Corps to return to flight duty. His son, who claimed to have had such an active childhood libido that he kissed the girl next to him on the first day of kindergarten, poured greater love and energy into model airplanes, styling many versions of Lindy's "Spirit of St. Louis." In old age the famed historian returned to making the Lindbergh model as if recovering a piece of himself lost somewhere along the way.[21]

Lt. Williams seemed to love his new life of male camaraderie and mechanized excitement. Mildrede and their son shared his excitement vicariously. The airman was scheduled to be given a permanent commission to Captain after the major war games of March 1929, although he still had private reservations about a military future. Mother and son made a special visit to him in Texas as he prepared to take part in the war games. One early morning of the games, he executed a dive and his plane failed mechanically. He crashed, mortally wounded with multiple skull fractures. It was unquestionably the worst moment of the boy's life. Many times later, Williams would return to the painful memory of seeing his father go off in the morning, cheerfully assuring the boy of his return— only to disappear forever.

Mother and son returned home to a funeral attended by much of Atlantic, and to a flood of sympathetic mail that continued for weeks. Nothing could console the two, abandoned in the world by a figure they had already learned to idolize at a distance. Young Bill had recurring nightmares which were so horrible that, decades later, he could still not bring himself to describe their contents even to his family.[22] Every child has dark moments, of course. But these anxieties may have not really passed, only gone into abeyance and taken other forms. Perhaps his later secretiveness, the inwardness masked by stern self-reliance, had its origins as much here as in Midwestern Protestantism.

Too stricken ever to marry again, Mildrede raised her boy with the help of her mother and father. Her in-laws, and the farm life outside Atlantic that they might have offered, never figured in her projection of the boy's future career track. He would visit his paternal grandparents from time to time and maintain a nodding friendship with an uncle who worked as a garage mechanic in Atlantic, but Mildrede's family had claimed him. He would become what she wanted, even if she could not be on the scene personally to supervise his rearing.

After her son's eighth birthday party she enrolled at Iowa State Teachers College in Cedar Falls, placing Billy (scarcely aware of any other name, he was uniformly called "Billy" throughout his youth) in a sort of parental limbo with her as an occasional visitor. His grandfather, Tossie, and his grandmother, Maude, would be Mildrede's surrogates.

Bill nevertheless thrived. As he looked back on this time, he could recount an early-twentieth-century Midwestern pattern of life slipping away even then. Caring for the root cellar, learning the mysteries of the ice box, using hand tools to make a soap-box racer, shooting a BB gun (he recalled that he had killed a sparrow and on the spot lost his love for gunning down living creatures), playing the piano, and vegetable gardening occupied much of his time and attention. He claimed in an autobiographical sketch to have been "reared in an extended family consisting of literally countless people" related by kinship or friendship, a "joyful and illuminating experience."[23] One can be skeptical of these claims without disputing the best of his small-town experiences. He spent little time with paternal grandparents or cousins, but neighbors and friends of the family were almost certainly sympathetic to the fatherless child.

A bright boy too active to be unusually studious, he later considered himself very fortunate to be situated in a town that believed staunchly in education. With his playmates, he often returned Saturday mornings from a film matinee to the public library, only later moving on to the ball field. At home, he poked through a stock of free thought–oriented family books unusual in Atlantic, from *The Well of Loneliness* by Radclyffe Hall, the first widely-distributed lesbian novel, to Margaret Sanger's birth-control volumes and Hemingway novels, to the standard of Poe or Tom Swift available in many Atlantic households. Probably the more avant-garde volumes had been bought by his father. At any rate, the family bookshelves were open with no prohibitions on what he might choose to read. Like so many future intellectuals, he browsed and absorbed what interested him.

Still, as his mother grew more deeply involved in school (so much so that an association of women enrolled in primary education at Iowa State made her their president), young Billy suffered another round of severe nightmares about abandonment. He imagined himself terrifyingly alone, missing the father who had rarely been present for long. He concluded later that Mildrede, driven by her need for a profession, had deprived herself and obviously him as well of the intimacy of a normal mother-child relationship. She, too, he now admired mostly from a physical distance. He must have felt, from early years, a need to be emotionally self-reliant and, more than that, to be strong for her.

Despite her career successes Mildrede suffered serious depression, and suggested unwisely in her letters to the boy that she believed her good life was over. During a mother-son driving trip undertaken to restore their relationship, Billy found her crying uncontrollably in a country outhouse, and he ran screaming to get help. Emotionally, the two recovered together, traveling all the way to California and enjoying each other's company. Meeting old flyers along the way, they had adventures memorable for the boy. A stranger in a hotel apartment in Long Beach, California, where they stayed for a few weeks, initiated him in the game of billiards. "The joy of being treated as an equal taught the boy to understand the true sense of skill and sport," he remembered.[24] One might as well call this experience the source of his later passion for the pool table and the pool hall atmosphere of male camaraderie, alcohol, stogies, and bloodless combat. At any rate he was growing emotionally, preparing for life without his mother again.

These episodes invite further psychological exploration, if only because Williams himself was so taken with the psychological theories of personality development in a later era. Williams strictly avoided Freudian theories with their inevitable Oedipal component. One of his favorite alternative prophets, Abraham Maslow, proposed the self-creation of the personality through "peak experiences," energizing moments which can reshape approaches to life. In Maslow, the instinct for creativeness and for meaningful existence possesses an importance at least equal to subconscious sexual desires. This species of existential psychology, a variant on the existentialism of such contemporary philosophers as Jean Paul Sartre and Albert Camus, permitted Williams to recast his youthful traumas as forced opportunities for personal growth. Gestalt psychology, another of Williams's preferred theories, viewed the surrounding environment and the subject's current situation as critical to development and reorientation. The "life-space" of mental and physical factors was decisive to life possibilities, helping to frame a self-actualization, the individual's growth toward what he (or she) might potentially be.[25]

There are other hints along the same lines. Little in the boy's family background suggested the self-conscious, sentimental Welshman that Williams's close friends claimed to perceive so clearly later. Any memories of the old country were generations back. Only his stature, which levelled off at under 5'10", and his sometimes almost maudlin manner evoked images of the popular sentimental film, *How Green Was My Valley*, with its singing coal miners—surely a nonexistent species in Iowa. If young William Appleman Williams needed to create a persona, he obviously drew upon and probably improvised resources deep inside himself. He wanted urgently to be *different*, to be special, as his first wife emphasized. To do so, he would assume *sui generis* identities sometimes quite charming and sometimes troublesome to those around him.

2

The next period in his life demanded all his psychic creativity for somewhat different reasons. By the time he and his mother recovered from their mutual crisis, the Depression of the thirties had struck. Like so many other American towns and cities, Atlantic was soon prostrate. The corn-canning factory, for decades the largest such enterprise in the world, went bankrupt. The fertilizer plant managed to stay open only by switching to synthetic fertilizer and drastically trimming its personnel. Atlantic rebounded slowly through a shift to growing cereals for feed cattle and other future meat animals. But Williams remembered best the rural desperation at the close of the day, when through the wild shadows flung across the barnyard by a swinging kerosene lamp, [one saw] the desperate fear and fatigue in the very soul of an uncle as he scuffed his shoes clean with a worn corn cob. And, sometimes, to see his deep frustration at not having the corn to feed the pigs, erupt in an angry outburst during a conversation with his wife or children—or myself.[26]

Williams's immediate family was only a little better off. Grandfather Porter lost everything, a terrible defeat that wiped out his various investments and left him mulling over his dog trophies and drinking to kill the disappointment. A tiny government pension, along with some military and civilian insurance, helped Mildrede pay for her own continuing education, and she made Billy's clothes with her foot-powered sewing machine.

In Williams's recapitulation of the period, these were also times of sharing and intensified community sentiment. No doubt he captured the best of Atlantic in his images of judges handing down suspended sentences for theft of food, theater managers looking away when kids opened the back door for their poorer friends, and storekeepers keeping a "tab" that they rightly suspected would never be repaid. As he also observed, "women were at the center of the community during the depression years" around America. Later feminists, he reflected, might see such women's lives as "limited, demeaning and destructive," but "the issue was survival."[27] He was proud of Atlantic's women (obviously including his mother and grandmother) *because* they used their strength to hold the family together, and not to assert their independence from it.

His memoirs were more frank. Grandmother Maude wearied of it all, falling into a deep personal depression. "So much for the claims of capitalism to provide opportunities for everyone to realize their full potential," Williams remarked with a rare suggestion of bitterness about his younger days. His grandparents, like hundreds of thousands of Protestant Midwesterners, left Republican ranks for the first time in their lives, if only temporarily. Crisis drove them into the arms of Roosevelt and the New Deal. The terrible price of economic recovery, when it finally came, would not be learned until later.[28]

Mildrede got a regular job teaching third grade in Atlantic. At that stressful time, more and more children appeared in class undernourished and sullen, their parents unable to understand what value an education might hold in a jobless future. She could only offer them hope of better times and more opportunities, for which education would serve them well. For her pains, she earned less than $800 per year. The family cut expenses to the bone. Any luxuries, such as athletic equipment, Saturday movies, a new model airplane kit, or music lessons were reserved for Billy. She took a better job across the state, bringing Billy along with her. But neither of them could adapt to the stress of single parenthood in an unfamiliar scene. He found himself alone and lonely in their apartment after school, waiting for her, imagining that his father was actually alive and destined to return.

The two came back to Atlantic, Mildrede reluctantly accepting a pay cut in order to see the boy through high school. Williams views this sacrifice as a mark of her personal maturity. But he adds that for himself, "life in the slow lane with Maude was more interesting and meaningful than life in the fast lane with Mildrede." He missed the quiet diversions of a relaxed home setting. His grandmother, with all her troubles, had been more of a mother to him than his own mother. In her struggles, Mildrede made an uncomfortably intense partner for a child who preferred security above all.

Strange memories rise up here, in this extended family reunion. Grandfather Porter, who had abandoned his customary drinking en route to home, now limited himself to a single tumbler of whiskey which he drank while playing cribbage and talking with the boy: he would fill a pitcher with water and then replace the imbibed whiskey, sip by sip. It was surely a discipline to drink in measured fashion. But to down a quarter pint in this rigorous fashion was at once self-justifying and self-deceiving in a deeply Protestant way, as if his grandmother had gone through liquor-tinged patent medicine by the case. Decades later, Williams confided (or rationalized) to a close friend, in the same vein, that alcohol taken at specific periods perfectly balanced his body's respiration; a scientific explanation that only a heavy drinker could take seriously.[29]

Intense adolescent family conflicts emerged, pitting mother against son over William's playing varsity basketball and drumming, rather than singing in the glee club and chorus. Grandmother mediated, and Williams emerged a small-town sports star, even an idol to younger boys—quite an accomplishment for a youngster of rather small stature. With sheer determination, fast hands, and the acquisition of good shooting skills, he made himself into the hero he had hoped to become. He acquired from his father's reputation the awesome importance of performing not just well but brilliantly if possible. And like many a lower-class or minority youngster successful in sports, he quelled inner demons if he could not eradicate them. Meanwhile, he excelled in English, Math, Physics, Biology, History, and Citizenship.[30]

Williams had also become a lifetime sports fan, however much he would later complain about the commercialization of athletics and control of play from the bench. Like so many youngsters, he admired the irrepressible Babe Ruth. But Red Grange, the "Galloping Ghost" from neighboring Illinois, also naturally caught his attention. Indeed, Grange was the first star of professional football, quickly putting the Chicago-area team on the map. A later Williams clearly appreciated athletic dexterity, but he especially liked to imagine himself in the leadership status of the coach or manager, quarterback or the captain of a basketball team.[31]

Jazz offered yet another dimension. By the middle thirties, dynamic developments in radio and record distribution had reshaped popular music, bringing in waves of black musicians and singers including Louis Armstrong, Mary Lou Williams, Bessie Smith, Count Basie, and above all, Duke Ellington, whom a later Williams considered "a master of the age." For a young Williams, jazz accommodated black contributions to American culture, even in little Atlantic.[32] Playing the drums was a way to literally tap into the excitement of American popular culture at its best.

Williams had thus gained an important measure of self-confidence all around, enough to be a winning personality comfortable with his recent success. Mildrede could feel satisfied that her boy acquired a good high-school education, even if he were considered popular rather than brilliant. He was regularly elected a class officer. Now and then he could shine academically, as when he wrote a prize-winning essay for the Daughters of the American Revolution–sponsored contest on "Citizenship." For his own part, he had begun to make plans. An Eagle Scout, he was selected for the Iowa delegation to the International Scout Jamboree at the Chicago World's Fair of 1933 with his way paid by philanthropic Atlantic businessmen.

There he fell in love with the buildings of Louis Sullivan, an architect he would later criticize for creating exquisite physical structures which symbolized centralized power and the triumph of the corporation over the individual. He almost certainly also glimpsed the work of Frank Lloyd Wright. One of the great and also typical intellects of the Midwest, Wright built on a human scale and, when he retreated, did so by embracing the organicism of the family and community that Williams held sacred.[33] The boy dreamed of going to Iowa State in Ames to study architecture.

He also began to earn his own first pocket money. A newspaper route was one of the few ways then for a boy in school to acquire an income. Desperate to get the job, he haunted the outgoing delivery boy until it was passed along to him. Williams later claimed that, while delivering the paper, he learned sociology and psychology by closely examining the daily life of his customers across the social spectrum and interacting withe them.

During his junior year, he struck up a serious romantic flirtation, his first, with Jeannie (or Emma Jean) Preston. Bright and spirited, small of stature like him, she was the daughter of the town's barbershop owner, a hard-working and kind-hearted businessman who dreamed of seeing his children acquire a college education. In a typical high-school romance, as he recalled later, the two could "make an ice cream soda last an hour."[34]

Ties went deep in small-town social life. Her mother and his mother, with birthdays on the same day, had once, in childhood, had a party together. Later, Bill's father had taken Jeannie's mother to the high-school prom, and still later Bill and Jeannie had shared music teachers and both attended meetings of the Bach Juvenile Society. Attending separate public grade schools, they lost touch; a year ahead of him, she had no classes with him and little contact at all afterward. But teenaged Bill, full of life and often dating several girls simultaneously, dared Jeannie to sit with him in a balcony of a movie theatre; then they began seeing each other regularly.

They shared many interests, from books to music, but especially Jeannie's writing for the school paper, *The Needle*, a year before Billy would be eligible as a senior to follow her as a cub journalist. The two naturally attended all social functions together. Her younger brother, Sam, became Bill's devoted follower, shadowing the older boy's trajectory from high-school sports to later military-school training. Perhaps by then Bill Williams had acquired at last the larger family that he had yearned for; he seemed more emotionally secure than ever before. He and Jeannie envisioned a married life together. Mildrede, more than protective, subtly and not-so-subtly resisted anyone threatening to take her Billy away. She suspected, as parents often do, that her son was well on his way to sexual adventures. She tried, without success, to limit his participation in dances and outings.[35]

In the most extraordinary passages of his memoir, Williams describes his mother ("a full-bodied, handsome woman") overinterpreting the courtship as a threat to chaste youth. Calling him to her room as she dressed, she put on her bra and her silky step-ins trimmed with lace, then the rest of her clothes in front of him. She warned him not to "play" with the sensitive part of a woman's body, and through sobs urged him to hold the line at some modest petting. "How she did it," he reflects, her son "will never quite understand. It was surely one of her bravest, most magnificent moments." A different interpretation would see a woman so desperate that she engaged unconsciously in borderline seductive behavior toward him. A half-century later, he claimed to hear the sound of her rustling silk in the rush of the Oregon tides.

She nevertheless readied him, and also herself, for the wider world. In the summer of 1938, Jeannie Preston prepared to leave Atlantic for Simpson College, a small coeducational liberal arts school in Indianola, Iowa, and Mildrede attended a summer session at Columbia Teachers College, taking an exuberant son along for the New York World's Fair. He heard Duke Ellington live and also Mildrede's own favorite, the debonair Cab Calloway. They were small-town bohemians at home in the metropolis.

Mother and son seemed, at last, to have put their troubles behind them as he passed from boy to man and she finished her degree, moving from Atlantic to a job at Central State Teachers College in Stevens Point, in central Wisconsin. Williams later took immense pride in her favorable graduate teaching evaluations as a tough but fair instructor who would go on to head the local American Association of University Women chapter. She was surprised but deeply gratified to hear that he had won a basketball scholarship in 1939 to Kemper Military Academy in Booneville, Missouri, grasping the only possible financial opening for a college education. Like his mother, he was leaving Iowa for good, returning only for family visits.

His grandparents lived on in Atlantic, the last of them dying in 1962, and his mother remained in Wisconsin until she died of cancer in 1978. Williams remained emotionally close to them and proud of them. But he had set his life on a wider course than Atlantic or Iowa or even the Midwest would allow. Many middle-class children from similarly small and generally prosperous towns had been prepared to leave home for wider opportunities. But few would spend so much of their lives intellectualizing the significance of it all.

There was another childhood issue which returned to him repeatedly in later life: his mother's struggle to bear the responsibility of the family and also to become her own person. He recalled that a friend of his mother's told him shortly after her death that "independence for a woman of [her] generation was a two-edged sword. We thought about it as members of a community, and [then] that [possibility] kind of disappeared."[36] This memory may have well been shaded by Williams's predilections, for Mildrede *was* an independent woman. But if she, the exceptional person, had won out, she had also been worn out by the fight. And so one can see the great themes of Williams's life: community and the individual, the achievements of the independent-minded American and the immense price imposed upon those who also yearn for peace and security.

William Appleman Williams later made much of the mixture of community and individualism that he had known in Atlantic. He believed that the country needed a specifically American brand of communal and regional socialism created by the kind of independent-minded, diligent, and determined "ordinary" citizens with whom he had grown up. How that vision related to his real home scene that Jeannie remembered as strikingly cold, where a youngster growing up read the newspaper at dinner to avoid conversation with the adults, remained to be seen. He pushed the frontiers of historical scholarship further than any other American of his time, but Williams always—at least in his own mind—remained rooted, spiritually, politically and philosophically, in his own idealized heartland. The great Pan-African historian C. L. R. James, like Williams an astute critic of Empire, once observed that the average American, while achieving an unprecedented degree of individual autonomy, for that very reason craved an elusive fellowship and community with others.[37] The Williams family could have been James's proof positive.

## 3

The fall of 1939 brought Williams into a happy moment of his life. He enjoyed the mixture of quasi-military discipline, rigorous scholarship, and competition at Kemper and did well. It exemplified, in many respects, what he admired most in Middle-American institutions. It had a good national reputation for academic standards among military academies, and its administrators and teachers encouraged students, as he recalled, to "play it straight," with "no crap" of the usual cliquish school kind or the artificial discipline that many military academies offered for troubled youngsters shipped off by their uncoping parents. A literature teacher might assign students to read pulp novels for weeks so that they could appreciate Shakespeare as a follow-up assignment; a math teacher had students read Descartes, Leibnitz, Spinoza, Russell, and Whitehead while learning calculus, spherical trigonometry, and differentials. Williams did especially well in Physics, English Literature, and various art courses, and almost as well in Composition and Calculus. Administrators treated the likeable Bill as a "fair-haired boy," Jeannie recalled from her visits for school dances.[38]

Williams found it a real pleasure to be trained and tested rigorously, to "do the best you could and then accept the losses, defeats, along with victories." A "very good" athlete by his own account, he quickly lost interest in organized sports, but had to continue in order to keep his scholarship. His interests had drifted elsewhere—to music, and above all, to reading books new and exciting to him. In this environment of limited distractions, where boys met girls only on specified weekends, his intellectual life blossomed for the first time.[39]

According to Williams's recollections, Spinoza meant the most to him, as the philosopher determined to see the relationship of the part to the whole, to grasp in each "ostensibly positivistic fact" the hidden pattern of connections which gave it meaning. It was during this period, Williams believed, that he became predisposed to something like Marxism, without grasping in the least any alternatives (or even the need for alternatives) to the social system as it existed.

The threat of war inevitably occupied the attention of military preparatory schools.[40] But as Williams mulled over his life ahead, corresponding on a daily basis with Jeannie, he managed to believe with millions of others that the U.S. might somehow stay out of the conflict. At the end of his two years at Kemper, he still inclined instead toward becoming an architect.

Fate intervened. Among the Annapolis appointments made available to each state's congressional delegation, one position opened up for Iowa. A Republican congressman, Ben J. Jensen, looked to Bill not only as the son of a late military veteran (and well-liked public figure), but also a young man obviously suited for officership. According to one version, his mother—now in Stevens Point—and his grandmother insisted that he accept the offer. He could not refuse such an opportunity. And he did not refuse. In September 1941, he entered the Naval Academy.

Looking back many years later, he had a reason to think that a larger inevitability had spoken. His great-uncle—a former apprentice seaman and later Captain Guy Kramer, with more than thirty long voyages under his belt—had told his story to youngster Bill Williams. Laying half-paralyzed in bed, carving an exact model of the final ship he had commanded, he conveyed "that eerie combination of exhilaration, dream and consummate fatigue" of ocean life to the "impressionable child" who also grew into a sailor.[41]

But Billy's first approach to the Navy was uneasy at best. For two years he suffered through classes and routines he hated. According to Navy records, he had especially deficient averages in Electrical Engineering and Foreign Languages, and these low grades meant that he eventually graduated 706th out of 915 class members.[42] Decades later, thinking aloud about how a renown scholar-to-be might have scraped by with mediocre grades, Williams reflected that he had learned so much about military discipline and taken so many similar courses at Kemper, he felt initially that he was only passing time. Classmates recall him as quiet, serious, completely uninterested in the routines of hazing and public hoopla, and intensely missing Iowa and his sweetheart. The couple wrote every day, and according to Jeannie's recollection, Williams had twin bracelets inscribed, "I BELONG TO BILL WILLIAMS" and "I BELONG TO JEANNIE PRESTON." A few years later, twin wedding rings read similarly, "NO ONE ELSE EVER."

He was also likely depressed at the prospect of active warfare, which some of his classmates anticipated with naive enthusiasm. Annapolis self-consciously prepared its plebes for active combat by this time. Instructors frankly described the preparatory stages taking shape in the Atlantic, American ships supplying the English and inevitably inviting German response. Mental escape seemed better to Williams than brooding about a grim future. "So," he recalls, "I laughed at it all and went off to read novels, economics, history, and in general, do my other things." Most memorably, he had fun as a jazz drummer, sitting in with the visiting bands of Benny Goodman and Artie Shaw (who he especially admired as a musician-intellectual), and serving in a warm-up band for Gene Krupa, who sauntered on stage with his characteristic Coca-Cola bottle in hand, complimenting the young man on his drumming skills.[43]

Gradually things changed, for reasons that Williams himself never made entirely clear. Certainly the courses got more interesting, the opportunities for real hands-on maritime training more frequent. He served as an assistant editor for the Academy's *Trident Magazine* in his final year and even wrote twice for the cadets' rather amateurish magazine: a short story which, according to its heading, would "prove once and for all, that midshipmen can write good fiction" on a wartime marriage and a naval war encounter; and an essay on the defeat of the Nazis by the Red Army. In the first, a flyer remembers his romance and hopes for a happy life together with his new bride while he makes a heroic, doomed bombing run on a Nazi munitions factory.[44] In the second—"A scholarly and interestingly written article giving valuable background on our little known ally"—he sees the "crimson flag of the Soviet Union . . . now maturing in . . . the blood of its men and women." Williams reflected on the background for the victory at Stalingrad in the rebuilding of factories amid wartime conditions, the breakdown of Nazi logistical lines inside Russia, and above all the heroism of the ordinary Red infantrymen. They had simply won the war, more than any other single force. "Thanks to them," Williams concluded, "we shall read of the Nazi Fashion rather than living as its slaves."[45]

With the passage of time, he also adjusted better to being away from Iowa. A close friendship might well have been decisive. Billy Bonwit, a rare Jew at Annapolis—not so much abused by that time as simply pushed aside from the military camaraderie—needed a roommate and Williams made himself available. They were a perfect match. One, from an economically privileged but emotionally damaged Jewish home, had been heavily exposed to artistic ideas including the art photographs that his late father had taken. The other, instinctively egalitarian, had plenty to teach his new friend in the worlds of jazz and sports. Novelistically, Williams described their relationship as a marriage of roommates who could each think the other partner was a bit crazy but also revel in activities together.

Williams had by now accepted the inevitability of participation in the war, and he assumed his prospective commanding role with the utmost resolve. He and his fellow future officers were "taken very damn seriously" by the instructors and, increasingly, by each other as well. They studied together, reciting on history, political theory, and English and American literature every weekday, writing small essays on sections of the blackboard—a great training in prose, Williams claimed later. They also trained together and above all "learned about power," including the moral necessity of accounting for one's actions. These leadership questions recalled Williams's sports days and seemed to bring out the best in his often steely character.

He thereby experienced a remarkable 180-degree turn in his attitude toward being at the Academy. He remembered his last three semesters as "exciting academically and otherwise," the basis for a lifelong pride in his Annapolis experience. Remarkably, the old-fashioned virtues of being "an officer and a gentleman," with emphasis on both parts of the equation, had become all-important. He improved his grades, but even more he changed his attitude. The yearbook described "Will" as notable for his straightfor-wardness and for "his hatred of poor organization and his determination to finish a job."[46] He might be forgiven for making a fictional version of him-self the best hands-on ship's officer of the class. He probably came close in real life.

The Navy had for generations wanted its officers to receive a well-rounded training and a sense for the culture of the military and diplomatic elites with whom they would interact. At least from the Victorian days of Alfred Thayer Mahan, founder of the Naval War College and himself a tal-ented historian, the Academy also aspired to make its graduates ready for global politics. Specialization would fragment the liberal arts tradition at Annapolis within a decade, but during the middle 1940s it remained strong. Having so doubted a vocation not of his own choosing, Williams deter-mined to be the kind of officer who exemplified the Academy graduate in the world of high politics and culture as well as war. He immediately bought "miniatures" (replicas) of his Academy class ring for the two most important women in his life, his mother and his fiancée. They married just before he shipped out, but Jeannie had to claim Bill's grandmother's ring, which had not been sent on to her by Mildrede. Williams wore his own Annapolis ring the rest of his life, unconsciously twirling or tapping it while making an important intellectual point, sometimes consciously fingering it to unnerve his left-wing graduate students.[47]

The sheer nautical aspect played a considerable role in his deep feelings for the Navy. As an executive, he learned to love the "beauty and the terror" of the sea from his very first cruises. He also formulated the vital environ-mental lesson, so important to him in the last decades of his life, "that man can survive only by treating nature as a senior partner in life." In a day when so many battle-wounded ships went down with their crews, he had no thoughts of conquering the elements, but instead set himself to learn how to live within them. Tactically or strategically, he absorbed yet another lesson that many fellow cadets somehow missed: it was militarily impossible for one nation to dominate the globe without making a mess of the attempt.

Williams broadened his intellectual horizons in remarkable ways. Having absorbed Spinoza, he now turned with growing curiosity to Marx and Freud. This choice of intellectual giants had a definite relation, he later recalled, to his classroom training in the science of engineering. He pressed scientific inquiry to the broad questions of society and the human mind. At a moment when Marx's star was soon to fall considerably in the West and Freud's to rise sharply, many intellectuals looked for a kind of synthesis or dialogue between the two. Thus Erich Fromm's *Escape From Freedom*, pub-lished in 1941, pointed the way by arguing that alienation from the soil and community of feudalism to modern capitalist relations had increased mass insecurity and fear. Socialism, in Fromm's perspective, would cure the alienation. Whether or not Williams read Fromm, this kind of thinking had begun to take hold in contemporary intellectual circles.

Williams also recalled first reading the English "guild socialist" G. D. H. Cole, who outlined a possible peaceful transition to a decentralized economic and social system based in autonomous communities. Cole's own inspiration had been William Morris, the famed designer, poet, and utopian novelist who led a wing of the British socialist movement during the 1880s. For Morris as for many late nineteenth-century socialists, capitalism was best seen as an interruption in the historical communities that advanced human society. The medieval era, with all its inequalities, its spiritual corruption, and its resistance to scientific advance, still had the important qualities of community feeling, pride of workmanship, and spiritual aspiration (no matter how cynically the ruling cliques regarded it all) toward a more worthy goal than the self-pride and possessions of this world.

Morris, Cole, and other such thinkers were never entirely welcome in formal Marxist circles, suspected of romanticism and similar heresies by communists and reform socialists alike. Yet they continued for Williams as a personal influence and as a style of thinking, a British counterpart in some important ways to the democratic and ecological regionalism of Lewis Mumford and other American enthusiasts of the Tennessee Valley Authority, as a model for social reorganization. Williams hints that he may have been grappling, this early, for a socialism influenced but not overwhelmed by Marxist ideas or Marxist organizations.

He had unquestionably come to a personal sense of the decisive importance of future relations between the United States and the Soviet Union. No far-thinking prospective military officer could fail to see the outline of possibilities. Indeed, millions of ordinary Americans but especially radicals and self-conscious antifascists felt an admiration and awe which decades later Williams described as the utter "dependence of the Western powers upon the courage of the Red Army."[48] The "worldly-minded" Williams, as the Annapolis yearbook called him, inevitably grew more emotionally involved in such quasi-political deliberations as his time for active service drew near.[49]

Annapolis graduated Williams's entire class a year early in 1944 to put them into the war. He later recalled that his classmates informally voted him most likely to reach the Joint Chiefs of Staff. He was someone they saw as possessing administrative skills and an unrelenting focus on detail.[50] Like his fellow graduates, he was immediately commissioned. He volunteered for the Amphibious Corps to avoid becoming an executive "errand boy" on a large ship and to be allowed a command of his own, however minor. He thus served the last fifteen months of the Pacific War as an

Executive Officer on board what he regarded as a mere splinter of a boat, a so-called Landing Ship Medium. His task was to ferry infantrymen toward battle while the Japanese tried to sink the ship from under him.

He never wrote at length about this period; nor did he recollect old war stories in the fashion of so many former military participants, nor mention the Purple Heart that he was awarded. He often commented, more generally, that with the military brass hard at work, the outcome nevertheless "all depended upon the men who went into combat," who "bled and died" and finally won the war against fascism.[51] Even his quasi-autobiographical novel about a Navy man said surprisingly little about the actual conflict. He had been chosen in the first wave of invasions, his protagonist claimed, because his task was like "tossing newspapers right on the mark while flirting with the girl three porches down the block." He had learned, through application of instinct, how to "handle a ship like it was flying a model airplane," letting the ship itself do most of the work. Alternatively, "reading" a ship was a Spinozan project, a model in political-scientific economy in understanding how the engine room and deck provide the base that supports the superstructure of guns and bridge, which in turn affects the function of deck and engine room.[52]

Williams offered no insights into the inevitable moments of terror, except to say, in a passage of *Contours of American History*, that modern war increasingly made targets into mere blips on the radar screen, and to add, in many private letters, that no novel yet written had been equal to the complexity of the World War's battle scene. Some of the most iconoclastic accounts, however, clearly appealed to him: Joseph Heller's *Catch 22*, Kurt Vonnegut's *Slaughterhouse Five*, and Norman Mailer's *The Naked and the Dead* all captured the "dehumanizing and undemocratic character of war and the armed forces."[53] Part of him wanted to remember, but part of him sought to suppress detailed recollections of battle gore.

Williams concluded several times later that an officer on a ship could create either an atmosphere of subservience or the framework for an "honest community." By self-consciously choosing the latter, he was clearly underlining a key value of his own life. He also said that life on shipboard was "not so much a chain of command as it is an interlocking network of mutually known and accepted responsibilities."[54] He admired those under his command, and by reading their letters as military censor for fifteen months, appreciated their clarity and insight as they struggled to explain their experiences to loved ones stateside. He also continued to read his favorite authors deeply, including Marx, and now also Kant and Faulkner. He claimed to have read Ernest Hemingway's own war drama, *For Whom the Bell Tolls*, at just the perfect moment in his life, when it gave him the political push he had been waiting for.[55] The fatalism, the romanticism, and the rugged antifascism with a leftward political tilt no doubt hit the right note in the captain's quarters.

As "Captain of the Line" in the secondary invasions intended to advance from the Philippines to Japan, he was thrown against a bulkhead in heavy seas during the closing months of the war, severely injuring his spine. Despite a determination to keep fit, he suffered discomfort and increasing pain for most of the rest of his life. Old age found him reliving the injury in nightmares, seeing himself as a helpless cripple. Had he not been injured and the atom bombs not been dropped, he might well have been part of the landing force on the Japanese mainland.

Williams nevertheless built parts of two novelistic chapters around bitter disagreement with his Annapolis roommate and a later Commanding Officer about the morality of using the bomb. He insisted decades later that "it is possible to be grateful that oneself and comrades were not killed in an assault on the Japanese home islands and yet have regret and remorse about how we were saved—and the consequences of being saved in that particular fashion."[56] The quest beyond victory had been Empire. He could not hate the Japanese, and unlike many who served in the Pacific, he could never justify to himself the use of the bomb to end the war. Like Lewis Mumford, the dedicated antifascist whose only son had died in the war but who nevertheless issued a manifesto against the use of atomic weapons ("Gentlemen, You Are Mad"), Williams felt the horror of the deed. There are some things, he often said later, that a right-thinking officer and a gentleman will *not* do. War crime was high on the list.

The war ended but Williams was still in service. Like so many other officers, he considered a military career. Self-consciously in his father's footsteps, he found the prospect of flying "very exciting and demanding," with the aircraft "unforgiving" to human error. He did not expect to be as good a flyer as the senior Billy Williams, but Naval flight school would let him see how far he could go. Corpus Christi was the nation's largest air naval training base, and there Williams's fortunes took several decisive turns.[57]

The first was marriage. After several missed trains and typical wartime confusion compounded by bad weather, Jeannie Preston joined him in December 1945. Williams probably captured his own mood accurately in the protagonist of his later, unpublished novel. Like so many other young men recently released from armed conflict, the fictional Williams was erotically inclined to an extreme degree ("the *second* thing I want to do when I get home" began a standard joke of the time) and very much in love with his wife. But he also loved flying, jazz, and alcohol. The couple made friends quickly and might have gone on together in any number of different career and personal directions.

Civil Rights and an accompanying radicalism made a sudden appearance, however, so sudden that Williams could never satisfactorily explain his remarkable shift of attention. Although race seemingly played no role in Atlantic as any kind of issue, he prided his grandmother on describing the dignity of Indian peoples, telling him that he needed to "walk a mile in their moccasins" to understand their unique and tragic experience. He would later tell students that the racial caste system of Annapolis and the surrounding area, with African Americans practically restricted to the servant class, had disturbed him. But he had no way to act upon inequity. Jeannie Williams recalled a burning sense of unfairness that she felt, too, because of the straightforward values of equal play she had learned, and because she felt a need for improving the world. She, rather than he, had been the aggressive leader of local and college clubs, the activist of the family, and now she urged him forward. She had not been politically active but was not to be frightened off, either. Henry Wallace's family had been patron saints of Iowa's farmers, and Jeannie's college roommate was the granddaughter of Milo Reno, the leader of 1930s "Farm Holiday" agrarian radicalism.

The antifascist and antiracist mood of the nation also played a large role. Williams novelistically reflected on the warmth of feeling by GIs who imagined an America with blacks, Indians, Jews, and others as equals. At this moment, *The House I Live In*, a short film feature starring Williams's (and the rest of the nation's) favorite crooner, Frank Sinatra, toured movie houses nationally, urging multiracial democracy and picking up awards. This marked a clear opening for racial change, almost a sanction for idealistic action.[58]

At any rate, a fractious local political campaign impelled Corpus Christi's black community leaders to seize the moment. They looked to the Supreme Court's *Smith v. Allwright* decision of 1944 to demand the opening of the voting process to all races on a non-prejudicial basis, and they followed in the wake of organizing by Corpus Christi's large minority population, the Mexican Americans. The potential advance in elections carried a hidden contradiction, the future use of black votes as leverage for payoffs by candidates to various ward leaders. But the local NAACP, headed by a respected black dentist and supported by a noted veteran southern white lawyer, spearheaded an effort to press the momentary advantage, raising a variety of social issues around segregation and employment.

Williams, now in his mid-twenties, had absolutely no experience in protest politics, even if his reading seemed to point him in that direction. But he had a new friend of the greatest importance to him. Air Safety Officer Herb Gilmor, an earlier Annapolis graduate from an abolitionist family background, was one of thousands of instinctive or simply unaffiliated American radicals. He had considered joining the American volunteers in the Spanish Civil War, with its Abraham Lincoln Batallion so clearly dominated by fearless left-wing (mostly Jewish), working-class youths. Gilmor had instead bided his time and served in the big war. At Corpus Christi he saw his latest chance to make a difference. The local African American community was small, certainly less than five percent of the total population. But black workers especially wanted access to jobs in the flight line as mechanics. Gilmor and his wife, Charlotte, threw themselves into the task of supporting integration just as they became the newlywed Williamses' most intimate friends.[59]

Williams later sought, in his unpublished novel, to capture the scene that he had lived. The fictionalized eye of the storm was a local Abyssinian Baptist Church, built by freed slaves with the assistance of whites in 1869. Serving as the nerve center of a community striving to transform race relations and in that sense the trajectory of the nation, it had been cheated of a historic opportunity. Populism, a quarter century later, raised prospects again, only to have them crushed by lynch law and the indifference of national business and political leaders. When another half century had rolled by, the struggle was joined here once more.

In chapters devoted to the eloquence of sermons and the excitement of political meetings there, Williams sought to recall and elaborate the historical lessons that he had been privileged to learn firsthand. In a rough but marvelously concrete way, black leaders understood the burden of American history. They also looked beyond their immediate suffering. They saw, for instance, the necessity to link their own fate to the "white niggers," however difficult poor whites had made that task. They could even appreciate that reformers firmly situated within the political system, like a young Lyndon Johnson, could play a positive role over time if given a big enough push from constituents back home. Williams thus grasped, or projected, a complex view of democratic transformation; it depended upon elites quite as much as grassroots action.

In the short run, black residents properly demanded elementary decency from the city. They insisted that buses run at night so that domestic servants could return home safely, and that at least a few of the local white merchants begin to hire them at decent wages. They also wanted an end to the climate of terror conducted intermittently by the Ku Klux Klan. Taken together, these changes along with similar ones for Mexican Americans would have transformed the racial climate of Corpus Christi. Racists, but not only racists, determinedly resisted.

Williams believed that a combination of giant interests had set themselves against major racial readjustments. The Navy brass and local officials of the immensely influential Catholic Church simply wanted no possible threats to their established hierarchies and rules. These were formidable foes, indeed. Meanwhile, General Motors and the King Ranch, two economic giants of the region, had hatched a long-range plan to pipe gas to Mexico and make steel there, barging it back up the Mississippi. Not only would this facilitate a "New South" economic initiative from the standpoint of regional elites, it would also undercut union-made steel for automobiles, weakening key union forces then considered a threat to capitalism's stability and its future. Indeed, it would not be hard to see in retrospect the emerging framework of a heavily populated, conservative Southwest dependent on oil dollars and on military subsidies. Racial minorities could not be permitted to upset the plan with too many early demands for civil equality—or, far worse, to pose any serious challenge to the power structure.

In the cold-war political climate, charges of "Communism" could be readily launched against anyone mobilizing African Americans for social change. Nationally, the FBI mounted a major campaign against "red" union leaders, by no coincidence the most aggressive supporters of racial minorities within the labor movement. Political conservatives and some liberals, again greatly assisted by the FBI, denounced and investigated civil rights groups guilty of left-wing associations. Across the South during 1945-50, pressure increased against organizations like the Southern Negro Youth Congress and the League of Young Southerners, whose activists would one day lead many local campaigns for integration. Corpus Christi was no exception. The local Catholic hierarchy reputedly favored modest and gradual improvements in the conditions of African Americans. But it sought to demonize those who organized for more dramatic and egalitarian shifts. According to Williams's own account, the regional FBI office was predictably reactionary on racial matters and unfriendly towards the most elementary demands for integration.

This set the dour political climate for Williams's first public political role. Using journalistic tools learned at their high-school paper and during Williams's days with *The Trident*, the newly married couple boldly produced a newsletter for the NAACP chapter, *CORPUS CRISIS*. Williams actually wrote most of the copy and Jeannie typed the stencils, with the shades of their apartment carefully drawn to prevent observation. In its scant pages, the newsletter mostly carried news items of the civil rights struggle that local newspapers were likely to ignore or distort. But by the second issue of the *CRISIS*, a contributor also warned that "baiting, whether race, labor, or red-baiting is distasteful to the more intelligent segment of our population," and it accomplished nothing positive. Very possibly Williams wrote this column himself, under a *nom de plume*. In any case, the author was careful enough to couch his remarks within the standard liberal argument that once justice truly reigned in America, "we shall see that Communism is fading away."[60] Catholic notables including a local monsignor and a prominent layman responded savagely. Criticisms of the Catholic Church and its behavior, they made clear, would not be acceptable in Corpus Christi in any form or for any reason whatever. A local integrationist who considered herself otherwise a social conservative wrote to the NAACP leader, "I [have] warned you that the person who is now publishing your bulletin . . . [has] expressed antagonism toward the Church." One of a "few transient Anglos who will frankly admit that they are here of short duration, have been allowed to take over the NAACP." The unnamed Williams, obviously a troublemaker and perhaps a red, obviously preferred "temporary zeal to slow but sure progress."[61]

Williams carefully suggested in the newsletter that the issues at stake were rather different than the empowered Catholics and other conservative integrationists imagined. He did not editorialize, but the *CORPUS CRISIS* urged major economic and social changes. A minimum-wage bill in Congress, acceptance of African Americans at all levels of professional life, and government adjustments of prices to the rising cost of living and an end to the arbitrary executions of African American prisoners constituted the primary demands.[62] This was a program considerably beyond mere racial integration.

The Gilmors, a handful of Quakers, and other white sympathizers backed these and local demands. Jeannie remembers drop-off points for the newsletter in small black businesses and churches, and the NAACP meetings in which copy for the next issue would be discussed at length. Looking back with pride, Williams felt that he had been initiated then and there into "the strategy and tactics of radical politics," building a community among otherwise ordinary, but extremely brave, people.[63] By his own estimate, the mimeographed publication was, within the limits of the medium, a grand success. Its appearance and continuation confirmed the growing sense of resolve in the black community.

Inevitably, at that place and time, intimidation and threats swiftly increased. The FBI, which probably warned the Williamses' landlord about harboring a dangerous radical tenant under his roof, harassed the young Naval officer at work by having his commanding officer call him in for a warning. He also recalled being pushed around a few times by local toughs and threatened with worse. The NAACP's local leader was assassinated a few years after the Williamses left town. "Yes, sir," Williams told an interviewer decades later about the ferocity of response to a modest campaign for equality, "that will make a socialist out of you. Unless you're dead."[64]

Williams almost certainly considered himself a socialist by this time. But he had to walk a careful line in public statements. He brushed off the red-baiting charges in the *CORPUS CRISIS*, for instance, insisting the newsletter was not in the least anti-Catholic or taking any political position about the world at large, but only for racial harmony, free speech, and dialogue on all sides. Any close reader could spot a modest socialistic slant, however. Williams published (and possibly wrote, under a pseudonym) a quite favorable review of James S. Allen's 1937 volume, *Reconstruction—the Battle for Democracy*, written by a former southern activist and published by the Communists' International Publishers. Critics charged that the National Maritime Union, at the time led by communists and active in the port city of Corpus Christi, infiltrated the NAACP via the national CIO's Political Action Committee and attached itself precisely to integration campaigns like the one around Williams.[65]

Williams, for his part, decades later unembarrassedly recalled having "enormous respect" for the handful of local communists who had bravely joined activities and had moreover "been down there a lot longer than I had."[66] They risked more, and went on risking their careers and their lives. Although he never became a member of any interracial Party-oriented organization, he intuited logically that subsequent FBI spying and harassment probably began in Corpus Christi. "Jeez," he reflected in a 1980 interview, "*did* I join the Communist Party? I mean it sounds strange, but [the local Left] had never been that formal an operation. Well, could anybody construct anything I'd done as proving that I'd joined the Party? Weird experience. You really get a sense of Kafka." There may possibly have been nothing local *to* join, in which case mere friendship and common political reform work were *prima facie* —proof of guilt.[67]

Williams was already apparently politically sophisticated enough to reject the national Communist position on race in 1945. Amidst an internal upheaval of their own, American Communist leaders that year dethroned Popular Front symbol Earl Browder and reintroduced a smattering of earlier "class struggle" themes (in many cases, mere symbolic slogans). For a decade, the Communists had stressed racial integration, winning over many black elites as well as white liberals to their programs. Now they returned to a partial version of an early 1930s plan for independent "black belt" states in the South where nonwhites constituted a majority of the population. Advocacy of this view was meant to stimulate an incipient black nationalism, but the real-life framework of political repression and rising individual opportunity made a shambles of the policy. "The party line in the South in '45 made about as much sense to me as . . . bah, humbug. That's not what these people needed, they were already an isolated community," reflected Williams decades later.[68]

And yet this rejection of communist views had nothing in common with either the anticommunism of local conservatives or with the emerging positions of prominent liberals in the newly founded Americans For Democratic Action (ADA). Indeed, just at the time Williams wrote against red-baiting, leaders of the ADA had opened a blistering propaganda campaign for blanket exclusion of all communists (and by extension, all opponents of anticommunist actions) from unions, political movements, and the entertainment industry, high and low culture alike.[69]

It was not the blunders of the Communists, in any case, that doomed the Corpus Christi campaign. Williams later described its best efforts as having been blunted by "prejudice, violence, and indifference."[70] Aided by both red-baiting and the indifference of the new Truman regime in Washington, local authorities foiled the prospect of any sustained African American social movement. Williams would probably have found himself on the outside if he had managed to stay in Corpus Christi any longer. He seems already to have been caught in the NAACP's own blacklist, which local or regional leaders often used to eliminate Communists and near-Communists. Indeed, over the next year he appealed repeatedly to national headquarters for formal membership and apparently got no satisfaction.[71]

Meanwhile, the Navy brass fully intended to send Williams upon the most unpleasant postwar mission they could imagine: to the little Pacific island of Bikini. There, he and others would personally test the viability (and safety) of post–atomic bomb land invasions through amphibious warfare games. Had they managed to order him to that location, Williams would almost certainly have been placed under an extended death sentence of radiation poisoning.

The recurrence of his spinal injury ruled out that plan for him. Dropping him from flight-training entirely because of the pain he suffered while in the cockpit, the Navy directed him to San Francisco's Treasure Island hospital for extensive treatment. There, doctors discovered he had been born with an extra vertebra. Evidently unnoticed at the time of his induction, the deformity should have ruled him out of Naval service in the first place, and might have made his injury grounds for litigation.

Navy doctors wanted Williams to undergo fusion surgery that had, however, left others he knew crippled for life. Refusing that treatment, he was covered in a cast from the shoulders down to the thighs for several months. As he wrote his mother (quoting from a letter he sent, and decades later rediscovered among her things), the pain during his worst days in the hospital was sometimes so severe that he wanted to "go elsewhere," i.e., to die. Instead, he brought himself back to life with thought, books, and Jeannie, who joined him after returning temporarily to Iowa to teach shorthand and business skills in high school while he was overseas. By the spring months of 1947 he had applied for and received a tentative medical discharge.[72]

Williams often said that the entire Naval experience had driven home to him the modern version of a classical adage, "Don't let bastards grind you down." In its good and bad features, it taught him the importance of unshakeable self-confidence. The Corpus Christi incident had given him a sense of mission, not necessarily to renew acvitity in the integration movement elsewhere but to do *something*. Ordered out of Corpus Christi, his novelistic protagonist tells a black Navy friend who has been through the civil rights efforts with him, "I keep thinking there are things to do down that lonesome road."[73] Elsewhere he noted that those who went to war hoping for a better world continued to do their best under difficult circumstances. "Some gave it up as a hopeless effort" but "others continued the struggle." He obviously considered himself one of the latter.[74]

But how could he act upon his newfound ideals? His mother, without necessarily advising him, helped him to decide what to do with himself. Then a teacher with a third-grade class at Stevens Point, she had for years put her visiting son in front of the classroom and walked out, saying something like, "I want you to give children a sense of what it is to be at the Naval Academy (or whatever) and what a commitment to quality involves." The experience, and her example, drew him to teaching. It was also his only immediate family role model in the world of wage labor.[75]

# MADISON AND HISTORY

SOMETIME IN THE EARLY 1940S, Williams considered becoming a mathematician but discarded the idea. He was not, a teacher informed him, destined to be an Einstein.[1] Neither did he take up a career in electrical engineering or thermodynamics, his majors at Annapolis, although he remembered being offered good jobs in several corporations.[2] He and some of his radical shipmates had clearly chosen Marx over (Alfred) Mahan, as he joked later. But how could he figure out what was really wrong with society? He had concluded that the nation needed "structural change as opposed to secondary reform," and the study of history increasingly seemed to thim the best means to "make sense out of what the hell was going on in the war and the way the world was going" with "the bomb and all that."[3] It may also have been the one discipline other than the social sciences where he could conduct the Spinozan search for interrelations or organic connections among apparently disparate elements. Surely, a study of history would make sense of his experiences in Corpus Christi. The key problems of

American democracy, becoming more urgent as the cold war intensified, were not new but deeply rooted in the national past.

Harry Truman's surprising victory in 1948, a year after Williams arrived in Madison, established the political and even the socioeconomic framework for decades to come. Portraying himself as heir to the New Deal's entitlement acts, the Missouri backroom politician effectively quieted his opponents by raising the twin threats of entitlement rollbacks and the Soviet menace. If his first administration proved the most publicly reviled since Herbert Hoover's Depression doldrums, Truman's second administration enjoyed a paradoxical success of expanding trade and rising productivity against a background of international tensions and unprecedented weapons spending. Truman had, in effect, discovered the formula for the consumer society. Muting the New Deal rhetoric of social equality, his Fair Deal simultaneously enshrined individual initiative and unprecedented growth at taxpayer expense. It also put the domestic impact of foreign policy on the national agenda.

Williams's graduate work and his life in the Madison, Wisconsin, of the late 1940s helped him locate the source of these developments more precisely, and prepared him to deliver his own unique responses to them. Williams, according to all reports, went his own way in almost everything. He was no professor's disciple, and no single thinker or writer could be credited with a decisive influence on his work. Still, the particular mixture of Beardian-American and Marxist-European professors, radical graduate students, free speech, and free thought offered the milieu in which Williams could consider and vigorously debate the various possibilities. A remarkable place at a remarkable time offered him lifelong friends, sponsors, and intellectual influences. He would bear the stamp of his graduate school days throughout his career, so much so that time away from Madison could be considered the exile periods of his life.

Later, Williams would look back and compare professors and students around the University of Wisconsin's history and sociology departments of the late 1940s to the Frankfurt School.[4] Circumstances did not permit the ideas discussed in Madison to come together in the way that those of Theodor Adorno, Max Horkheimer, Herbert Marcuse, and others did, he admitted. But the pessimism of the Wisconsin intellectuals about the prospects of radical change from below, and the consequent task of analyzing society through a radical perspective on the inner logic of the ruling system had important elements in common with the German Marxist (or post-Marxist) effort. So did the search for the reasons why ordinary Americans might passively accept that logic or even adopt it as their own.

Like the Frankfurt School, but with a much closer view of U.S. history, Madison intellectuals faced the exhaustion of traditional perspectives. The always schematic American Marxist notions of contemporary class conflict had already disappeared for all practical purposes into frantic and unrealistic hopes for another benign central administration, similar to patrician Franklin Roosevelt's, but improved. Applied to earlier history, American Marxism had referred to occasional heroic insurgencies and the misery of the oppressed (especially African Americans), but could not explain the sheer stability of the social system, let alone the economic recovery of capitalism after the war.

Williams's Madison intellectual circle came to grips with history's surprises in the best ways that it could manage. No Walter Benjamin was to be found here, with the dextrous dialectics to turn despair into utopian observations, and there was no Adorno to find solace in experimental modernism. But Williams, with his own disciples in the decades ahead, would almost be a school in himself.

I

Frustrated at receiving no satisfactory response from a series of letters to the University of Wisconsin registrar requesting permission to enter graduate school, Williams got through to longtime history chair Paul Knaplund. Williams lacked the necessary credentials, but his sense of determination struck Knaplund, who was then building up a departmental faculty and graduate student body. Knaplund's successor, Chester Easum, like Knaplund a political conservative, rapidly took the young man under his wing in a preliminary "undergraduate" seminar to make up coursework, and later wrote him sterling recommendations. So far as they understood Williams's political views, they had no sympathy for them, and simply admired his abilities. If Williams already considered himself a socialist— and he held his cards too close to his sleeve for any public reputation—he also had good reasons to take a distanced and scholarly approach.[5]

Madison, Wisconsin, proved the perfect place for him to study, at any rate. An isthmus situated among several lakes that had been praised by a visiting Henry Wadsworth Longfellow as jeweled diadems, the city was spectacularly beautiful if also bitterly cold for months at a time. During the late nineteenth century, the land-grant University of Wisconsin and its accompanying state institutions had become a center of social history and great scholarly influence. Frederick Jackson Turner, himself from rural Wisconsin, had transformed historical thought with his Frontier Thesis that the American character had been formed through continual westward movement.

Generations of historians debated the implications, but they uneasily joked that their entire profession was a "Turnerverein," a word play upon the *Turnverein*, the fraternal associations whose combination of gymnastics and free thought made them a center of nineteenth-century German-American social and intellectual life. From popular thought to the highest ivory towers, Turner's influence went forth. One of Turner's students, Algernon Simons from little Baraboo, Wisconsin, had gone on from 1890s Madison student days to edit the premier American socialist theoretical journal and to write a popular socialist history—arguably the most influential until Williams's work—of the nation, based conceptually on the virtue of the farming class.[6] Another of Turner's students, Merle Curti, had in turn spawned at Columbia some of the outstanding historians of the 1940s-50s, notably Richard Hofstadter, and had taught Williams's own mentor, Fred Harvey Harrington. With these giants on hand, physically in the classroom rather than perpetually on leave as in typical Ivy League schools, Madison's attractions proved irresistible. Besides, Mildrede was only a few hours away by car and wanted her son close to her.

The other notable feature of Madison's Americanists was their notorious loyalty to Charles Austin Beard, the great successor to Turner and to Madison's earlier Progressive scholarly tradition. Beard and his wife, Mary Ritter Beard, had written in 1927 *The Rise of American Civilization*, easily the most influential history of the nation ever published. Scarcely a home of educated Americans lacked it, a claim that could be made for no single scholarly or popular historical volume that has followed. It would be surprising, indeed, if the Williams home in Atlantic had not also possessed a copy. From the 1910s to the 1930s Charles Beard held forth on a wide array of political and social issues, in hundreds of newspaper essays, radio talks, and pamphlets. Never a socialist (although a definite ally of socialists on specific issues), Beard managed to appear somehow above all the particular controversies of the day. In the public perception, historical understanding had given him deep insights into the national mentality.

Beard's reputation suffered a monumental decline after the 1930s. Disillusioned with World War I, like so many fellow historians he had grown increasingly suspicious of the rise of the leviathan state apparatus. Taken up temporarily by archconservatives (like those at the *Chicago Tribune*) who had long attacked him, Beard argued against America's drift toward involvement in a second world war. The nation would be better served, he believed, by reliance upon its own resources. After Pearl Harbor, he accused Roosevelt of disingenuousness, a failure to place the issues before the public and to draw their approval for crucial war decisions. Thereafter, Beard's adversaries, notably in the Eastern schools and media, went on the attack. Once-eager publications and radio shows shunned him, and younger liberal historians, attaching themselves to Truman's policies, slashed at him furiously. He died in 1947 after a *Walpurgisnacht*—a burning of his private papers.[7]

But Beard retained the respect of many Madisonians, intellectually and politically. During the 1930s-40s, the History Department at Madison had become especially well known for its scholarly elaboration of Populist-Progressive themes close to both Turner and Beard. John D. Hicks, the foremost historian of Populism and himself a graduate of the University of Wisconsin, had returned to Madison at the height of the Depression. There, he wrote one of the most successful progressive-oriented U.S. history survey textbooks for generations. Beardian economic historian and colonial specialist Curtis Nettels, a former editorial associate of the Marxist journal *Science & Society* and later a campus leader of the 1948 Henry Wallace presidential campaign, was also on hand. Merle Curti arrived in 1942, the year that he won the Pulitzer Prize for the *Growth of American Thought*, and immediately expressed his deep sympathies for Beard. These scholars and others felt the continuing inspiration of Beard's emphasis on economic and social history, an outlook endangered along with Beard's own reputation. All a Wisconsin history student had to do for preliminary examinations, one graduate alumnus suggested jocularly, was to read Beard carefully.[8]

This generalization did little justice to the independent character of Williams's mentors, known by some as the "Murderer's Row" (after the Yankee batting lineup) of the history profession. Fred Harvey Harrington, a native of upstate New York, had arrived at Madison in 1937 after completing his doctoral studies at New York University under Henry Steele Commager. He concentrated his interests on the domestic sources of U.S. foreign policy, unlike the standard diplomatic historians of the time. His broad notion of foreign relations sought out a wide variety of influences and particular economic ones behind government policies, and not just the usual study of official diplomatic records. Harrington found himself inevitably at odds with the East Coast "court historians" who not only took a narrow methodological view of diplomatic history but seemed dogmatically determined to defend the State Department's record. Like other Americanists at Madison, Harrington took pride in challenging the well-funded and even better connected Ivy League establishment. His own history of late-nineteenth-century U.S.-Korean relations, written in 1940 but not published until 1944, focused upon the American imperial experience and the inevitability of competition from the Japanese. His biography of Nathaniel P. Banks, sponsored by the American Historical Association's Albert J. Beveridge Memorial Fund and published in 1948, was a study in political and military power.[9]

Harrington's scheme of graduate training shuttled some of his outstanding prospects into a preliminary year with William Best Hesseltine, a political historian who also rejected cold war imperatives (a decade later he would appear among "Sponsors" on the board of the pacifist magazine *Liberation*). A sympathetic soul who had also attended military school and whose father had died when he was two, Hesseltine trained a handful of the more distinguished historical scholars and popular history writers of the 1950s-60s, including Kenneth Stampp, Richard Current, Stephen Ambrose, and Gordon Parks.[10] Even more than Harrington, Hesseltine was a "scoffer" who liked to "say outrageous things and have people combat him"—a model for Williams's later style of scholarly-political provocations. In later years, when Williams joined the Madison faculty, he and Hesseltine spent many social evenings together; indeed, they were drinking and talking only a few hours before Hesseltine suffered a fatal heart attack in 1963.

During Williams's second year, Harrington invited the bright student to join his own more select crew of graduate advisees. He taught them, as might be expected, the nuts and bolts of research and publishing. But more notably, he had a ruthless way about his criticism of student papers, sitting across his old-fashioned green bridge table going over his comments, or slicing up an entire seminar with harsh criticisms of students for not having worked hard enough. Thus in seminar he would "dissect any decision, event, or movement into its constituent parts with a subtle, loving ruthlessness," qualities that earned him nicknames like "Mr. Cold" and "Fish Eye." This was not meant to be destructive except, perhaps, to the hopelessly thin-skinned youngster. Harrington conveyed through all his gruffness, as Williams later put it, "a great ability to let you consider his criticisms and then do it your way *and take the consequences.*" Warren Susman would later observe shrewdly that Harrington thereby offered an incentive to Williams's inclination to engage in his own methods of historical exploration, making discoveries all the time and "discovering America like Columbus."[11]

Harrington also had, Williams later recalled, a "genius for integrating biography and policy in a way that implicitly transcended interest-group analysis." He could analyze Theodore Roosevelt and other early eager architects of the diplomatic "Open Door" without falling back into vulgar materialism. Had he not chosen an administrative career, he might well have gone beyond Beard in the attribution of a worldview or *Weltanschauung* to America's elite, a speculation Williams frequently entertained in private letters. But perhaps Harrington had precisely coached Williams to do what he himself could not do or simply did not want to pursue further. The multitude of ways in which Harrington guided Williams's career and took enormous pride in its development gives good grounds for this conclusion.[12]

Finally, Harrington spent rare social time with the bright and ambitious Navy veteran, dropping by the Williams's apartment with his wife, Nancy, to talk about culture and history or sports or some other favorite topic. A future president of the University of Wisconsin who considered himself (according to persistent rumor) a serious prospect for a future Cabinet post, Harrington clearly had questions of power on his mind. That approach, as admiring young student and future American Studies notable David Noble has observed, was rare among scholars and especially radical ones. Williams, who freely remarked that he would one day have been an admiral if he had remained in the Navy, listened carefully.[13]

Hesseltine and Harrington had ample help in guiding Williams through the Progressive legacy toward new vistas. Colonialist Merrill Jensen created a school of young historians—the last Progressive historian to do so—sharing his view of the Articles of Confederation as the true democratic document, tragically overthrown by the centralizing Constitutional Convention. (Jensen's most noted protégé, Turner's grandson Jackson Turner Main, was another classmate of Williams's and yet another link to the historiographical legacy of the frontier.) Howard K. Beale, still another mentor, was a militant civil libertarian known to dramatize his cause by offering the Declaration of Independence *sans* title to passersby around the State House in downtown Madison to see if they would be willing to sign such an inflammatory document. Not by accident, Beale would soon be at work as editor of a memorial volume on Charles Beard, a most distinguished collection of essays by Richard Hofstadter, Max Lerner, Harold Laski, George S. Counts, and others. Another famous-to-be radical historian, Herbert G. Gutman, was Beale's research assistant.

These mentors all shared a penchant to see history as did Beard, a study of elites more than of social classes, and a study of "useable" history applicable to the need of the moment—from their viewpoint—to avoid another world war. At a methodological level, they also shared a deep commitment to the importance of the primary document. They felt a sort of aesthetic attraction to the *feel* of the document, examined with the belief that if properly viewed, it would yield up its secrets; and a firm confidence that great history could be built, brick by brick, from such documentation. These progressive-tradition Americanists gave Williams a framework or perhaps reinforced the one he had already intuited.

Williams also learned much from scholars indifferent to the Progressive tradition and conceptually far from the History Department. Economic historian Paul Knaplund, who had done so much to build the department, was a sympathetic scholar of the British Empire and gave Williams a framework for thinking about Empire in general. A later Williams called him "Madison's John Quincy Adams." English professor Fredrick Hoffman taught the novel, especially the radical novel. Paul Farmer, a brilliant but disillusioned former Marxist turned slightly cynical taught French history, did the basic historiography course, and imparted a sophisticated view of European ideologies such as Marxism and Freudianism, which few Americanists could then claim to grasp well.[14] Despite his formal politics, Farmer amply illustrated the appeal of European studies. Williams had actually considered, for a short time, a career in Russian history. He lacked the language skills, but more important, the doctrinaire cold-warrior Russianist at the University rejected out-of-hand Williams's skeptical intuitions about U.S. motives and U.S. responsibilities for world unrest. He would be a U.S. historian and a radical one at that. Yet Williams prided his graduate education as being marked by a dialogue with conservatives, the Socratic road to learning.

To Williams, more important by far than all the other non-Americanists was Hans Gerth. Harrington had advised Williams to minor outside history, and that may have been decisive in the young man's responding to the perceived theoretical deficiency. Williams chose the historical or dialectical sociologist, a brilliant but melancholy figure who had been repeatedly held back from promotion by the American-style empiricist sociologists around him and driven into a kind of internal exile. A German emigre and once a lesser-known member of the Frankfurt School, Gerth surveyed the totality of the social system's weight against free thought and activity. More than anyone else, he lent Williams an idiosyncratic Marxist social psychology and almost certainly a Weberian overview of system paralleling Williams's own admiration for Spinoza. Max Weber's influence, however indirect, offered additional clues to understanding the framework of a large and complex process. In later years, Williams simply described it as "the point of view of totality."[15]

Gerth directed the young man towards what Williams later called "a broad knowledge of the methodology of *Weltanschauung* (including serious study of Marx)" and helped him to apply it to foreign relations. Recuperating his Spinoza and reaching out for more, he responded to Marx as "a genius in social history and political economy," able to see "in one piece of evidence a set of relationships" at once economic, ideological, social, and political, at the root of "our alienation from our Humanity under capitalism." With this Marx, rather than the figure whose iron doctrines were purported to be guiding the Soviet Union, Gerth "took me by the hand . . . teased and pushed me into a confrontation with the central theory of reality into a manageable intellectual tool."[16]

Through Gerth, Williams became "deeply involved" with Hegel, Theodor Adorno, Max Horkheimer, Georg Lukacs, and philosopher William Dilthey, whose work actually explicated the notion of a worldview, or *Weltanschauung*. Sharing a bus bound for school, Williams sometimes saw Gerth reading a newspaper and then appearing with questions, based on his clippings, that he demanded his students solve by reading six or seven books in a single day. The sessions that followed were intense enough to be fresh in memory four decades later. So were the self-immersions in texts which posed "dialectical interacting world views" and the "tension" of an idea or concept "coming apart at the seams at midnight," practically demanding Williams stitch it back together in the wee hours of the morning.[17] According to Harrington, Gerth sent Williams soaring, while the job of the Americanists was to bring him back down to earth.[18]

It is more than likely that Gerth or Farmer directed Williams towards two important thinkers whose current works commanded considerable attention among those interested in large views of the world. Joseph Schumpeter, known in some circles as the "bourgeois Marx," was a sophisticated and somewhat cynical Austrian economist who found in the *Communist Manifesto* much that he could admire. Capitalism's impetus of "creative destruction," as Schumpeter wrote in *Capitalism, Socialism and Democracy* (1943), meant the replacement of the network of previous religious and secular, extra-familial ties with market rationality, when by any standard the "stock exchange is a poor substitute for the Holy Grail." In a political conclusion that Schumpeter would share with modern liberals and that Williams disdained, the Austrian insisted that ordinary people could never be trusted with the initiative that great leadership of nations and world society required. Schumpeter took no pleasure in the inability of capitalism to meet the test of pervasive social crisis; he simply expected some authoritarian form of socialism to triumph. Despite these differences, Williams often said that he found in Schumpeter someone he could admire.[19]

The other current thinker would very likely have been Karl Polyani, whose massively influential volume, *The Great Transformation*, appeared in 1944. The Polish economist elaborated a *sui generis* "organic rationality" to explain the evolution of capitalism from feudalism, and thus to explain the modern state and economy. Capitalism was not simply the latest social system but, as Schumpeter would have said, one completely unique in its social effects. "Modernity" signified disintegration of face-to-face working relations with a web of government systems and atomistic economic actors, together making a moral society increasingly difficult to maintain.

The sixteenth-century English "enclosures" which pushed the poor off the land for sheepherding prompted Tudor and Stuart kings to create labor regulations, church responsibilities for paupers, and other accommodations previewing the modern welfare state. People who felt themselves owed a living, however miserable, lost the conceptual means to grasp their own social significance and the role of labor in creating value. As mechanization continued, the historic traditions of guilds and of self-sufficient classes of farmers almost disappeared from memory. A society demoralized at its lower levels could hardly resist the completely commodified economy. The masses acquiesced helplessly or shared the dream of the emerging middle class in a market utopianism where competition of all against all would somehow become the happy route to freedom and prosperity.

Polyani could readily accept the Marxist view of twentieth-century irrationality, highlighted by horrifyingly destructive nationalism. But Marxism isolated the economic factor, in his view, when economics and culture had to be analyzed together. Classes might be seen better as functional groups distributing responsibilities. At their most productive, they struggled not for all-out class victory but to preserve and transform an increasingly self-destructive social order. Polyani looked, personally, to the promise of a moral tradition blending Christianity and socialism.[20]

Thinkers like Schumpeter and Polyani spoke to the felt need of Williams and his fellow graduate students for more theory than the Progressive historians could supply. As Warren Susman observed, they also had a gnawing sensation that the framework of political Progressivism was hopelessly outdated. These two gaps had much in common with each other. The frontier, which had supplied the key mechanism for the interpretation of American civilization by Turner and Beard, had rapidly faded into the historical distance. Neither the New Deal (regarded by liberal intellectuals as the culmination of national political evolution) nor the war, nor America's newly predominant place in the world could be satisfactorily and comprehensively explained from the older view.[21]

Grappling for a better methodological handle, they needed a larger view of culture, of modernization, and of social psychology. Their beloved U.S. history teachers could not offer much of this. But these professors were interested in such subjects themselves and eager for dialogue arising out of their students' challenges. Williams once described his fellow students (including the likes of future notables John Higham, David Shannon, Harvey Goldberg, and Wayne Cole, as well as a handful of eager intellectuals who never found a place in academic life) as "uncommonly intelligent and intellectually daring," enthusiastic about discussing historical questions inside the classroom and out, and especially hungry for fresh perspectives. No wonder that Harrington, Williams's faculty role model, remembered the graduate students as being the *most* influential on Williams's young intellectual development.[22]

They had an emotional support for this activity that they might not have had anywhere else in the country. The university and the Madison community together had also remained, in some ways, within a curious Beardian time warp. Defenders of free thought and of resistance against the national juggernaut state, Madisonians seemed at once quaintly outdated and yet almost recklessly courageous in the face of cold-war pressures. University administrations generally tolerated and even mildly encouraged the presence of left-wing dissenters. Otherwise conservative legislators had often agreed, despite recurrent grumbling, that the spirit of free opinion was a proven incentive to attract top figures in sciences and the liberal arts. Selective repression, such as the intimidation of controversial faculty and denial of facilities to controversial speakers, had taken place in times of national stress such as the 1919-21 Red Scare, but was considerably less severe than at most schools. And it always tapered off after a mood of national calm returned.

Williams often reminded younger generations of radicals that the teachers he admired and the colleagues he later embraced had not been so much radical or even political as simply the best in their fields. But the progressive, radical, and bohemian elements also had an unquestionable leavening effect. University President John Bascom, one of the nineteenth-century founders of the campus free-thought tradition, had embraced the Knights of Labor and woman suffrage before being cashiered by the Regents for opposing the state's liquor ring. Labor economist Richard T. Ely, fired by Johns Hopkins for his radicalism, espoused Christian Socialism in the Gilded Age. Twenty years later, "Fighting Bob" LaFollette built his brain trust here, a decade before he led the doomed Congressional resistance to U.S. entry into World War I. Close by, the daily *Madison Capitol Times* was launched in 1917 around an upsurge of popular antiwar sentiment. *LaFollette's Magazine* (later, the *Progressive*) kept the faith alive in hard times for the resisters against the monopolies and the big state that served corporate interests.[23]

Documenting the life and labor of ordinary people, the State Historical Society (practically an extension of the History Department) meanwhile rapidly outpaced the Ivy Leagues in the amassing of socioeconomic data. And this was not merely compulsive gathering. The first University of Wisconsin historian of note, Henry S. Allen, had himself collected slave songs in the Reconstruction South, in what might be described as early ethnographic or oral-history fieldwork. A succession of scholars, including labor economics giant John R. Commons, arranged for the Historical Society to gather an unprecedented volume of labor and radical materials. The democratic intent could not be misunderstood: the lives of ordinary people were *worth* studying.

Campus life was also unorthodox from the bottom upward. By the late 1920s, out-of-state Jewish undergraduates made their presence evident at Alexander Meikeljohn's Experimental College, where they imparted a distinctly bohemian and sometimes politically radical undertone to the usual Big Ten spirit. Student strikes might have rocked the 1930s campus but University President Glenn Frank personally greeted the strikers and declared the demonstrations a "peace assembly." The *Daily Cardinal*, the student newspaper, traditionally tended to be the voice of the avant-garde, liberal, and even radical students. A handful of well-liked professors, themselves bohemians or at least libertarians, encouraged the radical youngsters and drew the fire of perpetually enraged conservatives in the state legislature. By the late 1940s all this was a hallowed but also a living tradition, like the student dining cooperatives where left-wingers and other youngsters with small incomes gathered to share meals and talk about politics and culture.[24]

Williams the small-town Iowan with radical and modest bohemian leanings fit in easily here, even as he focused his energies upon his studies. Admitted for 1947, with his way partially paid by the GI Bill, Williams had to take extra undergraduate history courses to complete his preparation. Recalled to California in mid-semester for a last Navy physical and release, he left Jeannie behind to attend his classes and take notes. She loyally withdrew from the classroom once he was firmly enrolled, although she had been urged to continue her own studies. By spring 1948, Williams was extremely proud to be part of a great institution. It stimulated him, and it also gave him a sense of security.

He and Jeannie moved to an apartment next to one of the giant fraternity houses on campus, living just above another future campus legend, football star and later athletic director Elroy "Crazy Legs" Hirsh. Jeannie supported both herself and Williams by working full-time as a secretary in the extension school and later in the YMCA. Apart from an occasional play or concert they could share, the scant luxuries—notably the books he purchased for his own studies and separate interests—went to him just as they had at his boyhood home. They both pushed hard for him to race through his courses and his dissertation, graduating early to make up for time lost and in order to enjoy a post-military, post-college life together. He took his degree in a remarkable three years, en route impressing his professors with a seriousness toward his teaching, but even more with his ability to convey to undergraduates his enthusiasm about ideas.[25]

In the little time they had for extra activities, they made a small circle of friends, Bill's fellow history graduate students along with the Harringtons. They also went to church. Having been active in Presbyterian youth circles in Atlantic, Jeannie succeeded in interesting Bill during a wartime visit home, thanks to a dynamic young minister. Williams had himself baptized, and thereafter attended Sunday services irregularly. He evidently considered himself a sort of Christian socialist. During a summer visit to Madison in the early 1950s, he even gave a sermon at the new Unitarian Center, in a building designed by Frank Lloyd Wright.

They could not entirely avoid the glare of campus political life and its various cultural by-products. McCarthyism (not yet named) had begun to settle over American life. Hollywood moguls declared their unwillingness to hire anyone who refused to sign a loyalty oath. President Harry Truman moved somewhat hesitantly at first, then with increasing speed towards a massively coordinated attack upon suspected communists, homosexuals, radical dissenters, and potential dissenters in government jobs, labor, and public life. Colleges and universities, as purported centers of interracialism, homosexuality, and communist sympathies, received special scrutiny from the FBI and various other investigative agencies.

The local effects were oddly muted in part because Senator Joseph McCarthy was reluctant to attack an institution so close to home: such action could cost him votes and financial support. But several visiting scholars, including the famed German exile composer Hanns Eisler, found themselves barred from speaking in university facilities. A handful of young professors were also denied tenure on clearly political grounds. In many other places, opponents of such actions were intimidated into silence. Not infrequently, the FBI actually set up an office on campus and worked hand-in-hand with the administration to stalk and eliminate suspected dissenters. In Madison, however, even as state legislators sniffed and growled at purportedly subversive professors misleading youth, any hints of actual censorship and retribution met a volley of protests. Distinguished scholars on the faculty, including historians Merle Curti and Howard Beale, rushed into print to protect civil liberties. College administrators made mollifying noises, while trying to hold off the hotheads in the legislature. Student letters in the *Cardinal* warned that "we may kiss our liberties goodbye," and openly ridiculed the campus redhunters for sniffing out borscht and vodka (i.e., Russian agents) on every side.[26]

The crackdown intensified on other campuses across the country, but avowed Marxist discussion groups still met openly in University of Wisconsin facilities. Leftwing folksingers made regular appearances, and *Golden Boy*, leftist Clifford Odets's sardonically anticommercial drama, was staged amid great fanfare (the Williamses, too, enjoyed Odets enormously). Vintage antifascist European and American cinema, in an only slightly subtextual response to threatened fascism at home, played regularly at the student union. Like the 1948 election of socialist Frank Zeidler to the mayorality of Milwaukee, this was part of a definite anomaly in American life, but for the participants a happy one.[27]

Campus antiwar sentiment, which aroused the vitriolic denunciation of conservatives and cold war liberals alike, was pushed toward the margins at Wisconsin, but not quite beyond them. Visiting candidate Harry Truman, claiming to represent the New Deal tradition against the impending Republican backlash, met overflow crowds shortly before the fall elections. Yet Socialist Party presidential candidate Norman Thomas (introduced by

William Hesseltine) could still fill a good-sized hall, as could guitar-playing Idaho Senator Glen Taylor, running mate of Progressive Party candidate Henry Wallace. Compulsory ROTC was vigorously debated and rejected in a student straw poll. Most important, teachers who fled repression elsewhere, in Europe and New Hampshire alike, found a home in Madison and, especially if tenured, kept their voice. Gerth, who had coached the radical sociologist C. Wright Mills during the early 1940s, stressed in campus talks the desirability of planned economies in a democratically socialist postwar Europe.[28]

The intellectually curious and sympathetic Williams, notably absent from any such activities, made a crucial distinction between active politics and teaching so early, and so easily, that he hardly seemed to realize for decades that it had been final. Fellow graduate students and mentors remembered him in these years as a "gentle sort among the extroverts competing for the attention of the faculty," as Harrington put it. He opened up, if at all, only among close friends. Drawn to undergraduate students, he spent his public passions teaching. Merle Curti remembered him talking in private often and easily about Russia, but not about any real or potential American radical movement. David Noble recalls him blistering John Dewey and the tradition of Pragmatism as capable only of leading to superficial reform—as if Williams were seeking his own, more radical tradition. Williams still had no apparent particular interest in the history of U.S. diplomacy, but it seems clear that he would be drawn to a field which allowed a political slant but also some personal distance.[30]

There was still another reason, more idiosyncratic, for Williams's political inactivity. He and Jeannie had remained registered Republicans from their Iowa days, absentee voters still plugged into their home state's issues. From that unique perspective, they could appreciate Henry Wallace, whose family's magazine, *Wallace's Farmer*, had played a major role in Iowa life for generations and who personally visited Simpson College often. But such Midwestern sentimentalism played poorly alongside the issues surrounding the Wallace campaign of 1948. Conducting a fierce red-baiting campaign, Truman and his allies successfully drowned out what Wallace had to say about American life, making him into a mere stalking horse for Russian tyranny. Madison's own cold war liberals jumped on the Truman bandwagon, while a few professors joined Hesseltine in registering their affection for the Norman Thomas campaign, an acknowledged lost cause. The debacle of the elections rendered the progressive political tradition a memory which neither Republicans nor Democrats would now acknowledge. Thousands of other former GIs, many of them with young children, were like the Williamses, spending little time in campus political activities so that they could get through their courses and on to careers as quickly as possible. That said, they were still probably the most democratic and aggressive undergraduate body in history to that point and long after. Coming from virtually all social classes and groups, they had acquired a collective self-confidence during the war, and also a certain skeptical disrespect for authority. They—or at least most of them—doubted that they could stop the express train of history. Williams concluded later that they had ambivalently accepted the privatization of life that middle-class consumerism offered them. But they sincerely wanted to know what had brought the world from victory over fascism to the precipice of another and potentially more catastrophic war.[31]

If the hopeful elements in the intellectual radicalism sustained since the 1930s were faltering badly in the face of the cold war and postwar military-backed prosperity, if old versions of socialism seemed discredited as capitalism offered consumer pleasures galore, the prospects for a radical critique remained very much alive. Nowhere was this more true than in diplomatic history. At the historical moment when communist sympathies had become taboo and liberals celebrated the cultural pluralism of American society, Williams chose to focus on the power of corporations to control the perceptions and realities of international policies.[32]

2

Williams's master's essay and dissertation, his first two sustained pieces of writing, bore out the richness of his observations. He attempted to understand how the corporate-owned press limited the flow of available information on foreign affairs and reshaped data according to its own editors' interpretations; he also sought to interpret how perceptive and brave individuals could break through the web of disinformation, offering challenges to reigning diplomatic policies.

"McCormick Reports on Russia: A Study of News and Opinion on Russia in the *Chicago Tribune* from 1917-1921" (1948), grew out of his experience at newspaper work and his interest in responses to American views of revolutionary events abroad. Not surprisingly, he found the *Tribune* so editorially biased that it "ignored facts which would have modified this extreme hostility," contributing "both to the ignorance and error of American opinion and . . . exerci[sing] a negative influence on the possibility of the peaceful co-existence of the United States and Russia."

Tracing the controlling influences on the *Tribune*, Williams pointed to the internal "revolution of 1914" which placed Colonel McCormick at the helm. The *Tribune* had not been staunchly pro-war before 1914, but once committed, beat the drum for "virile" patriotism and declared, as early as 1915, the central conflict in American life as one "between individualism and communism." By 1917 the paper sharpened its knives against Bolshevism, and thereafter engaged in wild exaggeration and the dissemination of outright falsehoods about Russia and the Russian revolutionaries. Soon, the Industrial Workers of the World, incongruously became, by the words of *Tribune* writers, agents of Lenin within the U.S.; all manner of political repression was justified as patriotic duty. Havoc in Russia was attributed entirely to Marxist ideas, as revolutionary turmoil would be so often in the twentieth century. Finally, in 1919, the *Tribune* editors trained their hopes upon armed intervention in Russia, under whatever excuse could be mustered. As Williams might have added, the paper had established a prime motive for all future U.S. interventions.[33]

Much of the rest of the master's thesis documented the campaigns of distortion and falsification—Williams called the final chapter "The Poverty of Philosophy," after a manuscript by the young Marx—which took an increasingly racial character. Thus Bolsheviks became "hordes of barbarians, semi-Asiatic, pressing toward central Europe" aiming to "destroy . . . western civilization of Christianity, nationalism and property, the fountain of life as we live it." The *Tribune* editors thereby deprived their readers of any unbiased opportunity to learn about communism, or Marxism. They insisted that human behavior could not be based upon any motive but private gain. In the end, the paper identified as "red" any protest against its own particular interpretation of "nationalism, religion, political faith, and economics."[34]

In seeking a foil for the *Tribune's* disinformation campaign, Williams identified a protagonist for his dissertation and a twentieth-century radical after his own heart. "Raymond Robins and Russian-American Relations 1917-1938" (1950) told the story of a Midwestern progressive politician who devoted his life to Russian-American rapprochement. A descendent of early settlers, Robins grew up poor, became a coal miner and struggled to organize a union, and later caught gold-rush fever in Alaska and became a successful executive. Discovering rampant corruption in American business and political life, he shifted his goals from personal success to municipal reform. Relocating to Chicago, he emerged as a prominent reformer, close to Jane Addams and several leading philanthropists. He also quietly bankrolled socialist journalism. But his strongest sentiments ran to the social gospel, and he became one of Theodore Roosevelt's staunch supporters in the Progressive Party campaign of 1912.

But the war marked a turning point for Robins. From inside the philanthropic quarter of the elite, he worked to ease suffering as best he could. Part of the Red Cross Commission to revolutionary Russia, he felt at first an intuitive revulsion to the Bolsheviks and resolved to assist Alexander Kerensky. But he was impressed with Trotsky and eventually came to see the Bolsheviks as the only possible force for a stable government that could feed the people. The fact that Alexander Gumberg, Robins's translator and assistant, was the brother of a devoted Bolshevik hardly damaged the case.

Robins thus worked squarely against the Wilson administration and its furious efforts to mount a counterrevolutionary international crusade. But Robins also placed himself in close cooperation with major Wall Street figures who wanted to do business with the new government. By the 1920s, advising isolationist senator William Borah and sustaining close relations with Warren Harding and Calvin Coolidge, Robins sought to effect Russian–U.S. cooperation against Japanese expansionism in the Far East and against the rise of a resurgent German nationalism. Repeatedly stymied, he nonetheless influenced the Roosevelt administration's recognition of Russia in 1933. However he could not bring about a sufficient American desire for reconciliation in time to stave off Stalin's retreat into isolation and a desperate nonaggression pact with Hitler in 1939. Perhaps no force on earth, except a Franklin Roosevelt willing to confront prejudices and risk supportive alliances at home and abroad, could have accomplished this goal. But Robins was uniquely placed among world observers, American political figures, and businessmen to see how the world had again and again lost opportunities for peace.[35]

To get the full story, Williams made contact with Robins and interviewed him at length in 1949. Robins was, not surprisingly, eager to talk to a rare sympathetic graduate student in a society where any openness toward Russian experience had become inherently suspicious. He was also ready to turn over large quantities of his own documents. Williams buttressed his arguments with a thick folder of evidence—materials from the State Department papers of Wilson's Secretary of State, Robert Lansing; and the papers of William Borah, Woodrow Wilson, and others. Following Robins's logic, Williams insisted that even at the onset of the cold war, "the fact of German aggression and Russia's fear of Japanese encroachment provided a significant opportunity for Allied representatives to conclude an agreement with the Soviets." Tragically, "pride, fear, personal and official antagonism" had intervened.[36] Reexamining the intrigues of diplomatic history, Williams convinced himself that detente had nearly been achieved at a crucial moment in world history. The Munich agreement of Hitler and Chamberlain, and the appeasement of fascism by the antirevolutionary Western governments which opened the road to a second world war, had not been an inevitable consequence of the 1910s-30s. In a larger sense, the American twentieth century did not *have* to be one long antirevolutionary crusade.

Anticommunism had its way of course, and catastrophic events ensued. Williams's scholarship challenged the confrontational mood of the late 1940s. Eastern Europe had slipped into the Soviet orbit, and the last piece in the postwar puzzle was about to fall into place. Harry Truman had more than honored Republican Senator Vandenberg's advice to "scare hell out of" the American public to prepare them for unprecedented military expenditures and perhaps World War III. Between the superpowers, virtually all other possibilities had been excluded.

It was a moment for anyone, let alone someone of Williams's inclinations, to feel like a reluctant civilian combatant in an unwanted clash of titans. One part of the world still seemed, however, to be moving toward a higher form of society. The British Labour Party, taking over from war hero but dislikeable peace leader Winston Churchill, promised massive social reconstruction. The Labourites finally accomplished little more than an advanced welfare state. But they genuinely frightened the English wealthy class (and U.S. leaders) by threatening to go further. They also encouraged British workers and left-leaning intellectuals throughout the English-speaking world with the hope that they might expand their agenda. Britain was, then, easily the most exciting place for a socialist in the English-speaking world. Williams urgently wanted to go and learn, if only for a few months.

He applied for and accepted a scholarship to join a ten-week seminar at the University of Leeds on the Labour government's economics. The scholarship did not include all travel or living expenses, however, and an ever-dutiful Jeannie remained behind to supply the necessary funds. Williams, unburdened by any sense of guilt, had a wonderful time. Most of the Labour cabinet came up at some point during his stay, to lecture to and discuss programs with the seminar. A. J. Brown, an economist who ran the class, pointed toward decentralization as an alternative model to the nationalization of "sick" industries, like coal, then underway in Britain (and saddling Labour with impossible responsibilities).

Here in Leeds, Williams also received in person another dose of the non-Marxist but Marxist-influenced, non-Communist but also anti–cold war logic that had earlier reached him in G. D. H. Cole's work. Facing the cold war world, Cole repeatedly stressed, in ethical terms, how the Socialist movement *should* conduct itself and how the world *should* be. Freedom, individuality, equality, democracy, and fellowship created a continuity and web of values between them, antithetical to the perniciously individualistic values of capitalism. Cole's avowed Utopianism (calming, he insisted, the "Bolshevik soul" with the "Fabian muzzle") would realize itself in the "making of good societies."[37] Cole also stressed the importance of decentralization, or "devolution," as a step toward a more functional division of government's responsibilities so as to reduce the control over the citizen's life. He echoed Karl Polyani's plea to strip the class mysticism from Marxian pronouncements and to find an ethical antidote for capitalism's destruction of the common spirit.

Cole, a lesser minister in the British Labour government, had precious little opportunity to explore these possibilities in action. The other and more dominant impulse of Fabianism, toward a paternalistic State overseeing the welfare of the middle classes and the poor, fed into the worst of Labour's experiment with power. A watchful U.S. State Department, feeding Europe with the Marshall Plan and simultaneously warning against any move toward a much discussed "third force" of democratic anticapitalism, would not have permitted the Europeans anything more radical in any case. And yet Cole remained, for a certain type of Anglo-American socialist, a reminder of what might have been. Socialism *could* be based upon voluntary mixtures of collectivism and individualism, decentralized and cautious of state impositions. Thirty years later, the kindest compliment that Williams could hand out to a libertarian, anti-state think tank in Washington was that it represented the historical legacy of guild socialism.[38]

Williams had reportedly told Fred Harrington that he was going to England to "study Schumpeter," and that raises yet another intriguing possibility for the trip. Schumpeter, apart from his other theoretical inclinations, proposed that imperialism had relatively little to do with economics. Rather, he believed that it reflected the determination of conservative elites to find outlets abroad for domestic tensions. Schumpeter's thesis, pursued by several generations of German scholars, actually had an influence on Beard, and in turn, Beard's influence went through Williams to the younger Germans.[39] By refuting Lenin but offering a different and no less charitable description of the imperialist impulse, Schumpeter had helped make possible Williams's later perspective on the "open door" as capitalism's pseudo-solution to the threat of its demise.

As in other matters, the Labour Party was not about to adopt this or any critique of imperialism. The formal British Empire, like its French counterpart, was dissolving as nationalist movements grew. But the West's control over much of Africa and Asia would simply pass from London to Wall Street and the White House, maintained by financial aid or CIA operations. Russian sponsorship of anti-imperialist national movements projected the cold war around the globe in an endless waste of resources and ideals.[40]

Foreshadowing the heroic efforts of his later friend and fellow historian E. P. Thompson to break through the divisions still separating Eastern and Western Europe during the 1970s-80s, Williams took part in the last international peace conference of students from all of Europe. Meeting together in Paris at the end of summer 1949, they expressed a hope for amity that had been denied in both camps of cold war mobilization. As he must have guessed, his participation as a delegate (arranged from Leeds) invited just the kind of suspicion that fell upon so many other professors and graduate students at the time. Undaunted, Williams returned to Wisconsin in the face of the cold war, determined to apply the lessons he had learned.

3

Harrington arranged Williams's first major appearance at an academic gathering: the American Historical Association meeting of 1950, for a symposium on foreign policy. Williams's denunciation of American aggressiveness seemed to stun the audience. At such a moment, with the cold war turning hot in Korea, Williams seemed to many listeners either a spokesman for a hated national enemy or, more likely, a young man foolish enough to throw away his career on the most unpopular ideas imaginable.

Just a year earlier, AHA president Conyers Read had warned in his presidential address against historians thinking of themselves as "free agents." They should, rather, "accept and endorse such controls as are essential for the preservation of our way of life." Merle Curti, against whom this blast had been mainly directed, and Howard Beale, against whom it might as well have been aimed, answered with a stinging defense of historians' right and duty to write what they saw as the truth.[41] Madison professors and the British experience together gave Williams something more, or reinforced a determination deep within himself.

He had reasons for his self-confidence that his views might be taken seriously. His essay, "A Second Look at Mr. X," rebutted the theory of containment anonymously set out by George F. Kennan in a famed *Foreign Affairs* essay of 1947. Submitted to *Foreign Affairs* through a third party, Williams's rebuttal was much discussed by the editors at that journal until finally rejected as too sharp a criticism of the distinguished diplomat's views. Ironically, Kennan himself had meanwhile backed off from his "Mr. X" conclusions, convinced that a permanent threat of military confrontation with the Soviet Union was a terrible error.

The essay had been submitted, without his knowledge, by the editors at Rinehart, publishers of his first book, *American–Russian Relations, 1781-1947* (1952), for which it was originally written as a coda. An incisive and, for the time, extremely bold work, it practically invented the field of "cold war revisionism." During the early 1950s only a few other serious writers contested prevailing cold-war scholarship. Carl Marzani's *We Can Be Friends* (1952) was written behind bars by a victim of McCarthyism jailed on Contempt of Congress charges for refusal to testify. I. F. Stone's *Hidden History of the Korean War* (1953) actually inspired the establishment of Monthly Review Press because no other publisher would touch Stone's questioning of the war's causes and its course.[42] It is safe to say that Walter Lippmann's *The Cold War* (1947) was the only widely available critique challenging the

Truman administration claim that diplomacy with the Soviet Union had become impossible. "Cold War" studies tended otherwise to be left to the field of international relations, a field dominated by refugees and "Sovietologists" professionally hostile toward the Soviet Union, as well as by those close to the foreign services and to the current views of containment. Save for Williams, U.S. historians hardly played a role yet.

*American-Russian Relations*, a cautiously phrased but distinct challenge to accepted orthodoxy, was written with the undertone of a scholar who wished to focus the reader's attention on the historical backdrop of controversial current political questions. Compared to the style of Williams's later works or even his MA and PhD theses, its measured prose bespoke the dangers of the times. He could put across a message very similar to that of his dissertation, he seemed to suggest, only by stressing the lesser-known details of the subject.

It was above all else a remarkable performance in research strategies. *American-Russian Relations* drew upon a wealth of new material from official government documents and extensive private collections of the papers (some key sources gathered himself, from Robins and Gumberg) and personal interviews with such formerly high-ranking State Department figures and diplomats as Cordell Hull, William C. Bullitt, and Henry L. Stimson. Fred Harvey Harrington had helped make the necessary appointments with former State Department notables. But putting himself forward as a decorated Naval veteran and curious young scholar, Williams successfully drew out these men in the fashion of a skilled oral historian.

Williams thus detailed the opinions and activities of U.S. politicians, businessmen, and private individuals as well as diplomats involved in Russian affairs between 1900 and 1939. Less than fifty pages concerned events before 1904, and only seventy dealt with events following the Russian Revolution. Fully half of *American–Russian Relations* focused on World War I and the Bolshevik Revolution, i.e., the decisive moment when change might have taken place but did not. He stopped in 1939 because of the national security regulations placed on documents from World War II and the cold war. But within his scope, he wrote as if he had met the men as equals.

From the days of Secretary of State John Hay to the present, American policies toward Russia had remained remarkably consistent, notwithstanding the state form or the particular personalities of the two regimes. The influence of U.S. financial and industrial interests had been at all key points central. Expounding for the first time on Frederick Jackson Turner's "Frontier Thesis" and the expansionist ideas of Brooks Adams, Williams articulated his notion of an "Open Door" imperialism: the strong belief among policymakers and many other Americans that without ever-expanding markets and places for investment, the economy and society at large would surely collapse.

Thus, Williams found that after a long period of "loose and informal entente" with the Czarist empire, American economic interests seemingly collided with Russian interests. Such magnates as E. H. Harrington and strategists as Willard Straight aimed to build railroads in Manchuria, a challenge to the aims of Russia in northeast Asia after 1895. Presidents Theodore Roosevelt and William Howard Taft refused Russian offers of cooperation against Japanese expansion in Asia in order to play the two off against each other. A short-sighted strategy at the time, it foreshadowed later U.S. unwillingness to combine with the Russians against the Japanese forays of the 1930s and thus to forestall the terrible price paid in the Pacific (not to speak of the Korean peninsula and Chinese and Japanese mainland) during World War II. Williams did not say so, but he obviously spoke with the memory of his own battle days fresh in mind. Other veterans who became historians had by and large accepted the inevitability of the war; Williams had not.

The Russian Revolution understandably exacerbated anxieties on all sides, but American leaders had never seriously considered cooperation with the new regime as a way to relieve their worries. Indeed, Williams dated the cold war precisely to Woodrow Wilson's decision for military intervention in support of the dreaded White armies, intimate allies of royalists and anti-Semites. Most officials, especially at the State Department, had been staunchly, even unreasonably anti-Bolshevik from the beginning. But a number of well-informed observers, most notably Robins, had clearly pointed out that the Bolsheviks could not be driven from power, enjoyed great popular support, and were flexible enough to accept amicable relations with the West.

Williams retold the sad story of Robins's failures to persuade Wilson's successors, who, like Wilson, expected or vainly hoped that Bolshevism would somehow collapse. He recast from his dissertation the images of business groups and individuals eager to participate in Russian economic reconstruction and urging early recognition. Here, too, Williams recalled Robins's Republican allies, Senators William Borah and Hiram Johnson, who argued for a similar course on security as well as economic grounds.

The coda, "A Second Look at Mr. X.," spelled out the major conclusions and took risks avoided in the rest of the book. Kennan's unwillingness to credit the Russians' desire and need for security from 1917 onward (or even their attempt, through much of this period, to woo Washington) fatally undercut his logic. He could not perceive that Japanese and German activities could pose threats to Soviet security but insisted that Moscow threatened an America armed with the only atomic weapons in the world.

Kennan, at his most level-headed, advised a waiting game. But "freedom is not nurtured by nations preparing for war." Such a waiting game, Williams insisted, was the real treason to the ordinary people of the planet.

In pursuing Kennan's formulation of containment, Williams insisted, American leaders had conceded that Marx had been right: capitalism could not live with a specter of competition, even peaceful competition. By offers of cooperation and of encouragement to modify the Communist system into a political democracy, we might still prove the German master to be wrong.[43]

The reception of *American-Russian Relations* from the scholarly journals to the *New York Times* confirmed the value of Williams's first book. Almost all the critics praised his extensive research, although some felt that he had concentrated too much on economic interests. His political judgments also proved disturbing. Reviewers questioned, for example, whether an alliance with the Russians would have worked out better than closer cooperation with the Japanese in East Asia. Many other scholars, then and later, simply denied that Wilson intervened in Russia to crush the Bolsheviks, insisting that the actual reasons were more complex (but offering no convincing counter-theory). Few could accept Williams's plea for closer relations with the Soviet Union either before or after World War II. In their eyes, he had too easily overlooked the nefarious character of the Soviet regime and its aggressive designs. Hugh Seton-Watson, the first of many British scholars to take Williams very seriously, complained that he seemed for all his research to be "extraordinarily innocent of the way that foreign policy is made." Williams was not so much victim of the "illusions of Marxism," Seton-Watson suggested, as reflecting the American "anti-tycoon" tradition of blaming irresponsible millionaires for their national dilemmas.[44]

Writing in the *New York Times*, Dexter Perkins valued the book's detailed treatment of economic interests and admitted it "useful to know" that certain State Department interests had been ideologically fixed against Bolshevism from the beginning. He considered most of Williams's other conclusions debatable, especially the "dependency" of Russians as allies and associates. Those American leaders who actually wanted to get along, he argued, had been thwarted by "Russian obstructionism."[45] In the same vein, the *American Historical Review* found the book "decidedly uneven," with "infinite detail on numerous relatively unimportant items" but "not the answer to the need for a survey of relations between the two countries." The *Pacific Historical Review*, admitting that Williams's "many sweeping and undocumented statements" might possibly be true, nevertheless required "more adequate proof." The *Mississippi Valley Historical Review* praised the author's skillful tracing of economic rivalries in Asia, while not losing sight of many other factors, such as anti-Semitism in Czarist Russia. If

Williams's tone was at times "petulant and abusive," his interpretations nevertheless remained "within the bounds of scholarly comment." The *Indiana Magazine of History*, more typically cold war in its response, found the book "turbid and tendentious," an attempt "to present *Othello* without Iago," i.e., the protagonist United States without the villain, Russia.[46]

Catholic historians, at the time heavily under the sway of McCarthyism, were probably the most distressed. A Georgetown scholar pronounced the book a "failure" in every important respect. Williams had ignored or slighted "the innumerable Soviet violations of . . . legal and moral principles." For a Boston College professor, likewise, the "philosophy of communism, the imperatives of the third international," and the eagerness for "conversion by revolution" rendered amicable relations utterly impossible. St. Louis University's William A. Nolan conceded that the *Daily Worker*'s praise for the book did not necessarily make Williams a "party member [or] international sympathizer," but did "cast suspicion upon [his] objectivity." School libraries would "do well not to clutter up their shelves with books of this sort."[47]

Conversely, left-wing scholars, along with the effusive communist press, eagerly endorsed the volume. Richard Van Alstyne, another rare precursor of revisionist diplomatic history, called Williams a "forthright and penetrating" scholar, both "honest and courageous." He had, however, ignored the degree of "sentimentalism, missionary zeal and sheer naivete" involved in making policy, overemphasizing the economic content. British socialist E. H. Carr had likewise "nothing but praise" for the "real and original contribution" that Williams made.[48] The *Daily Worker*, the major public expression of a heavily persecuted Communist Party, USA, headlined its literary page "Crisis Laid to Anti-Soviet Policy by Oregon University Professor's Book." A stirring review described Williams as "one who faces facts with both courage and honesty," and proposed that "many more Americans" would "be able to struggle against a new war by making known the facts in Professor Williams's book—the facts which will destroy the Big Lie of 'Soviet Aggression.'"[49]

While few scholars could accept Williams's major suggestion that the U.S. should have established a closer relationship with the Soviet Union, few treated *American-Russian Relations* as Communist propaganda. Very likely many more professors, like Berkeley political scientist Ernest Haas, found it "refreshing and reassuring" to discover an author "willing to state the true implications of his source material" at a time of "rapidly vanishing tolerance" for research that did "not happen to fit the ideological needs" of the society.[50] Many others probably lacked the opportunity or the self-confidence to put forward such views themselves, but admired Williams's doing so.

Compared to his later and far more controversial works, *American-*

*Russian Relations* foregrounded the author's research. Williams complained in a letter several years afterward that he took little pleasure in writing monographs, already felt he had done his share, and wanted to turn to the extended essay as his favored form. Only once more, in the *Roots of the Modern American Empire* (1969), did he engage in similarly extensive archival work, and this book too was widely praised for its scholarship.

Other critics of the cold war pleaded for peace. But only Williams offered this peculiar "What If?" twist (also the most characteristically Williamsesque stroke of the book). While cold-war liberal writers drew a line, as he would say later, from Marx to Lenin to Stalin, Williams tried to encourage his readers to think the matter through in reverse, back to the origins of the conflict. Americans, regardless of economic station, who had real confidence in their system, he suggested, could only welcome an intellectual challenge offered in lieu of the arms race, proxy wars, and a potential thermonuclear disaster. Williams could not have expected to have his views adopted on Wall Street or in the White House. But he had struck upon the sort of appeal that American radicals had nearly forgotten, a way of speaking to conservative and patriotic instincts outside the adversarial framework of a common foreign enemy.

In the long run of two or three decades, *American-Russian Relations* practically invented the field of "cold-war revisionism." An area of scholarship that would eventually blossom into the central academic challenge of American politics during the 1960s-70s, it "revised" the orthodoxy of the cold-war specialists and with them the assumptions maintained from Truman (or perhaps from Woodrow Wilson) onward. Revisionism would also, from another viewpoint, become a major academic industry, with hundreds of monograph writers in various disciplines and thousands of teachers offering it to students of the 1970s-90s as the truth behind the national fictions.

The Williams of *American-Russian Relations* had established himself as the author of a well-researched and controversial scholarly volume, but nothing resembling the major figure he would become. He had hidden, or simply saw no reason to expose, the philosophical underpinnings of his study, or to reveal more of himself to the reader. In 1953, it is fair to say, he was just another promising young professor.

4

Looking back on the late 1940s, a crucial decade for a new generation of intellectuals, David Noble opines that the triumph of corporate capitalism as a national American ideology was not then nearly so secure as it would be a decade hence. "Marxism" in the communist sense had never really escaped marginalization in academic life. Just as a significant number of Marxist-influenced graduate students moved toward careers, cold-war pressures prompted them to camouflage their work; many of them abandoned it altogether. But the major liberal alternative to the Marxist view, the pluralist-universal model of consumer society, remained still inchoate. Grasping for a method to explain society and pursue their own research, most students found the remnants of the republican or Beardian tradition too contradictory and limiting to permit any reformulation of them as radical articles of faith. But most students were not William Appleman Williams.[51]

If Williams was strangely placed to improvise on socialist ideas, he was uniquely placed to revise radical notions of American democracy. A young man with a strong sense of leadership and a fascination with those in power, he had developed, he admitted later, remarkably little interest in such popular subjects for radical young scholars as "the negro in American society," or untarnished heroes like William Lloyd Garrison and Eugene V. Debs. Instead, Williams cultivated a strong and enduring interest in a certain type of dissonant, aristocratic mind which could consider the various options open to society on their merits. This was the discussion that Williams desperately wished to join, if it ever convened again.[52]

Writing a paper in William Hesseltine's seminar—the first piece of scholarship in which he took enduring pride—the young intellectual discovered for himself the immensely alluring observations of Brooks Adams. Scion of an American dynasty who in the nineteenth-century *fin de siècle* brilliantly grasped the *mentalité* of the time, Adams had squarely faced the available choices of the age. Bitterly disappointed by the unabashed materialism of the labor movement, Adams turned away from socialism, his first inclination, toward the promise of imperialism as a solution to the nation's political instability and recurrent depressions. Only something better—more exalted and more strongly suited to American idealism than Samuel Gompers's demand for a share of the pie—would have won over thinkers as vigorous as Adams. The intellectual who engaged in long talks in Cambridge with Frederick Jackson Turner after Turner's shift from Madison to Harvard happened to choose wrongly, but he was nevertheless a romantic melancholiac after Williams's own heart. Adams fortified himself against bad times and low morals with an exquisitely developed sense of irony. That might be the best option that American society offered.

Adams, seen perhaps through the lens of an imaginary radical Schumpeter, provided a model for the William Appleman Williams who all his life had believed in the "exceptional" or superior figure. He envisioned not sudden uprisings from below, but instead divisions among the ruling classes which would allow personal interventions and make possible grand political strategies at crucial moments. He could prepare the way for himself and for others by taking the elite at its word, judging its members fairly on their accomplishments within the existing system, and pointing out errors of logic and temperament. Their more intelligent members would listen to such a voice warning them against common disaster, if only in the collective self-interest of their class.[53]

Behind this quasi-aristocratic pose something else lay hidden, something more deeply personal and more enigmatic. Merle Curti, who had known the greatest U.S. historians of the age and not a few of the leading intellectuals, described Williams as heir to the "minor romantics," those who had carried on the dreams of the early nineteenth century in the face of diminished reality.[54] An important student of his, Thomas McCormick, describes Williams himself as an "incurable romantic."[55] Curti and others remember him evincing a wistful look, as if reality might not be at all that it seemed. Other friends said that specific issues appeared to assume a symbolic significance to Williams, just beyond explication. He was holding back something so securely that not even his wife Jeannie, an exceptionally intelligent and politically alert partner, could fathom it.[56]

Any number of reasons could restrain professor-to-be Williams from wearing his political heart on his sleeve. Perhaps this was a necessary guise for any radical during such a bleak moment of the century. No doubt it also reflected his personal experiences in Corpus Christi and in Madison: the dangers of open political activity and the rewards of finding a niche suitable to personal predilections. But Williams's small-town Protestant idealism and his background of childhood emotional insecurity, reshaped successively by the rigors of Annapolis, the horrors of war, and the driving need to make something special of his own life, could account for the energetic intellectualism and the personal elusiveness of the young man. Approaching his thirtieth birthday, he was still in the process of becoming the psychic offspring of that little boy from Iowa. He correctly anticipated glory, but he had a long, hard push ahead.

# A RADICAL PROFESSOR IN THE COLD WAR

BETWEEN 1950 AND 1957, William Appleman Williams gradually approached the *cause célèbre* status he would acquire in the following decade. In relative obscurity, he moved from job to job until he found a secure station from which he could issue manifestos, shaped as essays and reviews, well before his return to Madison in 1957. He worked at his teaching as he did at his writing, and raised the hackles of cold-war zealots in both liberal and conservative camps. He began to develop his celebrated persona, expressing positive and negative sides alike in his romantic, competitive character. He cultivated the *sui generis* literary style that later fascinated and puzzled readers, underpinning a typically Williamsesque analysis with an equally Williamsesque phraseology at once quaint, poignant, and as deeply American as the writer himself. Finally, and least obviously, he continued to work out his long view of societal development, the historical periodization and genetic examination of objective and subjective factors which would characterize *The Contours of American History*.

Williams's intellectual accomplishments were both remarkable and in some ways deceptive. He personally broadened diplomatic history in two ways: methodology and message. His extensive use of primary documents encouraged scholars to offer them to the scrutiny of nonspecialists in an age when foreign-policy elites (with their pet scholars) considered such materials unsuited for anyone outside a reliable coterie. Second, he deployed evidence and his own ruminations to pose large and troubling questions about deep continuities of U.S. policies over several centuries. Reigning foreign-policy specialists, assuming that American leaders were virtuous even in their Realpolitik, seemed stunned as well as outraged by William A. Williams's critical stance. These contributions, as much as the particular interpretations Williams set forth, made enemies aplenty in the academic world and the federal government. His presentation and their reception of his ideas threatened to disguise deeper purposes that transcended, in ways even his close readers often missed, the particular political divisions and parochial quarrels at hand.

The historical setting went a long way toward explaining the sources of Williams's complex analysis and also the possibilities of diplomatic history as a prestigious scholarly subject. Foreign news, as never before in peacetime, filled the daily press. While Americans stepped into the vacuum left behind by British and French spheres of influence from the Middle East to Africa and Asia, the success of the Marshall Plan in Western Europe seemed to presage the golden American future ahead. Even the Berlin crisis, threatening a third world war, provided Truman the welcome opportunity for a symbolic confrontation with the Soviet Union and the rationale to assume unchallenged leadership of the European allies under the new NATO banner.

Truman's own presidency did not experience the full benefit of his various cold-war moves, in large part because the Chinese Revolution and the Korean War unleashed forces that America could not control. By 1951 he had become a phenomenally disliked president for the second time in a few years, and yet he had launched (or perhaps merely propelled) apparently irreversible changes. Like the British Conservative government returning to office in 1953 after an era of welfare-state Labourism, the resurgent Republicans under Dwight Eisenhower accepted the broad outlines of Trumanism. Corporations ruled the economy virtually unchallenged, and business values ruled society. By the 1950s, however, they ruled at unprecedented levels of public funding and government participation.

The history of foreign policy, long considered the record of a mere exchange of diplomatic notes, now inevitably acquired a wider significance. International affairs had always been connected with domestic concerns, but never before had the connections been so dramatically outlined by events. In arguing that the battle against communism encompassed a conflict between ways of life, Truman had repeatedly warned against the loss of markets—just as his State Department promised assistance to governments which chose the American way over the competition. Despite some subtle differences of approach, Eisenhower's State Department continued this strategy and the accompanying rhetoric. As the old European-based empires continued to dissolve and superpowers assumed the reins on both sides, the globe had also become dramatically smaller.

Williams's "life of the mind," both his understanding of events and his personal experience, made remarkable sense of the bipolar world and America's prevailing intellectual currents. From a political angle, he could be seen as an outcast or underdog courageously locating himself among a relatively small constituency of anti-cold warriors. But from a methodological and, even more, a personal angle, he followed contemporary trends closely, in philosophy or psychology even more than in history. Alienation, the fragmentation of community, and the complex connections of social mobility with economic growth had hardly affected the historians of Charles Beard's generation. These issues quickly became central to the intellectual concerns of the 1950s as the threat of Armageddon receded into the long perspective of an extended arms race and cold-war prosperity.

Williams also reacted, in regard to the internal development of the nation, as forcefully against the prevailing myths of left scholarship as against those of the dominant right and center. He asked questions very different from the ones asked by the radical historians of the 1910s-20s or 1930s-40s. They had normally assumed as deep sources of progress what he reformulated as problems: the rise of the labor movement and the state regulation of the economy. If the New Deal seemed to swallow up the radical tradition, Williams sought to untangle a new radical conception from Roosevelt's legacy. Left-liberals and socialists had embraced the leviathan state and persistently held out the faith that a resurgent coalition of liberals and labor would someday, somehow outbid the Establishment in promising (and delivering) material benefits for another New Deal, a final happy ending. He had never thought so, and he began in this era decades of ruminating on alternative scenarios.

Williams protected himself through alliance and friendship, establishing the cooperation destined to make his later work possible and to broadcast its importance among a widening circle of devotees. More than that, politically, could hardly be done in the high cold-war years. But in another way, the context of limited political forms of protest suited him perefectly. Jeopardized by the undercurrent of repression, freedom of speech on the campus seemed more precious than it did later. In an age of cold-war sexual politics, with a rampant homophobia among liberals as well as conservatives, Williams was also a secret sharer of personal sympathies and deep friendship. The collegiality of administration, professors, and students, along with the interest generated by his writings, complemented his sense of himself as a public intellectual with private time for study, rumination, and family life.

I

Williams was above all determined to be a good teacher, and after several false starts he gained the kind of opportunity which would allow him a maximum of freedom in the lecture hall and seminar rooms. These experiences stirred him, and in some ways set the foundation for his engagement as a unique scholarly writer. He pushed himself to develop original approaches to problems, and he responded to students' eclectic interests by continually broadening his own intellectual horizons.

These were remarkably conventional aspirations, because Williams differed little from his generational cohorts who also entered academic life. The rapid growth of universities and the college town, the emergence of the suburbs for young faculty members, the tennis courts and golf courses had as much appeal for him as for thousands of other similar young men and a smaller number of women professors. His self-confidence soared as he reached for the good life that had eluded his Iowa family—even as he had increasing doubts about the price to be paid for it all.

Fred Harvey Harrington, in the best academic fashion of the time, found Williams his first position in 1950 at Washington and Jefferson College. Living about forty miles outside Pittsburgh, Williams seemed to have settled beyond any immediate political controversies, happy to do so at a time when McCarthyism rapidly intensified in academic life. He later remembered this year as a very happy one; his first marriage was still in bloom and he found, as he recalled later, "the happiest integration of academia and community I have ever known."[1]

The all-male college attracted many keenly motivated sons of working-class families whose members were employed by the local Corning Glass factory. Washington and Jefferson's young professors, whose own educations had been made possible by the GI Bill, vitalized various departments, from literature to economics and psychology to sociology. Williams made friends easily in a town-and-gown lecture series. Each Wednesday night a faculty member would read a paper and then the group would adjourn to a colleague's house for liquor and conversation. Here Williams's knowledgeability and charm found an ideal setting. Cautious on some current political issues, he was voluble on the larger subjects of American history.

Meanwhile, nothing could dampen the enthusiasm of a young couple surrounded by beautiful countryside. On weekends they loaded up their Crosley station wagon—America's version of the VW bug—with picnic materials and drove toward Wheeling, West Virginia, to shop and walk around. Or they headed to Pittsburgh for Pirates home games in slugger Ralph Kiner's heyday. Free of military and graduate school rigors, on their own at last, they simply and deliriously enjoyed each other's company: a fulfillment of expectations from the time of their teenage courting a dozen years earlier. Following in his father's footsteps, Williams took up golf seriously, a game he considered (as he wrote later) the utmost test of combined skills and dexterity and in which he repeatedly sought to instruct hapless protégés. With a little luck, Williams might have spent some years at Washington and Jefferson. But the cold war had turned hot.

The outbreak of military conflict in Korea had already shocked the quiet community a few months before the Williamses' arrival. The expectation of a renewed universal draft, threatening to deprive the school of its students, prompted the administration to give faculty newcomers their notice. A group of students wanted to stage a protest against the firing of their favorite professor, but Williams politely resisted. By the end of a post-midnight session, he convinced their leaders not to risk any student's status at the college for the benefit of his welfare.

The couple nevertheless spent a happy summer living close to Bard College in Annandale-on-Hudson, New York, where Williams taught in a seminar preparing Japanese and German scholars to teach in U.S. colleges—once again, thanks to Fred Harvey Harrington. On weekends, they would often travel to New York City and occasionally to Washington, D.C. Together, they sorted the personal papers of trade representative and unofficial diplomat Alexander Gumberg in the sub-basement of the Russian American Institute. These archives would be shipped to the State Historical Society of Wisconsin, like the papers of Raymond Robins that Williams gathered in Florida two significant caches of documents from important figures who opposed the cold war. Williams received a small but badly needed fee of several hundred dollars for his and Jeannie's efforts on the Gumberg materials, and he rightly thought of himself as being part of a Madison network of research efforts.[2] He even thought about returning to Madison to work in a bookstore, asking friends to find an apartment for the two to occupy if his academic career fell through completely. Jeannie, unaware of any such plans, remained confident of her husband's future success. They also tried, unsuccessfully, to begin a family.

By August, Harrington had come through again. He landed Williams a job at Ohio State teaching Western Civilization and Latin American history. This mix was not terribly close to Williams's specialty and only a nontenured instructorship at that, but warmly appreciated anyway. The couple moved into a made-over coach house in a small town ten miles from campus, and Williams cheerfully used his childhood-acquired skills to make furniture for them.

Williams renewed and deepened his friendship at Ohio State with a casual friend from his graduate-student days, French historian Harvey Goldberg. Brilliant, chain-smoking, animated, and affectionately gay, Goldberg seemed immediately to Williams "a great intellect, radical and teacher." Grandson of a rabbi and a native of Orange, New Jersey, Goldberg had spent three years after graduate school at Oberlin College and moved on to Ohio State. An outspoken professorial radical, utterly dedicated to undergraduate teaching, he shared more of Williams's intellectual enthusiasms than anyone except perhaps Warren Susman.[3] In Columbus, the odd couple set in place a foundation for decades of academic-political collaboration and comradeship, outlasting virtually all of their other personal relationships. For Goldberg in particular, it became the most important emotional relationship of a lifetime.

Friends of both men suggest that Williams possessed an open-minded appreciation of the gay intellectual rare outside bohemia (and uncommon enough within it) during those days. Like many other men, Williams adored women and needed them but felt intellectually drawn mainly to men. Unlike most other men, he was relaxed enough to extend this sentiment to his emotions: he could intuitively appreciate the gender-bending minority so quietly influential in the arts because he felt so drawn to a few of them. Strikingly unlike many leading liberal intellectuals of the age, he had no need to engage in homophobic attacks upon the "effeminate" traditions of caring reform and historic peace movements. Then again, politics and personality apart, Goldberg was to Williams an extended version of what his former professor Paul Farmer had been: the mentor in European ideologies like Marxism and Freudianism that an inveterate Midwesterner urgently wanted to understand.[4]

Williams thus characteristically recalled, after Goldberg's death, one "beautiful autumn day" in his and Jeannie's converted Ohio barn. "Off in the distance," as he sardonically put it, "we heard the primitive sounds of 85,000 men and women breaking wind about a football game," clearly the dominating spectacle of the day. Meanwhile, the three sipped bourbon and talked about virtue and history. Williams introduced Goldberg to a near namesake of his own, William Carlos Williams, reading him passages aloud of *In The American Grain*, on Aaron Burr and history. Decades later, Williams would similarly break bread and share wide interests in Aaron Burr with another friend and historically-minded gay intellectual of note, Gore Vidal, a more Henry Adams–type personality.

The communion of spirits demonstrated to the two junior historians the necessity and the possibility of devotion to historical discipline, as scholar and teacher, even in the face of overwhelming odds. "One way or another," Williams commented across a life to follow, "we were always seeking to free that Left hand that is history."[5] Real history, as Goldberg wrote in a sort of self-memorium before his death in 1987, could "destroy passivity" as few other intellectual acts, making a different future possible.[6] That was the faith they shared. Together they would offer a remarkable congruence, Williams teaching large classes and seminars through documents and Socratic dialogue, Goldberg through breathless detail and exhortation to revolutionary possibility.

Williams was not destined to stay at Ohio State in any case, but he refused to back off from his own notions of academic integrity. Football coach Woody Hayes, the most popular and arguably the most important figure on campus, had made himself widely known as both a Civil War buff and an extreme political conservative. In neither case was he likely to appreciate Williams. But the young professor did the unforgivable, assigning a dull-witted star halfback unacceptably low grades in successive semesters of Western Civilization. According to Williams's later account, Hayes came to see him personally, warning "*instructor* Williams" that Hayes's football team paid the faculty's salary and that the instructor would change the grade if he wanted to keep the job.

Many professors would have given in to the all-powerful Hayes. At that moment across the country, hundreds or thousands of former radicals bowed low to hold onto positions, and a large handful of beaten or opportunistic ones testified against former friends and mentors. Williams had too much integrity. He often said that he had already faced during military days far more frightening circumstances than joblessness. Heading for the nearest bar, he stoked himself with liquid consolation. Once again, Fred Harvey Harrington soon came through, this time with Williams's first sustaining position, at the University of Oregon in picturesque Eugene.

This was a fortunate development. Sparsely populated and heavily Yankee, Oregon had a strong reputation for libertarian acceptance of oddball types, Wobblies in the wheatfields and lumber camps, and a regional political radicalism that had flowered into a third-party movement of the 1930s. The Willamette Valley, including Eugene and Portland, had even known its "red" unions in various trades. From a less historical standpoint (and as Williams liked to call it), Oregon remained the "last frontier" of the American small businessman fending off high costs and franchise-domination. Statewide, liberal Republicans were often more critical of foreign policy than were Democrats. Eugene, along with Madison one of the most lovely of the nation's medium-sized towns, hosted a university once known best for its fraternity and sorority atmosphere but becoming steadily more diverse. Here, "radical" professors might be attacked and known Communists threatened with loss of positions, but outspoken dissenters were also widely admired, especially by the former GIs of Williams's generation. Like the University of Wisconsin if in a smaller way, the University of Oregon's freedom of intellect had value as a marketable commodity understood by moderates and even many conservatives of the state.

Williams spent five years there as an assistant professor (with an interim year of funded research in Madison), ultimately gaining tenure. Jeannie remembered these first few Eugene years as once more happy for the two of them together, pocket-poor but savoring the new experiences big and small. Williams found the most congenial physical surroundings that he could imagine. He loved the state's natural beauty, including the varied mountains, woodlands, and particularly its spectacular coast. "The sound and drive of the surf" inspired an almost unquenchable appetite for experience. The seacoast, as yet little touched by modern vacation housing and retail development, enthralled the couple, and they drove and walked their way along the ocean during many weekends. A Midwestern meat-and-potatoes man forever seeking something unique to say about himself, Williams now responded to a familiar question about his favorite food with the phrase "grilled swordfish"—his wife had just added it to her repertoire.

He ran his own large classrooms in "a truly *fine* small liberal arts environment." Frantically busy with his own work, he acquired no real protégés during this period, but many casual devotees. He also relished meeting outstanding people in various other departments, from the hard sciences to math. Like him, they felt certain they were making new discoveries. At first, living close to campus in a prefabricated housing development with small apartments but a large common space, he and Jeannie quickly made good friends. Several young historians not so different from himself, and even lower-level administrators destined to rise to considerable influence at the university, also drew close. The couple and their friends played bridge or golf, drank, and talked, enjoying each others' company enormously. "We were young, hot and rolling . . . having the time of our lives," notwithstanding the political hurricane outside.[7]

The two experienced the same difficulties as millions of other middle Americans. It had already become obvious that the couple could not bear children. Perhaps because of Williams's background as an only child and desire for his own flesh and blood, adoption would not do. As he created a campus charisma for himself, the great mind and the great radical, he claimed privately to have turned down numerous invitations for sexual liaisons. It is not difficult to read between the lines of this boasting. After a few years, Williams had likely begun the not unusual half-life of the young male professor, turning on the charm to women who attracted him. For the first time in his life, he had the self-confidence to do so. The couple meanwhile moved out to the foothills, enjoying a richer material existence. But they were headed for a marital crackup; none of his old friends doubted whom to blame.[8]

He was also en route to a controversial writer's life. For several years, he could not get his essays published in the two major journals, the AHA's *American Historical Review* or its Americanist cousin, the *Mississippi Valley Historical Review*. About one submission in particular to the *MVHR*, he recalled a "thirty page essay on American policy in Latin America from 1917 to 1933, with every single footnote from a primary source, and all but five footnotes . . . from archival materials," held by the editors for six weeks and returned as "insufficiently researched."[9] In another case, a noted conservative figure in foreign relations serving as referee had rejected Williams's submission to the *American Historical Review* on the basis that the young scholar had cited documents not ordinarily used, i.e., had called upon something beyond the characteristically self-apologetic State Department records to explain American policies.[10] Rather than belabor his effort or change his style, he went elsewhere with his extended historical essays, to *William & Mary Quarterly* and *Pacific Historical Review*. But these open-minded journals were clearly the exception.

Williams had ample reasons to complain of political prejudice, at a time when some of the highest awards went to shallow monographs proving the inapplicability to U.S. society of purportedly "Marxist" categories such as class conflict. The study of history was subjected to an unprecedented ideological assault even as notable historians rose to denounce ideologies in general. It was a high season of pseudo-objectivity.[11]

2

An attack upon historical relativism lay behind the overt politics of cold-war historiography. From Frederick Jackson Turner onward (and however much various historians might disagree with his particular conclusions), the utility of history was widely assumed to be discovered by testing the past against the questions facing the present. The ideological and personal enrollment of historians in World War II once again prompted commitments which seemed to render relativism suspect, if not actually treasonous. Important historians, conservative and liberal alike, determined that no return to "frame of reference" relativism should follow this war.[12]

These scholars had rising prestige on their side, and a popular press which readily accepted them as the ablest chroniclers of the American past. They also appealed to many historians who had wearied of one or another element in the Progressive synthesis epitomized by Turner, Beard, and V. L. Parrington. As economics-based history had riveted the Depression generation, intellectual history and a new stress upon the psychology or "myths and symbols" of society naturally attracted readers in an age of material comfort and mass anxiety. These factors alone might not have been sufficient to ensure a long-term hegemony. The emerging giants also had the cold war and McCarthyism strongly on their side.

Speaking to his fellow graduate students in 1953, Williams's friend Warren Susman described the war on relativism as a war against all scholarship which faced hard questions without ideological blinders. Shibboleths had become the marching orders of the day. Cold-war historians posing the history and fate of "Western civilization" against communism somehow managed to encompass "the teaching of a Nazarene who lived out his life in the Near East" and yet completely exclude "the teaching of a German PhD who wrote his monumental work in the British Museum"—Jesus but not Marx. Such monumental oversights typified a larger approach. As Susman warned,

> These vague notions of civilization have not helped us to more clearly define our position in the world. They have not given us any sharp insights that will enable us to overcome the many problems we face in dealing with people and nations, East and West. What they have made possible is . . . the obscuring of America and her internal problems. They have given us a perspective so high above and so far away from our own shores that we can no longer see our important section and economic divisions and problems; we can no longer see our nation with people of different races and national origins, different religious views derived from different cultures. By assuming the sameness of men, by refusing to examine the basic differences between cultures, it has allowed us to fall under the spell of Toynbeen mysticism and therefore to believe we—as part of some vaguely defined civilization—are citing correctly [whenever] we "respond" to the "challenge" of communism.[13]

In short, historians enrolled as cold-war soldiers could no longer act like citizen-scholars.

Susman, Williams's devoted correspondent over the decades to follow and a near companion in Oregon (he had helped secure Susman a position at Reed College, and the two couples spent many weekends together, where Williams and Susman loaned books to each other), keenly perceived what later historiographical scholars would detail. The political campaign within the world of scholars was shaded with an odd blend of conservative theology and dime-store Freudianism. Not many decades before, Social Gospel progressives and the moral avant-garde had made their own uses of religion and psychology to emphasize an openness to non-Western societies and a faith in the perfectibility of man; on the political backspin, these themes had become twin philosophical bulwarks of order.

The war of ideas that Susman described certainly commanded obeisance on foreign-policy issues, but it also commanded a parallel acquiescence toward a reverential view of American business history. Samuel Eliot Morison, in his 1950 American Historical Association Presidential address, savaged Charles Beard's "scornful attitude" toward American accomplishments and called for history to be rewritten "from a sanely conservative point of view" honoring the appropriate leaders.[14] Not only were the financial and industrial giants of the past to be seen as more virtuous than historians had often allowed; they were also admirably *manly*. Thus Columbia University's Allan Nevins repudiated in *Fortune Magazine* the "feminine idealism" of Progressive historians and called for a major reevaluation of the American past in which, for example, the "Robber Barons" of the late nineteenth century would be revalued as the virile "builders of an indispensable might."[15]

Nevins saw McCarthy-era America as glowing with the radiance "of the Periclean era," and this extraordinary myopia was freely adopted by other prominent historians to cast doubt about any and all excessive idealism of the past. If capitalism had brought capitalist America (in the encompassing vision of Henry Steele Commager) to its rightful place dominating world society, then the same America had been (as Daniel Boorstin put it) a "disproving ground for utopias" with any drastically different America or even a different world in mind. Boorstin, who zealously identified former friends and teachers as subversives at hearings of the House Committee on UnAmerican Activities, dismissed colonial Quakers as holding "bizarre" beliefs, their resistance to Indian-killing based upon "false premises about human nature." In the eyes of similar writers, agitator Tom Paine had become a "fanatic," the Transcendentalists "men without responsibility," and so forth.[16]

These judgments had a particularly coercive force because historians, like other professors, were often suspected as corrupters of innocent youth, possible subversives, or defenders of suspect activities including communism and homosexuality. To be guilty of a dangerous view of the past raised questions about one's trustworthiness in the present.

If not quite as glum as in many occupations, the situation for historians and especially young historians out of step therefore looked bad in the early 1950s. Untenured teachers identified as having left-wing organizational pasts often did not gain permanent places in the university. Hundreds more, including every scholar and graduate-student teaching assistant in the state systems of California, had to sign humiliating and conscience-searing loyalty oaths. The FBI also sought to interrogate privately and publicly, and often to engage students to investigate and report upon their fellow students, friends and professors. According to a recent study, an unknown number including undergraduate William F. Buckley, Jr., and graduate student Henry Kissinger, did so voluntarily.[17]

Prominent and ostensibly liberal historians as well as conservatives and ferociously anticommunist academics such as Sidney Hook demanded the firing of all identifiably left-wing professors. Arthur Schlesinger, Jr., among others, proposed what was then widely considered a moderate approach: only those teachers whose Communistic ideas had actually *influenced their teaching* should be eliminated.[18] The integrity of the profession thus suffered unprecedented blows, despite many instances of courageous resistance and an occasional outright victory for civil liberties, like the election of Merle Curti to the presidency of the Mississippi Valley Historical Association in 1953.

Hundreds of professors who did not lose their positions spent their time dodging red-hunters or only slowly gained the standing that would have allowed them to publicize controversial views aggressively. Campus life at large remained under the gun. Young Marxists felt they dared not speak the name of their doctrine, even as methodology.[19] Among Williams's fellow Wisconsin graduates, for instance, Herbert Gutman was singled out for his long-past teenaged activities as a counselor in a progressive summer camp and was interrogated by the House Committee on UnAmerican Activities. Others like William Preston had fled repressive environments by enrolling at Madison. At traditional centers of presumed academic freedom, such as Harvard and Yale, university administrations worked voluntarily with the FBI, combing faculty and student records, employing spies from classrooms to dormitories, and warning of severe sanctions against public dissent.[20] Even in civil-libertarian Madison, FBI agents closely monitored campus radicals and offered administrators details about current suspects. The administrators in turn informed department heads, who apparently made their own courageous or cowardly decisions.[21]

But perhaps most revealing, from Williams's standpoint, was the parallel delegitimation of a traditional conservative or libertarian perspective along with radical scholarship. During the 1920s-30s, as Gerald Nye's Congressional hearings exposed war-profiteering to public light, a small army of popular scholars such as Harry Elmer Barnes had reached great audiences on all sides of the political spectrum with accusations of abuse of power in the World War. Libertarians of the "Old Right" became after World War II the main supporters of Beard's and Barnes's heritage, while communists lined up to defend Roosevelt's pre-war actions. A "New Right" headed by young William F. Buckley, Jr., and his *National Review* quickly abandoned the Midwestern or isolationist Republican tradition, registering zealous approval of a massively enlarged military-industrial state with internal security forces working overtime at public expense. Scholarly supporters of the cold war described libertarian muckraking of the recent war effort as psychopathic and warned that revisionism could not be allowed a place in the sun again. Mired in charges of anti-Semitism both deserved and undeserved, the Old Right drifted into isolation and the atavism of the John Birch Society.[22]

No political issue was more crucial for the merger of centrist ideological forces across old boundaries than the preemptive powers of the Executive. Henry Steele Commager, in other days a noted civil libertarian, passionately defended Harry Truman's actions during the Korean War and argued that Congressional attempts like that of "Mr. Republican" Senator Robert Taft to limit presidential seizure of authority "had no support in law or in history." Thomas A. Bailey, senior authority on U.S. foreign-policy history, insisted in 1948 that Roosevelt had proved "because the masses are short-sighted, and generally cannot see danger until it is at their throats, our statesmen are forced to deceive them," and would indeed perforce have to deceive them more and more "unless we are willing to give our leaders in Washington a freer hand."[23] Williams would find himself decades later tilting at forces across the ideological spectrum, from Arthur Schlesinger, Jr., to Oliver North, for deceiving Congress and subverting the Constitution on the premise that only through such deception could a necessary freedom of presidential prerogative be retained.

This drift or concerted campaign had further philosophical implications for the legacy of Progressive historians. Charles Beard, it might be remembered, had based his vastly influential intellectual contribution on the premise that monopolistic capitalism was a foreign species and that Progressive American democracy had fought repeated battles to fend off a parasitic Europeanization. The intellectual revolution (or counterrevolution) of 1945-50, aimed at overthrowing and discrediting Beard, was devoted to interpret the American tradition as both democratic and capitalist, indeed democratic *because* it was capitalist in a special, productive, and individualistic sense.

Beard's chief antagonist of the 1940s-50s was Reinhold Niebuhr. Popular theologian and former Christian Socialist notable, Niebuhr argued in massively influential essays that innocent America, with no inherent expansionist or imperialist interests of its own, had been forced to respond to totalitarian Germany and Imperial Japan. Now it was likewise compelled to respond to totalitarian Russia. The United States had little choice but to defend both its own freedom and world progress through the particular program of massive militarization and foreign-policy strategies that

Truman, the State Department, and the CIA had chosen. Depicting communism uniformly as a "demonic religion" (in the phrase of his biographer), Reinhold Niebuhr generally neglected to account for the troubling details of massive human rights abuses and other dubious means taken by the U.S. for its own ends. Sometimes criticizing one or another facet of various U.S. policies, he used even his criticisms to defend the whole package. No wonder conservatives could hardly believe their luck at the defection of a leading left-liberal to many of their long-held theological and political positions. They were just as surprised to see liberals praising the very same conservative qualities of Niebuhr's vision.[24]

Niebuhr, as critics charged, was more than a little disingenuous. He not only refused to see the historic role of the U.S. in Latin America, for example, as that of a bullying power long before communism came onto the scene; he baldly denied that any such thing as American imperialism existed or even *could* exist. Niebuhr suggested repeatedly during these years that the historic extermination of Indians, the dispossession of Mexicans, the use of the slave system in continental America, and the massive overkill in a rebellious Philippines at the turn of the century, among other uncounted symptoms, were "honest" failures of morality in a young, expansive society, possibly to be regretted but certainly not to be used to judge American society or American capitalism.[25]

Nor would Niebuhr criticize in any fundamental way the theological implications of an unprecedented military-industrial complex at the center of the U.S. economy. Backpedaling furiously from his Christian Socialist days, Niebuhr had resolved that original sin could not be overcome through historical acts, nor a perfect society reached. Even the idea of "*potentially* innocent men" was best seen as "an absurd notion" in a world where "nothing that is worth doing can be achieved in our lifetime." Spiritual conviction required identification of the dark side of human nature (oddly enough not including business morality), and severe controls upon it. Niebuhr's remarkably one-sided moral views, adopted enthusiastically by many thinkers but especially by Arthur Schlesinger, Jr., offered a key trope to cold war liberalism.[26]

So did the marked gender tilt of Niebuhr's narrative. As conservative scholar James Nuechterline later grandly summarized, "it would be impossible to find a less feminized imagination" than Niebuhr's, less polluted by the "soft" and effeminate progressivism of the past.[27] Niebuhr's rhetorical hyper-masculinity captured the self-image of the 1950s pen-pushing intellectuals who fretted about the reputed omnipresence of homosexuals in the national life of the mind and sought to demonstrate their own political virility through muscular prose.

From the viewpoint of historical scholarship, as Susman put it, by defining reality in terms of the single great conflict with communism, Niebuhr calls the intellectual back into the fold of pessimistic, deterministic Christianity, which offers hope in a future world and no solution in this one . . . Niebuhr raises an impressive bulwark of Christian pessimism against the spectre of communism and in place of traditional history. For history, as we know it, has utilized the optimism, the rationalism, and the pretentious social studies that [Niebuhr] has discovered to be useless in Man's attempt to answer the problems that face him . . .[28]

Unable to see that Christianity, too, had a history (and that the great histories of the ancient world had been written before its appearance), Niebuhr negated many centuries of historical sensibility. The effect of his teaching, Susman concluded, would not simply be to damage any sensible view of the world but to destroy "the study of history itself."[29] Susman might have added the same for American democracy, because without perspective, ideology ruled all.

Arthur Schlesinger, Jr., was curiously positioned in all this. Destined for decades of intense conflict with Williams, he often seemed to represent the great radical's *doppelgänger* (as to many of Schlesinger's sympathizers, Williams was Schlesinger, Jr.'s *doppelgänger*). Schlesinger, too, had early in life sought to remake his own identity—but in the extraordinarily unique way of changing his middle name to *become* a "Jr." to Arthur Schlesinger, Sr., who was perhaps the most prominent U.S. historian after Beard. A precocious scholar and bestselling author of the *Age of Jackson* (1945), Schlesinger, Jr., quickly (and without any particular credentials in studies of the twentieth-century U.S. Left) took on the journalistic status of an authority on American communism. During the next decade or so, he used the popular press and the upper chambers of Americans for Democratic Action to urge the expulsion of pro-communists (or non-anticommunists) from public life and to warn against the return to respectability of noted Blacklistees. *The Vital Center* (1950) confirmed that role in the eyes of many observers. Some liberal critics, no less anti-communist than he, wondered why Schlesinger, Jr., had so very little to offer in values or vision beyond anticommunism. Perhaps, like so many others of his generation, he never found a replacement for youthful semi-socialistic beliefs.[30]

The Schlesinger, Jr., of *The Vital Center* had undergone a swift deradicalization directly parallel, one might say, to Williams's radicalization. Schlesinger, Jr., had as late as 1947 declared socialism "quite practicable" in the United States. A "series of New Deals" decisively expanding government ownership and control could create a postcapitalist state administered largely by intellectuals. Capitalists themselves offered little prospect of resistance, Schlesinger, Jr., insisted. In his mind's eye, Republican businessmen who lined up behind old-style conservatives like Robert Taft were so gripped by a death wish as to be foolishly eager to lower the U.S. military profile merely to balance the budget. They might indeed welcome a socialism which relieved them of their wearisome obligations. But liberals unwilling to confront the Soviet Union, men and women who seemed to Schlesinger amazingly influential in American life, could throw off this entire promising socialism-by-government scenario.[31]

If a young Williams looked to a sort of Social Gospel theology of redemption and perfectibility with an unacknowledged bow to homosexual friendship, Schlesinger, Jr., borrowed heavily from Niebuhr (borrowing heavily, in turn, from the current fascination with Freud and psychoanalysis) to demonstrate his main opposing points. The pro-communist liberals' moral softness had led them to credulously believe "man to be essentially good" and to offer incessant rationalizations of "why he does not always behave that way." Their consequent "addiction to myth," such as the Marxist or Populist myth of ordinary working people taking over society, was based in

> the intellectual's sense of guilt over living pleasantly by his wits instead of unpleasantly by his hands, the somewhat feminine fascination with the rude and muscular power of the proletariat, partly in the intellectual's desire to compensate for his own sense of alienation by immersing himself in the broad maternal expanse of the masses . . . [32]

The heavily gendered accusations of intellectuals' homosexual urges and childishness had arisen in wartime and powered a postwar drive to return women to the home or at least to the psychiatrist to recover their true roles. A large contemporary literature, led by Ferdinand Lundberg and Marnya Farnham's bestseller, *The Lost Sex*, blamed women for the sexual uncertainty of sons and directed a return to more proper behavior. Schlesinger, Jr., built upon the same basic analysis to create an edifice of larger political-historical points.

If man's *nature* was dark, depraved, and sinister, then a new equilibrium or control was the best that humanity could hope to see—even under a future democratic form of socialism. For the present, containment demanded measures that might at other times have been considered morally doubtful or undesirable, such as a willingness to "bribe the labor movement" by creating the military-industrial jobs of a "permanent war economy."[33] Ideological objections whether conservative or radical revealed an unpatriotic unwillingness to accept the basic framework achieved. Above all a strong national leadership was required, and ensuring popular support for foreign policy had become a first obligation of intellectuals.

Read back into history, this perspective became one of strong leaders and citizens loyal to the main thrust of the society, exemplified neatly by the expansionist policies of the nineteenth century. To question them raised doubts about loyalty, and possibly also sexual orientation. Tough cold warriors like Harry Truman added a "new virility" to government. Liberal supporters of Henry Wallace, by contrast, were likened to homosexuals in a boy's school enjoying the naughty secret of their shared support for Russia. Historians condemning the expropriation of Indians or Mexicans were guilty in a related way, childishly unwilling to accept at face value the material bounty that modern American society offered them.[34] Mature minds, realistic and firmly heterosexual, evidently saw their responsibilities better. They did not flinch at the use of force against those standing in the way of American progress.

Schlesinger, Jr., and his mentor Niebuhr also fretted, however, about an excessive or hysterical American response to the world situation. Niebuhr's *Irony of American History* (1952) thus remained somewhat troubled by the equation of the U.S. with Christianity (in the other half of the dyad, communism with deviltry), even while he argued that the threat of nuclear war and the economic tyranny of a permanent war economy were risks altogether consistent with Christian commitment. Late in his life Niebuhr, like Schlesinger, Jr., even turned against Vietnam War strategies that the two had earlier defended, admitting that American "innocence" in world politics might have led to Empire—but scarcely repudiating the various degrees of exploitation and human rights violations earlier rationalized or quietly endorsed as a necessary evil. The partial about-face also came decades too late to compensate for the treatment given to the Beardian legacy among a 1950s generation of influential intellectuals terribly eager to discount the virtues of past dissenters' ideals.[35]

Only when this darkest of scholarly eras had closed, and perhaps not even then, could the full measure be taken of the delayed or abandoned scholarship, broken lives, and the swift advancement of hardened cold-war ideologues into many positions of continuing professional authority and public prestige. Those seeking the threads of a future, more critical or reflexive historical study would find them scattered and very often at the margins of professional expression. In those margins, Williams found eager editors and his own public voice.

3

The glorious era of Progressive history had finished and could not be resurrected, Warren Susman concluded in 1952. Despite its many virtues, Beardian relativism could neither explain the key historical questions that its descendents wrestled with, nor even their own experiences in a growingly complex America. It consequently left behind "little but faith" in the possible uses of scholarship. The historian seeking to be of value today had to chart new courses boldly, improve his intellectual tools, and "do what he can . . . to aid man in passing from reality to even more meaningful reality."[36]

In this spirit, Williams took the first large risks of his intellectual career: he offered his controversial political essays to those few radical and left-liberal magazines willing to publish such challenges. When "A Second Look at Mr. X," the coda to *American-Russian Relations*, was refused by *Foreign Affairs*, he redirected it to the *Monthly Review*. Edited by former Harvard and New Deal economist Paul Sweezy and former labor educator and historical popularist Leo Huberman, the *Monthly Review* was the most notable independent Marxist journal published in the U.S. since the 1930s. It was also most notably the intellectual locus of a sustained economic, historical, and sociological critique of American imperialism.

Founded in the aftermath of the 1948 Henry Wallace presidential campaign, the *Monthly Review* located a "progressive" readership outside the ranks of the Communist Party and other left political groups. Cerebral but not academic, the monthly insisted on the continuing vitality of Marxism to explain capitalism's deep contradictions as well as the new problems posed by the cold war. To the discomfort of many Marxists, it refused to treat the labor movement as the potential savior of society, and increasingly focused its interest upon the African, Asian, and Latin American societies seeking to throw off the historic weight of colonialism and post-colonial controls. With the early optimism of growing nationalist forces, the Bandung Conference of 1956, and the creation of the "Non-Aligned Movement," a wing of American socialists had another star to steer by. For all their knowledgeability about Marxism, the *Monthly Review* following most resembled the Abolitionists and Christian antiimperialists of earlier days, passionate in their commitment to end white domination as the main principle of world order.

*Monthly Review* was eclectic, within limits. Welcoming into its pages Williams's favorite British intellectuals, the non-Marxist socialists G. D. H. Cole and E. H. Carr, it could also endorse Lenin's critique of imperialism and embrace the principle of state control of the economy while offering somewhat (many would say not nearly enough) critical descriptions of Russian or Chinese society. Never failing to assess the prospects for socialist transformation, it did not foresee any dramatic changes in that direction in America, at least not in the short run. This attitude matched Williams's own "cautious socialism." On the key question of the day, however, *Monthly Review* refused to support the West in its struggles with the Soviet Union and was therefore seen by liberals as worse than suspect. Communist leaders for their part regarded the journal as heretical. Still, anyone who contributed to its pages, emphatically including the young professor from Oregon, would certainly be tainted as an intellectual "fellow traveler."[37]

Williams saw in Paul Sweezy, by this time practically the only noted Marxist economist in the U.S., a kindred soul for correspondence and long conversations, which they held during Williams's rare trips to New York City and Sweezy's equally rare ventures to Madison. Genteel, handsome, and soft-spoken, Sweezy was every part the gentleman. Although Williams conspicuously failed to convince him of the virtues of American political aristocrats like John Quincy Adams, as Williams observed wryly later, and they had nearly opposite assessments of the New Deal, the two rebels nevertheless complemented each other's strengths.

Here at any rate Williams found a secure harbor and an outlet of last resort for some of his speculative essays. The magazine's own press, initially created to publish I. F. Stone's iconoclastic *The Truth about Korea*, put in print one topical volume of Williams's and an anthology with which he assisted his friend Harvey Goldberg. Among Monthly Review Press's small handful of other authors, Williams found himself placed with the likes of muckraker Stone, economist Paul Baran, and British historian E. P. Thompson—easily three of the most distinguished and intellectually heterodox critics of Empire anywhere.

The magazine's several thousand readers, academics and nonacademics from all walks of life, in turn constituted the first wave of devoted non-campus Williams followers. Veterans of older movements, but especially the scattered young radicals in the 1950s, found their way through *Monthly Review* to the future New Left's favorite historian.[38] Toward the end of the 1950s, as a small revival of intellectual radicalism began, Williams shipped off political essays and briefly served as an editorial board sponsor for a sister political journal, the *American Socialist*.[39]

The theoretically dense quarterly of the 1930s Left, *Science & Society* likewise welcomed Williams's contributions. Founded by a Harvard group close to the Communist Party, *Science & Society* drew in its early years upon such Marxist historians as W. E. B. DuBois, Broadus Mitchell, and Herbert Aptheker; also Turner students (and prominent U.S. historians) Curtis Nettels and Fulmer Mood, among others including Williams's future teacher Merrill Jensen. During the 1940s it had become politically isolated, many of its editors and writers blacklisted. But by the early 1950s major changes in its loyalties coincided with Williams's appearance. A break with the pseudo-scientific rationale for current purges of Soviet intellectuals led the journal toward the *Monthly Review*-style independent Left. Unlike most of the academic or professional journals, *Science & Society* editors also seemed eager to engage Williams privately in give-and-take—exactly the opposite of their supposedly "dogmatic Marxist" reputations. Williams appeared to them all the more welcome because he represented the rare Middle-American radical. He validated them, in short, as they validated him. For Marxists leaving the Communist Party milieu without abandoning their hostility to capitalism, he offered an open sesame to U.S. history.[40]

The *Nation*, organ of crusading Left liberals, afforded Williams's most public outlet. Having broken with the Communist camp in 1948 after many years of cautious support and occasional criticism of Russian policies, the *Nation* remained determinedly against U.S. military mobilization and the spirit as well as the practice of foreign intervention. For that, the magazine and its editor, Freda Kirchway, won the enmity of the other liberal weeklies such as the *New Leader* and the *Reporter* (both showing close allegiances to U.S. intelligence policies and at times a credulity bordering on complicity) and the undying support of anti-cold warriors. Kirchway happily published Williams's initial contribution in 1953 on the Russian "peace offensive," and Williams followed with four essays and six reviews for the *Nation* during the next five years.[41]

Carey McWilliams, taking over the historic magazine as editor in 1955, was himself a noted reporter on California's agricultural workers' lives and a talented popular historian. The academic historian had found a good friend as well as a serious and probing editor here, too. Writing widely on the cold war and on the major works currently appearing in U.S. diplomatic history and foreign policy, Williams rapidly emerged via the *Nation* as a major voice of foreign-policy dissent. In his middle thirties, he had thus identified himself with the Left as it began to piece itself together intellectually in the years of Communist disgrace, de-Stalinization, Third World independence movements, and unremitting U.S. interventions.

His favorite subject in nonacademic essays was the practical failure and the moral catastrophe of Containment. Following the death of Stalin in March 1953, many intellectuals in the western world argued that the subsequent mellowing of Soviet internal and foreign policies meant the vindication of U.S. assumptions. But for Williams, Stalin had been a reluctant revolutionist. He had proved himself most willing to cooperate with the West (for example, forsaking Greek revolutionaries by denying them material support in their civil war of 1946-47) in return for guarantees of stable frontiers in Eastern Europe, a six billion dollar reconstruction loan from the United States, and the major part of reparations from Germany. American leaders balked on each of these points, determined to isolate the Soviet Union politically and economically, evoking in turn an increasingly hard-line Russian response. Hence in Williams's view, Containment had actually tightened Stalinist control over Eastern Europe when a different policy would have brought an easing of pressures.[42]

Winston Churchill, whose evocation of the "Iron Curtain" in 1946 had been one of the principal manifestos of the cold war, inadvertently admitted in 1956 that Containment had boomeranged. The embittered Russians threw down the gauntlet of anticolonialism to a West ill-prepared to pick it up. The "narrow and militant anti-Soviet policy" had thus worked power-fully indeed, but mainly to "increase the power, influence and prestige of the Soviet Union throughout the world" as well as to reinforce the ideological and nationalistic forces within Russia. No doubt, Williams reflected, sounder results could be attained by reversing course.

Even better would have been never to have adopted Containment in the first place. By 1947, the United States clearly possessed superiority over the Soviet Union militarily, economically, and in every other way. Democrats and Republicans alike had nevertheless reviled both progres-sive Henry A. Wallace and conservative Robert Taft for pointing out this disparity. "Instead of long-term credits and candid negotiations" which together might well have moderated Soviet behavior, "the Russians got Kennan's Containment, Truman's doctrine and Dulles's liberation." The result was enormously costly and hardly "sublime," for Americans or Russians or the rest of the world. Perhaps Thucydides saw it best, Williams concluded, in analyzing an earlier war that also had catastrophic consequences: "'The greatest exercise of power lies in its restraint.'" Or at least it should.[43]

The hidden costs of the cold war to American society, Williams took pains to demonstrate, were far greater than they seemed. Despite liberal assertions that the nation had developed "beyond socialism," and Schlesinger, Jr.'s belief that everyone but "the nobodies on the Right and Left" had become part of the "vital center," the deep truth was that Americans enjoyed a modestly higher standard of living at the price of an eroded democracy. The cold war had served to "sustain, rationalize and tighten [the] corporate system," favoring certain large corporations (mainly those with military or military-related contracts) at the expense of many others. It threatened the delicate balance between labor and capital, and it glutted agricultural markets, forcing many farmers off the land. It also pos-sessed its own crazed logic, to the point where key players in the American economy fiercely resisted detente with the Russians despite all the obvious benefits of reducing world tensions. It thereby contributed greatly to the widely lamented psychological malaise and apathy, especially among work-ers, minorities, the poor, and the young.[44]

These tendencies reinforced an especially dark side of the American past. Since the 1890s, a corporate industrial model had been set into place, adopting from feudalism the idea of the organic model of society with interlocking freedoms and responsibilities, the principle of *noblesse oblige*, and the inspiration of a universal ideal (including "crusades" against non-believers). Despite its claims to success, the new system could not prevent the "recurring crises that plagued the supposed harmony of interests" and worked best only in wartime or under the threat of war.[45]

The internal dilemmas of corporatism had been compounded by those of imperialism as embodied in the ideology of the "American Century," enunciated in 1941 by *Time* magazine founder Henry Luce. This magnum figure of corporate journalism had urged Americans to "accept wholeheartedly our duty and our opportunity . . . to exert upon the world the full impact of our influence, for such purposes as we see fit, and by such means as we see fit." Such an intent or *Weltanschauung*, "shared by big corporation executives, labor leaders and politicians of every ideological bent," Williams noted, thoroughly dominated national thinking. Foreign-policy debates did not question the validity of Containment but only whether it "went far enough fast enough," while military debates concerned "which war should be fought [where] and at what time." Looking across the modern history of foreign policy, Truman's Doctrine had only paraphrased Theodore Roosevelt's "Corollary to the Monroe Doctrine," while Republican John Foster Dulles essentially renewed Woodrow Wilson's crusade. Williams later acutely observed that Luce and his "American Century" had successfully "contained" the discussion of American democracy within a very narrow range because the elites agreed with him: that was the deepest truth about Containment.

The bipartisan abandonment of any real difference between corporate and political ideologies increasingly limited American politics to the expression of mere rhetorical differences. Thus a "deeply conservative corporation director" such as Averell Harriman could campaign for the Democratic nomination "with the rhetoric of left-wing liberals," while highly touted liberal intellectual Adlai Stevenson (many of whose speeches were reputedly drafted by Arthur Schlesinger, Jr.) repeatedly reassured the corporations of their permanent leading role in U.S. society.

It was high time, Williams argued, to "abandon . . . bipartisan imperialism," to recognize that America was "neither the last best hope of the world nor the agent of civilization destined to destroy the barbarians. We have much to offer, but also much to learn."[46] A wise and far-sighted policy would create something like a small but progressive World Civilization Tax, to be turned over to U.N. programs for economic and cultural development of the undeveloped world without any strings attached. In turn, Washington would cease any unilateral economic and technical missions of its own. Hundreds of billions of dollars would no longer be directed toward right-wing dictators, and the U.S. could intelligently increase trade with the Communist countries. But Williams did not really expect this kind of enlightened development. He hinted at a more probable consequence, the historical axiom that imperialism, over the long run, destroys republican institutions.[47] These contributions in the *Nation* set the path, in a variety of ways, for *Tragedy of American Diplomacy* (1959).

Behind the journalistic thrusts informed by scholarship, a certain personal turn of mind could also be detected. This revealed itself best in an occasional shift of style, increasingly important to his self-expression by the early 1960s but present as early as his master's thesis. It might be described as his literary equivalent to John Dos Passos' famed historic montage novel, *U.S.A.* Thus his highly personalized view of the *Chicago Tribune* in the period of Joseph Medill's reign:

> Tribune Tower has withstood both rotten eggs and explosive verbiage. It is not the Tower of Babel.
>
> A detailed examination of the paper's history is not the present aim, and interested parties are herewith referred to the bibliography. It is necessary, however, to consider the structural skeleton if the outer form is to be understood.
>
> The shock of amazement upon entering the concourse at 435 North Madison Avenue is great. Size, scampering couriers, and indifference beget apprehension. An armed guard glares his challenge:
>
> "Are you on our side?"
>
> Once recovered, the visitor realizes that the walls are covered with various bits of information. Wind velocity and direction indicators, a barometer repeater, and a plastic weather map prepare one for his exit. On the north wall, however, is a more important indicator. In firm hard characters is engraved the testament of Joseph Medill . . . Perhaps it is the god Aelous keeping a date with the lake front, but a chill sweeps through the reader. Those are the words of a powerful personality calling for a high code of ethics. The glaring headline of a nearby *Tribune* underscores the apparent disparity between command and execution. Or perhaps the ethics were of a peculiar character. This heritage is important.[48]

Neither Charles Beard, nor Charles Francis Adams, nor any other obvious sources of inspiration for Williams contain this particular kind of counterposition, although the rhetorical strategy of a sudden turnabout was a popular nineteenth-century literary comedy device from Heinrich Heine to Mark Twain. Williams uses it often to speak to power and to the effects of misused power, a condensed stylistic metaphor of his view of American society's self-made tragedy.

Writing in the *Nation* with a freewheeling style, Williams whimsically synthesized his theories of corporate imperialism through a witty tale about the four personae of various *Weltanschauungen*: the crusading, moralistic, Puritan (most recently exemplified by John Foster Dulles); the paternalistic, aristocratic Planter (whose chief recent archetype was Franklin Delano Roosevelt); the conservative, mercantilist, industrialist Hamiltonian (the likes of Herbert Hoover, Dean Acheson, and George

Frost Kennan); and the liberal, populist, revivalist, expansionist Homesteader (both Harry S. Truman and Henry A. Wallace). They all had similarly covetous intentions, but carried out their plans in very different ways, with differing rhetorics. Williams's imaginary drama also included Virgins (land, markets) and a plethora of Devils (from Native Americans to Stalin). Through historical interplay, the collective cold warrior had gained a life of his own. So far, only a few of "Clio's own courtiers" had taken "a searching look into the mirror of history," and still fewer policymakers (mostly Hamiltonian conservatives) had come to the logical conclusion that "even the best foreign policy cannot convert all the *Heathens*."[49]

Published at a time and in a place destined to draw controversy, Williams's *Nation* essays marked something more than his personal courage or willingness to take the risks of exposing himself to McCarthyite persecutions in academic life. Williams was becoming a "public intellectual" in the last substantial generation of public intellectuals. He was also very different from virtually all the rest of them.[50]

The McCarthy Era and the coincidental rise of television dramatized the drastic narrowing of the public intellectual domain during the 1950s. With television sales booming, general magazines had become less numerous and less important. Meanwhile, economic and social issues discussed during the 1930s-40s as evidence of capitalism's gloomy future had been virtually banished from sight or turned miraculously into proofs of American superiority. The vast expansion of colleges and universities for the returning GIs foreshadowed further bursts of institutional growth for the approaching baby-boom generation, providing intellectuals the employment that the world of magazine culture and popular books no longer offered. A swiftly expanding class of professional thinkers, in other words, ironically had more political restraints and ever fewer means to reach people outside the classroom and the academic journals.

This sea change in intellectual life was disguised in important ways. If challenging either U.S. foreign policy or American capitalism in any fundamental way had been all but precluded, discussions continued and even accelerated during the 1950s on other issues related to the overall quality of life. A vital circle of urban critics (including Paul and Percival Goodman, Lewis Mumford, and William H. Whyte), for instance, struggled to defend urban culture from destruction by the expansive highway system and resulting inner-city decay.

A second set of more political-minded writers, including Irving Howe and Dwight Macdonald among others, conducted themselves carefully within cold-war political bounds but grew increasingly critical of many elements within the culture. They wrote for the flourishing paperback market and for such middlebrow magazines as the *New Yorker*, *Harper's*, and *Saturday Review*, directing sometimes bitter sarcasm toward mass society and "conformism." Fervent avant-garde literary radicalism also made an important *sub rosa* appearance, as in the surprisingly widely read poetry of Allen Ginsberg and Lawrence Ferlinghetti and in the work of a few of the Beat novelists. For the most part, however, those with a large continuing role in public discussion had moved rightward from earlier sharp criticism of capitalism and adeptly relocated themselves within liberal respectability. African American figures who had once been widely hailed, Paul Robeson and W. E. B. DuBois, were practically banned from print and public appearances because they disagreed with basic cold-war premises.

One exception to this large picture was most meaningful for William Appleman Williams: Madison-trained C. Wright Mills. Son of a Texas insurance salesman and the grandson of a rancher killed in a gunfight, Mills made his way via Madison and training by Hans Gerth during the early 1940s to New York City and Columbia University. His *New Men of Power* (1950) took apart the myth of idealistic labor leaders, one of the cherished notions of the 1930s-40s Left and a section of 1950s liberals. *White Collar* (1951) did the same for corporate employees and professors, pointing to their eager submission to the authority of hierarchies. *The Power Elite* (1956) paralleled Williams's critique of capitalism's corporate-military authorities; his studies within his own field of sociology had, for a time, the same kind of explosive impact that Williams's works would have among historians during the 1960s-80s. Finally, and on a personal level, Mills loved to play the Texas Wobbly among Eastern intellectuals, a motorcycle-riding bohemian who flaunted his differences from them. Williams often found himself, although less cheerfully, playing a similar down-home-American-radical role amidst New York intellectuals.

Williams the public intellectual was already, in some important ways, closer to the 1960s intellectual rebellion that Mills did so much to launch. As the political gatekeepers' influence eroded and dependable views on international issues were no longer assured, many would rush in behind him. But he had precious few outlets beyond the *Nation* to get his message across. And if he thought much about the ways that a citizen-scholar acted upon the processes of public discussion, he was more likely to see Charles Beard than Dwight Macdonald or Lionel Trilling as his model. He sometimes did well in the essay form, he had a great private interest in literature and music, and he studied the psychological theories of the time. But the close study of the historical document rather than the literary work was his home ground, and the epochal view of historical development his philosophical forte.

Looking back from a distance of almost twenty years, Williams remembered the winter of 1952-53 with several different research options. He could investigate the idea that "capitalism could not sustain itself without an expanding marketplace." That would lead him, eventually, back to questions of foreign policy and to the "problem of the relationship between the frontier thesis and the theory of marketplace expansion under capitalism." Whatever route he took, he would eventually come to the same nexus. But he had to choose whether to begin before the articulation of Turner's frontier in 1893, or afterward. In the short run, encouraged by finding so many references to a sort of frontier thesis in twentieth-century U.S. leaders' private and public documents, he turned mainly to modern history.[51] He sought to pin down the evolution of expansionist thought, and sought also to learn from the mirror image of the expansionist mentality, the dissidents who in taking a stand against the logic of the Open Door developed their own large views of American society.

*The Shaping of American Diplomacy* (1956), a hefty two-volume documents book with extensive editorial commentary, stayed largely in the areas of foreign relations, as in his earlier monographic volume. But Williams also offered the close reader a study in his own evolution. Published in a Rand-McNally textbook series edited by Fred Harvey Harrington, *Shaping* covered the two centuries after the 1750s, two-thirds of which concerned the twentieth century. Williams wrote over a hundred commentaries along with the two hundred documents, many of which had been previously unknown save to specialists.

Designed initially to train graduate students—he had personally mimeographed reams of documents for his classes at Oregon—the project had grown more or less organically from his own research. He complained later that he had not gained much through the labor-intensive method because royalties had been too low to cover the expense of preparing the volume. But the book played a large role in the classroom for well over a decade, offering sympathetic teachers a tool for engaging students with documents and exposing them to views that might be considered in other contexts to be dangerous propaganda. According to Harrington's testimony, Williams had to be urged to balance the selections with more liberal (and conservative) commentaries, but his basic analytical thrust served him well.[52]

All in all, *The Shaping of American Diplomacy* marked a bold new departure in the study of U.S. foreign relations. Traditional historians had analyzed foreign policy in terms of diplomatic exchanges but contradictorily suggested that democratic "public opinion" had ultimately determined U.S. policies—even when scholars knew better from the study of elites making the key decisions.[53] Williams stressed, on the contrary, how economics and ideology as much as the familiar political or military considerations affected U.S. decision-making. While the essays and editorial comments of the volumes avoided polemics, no sophisticated reader could miss implications about the baneful implications of imperialism, not excluding an imperialism overwhelmingly supported by the American public.

By the second volume, covering the period since 1898, Williams's essays and documents showed vividly how the pursuit of the Open Door led to military interventions abroad. Theodore Roosevelt looked like a belligerent bully, but Woodrow Wilson hardly seemed better (only such "isolationist" critics as Senator Borah consistently looked good). Basic U.S. policies had made involvement in both world wars deliberate and inevitable. Right down to the Eisenhower era, Williams suggested how very hard it was for diplomats and presidents to unshackle themselves from their own assumptions even when they could have benefitted personally and saved their nation from peril by doing so.

Especially impressive, because so little known elsewhere in academic or public life, was Williams's treatment of the U.S. and the Third World. Document after document revealed the continuity of Gunboat Diplomacy in Latin America from the 1850s to the 1950s. An evenhanded treatment of the Korean War, with the North no more guilty than the South, was especially daring for the time. The criticism of U.S. China policy that he reprinted similarly suggested how foolish had been the refusal to deal with the nationalism of the Chinese Communists. In all this, he declined the easy (and familiar Marxist, especially Communist) path of charging U.S. policy-makers with venality. A tragic shortsightedness, he indicated, had made their actions inevitable.

Beneath and behind all this, Williams's assumptions were disguised in plain sight, so to speak, in the volumes' introduction. "Human beings decide what will be done with the available resources," he wrote in italics, and added that "letters from American citizens to the State Department are just as important as the official diplomatic cables to another country," because finally, foreign policy stems from "domestic conflicts over what *should* be done and what *can* be done." These were ethical questions, he might have added—but did not.[54] Williams chose to be indirect throughout the volumes, from the bland title to the anonymous dedication ("For a friend who was very courageous," i.e., Harrington).

The reviews were few in number, as is usually the case with textbooks. On the Left, Charles Madison described in *Science & Society* a "rich and rewarding collection . . . pertinent and perceptive." A reviewer in the *Southwestern Social Science Quarterly* found it "very judicious," as did the many professors who assigned it in foreign-policy courses.[55] His Ohio

State friend and colleague Paul A. Varg was the most perceptive critic. Williams's introductory essays he considered "highly interpretative and controversial . . . provocative and imaginative . . . [containing] highly interesting analyses [and] enriching hypotheses." Although Williams might sometimes be charged with "reducing history to too schematic a basis," he was raising questions "which ought long ago to have been considered . . . [and which] provide "a healthy irritant conducive to the re-examination of stereotypes."[56] As a New Left commentator would write decades later, he had a knack for opening up "questions to which historians have generally paid little heed."[57]

Williams could not be pinned down easily, any more than the solidity of his source materials could be readily impeached. As the young professor's devoted new readership might say, Williams was busy shaking off orthodoxies of all kinds. He had borrowed enough from the current drift of historiographical debate to see the foreign-policy elite suffering its own crises of conscience or confidence, enough from the shifting history of expansionism to understand that motive to be rooted as much in what DuBois had called the "American Assumption" of endless land and business growth as the logic of any fixed capitalist class.

Williams collaborated in much that spirit with his friend Harvey Goldberg on *American Radicals: Some Problems and Personalities* (1957), published by Monthly Review Press; the book was one of a relative few new radical titles to appear in an era when publishers fled from dangerous ideas. It was, in many ways, the invocation of radical traditions in tough times. Close to a dozen of the standard Left or Left-leaning figures, such as Robert M. LaFollette, Eugene Debs, Big Bill Haywood, and even John Brown (considered in the conservative 1950s official scholarship and many college texts to have been a madman), found their place here.

But it was also very far from what a book on American radicalism might have been in other hands or other times. None of the standard Abolitionist intellectuals appeared, no African Americans, no women, no Communists, and few Socialists, and most obviously *American Radicals* lacked the sentimental evocation of the American Revolution so common to the Left of the later 1930s and the war years. Defenders of free speech, like newspaperman Heywood Broun and Illinois governor John Peter Altgeld, figured heavily here. A whole section was devoted to repression, to ex-left renegades and liberals who chose Empire and sought to coopt dissent for their own purposes. The most incisive section by far treated the deep thinkers, Thorstein Veblen and Charles Beard, who had little personal hope for American radicalism but described with an acid pen the civilization's destructive course. In short, *American Radicals* would not be considered the kind of text that a detached and distanced critic like Richard Hofstadter could call his own, but it was probably closer to that sort of position than it was to the familiar Communist-style celebration of Thomas Jefferson and Sam Adams, Populism and the New Deal.

Williams inevitably found his own version of the intelligent patrician in Beard, fellow Midwesterner of similar Protestant upbringing. In *American Radicals*, he wrote the nearest thing to a biographical treatment that he would deliver on the man he obviously admired most. Born in Spiceland, Indiana, to a family of conservative farmers and agricultural businessmen, Beard observed the hellish labor conditions of Chicago Stockyard workers and the degradation of politics by city machines. Somewhat like Williams, Beard spent three years traveling and studying in Europe, becoming particularly acquainted with the British labor movement and some Fabian Socialists. A graduate of DePauw University, he received his PhD from Columbia in 1904 and immediately joined the faculty there. Resigning from Columbia in 1917 after Nicholas Murray Butler had fired three faculty members for allegedly associating with subversives (i.e., opponents of the world war), Beard thereafter became the independent, public historian that Williams imagined as the ideal intellectual.

Williams had earlier come to know Beard's writing as an admiring graduate student, probably more than he realized, by way of osmosis through his favorite professors. He revisited the master a second and decisive time, in the mid-fifties, while crafting his mature methods of historical analysis. Here, Williams showed his fascination with the intellect which could balance radical insights with conservative caution, the historian who stressed the interconnectedness of economics to the rest of human behavior and who sought a general theory of causation. In each of these respects, Williams emulated the great man.

Williams wrote that Beard was a radical who went "to the heart of the matter," who insisted that "economics and morality [were] respectively the cornerstone and the keystone of a good life." While economic maladjustment would certainly undermine morality, "the lack of ethical integrity [would] corrupt the best economic system." This, according to Williams, was Beard's enduring legacy to American radicalism. Moreover, in all of this, Beard had not embraced an alien philosophy; he had been a quintessential American, showing the "Indiana common sense" which the prairie radical Williams could appreciate. Beard also refused to separate his intellectual from his political activity. For him, the ivory tower was "a refuge for the intellectual and moral coward—or scoundrel."[58]

While Goldberg edited the volume (no doubt with advice from Williams), the two collaborated on the introduction, a sober and not very optimistic account. American radicalism had failed, they opined, to meet the challenge of American expansionism. The deeply held assumption "that there was enough at hand, or within reach, to meet and satisfy the needs and desires of all segments of the nation" seriously circumscribed any "radical analysis of society." Radicals—and non-imperialist conservatives, they might easily have added— would first have "to wrench themselves [out of the expansionist] tradition before they could grapple with the central crises at hand." The self-proclaimed national mission of "carrying civilization and liberty to the benighted masses of the world" had only compounded the problems of democracy.[59]

So, ironically, did the Russian Revolution, an admission that no Communist or philosophical Leninist could ever have made. Although the Russian Revolution had greatly inspired American radicals, it had provided an extremely inappropriate model for the U.S. Left, while the unsavory aspects of Soviet rule had given reactionaries and liberals powerful sources for antisocialist propaganda. The ensuing repression of democratic traditions and of pleas for alternatives at home meant that radicals often had to establish their own freedom before they could begin to work out "a coherent and integrated radical program for America."

This presented a thoroughly daunting prospect. The "European radical, consistently sensitive to the difficulties of challenging a class system, could be broken and yet rise again." But the American dissenter, surrounded by those who shared the illusions of living in a near-perfect society, had a far harder row to hoe. Some "toughened their hides," while others "fell away when the reality replaced the dream." Not nearly enough had remained for a consistent tradition.[60]

The "unprecedented power of vested interests" and the "calculated manipulation of public opinion through the mass-communications media" frequently left radicals feeling so futile, afraid, and frustrated that they groped wildly for alternatives. Some knowing better but unable to find an alternative path accepted the liberal version of Empire. Others shared the alienation pervasive in society, demobilizing themselves from any useful action. Failing a proper reorientation, defeated radicals abandoned the field entirely to the hope for reformed Russian or Chinese Communists, or to "the new breed of men which will arise as a phoenix from a nuclear holocaust."

Perhaps most damning was the charge that American intellectuals had as a group grabbed the opportunity for personal advance in the prosperous society, trading their critical talents for unworthy ends. "The cutting edge of criticism can be easily dulled by the soft center of personal gain," Williams and Goldberg charged, and the "compromisers and hairsplitters . . . adorn themselves" with self-congratulation for their reasonableness. The authors were evidently describing former radicals who now dominated literary criticism and heavily influenced academic life through their prestige, connections, and their firm embrace of cold-war policies.[61]

Hidden in the text, well away from the concluding paragraphs, lurked another implication that had little to do with Goldberg's personal vision but much to do with Williams's. Perennially lacking solid "long-term popular support," the Left's programs paled in comparison with the "rational corporatism" of such enlightened conservatives as Herbert Hoover. A quarter century later, it had taken a "West Pointer and a General Motors executive [i.e., Eisenhower] to begin America's disengagement from the cold war."[62] One could almost say that the fascination of a critic like Lionel Trilling for the literature of the elite found its match here, albeit at the other end of the political spectrum. Or again, as a wing of former radicals turned to Adlai Stevenson as the best hope of the age, Williams (if not Goldberg) "liked Ike" with a similar mixture of fatalism and admiration.

## 5

In the less-read academic journals and in the free commentary of reviews, Williams experimented with theories of *Weltanschauung*, or worldview, to explain U.S. history and foreign policy. His classroom discussions with Oregon undergraduates, and his conversations with fellow Oregon historian Orde Pinckney and economist Robert Campbell, gave him a sense of historical background that made expansionism an epochal phenomenon. Williams was already thinking in large, long-range terms, utilizing "modernization" or periodization as ways to examine the stages of political economy and society at large.[63] Here and there he staked out a major position in foreign-policy research. For the most part, the conceptual experiments or trial balloons served as a basis for larger conceptualizations in his later works. Returning often to the writings of the classic historians, he prepared to challenge the dominant liberal historiography.

The prime American *Weltanschauung* of the twentieth century, according to Williams, was that of "Open Door imperialism," the right of the U.S. to enter all markets on formal terms of equality, in a relationship naturally favoring the stronger party. Reflecting on the development of this concept many years later, he insisted that it belonged to no particular school of thought, but had been advanced since the 1890s "by a disparate group of policy-makers and politicians, bureaucrats, nonacademic intellectuals, and university and college teachers."[64] Nearly all of them, it is fair to say, were elements of the ruling strata.

Scholars had been aware of the importance of the Open Door policy almost from its beginnings. Marxist Rosa Luxemburg had previewed the economic basis of it in *The Accumulation of Capital—an Anticritique* (1913), which argued that capitalism sustained itself only by extending its grasp of accumulation outward, absorbing lesser economies.[65] Several of the keenest interpretations of Open Door strategy as such, from liberal Englishman John A. Hobson's *Towards a Lasting Peace* (1916) to the Williams-influenced German scholar Hans-Ulrich Wehler's *Der Aufsteig des amerikanischen Imperialismus* (1974), were also penned from outside the U.S. An assortment of American historians appreciated the importance of the subject but failed to see it as anything resembling a comprehensive worldview, and the Marxist economists (including those around *Monthly Review* magazine) were preoccupied with the economic details of imperialism. Charles Beard and Mary Ritter Beard, along with Fred Harvey Harrington, possibly came closest to abandoning atomistic, interest group–based theories to identify a modern imperialist *Weltanschauung* as such.

In Williams's perception, the chain reaction that ignited his interpretation of Open Door imperialism took place in the History Department at Wisconsin shortly following World War II. Intellectual cross-fertilization helped, Americanists interacting with Europeanists and with scholars from other fields including sociology and literature. So did the ideas of the Frankfurt School, which seemed to be in the air at the time. The "particular genius of Harrington" had been to bring these people together.[66] It was also interesting that Williams should think of the milieu in these terms, especially because as successor to Harrington he would guide the work of a later and much enlarged generation of radical scholars. Williams's own work was the key link between the two generations, and his preparations went far to make that extended process possible.

His efforts in the 1950s and on American-Russian relations in particular, Williams admitted later, had only tested his new methodology. He was so far "not fully in command of the approach." He tried out the concept in specialized studies—Frederick Jackson Turner's Frontier Thesis and Henry Luce's articulation of an "American Century"— before analyzing the historical context and crucial consequences of Secretary of State John Hay's "Open Door Notes" of 1899-1900. Williams conceptualized these particular documents as the "basic formulation" of a general outlook leading to "a vast network of internal relations" that, taken together, integrated "economic theory and practice, abstract ideas, past and future politics, anticipations of Utopia, messianic idealism, social-psychological imperatives, historical consciousness, and military strategy." Guiding both "elitist *and* popular thinking (and responses)," the Open Door finally became "an ideology (even theology) and ultimately a reification of reality." Williams found little difficulty in delineating the development of this ideology with most of Hay's successors. Indeed, he remarked that one grew weary of repeated references to Open Door policies in published State Department documents alone.[67]

Charles Beard had doubtless understood best for his time that "empires are not built in states of absent mindedness . . . and expansion does not in and of itself solve problems but often complicates them." But he could never "pull the personal and group world views into one national *weltan-schauung* for the United States," and develop a comprehensive analysis of the mainsprings of American foreign policy. He moved in that direction during the 1930s, until the approach of World War II diverted him entirely.[68] The historical giant had nevertheless crystallized a philosophical framework that allowed Williams to develop further what his fellow Madisonians had so ardently discussed. Less concerned with raw economic motives than with hypothesizing about interests and ideas, Beard offered a working theory of causation.

Williams also admired and drew upon Thorstein Veblen, widely considered along with Beard one of the three leading intellectual influences of the 1930s (the third was Freud). Another fellow Midwesterner, born in Wisconsin and educated in Minnesota, Veblen had never been well accepted by the academic establishment. Although he read and admired Marx and became very sympathetic to the Bolshevik Revolution, he also remained outside Left party circles. And yet he was an anticapitalist and antinationalist who believed in fundamental structural changes and not merely reforms of the existing system. Williams particularly appreciated how Veblen connected foreign and domestic policies, and specifically how he understood the ways in which the U.S. could be ardently pro-imperial while generally anticolonial. Perhaps most of all, Williams appreciated Veblen's temperament: brilliantly iconoclastic, yet an idealist beneath it all.

With this timely return to Beard and Veblen, Williams plunged further into the synthetic interpretation of U.S. foreign policy outlined in *The Shaping of American Diplomacy*, but with a more keenly sharpened edge. In the *Nation* and a variety of scholarly journals, he directed his comments consistently and openly, for the first time, against the accepted wisdom of liberalism. He critiqued the existing historiography and in the process sketched out the alternatives he would detail in his masterworks, *Tragedy of American Diplomacy* and *Contours of American History*.

During the last decade of the nineteenth century, Americans had developed a set of ideas that had later become hardened into a worldview. Derived partly from Frederick Jackson Turner's theory that "America's unique and true democracy was a product of an expanding frontier," and partly from Brooks Adams's theses in his *Law of Civilization and Decay* that the struggle against entropy demanded a combination of Empire and corporatist coordination, this set of ideas passed on to John Hay and Theodore Roosevelt to subsequent presidents, secretaries of state, and assorted policymakers.[69] Turner's thesis achieved, meanwhile, great popularity with the general public. Writing during the 1890s, a time of serious socioeconomic crises, he gave Americans "a nationalistic world view that eased their doubts, settled their confusions, and justified their aggressiveness." Expansion would not only improve business but also extend white Protestant democracy. Far from a Republican or conservative project, it was evidently a bipartisan and even a consensual program.[70]

The liberal Woodrow Wilson seeking to "fit his conservative sense of noblesse oblige to an industrial society," thus articulated a "fundamental identity between the economic supremacy of American capitalism and [his] image of the good world." Contrary to the liberal orthodoxy of historians like Arthur S. Link, this Wilson was anything but an innocent idealist.[71] His ideological and military offensive against the new Soviet Union had been instinctive, as doctrinaire and unyielding as U.S. policy would be toward any society or ideology perceived as an obstacle to the Open Door.[72]

Williams decisively challenged the familiar notion that Americans had retreated into isolationism after World War I only to return to international responsibility as fascism threatened to overtake Europe. In a historical note and in a major convention paper (read to the Pacific Historical Association) that became the most reprinted essay of Williams's work during the 1950s, he sought to show that the prevalent historiography disguised deeper complexities. All the way back to the 1790s, Alexander Hamilton had proposed "no entangling alliances," but actually intended "a de facto affiliation with the British" rather than disengagement. If concerted opposition to U.S. entry to the League of Nations had been motivated not by isolationism but by the desire for unilateral options, and if the purported isolationism of 1920s Progressives like Senator William Borah of Idaho had included the very internationalist aim of the U.S. recognizing Russia, then mainstream interpretations of American leaders' international aims explained little.[73]

Liberal historians had, in fact, been stacking the deck by portraying a stagnant (i.e., Republican) 1920s against a dynamic (i.e., mostly Democratic) 1910s and 1930s. The contrast of Hoover and Roosevelt that would later earn Williams scholarly notoriety (and friends in ostensibly strange places, among conservatives and liberal Republicans) began properly here. The ruling group around Herbert Hoover, heirs to a wing of the Progressive Party, embraced shrewd capitalists, financiers, and labor leaders in a comprehensive corporatism aimed at "internationalization through the avoidance of conflict."[74] As a community of interests building upon the mechanisms established in the Wilson reign, they would guide the abandonment of the old territorial imperialism for a new economic Pax Americana.

This interpretation so thoroughly sliced through the liberal faith that it left the domestic economic interpretations as well as foreign policy in tatters. Bearing down on Arthur Schlesinger, Jr.'s *Crisis of the Old Order, 1919-1933* in the *Nation*, Williams argued that Schlesinger had not only fundamentally misunderstood Hoover but blunderingly misinterpreted the crisis of 1929 and its underlying causes. No nineteenth century–style, individualist capitalism had still existed to collapse. Schlesinger threw the blame on Hoover because to accept Hoover's rationalization of the system would be tantamount to admitting that corporate capitalism and not its predecessor had failed in 1929. Schlesinger had better described the crisis of the 1890s or even the Panic of 1873 than he did 1929, so much did he fear coming to grips with the implications that the key problems of the society had remained unresolved except by war and Empire.[75]

If Williams had set his enemies to sharpening their knives for him, he prepared himself for his next great conceptual leap forward. He had also shown some of the idiosyncratic edges which inspired curiosity and amazement from political observers, Left to Right. His rehabilitation of the 1920s in general revealed something about Williams and his Wisconsin milieu. Warren Susman later devoted considerable energies to debunking the 1930s as the supposed "red" or radical decade. Like Williams, he sought to upturn the standard liberal historiography which portrayed the New Deal as the apex or end-goal of political accomplishment; like Williams, Susman found himself working upstream all the way in the existing climate of scholarly sympathies, his task better conceptualized in essays than argued in monographs.[76] Williams's twist of this radical revision, making Hoover a political centerpiece and sentimentalizing the conservative gendered family-centeredness of 1930s life, found him at odds with almost everyone among a liberal and socialist cohort, but not so distant from his Iowa Republican background after all.

6

Suspiciously publishing in "red" journals and almost certainly tracked by the FBI since his Corpus Christi days, Williams was ripe for victimization. In 1954, Arthur Schlesinger, Jr., added an accusatory phrase to an otherwise unrelated letter to the executive secretary of the AHA, attacking Williams as a "pro-communist scholar."[77] At that moment in the profession, such a letter from a distinguished scholar and famed writer could easily have been taken to be an invitation to banish a possibly subversive writer and teacher. Offered very few grants, fewer jobs, and no particularly prestigious ones over the course of his career, and awarded only one honorary degree (by a black community college) despite his later presidency of the Organization of American History, Williams evidently never entirely escaped an informal blacklist.

Whether by coincidence or not, he also faced a modicum of harassment in liberal Oregon. After the departure of a trusted and powerful ally to Berkeley, the senior figure of the history department decided to make life difficult for the young radicals. One day at the water fountain after a day of work, the elder professor demanded, "Are you a Communist?" It was not an innocent question. Williams recalled he replied simply, "I consider the question as an insult," and turned on his heels.[78]

This dour chairman did not and perhaps could not prevent Williams, one of the most intellectually productive members of the department, from gaining tenure. Oregon, moreover, lacked the kind of state legislation which would have allowed a public political hanging. But the issue of his real or possible political connections and inclinations floated around campus and became an obstacle to his further advancement as well as a cloud over his general status in the community. In an academic novel about Oregon by Williams's colleague and friend, Bernard Malamud (who reportedly considered Williams the only one to have correctly interpreted his baseball novel, *The Natural*, as a metaphor of American life), a professor unravels the tale of his predecessor's firing as a confused, heavily personalized, nightmarish mockery of political struggle. Drawn by the beauty of his surroundings despite the almost constantly overcast skies and deep sense of geographic isolation, the protagonist triumphs—but only by leaving. Williams himself moved out of his home, albeit for more personal reasons. The same year, he had been offered an untenured position at the University of Illinois in Champaign-Urbana, which he turned down. It is likely he simply felt little desire for a position no better than the one he had. Perhaps he had other reasons.[79]

From Williams's point of view, his marriage with Jeannie had gone bad, and after a trial separation, the two had decided that they were "doing . . . each other more damage than good."[80] Jeannie could not see matters so nonjudgmentally. From her perspective, he was an adulterous husband who had already made his life decisions without giving her the dignity of a sincere explanation. Between his second and third marriage there would be talk of a reconciliation with Jeannie. He wrote to her in great detail about his further experiences and marital troubles, evidently feeling guilty for wrong done to her.

Drawn into what some later described as "a Great Passion," he had meanwhile struck up a relationship with Corrinne Croft Hammer, an Oregon-raised radical who had returned to graduate school after bearing two children. A decade earlier, fleeing the conservatism of small-town Oregon and of her southern-born parents, the bright and rebellious Corrinne had attended Portland State College and joined the United World Federalists. Later, trapped in an abusive marriage, she set her heart on becoming a social worker with an advanced degree, and had managed to secure a teaching assistantship in Sociology at the University of Oregon. There, Williams swept her off her feet.

Corrinne put aside her aspirations for a love match. The similarly stubborn temperaments of the two should have set off warning bells, many friends concluded later. But they plunged ahead, marrying. She accompanied him to Madison for a Ford Fellowship in research from the fall of 1955 to spring 1956. Having finished *The Shaping of American Diplomacy*, he could seriously begin work on *The Tragedy of American Diplomacy*. They lived in a house overlooking picturesque Lake Mendota, and he renewed his many acquaintances, especially a warm friendship with a noted scientist, the emigre German socialist Karl Paul Link. Williams had enjoyed his life in Oregon, but Madison offered him incomparable intellectual excitement.[81]

The national mood of McCarthyism had also eased significantly, even as generalized blacklisting, roundups of Communists, and the jailing of unwilling witnesses before Congressional committees all continued to chill free speech. Meantime, flagrant U.S. misdeeds abroad began to provoke a skepticism and even a protest unthinkable in the anticommunist liberal press only a few years earlier. Norman Thomas, still "Mr. Socialism" to *New York Times* reporters, would soon be heard denouncing the "New American Imperialism" and omnipresent, unquestioning American support of "corrupt, reactionary cliques so long as they [are] anti-communist."[82] Williams could rightly anticipate in Madison an arena for relatively free, open discussion of America's Empire past and present.

In 1957, Fred Harvey Harrington was elevated to Chair of the History Department in Madison and made no secret of his aspiration to climb higher. Well respected on campus and around the state, he would become university president five years later and preside over the most rapid growth the school had ever known. With his influence looming large, he bypassed the normal controversies of new appointments and asked Williams to replace him as historian of U.S. foreign policy.[83]

Wisconsin policy prevented an immediate tenured appointment, but Harrington made Williams the tentative promise of tenure, promotion, and a significant salary increase at the end of the first year. The younger man might have preferred to stay in Oregon for another year or so. But Wisconsin offered $7,600, four hundred dollars more than his present pay. When he asked Oregon to match the four hundred dollars, his department adversaries made sure the Dean would not budge. Williams seized the moment. By the time he, Corrinne, and her own two children left Eugene permanently for Madison, she was pregnant with their first child. A new life had begun in more ways than one.[84]

# High Times in Madison, 1957–1963

THE RETURN TO WISCONSIN HELD PROMISES and hazards that Williams could not have fully anticipated. He had waited as he had worked and lived all along, since the late 1940s, for the revival of a political Left. If he guessed that he might be its chief scholarly avatar, the one who could point to the crucial developments in national life, he betrayed no advanced knowledge of this possibility. His key books, in no way styled for a new generation, resonated with that tone of the 1940s–1950s which brought his powerful intellect to bear upon the large saga of democracy and Empire. More subtly, they also resonated with the memories of the 1930s that encompassed his childhood and the diminished promise of modern times.

The resulting intellectual edifice, in style as well as content, was unlike anything that U.S. historical scholarship had seen before or would likely see again. Idiosyncratic to the core, Williams's *Tragedy of American Diplomacy* and *Contours of American History* overviewed the national saga from the standpoint of a bereaved patriot. He offered at different moments, occasionally within the same paragraphs, grand syntheses of historiography, insights entirely outside existing scholarship, and witty observations about the nation's giants. Unlike those nineteenth-century "comic histories" (the most famous by Eugene Debs's friend Bill Nye), which ridiculed American statesmen for their looks and behavior, Williams reconstructed these giants as leviathans indeed, but not as Americans had ever seen them. In this way among others, Williams the patriot escaped being a mere iconoclast. He challenged not so much the details of the existing canon as the very root assumptions of the liberal-conservative coalition which had held the commanding towers of prestige and influence since the defenestration of Charles Beard.

He did not entirely escape the suspicion, especially among younger historians, that he nevertheless held to some certain very conventional assumptions: a small number of great, white men make history; and the rest of society acquiesces to their rule, not only from powerlessness but from a widespread agreement with their purposes. Nevertheless, he proposed an extremely radical way of viewing that history. In short, he came at his subject from various perspectives that would in others have been merely contradictory or confusing. For all his weaknesses, he dazzled again and again.

For a moment in time Williams also made himself into a major exemplar of Madison, Wisconsin's progressive tradition, as its revived importance in the beginnings of national dissent was reflected in him. Of course, merely a sliver of campus knew much about Williams, took his courses or cared; outside the university only the circles of progressive intellectuals and casual readers of local press articles mentioning him from time to time would likely even have known his name. But history popularized for the common citizen had been a significant claim in the land-grant university and in the much-utilized State Historical Society of Wisconsin with the mural of "Fighting Bob" LaFollette painted on its interior stairwell. Within that tradition, Williams personified progressive Midwestern citizenry self-realized. No better candidate, at any rate, could be found since the death in 1925 of the legendary idealist and third-party Presidential candidate.

In that spirit, Williams trained a legion of future professors. These democratic-spirited youngsters in turn sought to give the nation, beginning with their own students, a more realistic picture of American society, its deep problems, and its vast possibilities. Williams also encouraged the formation of a sort of brain trust, like-minded youngsters brought together around his ideas as a method of approaching the complexities of the Corporate Age. Working in this atmosphere, he developed the crucial insights into "Corporate Liberalism," the historic view popularized by his devotees in conscious preparation for the momentuous social movement arising a few years later.

Behind the bold front, a certain pathos might be detected, but only by the very perceptive observer. Williams disguised the ample private weakness hidden in the strength of many a remarkable public figure. A slap at him in *Time Magazine* and ferocious personal attacks upon him by veteran cold-war operatives like Theodore Draper did not daunt him; nor did the cancellation of book contracts on political grounds, nor even the chilling experience of persistent harassment by the U.S. House Committee on UnAmerican Activities and the Internal Revenue Service. But a certain political and emotional inconsistency, the difficulty of reconciling current hopes with an unsentimental interpretation of American history, cast a shadow over his efforts. Beloved and admired, he frequently seemed in private a radical alone with his own soul.

I

Madison was ready for Williams's return. Ground had been broken for a new library the year he left, across a mall from the Historical Society, with a magnificent collection of volumes opened in 1953 to students and all state residents. The University of Wisconsin's national and international reputation across many departments grew steadily as well. By the late 1950s, it had entered an era of good feelings with a state legislature markedly proud of its rising stature and almost eager to fund its continuing expansion.[1]

In the seven years since Williams had departed, the political atmosphere had changed considerably and almost welcomed the pre-dawn of a new Left. Numerous students and prestigious faculty members would become his natural allies, shielding this public intellectual when necessary and lauding him as their own radical champion *qua* historian.

The dissipation of cold-war gloom had begun, in small ways, just as Williams and his graduate school cohorts left graduate school in 1949-50 to take up their first faculty positions. New graduate students with the experience of Left summer camps or the Henry Wallace campaign behind them arrived with their ideologies battered but their scholarly hopes high. In American history, Warren Susman, David W. Noble, Herbert Gutman, William Preston, and George Rawick, among others, were just beginning their momentuous work of redefining modern cultural studies, working class immigrant and African American history. Some of them were also at the heart of the failed but heroic "Joe Must Go" campaign aimed at defeating Senator McCarthy in his home state. Susman, the speaker-system expert for the campaign, would remain one of Williams's intimates in the decades ahead, and Noble one of his keenest interpreters. Together with a few beloved professors, this intellectual cohort created the "Smoking Room

School of History," an informal but dynamic round table of historical discussions in an alcove of the State Historical Society.[2]

These graduate students, even more than their sympathetic professors, made Madison an increasingly vital locus of historical study outside the political mainstream. Their devotion fostered a small-scale political renaissance that predicted the distinctively cerebral character of Madison radicalism during the 1950s. As teaching assistants for such favorite professors as Howard Beale or Merle Curti, they cultivated the circle of undergraduate students who would form a crucial link between Williams and the New Left.[3]

A dozen or so precocious Jewish undergraduates, mostly from the New York area and deeply interested in history, quickly made themselves an active political group on campus, stirring controversy and driving liberals into action. The communist-linked Labor Youth League (LYL) offered cultural variety to a student body otherwise heavily inclined toward the beer guzzling of the "frat-rats" and the plodding of the upwardly mobile engineering majors. At the very depths of McCarthyism, they and a circle of radical pacifists protested compulsory ROTC and the presence of racial discrimination in campus housing, and they formed support groups for local strikers. Professors like Beale and Curti defended them in print, insisting that even communist views deserved free-speech protection.[4]

Madison thus remained a remarkably lively place during the national nightmare of political paranoia and bomb shelters. Elsewhere in the country, unions were demobilized and purged of suspicious members, thousands of Americans considered either subversive or homosexual lost their jobs, and Hollywood enforced its blacklist of those who refused to testify against their colleagues. But on the University of Wisconsin campus, Marxists like slavery scholar Herbert Aptheker or Shakespeare scholar Annette Rubinstein spoke freely. Meanwhile, the civil rights movement elicited wide local sympathy, with visiting southern activists drawing enthusiastic audiences and volunteers determinedly raising thousands of dollars on Madison street corners. As usual, radicals were among the most active in their sympathy, the most eager to draw the campus into the national integrationist effort. In this odd moment, history had almost caught up with the William A. Williams of 1946.[5]

Dramatic international developments propelled the young University of Wisconsin intellectuals in new directions of their own. The 1956 Hungarian Revolution and the brutal Russian response, along with the Twentieth Congress of the Soviet Union and Nikita Khruschev's revelations of Joseph Stalin's misdeeds (including horrendous anti-Semitism), abruptly ended Communist sympathies on campus. Joining with other campus radicals, former Labor Youth League members created a portentous post-Stalinist entity: the Socialist Club. Heavy with history enthusiasts, the SC would provide Williams's prime forum outside the classroom.[6]

Parallel developments in Britain set the pace for a revived Anglo-American radicalism with its roots in fresh historical interpretations. A group of brilliant young scholars with a shared background in the British Communist Party, including E. P. Thompson, Eric Hobsbawm, Christopher Hill, and George Rudé, founded the journal *Past and Present* in 1953. It aimed to move beyond Marxist generalities and old dogmas to a close investigation of the national past, underpinned with a certain moral reverence for the anticapitalist and antimaterialist sentiment of the English Revolution's Diggers and Levellers. In the following few years, Thompson founded the more political-minded (but scarcely less historical) journal, *The New Reasoner*, and joined others in a massive "Ban the Bomb" movement. Young intellectuals on various British campuses called themselves the "New Left."[7] The initial U.S. response was fairly anemic. Groups actually formed at a handful of colleges or universities, but only Wisconsin's Socialist Club was both scholarly and intently historical-minded.

By the later 1950s, the combined Left of ex-communists, pacifists, and independent radicals began to reach considerable chunks of an apathetic campus majority. The 1959 Anti-Military (shortened to "Anti-Mil") Ball, a counter-spectacle to the ROTC annual event, actually had more participants than the high-heels-stars-and-braids showcase. Talented young impresarios like Marshall Brickman (later collaborator with Woody Allen in several films, including *Annie Hall*) prepared witty left-wing theatricals.[8] In this burgeoning cultural climate, Williams the Midwest bohemian and amateur jazz musician was especially valued as a link between the youngsters and World War II's radical generation.

Williams, in his return to the University of Wisconsin, was thus somewhat larger than life. Inevitably the Socialist Club's favorite speaker on such immediate political subjects as the "test ban" that leading scientists had proposed to halt the proliferating nuclear weaponry, he spoke also on Marxist philosophy as well as foreign policy in general. If conservative undergraduates of the time complained to the *Cardinal* about a dark force throughout the campus, manifested in the denunciation of imperialism inside the classroom and out, it could be traced directly or indirectly to Williams. Student political rallies renouncing U.S. policies in Latin America naturally sounded like popularizations of the ideas pronounced by the speakers' favorite professor.

Williams thereby found himself unexpectedly a public figure. As several of Williams's students openly supported the right of Cubans to make a revolution, the *Chicago Tribune* warned of subversion on campuses. A worried University of Wisconsin Dean of Students added to the atmosphere of intimidation, pointing to the probability of future damaged careers among undergraduates who joined certain left-wing student groups. Williams, for his part, simply defended his students against a former state assemblyman's charges that they were being made "dupes of the Communists." But when the campus Young Democrats—led by Williams student Henry W. Berger—denounced the red-scare atmosphere and boldly passed a resolution calling for the abolition of the House Committee on UnAmerican Activities (HUAC), conservative legislators hungered for revenge.[9]

A judicial-committee hearing of the state legislature summoned in 1961 to urge Congress to continue HUAC inevitably sparked political fireworks. American Legionnaires and liberal undergraduates demonstrated and counter-demonstrated outside the Capitol, adding further drama to some of the best-attended sessions in decades. Called to testify before the committee, Williams charged that HUAC wasted money, usurped legitimate constitutional powers, and provided biased information to leaders. "Proud to be an intellectual" who could dissent, he boldly avowed that "among man's rights is the right to revolution."[10] Asked what he taught his students, he answered, "I teach people to think," bringing down the house in a veritable explosion from the galleries.[11]

Such courageous theatrics could not be staged entirely without cost. Conservatives insisted, just as they had about other campus radicals for generations, that Williams's supporters in the capitol were out-of-staters, mainly from New York—another way of saying that they were radical Jews. A doughty American Legion commander and frequent letter-writer to the local press charged that Williams, known to encourage disloyalty, had rapidly been "amassing a reputation as a fellow traveler."[12] Madison Peace Center pickets holding up signs at a Civil Defense exercise were heckled with shouts of "Jews, go back to New York and the Soviet Union!"[13] The familiar anti-Semitic undertone to local red-baiting only hardened the determination of cold-war critics. Williams, the professor-as-war-veteran and an officer at that, offered his person as evidence that dissent was deeply American.

Williams meanwhile placed himself comfortably among colleagues in the History Department and the university at large. More perhaps even than he expected, he had come home. As veterans of that time recall, the great changes brought by the 1960s had not yet taken place. U.S. history still seemed to be taught here largely "from the view of North Dakota," as one of Williams's colleagues wryly described the continuing Beardian or regionalist outlook. Professors continued to be valued on the basis of their teaching (it was a commonplace to say that each historian had one good book in him) rather than on their literary output. William Hesseltine was still around to say that real historians "eat and drink history," properly devoting much of their leisure conversation to points raised in classes. Williams was unusual in this crowd only because he seemed also to eat and drink research, so enthusiastic about his discoveries that he could hardly stop talking about them off duty.[14]

The close-knit Americanists included Alan Bogue, a Beardian agricultural historian from Iowa, and a small circle of the familiar 1940s Progressive crew, most prominently Merrill Jensen and Merle Curti. Former mentor William Best Hesseltine and university administrator Fred Harvey Harrington were Williams's special colleagues and friends. The European side featured historian George Mosse, destined to be another of Williams's closest colleagues. A gay, Jewish refugee from Germany—the scion of a vanished dynasty of influential newspaper publishers—Mosse synthesized and reinterpreted the modern European cultural legacy for generations of students. Quickly, undergraduates and graduates alike learned that by taking Mosse, Williams, and sociologist Hans Gerth in tandem, they could acquire knowledge that no book held and insight into European and American life that no other university offered. Such students would also have encountered three of the most atypical professors in the American academy.

History students knew little about Williams before he arrived in Madison except the "larger than life stories" that they heard on the grapevine. Some had read *American-Russian Relations* and found its epilogue in particular to be unsettling and exciting. But its author was also supposed to be "crotchety," altogether "difficult and opinionated," a "kind of Socrates as Socialist who habitually got up on the wrong side of the bed," eager for dialogue but also cranky and stubborn. They could not miss the element of distance he demanded to keep his spare time free for research and writing. Few of them could fully appreciate that Williams had been groomed in the stern school of historiographical training and was mainly trying to pass on his own experience.[15]

In the seminar or one-to-one encounter, Williams was quietly charismatic, his presence in one recollection "the irresistible attraction of a commanding, creative intellectual, who possessed such a robust and essentially healthy ego that he would knowingly make himself vulnerable." He commanded respect and yet also invited personal attachment. His syllabus for an undergraduate course thus typically read:

> I teach this course on the assumption that History is a way of learning about how we humans operate: in thinking about what we have done and what have been the consequences; and in thinking about how we can learn from that vicarious experience in making our own history. I look upon the lectures as a way of giving you information that you can use in your own thinking, and as a way of showing-by-example how to

make sense out of the information you gather. If you find that my way
of making sense out of the information convinces you, that is fine, but
I am not primarily interested in persuading you I am right. The object
is to help you make your own sense out of our history.[16]

Williams's lecture style was also fascinating, if not as dramatic as that of
some colleagues. "You were seeing a world-class intellectual thinking on his
feet; you could see the wheels turn and grind and mesh," according to
Thomas McCormick. Williams's graduate assistants found a certain
"Thomistic logic" inherent in what he said. His train of argument, once set
into motion, had an almost irresistible appeal.

If America were a self-conscious empire rather than the idealistic
democracy it claimed to be, angling for power rather than compelled
against its collective will to seize world influence, then everything else followed. McCormick, former undergraduate president of the Young
Republicans at Cincinnati, remembered fighting "tooth and nail over those
first premises for a full year before finally succumbing. But thinking back, I
realize that the battle was both shorter and more one-sided."[17]

Almost immediately, three of the more promising graduate students in
diplomatic history, Walter LaFeber, Lloyd Gardner, and McCormick
invited Williams over to dinner to "decode" him. In the discussion which
lasted until the wee hours of the morning, he gave them "a private screening, as it were," of *Contours of American History*. It took weeks "to sort out
what had happened," Gardner recalled. But the graduate students had the
feeling that the field of foreign-policy studies would never be the same, and
for them personally, "life was never going to be the same either."[18]

Williams brought them from foreign-policy issues as such, and the
methodological breakthroughs of the time (mainly the process of traveling
abroad to use non-U.S. archives) toward something far off in the intellectual horizon. If they studied and learned from Thomas Hobbes and John
Locke, understood the counterpart theories of social organization worked
out by Thomas Jefferson and James Madison, and grasped how the capitalist market plunged society from one age to another, then they could study
with some facility the various internal developments that had traditionally
been outside the scope of diplomatic history. Above all, they could understand something about how the society worked organically and evolved as
a dynamic unit. In that light, foreign policy became a vantage point to view
the past as no one else but Williams had done.[19]

For many graduate students, Williams also offered a model of the way
they might strive to conduct their lives. He always seemed to have "a new
slant on things" and his open-forum Friday afternoons quickly became "a
weekly mecca for ever-growing numbers of students—some coming to
praise him, others to bury him."[20] Walter LaFeber recalled that "sitting in

that classroom and listening to him lecture, I understood for the first time what a teacher . . . was supposed to do." Williams time and again compelled students toward fresh perspectives, "from a broader perspective and more critical in context" than they could reach by themselves. The capacity to teach in that fashion constituted, for the professorial trainee, "the test of a great historian."[21]

Williams's ability to stimulate unorthodox thought located a particular soft spot in twentieth-century U.S. history. As Lloyd Gardner recalled, the New Deal was then generally seen as the climax of contemporary history. World War II, and then the Truman and Eisenhower presidencies reshaped but also reinforced that legacy as an adopted "Americanism" of government entitlements for citizens and business. A flood of prestigious academic monographs during the 1950s and early 1960s on a variety of subjects, from Teddy Roosevelt to Woodrow Wilson to Franklin Roosevelt, drove home the uniform message and effectively marginalized any alternative, Left or Right.

Williams came at this seeming historical truism from all sides, including among his favorite authorities Marx, Sartre, Herbert Hoover, John Quincy Adams, and science fiction writer Arthur Clarke, and adding random shots from mass-culture genres from jazz to sports. According to him, even those self-consciously elitist and perennial world-champion New York Yankees, showed the excellence that modern liberal bureaucratic mediocrity so palpably lacked. The use of such sources unexpectedly demonstrated, through Williams's unique interpretations, that the New Deal had actually brought forth monsters, and that America could do better.[22]

Conservative undergraduates, who might otherwise have found this line of thought tantalizing, tended to view criticisms of U.S. foreign policies as bordering on treason. (A later generation of young libertarians, bitterly opposed to the Vietnam War, would find in Williams penetrating criticisms of liberalism and the imperial agenda it shared with neoconservatism.) Williams's very command over his teaching assistants appeared to the same suspicious minds as a concerted conspiracy against America. Still others were put off by his high-flow conceptualizations, his occasional abrasiveness, and his toughness toward students he considered lazy.[23]

But Williams found himself mostly admired, and he worked hard to reinforce his influence. In the ethos of the period, the professor who generated the greatest interest among graduate students gained maximum status, and at this project Williams rapidly excelled. On the level of sheer concentration, he scouted graduate school applicants who had less than exemplary undergraduate academic records but who showed signs of promise and determination similar to his own a decade earlier. Through untiring attendance at department meetings, he also usually obtained funding for his favorites. Many of his colleagues indeed felt he pushed too hard in this respect. To the end of his career in teaching graduate students, when he claimed to be bored and exhausted by it all, he remained extraordinarily patient in coaching his charges and then prompting them to go off in their own directions.[24]

He also assiduously promoted his students' postgraduate careers by making sure to find available jobs for them a first and even a second time. In an era before more formal procedures and affirmative action programs, this kind of informal networking practice was normal, although it demanded so much effort that not many professors had the influence or energy to carry through continuously. Within a decade, Williams produced thirty-five PhDs, far more than an average historian, and with considerably more individual attention per student than was usual.[25]

The effort took its toll on his energy and patience. By 1960, he wrote his old friend Warren Susman that he desperately needed more time off, and that the young radicals' demands for less emphasis on elite class consciousness and more on lower class consciousness drove him to distraction.[26] Within a year, he had already begun to look for another job, hoping to find some picturesque and distant place where he could escape graduate students altogether and work out his ideas to his own satisfaction.[27]

Still, he found much of his renewed Madison life very enjoyable, especially in these early years. He worked furiously in his garden, played tennis until his back began troubling him too much, and above all zealously guarded his home life from student interference. He returned home from school by 4:30 p.m. as often as possible and gave himself over to his children (two girls and a boy born in Madison, in addition to Corrinne's boy and girl) until they went to bed, then retreated to the study he had built under the clothesline in the basement. There, puffing steadily on cigars, he would write until 2:00 a.m. or so. Between the pleasures of family life and the atmosphere at school, "I had so much energy [that] I didn't know what to do with it."[28] He had accomplished mightily in the extraordinarily favorable circumstances Madison afforded. The draining unhappiness of marital and family troubles, increased drinking and a deepening sense of urgency to leave Madison were all still years away.

2

Williams formulated the major syntheses of U.S. history that he had been mentally preparing in the 1950s through two book-length studies, *The Tragedy of American Diplomacy*, which first appeared in 1959, and *The Contours of American History*, published two years later. *Tragedy* concerned foreign policy and *Contours* focused on domestic developments leading to the corporate state, but the two books can be read together as Williams's foremost intellectual expression.

*Tragedy*, his most widely read and certainly most influential work among the general public, traced the development of Open Door imperialism from the 1890s through the early cold war. As a sort of point-counterpoint to the claims of George Kennan's *American Diplomacy* (1950) that expansionism had been a product of State Department naivete fumblingly continued afterward, Williams showed that the notion of Empire arose as a solution to late nineteenth-century social crisis and became the *deus ex machina* for national well-being.

U.S. policy-makers sought initially to halt the ongoing division of the globe by existing imperial powers, encourage an increased international volume of trade and production, and promote development American-style in pre-capitalist societies and cultures. The globalization of American economics, antidote to the domestic clash of farmers and labor with capital, demanded an Open Door. Thus, the U.S. could (with only a few exceptions of its own, such as Hawaii and the Philippines) declare itself anticolonial and still become the leading counterrevolutionary force of the twentieth century. Throughout, Williams stressed the importance of economic factors influencing foreign policies, although he did not ignore politics, culture, or psychology.[29]

Many particulars in *Tragedy* had already been expressed in previous articles, but Williams amplified some areas and added new ones. There was more, for example, on Woodrow Wilson's responses to various revolutions (Mexican and Chinese as well as Bolshevik) and the economic imperatives that led him into World War I. Also new were Williams's discussions of Franklin Delano Roosevelt, the New Deal, and how "the nightmare of depression and visions of omnipotence" had led the United States to engage in a world "war for the American frontier" and then into a cold war to preserve and expand the Open Door. Particularly irksome to critics was his continued insistence that the United States should have better accommodated the Soviet Union during and after World War II.

Behind these particulars, Williams had begun to work out his own version of the Spinozan, Frankfurt School, or Diltheyan wholeness as the notion of inner unity within the events, institutions, and personalities of a historical epoch. He did not yet develop the concept of *Weltanschauung* as he would in *Contours of American History* to express the worldview of a time and place. But in analyzing the rise of American imperialism, he argued that it involved a deeply held philosophy, embraced by almost all sections of the community (politicians, intellectuals, farmers, workers, industrialists, and financiers). National prosperity and freedom, these groups had agreed, depended upon unlimited economic expansion. The creative originality of the Open Door policy, that "brilliant strategic stroke" that he had pioneered earlier, reflected a belief that America's economic might was so great that it could conquer without European-style military occupation. The broad outlines of this policy had been conceived well before the Bolsheviks took power in Russia and required only a shift of ideological strategy. But American leaders were not entirely disingenuous when they contrasted communism with the "American System," rather than capitalism as such. Open Door imperialism *was* modern America's capitalism.[30]

The United States could for the moment avoid Europe's far-flung colonial wars of invasion, conquest and repression. But the premise of the Open Door brought the nation into ever increasing conflict with any and all "closed systems," whether European colonialism, fascist hegemony, or popular revolutionary uprisings (Communist or not) to shut national doors and thus permit autonomous economic development. Herein lay the story of most of the history of recent American foreign relations, including participation in two world wars—one completely unnecessary and the other precipitated by a failure to cooperate with the Russians in joint pursuit of collective security—and a ruthlessly destructive cold one. Americans had in the process vitiated their own values and ideals. The nation could reverse course, bring the world back from the verge of nuclear destruction, and allow other peoples to develop as *they* best saw fit. But this broad change would require detaching American democracy and prosperity from imperial economic expansion, much as Charles Beard had envisioned decades earlier.

A good part of Williams's originality in this by-now-familiar argument lay in his presentation. He began his introduction, "History and the Transcendence of the Tragic," by describing the history of U.S. actions in Cuba leading up to the Bay of Pigs invasion. These policies were "not caused by purposeful malice, callous indifference or ruthless and predatory exploitation," and *for that reason* they "contained the fundamental elements of tragedy," a destruction that the hero or protagonist brings upon himself.[31] In the book's conclusion, he returned to this thought, offering a sharp critique with an unmistakeably moral center:

> The tragedy of American diplomacy is not that it is evil, but that it denies and subverts American ideas and ideals. The result is a most realistic failure, as well as an ideological and a moral one; for in being unable to make the American system function satisfactorily without recourse to open-door expansion (and by no means perfectly, even then), American diplomacy suffers by comparison with its own claims and ideals, as well as with other approaches.[32]

Many younger historians who owed Williams serious debts later complained that he had naively suggested American interference could be anything but manipulative and predatory, or was ever intended to be.[33] But he needed this proposition, and not merely for political reasons. His belief went to the heart of his style, epitomized in his proposal to replace the Open Door with "a program for helping other people that is closer to American ideals and also more effective in practice" in bringing world peace and cooperation out of the current destructive chaos. He thereby offered readers an idealistic challenge to "transform the tragedy into a new opportunity for great achievement."[34]

Near the end of the book, Williams similarly posed a series of questions beginning with the phrase, "Isn't it time?" as in time to "stop saying that all the evil in the world resides in the Soviet Union and other communist countries." He desperately wanted to encourage policies that would help reform communism into the real rather than the merely rhetorical pursuit of utopian possibilities; by the same token, he wanted the U.S. to abandon the cold war so as to come to grips with its own internal dilemmas. If Kennan and Schlesinger, Jr., were elitists and moral cynics, as many students comparing relevant texts easily concluded, Williams the heretic was the true patriot and the democrat.

He offered no primrose path to freedom. Only an "open door for revolutions" could achieve what Williams had in mind, and only by "having achieved maturity" could Americans cope with the complexities and dangers that lay ahead. They had every reason to aspire to a "radical but noncommunist reconstruction of American society." But in the short run they needed to evoke and even to assist the "calm and confident and enlightened conservatives" at the centers of power to see the light and steer the nation away from disaster.[35]

The unusual appeal to a mixture of radical ideals and enlightened conservatism had great possibilities. But in 1959, Williams's ideas were daring indeed. The contracted publisher, Braziller, gave Williams a twenty-five hundred dollar advance for the work. But one of the readers, Max Ascoli, editor of the staunchly anticommunist magazine *The Reporter*, "went through the ceiling." Cowed by political pressures, Braziller cancelled the contract but did not demand return of the cash. "You're damn right I'll keep the money," Williams responded. He turned to an agent who got World Publishers, a lesser but reputable house known mostly for their textbooks, to accept it. A second and expanded edition of the book, released in 1963 by Dell, had great success on campus and off.[36]

Initial reviews by professional historians were surprisingly positive for a book that would elicit so much controversy and hostility. *Tragedy* was not yet associated with a major movement to revise major tropes of U.S. history and hence did not challenge or particularly threaten the historical establishment. Nor had broad student and New Left movements, politically receptive to the findings of *Tragedy*, coalesced as yet.

Foster Rhea Dulles, one of the leading traditional diplomatic historians, wrote in the *American Historical Review* that Williams was "brilliant but perverse," a scholar who despite "extensive knowledge" in other disciplines was "obsessed by an almost exclusively economic interpretation" and who "arrogantly dismisses rather than answers what he considers the mistaken ideas of most of his fellow historians." Nevertheless, the book was "stimulating and provocative," enlightening, and in all a "highly interesting contribution to today's great foreign policy debate."[37] Academic blacklist survivor Armin Rappaport, writing in the *Pacific Historical Review*, saw Williams as an "original and decisive thinker" whose thesis of Open Door imperialism, while "plausible and interesting," nevertheless led to "some tenuous if not bizarre and distorted conclusions." And yet the historical profession could use more such "bold and stimulating analysis."[38] Gordon M. Craig, later a president of the American Historical Association, complained that Williams made too many "flat, unsupported," and ultimately unconvincing statements, but was "on solid ground" in dismissing the accepted explanations of American diplomacy as "superficial and naive."[39] Williams had thereby already earned the sobriquet that the *New York Times*, reluctantly respectful, one day hung upon his obituary: the great gadfly or iconoclast.

At least a few major observers outside the academic mainstream but prominent in public life caught Williams's larger importance. James P. Warburg, veteran critic of foreign-policy issues, argued that Williams deserved "the widest possible reading by those, alas, all too few American citizens who are deeply concerned over the future of their country and the future of mankind." If only Williams had included "the impact of the corporation-dominated machine age upon democratic citizenship . . . the failure of religion to sustain a sense of moral responsibility," and the failure of an educational system that now served only "the needs of a parochial, self-contained" society, his work could have been broader still. This, at least, was a warning that Williams sought to heed.

*Tragedy*'s most important reviewer, former New Deal think tank veteran Adolf A. Berle, saluted Williams in the *New York Times Book Review* section for a "brilliant book," one marked by "provocative insights" and a "courageous and essential" attempt to grapple with a vast problem. He particularly agreed that U.S. foreign policy to its discredit did not "accommodate . . . revolutionary changes elsewhere in the world," and that it should learn to work with "social systems different from our own." At the same time, he thought Williams wrong in assuming that America *could* have developed otherwise. He also regretted Williams's adopting certain words—notably "imperialism" and "colonialism"—so far outside the boundaries of the permitted discourse that they hinted at communist propaganda.[40]

Berle countered Williams in terms that would seem curious to scholars generations later, but had long been assumed by 1960. America did expand earlier, Berle readily admitted, but only "to occupy vacant real estate" (thus neatly cancelling out the centuries-old presence and culture of Native Americans). It did acquire overseas influence at the turn of the century, "when real (not semantic) imperialism was rampant," but did not conquer vast populations (likewise cancelling out the Philippines and the various Latin American societies made victims of Gunboat Diplomacy). Former New Dealer Berle insisted that the New Deal had not been designed to "'rationalize corporate development,'" even if the results had gone in that direction. Finally, Williams's recipe for an "Open Door for revolutions" was and had to be "uncritical nonsense." The U.S. could hardly be expected to keep an Open Door to revolutions which went against its own or the larger human interest. Despite these caveats, Berle "anticipated with lively hope" the "more mature development" of Williams's thinking.[41]

Others would say about *Tragedy* that Williams's ideas had actually reached maturity decades earlier, i.e., in the mind of Charles Beard. There was a degree of truth in this observation, for the Beard of *The Idea of the National Interest* (1934), written with G. H. E. Smith, had carefully articulated the economic interests of American nationals leading to involvement in war and had spelled out that war was in essence "one of the fruits of the system" at large rather than a disruption to the system. *The Devil Theory of War* (1936), a very popular essay, dismissed conspiracy theories so as to treat seriously the "impersonal," economic, and social underlying causes of conflict. Most of all, Beard's essays of the late 1930s asked why the U.S. should "have the effrontery to assume that we can solve the problems of Asia and Europe, encrusted in the blood-rust of fifty centuries?" In short, Americans should not deceive themselves with rhetoric about the power of their own ideals. Leaders and especially presidents, as he urged in his final work, *American Foreign Policy in the Making, 1932–1940*, could lead properly only if they dealt in candor with their citizens about what they intended to do and why.[42]

Williams's responses generally, and *Tragedy* in particular, followed this logic only up to a point. Beard had been more concerned with internal developments than foreign policy until the 1930s. He lacked Williams's psychological approach to the mass support of Empire and he did not foreshadow Williams's analysis of the democratic-imperial contradictions in the dreams and strategies of the Founding Fathers. Beard's general attempt was to assess economic influences and the framework of public history and the citizen-as-historian, far more than the particulars of analysis, carried over to Williams. The younger man still might be seen as Beard *revividus*, but mainly in the matter of personal bearing.

In any case, Berle's response and Williams's sudden prominence in the *New York Times* meant that the scholar, not yet forty, was making serious headway and also making waves. A few months later a *Time Magazine* writer attacked the book in no uncertain terms, describing Williams as an unlikely Annapolis graduate.[43] An occasional rising state politician, like future Milwaukee Congressman Henry Reuce, would now spend hours discussing *Tragedy* with the controversial Madison professor.[44] The *Foreign Policy Bulletin* meanwhile asked him for eight hundred words to respond to an essay by Dean Acheson.[45]

More important than all this was Berle's continuing interest. He had used *Tragedy*, Williams recalled, "to begin to get off the containment bandwagon."[46] So he responded with enthusiasm to Williams's invitation to speak in Madison and the two enjoyed "an absolutely magnificent seminar" with graduate students. Amazingly, a year later Berle invited Williams to be his "personal first assistant" dealing with Latin American Affairs in the new Kennedy administration. He was told that he would also sit on the Council on Foreign Relations.[47]

This was a remarkable proposal for several reasons. Understandably, Williams had enormous mistrust for Kennedy's "New Frontier" as yet another "frontier" to conquer, more so as Kennedy intensified the confrontationist cold-war rhetoric in his presidential election drive. "He scares the hell out of me," Williams reflected privately at the time. In mid-campaign, Williams actually wrote a long note to candidate Richard Nixon about the New Frontier, and received an intelligent reply—obviously not from Nixon himself but from someone who understood Williams's point.[48] In the end, according to George Mosse, Williams himself voted for Nixon as the "lesser evil."[49]

Second and more to the point, Kennedy quickly adopted Arthur Schlesinger, Jr., as a house intellectual (or court jester, as some wags suggested). The new president could hardly have brought to power a more violent opponent of the views set out in *Tragedy*. Perhaps, as Williams suggested privately, Berle was warning him in the *Times* to "mature" (as Williams put it, show himself "ready to 'join the system'") and then rise to the top. Schlesinger, Jr., himself had obviously done the same almost fifteen years earlier, with great personal success.

But with Berle and Schlesinger, Jr., in charge of Latin America, "maturity" would have meant joining the Alliance for Progress team, whose plan aimed at dramatically increasing the rise of a Latin American middle class, expanding these nations' export economies, and accelerating the transfer of subsistence lands, inevitably driving rural families from the countryside and encouraging wider use of chemical pesticides as well as toxic industrial substances. This move neatly predicted the course of future U.S. programs for the region, where "economic growth" and regional integration replaced serious attempts at redivision of the highly concentrated pockets of national wealth.[50] In the immediate future, Williams's tenure would clearly have depended upon his quiet acceptance of the Bay of Pigs adventure and Kennedy's personal sponsoring of an imperial counterrevolutionary strike force, the Green Berets. To stay on the team, Williams would have had to accept U.S.-paid and -guided "counter-terror" methods which previewed in the devastated rural villages of Latin (and especially Central) America the widespread military abuses against civilians during the Vietnam War, and even more galling, to accept the flat-out lying denials of covert wrongdoing.[51]

Williams also hesitated for personal reasons. Fred Harvey Harrington urged him on, promising "if nothing else you'll get to read a lot of stuff you wouldn't get to read for thirty years." But he feared uprooting his family. Above all he did not trust the Kennedy clan: "Don't ask me why, I just don't trust them." In light of the Bay of Pigs fiasco and Schlesinger's ignominious role as scholar-activist summoning his talents to deceive the public, Williams later reflected, "Thank God! I would have had to resign before I'd even found an apartment to live in!"[52]

An ugly political sequel followed this refusal to serve. In 1960-61, the House Committee on UnAmerican Activities demanded to examine the still-unpublished manuscript of Williams's next book. The Committee never revealed its reasons for this extraordinary demand, but some members had apparently been inflamed by Williams's public testimony in front of the Wisconsin legislature. They viewed his grant from the leftish Rabinowitz Foundation as an excuse for an intellectual fishing expedition through the troubled waters of one campus, perhaps to chill once more the warming campus political climate nationally. It was a curious moment, as White House initiatives simultaneously moved out of the dreary fifties moods by encouraging an end to the Hollywood Blacklist (John and Jacqueline Kennedy personally attended a premiere of the film *Spartacus* despite American Legion calls for a boycott).[53]

HUAC was not the all-powerful force it had been during McCarthyism's better days. Leading members had disgraced or exposed themselves by their bitter resistance to racial integration as well as their moral turpitude, and civil libertarians, including some who had made appearances on the Madison campus, boldly urged the Committee's abolition. But in an age when the FBI continued to launch furious plots against civil rights leaders and occasionally made spectacular public "discoveries" of current professors' earlier political identities, HUAC and its allies still successfully engaged in intimidation. They certainly remained capable of creating much personal grief for particular victims. Williams had just cause for concern.

Fred Harvey Harrington, by this time en route to being president of the university, assured Williams that he would not be fired, but suggested that he conduct his own defense. As Williams wrote to his intimates, he personally shunned any orchestrated public campaign as a bad defense tactic. Young radical admirers and their older supporters, eager to dramatize his "martyr" status, would doubtless call national attention to the case and do him more harm than good.[54] Friends in the Law School put him in touch with Paul Porter, a major Washington attorney for the labor movement.

Porter "took me up and down and sideways and backward," trying to figure out the logic of the Committee and the proper response.[55] Porter advised him to refuse to hand over the manuscript. HUAC then played him "like a yo-yo," issuing a summons and then, after he had boarded a train from Madison to Washington, cancelling the order. That way his time had been lost and he could not collect any money for the trip. When he finally did get to Washington, Porter's partner Thurman Arnold handled the case. A former New Dealer of note and author of the iconoclastic 1930s classic, *The Folklore of Capitalism*, Arnold advised Williams to get himself off the hook by "paying his respects" to the Committee. Williams dutifully complied, appearing for about ten minutes privately in a "little tête-à-tête" and offering no information beyond himself and his work. Arnold told him that he had "handled it perfectly."[56] The subpoena for his manuscript was dropped, and he left Washington a free man.

Unlike less fortunate witnesses of an earlier era, Williams had not gone to prison nor had his career been ruined. Still, his treatment during a notably liberal Washington administration warned him that intrusions of the state upon dissenting individuals did not ever really go away. If he needed more warning, his treatment at the hands of the Internal Revenue Service, the auditing of his tax records year after year, showed the government had not finished with him.

Back in Madison, the publicity for *The Tragedy of American Diplomacy* and Williams's treatment by Washington had the converse effect of solidifying a radical, dissenting scholarly climate of opinion around him and probably pulled Williams further to the Left. His work and notoriety convinced scores of graduate students that diplomatic history "could have real meaning for the present and could be a pioneering field," as one put it, and that the story of history could be "a vital part of creating, sustaining, and changing a culture," work which required "serious and consequential labor."[57]

Within the decade, he and his doctoral protégés (including Lloyd Gardner and Walter LaFeber, who actually finished under Harrington) earned a national reputation as the "Wisconsin School of Diplomatic History." In the Anglo-American world of historical studies, only the influence of social historians around E. P. Thompson had a more long-lasting effect in any field; it would also be difficult to imagine any other U.S. school of studies (such as the social histories of labor, or women's histories, or the black history field) which continued to have so much effect on scholarship at large.

The reasons for this are not mysterious. Williams created a scholarly following guaranteed to grow steadily in public prestige as well as intellectual importance when the Vietnam conflict and a series of U.S. misdeeds elsewhere drove Williams's points home.

The year of the publication of *Tragedy* saw the appearance of *Studies on the Left*, the first of the U.S. "new left" publications, engineered principally by Williams devotees in the Socialist Club. *Studies* might properly be seen as the delayed political response to the British New Left and to the U.S. civil rights movement. But *Studies* could also be seen as an expression of wider academic stirrings, a profound break from the claims of scholarly "objectivity" so popular among social scientists of the 1950s.

*Studies's* opening editorial, "The Radicalism of the Disclosure," could easily have been written out of a Williams seminar. In the current climate, so-called "objectivity" was finally "reducible to the weight of authority, the viewpoint of those who are in a position to enforce standards, the value judgments of a not so metaphorical market place of ideas." The editors mounted no claims of their own for scholarly dispassion. On the contrary, they had entered the "scholarly racket" because they wanted to deal with the problems of the real world, not merely to gain a "means of livelihood and security." Their task was not, however, to change society directly, but to commence an "investigation of the origins, purposes, and limitations of institutions and concepts" along paths where liberals and conservatives alike obviously feared to tread. They determined, in a phrase, to create a real community of intellectuals.[58]

The tone was especially consonant with Williams's own self-distancing from the Old Left. *Studies* did not claim to speak for (or to) the "struggling masses," workers and the poor. It obviously did not identify itself with the Communist Eastern Bloc, even while bitterly criticizing most U.S. intellectuals' supine posture before demands of their own security state. It did not look upon the ultra-Right of the Republican party (active in the Birch Society and other such institutions, but soon triumphant in nominating Barry Goldwater for President in 1964) as the main enemy or describe current liberalism as betraying Franklin Roosevelt's heritage. Instead, it pinpointed "corporate liberalism" as the hegemonic ideology of the cold-war age.

If a future Socialist movement were to play a vital role, it had to "cut itself free from the stifling framework of liberal rhetoric and recognize that at heart the leaders of the United States are committed to the warfare state as the last defense of the largescale corporate system." The task of Socialist intellectuals, formulating a "new system of political ideas . . . capable of serving an effective movement for the good of society," could best be accomplished by acknowledging their special status as intellectuals. Unlike the ideals of previous (and future) radical generations to go "to the people" as organizers of unions, civil rights movements, and the poor, they had to stay in the universities.[59]

Williams later warmly recalled his association with these young intellectuals as one of his most fulfilling moments. The members of the Socialist Club and the editors of the journal *Studies On the Left* had made important contributions to the understanding of important concepts like "corporate liberalism," and to the dialogue about the intellectuals' possible contributions to the civil rights and early anti–Vietnam War movements. As much as anyone, they had been responsible for the intellectual side of the New Left. For the young participants, as Saul Landau noted later, it was Williams himself who created the intellectual excitement, stirred young radicals to serious study, and convinced them of the possibility of a conceptual breakthrough that could have large implications for the world beyond the universities.[60]

Williams could certainly have played a direct role in *Studies*, but he chose very consciously to remain in the background. In part, he wanted to give the new generation its own opportunity to make mistakes and learn. Secondly, he had his work to do, and it kept him hopping. Thirdly, as he wrote privately to Warren Susman, the *Studies* editors had too much of the "left-over nuttiness of the 1930s image that they carry around in their bones," with a built-in proclivity to believe that they had to shock in order to be radical.[61]

Still, he felt he had "calmed them down" on some issues, and that his presence had a special effect upon the magazine's leading figures. Martin J. Sklar, former hod carrier and later major theorist of "corporatism," was a particular Williams favorite and a moving spirit of the publication, raising money and gathering subscriptions on the road. Saul Landau, a national leader of the Fair Play for Cuba Committee, was another fundraiser as well as editor. Nina Serrano, Saul Landau's wife and yet another Williams devotee, worked in the *Studies* office with Gerth student and cultural critic Eleanor Hakim. James Weinstein, destined to be one of the more important older intellectuals of the 1970s-90s Left, had moved to Madison after dropping out of Columbia graduate school, made himself *Studies'* leading editor, and provided his own funds to the magazine. He recalled meeting casually with Williams over coffee to talk about the direction of the journal. Weinstein's well-received monograph, *The Corporate Ideal in the Liberal State, 1900-1918*, like Martin J. Sklar's notable essays on the rise of corporate government, came out of a collective dialogue in which Williams traded ideas and, more than anyone else, reformulated them for an increasingly large intellectual following.[62]

The importance of *Studies on the Left* was far greater than its circulation of a few thousand. *Studies* reached out to encourage the creation of intellectual networks across the more liberal campuses and major cities. Occupying this historical juncture, *Studies* was perfectly placed to shape the intellectual development of the New Left. Indeed, many of the emerging political leaders were connected with it in one way or another, as writers, editorial associates, or full-scale editors. By the early 1960s, Williams had thereby founded a "school" twice over.

The journal also had a more immediate function. Like Williams himself, it first of all attracted respectful interest from a section of liberal academia tired of the stifling intellectual atmosphere of the 1950s. Thus political scientist Andrew Hacker offered a positive, if patronizing, estimate in 1960 for the well-read *Commentary* magazine. Trained at the University of Wisconsin where "the radical tradition runs deep," the editors, "serious about their radicalism," would likely have an "important influence" over American scholarship in the years ahead.[63] *Studies* writers sought not "the abolition of private property or the establishing of human equality by political means" so much as a "rational social order" through better education and knowledge. Hence they remained safely "theoretical" or "utopian" Marxists. These graduate students, Hacker predicted, would soon enough find well-paying positions from which to launch "recognized and acceptable" careers.[64] C. Vann Woodward, highly esteemed author of *The Strange Career of Jim Crow*, similarly welcomed the journal a few years later as a "sign that graduate students are still alive and kicking in spite of all the professors can do to anesthetize them."[65] If only a few years earlier Turnerian historian Lee Benson had feared to articulate his Marxist predilections, *Studies* made radicalism, or at least cerebral radicalism, respectable, allowing many students to discuss and publish in their areas of interest without fear of sanction.[66]

3

A subtly subversive element within historical revisionism of the 1950s meanwhile made possible the boldest moves by Williams and his students beyond the realm of foreign policy. If Arthur Schlesinger, Jr., had shifted from a model of bureaucratic socialism to guided liberalism in the post-Progressive mode, others influenced by Marxism in their youth rebutted Progressivism more definitively and in so doing opened up new conceptual territory.

Political scientist Louis Hartz's *The Liberal Tradition in America* (1954) was seen at the time of its publication as an exemplary text of anti-Progressive thought. By removing from consideration the same historical phenomena that Reinhold Niebuhr had dismissed as irrelevant to American experience—expropriation, exterminism, slavery, and international forms of exploitation—Hartz managed to create the picture of an American social order based almost wholly upon the principles of classical liberalism. American society had been so free of major conflicts (rather amazingly putting aside the Civil War, labor uprisings, and continuing race conflicts as well) that Americans had not even recognized their freedom from European ideologies. Hence, on the conservative side of Hartz's critique, the Populists' strictures against greedy capitalists had indeed necessarily been irrational "demonology."

But if, in Hartz's account, nearly all Americans were white and actually or potentially middle-class, they had nevertheless thrashed about in the psychic threat of personal failure that individualism imposed upon the national mentality. Influenced by a background in Marxism but even more by a detached iconoclasm and the contemporary predilection for psychologizing, Hartz also implied (though he did not state openly) that the seamless "Americanism" prompted international crusades with no clear positive purpose, like Woodrow Wilson's entry into World War I and perhaps even the current crusading anticommunism.[67] This was not at all what Schlesinger, Jr., and Niebuhr had in mind.

Richard Hofstadter had already gone still further in several key respects. Without doubt the most widely read American historian of his generation (although by only a small fraction of Charles Beard's earlier public audience), Hofstadter carried his own sense of high irony into a major new interpretation of history. He later insisted that his *American Political Tradition* (1948), essentially a series of biographical essays, stemmed directly from his earlier Marxist training. In youth he had been a Communist, albeit keeping this secret from his academic advisor and mentor, Merle Curti. From his first published essay, on Charles Beard, he had worked with the tradition of the Progressive historians, raising sharp questions about them and revising their interpretations. He responded more to historiography than to historical evidence.[68]

In the *American Political Tradition* he had, by and large, reversed the Progressive optic. Hofstadter's America was in fact no democracy corrupted by capitalism, but rather a business-minded society from top to bottom—Hofstadter also conveniently ignored the bottom, for the most part—with the elite being the only truly "class-conscious" sector of it. This "democracy in cupidity" need not be admired, but it needed to be understood without the old rose-colored glasses of the Popular Front's historians who had always seemed to see the heroic plain folk rising somewhere in the distance. The real heroes (and he saw a few, notably the abolitionist Wendell Phillips) had worked against the grain. Arguably, they were the real radicals. *The Age of Reform* (1955), however, pushed the conservative edge of this perspective further. As he had earlier praised slavery spokesman John C. Calhoun's shrewdness and intelligence, Hofstadter viewed reformers like William Jennings Bryan altogether unsympathetically as frustrated capitalists, and the Populists as prototypes for anti-Semitism and McCarthyism.[69]

Appealing for an "intelligent conservatism," Hofstadter seemed, like Hartz, also to be warning vaguely against the illusions of liberalism, in suggesting that the perpetual scramble for materialistic advance had not necessarily been worth the effort. But he suffered the defects of his status as the cold-war liberals' favorite historian, so much so that he appeared to accentuate just the aspects of his theory that they endorsed. He gained entrance into their inner circles of influence and prestige, but at a heavy cost. *Their* Hofstadter (an interpretation which he did not at the time resist) looked suspiciously upon the American masses as responsible for the dangerous drifts in national life, and hoped for a far-sighted elite to hold them in check.[70] The rightward-drifting liberals of the opinion magazines were not alone. If some sophisticated graduate students read the *American Political Tradition* and the *Age of Reform* as subtly radical critiques of liberalism, cold-war liberal professors taught them to a generation of undergraduates as clever proofs of America as a business civilization and of radicalism as perhaps interesting but finally irrelevant to the main process.[71]

This perspective had its own internal limits. Hofstadter's work and that of other contemporary revisionists remained essentially a revisionist critique of Progressive history. It therefore never gained the solidity and finality of the Progressives' effort, except as it tended toward vulgar celebration of America in the writings of Daniel Boorstin, for instance, that Hofstadter himself disdained.[72] Few of his readers or even his academic colleagues realized how unstable Hofstadter's ideas were and how greatly they changed over time.

Hofstadter swam for more than a decade in a current of fervently anti-Beardian publicists destined to become key neoconservative operatives, corporate fundraisers for conservative think tanks, and "Reagan Revolution" favorites such as Irving Kristol, S. M. Lipset, and Nathan Glazer.[73] But when he reevaluated his positions on Beard, Turner, and literary historian V. L. Parrington during the later 1960s, he found them far more insightful than he had remembered. They had something extremely important to say, even if their views might be outdated in historical particulars. Always prone to considering himself politically detached, telling friends he had "nowhere to go," Hofstadter suggested late in life that consensus theories failed to explain American life and that radical historians (including some of his own favorite students) were destined to have an important impact on historians of the future.

Unlike his former associates who became steadily more vulgar in their conservative views and rabidly opposed the New Left scholars, he had actually drifted through conservatism, never really recovering from his youthful disillusionment. Yet he had never lost faith in the possibilities of historical scholarship. For Hofstadter, it had always possessed the great virtue, in an age of increasing nihilism and academic positivism, of a potentially humanizing art.[74]

Williams had sharply criticized Hofstadter's *Age of Reform* on its publication. He was too kind to accuse the book of disingenuous rationalizations for Empire-building. But he argued that the so-called "psychic crisis" to which Hofstadter attributed the late nineteenth-century surge of U.S. expansionism could hardly explain the "relationships between a given conception of the world, entertained by individuals and groups with power, and subsequent events." Whether or not Americans of the time had been locked into a "general neurosis," one had to explain specific economic and functional forms taken, and the consequences as well. Hofstadter had clearly failed to do so, a flaw that applied to much of his work.[75]

But Williams shared more space with Hofstadter than seems obvious at first. He dealt with many of the same subjects and treated more than a few from a roughly similar angle, the analysis of *mentalité* in the leading figures of the time. Indeed, as in the case of Abraham Lincoln, who they both criticized harshly, they often stood remarkably close. They created a perspective at equal distance from the cold-war liberal re-reading of history by Arthur Schlesinger, Jr., however much they might carry the implications in different political directions. Williams, far more than Hofstadter, moved beyond critique of historiography and toward synthesis. There was another key difference, however. Hofstadter was the veritable bridge between the New York literary world and the university. Williams was by contrast the outsider, the non-Easterner at large.[76]

Taken from yet another vantage point, the turn of Hofstadter, David Potter, and other noted 1950s historians toward a quasi-psychological view of an American "character," had its origins not only in the abandonment of Beard (or Marxism) but also in the commonplace reading of Freud, as in the influence of "culture and personality" interdisciplinary studies of the 1920s-40s. Influenced by anthropology and psychoanalysis, its practitioners, especially anthropologists and sociologists such as Columbia's Margaret Mead and Yale's John Dollard, sought to understand the origins of group behavior and tradition. During the 1930s the influence of such anthropologists as Mead and Ruth Benedict had been heavily antiracist and relativist, suggesting that America had much to learn from other cultures, especially in regard to gender roles and racial attitudes.

Cold-war intellectuals, placing the United States at the pinnacle of human possibility, of course abandoned and often condemned such relativism, viewing American achievements and even the American character as models for other societies to follow. But they strived to encompass interdisciplinary methods as a major step forward in historical understanding. On the overwhelmingly positive side for optimists such as Potter, the "culture of abundance" had shaped the American character for the better. Although they feared the alienation in contemporary America, and they bemoaned the poverty of African Americans, they regarded both these developments as products of specific cultural and psychological dysfunctions rather than the effects of capitalism.[77]

A younger generation of scholars used the available cultural methodologies for another and very different purpose: to escape the economism of the Progressive historians without lapsing into cold-war ideological assumptions. By the later 1950s and 1960s, the "new social history" sympathetically investigated the lives of the lower classes, minorities, and women. Adopting anthropological methods, it argued for a complexity and a humane nobility of ordinary people, even those ill-placed to transform society from below. Herbert Gutman, who entered the University of Wisconsin graduate school just three years after Williams (and with many of the same mentors), would become the major proponent of this view and for a time the most admired U.S. radical historian after Williams.[78]

Williams, caught between radical generations, retained the economistic frame of the Progressives but styled within it a psychological version of national character and the individuals who epitomized its workings. In this way, Williams depicted expansionism taking shape not as (in the crude Marxist version) the scheme of wicked capitalists but as a common belief of Americans that expansionism would somehow resolve or at least postpone serious social problems.

Still another distinct and seemingly unrelated trend in scholarship also facilitated Williams's personal growth and potential impact. In the unlikely district of Western history, long dominated by perhaps the most triumphalist believers in democratic expansionism, the definite beginnings of a political shift could be felt. Walter Prescott Webb, dean of scholars of the American West and in most of his past interpretations a great devotee of the white settler, cast a remarkable shadow with *The Great Frontier* (1952). After a lifetime assessing U.S. expansionist assumptions beyond the given territorial limits, Webb had quietly and on his own come to the rather staggering conclusion that expansionism had its own inherent logic beyond any economic, or social, or ethical purpose. Americans were hooked.[79] This conclusion implicitly challenged the entire weight of the cold-war liberal enthusiasm for Schlesinger, Jr.'s model Democrat, Andrew Jackson. Perhaps, as a small but significant trickle of "good Indian" Western films seemed to suggest, expansionism had actually undercut the democratic ethos.[80]

The Williams who gave his wife a three-volume set of Freud and who referred repeatedly in later years to psychological symptoms in society and the individual shared many of the same sources as his cold-war liberal intellectual critics. But he saw the issues through different eyes. The deep criticisms of American culture that he and Warren Susman derived from Frankfurt School theorists like Theodor Adorno and Max Horkheimer, whose few translated works they had traded in Oregon in the early 1950s, fell onto rocky soil among most of the intellectual elite. Complaints about the Frankfurt School often followed the view of David Riesman: America was not at all "authoritarian," big business was certainly not "ruthless," and criticisms of the anticapitalist kind made by Adorno and his colleagues were completely outdated, if ever relevant to American society.[81] But what if Williams tied the Frankfurt School to Webb's revised history with a new conceptual knot?

The implications of this for Williams's published work lay years away. But to judge from scattered correspondence, Williams was reading Marx, Thomas Hobbes, John Locke, Emmanuel Kant, and the writings of American leaders like Jefferson and Madison, classical economic theory, sociology of knowledge, and social theory, always searching for his own synthesis. In the future, he would make the argument openly that the market society (to which Richard Hofstadter's circle of future neoconservatives naturally attributed the democratic virtues) was in fact the "Great Heresy" in human history.

4

Williams's *Contours of American History* (1961), his magnum opus, confirmed his status as the controversial and unpredictable leader of the budding corporate critique from the *Studies On the Left* circle, and in doing so applied the insights of *Tragedy of American Diplomacy* to virtually the entirety of American history. But in attempting a major synthesis of historical information and psychological or behavioral insight, *Contours* did still more. Little understood at the time, it set a final note to the critical revisionism of the historical revisionism of the 1950s by recuperating crucial threads of Progressive history and reaching far into the future interpretations of Western history. With all its abundant flaws, it is one of the most remarkable U.S. history books ever written.

Turned down repeatedly by major commercial presses, *Contours* saw light from the same World Publishing of Cleveland that had brought out *Tragedy*. A tiny left-wing press, Prometheus Books, quickly bought up several thousand copies and stamped on its own imprimatur, expanding the book's circulation widely among the existing "progressive" (i.e., Left) circles outside the university.[82]

*Contours* was Williams's most ambitious work, his most enduring and influential among historians, if too difficult for most of the popular readers of *Tragedy* as well as for many intellectuals in other fields. At a time when observers of historical interpretation began to complain sharply of excessive specialization and lack of synthesis, Williams offered a big-picture approach. Just as newer scholars from all sides commenced to pummel the 1950s consensus history which saw America (in John Higham's words) "coming to seem a much more homogeneous country, more uniform and more stable" and also more cheerful than any previous historian had imagined, Williams confounded critics by embracing aspects of consensus history only to shift the interpretation decisively. Indeed, if Frederick Jackson Turner and Charles Beard had sketched out the major interpretations of U.S. history, Williams was arguably their proper successor, for the good reason that he had them always in the back of his mind.

To change and update the metaphor, no other contemporary radical scholar in any field, not Marcuse and not even Mills, had sought to systematically apply a critique to the national experience.[83] As James Livingston observed, writers as different as Mills, Marcuse, Hannah Arendt, and Norman O. Brown found their various trips through the American mind "only cause for debunking and despair."[84] Williams discovered a useable past, as the Progressive historians used to say, because he knew what he was looking for.

Williams sought to periodize American capitalism in ways that economic historians considered overly bold and to interpret that periodization through the thoughts of the ruling classes as the ruling thoughts of the age (hence taking a page from Marx). He therefore took American thought as a whole seriously, in ways that American historians had rarely done and that the Ivy League intellectual historians in particular had studiously avoided. Writing of "freedom," the Founding Fathers and others had not meant something abstract as the intellectual historians suggested, but something definite, concrete, economic, and social in the ways the age had allowed them to see complex issues.

If U.S. history could be described in that way, without the flagrant use of the Marxist theoretical apparatus so obvious in the hands of the greatest European historians, something large would have been accomplished. Williams did not see, or perhaps could not have recognized, that in the attempt much of the precision of overall coherence might slip away. Readers often had to stumble across large thoughts, as Williams did himself. Many of his students, primed by assignments in Hegel's *Phenomenology of Mind* for George Mosse's European history classes, had learned to move from one page to another hoping for insights rather than expecting to understand every word. Others simply felt befuddled and gave up the effort.

*Contours*, even at its weakest, possessed another large virtue that disarmed many would-be critics in advance. Placing individuals within an all-encompassing and increasingly destructive system, Williams nevertheless treated them with personal sympathy—at least until the early decades of the twentieth century. Once again as in *Tragedy*, students and others could read Williams as "pro-American," a radical who saw great potential good in his society even when he viewed the outcome of their actions with distress.[85] Williams thereby went far to reinvigorate the history of ideas in U.S. historical scholarship at large by recasting the dialogue about liberalism and conservatism, showing the similarities of the two intellectual systems as no one had earlier. In all this and despite his stress upon *system*, he seemed always to suggest that with sufficient knowledge and sympathy, individual actors *could* have exerted themselves toward better ends—just as the reader might, whatever his or her place in the nation.

If *The Tragedy of American Diplomacy* had drawn heavily on the legacy of Beard, *Contours* was determinedly original. In his sweeping panorama, Williams detected three *Weltanschauungen* informing the national experience, beginning with the colonial and early national periods (1740-1828) and their "mercantilism," the favorite Anglo-American system of economic growth and regulation.[86] This age was succeeded, or subverted, by that of "laissez nous faire" (1819-1896) which led, at the end of the nineteenth century, to the present system of "corporate capitalism" or "corporate syndicalism."[87] As usual strongly iconoclastic, Williams praised certain individuals often criticized in standard liberal historical accounts—such as John Quincy Adams, Henry Clay, Thaddeus Stevens, Charles Evans Hughes, and Herbert Hoover—who despite their limitations saw the American dilemma and appreciated the need for community. Williams consequently looked darkly at those other national heroes, including Jefferson, Jackson, Lincoln, Wilson, and Roosevelt, who avoided the nation's fundamental problems by turning to expansion and/or war.

But one can approach the dense historical details of *Contours* more easily, perhaps, from the ethical or philosophical standpoint that Williams brought to the text. He began with the proposition that market values had to be seen as the "great heresy of human history" rather than (as in the standard Marxist accounts) an unhappy progenitor of the growth that would lead inevitably to a deferred communal gratification. Williams's own perspective would have been most familiar to late nineteenth-century social-ists, especially William Morris, and it permeated the popular perception of capitalism's special cruelties. Memories of the handicraft tradition and the evocation of a vanishing communal warmth filled the iconography of European socialism and overflowed into the various rituals, from choral choices to holiday costumes. Morris's favorite illustrator, Walter Crane, captured this sensibility, and Williams must have seen Crane's illustrations of British and American socialist volumes. The popularity of early anthro-pologist Lewis Henry Morgan's work among socialists, attributing communal values to neolithic societies, deepened the sentiment.[88]

Discredited or displaced by fascination with industrialization and by the accessibility of consumer goods to the Western working classes, the mood passed but never entirely vanished. Humanity, according to an argument renewed by liberation theologians shortly before Williams's death, had required a considerable degree of cooperation throughout its eons of social evolution or it would simply not have survived. Humanity would finally recover its capacity for cooperation or surely destroy itself. Not susceptible to proof or disproof, this sentiment might be called the Christian Socialist kernel of Williams's historical perspective.

But unlike other Christian Socialists, including the Reinhold Niebuhr of younger days, Williams looked sympathetically through the prism of his-toric development at the ways the system had been successively reordered. In *Contours*, mercantilism was seen as the last of the somewhat cooperative systems, compromising its sense of community or common values with nationalist imperatives (such as expropriating the wealth of other nations) and the large-scale African slave trade, but still retaining a notion of com-monweal and a belief that the social elite *could* rule judiciously.

Williams had grappled to comprehend how the American break-through into new dimensions of freedom had also engaged the opposite possibility, conquest beginning with indigenous societies at hand. He had been ruminating on questions of pre-capitalist expansionism since his days in Oregon with his friend, economist Robert Campbell, so the interest he now had in mercantilism was not strictly new. But as he wrote to Warren Susman in 1958, he discovered in an essay by economic historian Curtis Nettles (which he had reprinted in *The Shaping of American Diplomacy)* a suggestion that he had not pursued before, the role of British mercantil-ism in creating an *American* mercantilism. And he added with a sense of difficult accomplishment:

> Well, the fiftieth time I read that[,] it finally got through my skull: this is a key insight to the whole period from 1776 to 1825. [The] Articles of Confederation represent a treaty between 13 bunches of damn fools who think each of them can have their own mercantile

empire; [the] constitution is the mercantile state; and the foreign policy is beautiful, concluding with the War of 1812 as a classical
mercantile war for trade and the colonies (see Jefferson's change of
heart on land policy, et al.) and the Monroe Administration with John
Quincy [Adams] as Sec[retary of] State and the Monroe Doctrine as
the document of mature American mercantilism. Then we get the
wild spell of laissez faire, and back to corporate capitalism in the
1893-1903 era. Suddenly Madison becomes comprehensible as the
American mercantilist philosopher: so ideas and economics come
together in a fascinating way in the minds of the characters themselves as well as in ours. And Johnny Locke, of course, suddenly
makes sense as the mercantilist natural law philosopher. I am excited
about this, as this paragraph indicates . . . [89]

Williams used this shrewd and original interpretation to set the philosophic
linchpin or mainspring for *Contours* with the compromise of democracy
and Empire. Arriving at the end of the Age of Mercantilism when ideas of
national welfare had turned into corruption and special interest, the
American Revolution definitely espoused the values of liberty and democracy. It also opened a Pandora's box of individualism's potential effects. In
doing so, it recuperated the "modernization" theories proposed by
Schumpeter or Karl Polyani, but with a twist. A shadow American socialism lay always, even in the most unexpected places, within the opposition
to the imperial option.

Lord Shaftesbury, an aristocrat after Williams's heart, had accepted the
framework of British mercantilism but sought to curb its excesses. A political and intellectual Renaissance man with real literary style and a typically
Tory Radical verve, he hoped to establish a system of Empire that would
ease Britain's internal pressures. He also sought to create a workable relation with the colonists, and on that basis showed a remarkable toleration for
religious dissenters, arguing that they made good economic citizens. He
demanded the supremacy of elected parliaments even while clinging to the
monarchical form. And he rejected firmly the emerging notion that poverty
was caused by sin rather than economic maladjustment.

Of course, expansionism and mercantilism had their own deep logic.
Shaftesbury's intellectual successor, John Locke, disdained the very notion
of corporate responsibility. With Locke (Merle Curti had called him
"America's philosopher"), individuality became the highest virtue, even
while it rested upon the twin foundation of Empire abroad and conform-
ing citizens at home. This vaunted individuality was, then, defined mainly
by a near-absolute control of personal wealth. Pleasure and the avoidance
of pain, a sort of working definition of what would become Pragmatism,
measured the narrow parameters of secularized Puritanism.

Mercantilism in either guise demanded taking the resources from one nation or empire to enrich another: Britain had to best the competitors for the New World. But the North American colonies that the British created would soon enough consolidate their own system sufficiently to prompt the rise of an independent-minded American mercantilist class with a nationalist Lockean orientation. Until the last historical moment before the Revolution, future leaders of the new nation fervently wished to exercise their colonial prerogatives within a broad, Shaftesbury-like definition of the British empire. When this became impossible, the rhetoric and the experience of the Revolution carried them in a new direction. The determined decentralism of the Confederation pointed away from the national consolidation and expansion that mercantilism demanded. But historic logic dragged the actors, some of them uncertain of their own loyalties, in another direction.

Throughout his narrative, Williams had an almost obsessive determination to overturn the accepted hagiography of American heroes, including many of the traditional favorites of liberals and radicals. Examining their rhetoric and action carefully, he found the impulse for national expansion near the kernel of their political being. He offered interesting asides on the worldview and tactics of the Quakers, of Massachusetts' Puritan descendents, of Benjamin Franklin's Philadelphia milieu, and of the various rebels like Nathaniel Bacon who seemed to threaten stability. In the colonial era, Calvinism's heirs held a special fascination because they "asked the right questions and struggled for the right answers" in their struggle for a kind of community. But in Williams's folksy vernacular, he added that

> like the little girl with the curl in the middle of her forehead, these early Puritans had a kink in their ideology; when they went wrong, they went very, very wrong. Devoted to the ideal of a corporate community guided by a strong moral sense, they developed a great talent for misinterpreting any opposition. From the outside, for example, they were prone to view the Indians as agents of the Devil . . . . The propensity to place Evil outside their system not only distorted the Puritans' own doctrine, it inclined them toward a solution which involved the extension of their system over others.[90]

This interpretation actually marked a return to the critique of Puritanism by the avant-garde crowd around the *Seven Arts* magazine of the late 1910s, fleshed out by Lewis Mumford during the 1920s and 1930s when a young Williams had been reading omnivorously. The cold-war years saw a revival of the Puritans' reputation by Perry Miller and others. Williams sought to preserve their ideal of community while revealing the dangerous implications in their thought that Mumford's generation had noted.

The Virginia dynasty naturally had a special fascination for Williams as the closest approximation to an American royalty. Thus Thomas Jefferson, long honored by radical scholars as the champion of liberty, came to be seen in this light as the key visionary of Empire. He and James Madison buttressed their plan for the American future with the vision of endless expansion. They created the working ideology that W. E. B. DuBois later named the "American Assumption": with sufficient resources every white man could create his own sphere of freedom. Millions of practical-minded settlers lived out the paradox of possessing the liberty to expropriate at will and, if necessary, to destroy everything in their path that they could not turn to profit.

It would be difficult to overstate the originality or radical quality of this interpretation for the field of U.S. history. Previous radicals' attempts had often reduced great national conflicts like the Revolutionary and Civil Wars to raw class interest, a favorite conclusion of turn-of-the-century socialist classics. Or they had, like Herbert Aptheker and other Communist writers, chosen a pantheon of heroes to cheer onward, insisting that the side of the angels would one day be that of class-conscious socialists and communists.[91] Williams would have none of this. Reading the American saga as Greek tragedy, he once more sought the errors not mainly in venality but in human weakness, reading into the minds of the Founding Fathers a well-nigh irresistible temptation offered by "empty" land and the vast economic productivity of the slave-plantation system.

Williams's view of the Founding Fathers, in particular, was an engaged view of major personalities and their dilemmas. John Jay had promoted the idea of expansionism as the road to prosperity and republicanism, even perhaps temporarily abandoning claims to the Mississippi River and New Orleans in return for access to the Spanish Empire and Asia. He could admit that whites had done wrong to Indians but insisted nevertheless that the mercantilist system worked that way. ("It would seem," Williams observed in an ironic offhand parallel to U.S. policy during World War II, "that the principle of unconditional surrender and total war appeared rather early in American history."[92]) Jefferson evaded the problems while Monroe saw the implications clearly. Jefferson's own steady move toward the imperial solution made him seize, unwontedly, what Jay intended. And Madison recognized that republicanism degenerated into conflict when state grew into Empire, without ceasing his own contribution to the direction of things. The point of postrevolutionary settlements had been to try to square the circle of mercantilism, to bring in the new order with efficient upper-class leadership. As Merrill Jensen might well have taught Williams more than a decade earlier, that was the main point of the Constitutional Convention.[93]

In its own waning days, two generations later, mercantilism yielded to a *laissez nous faire* principle that relied flatly on expansion to resolve internal contradictions and conflicts. Echoing the arguments of Lewis Mumford's almost-forgotten *The Golden Day* (1927) with its apotheosis of small-town New England, Williams insisted that the frontier had mainly offered opportunities for self-barbarization, and that Andrew Jackson epitomized the malignantly burgeoning individualism. Williams thus turned upon its head *The Age of Jackson*, Schlesinger, Jr.'s sentimentalization of the Democratic Party alliance of working people and entrepreneurs. Apart from ignoring Jackson's well-earned reputation as one of the most murderous enemies ever faced by American Indians and his deep personal attachment to the South's "peculiar institution," as many other scholars would point out, Schlesinger, Jr., had willfully refused to see how cupidity had triumphed over commonwealth.[94] The same transparent parallel which led Schlesinger, Jr., to view Franklin Roosevelt (and later in his own writing, Harry Truman) as rightful heir to Jackson's regime obviously propelled Williams toward his own, nearly opposite conclusions.

When he turned to the later nineteenth century, Williams added even more remarkably to the changing currents of historical sympathies. As the contemporary civil rights movement stirred imaginations, the historical reputation of Abolitionism had sharply revived among scholars and the public at large. Passages were quietly withdrawn from reputable textbooks which for decades had portrayed Abolitionists as madmen and southern blacks as happy children. Leading historians' hostile portrayals of Abolitionist leaders as neurotic malcontents likewise fell out of fashion. Williams pointed out what few on either side of the argument about Abolitionists had noticed. No one had so thoroughly glorified individualism as had the Abolitionists. To an unsympathetic eye, they had urgently wanted to free the slaves but did not put equal effort into providing them with the land they needed to ensure their independence.

Williams touched the most sensitive patriotic chords in his portrait of Abraham Lincoln. Hardly anyone but loyal Confederates had pilloried the Great Emancipator, not even those anti-Reconstructionists (such as film-maker D. W. Griffith) who made Lincoln's assassination into the occasion for a supposedly brutal treatment of beleaguered southern whites. From the Left, boy socialist Carl Sandburg had grown into a beloved popular biographer of the Illinois lawyer. And in the liberal-conservative mainstream, Lincoln had been canonized as the spirit behind U.S. entry into two world wars (and the cold war), the veritable father of the Republican Party. Only in the iconoclastic historiography of moderate conservatives like Richard Hofstadter and David Donald had any respectable scholar dared puncture Lincoln's aura.

But in Williams's eyes, the corporate railroad lawyer become president was, mainly, an empire-builder par excellence. Rather than accept the logic of the Declaration of Independence and the Constitution, which all but promised the right of secession, Lincoln had pressed his goal of national unity at any price. He thus set in place two foundation stones for an unceasing world crusade. The corporation would become the mechanism and rationale for that ultimately self-destructive venture.

Williams brilliantly characterized the rise of the corporation as the emergence of a new model for the social compact. He hit his stride with an analysis of overseas Empire, seen through the eyes of the diplomatic elites and political leaders at the end of the nineteenth century. Unlike traditional radicals who saw American leaders solidly in favor of expansion, Williams detected subtle fissures and hesitations. He also hinted at the premise of a later volume, that farmers' own demands quite as much as corporate interests and sheer nationalism had powered the conquest of Hawaii, the Philippines, and Cuba, as well as influence in China and elsewhere. He showed his strongest card in demonstrating the fallacy of the common assumption that the United States had acquired an empire "in a fit of absent mindedness" (according to the popular phrase about England), almost against the national will. No great empire had ever been created with inattention or ease, he observed.

Williams carried this perspective forward in a savage critique of Woodrow Wilson, and of the U.S.'s entry into the First World War as the act of a reckless empire-builder. As much as Harry Truman would be for neoliberals of the 1990s, Wilson had been granted iconic status among 1950s cold-war liberals through discrediting the popular ignominy heaped on him in his last years of office. Wilson biographer Arthur S. Link, a severe antagonist of Williams, portrayed the president as a finely tuned intellect, a magnificent reformer, and a dedicated idealist doomed by a tragic turn in world events. Link made just as little as possible of Wilson's other side, quite apart from the war: his racial policies, the very worst in generations of the presidency; his antienvironmental giveaway, the release of massive federally protected lands to Western states' developers and the consequent drastic reduction in future national parks; his imperial invasion of Mexico; and his direction of the nation's most violent and repressive red scare ever.[95]

Williams saw Wilson as a fellow historian who had, however, early set his sights upon Empire, struck a grand deal with the corporations for a refined profit system, and brought his overweening ego into the catastrophic world scene. Wilson had determined to make the world safe for U.S. economic expansionism, committing vast lives and resources to that goal. Above all, he made the U.S. into a formidable counterrevolutionary world power from Mexico to Russia, meanwhile turning his back on

Chinese nationalists and repeatedly invading the smaller nations of Latin America.

Williams used Wilson once again to delve more fully into the theory of corporatism as the major *Weltanschauung* of modern American society.[96] From the end of the nineteenth century, American leaders had drawn drastic conclusions about the change they intended to bring to the society at large. In a drive to rationalize the economy and increase production, a kind of oligarchic rule had encompassed government, big business, labor leaders, and large farmers. Individualism had indeed been subverted by this change, but without creating a genuine community.

The core idea of this perspective was not new to Williams. Herbert Croly had advanced a version of it early in the century, glorifying in its triumph during World War I. A host of *New Republic* writers gleefully greeted Wilson's War because they believed that corporatism consolidated a system of potentially benevolent elites, guided by the best minds (obviously, their own). A few keen-eyed socialist theorists saw the same phenomena of consolidation but from a harshly critical perspective, outlining the passage of private capitalism to a corporate-led state capitalism with the collaboration of craft workers and the petty bourgeoisie. These socialists had even noted the critical connection of state hegemony with the acceleration of postcolonial, economic imperialism, and in that specific sense, they foreshadowed Williams, more than any others.[97]

A school of rather conservative business historians had subsequently, especially since the 1940s, tended to use corporatism as a way to explain the logic of business organization as the proper model for an evolving society.[98] Traditional left-wing scholars less interested in "system," or casting it in familiar Marxist dichotomies of class interests, had been inclined to write off this business history as mere apologism. Williams took it seriously enough to borrow the logic while shifting the interpretation.

Several of Williams's students were to elaborate better than Williams himself some of the main implications of corporatism for the twentieth century. Labor unions, for instance, achieved recognition as part of a corporate system. Their leaders, such European immigrants as Samuel Gompers and Sidney Hillman, could be made an important part of the corporate order.[99] Wise businessmen, from the National Civic Federation to electronics magnate Gerald Swope, had foreseen the process, and even encouraged unionization under certain circumstances.[100] A psychological or ideological penetration of Woodrow Wilson showed how the system came together at its administrative center, with Protestant values merged into the marketplace and expansion as the only possible American system.[101] McCormick and Michael J. Hogan, in particular, later applied corporatism to explain twentieth-century U.S. foreign policy, thus providing a more complete explanation than Williams supplied with his Open Door thesis in the *Tragedy of American Diplomacy*.[102]

Williams himself added the conceptual final touches, in a sense, by portraying Herbert Hoover as the last of the maximum leaders to seek a kind of internal solution to the problem of business's expansive needs, rather than looking to Empire. In that light, Hoover, the goat of the Depression, looked better, while Roosevelt (still seen by liberals as the greatest figure of the century) looked far worse. One could suggest—as Communist historian Herbert Aptheker did—that Williams had in this sense finally come home to Charles Beard; indeed some ironically concluded that Williams was "more Beardian than Beard."[103]

This was not entirely off the mark, but Williams took Beard for the larger thought of an age and a mood discredited by later liberal and conservative thinkers. Lewis Mumford, Van Wyck Brooks, Waldo Frank, and other heterodox radical intellectuals of the 1920s-30s had rejected the Wilsonian solutions and strove in a variety of ways to project images of possible communities. Dreading the prospect of another world war, they had hoped that historic recollections of realized communities or small-scale models of cooperative living (such as the new towns of the Tennessee Valley Authority, or the "garden cities" planned for several states) might provide ways to turn America's best energies inward. Only the pressure of fascism, and the popular support of the New Deal, had reconciled them to Roosevelt's programs.[104]

The last few chapters of *Contours* touched oddly on various aspects of American life reshaped by imperial ends, such as the ways in which labor leaders (including Walter Reuther, often idealized by cold-war liberals) shared basic international objectives with business leaders. Or the mighty moralists of the age, like theologian Reinhold Niebuhr, who had blessed the emerging military-industrial complex as a work of righteousness, concluding that Americans could retain their morality by accepting the logic of business, i.e., endless expansionism. "But Christ, and Marx and Freud as well," wrote Williams in a characteristic passage,

> had insisted that the only important frontier was man in society—not man on a frontier. To them, the frontier was harmful not merely because it offered an escape from difficulties that needed to be faced and resolved; that was but a minor point. To them, the frontier was harmful because it was precisely what Turner called it: an escape from even the chance to become fully human. Hence Christ and Marx and Freud quite understood the vital function of a Utopia. Unlike Dewey and Niebuhr, they put stars in their philosophic sky. Such an ideal was essential if men were to move beyond the enervating and ultimately dehumanizing stalemate of existence.[105]

That passage fairly encapsulated the peculiar writing style and moral vision of Williams, which along with an absence of footnotes puzzled his sympathizers and offered his critics fuel for counterattack on various grounds.

Hardly anyone noticed the other oddly significant methodological note in the volume. In his acknowledgments section, alongside credits to Mosse, Gardner, Warren Susman, Harvey Goldberg, Hesseltine, Jensen, and Hans Gerth, among others, Williams offered a paragraph tribute to Marx, adding that a passage in the Socialist giant's correspondence concerning the concept of "feudal socialism" had "probably" moved him toward "the questions and research that produced this interpretation of American history."[106] He did not identify the passage, but he apparently referred to a mention of the concept in Engels's correspondence with Marx, finally published in English in 1955. Here, Engels describes Marx's distinction between different kinds of socialism, essentially feudal, utopian, and "scientific."[107]

But something was decidedly lacking here in Williams's own logic. His "reactionary" statesmen, like John Quincy Adams, earn the highest praise and not only because they identify the ills of the rising bourgeoisie. Marx and Engels (with perhaps the exception of their literary tastes, as for the pronounced French royalist Honoré de Balzac) had relatively few flattering words for Tory radicals or Tories, and then only in contrast to capitalism's apologists. Williams, understandably lacking Marx and Engels's confidence in a future proletarian revolution, by contrast actually identified with "feudal socialism" as superior to the development of anarchic individualism.

One critic suggested, decades later, that Williams had repeatedly missed his best opportunity to clarify his methodology and his philosophical assumptions; his impact upon historical study and especially Marxist-influenced study would suffer as a result.[108] He could be blamed too easily, however. If Williams remained vague, Marx and Engels had been almost as vague in references to the meaning of pre-capitalist collectivism and its significance for the post-capitalist future. At most—and Williams would repeatedly use this insight—Marx had noted that capitalism dissolved the older forms of village life. Yet, the aging Marx struggled in his notebooks with the possibility that capitalism could possibly be overleaped by backward societies in revolution.[109] Williams echoed the popular views of late nineteenth-century socialists like William Morris that capitalism had been a monstrous interruption in human development. But this insight or belief related approximately at best to Marxism or to most of white American experience.

*Contours'* critics hardly noted these fine points, however. According to Williams's recollections, Henry Steele Commager called Williams and they spoke for some time about the book, but the *New York Times* killed the review that had been commissioned from him.[110] The first noted com-

mentaries came from conservatives, and were characterized by a vitupera-
tion rare to scholarly discourse. Williams had plainly made nervous the
self-avowed pluralists who celebrated 1950s America and looked uneasily
upon the fast-changing scene. If they had earlier failed to demonize him as
a pro-communist, they sought now to drum him out of intellectual
respectability. "One cannot exclude the possibility that [this book] was
intended as an elaborate hoax," declared Oscar Handlin in the *Mississippi
Valley Historical Review*, and "that its author has been enjoying himself by
ingeniously pulling the legs of his colleagues." Williams's interpretations
were simply "perverse," his writing style parodied "the literary striving of
unskilled freshmen," and large sections of the book were "altogether farci-
cal." The book, in short, was a "total disaster," permeated by "pervasive
wrongheadedness," and inviting "no form of rational discourse." "Enough,"
Handlin concluded woodenly, "This much can certainly be said for the
book: it is original. There has never been anything like it before."[111]

The acceptance of Handlin's polemic at face value by the editors of the
*Mississippi Valley Historical Review* suggested how far a wing of the scholarly establishment might go, and how far others would permit them. Critics
wondered aloud if Handlin's own maudlin treatments of American history
would have been turned over to a radical historian for review, or whether
those of various other respectables, Samuel Eliot Morison to Arthur S.
Link to Arthur Schlesinger, Jr., would have been allowed to be attacked in
such a scurrilous fashion in the leading journal of Americanists. Not likely.
Indeed, the subsequent shift of the profession leftward brought nothing like
the crudeness of these attacks.

Younger historians in particular considered Handlin to be overstepping
the bounds of scholarly propriety. "Cheap ridicule," "bullying," and "a scan-
dalously intemperate polemic" had no place in a professional journal,
according to immigration historian John Higham.[112] Williams's fellow
graduate student at Madison but also a staunchly anti-Communist liberal,
Higham even took to the pages of *Studies On the Left* to celebrate
Williams's "patriotic radicalism" and his originality, and to rationalize the
"almost vertiginous complexity of application and incident" involved in the
writer's unique thought process. If not entirely persuaded—as a self-
described liberal, Higham could hardly be persuaded by an "anti-liberal"
text—he nevertheless insisted that Williams had the merit of dealing "more
extensively and strenuously" with the relations of freedom and community
that any previous writer hitherto.[113] In his insightful letter to the *Mississippi
Valley Historical Review*, Higham also pointed out Handlin's real intent
besides blackening Williams's reputation: he meant to deliver a blow at
Charles Beard. Although a student of Beard's own pupil, Arthur
Schlesinger, Sr. (a relation fraught with still more ironies), Handlin had as

early as 1942 dismissed Beard's influence on subsequent U.S. historical scholarship, as if engaging in scholarly wish fulfillment.[114]

Other conservatives tended to be equally hostile and only slightly less polemical. Williams, according to John Braeman, was simply "naive and wrongheaded." As a historian, he failed by attempting "to force the whole of the American experience into the straitjacket of an economic interpretation of history," making it appear that only "the dollar sign" counted as "a dominant motif force" in American history.[115] James Malin, who had hosted Williams at a Kansas regional history session in 1957 and was himself known as a vituperative critic of big-state liberalism, could not get past his impression that Williams proposed unfair limits upon the American magic of success. The pragmatic national confidence that "both parties to a business transaction may gain, and that there are no known limits to natural resources, except that man's contriving brain may fail him," were clearly missing from Williams. Malin's attack pointed to a deeper difference which passing time (with the ever worsening environmental situation) and future historians would further illuminate.[116] Williams's estimate of limits, his kind of Christian Socialist corporatism, ran up against a liberal conservatism whose central logic was the absence of natural restraints.

And this question in turn raised an important point made decades later by Williams's former fellow graduate student, David Noble. For many of the young radicals of the 1940s, including John Higham and even to a degree Warren Susman, the materialistic cornucopia and the ethnic pluralism of the 1950s had become a rather successful substitute for the socialism they had embraced in their youth. It offered a utopia of sorts if not a cooperative model. The *Tragedy of American Diplomacy* remained ambiguous on the matter: if Americans could abandon their expansionist fixation, they might all enjoy the middle-class ideal that the author embraced in his private life. The Williams of *Contours* was closer by contrast to Noble's own conclusions in *The Eternal Adam and the New World Garden* and to later ecological observations: the apparent cornucopia was a nightmare in disguise, a vast misuse of natural resources; and the consumerist pluralism was less a happy outcome than a flattening of character.[117]

It remained to Herbert Aptheker, the best-known and most politically influential of communist historians since W. E. B. DuBois (and indeed, himself the designated editor of the DuBois Papers) to pronounce a definitive view from the Old Left. Asked to write a second review for *Studies*, Aptheker the seasoned politico was uncharacteristically judicious. If Williams's sweep of all U.S. history did not fully succeed, the partial failure "does not dim the reviewer's admiration for the boldness of the effort, the brilliance of its insights, the humanism of its commitment, and the transparent honesty with which the case is offered."[118] Aptheker criticized

Williams's American-centeredness, his often narrow focus on the machinations and mentality of the ruling classes, his indifference to the contributions of Abolitionists, and his converse unwillingness to consider the dangers of fascism. Behind these particulars lay a sense that in failing with black history, the Civil War, Reconstruction, and all their historical implications, Williams had missed a very large trope in national experience. This was the other side of Williams's single-minded concentration upon expansionism.[119]

The Pan-African scholar and culture critic C. L. R. James, reading *Contours of American History* in the final years of his long and varied life, analyzed the problems raised by Aptheker more simply. Urged by a youngish devotee to read Williams, he pored over the pages, and putting the book down asked only: "Where is DuBois?"[120] Had James known that Williams began his political life in the civil rights movement, his puzzlement might have been greater. Somehow, the impulses which helped to set Williams's ideas in motion and prompted him to become a historian had gotten left behind. Perhaps he felt, as his British counterpart E. P. Thompson was wont to say about the limits of his own work, that there was a larger historical/intellectual conversation going on and no one scholar could expect to encompass it all in his own writing.[121] But this would be something of an evasion. In moving toward a synthesis (as his contemporaries moving into social history rarely attempted), he could create a sense of unity only from above, drawing from below those who, like labor leader Samuel Gompers or Populist leader Jerry Simpson, had been admitted to the club. Williams lacked the capacity or the energy to go any further with an alternative line of thought.

Decades later, when Williams devotees and former students reflected on the meaning and significance of *The Contours of American History*, they came to very different conclusions. Thomas McCormick was still impressed by the text's holistic "integration of domestic and foreign affairs," its providing "radical ways to think about whole epochs . . . and fascinating new notions about corporate liberalism" thoroughly overturning the familiar "liberal notion of cycles of history." Black historian Manning Marable found the treatment at its weakest points utterly lacking in social dynamics, an "old-fashioned, elitist history from the top down," ignoring "the dynamic, creative role of social protests by African Americans, working people, women and other oppressed groups . . ."[122]

These differences were instructive, for in a slightly earlier or later age when Williams's plain radicalism or his clumsy grappling with social history would have been far more defeating, *Contours* might have passed quietly as an eccentric work with some interesting insights. In the half dozen years after its publication, however, it was the open sesame to the younger radical historians, graduate students, and undergraduate students who wanted to take a large and long view of the national experience. As interesting and valuable (also better documented and more smoothly written) as synthetic accounts by other radical historians might be—and there were still relatively few of the species—none had the sweep of social formations and personalities in the historical process, and none had the intensity of identifying the specific role of ideas. By a large but not illogical leap, Williams's readership proved themselves as the core group who could explain the historical origins of the gigantic U.S. war upon the tiny jungle nation of Vietnam.

5

By no accident, the developing perspectives of the 1960s social movements seemed to coincide, for a time, with Williams's own. The Old Left, which the *Studies on the Left* editors avowed that they had outgrown, had hidden its socialist ideas inside a liberal casing and identified the enemy as the Far Right, when in reality a bipartisan corporate liberalism had long guided the State. The same Old Left had romanticized the top-heavy labor movement, and in true bureaucratic spirit urged youngsters to attach themselves to centralized institutions. Research and active discussion, according to the *Studies* editors, could make known alternative truths. Hence the journal bristled with the vision of the "citizen-scholar" that Williams more than anyone else had laid out for them. James Weinstein, soon to become the journal's leading political spokesman, pointed to Williams's understanding of the decision-making capacity of ordinary people as an inspiration for the New Left's commitment to "participatory democracy," even as he called for greater clarity and outright socialist organization.[123]

The political and tactical originality of this position was striking for the times and for the development of the American Left, precisely because the political dinosaurs of earlier eras—the fading Communist Party and the nearly defunct Socialist Party—had shared for decades a basic commitment to liberalism and the enlarged federal government. While various leftists continued to quarrel over foreign-policy questions decades old, they nearly all saw the levers of power and mass influence as lying within the Democratic Party and the AFL-CIO.

The peace movement, dominated by pacifists, had injected something new during the 1950s, leading demonstrations against nuclear testing as well as providing tactical models and volunteers to a determinedly nonviolent civil rights movement. Along with the aura of Martin Luther King, Jr., then drifting leftward (or acknowledging socialistic positions he had held privately for years), the passionate protests against the arms race and against the ceaseless maneuvering of Russians and Americans to control the rest of the world went far to define what "radical" meant. Williams's mentor and friend William Hesseltine was a sponsor of the pacifist *Liberation* magazine, and although disclaiming his own capacity to become a pacifist, Williams quietly sympathized with these most American of left-wingers.

But Williams, *Studies*, and the pacifists alike suffered major disadvantages in defining the changing radical turf. Scions of the Old Left still held charge of many institutional mechanisms as well as access to major media. Liberal Socialist Irving Howe, a talented scholar and cultural critic with rising influence among liberals, for instance joined sociologist Louis Coser in denouncing militant opposition to U.S. adventures abroad as "New Styles in Fellow-Traveling."[124] Tom Hayden, a *Studies* editor who sat in on editorial meetings of Howe and Coser's *Dissent* magazine, later reported laconically that Howe repeatedly asked him "how he could be an editor of a journal that was part of the Soviet world."[125] *Studies On the Left* might inspire campus intellectuals, but Howe's protégé Michael Harrington wrote *The Other America*, reputedly inspiring Lyndon Johnson's War on Poverty and winning for himself a special status as moral spokesman of a socialist politics determinedly loyal to those cold-war liberals despising Williams. Compared to the kind of celebrity so obvious in the pages of the *New York Times* and in the high-profile liberal organizations' banquet circuit, the New Left and Williams could only be suspect outsiders.

Busy with his teaching and local appearances, Williams barely bothered himself with such matters until the Cuban Revolution's sharp leftward turn in 1960-61. C. Wright Mills issued in his *Listen Yankee!* (1960) the most stirring and popular manifesto of anti-interventionism since at least the middle 1930s. Williams's own short volume, *The United States, Cuba and Castro: An Essay on the Dynamics of Revolution and the Dissolution of Empire* (1962), seemed in ways an echo of Mills's far more successful work. Williams's publishers, Monthly Review Press, lacked the outlets and cash for a major promotion even on a most topical theme. Besides, Williams was not entirely at his best writing current or international history, where the impish or unexpected side of his work was least effective.

Still, *The United States, Cuba and Castro*, written in the aftermath of the failed Bay of Pigs invasion, cried out against the long legacy of U.S. bullying in the hemisphere. In offering a critique of the several current popular treatments, it appealed most uniquely to the enlightened conservative tradition of voluntary restraint. "Had American policy in action between 1859 and 1959 actually been successful according to its own standards," Williams argued,

> then there would have been no Castro and no CIA invasion. The current argument about whether or not the United States should intervene in Cuba and other Latin American countries is ridiculously

irrelevant. It has been intervening ever since the 1780s and is still doing so today. The real issue concerns whether or not any kind of intervention is capable of effecting the traditional and existing American objectives.[126]

The error or deception of the current literature, especially Theodore Draper's *Castro's Revolutions: Myths and Realities* (1962) was, indeed, its studied indifference to the weight of history. Draper's determined compartmentalization of post-1959 events troubled Williams most. An affront to larger vision of "interrelatedness," it was also the hinge of the liberal-interventionist argument that any Latin American revolution which refused to accept the U.S. economic-political model (and State Department guidance of its functioning) had been "betrayed." An argument that forever displaced the facts of American wrongdoing into a disposable past, it neatly avoided the difficulty of U.S. business interests' resistance (with State Department and CIA support) to popular calls for expropriating the expropriators of national wealth. Williams insisted that the issue was inevitably more complicated.[127]

Patiently, and familiarly to many of his regular readers, Williams traced U.S. rule from the 1890s onward, stressing the ways in which American leaders had raised and then dashed the expectations of Latin middle classes. In passing, he revealed how deceptively American "non-recognition" had been used to block Cuba's ability to gain acceptance by any major power. That kind of tactic, to "intimidate a society through the belly," had been scarcely recognized as "intervention" unless Marines were sent in to protect American investments. Adolph Berle himself described the consequences of U.S. hegemony as "great luxury for a relatively small group in Havana and a small rise above the starvation level for the masses."[128] Yet nothing had changed significantly until 1959. Efforts by Draper and others to paint Cuba as a semi-prosperous nation on the basis of a relatively high (for Latin America) per capita income entirely passed over the actual division of wealth, as well as the overwhelming control of the Cuban economy by American interests.

Seen differently, *The United States, Cuba and Castro* suggested in one case study that when New Deal–style liberalism collided with Third World nationalism, the world had come to the brink of nuclear catastrophe. In that light, Williams was surprisingly sympathetic to Castro's predecessor, Fulgenci Batista, for seeking to establish a corporatist balance of interests against overwhelming U.S. hegemony. At a time when liberals and Castro supporters alike portrayed Batista as a monster, Williams went out of his way to praise the dictator's 1940 Constitution and suggest that Fidel Castro had sought to "honor" its radical possibilities. Castro the declared communist was therefore also, to Williams, the Cuban patriot that many radical nationalists of the

Caribbean and Latin America took him to be, a left-wing *caudillo* in a long line of conservative or politically ambiguous *caudillos*.

Williams envisioned, in a conclusion that must have flabbergasted real-life Cuban revolutionaries, Herbert Hoover ("the last great conservative to honor the bedrock principle of self-determination") having appreciated the notion that crusades to shape other peoples in the U.S. image violated fundamental American ideals. He sincerely, but not very realistically, hoped that America could withdraw gracefully from Cuba, as England had from its colony, India. Williams had made the right argument for the wrong audience, or the wrong argument for the right audience. The readers of Monthly Review Books wanted something very different about the hopeful new beginnings in Latin America, and the book reached hardly anyone else. Williams came off as well-meaning but definitely eccentric, offering the first of a number of volumes to strike off center. Within the academic world, *The United States, Cuba and Castro* was scarcely reviewed at all.

If Williams stirred little radical or mainstream interest, he ran squarely up against the steamroller of cold-war liberalism. Theodore Draper, a former Communist functionary with a reputation for hard-nosed Stalinism and for hardball tactics against dissenters, had changed political camps but maintained his style of invective.[129] Draper's essay, "The Strange Case of Professor Williams," was an attack on Williams's scholarly integrity disguised as a complaint against factual errors and mistaken conclusions. In the main, Draper debated particulars, showing himself a true master of the selective quotation. Here and there, his complaints found their mark. Williams had carelessly referred to a book that Castro did not write; his treatment of Cuban history was occasionally erroneous, stemming from his attempt to wrestle with the past as Draper himself had not. Most of all, Draper pointed to a familiar ambiguity in Williams's writing: he wished to insist upon the possibility that in spite of all the crimes committed by administrations in the past, the U.S. might still have made peace with the Cuban revolution, giving Castro the opportunity to backstep toward constitutional democracy.[130] It was not a realistic expectation, but Williams obviously hoped against realism that a crisis of conscience might prevail.

In pursuing a somewhat tortured logic, Williams had indeed mangled his argument, but not in the ways that Draper suggested. Draper's choice of the *New Leader* for attacks on the Cuban Revolution, a sort of mirror-opposite of the communist *Political Affairs* in its hard-line impulses and its enthusiasm for superpower hegemony, tended to confirm this expectation. Remembered especially for its ideological assault upon the reform Arbenz government in Guatemala and its enthusiasm for a U.S.-guided 1954 coup, the *New Leader* had its own unmistakeable agenda for the Americas. "Liberal democracy," very much like "People's Democracy" in the Soviet lexicon, meant nonresistance to the large neighbor's wishes. In a small-scale special operation directed against Williams and the post–cold war radicalism that he seemed to represent, the *New Leader* sent out extra copies of the Draper issue far and wide. Noting with the original publication of the Draper piece that "too little space is being devoted these days to serious dialogues," the *New Leader* editors predictably refused to publish Williams's response. The "dialogue" was only one-sided after all.[131]

On the other side of the political fence, Williams had also begun to experience serious difficulties with the New Left. The non-historians at *Studies On the Left* had always been somewhat restive. "Our readership," the managing editor complained in 1960, "is getting a bit irritated by the Williams-crowd American history, diplomacy and foreign policy surplus of articles in *Studies*."[132] The shift of the journal from Madison to New York in 1963 coincided with a modestly growing radical movement. True to the history of American social movements and notwithstanding the campus base of most current enthusiasts, the "Movement" was more activist than intellectual. Inevitably, the need for "relevance" grew steadily and Williams's influence in the more narrow political sense sank, more or less as he had gloomily anticipated.[133]

Williams mourned in advance the larger consequences of these shifts in political taste. While *Tragedy of American Diplomacy* and *Contours of American History* carried his intellectual reputation to higher and higher levels, he would soon be trapped between the New Left and the Old Liberalism. The Vietnam War, which proved the validity of his insights more than did any other development, almost seemed to preclude any other possibilities. These two forces, in Williams's eyes, had altogether too much in common. Neither constituency had any appeal to or even clear perception of intelligent conservatism; neither could anticipate a Middle-American crisis of conscience over Empire or win people over to a different politics.

### 6

Things were not all that good at home. By 1960, fractures had begun to develop in his second marriage. As happy as Williams could be at times, he could also feel at loose ends over a series of problems with child-raising. These tensions, and Corrinne's suggestions that she would want to return to school at the first realistic opportunity, precipitated conflicts that would stretch out for nearly a decade. Determined to be head of the household, he could brook no open opposition, but the conflict inevitably reappeared in one guise or another. By 1964, his adopted son had been sent to a private school in LaCrosse to deal with various emotional problems. A daughter appeared to be plagued with something similar. Both children seemed so troubled that Williams considered shipping them off to Oregon grandparents. "God," he wrote his friends,

> What an endurance test this is. I think of those nuts who used to fly airplanes around and around and around over some city for days on end, and decide that I am in a similar situation . . . this has been a three weeks to cap six years.[134]

The problems had only begun. Once the memorable part of the new era had arrived, his daughter recalled, the fighter for a socialist worldview in the previous dark age simply did not know what to do with unloosed energies beyond his ken.[135]

# 5

# TROUBLE, FOREIGN AND DOMESTIC

WILLIAMS THE DEEPLY AMERICAN RADICAL could not have met the late 1960s without a considerable degree of stress. Not so different from Irving Howe, a socialist at the center of the New York Intellectuals and at nearly the opposite end of the cold war debate, Williams had weathered the 1950s with verve and a large degree of satisfaction. Not much could be done politically, but that dismal fact had reinforced the scholarly vocation. The universities had been in some places quite accommodating, the younger dissenting intellectuals hopeful if not numerous, and the civil rights movement offered promises of better things ahead for American society at large. If the early 1960s revealed the discomforting prospect of a bohemian undercurrent rising above ground and threatening to capture the attention of the college crowd, the steady growth of student idealism in general still augured well for senior radical savants.

For many of those who came of age at this time, Williams had captured exactly the logic that they intuitively grasped but could not fully comprehend. Orators against the Vietnam War on campus and in the community, it is fair to say, crammed the *Tragedy of American Diplomacy* before mounting the stage and calling for the nation to consult its sleeping conscience. In their free time, the same student leaders often turned to *Contours of American History*, along with Herbert Marcuse's *One Dimensional Man* and a small handful of other vital books. Williams's stature notably rose as that of the cold-war liberals fell; Vietnam proved him right, and showed them by contrast to be hypocritical and self-serving or (at a generous estimate) simply dead wrong. The University of Wisconsin at Madison was only one spot on a large national map of rising antiwar and generally radical political activity. But it played a special role in providing Williams a supportive milieu and an intellectual sounding board.

In Madison and far more elsewhere, however, the young radicals took from Williams only what they wanted or what they understood. Even as they underlined key passages of his books, they rendered him into a monument and sought to move beyond the particular prescriptions for change which they viewed as either quirky or outdated. As the too-well remembered "Summer of Love" days of cheap dope and free love (or loose sex) unfolded, Williams was confounded. This was not at all what he had in mind.

Suddenly, the generation barely coming of age during the last major phase of radicalism in the later 1940s felt old, indeed. Their presumed constituencies continued to listen to them in the classroom (when the universities were not on strike), but as if from increasingly far away; the drumbeat of the times sounded action and more action. The more adept or adaptable ones rode the tide, but often felt in danger of being swept away.

Nothing in this development *should* have surprised Socialist intellectuals. The American Left and radical reform movements had never been especially cerebral, a reality that had often caused theoreticians to wring their hands and wish that they had been born (or stayed) in Europe. At their best, generations of radicals published newspapers, staged lecture tours, organized unions, and generally agitated against the status quo and for "the good time coming" (as a nineteenth-century "movement" song put it). Even college students, extremely active for a few years during the 1930s, spent most of their political time on the picket line; if they had serious intellectual aspirations, they wanted badly to write novels, not analytical studies. A handful of intellectuals had by that time good-sized followings; nearly all of them were novelists or review mavens in the *Nation* and *New Republic*. Few professors of those days could afford to risk being activists themselves, but not many had ever aspired to roles beyond teaching the young and testifying at public hearings on social issues.

Thirty years later, amid the largest college generation by far, the majority of professors had probably not changed so greatly in the role they saw for themselves. But many of the academically situated 1940s political veterans, who had gone on to support civil rights movements, now increasingly found routes to bolder action. National personalities like Howard Zinn and Staughton Lynd mirrored the lesser-known hundreds active on the lecture platform and, where permitted, in the television studios as the movement against the war spread. Many of them roughly the age of Williams or Howe had long hoped for still more, the fulfillment of their life's work in a solid, popular radical movement which heeded their intellectual contribution. These experienced the keen disappointment of having waited, planned, and prepared themselves for a big personal letdown. Even the 1950s had been personally better, certainly happier for those who had had good jobs and eager protégés.

Williams had his own sources of frustration. Dissidents of considerably less standing than himself became overnight celebrities, often borrowing his ideas wholesale. At antiwar marches and rallies, orators intoned unmistakeably similar ideas, hailing a children's crusade which older people joined sheepishly, feeling always somewhat out of place. The ordinary middle-class and working-class Americans that Williams had hoped to convert were sometimes on hand, but rarely in numbers. Increasingly skeptical toward the brutal and seemingly senseless war, a large part of the nation remained unable to break with gung-ho patriotic traditions, the bread-and-butter logic of defense-related employment, and the feeling that irresponsible young people had no right to challenge the morals and the politics of the older generations.

Unsettled by such events and dragged down by intensifying back pain and deepening personal problems, Williams sometimes acted the part of the disappointed parent who, feeling betrayed by apparently uncontrollable teenagers, rages into the night. But even that sentiment would be hard to separate from his gut feeling that some vitally important moment was passing and that the one splendid chance for social transformation was being lost. Like so many other writers, but always with his own distinct mark of originality, he tried repeatedly to work out in print what he could not resolve in his own life.

He also continued to go his own way, managing often enough to make the best of a bad situation. He rose to the occasion when increasingly large numbers of students came to believe that knowledge *could* facilitate structural change in society—so long as they kept their quest to the classroom. He also reached out politically, even as he expressed his resentment at the direction of campus and New Left politics generally. In contrast to some other sharp critics of contemporary social movements including Howe and a host of erstwhile liberals or former socialists, Williams never sided with faculty conservatives who urged a crackdown on student demonstrators.

Nor did he follow them in cursing the antiwar movement more fulsomely than the Vietnam War itself. As in so many other instances, Williams continued his own way alone, paying the costs in his own fashion.

I

Until at least the middle 1960s, tensions between Williams and his youthful admirers were held in check by a variety of common sentiments and common foes. The political scene intermittently simmered toward a boil, but the classroom remained the focus for the great majority of sympathetic students. A professor extraordinarily hard at work packing the lecture halls, guiding seminars, and directing graduate students, Williams attracted attention and gained support.

He had many local sources of satisfaction and encouragement. As Fred Harvey Harrington moved further into administration, he saw Williams less, and the rest of the older generation of Beardians including a beloved Merle Curti gradually faded from the central avenues of intellectual life. But Williams had two intimate colleagues who, together, helped him realize his aspiration for a larger view of the world, and who with him set the pace for the extraordinarily rich classroom experience shared by thousands of undergraduates. In a way, he had found his own successor to the Beardianism of the 1940s-50s, this one not American-centered or heavily Protestant but cosmopolitan and disproportionately Jewish.

The older of the two colleagues was George Mosse. Active in the liberal wing of the local Democratic Party, Mosse was not a Socialist much less a Marxist, but prided himself on his continual dialogue with the faculty and student Left. Warning against the seductive power of ideologies, Mosse analyzed Marxism as one avant-garde trend among many, several of the key ones set in motion by a Hegelianism that he described carefully and sympathetically in his packed lecture courses. Personally more approachable than Williams, Mosse charmed even those pained by his long-standing ties with certain cold-war intellectuals.

The second figure was Harvey Goldberg, hired away from Ohio State in 1963 at Williams's initiative. If the ever worldly and amiably cynical Mosse taught European ideas, Goldberg taught European (and other international) social movements with a markedly different emphasis. The plump and gentle Mosse impressed students with his range, his genial and provocative ironies, playing especially upon the middle-class backgrounds and radical visions of Jewish undergraduates. Goldberg, by now terribly thin, cigarette chain-smoking and coughing, orated with torrents of narrative detail, wild hand-waving, and generally spellbinding sincerity. In a sense, much of the best of Mosse was reborn in his many books, and those of dozens of graduate students. Goldberg, who wrote little, put everything into his presence, and fairly swept the campus in the first year of his appearance there. As if that were not enough aura, he went out with students for coffee and drinks, frequently in public and always seemingly "on." After a few years, he employed half the teaching assistants allotted for all the European historians, and enrolled ten percent of all history majors of the Europeanists in one or another of his courses. He also marshalled his graduate students (forty-nine took PhDs with him over the decades) to write a veritable collective history of the French Left, touching on many other subjects.[1]

Office mates for several years, Goldberg and Williams also spent countless hours in less formal conversation. Delivering the first Goldberg Memorial Lecture after his close friend's death, Williams recalled the two throwing their arms around each other after characteristically long days of lecturing and meeting students. Williams had a family, of course, and a circle of other friends from the faculty and elsewhere. Goldberg shunned most faculty events, spent time with students, and had many lovers (some of them bailed out, after minor legal violations, by Mosse or Williams). Emotionally, Williams was Goldberg's sustaining intimate. And so the straight and gay man had a kind of "marriage," not unlike that of Williams and his wartime Jewish roommate at Annapolis. They could be gruff with each other, but the degree of love they felt can hardly be overestimated. Their relationship can surely be appreciated better from today's more sympathetic perspective on the hidden roles of gays in America's intellectual and cultural worlds.[2]

Williams, Goldberg, and Mosse at any rate made up a magic trio, in tandem unexcelled anywhere for the young cerebral leftist or attentive activist. Compared to the earlier triad of Williams, Mosse, and Gerth, it was less introspective and more directed to dynamic social developments. It might be said that hundreds or perhaps thousands of students lived the political excitement of the later 1960s a few years in advance, a more fulfilling experience in some ways than the real thing. Over-enrolled lectures and seminars, wildly enthusiastic undergraduates, and deeply committed (and usually radical) teaching assistants created an atmosphere of perpetual excitement. Many professors and not a few students remembered these as their happiest, least conflicted days, after the glum fifties had passed and before the confrontations ensued.[3]

A changing spirit gradually infused the scene. The students most enthusiastically devoted to the trio of Williams, Goldberg, and Mosse also responded to early stirrings of political movements. Madisonians' trips to Cuba had inevitably stirred conservative legislators' wrath, but actually involved few students and no professors. The Congress of Racial Equality (CORE) campus group, like the Friends of SNCC, at first engaged mainly in support work for events elsewhere. Some of the most eager radicals indeed soon left town for the South, in order to be part of the real action. In 1963 the CORE chapter launched a campaign against the local Sears and Roebuck, which refused to hire local African Americans in sales positions. Hundreds of students and community members joined picket lines, and some were arrested. But so clear were the moral issues and so marked the links between community and campus liberals that the university seemed to be resuming its legendary moral leadership familiar to the 1930s or 1910s.

Williams, too, welcomed this activity, albeit ambivalently. He believed strongly in the division between the classroom and society, and seemed to anticipate that with the continued rise of activism he could easily become an increasingly distant figure, more icon than palpable presence. He complained privately that young radicals seemed too eager for political shortcuts. He probably sensed already that he would not be in on the action or even urge it forward dramatically as Harvey Goldberg did in public orations to demonstrators and in countless private chats with students.

Other changes left him still more uneasy. Increasingly restive undergraduates, not yet very many but a considerable portion of students attracted to Williams and Goldberg, adopted habits and personal mannerisms somewhere between the Beat Generation and the later counterculture or New Left. Like Williams they often loved jazz, but Count Basie and Duke Ellington interested them far less than the more avant-garde varieties of free jazz and musicians like John Coltrane. They were likely to find Williams's great vocal favorite, Frank Sinatra, downright repellent.

These young radicals also dressed down with cultivated scruffiness, sometimes experimented with marijuana, and generally placed themselves outside the cultural mainstream that Williams regarded as politically mistaken but morally decent. They experienced major elements of the Sexual Revolution and even (more selectively) an early Women's Liberation. The tough-minded young women were not his type, in any sense. They raised troubling questions about male authority in political and intellectual life. Above all, by distancing themselves from their families they deeply offended Williams's socially conservative sensibilities.

Williams made no public issue of his disdain. Indeed, the avant-gardists who had direct contact only with his teaching assistants could simply admire the 1940s version of nonconformity (his red vest or tie, and rumors about his jazz drumming) as part of the fascinating character they loved to hear lecturing. Graduate students were at this point likely still more conventional socially if not politically, pipe-smoking family men en route to respectable jobs.

He surprised many devotees and close readers, then, with the undercurrents in his next book, bearing the whopping title *The Great Evasion: An*

*Essay on the Contemporary Relevance of Karl Marx and the Wisdom of Admitting the Heretic into the Dialogue of America's Future*. Published in 1963 by his friend Ivan Dee at Quadrangle Books of Chicago, it was in no small part his response to the young radicals' anticipations of a New Left.

He had nurtured the idea of a "Marx Book" for several years, but the outline had actually emerged through his participation in a seminar during 1962-63 directed jointly by himself and George Mosse. According to Mosse, the writing coincided with Williams's rediscovery of religion through the reading of a few British Christian Socialist texts on loan from Mosse. It was for Mosse, who listened carefully as Williams developed his ideas aloud, a "very American" book in the sense of a moral quest or pilgrim's progress toward the horizon of Marxism but settling for a decidedly non-Marxist oasis.[4] For himself, Williams characteristically saw the manuscript in Spinozan terms. As he wrote Merle Curti shortly after its publication, *The Great Evasion* gave him true satisfaction because it had integrated "all parts of the story" in modern society by tracing central ideas about capitalism back to Marx.[5] Or so he believed.

In another sense, Williams had been anxious to do something on politics and theory rather than history, both because of his long-standing interest in Marx and his weariness with the usual professional demands for more and better monographs. He often expressed the feeling that as far as foreign relations in particular went, he had already trained his students to do better, to work on documentary sources more intensively and extensively, than he chose to do anymore.[6]

Serious students of Marxian exegeses could immediately recognize that Williams was espousing something closer to a Socialist Americanism than an American understanding of socialism—let alone Marxism. Like a later generation of texts but without their cumbersome language or psychoanalytic theoretical underpinning, the *Great Evasion* contained a very particular "reading" of Marx. It recalled Edward Bellamy's utopian novel, *Looking Backward*, the best-selling American Socialist work of all time and the third-best-selling book of the nineteenth-century United States. Both Bellamy and Williams were pained by social disorder and believed that citizens of all classes, properly educated to their real interests, could move towards a cooperative order. Bellamy, writing at the end of the nineteenth century, never suspected the dark potential of the behemoth State. He also found a better medium to express ideals than Williams's attempt at sophisticated social criticism.[7]

Williams began with the remarkable premise that "America's great evasion lies in its manipulation of Nature to avoid a confrontation with the human condition and with the challenge of building a true community." The ecological suggestion here, which Williams scarcely pursued, would alone have made this volume farsighted for 1963. But he also struggled with a unique interpretation of why Marxism had historically seemed unnecessary but become increasingly vital for the Americans to confront and accommodate. Unfortunately, as critics noted, his method of placing moral pleas and materialistic analyses side by side puzzled more than satisfied.

Williams spent about half the book detailing the means and byways through which Americans had evaded Marx's telling criticisms. These evasions rested upon the fertile but familiar idea that the "frontier is a cast of mind as well as a stretch of open territory," an "escape hatch" that eventually stretched around the world and now threatened to reach the infinity of outer space. Expansive America conquered everything in its path, but could not create community, and—as the young Marx had predicted about the upward climb of industrialization—produced estrangement and alienation among its citizens. With their own version of collective amnesia, Americans had ignored serious criticisms of capitalism, making "Marx into Lenin" and "Lenin into Stalin," and thus "Marx into the Soviet Union." They did not or would not see that Marx had "challenged capitalism's ability to honor the West's historic and declared values and to achieve its avowed objectives."[8]

Williams had said much of this earlier, if not in quite the same terms. The unique methodological hinge of *The Great Evasion* could be traced to that indirect reference to "feudal socialism" that Williams mentioned in passing in the acknowledgments section of *Contours*. Here, he wanted to explore the possibilities more theoretically. Williams's leap from Marx's concept to the mental world of the Founding Fathers was a big one, based upon a few phrases in *The Communist Manifesto*. He insisted once more that Jefferson and Madison, among others, could be fit perfectly into the Marxist model because mercantilism, as Marx and Engels had noted polemically, "appears as a higher form" of precapitalist self-organization. Growing out of a particular view of Christianity, it contrasted with the dog-eat-dog realities of modern industrial society. In Williams's words and not Marx or Engels', mercantilism thus

> acknowledged its avowed commitment to the ideal of the whole man based on an aristocratic model, and recognized its political, social and intellectual achievements as well as its success in organizing and carrying through the crucial first steps in developing a capitalist political economy at the national level.[9]

The quasi-feudalism that Marxism's own Founding Fathers offered as an immanent critique of capitalism, Williams cited almost reverentially as the best of the American promise. Rather like Staughton Lynd's *The Intellectual Origins of American Radicalism*, published a half dozen years later to a wide readership, Williams proceeded to insist that Marx's recognition of moral values (and their erosion by invading capitalism) was mirrored in the best of American thought. But Lynd cited the Abolitionists and Thoreau, traditional heroes of radicals; Williams had instead looked to John Quincy Adams.[10] Williams also suggested that Marx had seriously underestimated the *continuing* importance of mercantilist criticism, a most critical point of Williams's heterodox Marxism. And yet with its limitations, Marxism alone was capable of "bringing our capitalistic ego into a confrontation with our capitalist reality."[11] Somehow, the ego as reality principle in Freud's system had slipped into the ego of street parlance, as in "egotistic." The back cover sported a quotation from the *Library Journal* comparing Williams to Erich Fromm as a "non-doctrinaire student of Marx."[12]

In this queer theoretical setting, more Frommian than Marxist or Freudian, Williams bore down on familiar themes. The "bourgeois Socialists," Abolitionists, and Populists thus spoke for freedom but failed to grasp the increasingly divisive influence of the marketplace. Again in street or perhaps pulpit parlance, Williams declared that by looking at the marketplace, "the rich as well as the poor white can verify [that it] does not transform the ego into the soul."[13] All classes alike were trapped, he insisted, by sharing key assumptions of expansionism consciously or unconsciously. The "Corporate Socialism" of the New Deal, widely and mistakenly believed to be the highest degree of idealism reached by the national polity, likewise presented no serious alternative. Williams inevitably preferred the caution, and the social criticism, of Herbert Hoover.

These would be odd formulations for any other writer, but Williams needed them to repose the question of alienation, then popular among the readers of Fromm's *The Sane Society* and the "Young Marx" of the *Economic and Philosophical Manuscripts of 1844*, newly translated into English only a few years earlier. Others made much of the "lost" feeling widely prevalent (but especially keen among the young) under contemporary capitalism. Williams's own Marx became the "paradoxical prophet of affluence and of the irrelevance of affluence once it is attained," anticipating the possibility of a realized community in a fully technological, i.e., cybernetic society. Carefully calibrating the implications of industrial production and human needs, Williams insisted that "the issue is not whether to decentralize the economy and the politics of the country, but rather how to do so" through an inevitable but also "exhilarating" new constitutional movement. *That* America could truly aid the poor countries of the world, and even project "the rational (as opposed to political) exploration of space."[14]

Easily the oddest sections of the book identified—but never admitted as much—the problems in his own campus and family with the presumed ravages of alienation and consumerism. Under the heading of "Increasing

Misery and Increasing Proletarianization," he bemoaned the fate of mechanized labor, the loss of familiar jobs, the spread of psychological ailments among African Americans, women, and youth. But he chose campus sexual promiscuity as "the most dramatic sign of a sad and desperate search for a human relationship," the devaluation of sex as a commodity. Changing partners in bed now substituted for changing the society, he observed, and obviated hopes for the honest relationship of two adults within a real community. He could appreciate the young hot-rodder (like his adopted son) for using the mechanical means at hand to revive an almost handicraft creativity. But he castigated the struggle for women's emancipation in a male world, on male terms of equal access or competition for jobs and services. To Williams, this last was clearly an unendurable extension of community disintegration. Judgments like these, common enough among intellectuals during the 1950s, could not have been more ill suited for the era ahead. Within a few years, when so much had changed, Williams's sexual and gender observations could only be taken as eccentric or idiosyncratic, part of a larger problem in the volume.[15]

Williams had evidently drawn deeply, over a long relationship and correspondence, upon Warren Susman's work seeking to interpret the personality type that predominates in mass society.[16] In turn, Susman and others had culled ideas from neo-Freudians like Karen Horney, Fromm, and the anthroplogical followers of "Culture and Personality" studies analyzing behaviors in all societies as variants of distinct "factors." The perceived problem for these clinicians and writers was not "interpsychic," the individual mind wrestling with the innate drives described by Freud, but rather interpersonal, in conflicts which could be socially understood and hopefully resolved. But unlike Susman (who published little in his lifetime), Williams had no sophisticated critique of consumerism except as a form of alienation. And unlike *Contours of American History*, *The Great Evasion* did not surround its social-psychological assumptions with historical interpretations but instead exposed them in their fragile state.

Williams was also almost certainly drawing upon a Frankfurt School theorist's very particular observations on family authority, a side of the Frankfurt theorists conveniently neglected by radical devotees but later vividly recalled by intellectual historian Christopher Lasch. During the late 1940s, Max Horkheimer had attributed the rise of fascism to the decline of the patriarchal family. In an earlier era, boys internalized authority and grew up properly. The self-control of the individual, the ability to take pleasure in constructive activity all depended upon the mixture of fear and authority that the father provided. The undermining of that authority in the twentieth century had produced a growing insecurity for the whole family, encouraging the retrograde impulse of "unsatisfied, spiritless," and fearful women.[17]

Merging a critique of consumerist materialism with a hand-wringing complaint at the loss of paternal authority was so commonplace in intellectual circles during the 1950s that one might almost call it the thread connecting critical theory to cold-war liberalism. But it had slipped down several notches by the time *The Great Evasion* was published and was doomed to slip down many more before the 1960s had ended.[18] As the political lines on race seemed to coincide with generational tastes in music, so did attitudes on the war in Vietnam; those on the other side from Williams in age and culture had no reason to bemoan the crisis in family authority and growing reasons (with the rise of feminism) to celebrate the attack on Father from all sides. In one more way, Williams had written a book badly out of time. It might be contrasted, finally, with another reading straight out of the Frankfurt School: Herbert Marcuse's *Eros and Civilization* (1955) which anticipated and shaped young people's changing attitudes toward intimate subjects which interested them at least as much as political events.

The critics were in any case far from kind to the *Great Evasion*, and no major historical journal even bothered to review it. Many commentators already unfriendly toward Williams leaped at the chance to nail him. Among the most mean-spirited, Robert Heilbroner in the *New York Review of Books* found the *Great Evasion* "vulgar, self-serving, imprecise and shallow."[19] Political Scientist Floyd A. Cave called the book itself a "great evasion" for misunderstanding Marx's scientific socialism and for evading the doctrines of class warfare and the dictatorship of the proletariat.[20] Even in the columns of the *Nation*, Williams's long-reliable ally, labor historian Milton Cantor, described the volume as "disappointing," marked by idiosyncratic formulas and "careless generalizations."[21]

Eugene Genovese, the leading scholarly light of *Studies on the Left*'s New York–based operation, was considerably more impressed, but for reasons that would finally do Williams little good. He saw in Williams mainly an antidote to permissive individualism at large and to the emerging New Left in particular. Despite its plain ignorance of Marxism, the *Great Evasion* was to Genovese "both instructive and urgent" because Williams had "masterfully [exposed] capitalism as a process of dehumanization." Williams's desire for an organic community might just as easily have been a vision of a Catholic feudalist, a patriachal slaveholder, a utopian socialist, or even an Italian Fascist; it was, as other critics had said about *Contours*, more Hegelian idealism than real Marxist thought. But Williams had grasped the failure of the modern welfare state, and above all its encouragement to false emancipation of women through their participation in the marketplace.

Most tantalizing for Genovese, Williams had denounced those "quasi-beatnik anarchists" (in Genovese's words) of the New Left. He had restated the "spirit of Puritanism—of discipline, civil responsibility self . . . a respect for order" and genuine family values that Americans could appreciate. Contrary to the young radicals, Williams did not "expect [America] to jump into revolutionary transformations of any kind." Genovese obviously hoped, with Williams, that Americans could "reclaim their soul" in ways distant from the present young and rebellious generation, i.e., with a firm sense of admiration for their patriarchal-minded elders.[22]

George Mosse would later reflect that when he asked students,

> why on earth they were not reading *The Great Evasion* instead of Herbert Marcuse's books, they replied that Williams did not give them the kind of theory into which they so much wanted to fit the American situation. They had this hunger for theory, and the only theory that answered their needs was European. Williams's democratic vistas should have appealed mightily, but the radical students were in love with the philosophy of history of Marx, and with a sort of Kantian moral imperative that meant to be politically active while harmonizing means and ends.[23]

Mosse did not quite go to the heart of the problem, but he had detected the source of a significant misalliance. As an intellectual progenitor of the New Left, Williams resisted not only the student radicals but the drift of scholarship as well.

If the 1950s and early 1960s mainstream theorists of alienation such as David Riesman stressed the importance of norms and roles, seeking above all psychic adjustment and the restoration of social stability, the students and radical scholars of the later 1960s and after placed their main emphasis on creative destabilization and the dynamic elements in American history and society that seemed to disprove both the permanence and the desirability of consensus. Warren Susman, writing in 1979, would propose that as the late 1940s Age of Anxiety had given way to an Age of Identity (delineated in the writings of psychoanalyst Erik Erickson), the successor mood had yielded, in turn, to an Age of Liberation.[24] In a way, Herbert Marcuse had provided the middle term between the last two psychological "ages," and Williams had indeed used Marcuse's *One Dimensional Man* extensively in *The Great Evasion*. But far from doing so in ways that Marcuse (who looked favorably on student radicals and women's liberation) would have imagined either likely or desirable, Williams transported Marcuse's ideas back into the theoretical framework of the 1950s.

If students now wanted "theory" much as Williams fifteen years earlier in Madison had wanted it, they would get a great deal more, from Mosse, Goldberg, and others. Still, the accumulation of theoretical hints did not meet the scale of the problem they perceived, perhaps because no solutions existed. *The Great Evasion*, in any case, was left swiftly behind, a kind of marker to unsuccessful transitions. Most ironically, Genovese and Williams's later defender Christopher Lasch both would ride the antifeminist backlash of the 1980s-90s by renewing theories of family disintegration that Williams had found so absorbing.[25] By this time, socialism was no longer seen as an antidote but an impossibility. The envisioned organic society had become, for this day's ideologues, something closer to the market liberalism with individual solutions that Williams had shunned all his adult life.

2

Campus disruption came relatively slowly to Madison, in part because the Left could operate so freely already and in part because the forbidding Wisconsin winter limited demonstrations to early fall and spring. The explosion of the free speech movement in Berkeley during 1964-65 took everyone by surprise, thoroughly unnerving cold-war socialists (or former socialists) like sociologist Seymour Martin Lipset, who imagined omnipresent communist infiltration and urged a tough-minded response. At a distance, Williams and Mosse surely didn't like campus uprisings much more than the Lipsets did, but the generally relaxed atmosphere of Madison and its wise administrators both minimized the periods of unrest and kept the ardor of students for their classes high. The preliminary stages of the Vietnam protest movement, moreover, gave Williams an early sense of the ways in which his intellectual contributions had shaped the emerging radical thought. As a political (rather than intellectual) hero of the day, he now enjoyed his last moments of high visibility.

By March 1965, a month after Lyndon B. Johnson ordered intensive bombing of North Vietnam, the first Peace March on Washington occurred, sponsored by the Students for a Democratic Society. With twenty-five thousand on hand (more than twice what organizers had expected), it was the largest such demonstration in U.S. history, however small by standards soon to come. For the first time, a New Left was projected onto the nation's consciousness. SDS president Paul Potter, the rally's chief speaker, went beyond war and peace issues as such to say that "we must name the system" which produced brutal war-making.

A decade or two earlier, leftists would have concluded that Potter simply meant capitalism but had been too cautious to say so openly. The SDS leader hinted, however, at something far closer to Williams's concept of a *Weltanschauung* that categorically and irrationally rejected Third World revolutionary aspirations. SDS's next president and most popular orator, Carl Oglesby, was yet closer to Williams's way of thinking. An advocate of "decentralized socialism" and somewhat of a Christian Socialist, Oglesby agonized visibly on platforms about the betrayal of national ideals.

America, he often averred, had broken his "liberal heart." Only a kind of spiritual rebirth, he seemed to suggest, could salvage America from the sins of avarice plainly apparent in its international policies.[26]

Williams's articulation of "corporate liberalism," a phrase introduced by Martin J. Sklar, offered young radicals a major insight into how Lyndon Johnson could combine a Great Society at home with a senseless war in Southeast Asia and how an apparently left-of-center Democratic Party could be an integral part of bipartisan corporate control of politics. Sklar was himself seeking to distinguish various forms of corporatism, some of them considerably more consensual and, he believed, more benign.[27] Study groups on "Corporate Liberalism" became a fixture for several years on the Madison campus. Caught up in protesting the war, few young radicals elsewhere perceived the historic complications, and still fewer could likely have correctly identified the sources of the insight.

Later in the spring of 1965, teach-ins swept college campuses and found professors at the center of antiwar attention for perhaps the last time. Hundreds of students in Madison listened as speaker after speaker recounted the causes of the war and proposed peaceful solutions. Williams told the crowd which had waited until after midnight to hear him speak that they had the "makings of a community" forced to "assemble as citizens" because the government was violating America's "best traditions" and "threatening grave harm to [its] highest moral ideals and aspirations." The duty of those assembled was to try "to bring [the] government back into a dialogue with its own citizens . . . to transform America into a more humane and creative community."

Williams saw two alternatives to the present disastrous policy. One was to "embark upon a sober and informed imperialism designed to establish and maintain an American Empire of optimum size, efficiency and benevolence." The other and better solution was "to honor our moral commitment to the principle of self-determination . . . . We can clearly learn a good deal from others if we will only give them a chance to teach us; if we can only give ourselves the chance to learn."[28] Notably, he did not denounce the commander-in-chief of current U.S. policies. In private, he expressed admiration for Lyndon Johnson's domestic program of inclusiveness, especially the Civil Rights Act of 1964. He hoped almost desperately—and contrary to his own system of thought—that the New Deal liberal Johnson, outsider from Texas, would extricate the U.S. from Vietnam and go on to prove that an adopted *noblesse oblige* could point the way toward a better future.

In public, Williams could still seem close to the young radicals. At the annual banquet of the weekly *National Guardian*, in New York City, twelve hundred attendees watched pacifist David Dellinger and community organizer Tom Hayden, along with Eugene Genovese, Carl Oglesby, civil rights leader Fannie Lou Hamer, lawyer William Kunstler, and Williams together on the dais, the last four as speakers. Complaining at the exhausted visions of the Old Left and insisting upon the necessity of going beyond antiwar activism, Williams urged the new generation forward toward a decentralist vision of socialism, rebuilding in practice "an inspiring and exciting and practical alternative for a different and better America."[29]

But mostly, Williams seemed prepared to withdraw from the centers of action himself. In New York during the same fall of 1965, a handful of prominent academics formed the Socialist Scholars Conference, dedicated to holding large, annual meetings for intellectual and political exchange. Williams was notable for his absence among a circle of rising intellectuals who owed a great deal to him.[30] Neither did he participate in the Madison Teach-in of 1966. Already the local political scene had soured for him, and he was not sorry to be on leave in Oregon for the 1966-67 academic year.

In Madison as across the nation, liberals gave up on Johnson, and ever larger groups of students determined to express themselves against the war at any cost. In the spring of 1967, activists warned against the use of campus facilities by the Dow Chemical Company, notorious for its production of napalm, jellied gasoline dropped by airplane and used notoriously to terrorize Vietnamese civilians. A small group of Madison intellectuals and graphic artisans, disproportionately history students, set up an engaging campus "underground" newspaper, *Connections*, whose journalists enormously admired Williams but also ridiculed college administrators and urged mass action against both the war and the university's role in it.[31]

University officials now found themselves in a quandary which Williams largely shared. From Fred Harvey Harrington down, many and perhaps most of them personally opposed the war but felt compelled to obey the wishes of the regents. The contradictions sharpened further as a crisis emerged. Scholarship into the university's "power structure" by graduate students and others offered convincing proofs of how thoroughly the university had become enmeshed, over the years, in research destined for use in unconscionable anticivilian activities. Specific sections of the university also had records of long-standing cooperation with intelligence agencies guilty of widespread human rights abuses.[32] Those who opposed the war found it harder and harder to accept without question the university dissimulation of rights and wrongs, even as the university administrators proudly defended their own record of protecting antiwar freedom of speech against demands of conservative state legislators for a campus crackdown. Each side had important points to make, but could not hear the other.

Williams returned to Madison in this tense atmosphere for the school year 1967-68. Once again the Dow Corporation promised job-placement interviews, foolishly (or brazenly) coinciding with a declared "Vietnam

Week" nationwide, October 17-18. Antiwar demonstrators in many cities sought to halt the escalation of the war, which included a half million GIs stationed in Vietnam, with hundreds of resulting U.S. casualties and thousands of Vietnamese victims every week. Madison rallies appealed for nonviolent action against Dow. The peaceful sit-in of the building where the interviews were to be held might easily have ended in a draw, with Dow cancelling interviews or quietly moving the location. Instead, city officials unwisely called in by the university's chief of security ordered local police to clear the area by any means necessary. Given the esprit of uniformed student-haters unleashed to be bullies, a police riot was predictable. Swinging their clubs wildly, breaking glass doors, and dragging bloodied students out, they meanwhile fired tear gas and mace at the assembling crowd of incredulous and increasingly enraged bystanders. As the melee continued, the campus exploded.

A student strike quickly became inevitable. That night, after a stormy session in the Memorial Union auditorium, the attending faculty meekly voted to support the administration's decisions rather than join the strike. Students stood outside singing "Solidarity Forever" and watching disappointedly, sometimes whispering, "Shame, shame" as the faculty members filed out. Harvey Goldberg later addressed the crowd of embittered students in strident tones, offering no tactical advice but reminding them of their responsibilities to history. Williams was noticeably absent.[33]

Instead, he had been corralled by a young *New York Times* reporter, Nan Robertson, and over more than a few drinks he spilled out his anxiety. While student leaders appealed for idealism and set themselves to educate intensively within the dormitories (as Williams himself had long urged them to do), he described the era's undergraduates as the "most selfish people I know," determined to create a society which "an orangutan wouldn't want to live in."[34] The next day, as energy continued to build, a half dozen graduate students passed out bananas at the door of his diplomatic history lecture class, as if they were leafletting in the fashion of the day. Williams mounted the stage slowly, looked out at the banana-laden students, and smiled sheepishly. Rumors of his drinking spree had been passed around with copies of the *Times* article, and students accepted with compassion their beloved mentor's obvious moment of weakness. He went on that day to give a characteristic denunciation of U.S. foreign policies. Although he observed the week-long strike at close range, Williams kept a low profile while his friend Harvey Goldberg sparkled.[35]

The strike soon passed, the winter freeze set in, and students returned to the libraries until spring—a veritable fixed pattern in Madison's campus political life. Some professors melodramatically spoke of being "terrorized" by student activists. Aging refugees among them with memories of fascist

Europe knew better what terror meant and did not mean. Many committed faculty found these years a time of constant troubles but also of idealism, high cerebral energy, and above all, little apathy.

Williams continued to make personal gestures towards those student radicals who sought intellectual and political alternatives closer to his own heart. When a "free university" atmosphere encouraged the proliferation of study groups, especially active in times of campus strikes but often lasting for entire semesters, Williams readily arranged reading credit for a circle of choice graduate students analyzing liberalism. He also devoted entire days to a serious critique of a community organizing program set out by a new off-campus group, the Wisconsin Alliance.[36]

But for the most part, Williams did not have the heart for an active response. He could not reconcile himself to the politics of student demonstrators or to the response of the administrators, but he was disturbed even more by the cultural atmosphere emerging around campus. Madison rapidly became a center for counterculture or "youth culture," a Midwest-style, small-scale Haight-Ashbury with the full complement of marijuana, LSD, poster-and-incense stores, and even transgressive gay bravado. Bohemian in his own mind and intimate with gay intellectuals, but happiest when he could talk and drink with faculty and neighborhood friends, Williams felt more and more alienated.

Moreover and more personally, the rise of youth culture literally hit too close to home. He had developed problems, almost from the beginning, with his own sense of authority in the family. He wanted or demanded the kind of respectful attention that he imagined he might have given his own father. Like so many other parents in the 1960s, he found rebellion in the domestic setting impossible to accept. According to his ex-wife Corrinne, he typically sought to subject his (and her) children to absurd Annapolis rituals such as shining their shoes and holding them up for inspection when he came home. His Frankfurt School readings bolstered him theoretically in the belief that he deserved a respectful order.

Naturally, these kinds of demands elicited the very reverse of what he had hoped. The small and large rebellions of his stepchildren and children as they reached their teen years in turn hardened a view he had already developed, that somehow the harmful breakdown of authority was due more to the selfishness of the rebels themselves than to the failure of established institutions and leaders. Drugs, to take an obvious case in point, seemed as repellant and destructive to him as alcohol appeared benign or at least controllable in his own increasingly hard-drinking personal life. He simply could not acknowledge any link between his own alcohol consumption or his addiction to cigars and the larger addictive patterns in society.

A double irony pervaded these confused and sometimes strident generational conflicts. In the first place, a belief in decentralization that Williams viewed as the *sine qua non* of a democratic socialist society had continued to grow apace in the New Left from 1965 to 1968. Madison, partly because of his presence, was one of the intuitive centers of this kind of perspective. Despite the heavy influence elsewhere by the Leninist-style centralism of Trotskyists and Maoists, the vast majority of New Leftists and "movement" activists here continued to believe deeply in the potential power of the "community" (however it was defined) to meet individual and collective needs.

Unfortunately, the war and the particular forms that rebellious culture assumed inevitably continued to polarize opposing sensibilities. The inclination of the radical youth "community" to define itself as a counterculture against the dominant moral order (especially against the guardians of order) inflamed Williams. He believed that the mass of ordinary Americans *could* be won over, and no doubt he also resented the generational lines of division. Speaking in largely working-class Madison East High School once or twice gave him the kind of audience he wanted far more than the middle-class campus did. Without doubt, he had mastered the art of opening the minds of instinctively patriotic youngsters to the possibility of a patriotic anti-imperialism. But such opportunities remained rare. The New Left emphasis on the more impoverished, the lower layers of the working class, and the ghetto minorities left Williams cold, probably because he saw marginal classes as unable to lift themselves out of their misery.

In a second irony more obvious outside Madison, Williams's writing grew steadily more popular among political circles with which he found little or no spiritual common ground. The "anti-imperialist" wing of the New Left, concentrated in the coastal universities from Columbia and Harvard to Berkeley and San Francicso State, tended toward versions of Leninism, but schooled themselves in *The Tragedy of American Diplomacy*. Institutions like New York's "Alternative University" (the very idea of free-floating classes teaching "revolution" could only dismay Williams) considered I. F. Stone and Williams their patron saints, for these two had opened wide the book of American sins abroad. If liberals and conservatives increasingly viewed Williams as an "America-hater", the self-defined anti-imperialist activists, never a large section of the Left but increasingly present, manifested adulation precisely because they sought to overthrow what they usually referred to as "Amerika" or even "Amerikkka." It seems hard to imagine that the same readers could have comprehended *Contours of American History*—but hardly impossible in those strange days, either.[37]

For these contradictory reasons among others, Williams's familiar successes continued. His undergraduate course was larger than ever. He had not changed his political-minded critique of the past, nor his critique of the war in Vietnam. He maintained his graduate seminar at a high level, commenting privately that he had had enough of this work for a lifetime. He complained that even the graduate students had become rabid activists (indeed, in large numbers around the history department they set themselves to organizing a Teaching Assistants Association whose leaders would eventually guide the state federation of labor). Meanwhile, his private generosity included a helping hand to *Radical America*, a new graduate student radical history journal on campus and successor to *Studies On the Left* but distinctly drawn to the history of radicalism and labor rather than the history of elites. He successfully lobbied the Rabinowitz Foundation to offer a small grant making continued publication of the journal possible.[38]

One route out of the frustrations that seemed to surround him was an academic career move. He received in 1966 an offer from the University of Rochester, which had a strong history department with important Madison connections (notably his graduate school friend Loren Baritz, but also Herbert Gutman, a former teaching assistant to Howard Beale and a promising labor historian) and two new professors of note, Eugene D. Genovese and Christopher Lasch. Williams was drawn to and uncertain about Rochester for almost the same reasons. He would have plenty of intellectual stimulation but would also be swamped by another crew of ambitious young men (and a few women), determined to get him to lead seminars, read dissertation chapters, and write endless recommendations. He admired Genovese not least because the expensively dressed, cigar-smoking, self-defined gentleman on the Left shared many if by no means all of his values. He may also have suspected that Genovese's important works on slavery, *The Political Economy of Slavery* (1965) and later *The World the Slave-Holders Made* (1969) were, notwithstanding Genovese's greater Marxist theoretical acuity, in large ways shadow versions of *The Contours of American History*.[39]

Both scholars felt a repugnance at feminism and the activist campus New Left, with sentiments that grew steadily stronger. But Genovese, a rising master of the academic power play, also made Williams nervous. Williams had taken real pride in his various roles in the University of Wisconsin History Department, from training students to editing the department newsletter. But like a man who has raised a family, divorced, and had no wish to start over with a new wife, Williams did not intend to begin graduate training again. Nor did he want to take the time and emotional effort to become involved in Machiavellian professional maneuvers that he suspected Genovese probably had in mind, all the more because he guessed that he would be used as a symbolic chess piece for unspecified ends.[40]

Williams visited Rochester twice with Corrinne, and postponed until the last minute a final decision. He sought to blame his reluctance on her wanting to commute to Buffalo for courses toward a social work degree, thus fragmenting their family life. By staying in Madison, he concluded, he would do the best thing for them all. But he confessed to having other motives as well. The University of Wisconsin came through with a better salary offer, including some paid leave. He and Harvey Goldberg had worked long and hard in the department to win a special kind of freedom for both of History's stars (thereafter Goldberg regularly commuted to Paris for alternate semesters, as Mosse would similarly alternate with appointments abroad, years later). Williams thought he would stay.[41]

Williams also had a backup plan. He had wanted to return to Oregon's climate and its beautiful coast almost from the day he left. Now he could do so for an entire year. He thought that it would be good for the troubled marriage, which he insisted he hoped to save for everyone's sake including the children's. But it was also an unmistakable control move. He meant to take his teenagers and near-teenagers out of the rampant youth culture environment into the small and insular town life of Oregon. The implications for Corrinne were still more one-sided. She would not be able to continue coursework en route to a career. Although Williams rationalized that Corinne could now be near her own extended family, she simply did not want to leave Madison. He made the decision for everyone.

Renting a home in Newport, Oregon, for the school year 1966-67, the Williamses quarreled often. They also socialized, danced, and drank heavily with two other couples: all three were later divorced. On the positive side, Williams and Corrinne enjoyed the natural beauty of the scene and revisited, together, something of what they had experienced in their courting. But basic conflicts could not be avoided for long. As Williams angled for a job somewhere in the state, Corrinne felt trapped and looked forward to returning to Madison and going to school.

Williams owed the University of Wisconsin a year in any case. The return to Madison was fraught with emotional tremors on all sides. Daunted no longer, Corrinne applied and was accepted into the social work section of the sociology department at the University, and she completed her first semester more than satisfactorily.[42] Williams, on the other hand, told himself and his friends that he wanted to set down roots in small-town Oregon while he still had productive years, sparing himself both Wisconsin winters and the university-urban setting. Further problems with his back, which demanded he virtually give up active sports, also prompted him to think about his retirement still almost twenty years away. These perfectly logical reasons, however, also had the sound of a man frantic to control the elements of his marriage and, in other ways, tired to the bone.[43]

Williams measured his withdrawal from the New Left with a sort of anti-manifesto published, significantly, in *Liberation* magazine. There, the "Movement" (at least beyond civil rights) had arguably begun, recorded in the words of participants. *Liberation* had subsequently become more and more a magazine of direct (albeit nonviolent) action, raising the extreme ire of anti-Communist Socialists loyal to the Democratic Party and ambivalent about Vietnam. But for Williams, it undoubtedly displayed a more promising side. *Liberation* had been resolutely anti-imperialist without succumbing to Leninism, an ideology very suddenly gaining popularity within the New Left. It was also never anti-intellectual.

Thus Williams delivered, in early 1969, the damning complaint that the movement seemed incapable of forming around itself a social bloc capable of compelling structural change in capitalist America. Worse, in Williams's eyes, it had in many cases invited political repression through pseudo-militance and wild rhetoric. It showed little ability to discern conflicts among dominant groups of society (he would later say that any effective Left had to figure out how to split the ruling factions), and it had no sense of what kind of order should emerge from the chaos. Its utopian counterculture offered ordinary people ("the straights," and he counted himself among them) nothing but put-offs and put-downs. Williams unfailingly referred to this "do-your-own-thing" behavior as particularly destructive, mirroring marketplace individualism. Demonstrations, more and more followed by bloodlettings, could not convince in the way that quiet door-to-door or dormitory-to-dormitory dialogue could do. Unless and until the New Left found a way to reach the majority of the population with a vision of a better society, unless it learned how to use the campus for the testing of ideas, and unless it abandoned its sheer arrogance toward others, all the energy expended in protest would bring no significant, structural change.[44]

The young radicals needed more than anything else a positive vision of "what it means to be an American," and how Americans could make "their lives . . . richer and more purposeful." This demanded not only a better attitude (another age would say, less of an attitude) but also a blueprint of some kind: "how will  socialism be any better than a capitalism without the Vietnam War, and with a continuing (and improving) pattern of permissive welfarism."[45] In short, he demanded more than Marx or Lenin, Trotsky, Mao, Castro, or the existing New Left had to offer.

Williams raised serious questions about the frantic pace of demonstrations against the war and the absence of any other apparent strategy. He pinpointed quite accurately the failure of New Left intellectuals to put forward some kind of long-range perspective. But in truth, such strategy (or nonstrategy) from the Left had evolved during the wild escalation of the war against the Vietnamese, and in a virtual vacuum for his kind of thinking.

The campus might well be considered, as Williams insisted, so precious a "center of serious intellectual activity" as to be sacrosanct from potentially destructive protest.[46] But such an attitude—if the many hawkish administrators away from Madison could be forgiven their own sordid intentions of keeping the campus a cold-war intellectual reserve—did not neatly resolve the problems of university complicity. All the free speech of professors and students together could not blunt the harm done. As Harvey Goldberg had said, you don't call it free speech when an island of truth is surrounded by an ocean of lies. Nor was it self-evident that student activists taking their visions of peace into working-class (or middle-class) communities would have any particular success reaching people.

Those who determinedly heeded Williams's advice shaved off their beards or put on dresses and went door to door in Madison. They usually had the doors slammed in their faces.[47] No doubt they and many more like them should have persisted. But as the death toll mounted in Vietnam, antiwar activity remained centered in the one place where students could not only avoid being ignored but actually effect a sense of national crisis. Various liberal politicians including future candidate George McGovern offered peace proposals while vigorously condemning student actions. Hubert Humphrey, whose career-long behavior rendered his peace proposals entirely suspect, staged a dramatic appeal late in his 1968 presidential campaign to be given his opportunity to halt the American mayhem in Vietnam. But meanwhile the military machine moved onward, troubled more by drugged and rebellious GIs than by conflicts within Congress. Demonstrations at least brought the nightmare back home in small doses.

There was also a larger issue which Williams left unresolved. The intellectual guidance behind a new blueprint for socialism belonged properly not to undergraduates nor even to graduate students but to the mature intellectuals whom they most admired, including Williams himself. His appeals for a new constitutional convention attracted few listeners. Discussions revived along somewhat similar lines in many intellectual circles during 1968-70, including those of former *Studies On the Left* editors, by this time placed highly in the history profession. Various groups struggled for a perspective, a statement on where a socialist movement should be going. None succeeded in doing more than launching new journals.

Unable to reach beyond its limits on the campuses and in the ghettos, the social movements exploded or collapsed. They had considerable help in both regards from the largest national intelligence and local police "Red Squad" campaign in American history. As Williams might have recognized from his personal experience, episodes of violence very frequently left the telltale print of outside provocation. FBI, Cointelpro, and police groups offered weapons and explosives—or as in Madison at the time of the Army

Math Research Building bombing in 1970, apparently watched quietly as the plot was hatched by politically naive youngsters, shrewdly calculating that it would discredit the radical community.[48]

The severe repression of the Black Power movement, including the police assassination of Chicago Black Panther leaders, the wild factionalism of the Students for a Democratic Society, and the disintegration of the larger student movement had many causes but one result: they left almost nothing behind. As Williams would have predicted, the counterculture survived for the most part only in commodified forms, style rather than substance of rebellion. The underground press dragged on despite a continuing and highly illegal goverment campaign of harassment, but largely succumbed by 1973. The Women's Liberation Movement loomed steadily larger and the Gay Liberation Movement took shape as a social force. But Williams evidently looked askance at such phenomena (he never actually commented on the Gay Movement) as a further individualization of "freedom" at expense of community values.

Besides, the appeal of moving a consumer society off the mark of individual material pursuits had rarely reached beyond the middle class and other milieux who perceived a *need* for America to change gears. Outside those groups, relatively small numbers ever felt anything like the Depression-era sense that American capitalism had failed in some deep and fundamental way. Most other whites at any rate wanted to protect what they had gained (or might gain) from the real or imagined threats of communists, student protesters, enraged racial minorities, and liberated women. The suburban home and second car beckoned, not to the materialistic wife as Williams imagined but to the whole family. As Kevin Phillips later observed, these were the real "silent majority" of voters increasingly strong in the Southwest and West, often scarred by Vietnam but in no large way disillusioned with what capitalism could bring them.[49] Williams himself grasped, quite brilliantly, why liberalism had no more appeal for them. But neither he nor anyone else offered a serious plan to get them to move leftward from liberalism rather than moving rightward.

3

By the time he left Madison in June 1968, Williams had almost put the finishing touches on his next volume and final monograph. He had ruminated on the project since the *Great Evasion*, convinced that conservative and radical scholars of Populism alike had failed to give credit to the sophistication and unique insights of Populists as reflected in their own press. His letters to friends had for several years described with excitement his criticism of the polar positions taken by Richard Hofstadter and Norman Pollack.

Hofstadter, who coincidentally died in 1968 of a heart attack at age 52, had of course portrayed the Populists as irrational and often anti-Semitic agrarian losers who simply could not adjust to the realities of the market economy. Pollack, a victim of academic politics at Harvard, quoted many Populist newspapers to demonstrate a semi-socialist idealism and a solid economic consciousness hard at work.

Williams, as he eagerly wrote his friends during the middle 1960s, concluded after looking at many newspapers and the personal archives of key agrarian leaders that these estimates were equally off base. Unresolved questions in *The Great Evasion* prompted further inquiries and an extremely odd defense of the farmer. Far from irrational, backward, and untutored, farm folk were keenly aware of the changing shape of the world as well as the domestic economy. Far from renouncing competition and conquest for a cooperative or socialistic perspective, they actually previewed the idea of overseas colonies.

Confirming this perception played several other parts in Williams's long-term projects. If he had spent his time in the middle 1950s working out U.S. foreign relations since the 1890s (and especially since 1917), he had remained committed to an earlier notion of the "frontier" thesis as an American outlook developed before Frederick Jackson Turner's explication of it in 1890. *Contours* had of course been the major theoretical outgrowth of Williams's wider view. Expansionism, indeed, had been a *leitmotif* since well before the nation's Founding Fathers. But something of Williams's own sensibilities, along with the work of a student on a master's thesis under Williams at Oregon, sent him searching for evidence he had long intuited to be present.

*The Roots of the Modern American Empire: A Study of the Growth and Shaping of Social Consciousness in a Marketplace Society*, published by Random House in 1969, was also without question a response to critics' complaints that he could not (or at least did not) "do footnotes," i.e., serious archival work. The dense documentation proved, really for the last time in his career, his eye for the archival detail when he made up his mind to find it. The book also offered yet another flash point in his relationship with Corrinne when he sought to transform her career ambitions into wifely research assistance. He reveled in his findings in the National Archives when they took a family trip to Washington, D.C. By all accounts she found the work intolerably boring. More likely, she saw no good reason to do *his* work when she had waited so long to begin her own.

Modifying some earlier views, Williams now sought to prove that during the three decades following the Civil War, farmers (i.e., the majority of Americans) rather than financiers and industrialists were in the forefront of the campaign for foreign markets and overseas expansion. Extensive economic summaries of agricultural exports, along with plentiful quotations from the agricultural press and farm state politicians, provided ballast for his argument. In a logic less theoretical or sweeping than *Contours* but just as hard to follow, he drew out the steps leading to his conclusions. His argument hinged on the growing surplus of grains, animals, and other farm goods, and the crisis posed for the farmer.

Decades of troubles had dogged agricultural businessmen, frustrating their efforts to succeed by more intensive and extensive production. Higher capital costs, more expensive transportation to market, and the increased difficulty of obtaining inexpensive farm locations put agriculture in an intermittent squeeze despite the farmers' best efforts. Government action, moreover, had never been on their side. Tariff laws intended to boost national manufacturing by keeping out low-priced foreign goods had penalized them without compensation. Likewise, federally funded internal improvements had been devoted largely to railroads, benefitting elite shareholders. As European nations sought to restrict American agricultural products, farmers concluded that a shift of markets from Europe to Latin America and Asia offered the best and perhaps the only way out. Empire held, in short, their deserved slice of the pie.[50]

If not perhaps convincing readers that various pro-imperialist political leaders of the time actually represented farmers, *Roots* had made a strong case that the ruling groups of the nineteenth century had shrewdly turned an impending social crisis into its opposite. They responded to the agrarian demands creatively and boldly. Farmers and workers supported Empire because they had accepted the large program of materialism offered them. Indeed, farmers at the least had demonstrated their acuity by insisting upon such a solution! Put differently, a culture driven by expansionism would produce imperial ambitions, whoever made the decisions.[51]

Williams was on his strongest ground when he tackled symbolic or emotional issues, such as the struggle over currency issues that had long puzzled observers. He could show that the debate between "goldbugs" (those who sought to maintain gold as the exclusive basis of currency) and "silverbugs" (those who wished to move the treasury to a parity of silver and gold) really rested upon the best means of facilitating expansion. As in the study of so many other great or obscure figures of American democratic history, contemporaries and scholars debating various sides of the issue had failed to keep their collective eye on the ball. William Jennings Bryan in particular, long seen as a forlorn moral leader of rural mores, might be better seen as the spokesman for a relatively conservative Democratic outlook which hoped to bring prosperity without armed activity abroad. But he, like his constituents, had his own plan for advancing America's world interests. William McKinley, long condemned for his consolidation of industrialists' political power in the Republican Party, might be better seen as a competent manager of the emerging world economic relations. Williams thus agreed with mainstream or conservative historians' historical accounts of McKinley's 1896 victory over Bryan as a successful appeal to the self-interest of urban dwellers, businessmen, and working people alike. He confirmed this conclusion in a characteristically Wisconsin way: Robert LaFollette had been a loyal follower of McKinley, bolting the party only with the later mismanagement of Empire.[52]

All this led Williams to an extremely strange conclusion in *Roots*, one as deeply personal as political or historical. He warned that the "schizophrenic discipline of the historian is a harrowing way to stay sane," the effort to tell the absolute truth despite recognizing the egotistic weight of the scholar's own opinions.[53] The aphorism of Max Horkheimer (which Williams must have read in graduate school) that "Again and again, ideas have cast off their swaddling clothes and struck out against the social systems that bore them," he evidently grasped as a saving grace. The imperialist consensus had determined the American past, as he believed he had demonstrated so clearly. But he hoped, if perhaps he did not quite believe, that the future remained open.

Americans should not want to create a different society still ruled by the dominant logic, he insisted. His grandmother long ago warned him to beware of what he wished for, because he might get it. The counterculture idea of "doing one's own thing"—once more that phrase and notion that he loved to hate—seemed to Williams a travesty because it reproduced the irresponsible market way of thinking. Americans desperately needed real models of decentralized, autonomous but interrconnected communities, and the political movements to create the necessary support systems.

Williams urgently asked, in closing, "whether or not there is time to accept short-run defeat rather than win a minor battle by becoming more like the enemy."[54] This was not a rhetorical question. He seemed to be suggesting that the New Left and all the associated movements (especially, perhaps, Women's Liberation) would be better off defeated, so that a more worthy challenge to the system could take shape. That was not so different from (if far less harsh and vituperative than) the curses that Irving Howe hurled at the New Left from the pages of the *New York Times Magazine*, suggesting that liberal college adminstrators joining pro-war conservatives in ordering police sweeps against antiwar students and other disruptive demonstrators could bring a sane and sensible liberalism back to light.[55] Williams remained unwilling to go this far or he was simply vague on the implications of his proposals. Unlike Howe, he viewed the American Empire as an unambiguously ominous force and had no reservations about the positive value of GIs getting out of Vietnam. But he, too, felt the passion of the moment turning against the ordered process of structural reform.

Subsequent scholarship on Populism and agrarian movements of the late nineteenth century confirmed what many critics of *Roots* had immediately suspected. Williams's eagerness to generalize from what he took to be his Iowa legacy, his consequently one-sided focus on a conservative or business-oriented Populism, could not be sustained as an accurate view of Populism as a whole. Meanwhile, the various odd implications of the book from premise to conclusion placed him at odds with his most likely sympathetic, i.e., radical reviewers. This probably was an advantage within the mainstream and would have been more so in any time but the height of the Vietnam War. But it left Williams's latest work, if not the larger body of his *oeuvre*, at odds with those who had loved him best.

Judging from reviews alone, it ranks as Williams's third most important book, after *Tragedy* and *Contours*. Indeed, a few of his closest friends such as Lloyd Gardner consider it his most original and important volume. Yet *Roots's* lengthy introduction and a broad overview of his conclusions might have been easily excerpted into a separate essay with more thematic clarity, in the manner of *Tragedy*. The unnecessary difficulty of the text pointed to other internal problems.

The sheer volume of the research certainly impressed reviewers, even if they usually could not agree with Williams's analysis. Patient readers delved into the bulk of the book, either to note how well-anchored the arguments were or to point out contradictions and omissions. Even the most severe critics took Williams's effort seriously. As the nation agonized about its imperial overreach and familiar cold-war liberals sought desperately to separate apparent errors from the generally proper course of post-1945 strategy, Williams offered at least a well-documented fresh view.

The *New York Times*'s Christopher Lehmann-Haupt, in the book's banner review, found it "certainly among the profoundest and most important books of the year," considering *Roots* to be a contribution "beyond mere concern, beyond protest, beyond tears, beyond politics, and beyond hope that what is troubling this country these days can be cured by minor surgery." Unfortunately, *Roots* had concluded with "an almost idiotic faith that by understanding history, we can reverse its course." Other reviewers showed more ambivalence. Writing in the *New York Times Book Review*, Amherst College historian John William Ward complained that the volume was "tedious, dull and repetitious," with little consideration of other hegemonic factors than market forces. Still, Williams had pointed in a direction which alone could save historians from irrelevance, an "admirable" stance of both courage and insight.[56]

A handful of the academic reviews revealed a resentment, even an envy of Williams's acquired status, mixed with a sometimes thoughtful series of criticism of his methods. The distinguished liberal historian Carl Degler, widely known for his condescension toward Old or New Left scholars complained that Williams was too narrowly economic and ignored sentimental, psychologial, and political factors.[57] Minnesota historian Gretchen Kreuter struck hardest from a methodological standpoint, questioning whether Williams was imposing a thesis upon his research and in the process dismissing twenty years of scholarship on farm protest and reform movements, especially by sympathetic scholars of Populism. David Pletcher found that Williams's sources spoke less for farmers than for rural congressmen, farm journals, processing industries, and the Midwestern press, while ignoring the significance of the millions of dollars of investments abroad by corporations in railroads, sugar plantations, and refineries.[58]

Other American reviewers divided along political lines more predictable than the ambivalences of *Roots* should have allowed. His reputation preceded and suffused the reading of his book. Among economic historians, for instance, J. R. T. Hughes deeply resented Williams's suggestion that the desire for economic growth was "sinister" and business itself a "grand conspiracy against the people"—quite a remarkable misreading of his work.[59] Liberal opinion magazines, relying upon former Marxists accustomed to defending the general outline of cold-war policies, used Williams to refine their own approach in light of the Vietnam debacle. In *Dissent*, which until 1970 supported the U.S. presence in Vietnam while opposing the particular course of the war, Henry Pachter approved Williams's special innovation of calling attention to the rural roots of the imperialist impulse. In that way, the fault could be generalized to a culture at large rather than attributed to a certain stage of capitalism, as New Left writers often asserted.

*Partisan Review*, favorite magazine of the New York Intellectuals in their aesthete and anticommunist mode, had surely rejected an earlier Williams outright. Grown temporarily shaky about the familiar justifications of military overreach, it devoted a roundtable over two issues to a remarkable discussion of *Roots*. Socialist intellectual Michael Harrington framed his response to *Roots* in terms of his own current political imperatives. A Catholic moralist by background, he might well have found a common ground with Williams on other issues. But he was personally close to Arthur Schlesinger, Jr., (who praised him, in turn, as one of the very few intelligent commentators on the Left) and characteristically muted his own criticism of the Vietnam War in order to maintain his influence among the upper bureaucratic reaches of the extremely hawkish AFL-CIO. Harrington could not abide Williams's description of a consistent American imperial tradition. Simply to acknowledge its existence, Harrington insisted, negated the possibility of significant change, much less a Socialist transformation. Williams thus lent ammunition to the "fifth column guerillas of the Third World" living in the United States, presumably those who celebrated the victories of

Vietnam's National Liberation Front or disdained the electoral process—just the New Leftists that Williams despised.

Harrington saluted Williams's *Contours* (as he had never done previously) for a dialectical complexity absent in *Roots*, and observed that farmers had actually shown more hostility to commercialism, more interest in the possibilities of socialism (this was surely a stretch on Harrington's part) than in the potential benefits of imperialism. But Harrington's main complaint had an unmistakeably personal tone: Williams was a "Leninist," code word among democratic socialists and liberals for a communist sympathizer who willfully excluded himself from respectable debate. Williams's longtime self-identity as a Guild Socialist or decentralist was once again drowned out by his impermissible view of cold-war history.[60]

Decades later, Williams still smarted from the sheer unfairness of Harrington's comments. He had even written Harrington personal notes and received no response.[61] The nearest successor to Norman Thomas, a sort of lesser-prestige "Mr. Socialism" in popular books and on the lecture trail, Harrington might have drawn Williams in to a pact against the confrontationism of the campus New Left and toward a different politics. But Harrington had his roots in the Democratic Party and New York Intellectual circles; to these, Williams remained an unrespected outsider. Perhaps he was seen most hatefully as mentor to younger Jewish radicals who had turned against liberalism and toward some suspect populist spirit west of the Hudson.[62]

Howard Zinn, the historian and civil-rights and peace movement veteran, might well have been another scholar at the leftward fringes of academic life to draw Williams into a different intellectual orbit. Unexpectedly invited to add his perspectives to this discussion, Zinn complained that Williams was actually losing his radical edge and becoming too much like other professional historians. Assembling a "barricade of citations against the assaults of fellow professionals" and posing academically interesting questions (such as which classes had originated imperialism), he had failed to ask what the radical readers wanted to know. *Why* had change taken place, *what* changes should take place, and *how* could such changes be brought about? Placed as few other contemporary scholars to exert a wide political influence, Williams had failed to seize the time.[63] Zinn, whose own radicalization as a pilot during the Second World War had prompted him to become a civil rights activist while teaching in the South, could not manage the scholarly detachment Williams sought and did not want to make the effort.[64]

If Harrington considered Williams a dangerous figure and Zinn considered him not dangerous enough, the inevitable *Partisan Review* choice for Williams critic, Arthur Schlesinger, Jr., sought to outmaneuver his *bête noire. Roots*, he argued, was no proper Marxist text at all (a claim which Williams never made) "except in an épater-l'académie sense," the same canard that Schlesinger, Jr., had hurled against the New Left historians. Marx himself had believed that imperialism and colonialism were necessary if often atrocious stages in world development; furthermore, Williams had miscast the eighteenth-century legacy. What the Founding Fathers meant by Empire ("secure national sovereignity") was wholly different from the twentieth-century connotation ("territorial expansion"). Williams had overstated his case and manipulated evidence to suit his thesis. The empire, if it could be called one, had been created for reasons of state, not economics. The Open Door, Schlesinger, Jr., reiterated, was merely a benevolent free-market system for equal trade.[65] As usual, Schlesinger, Jr., exercized a remarkable capacity for denial in place of dialogue.

Williams had ready answers for his critics. If one wanted to build a social movement, it was "crucial to know a great deal more than we do about the *Weltanschauung* of the majority." Only then could a dialogue begin to change it. He dismissed Schlesinger's "hyperbole and gingerbread," noting that Otto Bauer, Rudolf Hilferding, and Rosa Luxemberg, and not Lenin, were the major Marxist theorists of imperialism. The notion that key American imperialists of a kind of "warrior class" identified with the state rather than the economy made sense only if such men had rejected the belief that marketplace expansion was necessary to sustain the economy. On the other hand, Williams accepted the criticism that he had ignored subsistence farmers, migrant farm laborers, tenant farmers, sharecroppers, and the huge black rural population of the South generally. These, he added in a telling admission, had simply not been central to his work.[66]

Foreign reviewers, no doubt reflecting the appearance of several of his books in translations and the general growth of his international reputation, saw the issues of American town and country more clearly. Edmund Ions observed that going all the way back to Schlesinger, Sr., "historians East of the Appalachians—even East of the Hudson Valley" had fashioned the traditional perspectives on the nation. Williams spoke for the other America, and thereby for a larger truth. The *Times Literary Supplement* complained at his emphasis on imperialism, but congratulated Williams for supplying a healthy corrective to traditional views of the American "agrarian myth." Noted foreign correspondent David Schonbrun was effusive: *Roots* had challenged the "cherished and firmly held self-image" of Americans as "descendents of freedom-loving people who have cast off the yoke of Empire and set themselves to build a model of demoracy for all the world to envy and emulate." Who else but Williams had ever been willing to characterize U.S. foreign policy as "interventionist, imperialist, or anything but freedom-seeking?" Many had, of course, although usually without being heard. But Williams the prestigious scholar had found a *sui generis* mode of puncturing national self-delusion.

For non-historians in the United States who could wade through the tough academic prose, Williams was likewise very much the phenomenon that he took himself to be. In the liberal Catholic *Commonweal*, Richard H. Miller proposed *Roots* for the 1969 Pulitzer Prize. While the "practicioners of establishment self-deception . . . led by a lesser luminary of the Pulitzer emiriti, Oscar Handlin . . . continue to denounce . . . revisionism et opera omnia," raining their polemics on Williams, he had "helped train more important diplomatic historians than the rest of the profession combined."

One of the shrewdest reviews of all, by fellow historian Richard Leopold, spotted in between the lines of the text "a revealing self-appraisal of the author's previous writings," as if Williams were courageously seeking to come to grips with the limits of *Contours* and the rise of social history. Whatever his weaknesses, he had also fashioned a "laudable attempt to make history relevant" to a traumatized age.[67] Williams, never quite predictable, had done it again. But *Roots* could not achieve the political force of his earlier texts both because he had arrived at uncomfortable views for radicals and because the fruits of his narrowed purpose had to be judged on their analytic merits alone. The Williams of *Roots* was neither the bold anti-cold warrior of *Tragedy* nor master of the synthetic overview.

Williams had taken up, consciously or otherwise, that sector of Populism most clearly expansionist-minded. He had ignored the militant antiracist action of southern Populists which threatened for a moment to tip over the post–Civil War reestablishment of the caste system, and he also ignored the vast intimidation and illegal procedures required to prevent a multi-racial victory. Williams made no sense of the sometimes ardent Populist support of anticapitalist workers' movements and mass demonstrations of the unemployed, the interest of many thousands of Populists in utopian socialism and their later membership in the Socialist Party. Nor did he connect Populism, looking further backward, with Radical Reconstructionism and its remarkable moment of shared black and white political history of the South.

More important by far, as Lawrence Goodwyn argued so carefully in *The Democratic Promise: The Populist Movement in America* (1976), the vast enterprise of agrarian cooperatives, especially in the South, pointed in another, very different direction. The Farmers Alliance, embodying an "ethos" in Goodwyn's term, sought to integrate elements of capitalism and what can be called socialism into a "belief in the power of man as a cooperative being," potential agency of a "cooperative commonwealth." To do so, the Populists knew they needed to overcome the thickening web of finance capitalism which took control of them through the railroads and the wholesalers. To be sure they faced overwhelming odds, they lost everything in 1896, and many of their adherents embraced the emerging system that they had so abhorred.[68] The party of business successfully "created in the larger society the cultural values" dominating the twentieth century.[69] The centralization of farming steadily eroded remaining pockets of autonomy. The very idea of popular control over the banking system, however poorly expressed by agrarian radicals, now fell to the ground forever.

Williams came close to admitting the *possibility* of this interpretation in acknowledging his failure to treat the lower-class element of Populism. Goodwyn reflected enough of the marketplace reality of the farmers' cooperationist vision to offer a conceptual bridge. But if the evidence laid out by Goodwyn should have persuaded him, Williams offered no significant reinterpretation of the subject in his later, mostly passing remarks about nineteenth-century agrarian movements.

For Williams to have accepted a fundamentally different view would have been to contextualize his particular organic vision of Midwestern America within a larger rural frame, limiting its universal significance. But his system of thought was buried as deeply in him as the rectitude of massive cold-war militarization and unchecked presidential prerogative was in the mentality of Arthur Schlesinger, Jr. Not only childhood recollections and subsequent projections, but a large portion of Williams's energies since 1953 had gone into demonstrating the validity of Turner's thesis before Turner, i.e., how much expansionism had been a popular doctrine.[70] He could not encompass an opposite view, even a partial one.

On the markedly positive side, as Williams's friends and devotees argued, *Roots* was important less as a book about agrarian politics than as a book about American life at large. Richard Van Alstyne insisted in the *Nation*, with pardonable exaggeration, that Williams's "intellectual tour de force" hit traditional interpretations of American domestic history with almost the same force as his earlier work had hit foreign-policy history. Michael Meeropol, who had come to Madison hoping to study with Williams and subsequently sought to draw him into local neighborhood organizing projects, concluded similarly in the pages of *Radical America* that Williams remained the "great myth-destroyer" clearing away the "mechanistic Marxist cobwebs." Thereby, he had fostered a "creative Marxism" far larger than himself. A well-circulated special issue of the same journal, *Radical Historiography*, which sold widely at the 1970 American Historical Association convention, accorded Williams the honor of having laid foundation stones for the ediface of a reinterpreted national history.[71]

In that specific sense, *Roots* was the logical successor to the *Great Evasion*, *Contours*, and *Tragedy*. Those close and distant who believed that they observed his work falling off in pertinence to contemporary politics and historical scholarship and found themselves reading each volume with less interest after *Contours*, missed an elusive but all-important point. Very much like a novelist who creates works that cover various fields but always refers back to the deeply personal experience of youth, Williams continued to work out the place of Atlantic, Iowa, within the Empire at large, and to pose the moral dilemmas of American success. Karl Marx's theories and "Sockless Jerry" Simpson's personal version of Adam Smith alike offered grist for Williams's particular mill. He simply could not have written *Roots* any other way than the particular way he wrote it.

4

*Roots* also completed a major *modus operandi* and even a way of life for Williams. He would never work on another full-scale monograph, devoting the remainder of his intellectual energies to moneymaking textbook projects (however little money they actually made), synthetic essays, and autobiographical ventures. Only rarely did he acknowledge any regrets over unfinished projects or ones never begun; often he confided to friends, inaccurately as it turned out, that he had written his last book.

But now personal troubles became more and more overwhelming. Williams had enjoyed enormously the early years of his own three biological children, set off in a sense from problems with the older ones. He wrote close friends repeatedly relating, in passing, his special delight with his girls. But troubles were never far away. Almost predictably, one of his grown children, moving into her own apartment in Madison, was arrested hiding a substantial "stash" of marijuana: the most transgressive nonviolent behavior imaginable. Williams, like so many other parents in the 1960s, continued to resist the implications. He could not help feeling that he had provided luxuries and security that he had never enjoyed, but that he received in return no gratitude and precious little acknowledgment.

He naturally blamed Corrinne and Madison for the growing problems that he experienced with his children and hers. Close observers might have detected that while he had bragged of changing diapers, he took little role in the considerable household duties, such as cleaning, and he could hardly boil water let alone cook. He considered the gender roles of parents as fixed and satisfying. No doubt, in his own mind, he had achieved after great effort what had been denied his mother's family after his father's death.

In 1964, as Corrinne Williams tells the story, she tuned in state radio station WHA while doing the family ironing. On a show of daily readings, the narrator offered chapters of Betty Friedan's *The Feminine Mystique*.[72] Corrinne's consciousness, like that of millions of other American women, had already begun awakening. By the middle 1960s, middle-class Madison's faculty-heavy and politically progressive West Side fairly buzzed with doctrines foreshadowing the Women's Liberation Movement. Several of Williams's social circle, wives of faculty friends, took part in local chapters of the International League for Peace and Freedom or Women Strike for Peace where such doctrines quickly took root.

Williams met this ideological invasion with a sense of intellectual scandal and personal outrage. He needed someone or something to blame, a superstructural theory to explain his own growing discomfort. Feminism, as he wrote often privately and a few times publicly, was not a true theory of emancipation but only a theory of individualism. It had no spirit of community, and indeed it aimed at breaking up that most fundamental community, the family itself. He had *always* made the large decisions on family funds, and preferred (as he had with Jeannie) to view his withdrawal from emotional closeness as the result of mutual differences rather than a power play with nearly all the power on his side.

Corrinne, who had announced early in the marriage her determination to return to graduate school when her youngest child was enrolled in first grade, now made clear that she intended to follow through. Williams viewed this move as a further effort to undermine his family status. An extremely revealing passage in a later book intellectualized the quarrel by trivializing its origin. Note the almost bizarre shift of subject from the 1890s to the present and back again:

> [President Grover] Cleveland's almost obsessive concern with the silver question serves to illustrate a more general aspect of interpreting the raw facts of history. Even at the individual and highly personal level, major confrontations often become displaced—symbolized—by secondary aspects of the crisis. Two people who are living together and who have come to understand their potentially destructive differences often argue about their fundamental incompatabilities (a matter of value systems), for example, in the language of who earns the most money and how it is spent. That also happens on the social level, between two or more groups of people, and just such a debate was well advanced in 1892 in the United States.[73]

No more transparent passage had ever been written, at least by Williams. He was right about displacement but dead wrong about what was being displaced.

Drinking more steadily, throwing himself into secret sexual liasons, he seemed to lose the personal control that he valued so highly in himself and others. It was, above all, time for a fresh start. But no midlife renewal is ever really free from the ghosts of the past.

# At Home in Oregon

WILLIAM APPLEMAN WILLIAMS SPENT MORE than a third of his adult life, twenty years, in the relative seclusion of the Oregon coast, living in the manner he planned well in advance of his retirement. As he later wrote in the outline of a never-to-be-published autobiography, he wanted to give himself the "chance to get beyond History into dealing with alternatives for a better America."[1] His reputation grew and his scholarly influence spread. With the publication of several more popular and well-received books (and despite several others that could qualify on neither count) he became an admired senior figure. New generations of historians seeking fresh insights into the large picture of American development found, at any rate, no equal to his work.

Yet it was intermittently a bitter time rather than the well-earned rest and reinvigoration he had anticipated. He imagined himself happy in the small town of mostly working-class people, and he was certainly so at times. He could hardly avoid the national dialogue that he, more than any other scholar, had helped to generate along historical lines. When he sought to intervene directly in questions of foreign policy and its domestic consequences, however, he found himself more and more at the margins, both geographically and politically.

Williams's best books continued to carry considerable weight, but he somehow never received the high academic status virtually automatic to others who had refigured major paradigms. He reached the wide-circulation periodical press only briefly, in a series of *New York Review of Books* essays, while confronted with continual attacks from various critics and afforded scant opportunity to respond. He also rightly suspected that new careers in academic and public life had been based on the mining of his ideas, often without the proper acknowledgment. Finally, he felt hemmed in by the self-defined secondary status and intellectual mediocrity of Oregon State. He acknowledged what he had suspected for a long time, that he had depended upon the excitement of intellectual exchange and intimate friendships of Madison more than he had realized.

More than all this, he suffered from the growning awareness that the hopes of changing U.S. foreign policy and U.S. life in general had almost certainly been lost for a generation or more. Liberals at or near the apex of the Democratic Party establishment had learned almost nothing, despite the presence of a few intelligent diplomatic figures like Cyrus Vance. After the Vietnam episode passed, the party center tipped steadily back toward military-industrial economics and the centrist effort to outbid Republicans as swaggering cold warriors. Intelligent conservatives, if they existed at all at the upper levels of government—a few surely advised Nixon's China policy—folded ignominiously before the New Right of Jesse Helms and Ronald Reagan. Through recession and better times alike, many millions of Americans appeared to thrive psychologically in a fool's paradise of knee-jerk nationalism with no need for the likes of a conscience like William A. Williams.

Increasingly pained at the irrelevance of the Left in this dreary slide, Williams drew his own predictably idiosyncratic conclusions. The great historian seemed at times very wise, at others almost misanthropic and convinced that the "new social movements" such as feminism only contributed to the national dilemma by diminishing resistance to ever advancing individualism. His continued troubles with publishers reinforced his sense of frustration and isolation as a prophet in the wilderness of intellectual fads and political regression.

Seen from a longer view, he still had much to contribute. Nothing could have offered a clearer picture of government conducted behind closed doors than did Watergate. The widespread disillusionment with government, the energy shortage, the slow perpetuation and sudden flare-up of the cold war when the Russians clearly wanted peace, the accelerating environmental degradation and other such developments could not have surprised veteran Williams readers. The "overextended society," as the 1970s came to be called popularly, had the unmistakable look of a characteristically American self-made national tragedy. Such vindications, however, consoled him little when his mood was dark.

Williams was nevertheless personally resilient. Publishing important books at the center of acrimonious debates during the final years of the Vietnam War, he remained an intellectual inspiration to antiwar intellectuals and cold-war revisionists. Despite growing physical ailments, he lectured widely in the U.S. and on occasion abroad. On the platform and in the seminar room, if not in the *New York Times*, *Harper's*, or the *Atlantic*, he reached audiences willing and eager to listen.

I

Williams started his return to Oregon on a high note. *The Roots of the Modern American Empire* was published almost precisely as he reached campus, and he seemed to be cruising along toward ever greater heights. Critic (and literary agent) Clifford Solway, writing in the *Saturday Review* in 1970, hailed Williams as the nation's "leading radical historian." Occupier of a "special, soulful niche of Great Teacher" and an author of vital works, Williams had brilliantly articulated the widespread but mostly inarticulate desire to "find a moral substitute for the market place in American society." He had made himself the grand narrator of a society which failed to realize its original aims but might still turn "in on itself, responsive to its own needs . . . harmonizing its conflicting interests, redeeming citizens from alienation, giving them a handhold on their own destiny."[2] Eugene D. Genovese, in an interview, described Williams simply as "the best historian that the Left has produced in this country."[3]

In 1970, the *New York Review of Books* had solicited from him a series of lengthy essays on various topics, producing the largest immediate circulation his writings had ever achieved. The *Review*, then at its peak readership of perhaps 200,000 and at its peak political prestige as an intellectuals' journal opposed to the Vietnam War, had unique highbrow cachet as a kind of American *Times Literary Supplement*. In the *New York Review*'s pages, Williams seemed to hold court. Much as his later friend and correspondent Gore Vidal would do there decades later, he wrote as quirkily as he chose on a given topic, challenging Americans to think about their mixed legacies. To some of his old friends, it was the oddest Williams yet. But by flaunting orthodoxy on all sides, Williams successfully disarmed in advance the stock conservative complaints while compelling many sympathetic readers to rethink their assumptions—and once more inflamed liberals who, despite their shaken confidence and the generational downward drift, still dominated U.S. political history. All in all, it was his most public performance and (along with his late-life classic, *Empire As a Way of Life*) his most eloquent text in the typically Williamsesque mixture of horse sense and moral pleading.

Williams insightfully imagined a mercantile America run by Alexander Hamilton–type conservatives choosing a smaller land empire and thereby leaving large numbers of Indians (along with the environment) to a better fate. He further imagined the North letting the South go to its own destiny, presuming with more than uncertain judgment that slavery would have to fall. He imagined Herbert Hoover rather than Woodrow Wilson setting the tone for post-1930 politics and diplomatic engagement, with open candor about the proper and practical limits of international influence. He imagined that the paternalism of Wilson and Roosevelt once done could nevertheless be undone, and that Dwight Eisenhower had begun the process by exposing what Roosevelt had hidden, the economic agenda that the military had been ordered to carry out in alliance with giant corporations.

Williams's views of many subjects, particularly Wilson and Hoover, would be familiar to his readers, if reworked here in terms of current books. He had no difficulty explaining Wilson's commitment to "an organic, conservative, corporate America in which all constituent elements would be integrated under the leadership of a benevolent elite."[4] Doing so cut neatly through the standard liberal interpretation of the old-fashioned individualist Wilson poised against the corporate giants which, of course, he aided enormously. Likewise assessing Wilson's preparations to invade Mexico ("the first Cubans, the first Russians, even the first Vietnamese," Williams called the Mexicans), the essayist plucked an appropriate gem of true American imperial psychology in Wilson's phrase that *"when properly directed*, there is no people not fitted for self-development."[5]

Williams had only a bit of trouble with Hoover, convincing himself if not many readers that the much-maligned president was "done in by his faith in the dream of a cooperative American community, and by his ruthless intellectual analysis of what would happen if the dream was not honored."[6] The crusader against paternalism looked to Williams like a philosopher, holding off various versions of state capitalism and state socialism. Williams could barely conceive that Hoover's faith in the redeeming power of business might have vitiated his other admirable qualities or prepared the way for other kinds of business-centered presidencies.

In his most creative stroke, Williams took up military questions as a radical or merely sensible military man might. The Second World War looked different when the historian considered that Eisenhower and

Marshall had been eager to assault the Germans in 1942, so as to assist the Russians actually doing the vast bulk of the fighting. Ike boldly resisted the temptation to look at war as a vast engineering project, an idea fostered by those convinced they could win easy victory through more and more intense bombing strikes against German industrial (i.e., urban) centers. Eisenhower knew better, and with the same wisdom refused Churchill's plan to "end World War II by forming a skirmish line for World War III in Berlin" and confronting the Russians.[7] Ike's wisdom recalled John Quincy Adams saying "no" to the annexation of Texas, and even to George Washington declining a chance at kingship. He looked bigger and bigger in Williams's eyes, morally much larger than the golf-playing former general could to those who recalled that the arms race had never slowed under his regime nor had the CIA or FBI hesitated in their heavily funded pursuits.

Against the benign image of Eisenhower, Douglas MacArthur offered a study in personal arrogance. But Williams managed to see him sympathetically as warrior trained for no other purpose than the acquistion and expression of authority. More to the point, MacArthur had seized only the opportunities for overreach that the civilian authorities had eagerly handed him. The ominous "military industrial complex" of Eisenhower's phrase was for Williams actually "but one facet of the industrial-political conglomerate that has dominated the political economy throughout the twentieth century." In function if not personality, MacArthur was a creature of their making.[8]

A proud military veteran responding to the Vietnam-era revulsion at violence, Williams likewise suggested that the exposure of the U.S. massacre of Vietnamese civilians at My Lai and other American war crimes should prompt not the scapegoating of the military (which, as usual, carried out civilian orders) but an investigation of where the abuses originated. He thought that military officers, imbued with the concept of Duty, might take the course of public resignation when orders conflicted with constitutional responsibilities—if only they were honored for that brave act as they had been honored for battlefield heroics. Arguing against a national exercise in public trials he proposed eloquently:

> It would be tragic to externalize all moral energy in a righteous trial of what we all now know is wrong. It is not really to the point to say simply that if all of us are guilty, then no one is guilty. The trouble is that when all of us are guilty we much prefer to shovel it all off on a few so that we can go on with business as usual. It is time we recognized the potential health in honest guilt, acknowledged our mistakes, and healed ourselves through political action to create an America that will no longer be hated and feared. That is, incidentally, the only

sure way to solve the problems of the military. And, also, the problem of law and order.[9]

This reasoning had its limits, mostly those of class and race within the armed forces. Rather than an orgy of blame, the chief danger was that America would brush aside the war crimes issue entirely. (Indeed, Oliver North first emerged here as a public figure, sponsored by William F. Buckley and denying that any massacres had taken place.) Vietnam Veterans Against the War offered more stark and better testimony about the nature of the war, returning their medals and marching on the White House with broken bodies, than Williams with his references to Duty and constitutional authority could possibly provide. Active officers knew that terrible orders had been given or implied, and many of them carried that consciousness into later civilian and military life. But the effective acts of conscience or passive resistance took place with the rarest exceptions only at the lowest military levels.

That said, Williams made his points with an authority that no one else in public life could match in this respect. For the last time, he was the war veteran who glimpsed the big picture from within the field of battle and lived to develop the immanent critique of the civilization that had programmed conquest without admitting the cost in blood. Other future historians had certainly gone to war and returned both sadder and wiser, but none had brought back this kind of eloquence.[10]

Williams waxed eloquent on Lyndon Johnson and John F. Kennedy because he had found a remarkable foil for his favorite villains. While Johnson was never much respected by Eastern liberals and was regarded by 1968 as a lower form of life (perhaps only a bit higher than Nixon), Williams did not approve of "the computers . . . overheating under the load of all those Brownie Points coming in from the Ivy League" calibrated for comparing Johnson unfavorably to Kennedy.[11] A vintage Williams passage, in form as much as content, followed:

> If the Liberal Establishment were prepared to lead us plebs into the Golden Age, it would have neither the time nor the need to belabor Lyndon and his merely human torments. Having won the battle at the crossroads with their shiny new crossbows, the prodigies would be fingering the Grail.
>
> Alas.
>
> Rather, thank God. (Remember the Bay of Pigs, the Green Berets, the Missile Madness, and the noble call to Define Ourselves in Terms of the State.)[12]

Johnson, he insisted, had been sucked into abandoning the best vision of any president in the century. He had been duped or self-duped into believing that enough economic growth would solve any problem—if only he could explain water power to the Vietnamese, he honestly believed that they would halt their rebellion—and he had simply continued down the primrose path of New and Fair Deal liberalism. He had been miseducated in diplomacy by Kennedy advisors in particular. One final time Williams recalled Herbert Hoover's public objection of 1950 to the famous Truman global overreach. Eisenhower was, at his best, closer in spirit to the Iowa-born engineer than to the former Missouri haberdasher that he succeeded. But Kennedy revived Truman-style international "activism." He initiated the new arms buildup and computerized the counterrevolutionary apparatus at the Pentagon. He opened the door to Asian war in Laos, nearly provoked a military confrontation with the Russians in Berlin, sprung the Bay of Pigs (Williams was convinced that in this matter, anyway, Nixon was worse: he would have followed up with the Marines), and learned nothing from all this except that he *really* wanted to win:

> He gave serious consideration to any proposal that seemed likely to blot out the defeat. There was open talk of another invasion, and he persistently discussed the assassination of Castro.
> Irony of ironies.
> Terror of terrors.[13]

Khrushchev had been expansive enough to grasp, at the crucial moment of the Cuban Missile Crisis, that Kennedy could not psychologically make the first gesture pulling back from the nuclear brink. And Kennedy learned something from near-catastrophe. But he did not not learn enough, certainly not the lesson that "a social movement can unzip a nuclear empire."[14] Thus Vietnam.

Even here, on an issue where millions of words had been spilled by 1970, Williams had something original to say. Johnson had (in Williams's familiar terms) failed to honor his own commitments and thereby failed the nation. He actually went to Congress in 1965 with the war issue, as Roosevelt, Truman, and Kennedy would surely not have done. He grossly misrepresented the Gulf of Tonkin incident there, as Williams did not note. But the North Vietnamese handed him a rationale by launching ground attacks in February 1965. Aroused, Johnson set out to finish an awful job. Only much later did he begin to understand the full measure of the harm he had done. The Kennedys, minus two assassinations, might have somehow given a credulous public the illusion in Southeast Asia of "another classic American victory." Johnson, in his blunders, had prompted Americans "to the visceral confrontation with ourselves that offers us a chance to break out of our traditional outlook."[15] It was an enormous potential contribution, if only Americans could take their opportunity.

But the great chance for change had been squandered in the sixties, twice over. The racial egalitarianism that white southerner LBJ proposed at home would, in itself, have been a magnificent democratic leap forward decades earlier; by 1964, and notwithstanding the Civil Rights Act, it was simply inadequate to the social problems at hand. When Johnson went down, Nixon came up a colorless figure who might possibly have made himself an American Disraeli but instead became (under the tutelage of Henry Kissinger) just another would-be successor to Woodrow Wilson. Williams still hoped Nixon would reconsider his course and become a statesman and even an intellectual, although he had few illusions on that score. Williams obviously did not foresee Watergate ahead, although he would have been the last one surprised at presidential debacle rooted in the unconstitutional imperatives of the security state.

Reprinted by the *Review*'s own press the next year as *Some Presidents*, the essays had little further distribution (as the publishers anticipated when they informed Williams they could offer only a small advance for the book). Nor was it much reviewed, a process which might have found critics unraveling the fascinating contradictions within Williams's narrative. One could imagine friendly commentators showing that Williams had tried more than ever before to speak for himself, not the foreign-policy expert or professor so much as the military man, the non-Easterner, the citizen.[16] The book seemed to fall anomalously from sight, probably because anyone interested in it had already read the contents serially in the *New York Review*. Its impact had been, for Williams personally, important nevertheless. As the U.S. involvement in the Vietnam War reached a climax and wound down, he seemed to have gained stature continuously, and by now, not quite fifty years old, to be at the top of his game. He was properly prepared for the stiffest challenges he would receive from cold-war traditionalists.

2

Behind the accolades and general wide appreciation for Williams with all his warts, a geological shift had taken place in the teaching and writing of U.S. history. The Vietnam War and the rise of social movements dampened the aging cold warriors' spirits as bright youngsters researched dissertations on "radical" subjects and looked to favorite historians to oppose once orthodox views in the public arena. On the merits of the arguments as much as the political shift of the profession, the antiwarriors won much historiographical ground, but not without facing well-placed challenges. For the last time, Williams seemed to be in the middle of the controversy, even when personally on the sidelines.

Defections from the erstwhile scholarly mainstream counted heavily at the end of the 1960s. As a handful of neoconservatives and traditionalists rushed into print condemning the rise of "New Left" history generally (and in particular the early volumes produced by scholars of women's history), other notables showed remarkable signs of rethinking their positions. Richard Hofstadter's *The Progressive Historians* (1968) suggested that historians needed to ask new questions about "the complex texture of apathy and irrationality that holds a society together." Thinking aloud about the radical historians, some of them his final graduate students, Hofstadter observed that scholarship *should* restore "our slave insurrections, our mobbed abolitionists and lynched Wobblies, our sporadic, furious militant Homesteads, Pullmans, and Patersons; our race lynchings and ghetto riots."[17]

Hofstadter more than answered the sputtering critics such as Oscar Handlin, who had insisted that the radicals were forcing a political agenda upon scholarship. Admitting that developments themselves had changed the agenda, conservative David Potter lamented that historical studies became irrelevant in the "intellectual riptide" which occasionally swept through society at large. Scholars who had once forced their own agendas upon the profession during the not-so-distant 1950s found themselves demoralized, bitter, and often uncomprehending. Others like David Donald, in 1940s youth a radical sympathizer and in early middle age a doughty conservative, began to see the history that they wrote with new eyes. Radical fanatics had become heroic fighters for black rights. New scholarship in their fields, rather than enraging them, prompted admiration and rethinking.[18]

This flexibility remained more rare on issues closer to the present such as the cold war. Rather than altering their views, hardliners found themselves displaced in prestige, and replaced at lower levels of academic privilege by younger men and women with strikingly different assumptions. The "realist" Norman Graebner, one of Williams early admirers, discovered in distributing a questionnaire to several hundred colleagues about the "success" of U.S. foreign policy in the nineteenth and twentieth centuries that the old questions could not be posed in the same way. A great number of teachers had come to the conclusion that "success" in attaining standard U.S. national objectives might well be moral disaster for the world. When the work of younger scholars began overturning some of the most basic assumptions of the cold war (such as Stalin's supposed aggressiveness on Greece, which in actuality was an acquiescence to Western interests), and when even George Kennan's *Memoirs* showed an anguished diplomatic veteran seeking to grapple with the nation's obsessions and errors, traditional positions simply could not retain their familiar credibility.[19]

U.S. escalation of the bombings and the war generally played a central role in turning minds, but before Vietnam's effects had been fully realized, Williams had one more round of spirited debate with his major critics. Arthur M. Schlesinger, Jr., early on signalled the beginning of an intensified controversy with a letter to the *New York Review of Books* in 1966, declaring it was time to "blow the whistle before the current outburst of revisionism regarding the origins of the cold war goes much further."[20] Within a year, the debate had attracted the attention of the *New York Times*.[21] A month later, Schlesinger, Jr., fired a major broadside in *Foreign Affairs*, the voice of the Council of Foreign Relations. Although historiographical revisionism had occurred after every major war, he noted, "past exercises in revisionism have failed to stick." This time, however, the challenge appeared to have a dangerous staying power. The United States no doubt made some mistakes, and the failure of communication on both sides had been harmful, but Marxist ideology and Stalin's paranoia made certain that even the "most rational of American policies could hardly have averted the cold war."[22]

Williams countered wryly in the *Nation* that Schlesinger, Jr., lacked the professional training to make psychiatric judgments. Besides and more importantly, no major U.S. policymaker between 1943 and 1948 had dealt with Stalin as a paranoid. Cold-war psychologizing could have found plenty of unbalanced minds at the top of both superpower governments, as subsequent studies of the James Forrestal (one of Schlesinger's early favorites), John Foster Dulles, J. Edgar Hoover, and arguably also Truman in his public tantrums suggested. In any event, Russian leaders need not have been paranoid to be upset by the way the U.S. flaunted its atomic bombs. Besides all this, Schlesinger, Jr., ignored the real historic origins of an ideologically driven anticommunism: not the 1947 of Stalin's misdeeds but 1917, when the Russian Revolution struggled for life.

Historian Christopher Lasch, who admired Williams while assailing New Left historians as a group, followed the Schlesinger, Jr.–Williams exchange with an extremely odd essay in the *New York Times Magazine*. It was good, he suggested, that revisionists could continue their work "(inconsequential as it may eventually be) without fear of being whistled to a stop by a referee." Historians should take such arguments more seriously in any case, not only to expose the "inadequacies" in orthodox positions but also the "ambiguities" in the revisionist cause. This lefthanded defense of Williams and the revisionists was weak enough. Lasch added that due to Williams, young radicals now foolishly considered it "axiomatic" that U.S. foreign policy had been counterrevolutionary and that no fundamental change was possible short of domestic revolution.[23] Even most of Williams's critics would consider this a bizarre caricature, closer indeed to Lasch's own position that the Empire could not be halted short of socialism.

The distinguished European intellectual historian and sometime peace candidate, H. Stuart Hughes, also weighed in to defend the intelligence services and anticommunist public opinion from what he took to be Williams's slights. Offering in *Commentary* magazine some personal testimony from the time he had served with the Office of Strategic Services during the world war and later with the State Department's Division of Research for Europe, he insisted that the revisionists simply lacked the "feel and taste" for the complexities of the 1940s. Although they had properly rehabilitated "those of us who originally opposed the cold-war mentality," they wrongly believed that the U.S. leaders could or should have seen the world in terms of spheres of influence, with Russia's unique history and its needs given special consideration. They also improperly saw anticommunism as "evil or misguided," when on a case-by-case basis "hostility to communism made sense in certain contexts and was blind and self-defeating in others."[24] Hughes could not account, however, for the out-of-control quality of the state security apparatus, or for the failure of presumably moralistic insiders to speak out early and often against the clear violations of international law and morality—to say nothing of the corrupting influences that secret funding exerted within American academic life.[25] While offering what seemed to be a balanced and personal perspective, Hughes actually anticipated a revulsion at anti-imperialism fully realized in the neo-conservative tilt of *Commentary* editors and contributors during the 1970s-80s.

Meanwhile, Williams emerged an admired figure in steadily wider academic circles. A poll of members conducted by the Organization of American Historians in 1971 showed that the *Tragedy of American Diplomacy* was one of the most influential books of any kind on college campuses. By this time, revisionist interpretations had begun to find their way into college textbooks, and even many traditional scholars had shifted ground to some degree on the cold war.[26] Gar Alperovitz, Gabriel Kolko, Lloyd Gardner, Diane Shaver Clemens, D. F. Fleming, Thomas G. Paterson, and non-campus intellectuals Carl Oglesby and David Horowitz were only a few of the heavily read revisionists caught up in scholarship, popularization, and controversy around views often heavily influenced by Williams. A *Wall Street Journal* reporter called him the "dean of leftwing diplomatic historians."[27]

Williams must have found the Congressional summons for 1971 on the origins of the cold war psychologically fulfilling. Only a decade ago, he had been hauled in front of HUAC. Now, he joined experienced cold warriors like Schlesinger, Jr., and Adam Ulam, fellow revisionist Richard Barnet, and the dean of revisionism, D. F. Fleming, in the spotlight. Schlesinger, Jr., restated his familiar perspective, insisting that the Truman administration had conducted no "crusading policy" until the Korean War and that the U.S. had never overreacted until 1953, when John Foster Dulles came to power at State—conveniently forgetting NSC-68 and the largest peacetime military buildup in American history. From that point on, Schlesinger, Jr., now saw what he had missed before, a runaway conflict with nationalism gradually undoing the assumptions of a bipolar world. Cold-war institutions were viewed ever more skeptically, now that the "old Stalinist Russia had gone," and that was "immensely to the good." No world power should continue to insist "that it has exclusive possession of the truth . . . [and] that it looks forward to the day when its absolute truth obliterates competing truths in the rest of the planet."[28] It would be difficult indeed to find a more forceful vindication of post-1953 relativism. If only Schlesinger had been expansive enough to admit the Kennedy administration's large burden of guilt in its dealings with the Third World as well as its escalating arms race with Russia, he and Williams might have found valuable common ground for the decades remaining to them.

Williams seemed for his part determined to be as cooperative as possible, almost as if to build upon Schlesinger, Jr.'s tacit admission of earlier errors of judgment. Because the U.S. had insisted upon a "world marketplace on capitalist terms" and wrongly analogized the Soviet Union with Nazi Germany, it had projected unrealistic expectations, including the long-term dominance of the Third World. He proposed that "Professor Schlesinger is absolutely correct . . . that the government generally engaged in a kind of massive overkill in its selling" of cold-war views to the public—but added politely that the exaggeration had come "much earlier than Professor Schlesinger allowed." The U.S. had thereby become locked into policies that misallocated resources, disregarded anticolonial and postcolonial nationalism, and harmed America. Stepping "outside my defined role as a historian," he concluded with a citizen's appeal:

> I am very pleased by what this subcommittee is doing. I think you have a great opportunity. I would like to see it be the beginning of Congress reasserting its role in the active ongoing dialog about foreign policy. I would like to see it as the House of Representatives, close to people every two years, broadening and deepening the debate about foreign policy. And I would like to see and like to hope, finally, that out of these hearings would come a decision and a will by the House of Representatives to take the lead in reallocating our resources and reordering our priorities.[29]

There the discussion practically ended, with a series of reiterations. Schlesinger, Jr., rebutted that capitalism played no "kind of significant role" in American postwar policy, and that the U.S. had simply been compelled to act; Williams responded that patience and understanding had never been tried, especially not by the "terribly impatient, hurryup" Truman who wanted everything settled in America's favor at the outset.[30] The two decades-long antagonists had obviously not reached agreement. But the fact that he and Schlesinger, Jr., found each other on the same platform and at an equal level of public acceptance was a great step forward. Within the profession, meanwhile, there was no doubt where the sympathies of the younger intellectuals lay.

Other scholarly assessments of the revisionist controversy dragged on mainly among specialists in the academic journals. Daniel M. Smith, for instance, hoped that revisionism would initiate a "scholarly dialectical process" that would ultimately yield "a more intellectually satisfying historical synthesis." If current revisionism had emerged in reaction to the "alleged failures of an affluent middle-class society, disillusioned by cold-war rhetoric, and appalled by the dangers of thermonuclear destruction," Smith complained, then the "moralism" of the New Left that prompted its members to embrace foreign revolutions tended "merely to substitute one kind of interventionism and American concept of mission for another."[31]

Charles S. Maier was more typical of intellectuals defending their familiar turf from scholars who seemed to represent the troublesome student activists. Revisionists had showed themselves "interested in certain specific modes of explanation and no others," with a value system and vocabulary that made meaningful dialogue impossible. Just as guilty as traditional cold-war historians of producing tautologies, they offered propositions that could not be proven or disproven. Others who styled themselves "realists" lamented similarly that New Left interpretations perceived "only evil in U.S. motives rather than merely setting forth the facts and explaining them."[32] This line of argument had the strangely reminiscent sound of the 1950s, when cold-war defenders had cursed criticism of America as based in "ideology," defending their own views as disinterested logic.

Lloyd Gardner, Hans Morgenthau, and Schlesinger, Jr., made what might be regarded as one final effort at dialogue or scholarly detente between cold warriors and their critics, setting forth respectively the revisionist, realist, and liberal perspectives in a roundtable. The discussion foundered when Schlesinger, Jr., could accept no element of the "spheres of influence" position. Had the West equivocated, Stalin would have "used Eastern Europe as a springboard for further leaps to the West," a view Gardner easily rebutted by pointing to specific instances of calculated and restrained Russian actions.[33] Seemingly, the differences of historical interpretation had proved irreconcilable.

For a brief moment in time, the various players nevertheless shared an opposition to the current Southeast Asian conflict. The logic of escalation had led to massive U.S. bombings (including unprecedented use of chemical warfare, with the volatile herbicide Agent Orange dumped on millions of biologically rich acres of rainforest), "free fire zones," and the "secret" invasion of Cambodia. Jolted by the opening of a technological nightmare and the popular response in protests across the U.S. and Europe, Schlesinger, Jr., joined Morgenthau as a prominent if cautious critic of the war. But Schlesinger, Jr., and most of his old-time colleagues in the leadership of Americans for Democratic Action (ADA) found the implications hard to swallow. During a heated White House meeting of 1967, when Schlesinger called for the replacement of the State Department team around Dean Rusk, Vice-President Hubert Humphrey (himself absolutely convinced that the Vietnam War was an extension of a Chinese Communist plot) reportedly shot back, "Arthur, these are your guys. You were in the White House when they took over. Don't blame them on us." Schlesinger, Jr., went silent.[34] Liberalism was in disarray, and would remain so for a long time, arguably because it could not handle the contradictions of its own conflicted history.

Later, the traditionalists' mood turned vindictive. After the high point of military conflict and the antiwar protest had passed, counterrevisionism entered full swing, both conservatives and liberal hardliners determined to shrug off the significance of recent events. Oscar Handlin, for instance, blustered in the conservative press at the publishing houses, attacking the media and fellow historians for "flaccid acceptance" of the "shoddy work" of the revisionists. Although the claim that the U.S. had the principal blame for the cold war was "inherently absurd," the revisionists had somehow "persuaded a considerable segment of liberal opinion" by supplying "a pseudo-historical basis for the wishful thinking of present-day isolationists."[35]

In the now swiftly rightward-drifting *Commentary*, veteran ideologue Walter Laqueur went for the jugular. Cold-war revisionism smelled to him like the German revisionism of World War I that had produced the myths upon which Hitler had been able to capitalize. The possibility that these myths reflected a revanchist, military-minded conservative nationalism far closer to Laqueur's own sentiments about America's war on Vietnam—which had supposedly been sabotaged from within—did not seem to occur to Laqueur at all. The Germans themselves had no revisionist views of the cold war, Laqueur insisted—overlooking the very considerable New Left influence in German scholarship—because Germany had experienced communism at close range and Germans were "more likely to trust their own recollections than the work of historians from . . . Madison, Wisconsin." The American New Left writings contained "a good deal of inanity, misjudgment and even hysteria" like that of the anticommunists they condemned (Laqueur obviously did not include himself). One could respect William Appleman Williams "as a writer on American history . . . but once he ventures outside his field, as in *The Tragedy of American Diplomacy*, the result is often embarrassing, if not laughable."[36] Just what did Laqueur think Williams's field of history was?

The indomitable Schlesinger, Jr., meanwhile moved his assault against the revisionists into the *Wall Street Journal*. He recalled, with only a trace of irony, "those brave days when America was manning the battlements of freedom against the wicked communist hordes." He now admitted that the Soviet Union had some "clear and legitimate concerns" and had been "acting more on defensive grounds and on local considerations" while the U.S. replied with "universalist principles." Nevertheless, the Soviet scheme for expansion had been heroically met with the Marshall Plan and NATO. Reiterating his familiar positions, Schlesinger, Jr., also previewed the coming attraction of a new book that would be "a quiet but devastating indictment of revisionist scholarship," showing the revisionists' "unscrupulous manipulation of documents."[37]

The book that Schlesinger, Jr., glowingly (or perhaps gloatingly) described was *The New Left and the Origins of the Cold War*. The scholar behind it, Robert James Maddox, not only began as a Williams student but owed his career to Williams's personal intervention. One of his graduate school classmates remembers him as a thoroughly cynical young man with a great sense of humor. After Maddox twice failed his comprehensive examinations, Williams got him into the doctoral program at Rutgers (through Warren Susman) without penalty or delay. Maddox later got a job at Pennsylvania State University and wrote a volume on William J. Borah with a distinctly Williamsesque revisionist flavor.[38]

Souring on his own views and seeing a unique literary opportunity at hand, Maddox carried an antirevisionist manifesto to Princeton University Press, which successfully solicited the endorsements of Schlesinger, Jr., Handlin, Kennan, and the noted Vietnam hawk, Eugene Rostow, for the contents of the book.[39] *The New Left and the Origins of the Cold War* examined accounts by seven revisionist writers (Williams, Alperovitz, Gardner, Fleming, Horowitz, Kolko, and Clemens) as they treated the four-month period of diplomatic history in early and mid-1945. Maddox believed that he struck gold finding discrepancies between the original documents and how the seven writers used or interpreted them.

Right-wing reviewers and embittered liberals were initially delirious. Writing in the *National Review*, Jack Chatfield declared that Maddox had literally "done in" Williams, showing up *Tragedy* "for what it really was: a novel rather than a work of history." Claire Z. Carey in the *Intercollegiate Review* congratulated Maddox for uncovering an "academic Watergate" (an unconsciously hilarious criticism coming from part of erstwhile Nixon enthusiasts, but also from defenders of presidential prerogative at large) which had jeopardized "the effort of honest and genuine historians." The *New York Times Book Review* assigned the review to the undistinguished Francis Lowenheim, who expectedly concluded that New Left histories were "filled with systematic omissions, unwarranted insinuations, misstatements of fact, gross misconstruction and misrepresentation, and quotations wrenched out of context." Williams in particular, Lowenheim claimed, "unable to locate evidence to support this or that of his basic premises, has engaged in an unscholarly manipulation of the evidence," by splicing documents together.[40]

The *New York Times* uncharacteristically permitted seven "culprits" to respond in the same issue. Each of them refuted a specific charge or two. Horowitz and Kolko complained that Lowenheim was a lazy reviewer for not checking the accuracy of Maddox's charges. Williams responded methodologically, defending the use of "seriatum quotations to document, illustrate, and communicate to the reader the substance and texture of the *Weltanschauung* of the protagonists." Even if Stalin's precise words referred to the Italian situation, Williams explained, they accurately reflected Stalin's sentiments (corroborated by other evidence) about German reparations. A literal reading of documents certainly had its place in historical scholarship, "but that place is at the beginning—by no means at the end—of historical understanding."[41]

A wave of pro-Williams sympathetic commentary followed. Writing in *Commonweal*, Richard H. Miller accused Maddox of having "committed a verbal mugging on behalf of the cold-war liberals," using the "technique of obscuring the message by slandering the messengers." Those "who gave us McCarthyism years before the Wisconsin demagogue," by which Miller obviously meant Truman, Schlesinger, Jr., and company, had resorted once again to slander. After all, Miller concluded with pardonable exaggeration, "Schlesinger's *Vital Center* and the professional anti-communists in the American Committee for Cultural Freedom . . . [had done] more than the FBI to stifle intellectual freedom on the nation's campuses."[42]

From the *New York Review of Books*, Ronald Steel likewise found Maddox's book "highly disagreeable," marked by "personal vindictiveness" and "nastiness." The author had suggested through innuendo, but could not prove, that the revisionists' arguments were actually false. Maddox had also proposed an amazing degree of "collusion and conspiracy" among a disparate group of historians who often disagreed sharply among themselves. Certainly the revisionists had "sometimes been inaccurate in their use of source material and unduly eager to jump at predetermined conclusions," but this was also true of orthodox, liberal, and reactionary historians alike. Naturally historians interpreted "the same evidence differently, depending on their own time, place, and view of the world," but this did "not prove distortion." Nor was Maddox in the least immune from wrenching quotations out of context.[43]

Mainstream historians delivered the real *coup de grâce* to Maddox and to his defenders' influence in promoting the book. From the *American*

*Quarterly* to the *Journal of American History* to the *American Historical Review* and the smaller venues, Williams was defended against what the distinguished foreign-policy historian Norman A. Graebner called the "spirit of vindictiveness." Robert D. Schulzinger found Maddox's work "irrelevant, nasty [and] boring." He recalled that following World War I, an entire generation of scholars, following von Ranke's dictum to tell history "as it actually happened," had "exhumed letters and treaties from every European depository" to explain the causes of the world war. Only later did historians realize that "merely rummaging in the archives until the last mis-filed memorandum had been found" did not necessarily lead them any closer to "the Truth." Maddox likewise seemed "incapable of believing that documents [could] reveal anything about any subject other than the one under consideration in a particular memorandum." Graebner concurred, insisting that distinguished historical work embodied a framework "often based on contemplation and not easily documented, which creates the meaning that transcends the immediate sources themselves."[44]

The most middle-of-the-road or diplomatic history establishment assessment, by Warren F. Kimball in the *American Historical Review*, admitted that while Williams's use of *ad seriatum* quotations sometimes troubled historians including Williams's own students, he certainly had the scholarly prerogative to employ "stream of consciousness arguments" and an "intuitive ordering of the facts."[45] On this understanding, the worst charges against Williams collapsed. An enraged Handlin responded by charging "the ultimate betrayal of the discipline" in which "truth and untruth become matters of choice; and fact yielded to intuition." Hard put to defend himself, Maddox answered weakly a decade later that orthodox historians had obviously felt too much guilt and frustration over Vietnam to confront the abandonment of critical analysis for "ideological preferences."[46] These kinds of arguments steadily lost force save among neoconservatives, often the former colleagues of Schlesinger, Jr., and Hofstadter from the intellectual circuits of the 1950s, now housed in private institutes and seen in magazines like Irving Kristol's *The Public Interest*. And for the time being, they had other fish to fry.

Williams himself offered a parting shot in "Confessions of an Intransigent Revisionist," a paper given at the American Historical Association in 1973 and published in *Socialist Review* (its then leading editor, James Weinstein, was a friend from Madison and *Studies On the Left*). He admitted to honest occasional errors in taking notes from documents, in condensing them into summaries and those into narratives, as well as to being a poor proofreader of his own books. But he avowed his fundamental identity as a revisionist, "one who sees basic facts in a different way and as interconnected in new relationships." Just as he did not believe that his errors subverted the values of his work, he insisted that his critics "have yet to respond to the fundamental issues that I have raised."[47]

He could easily have been rephrasing Jean-Paul Sartre, who answered critics by proposing that they had not begun to comprehend his contradictions. But he intended something more. Challenged to explicate his worldview, he confessed to being a "Gestaltian who does not think that Freud or Jung or Adler wiped the slate clear of Dilthey or James—or even Marx."[48] In other words, if he believed that empirical examination remained the essential work of the scholar, he also had his own distinct framework for looking at things. He frankly sought the particular documents and the precise intellectual perspectives that allowed him to interpret the big picture in his own way. Seeking to "explore and reveal all the internal relationships that give meaning to a group of positivistic facts" had sometimes produced logical gaps or redundancies in his narratives, raising hackles for instance when he explained one era by a piece of evidence from another. But he was doing "my best to encapsulate the history that I then explore."[49] If he were proven wrong on this or that point, if scholars disagreed, he still saw things where other people did not. For sympathetic readers, this *mea culpa* would be sufficient. He did not seriously expect to convert the inveterately hostile.

By the middle 1970s, at any rate, no one appeared eager to challenge him or his methods any more. For that matter, the whole revisionist controversy seemed to wind down. Perhaps both sides had simply wearied of writing polemically, or perhaps the Watergate fiasco, the end of the Vietnam War, and the collapse of the 1960s social movements had left so little behind that the edge of expectations had dulled all around. Williams meanwhile plunged himself into private life.

3

Williams's return to Oregon was almost as rocky and uncertain as its famous coastline. A friendly and insightful colleague later recalled the "man with the compact frame, with oversize hands, a generous smile, and the smell of cigar smoke" meeting with Oregon State's history chair in November 1966. It seemed unlikely that an acclaimed genius at mid-career peak would choose an agricultural school. But new friends vigorously lobbied departmental colleagues on Williams's behalf. As the college's bureaucratic procedures suddenly slowed to a full stop, Williams looked elsewhere in the region without effect. Administrators at Portland State made clear that they wanted nothing from a man bearing Marxist credentials, and at his former home base of Eugene, University of Oregon historians seemed astonished that he could even consider OSU—not that they had anything else to offer. One of the nation's most influential scholars had seemingly run out of luck in the Northwest.

Then OSU moved ahead. The liberal arts dean, gazing at Williams's credentials—he had carefully listed his involvements, including his early campaigning against the Vietnam War—wondered aloud if the candidate were "safe." Madison Chancellor Robin A. Fleming reassured the dean on that score.[50] A lone hostile letter of reference among the laudatory ones described him as "abrasive," "dogmatic," and "stubborn." The History Department's initiative now almost fell through again, but not quite. The acting chair reassured the dean that Williams would not be an "uncooperative" faculty member, and OSU made him an offer.[51]

His old friends and Madison admirers were deeply disappointed by his decision. Merle Curti grudgingly supplied a "damnable letter" which facilitated the departure of "a man I admire as much as anyone I know," and the further prospect that "Wisconsin would suffer an irreparable loss by his departure."[52] Madison's graduate student Americanists regarded Williams's disappearance as the end of an unforgettable era, in no small part because it climaxed the retirement and disappearance of the once-dominant Progressives as a group. Williams's relocation did not mean the end of the Wisconsin School as a body of thought, for it was renewed in virtually ceaseless diaspora of individuals and generations. But it no longer had a center.

Williams's decision meant for him, a family head and a proud man, both a sharp reduction in salary to less than $20,000, and starting over without tenure for at least a year. He dickered, first on salary and then on moving expenses. He made it clear to OSU officials that he could not be expected to be present more than three days (it later became two days) per week. And he soon let his prospective colleagues know that he wanted no early morning courses. Those concerns answered, he eagerly made the leap, both because he had resolved to live at the ocean and because he hoped that his marriage might be patched up. Newport was indeed as spectacular as he remembered. A few blocks from the Corvallis campus, a cousin on his mother's side worked in the downtown candy store. In short, he felt he had come home.

But for a number of related reasons it was not, at least for some years, an especially happy homecoming. Above all, the move away from Madison not only failed to heal the damaged marriage but made matters worse. Williams saw his plan to halt his wife's career stopped cold when Corrinne announced that she was determined to return to school. She could manage by commuting for several days each week, she insisted; he took this as an outright attack upon the family and attempted to forbid it. She moved out, accepting his custody of the children and expecting them to return to her eventually (as they all did but one).

In an outline for a never-to-be-written autobiographical volume, he referred to "marriage in the midst of social traumas," and the "frustration of trying to be a historian writing books from 10 p.m. to 2 a.m." Only once, in a personal reference to his first marriage decades after its ending, did he acknowledge that he might have been partly at fault for his repeated and now enveloping problems. He considered himself a martyred single father. He drank much more heavily, swore he would cut down or cut out—and then returned to pattern.

In a still less mellow vein, Williams addressed a handful of students in the Home Economics Auditorium in 1973, decrying the women's movement for misconstruing the task of liberation as freeing the individual rather than women joining men to break away from "the miserable and dehumanizing system which defines freedom as the opportunity to do battle with each other, man against man, man against woman, adults against children."[53] Sometimes in letters he also railed against the new and exciting field of women's history, even as he sought increasingly as a scholar to grasp the importance of women's various roles in U.S. history.[54] He must have been relating larger social developments to his own life, consciously or unconsciously, with its two failed marriages. Far too much like the stuffier senior members of the profession whose elitism he had long disdained, he took personal offense at the idea of a women's experience as somehow distinct from or even opposed to that of men.

Despite his determination to be positive about the regional tilt to life in the Northwest, it was hard to deny a certain intellectual-political sense of absence. What attracted him to Oregon, the joy of daily life rather than cerebral competition, had a definite down side as well. If he had complained that in Madison he often felt "trapped half-way between the 1920s and 1940s, reliving all the strange individualism and the brittle leftwingism of that period," he might now in Corvallis and Newport have felt he had slipped in somewhere between the blue collar 1950s and the earth-toned 1970s, with very little conscious political sensibility to speak of.[55] He also felt intellectually unchallenged and at times just plain lonely.

His new geographical locus also seemed to finalize his tendency, evident since the mid-1960s, to withdraw from things national. In 1969, for instance, a dozen radical historians including Eugene Genovese, James Weinstein, and Warren Susman, nearly all of them heavily under Williams's influence, gathered privately in Chicago to discuss the formation of a new Socialist Party or intellectual nucleus for one; Williams chose not to be on hand. The next year, some of this group formed the journal *Socialist Revolution*, a successor to *Studies On the Left*, published not so far from him in San Francisco, with many of the familiar *Studies* editors and a perspective seemingly quite close to his.[56]

The new journal occasionally published him and drew considerable inspiration from his intellectual framework; indeed, it might be regarded as potentially forming a third "Williams School." But he drew no closer. Nor did he make any effort to hook up with the post-New Left New American Movement founded in 1970 and aligned with *Socialist Revolution*, and the subsequent merger of NAM with the Democratic Socialist Organizing Committee to form Democratic Socialists of America, the largest non-Communist Left entity in the U.S. for some time. At an editorial meeting of *Socialist Revolution*, or at the founding convention of NAM in Davenport, Iowa, welcomed by the progressive mayor, he would surely have been accorded a central spot, his views considered an inspiration to begin again with Socialist education. Feminism aside, he would have found wide agreement with his vision of a decentralized socialism and appeal to a Socialist Americanism. Yet he opted out, perhaps correctly judging the sharp limitations in advance or perhaps simply leaving all of it behind.

He instead adapted himself and his aspirations, not without losses, to his Oregon life. He made friends and lovers, and especially when his health was good, he relished out-of-door activities like hiking in woods and along the shoreline. He rarely complained about being far from the national scene. But the longer he was away from Madison, the sweeter that camaraderie seemed to have been and the more he treasured visits from old friends stopping by to drink and swap stories with him. The University of Wisconsin, as he unintentionally revealed in interviews of the time, had joined Iowa and the Navy as sources of his own political and intellectual vigor, steadily idealized the further he grew away from them.[57]

He made one last, major change in his life during the early 1970s. In late 1973, he married Wendy Margaret Tomlin, a returned student fifteen years his junior who had emigrated from the UK to the United States via Canada and who met him on the OSU campus. At last he had made what he considered, according to frequent and effusive descriptions in his letters, a soul match. A peacenik or anti-imperialist of nonconformist family background with anthropological training and a keen sense for the dangerous expansiveness of American life, she understood his political worldview perfectly. She helped him raise the children still at home; and, in time, she returned to work. This time, a wife's career seemed to him a reasonable choice, and he began to feel more comfortable with the growing independence of American women.

The family moved up the coast from Newport to Waldport, a still smaller town of about 1,500, where Williams bought a very modest house near the water. There he nursed his spinal ailments and mulled fusion surgery, choosing instead the path of "reasonable control with exercise, some good sex, and once in a while an extra drink or two."[58] A few years later, with all the children gone, he did the carpentry for an expansion and took considerable pride in his work. From a captain's chair just outside the house, he could survey the cliffs and the water below, somewhat sheltered from the steady winds and from the drizzle which fell intermittently. As a skilled and occasionally prizewinning amateur photographer, he relished the opportunity to snap cormorants sunning themselves, or capture the shading of the light in different weather or seasons. Above all, he loved to catch fish and to eat them fresh. Development arrived slowly to the roadside in Waldport, so gradually displacing a feeling of insularity that the changes seemed, as so often elsewhere, almost welcome at first. The coming strip malls and the significantly heavier volume of traffic (much of it former Californians seeking a new retirement haven) with its accompanying noise and pollution were still years away.

The coast and Corvallis now suited him better and better. He genuinely loved spending time with locals, from truckdrivers to fishermen to lumberjacks to small business people to students and like-minded academic colleagues. A bit like the legendary idealists Gene Debs and Wendell Phillips, he was known to empty his wallet occasionally to a destitute oldtimer on the streets of Waldport. He wrote self-effacingly to his in–laws about his professional life, claiming that it was "satisfying to have superior students and create books which were translated into six languages." But "compared with finding the way to create sound and happy and even passionate relationships with other human beings," writing seemed only "a kind of finger exercise."[59]

This sentiment fit well with his happiest sense of life among colleagues in the OSU History Department. A fellow historian wrote, apparently without exaggeration, that Williams had "reached out right and left with words, gestures and manuscript assistance." After four years the chair could say that "no one in his experience, so well qualified to play the role of prima donna, resisted the temptation so completely." A small circle of colleagues drew close, shooting pool with him, sharing a drink (or several) during his days in Corvallis and occasionally visiting in Waldport. Of all these, a young labor historian with a Connecticut working-class (and military) background and a growing interest in environmental history earned Williams's greatest affection. William Robbins, in turn, became Williams's first in-house historian, peppering him with biographical questions and laying the groundwork for the most personal sections of a *Festschrift* published in 1986. To Robbins's wife, Karla, he became a rare male confidant, and to their children he was "Uncle Bill," a frequent playmate and sometimes correspondent.[60] He had become part of another family.

Williams also became something of a public personality. He wrote sharp political letters to the statewide and local press, took part with congressmen and other politicians in public hearings, appeared in a wide variety of other venues from church-sponsored lecture events and demonstrations against U.S. imperial adventures to an occasional tribute dinner for himself (such as a 1981 event at the Corvallis Country Club). He was seen much as he wished to be, an adopted Oregonian with a national and even international reputation. Even if the business community ignored him and the OSU administration remained indifferent to the true value of their noted faculty member, other elites were not entirely blind. Liberal Republican senator Mark Hatfield, with a reputation for mild anti-imperialism or at least international caution, avidly shared Williams's enthusiasm for Herbert Hoover and proudly announced that he regarded this adopted Oregon historian as the finest practitioner in his chosen field.[61]

Williams meanwhile made good on his promise to devote his main energies to undergraduates. Although few of his students were aware of his full stature, they quickly got an idea of his commitment to learning. Especially in the early years, he found many eager to take all he had to give. He set himself to "design a course that would engage students with the teacher and yet enable [them] to experience the excitement and relevance of history by beginning to act as their own historians involved in an on-going dialogue with other citizen-historians." To that end, he devised elaborate experiments in pedagogy to interest students into doing serious reading, dividing them up in groups to consider documents and to make up their own minds about what historical interpretation meant. He also "learned once again how difficult it is to prepare and deliver one good lecture a week."[62]

Williams also reaffirmed his belief that students digging into original sources and arriving at their own conclusions remained their own best teachers. Especially at a school like OSU, however, "they were not disciplined or engaged enough" to do it rigorously "unless it was required and unless I was involved."[63] Over the years, such demands proved more and more tiring, especially in the foreign-policy course that he sometimes felt he had done to death. He was also saddened when Greyhound cancelled its bus service on many less-traveled routes, including Corvallis to Waldport (the camera team for PBS's McNeil-Lehrer Report just happened to catch Williams on the last ride), forcing him to make a wearying and, after dark, a potentially dangerous drive. But even when his energy level and his interest in school waned, he still had his moments. One day walking across campus, he stopped to watch an undergraduates' pickup softball game and a couple of his students yelled "Come on, Prof, have a hit!" He knocked a series of long balls and then gave them a demonstration of old-fashioned, windmill-windup fast-pitching, to his own immense satisfaction.[64] He had, perhaps, delivered a blow against the self-perception of advancing old age.

The administration's lack of commitment to excellence, however, particularly frustrated Williams. The state had never "mustered the sustained will to act on its peculiar kind of incipient radical ethos," taxing resource production in timber or water power to pay for education as some Midwestern states had.[65] Oregon State got the worst of a bad deal. He believed the school should either fight for more stature and funding within the state system or else simply merge with the University of Oregon. The administrators reciprocated his criticism by refusing to defend him against occasional public attacks on "the radical professor." For all this, he had no patience. "In typed and scribbled messages," a colleague recalled, Williams "bombarded the administration from top to bottom," sometimes on behalf of himself but mostly on behalf of a better learning environment at large. He occasionally suggested that certain administrators deserved a good old-fashioned ritual humiliation of having a scholar's hood torn from their heads and ground into the mud.[66]

4

His frustrations in Oregon were minor, in the larger sense of his career, compared to the consequences of his writing. He had always felt, as most authors do, that he lacked a certain creative control over marketing and had probably been too gullible in dealings with publishers. Increasingly, however, he considered himself cursed with bad luck and perhaps swindled to boot by the arrangements he had made. Asked by his agent in 1978 to "go public in the marketplace," he responded that he could not "take it very seriously because my books are not earning anything at all any longer," nor did he expect they ever would again.[67]

For years, he exchanged anxious and occasionally exasperated letters with his literary agent and with publishing house editors. He cajoled and threatened, even filed legal briefs to get what he considered his due. But his new book projects seemed stymied while royalties on his old books were steadily diminished by changes in scholarly fashion and by corporate takeovers. He swore repeatedly never to write another book. Although he did attempt half a dozen projects and completed several, he almost certainly earned more through the sale of his mother's modest property than he had from all his books together.[68]

It was an old story. Going back to the middle 1960s, he consistently failed to get the kind of publishers' attention and healthy advances that one might have expected for the author of *Tragedy* and *Contours* as well as an earlier successful classroom text. Nor did he get any lucrative fees for journalism and commentary. *Tragedy* continued to return several thousands of dollars each year in paperback sales, but by no means large sums. *The Roots of the Modern American Empire* garnered a thirty-five hundred dollar advance from Random House, with an additional five hundred dollars for publication of the Vintage edition.[69] But it faded after a strong beginning, never to reach the status that he had anticipated for it.

To a degree, Williams resisted suggestions to frame his work in the ways sympathetic editors thought the most propitious. Even a radical editor like Knopf's Angus Cameron expressed frustration when Williams refused the timely notion of carrying the vision of community into a popular history book devised with that purpose squarely in mind. Perhaps the *Great Evasion* had been his one "concept" book and he had no more patience for a nontraditional narrative style.[70]

But there was always another element, quite despite the apparent success of Williams's writings in the *New York Review* and the *Nation*. The response of the influential Theodore Solotaroff, liberal but firmly nonradical editor of the *New American Review*, might be taken as characteristic. Without quite saying so, Solotaroff politely rejected Williams's work as simply unsuited—as it certainly was to the New York Intellectuals' literary and political tastes alike.[71] They might be under severe attack from the younger generation, but they and their heirs still held the majority of the prestige literary cards. Neither the *New York Times*, *Harper's*, the *Atlantic* nor other high-profile magazines like the *New Yorker* or *Saturday Review* ever invited the extraordinarily talented historian and essayist to contribute. The efforts of his agent to land his essays in such magazines were hopeless.

At any rate, Williams had a bad publishing decade after 1970, partly but not mainly of his own making. According to his hardworking agent Gerald McCauley, Williams was perennially "overcommitted to publishers in what he wanted to write." Flattered by the attention and drawn to even comparatively modest financial offers, he then felt tortured by the response of editors to what he was actually trying to do. He signed contracts overhastily for several trade books including a survey text of U.S. history and another overview of foreign policy, in addition to revisions of both the *Shaping of American Diplomacy* and *Tragedy*. It was an unrealistic and, for a normally slow writer (in his own opinion), a simply unmanageable pace. As the seventies wore on and he found himself increasingly wracked with spinal pain and facing unexpected bills, he pressed publishers to pay the full advance, scheduled on delivery, while he still worked on the manuscript. In this, too, he had little success.[72]

The sudden transformation of the publishing industry, from a low-profit-margin but high-prestige field of capital to a rapidly changing corporate shuffle of ownerships and staffs, badly undermined his confidence in editors and book production generally. Sinking college history enrollments steadily eroded the commercial market that Williams had rightly expected his reputation and accomplishments entitled him to reach. The Franklin Watts company, for instance, took over his books that had been originally published by Quadrangle, on the sale of that latter company to the *New York Times*. After delays in payments and other frustrations, Williams demanded to buy back his contracts. In turn, a Watts editor wrote him peevishly that *History as a Way of Learning*, the collection of his older essays that Franklin Watts published in 1972, was mainly considered a stimulant to get him to write a popular book; they thought of *Way of Learning* itself as a born loser. He was not wrong to conclude that the book had been written off rather than promoted seriously.[73]

This was not only a personal disappointment but an editorial and political injustice. From the highly personal preface to the eclectic contents taken from virtually every phase of Williams's life and interests, *Way of Learning* should have attracted attention due to Williams's stature alone. Even the thinnest collections of essays by adversaries such as Handlin and Schlesinger, Jr., had been promoted heavily and given ample attention in the commercial press.[74]

By this time, an increasingly frantic Williams implored his agent and publishers about his needs for cash due to family medical bills and his children's education. He complained about the unwillingness of foundations to underwrite radical explorations, and joked about going on welfare when he was faced with a loss in salary if he accepted a Fulbright to Australia in 1976. He contracted a local bank loan in order to take a semester off to finish a volume and thanked the banker personally in his acknowledgments.

Soon, even the once-regular returns from *Tragedy* and *Contours* melted away in the corporate shuffle. What small royalties he received had passed through three or four hands en route, leading Williams into continual uncertainty and the ironic reflection that he was "becoming dim-witted" with the strain of figuring out the cash flow. To make matters worse, younger scholars had by now produced highly readable texts and collections of readings on foreign policy with a strong revisionist bent, adaptable for classroom use. Indeed, several of Williams's own students turned out their own foreign-policy overviews. These texts inevitably made *Tragedy* less useful.

More than once, Williams had in hand what he mistakenly took (from the responses of his former colleagues or friendly locals) to be a "mind-blowing" set of chapters. The publishers rarely thought so, and his work interested them less and less as the sixties grew further away.[75] Perhaps the worst experience for Williams involved trying to write a mainstream textbook. He signed a contract for thirty-two thousand dollars and promptly collided with editors fixed in their ideas about how to reach a rapidly diminishing market. Williams wanted to experiment with the text, including a radically different design with many illustrations, from photos to

Beatles sheet music. He also wanted to use documents alongside text in different and (for the publishers) unexpected ways. He aspired to produce a unique text prompting "more creative . . . more oral, more ecological, more playful . . . more responsible, and more equitable" responses of young readers to events around them. He was, perhaps, a generation ahead of time with a CD-ROM vision of how history might be taught beyond the limits of traditional texts.[76]

But the manuscript that he produced in 1975 did not satisfy the editors at all; one of them pronounced flatly that it would not "play in Peoria." He parted with the ostensible publishers, Wiley and Sons, in what he considered a spirit of mutual resignation, ultimately returning two-thirds of the advance. He complained that his out-of-pocket expenses during the protracted revising process did not figure into the financial settlement. He had been treated like a bush leaguer rather than the world-class historian that scholars and many popular readers believed him to be.

*Americans in a Changing World: A History of the United States in the Twentieth Century*, finally published by Harpers in 1976, was certainly an odd volume, and a measure of Williams's difficulty meeting the changing times. At its best, the text had the feel of lectures to undergraduates, probing for ways to clarify large ideas without patronizing the reader. He insisted, for instance, that the text be considered an argument rather than absolute truth, and Williams ended each chapter with references to books with opposing arguments. At worst, the main historical figures chosen in the chapters seemed to appear almost from nowhere and then again disappear, as a friendly critic observed, unexpectedly bearing and then deserting the large historical tendencies that they represented.

Williams also weighed down the book with judgments that otherwise sympathetic readers found doubtful or downright repugnant, such as a condemnation of late-nineteenth-century women's "false choice" for either marketplace equality or satisfying family life. Privately, Williams was increasingly fascinated and impressed by the contribution of women's history to scholarship. But he lacked the sensibility to make the emerging research and insights his own.[77] On the other hand, he appeared eager to congratulate contemporary corporate leaders such as George Perkins of the House of Morgan for being "honestly paternalistic," keenly aware of the need for reforms to preserve the system. He seemed to ask a greater sagacity of reformers than he demanded of genteel thinkers or politicians.

From the viewpoint of younger historians slated to assign or not assign the text to undergraduate classes, the book was also plainly short on social history. Historical conceptualizations had changed drastically since Williams had himself first taught surveys during the 1950s, and since his own cutting-edge work had changed the diplomatic-scholarly map. A large new literature had meanwhile appeared on black history, women's, and working-class history, with important contributions to Asian American, American Indian, Chicano, and other minority history fields as well.

It was not so much that he lacked the requisite sympathies. He expressed admiration for leaders of various downtrodden groups, especially the Socialist idol Eugene Debs. But the detail in the newer social history simply overwhelmed him. As he mulled with various former students the question of American labor, for instance, he returned repeatedly to the absence of imagination on the part of labor leaders, their inability to envision any other possible system of social organization.[78] The emerging labor historians would hardly have disagreed with this estimate. But they sought imaginative possibilities where Williams did not look, in the lives and day-to-day culture of ordinary people. This was simply not to Williams's taste. Feeling provoked, he lashed out in private at the scholars who somehow thought the people at the bottom of society were morally superior, or would operate the system more effectively than the people currently on top.[79]

He had wanted to make a very different point, that a consensual belief in expansionism drew even dissident groups, with few exceptions, into that strategic posture. Class and race conflict had never overridden this fundamental fact in his reading of U.S. history, and he would be hard put to accept the idea that any other sort of difference (the contemporary assault on male privilege, for instance) short of a community vision of socialism or at least of international restraint could change matters fundamentally. He confused the issue by teasing friends and especially younger historians with jibes against social history that he knew would get under their skin. But in truth, he could not transcend the limits of his fundamental perspective, including his fascination for elites and a certain reverence for "enlightened conservatives." He was plainly out of fashion, but also badly limited in his understanding.

To be fair, Williams was in this last respect among abundant and prestigious company even at this late date of historical revisionism at large. A host of traditional liberal historians in mid-career or a bit older continued to turn out fresh editions of survey textbooks devoted to political history from the top down, with a staggeringly familiar cast of heroes and a far less interesting or original treatment than Williams's. For them, the shock of the sixties and the emergence of social history had not changed anything interpretively, even as they made minor adjustments to include more material here and there on women, minorities and sports history. These books had their fixed constituencies among the older historians, with the further advantage of the standard textbook format and a large sales force. Williams's challenge to cold-war assumptions effectively barred his book from the classrooms of traditionalists, while the younger radicals who might have assigned it were not yet sufficiently numerous and besides, had other objections or reservations.

*Americans in a Changing World* can also be read in an entirely different way. It was a book written consciously or unconsciously about himself, his personal sources of influence, and his ostensibly private tastes. The novels, films, music, and sports he described from the 1930s onward were clearly part of his own experience, the older fiction he lovingly described mainly the books that he had learned to cherish. He finally had something good to say about Franklin Delano Roosevelt who, having established an intimate rapport with the American people, died "deeply mourned." But something fundamental in Williams's world had obviously ended with the loss of faith in Herbert Hoover's vision of dynamic equilibrium. As Warren Susman once observed, the outbreak of the Depression marked the end of Turner's thesis as an explanatory device: the meaning of the frontier, at least in its original form, had been exhausted, and nothing else equally clear followed. Williams was clearly out of his depth in domestic history at large after that point.[80]

*Americans in a Changing World* had its moments in the post-Hoover society only when the text seemed to speak directly from Williams's personal experiences. He wrote feelingly about the Second World War, the terrible sense of battle, and its effects upon the survivors. He analyzed the GI Bill's effects as greatly assisting a large generation but also prompting in most of them both a desperate quest for middle-class status and the abandonment of any political lessons they had learned in the war. He predictably seared Truman, but not without crediting even this prime agent of the Imperial Presidency with serious desires to enact needed domestic reforms.

American history had no apparent happy ending in sight. For almost the last time, Williams showed a certain respect for Dwight Eisenhower and how Ike had tried to ease the cold war. But more recent events, from at least the middle 1960s on, looked terribly disappointing. By no accident, these were historical moments when the actors might conceivably have taken heed from Williams's writings. As the possibility of U.S. hegemony disappeared, administrative leadership had been utterly unable to respond to the challenge; Kissinger and Nixon disguised their blundering through bluster. Williams could still not believe that a "Class B movie actor" and rising candidate for the Republican nomination during the 1970s would prove to be the culmination of all the turmoil. In Congress, the rising political influence of neoconservative academics like Daniel Patrick Moynihan, whose "new" ideas were both wrongheaded and mean-spirited, showed that the same mental bankruptcy prevailed among supposed moderates. The dream of a democratic citizenship receded ever further from reality. Sounding like an aging but radical World War II veteran remembering a strip show seen in youth, he concluded that America by the mid-1970s just "continued to bump and grind around the dead center: a once revolutionary society unable to break free of the status quo."[81]

He had apparently intended to say something more grand, but could not quite find the words. Nothing quite so characterized the better moments of *Americans in a Changing World* as much as his motto-like insistence that

> As you begin history, you will develop a feel for the ironies related to a sense of what might have happened at those moments known as turning points at which nobody turned, those instants when as a society, as well as in our individual lives, we came to a fork on the road and choose to go down the path that seemed safe and secure.[82]

Unfortunately, American history now seemed littered with almost nothing but such disappointments. Even as an exercise in mordant observations, his literary efforts got lost in the effort to render his polemical, almost novelistic approach into a textbook narrative.

The in-house reviewers of the manuscript who described the text as off-center for a course book had thus not been all wrong. His effort to "make sense out of the American experience" and to "give the student some meaningful essence of where he is today," had not succeeded despite what Williams regarded as the crucial test of the classroom setting. His self-belief of being keenly prepared, "the same sense of being ready to work that I had when I did the readings-and-documents text in foreign relations," had ingloriously let him down. Or the publishing world had let him down by not encouraging and promoting a format in which he thought he could exploit his best talents and create a text which somehow spoke directly from the writer's soul to the student's mind.[83]

For the Bicentennial, Williams produced *America Confronts a Revolutionary World, 1776-1976* (William Morrow, 1976) in which he argued that the nation had been counterrevolutionary from its inception. Fearing the "Future" and unable to examine the "Past" fearlessly, American leaders had with few exceptions sought to freeze the national experience into a mythical "Present" (all three concepts capitalized), continually denying the right of self-determination to other peoples. Although most of the book reiterated familiar themes, e.g., how Empire had negated community, at the end Williams proposed a return to the days of the Articles of Confederation so as to break down the continental U.S. into units over which citizens would have effective political and economic control. Williams's own chosen region, including Washington, Oregon, Idaho, Montana and perhaps part of Canada, might, he thought, assume the Indian name, "Neahkahnie."

Williams had imagined himself writing a lucid, conceptual, "what if" book-length essay dealing with his favorite subject: the Open Door. It turned on the crucial moments—the Constitutional Convention, the Civil

War, the Spanish American War, two world wars, and the Asian conflicts—when U.S. leaders might have said "no" to Empire, and prepared American society for a decisively widened democratic practice.[84] All too aware of the rightward current drift of the nation, and alienated from the post-McGovern drift of liberalism both to the Left (toward feminism) and to the Right (toward a renewed acceptance of military Keynesianism and cold-war diplomacy), Williams made a valiant effort to cut through traditional lines of division. Not only did he appeal repeatedly to conscience conservatism, upholding as models J. Q. Adams and Henry Adams along with Herbert Hoover and Dwight Eisenhower; he directed his invective almost exclusively at the traditional heroes of the liberals. If only the Founding Fathers had chosen the ideal not of Empire but of the Republic, or if their successors had heeded the danger signs of its subversion by liberal mechanisms, he repeatedly suggested, America would be a different place.

Williams took exceptional risks by expanding his critique of Lincoln and Franklin Roosevelt. Cold toward the Abolitionists for decades, he now nearly suggested that slavery would have been better left alone, or at least its life would not have been significantly longer without a Civil War. Lincoln, who indeed exceeded his constitutional powers more than once, came to be seen as a railroad lawyer who desperately *needed* Southern rebellion in order to justify and extend the imperial presidency. Never had Beard's view of the Civil War as the "Second American Revolution" been recreated quite so starkly, nor had a prominent radical historian made so little of slave and free black activity before, during, and shortly after the war. Once again, as in *Contours* but with a generation of further research available, he seemed to have missed entirely W. E. B. DuBois's point about the possibilities of Black Reconstruction. Not since the relatively conservative historiography of the 1950s, when former Marxist David Donald held Lincoln up to scorn, had so distinguished a scholar confronted the favorite American president of the nineteenth century.

Williams had once again chosen to be outrageous. A wiser rhetorical strategy for his antebellum nineteenth-century treatment, such as attacking the ever familiar sentimentalization of Andrew Jackson the slaver and Indian-killer by Arthur Schlesinger, Jr., and the traditional liberal historians, apparently did not occur to him despite his increasing stress upon the plight of the "First Americans." He needed to make Lincoln the empire-builder as he much as he needed to hammer once more at Woodrow Wilson.

Tackling Truman was elementary, especially as the Wisconsin School of Williamsesque scholars made the case against the cold-war leader in ever increasing detail. Savaging Franklin Roosevelt meant risking the wrath that fell upon Beard and continued to fall upon Harry Elmer Barnes. Williams carefully pointed out that Roosevelt's long-term policies had encouraged Germany and Japan against Russia and then failed to articulate the consequences to the American public. Unwilling to undertake fundamental reform at home, Roosevelt had actually opened the door to the frightening atomic arms race that followed. By contrast to Truman, Roosevelt still looked pretty good; by contrast to Hoover, he looked terrible. Behind these particulars lay Williams's familiar credo: "the act of imposing one people's morality upon another people is an imperial denial of self-determination. Once begin . . . and there is no end of Empire except war and more war."

If the *Philadelphia Inquirer* hailed it as an important and fresh look at U.S. history, *America Confronts* had few other unequivocal enthusiasts. One of these, Robert M. Senkewicz, in the Jesuit magazine *America*, hailed the "well-written and eminently readable volume," which made "the basic premises of a very sophisticated argument available to a wider public" than just the younger historians who had been enormously influenced by Williams's creative inventions.[85] Michael Zuckerman, writing in the *Nation*, was by contrast plainly disappointed. Unlike the "White House-broken" Arthur Schlesinger, Jr., Williams had "affected the tenor of public affairs where the Presidential chroniclers and court jesters have not." He was "probably the most influential—and perhaps the only influential—American historian of our day." But if his present narrative was "often convincing, occasionally outrageous, and always engaging and alive, his judgments . . . fresh and provocative," much of the book was "certainly problematic if not preposterous."[86] Thomas G. Kennedy likewise believed that many scholars would agree with Williams's description of the "ill effects of the sense of national uniqueness and destiny or the penchant for crusades," but not his oversimplifications or "assumptions of a calculated rationality and consistency on the part of policy-makers."[87]

Other reviewers were less than kind. Yale diplomatic historian Gaddis Smith attacked the book on the front page of the *New York Times Book Review*. Subtitled "the United States as Villain," Smith's essay (which also covered a recent volume by Gabriel Kolko) made Williams into a mere "pamphleteer." Smith's view was hardly surprising; he would continue to attack Williams's positions well after the latter's death, as an obstacle to the triumph of the neorealist scholarship that Smith represented. The assignment of Smith to the book demonstrated that the somewhat favorable tilt of noted liberals toward Williams in the Vietnam years was swiftly coming to an end. The *Times* had returned to a center from which Williams was an unwanted heretic or perhaps the relic of a recent dissenting past.[88] The reaction of the *New York Review of Books* was similar, where the most charitable thing Edmund S. Morgan could say was that *America Confronts* seemed "eccentric."[89]

Roscoe Drummond in the *Christian Science Monitor* saw the book only as an intended "total antidote against any reverence or warmth of the nation's Bicentennial." Williams had "set out to prove that just about everything the United States could do wrong, it has done wrong year after year for the first two centuries—deliberately, eagerly, grievously wrong." Noting that "the kindest and most complimentary works in the book go to Marx, Mao and Castro," Drummond expected that the book would "please the communists and may win some allies and recruits." He warned, "We had better know what they are up to."[90]

Professionally, Williams's stature nevertheless continued to ascend, even as the dialogue among differing scholars that he had always hoped to see now disappeared from any foreseeable future. The American Historical Association devoted a second session to his works at its annual meeting in 1973. Antirevisionists attacked Williams personally for perpetrating a "historical fantasy," while David Horowitz, the author of the popular anti-imperialist volume *Free World Colossus*, lashed out at other panelists and the audience. Obviously, the panel had made no progress in facilitating discussion across political lines.[91]

The Organization of American Historians offered its own version of a collective critique of Williams in 1978. William Leuchtenberg, widely regarded as a dean of liberal historians and who served shortly as OAH President, presided over a panel of Christopher Lasch and N. Gordon Levin, Jr., with Williams himself and peace scholar Martin Sherwin serving as commentators. Lasch stressed the importance of Williams's contributions to U.S. history at large—and also why Williams's roots in Progressive history prevented him from moving beyond the limits of his own remarkable views. Although Levin had himself earlier followed revisionist leads in studies of World War I diplomacy, he now typed Williams a "radical isolationist" who inexplicably refused to acknowledge the heroic "strategic and moral roles" played by the U.S. in assisting world democracy. Martin Sherwin deftly noted that Williams had moved scholars from peripheral questions about public postures to unstated assumptions of U.S. policies. Right or wrong on details, he had aimed bravely at explaining Americans' various contradictory and conflicting assumptions and urging them to accept change as progress, not capitulation.[92]

In the most prestigious presentation of the panel, a definite irony prevailed. Lasch praised Williams's "distinguished work" and insisted that no other historian had "taught so many outstanding students or imbued them with such a passion for critical scholarship," effectively defining the questions asked by diplomatic historians. He had made clear that "American liberalism cannot be understood as an anti–business creed" and liberalism had been shaped in part by corporations, and that Progressivism and the New Deal had stabilized society rather than "revolutionized" it.

But Lasch also had in mind a very different purpose. Williams the "lonely radical" of the 1950s-60s had inspired so much ridicule that many young scholars (including, Lasch freely admitted, himself) had ignored his work. After the "brief rise of radicalism to academic respectability and even fashionability," many of his erstwhile opponents had become supporters. Now, his work could be "acknowledged not as a formative influence on a nonexistent school of New Left historians but as an inescapable influence on American historians in general."[93] Useful radicalism had been absorbed, transcended, or extinguished, as proved by Williams's own case.

This was certainly an odd formulation, all the more so in the doldrums of the 1970s, and it had far more to do with the conflicts Lasch felt within academic and public life than with Williams's work. If, indeed, the New Left scholars of foreign policy, women's labor, and minority history had originated with Williams more than with anyone else, and if they taught his ideas with a fury when entering the classroom (as well as launching local public history forums), it would be strange indeed to imagine these ideas vanishing into thin air. A better case could be made, as Jon Wiener did a decade later, for declaring that their influence had been stamped upon virtually every corner of the profession and had shifted it leftward in a variety of important ways. If many of Williams's former critics had come to agree with him, it was hardly their amiability or his growing respectability but surely the Vietnam War that broke their faith in cold-war liberalism's narrative of the American saga and found them accepting many criticisms set forth by Williams and the New Left.[94]

Lasch could accept Williams's view of Empire as an extremely useful reformulation of Progressive history. But Lasch focused his hostility upon Charles Beard and Beard's demand that American capitalism solve its own problems without expansionism. An inner-focused capitalism could only bring fascism, Lasch insisted; rather than criticizing Franklin Roosevelt, Williams should have congratulated Roosevelt for aiming outward and setting the pace for administrations to follow. So long as capitalism survived, Lasch seemed to be suggesting, expansionism was at least an outlet for its aggressive energies. Any attack upon expansionism which was not an attack upon private property could only assist in creating a regionalist democracy in place of the imperial state, and end up encouraging "the very escapism it condemns."[95]

Thus Lasch had reversed the logic that Williams urgently sought to extend beyond the barriers separating the Left and Right, ruling out in advance the vision of a medium-range strategic alliance of students, minorities, workers, citizens at large, and small business united against the expansionist-minded Establishment. In levelling his attack on Beard, Lasch also seemed to rule out any final vindication of the Beardian circles where Williams's worldview took shape. Believing himself also an heir to Frankfurt School themes and insights, Lasch (as he would detail in a few years) had actually assimilated Williams into his own sense of a moral tradition armed against consumer society and feminism alike. Williams thus became, most oddly, a prime source or at least a scholarly reinforcement for Lasch's *The Culture of Narcissism* (1978) on which President Jimmy Carter was said to have based his disastrous speech lamenting the American "malaise." [96]

At any rate and for apparently contradictory reasons, Williams continued to pick up admirers within the scholarly mainstream. In 1976, he was nominated for but narrowly lost the presidency of the OAH to noted slavery and Civil War scholar, fellow Hesseltine student Kenneth Stampp. Responding to disaffection of younger members, OAH officials grudgingly permitted a sweeping rules change. Rather than the officers of the organization only, the entire membership now voted. In 1980 Williams swept easily into office. Williams was not the first radical historian to be named president of a major historical association. Merle Curti had served in the depths of the McCarthy era and unabashed Marxist Eugene Genovese occupied the OAH presidency in 1977. But unlike these others, Williams clearly represented a new constituency, the antiwar generation of the 1960s. As unlikely as Williams was to represent their main scholarly interests—by this time, women's, labor, and minority histories—he readily offered them the chance to legitimate their growing claims upon the profession. [97]

His election could be properly seen as a happy climax to his decades of work with colleagues in Madison and his participation in the far-ranging controversies among historians. According to his student Edward Crapol, Williams had always felt "the ambivalence that all self-defined mavericks and outsiders have about a community that shuns them and considers them and their work beyond the pale." He had rarely showed up at conventions unless on committee work, and often expressed disdain for the hierarchical, individualist attitudes that belied the ideal intellectual community of peers. And yet naturally enough, as the generational shift brought more and more of his admirers into the mainstream, he was flattered and honored. [98] It was also, if he cared to think of his election in this way, his personal vindication over the cold-war zealots who had so often sought to belittle him. He had long since developed definite ideas about what scholars could do to remedy their collective failings. This was his opportunity to make a difference in the way historians practiced history among themselves and in public.

# VINDICATION IN DEFEAT

WILLIAMS'S FINAL DECADE COULD NOT very well have been a happy one, given the triumph of a demonstrably unenlightened conservatism in Washington, the rapid acceleration of military spending, the unembarrassed plundering of natural resources, and a mean-spirited celebration of wealth that seemed to bring out all the worst in the American character. While these events unfolded, Williams's health slipped downward. He occasionally mulled over projects that he thought he might have tackled under different conditions, if he were younger and unmarried. He thought he could have written a biography of antiwar senator J. William Fulbright, the "Rhodes Scholar from Arkansas [who] was the best we had to offer, but . . . failed."[1]; this exercise would have returned him to several interests of his graduate student years, including biography and a Raymond Robins–like statesman who looked beyond the cold war. By now, however, Williams had accepted narrower limits. His projects and plans remained closer to home.

Williams began to project himself somewhat beyond the passions of the times, taking the long view of the nation and, increasingly, of his own life as well. He found new interests, scholarly and pedagogical, as he approached retirement. He also re-learned how to play, devoting himself to building model airplanes as in childhood—including replicas of Charles Lindbergh, Jr.'s *Spirit of St Louis*, which had flown over his family's home. In tune with all this, he struggled to reap the benefit of accumulated wisdom. If he could not hope to turn back the incoming toxic tide of politics, he could tell those listening how they could get a better sense of the world before their eyes, and how they might act upon the hopes of coming generations.

Here Williams found the strength for his remaining work. As a former student wrote in an obituary, Williams had the talent and, even more, the will to dialogue with ordinary people about the nation's dilemmas.[2] If he appeared at times to throw his hands up at the sight of a "weary and nostalgic Empire," he still had mental resources aplenty to prompt fresh views of liberalism, conservatism, and radicalism. As Warren Susman remarked about the Williams of graduate school days, he seemed ever ready to "discover America" in ways that others did not. And in this crucial respect his vision grew keener at the end of this life. Even while attacks by unrepentent cold warriors continued in high-brow venues generally closed to the dissenter, he refused to be dragged to their polemical level, taking the high road instead. And there he could be found, to the last day.

I

Williams rounded out his public life in two distinct ways during the early 1980s. Controversial scholar one last time, he briefly placed himself near the center of intellectual challenges to the rising imperial arrogance of the age. President of the Organization of American Historians, he worked at the center of a profession which had moved beyond his generation's mindset but desperately needed its administrative support.

Williams had long since ceased writing monographs by the time of his OAH presidency, having made his mind up to work on projects more intimate to his memories and to his unfulfilled aspirations. If his scholarly reputation continued to grow, it was due to past accomplishments and to one more volume, his last: *Empire as a Way of Life*. Urged by his agent to meet the requests of publishers for a cogent overview, he delivered to Oxford University Press in 1979 an extraordinary book-length essay.

By the time it reached publication, the 1980 election season had begun and the *Nation* decided to publish a longish section of a chapter with responses. Lawrence Goodwyn, the leading historian of Populism, and foreign affairs critics Richard Falk and Norman Birnbaum starred among the commentators. Copies of that issue, as planned, were made available to delegates and attendees of the Democratic party convention. "Devoting this special convention issue to Williams's manifesto," the *Nation*'s editor commented, was intended not to undercut President (and candidate) Jimmy Carter but to show "the limitations of the sameness" among the various presidential hopefuls on the central issue of Empire. This examination would highlight the necessity of coming to terms with the "vital work of internal reconstruction" as well as a better international policy. From the standpoint of America's outstanding left-liberal weekly, no one put the issues better than the Oregon anti-imperialist. From the standpoint of a Williams who had first made his name in the *Nation* nearly thirty years earlier, it marked a satisfying return.[3]

Carrying the Williamsesque subtitle of *An Essay on the Causes and Character of America's Present Predicament Along with a Few Thoughts About an Alternative*, the book was Williams's most cogent and artistically complete. Published shortly before his sixtieth birthday, it was also, very self-consciously, his last major salvo. Here, Williams examined every major action in U.S. history, from the nation's origins in Elizabethan England to the present, as premised on unlimited expansion and imperial dominion over internal and external foes. American politics and ideals and the American way of life itself had been premised on endless abundance, making expansionism almost literally an "opiate of the American people." By the 1970s, the world seemed to be closing in, and Americans needed urgently to reassess their traditional values and assumptions. While most of his arguments were familiar to Williams readers, he revealed a fresh grasp of current studies in the cultural dynamics of imperialism. He subtitled his second chapter in a way unimaginable to the Williams of the 1950s: "The Myth of Empty Continents Dotted Here and There with the Mud Huts, the Lean-tos, and the Tepees of Unruly Children Playing at Culture."

Williams also responded to critics, and added some subtle methodological touches to his earlier formulations. He now saw the drive toward a worldwide Open Door as shaped not only by economics but also by a mix of politics, culture, and even sheer diplomatic energy. In response to critics who had challenged not so much his focus on economics as his basic interpretations, Williams once again stubbornly declared himself an "intransigent revisionist." As far as he was concerned, Henry Kissinger had summed up an entire school of official diplomatic thought with the observation "I don't see why we need to stand by and permit a country to go communist due to the irresponsibility of its own people," rationalizing the U.S.-choreographed overthrow of the elected Chilean government in 1973. But Williams's book was no narrow indictment of State Department officialdom. The collective psychology that demanded intervention somewhere or anywhere to stroke the national ego, and the apparent voter willingness to incur a matching federal debt from past military-industrial waste, were scarcely better than Kissinger's personal cynicism.

Perhaps more effectively than ever before, Williams told the familiar story as Greek tragedy and self-evasion. Each chapter ended with a detailed chronology of intervention from the first days of the American Republic, but the narrative disputed any Manichean interpretation of the virtually uninterrupted warfare. White Americans accepted the Empire because, for a long time, it had worked for them—whatever the price to others. "Marx would very probably have shrugged his shoulders (and ideology) and said only that socialism is *unimaginable*, let alone pragmatically possible, until capitalist Empire has run its course," Williams reflected laconically.[4] The crusading expansiveness of the Spanish American War (against the colonial Spaniards, and then against the presumably liberated Cubans and Filipinos) had established a fresh precedent of extra-continental warfare, creating a demon which no subsequent administration could readily exorcize.

Williams gave new exactitude to the self-image of Americans as benevolent rulers of the planet and of themselves, offering various definitions of Empire's key terms and noting how the images blurred with each other and with reality. Bullies looking at their image in the mirror imagined they saw Greek gods staring out at them. The vision of the imperial chase thus became larger and more satisfying than any possible reality, occluding hopes for a wiser "philosophy that viewed . . . restraints as part of a community of reciprocal benefits and obligations."[5]

The State filled the gap between imperial grasp and desiccated democracy. World War II, seen afresh, offered the chance for American leaders either to admit to Empire and pay the cost, or to give up their imperial designs. Letting the Red Army and other exhausted allies pay the cost in human terms while asserting U.S. leadership of world democracy, Roosevelt sowed dragons' teeth for the postwar world. Having lost only four hundred thousand to Russia's twenty million, the United States emerged unquestionably the strongest nation on earth. But faced with the challenge of a postwar world slipping out of the U.S. grasp, leaders fell back upon NSC-68, written *before* the outbreak of the Korean War to rationalize a massive military buildup against potentially revolutionary changes everywhere.

Imperial optimists of the 1990s would insist that Williams had badly misjudged the future balance of power when he labeled the cold-war era "the Empire at Bay." The cold war had tested the U.S. ability to outspend and outlast its opponents across a planetary graveyard of threatened, war-torn or starveling populations (not to speak of devastated flora and fauna). But Williams would not likely have been put off and certainly not satisfied by this victory-through-exhaustion. He admired most the peaceful pioneers who had been able to challenge their own assumptions and had taken the measure of alternatives to Empire: former advocates of Empire, like W. E. B. DuBois, Eugene Debs, Robert M. LaFollette, or Congresswoman Helen Gahahan Douglas (defeated by young Richard Nixon in a 1950 campaign notable for its red-baiting smears). Extrication would not be cost-free. In getting out of the Empire and paying the price long overdue, "some of us will die. But how one dies is terribly important. It speaks to the truth of how we have lived."[6]

Not surprisingly, the last page of his last book brought Williams back squarely to the Atlantic, Iowa, of his childhood where "we did miss much of the so-called American Way of Life" in materialistic terms but believed in the ideal nevertheless. Becoming a part of the imperial ethos which "informs one with the assumption that the goodies should be here and now—and forever," young Billy had stolen an expensive knife from the best hardware store in town. His grandmother discovered the knife and told him that he had not earned it and had to take it back. He resisted, insisting that he couldn't return it now. Around her response and the following action, he framed his last parable:

> She said: You *will* do that. *Now.*
>
> Oh, my: the power of the declarative sentence.
>
> And so I walked back along those long and lonely blocks to the store. And in through the door, and up, face to face, with the member of that small community who owned the store.
>
> And I said: I stole this knife and I am sorry and I am bringing it back.
>
> And he said: Thank you. The knife is not very important, but you coming down here and saying that to me is very important.
>
> Remembering all that, I know why I do not want the Empire. There are better ways to live and there are better ways to die.[7]

Did the incident really happen this way, if it happened at all? Perhaps the "facts" do not, as usual with these things, matter so much. The vividness of real or mythical small-town Atlantic of the 1930s to Williams's wide view of American and international life allows the reader a parting glimpse of the patriot appealing to the public as eloquently as he can. It was also a last testament, from a man who still had no apparent inkling of the cancer that would strike him down in a few years.

If *Empire As a Way of Life* was a remarkable book and a courageous personal statement, it brought Williams's enemies out of the woodwork and into the columns of the *New Republic*, among other places. But for Williams admirers from the U.S. to Europe and Latin America to Israel and Asia, he had reaffirmed his stand like a Biblical prophet of old. "Might

Makes Wrong," proclaimed the Oxford University Press advertising campaign, inveighing against the "binge" of consumptionism, expansionism, and militarism.[8]

It was tragically a message out of time, an effort that an admiring German historian called a "farewell song . . . just at the close of that short period of postwar history during which the political mood of mainstream America could permit critical reflections on premises, judgments and results."[9] Some Americans were indeed ready to hear. But the Carter re-election campaign, running scared, drifted steadily rightward as Carter himself had done during his final two years in office. Already the vision of a reduced cold-war budget and the modest social alternatives that George McGovern had endorsed were long gone from the Democratic party centers of influence. Worse still, the future belonged to Reaganism, an immoderate Republicanism which allowed no guilt or self-doubt whatsoever. As the same admirer of Williams wrote, the "rhetoric of national revival" was now full-tilt, with revisionist criticism reduced to "one more bit of postmodern pluralism easy to ignore in the halls of power."[10]

Critics tended to be deferential toward Williams's new status, even when they were sharply critical of his arguments. Historian Lawrence S. Kaplan complained that the book distorted materials to fit a pattern, but he nevertheless admired its "folksy ways, pungent expressions," its "well-turned phrases" and the author's imagination, revealing Williams to be a "deeply caring person who wants to purge the nation of its original sin." Diplomatic historian Robert H. Ferrell likewise admired Williams's "intense humanity" and could "share his apocalyptic feeling for the present-day confusions . . . compounded with ignorance and pat phrases out of the distant past." He had indeed made himself a modern-day Beard. Intellectual historian Rush Welter charged Williams with "imputing consistency of purpose to actions that were at best confused responses to a variety of circumstances," further burdening the argument with "allegation, insinuation and indignation." Yet he admitted that Williams's "theology is probably true" and his argument "highly persuasive" on at least some level.[11]

Conservatives predictably waxed wroth. A. J. Beitzinger considered the book "an embarrassment to read," the manifestation of a "'rap session' leader" spouting the puerile language of a "righteously indignant Marxist populist." Joseph M. Siracusa, borrowing a phrase from Oscar Handlin, wondered if Williams had prepared yet another "elaborate hoax," with a concept of community resembling "the ancient Greek city-state with Williams himself as philosopher-king, surrounded by a chorus of former graduate students."[12] This was normal fare for Williams.

Those journals which might be called cold-war social democratic or neo-liberal offered the most vicious attacks outside New Right circles. The attack upon *Empire* in the *New Republic* easily exceeded the usual dosage of that magazine's political venom. For reviewer John Lukacs, Williams had in the twenty years since that "artless book," the *Tragedy of American Diplomacy*, "learned nothing and forgotten everything. Truth has further decayed, and lying has become worse." Williams was no "American idealist," as his devotees claimed, but a "vulgarian and a pedant." Henry Pachter, a familiar figure around *Dissent* magazine (and once an admirer of Williams's *Roots of the Modern American Empire*) writing in the *New Leader*, hit a similar low note of intellectual abuse.[13] Not much else could be expected of erstwhile moderates never especially regretful of U.S. misdeeds and now furiously backpedaling from the 1960s—although Williams claimed to have received an apology from the *New Republic*'s review editor for the sheer crudeness of the attack.[14]

With *Empire as a Way of Life*, at any rate, Williams had offered his last and his most cogent overview of American history and its meaning, to the nation and to the world. He could be satisfied that those who sought to understand his message *sans* the troubling complexity of earlier works would find it here.

2

A sympathetic writer in the *Manchester Guardian* observed that the influence of the "deeply American figure" had found "readier and wider acceptance among non-Americans than among his own countrymen."[15] This view, perhaps a bit exaggerated, had the same perceptive insight as Gerda Lerner's *bon mot* that each reader took away from Williams what he or she had come to search for, rather than the author's whole *oeuvre* and driving purpose. Williams's work reached different cultures at different times, touched academic and activist, and its effect varied at least as much with the political situation and academic interests as with the particular text adopted. Altogether, it was a deep international penetration for a dedicated Americanist, with no end in sight.

The Williams influence had been felt earliest, and perhaps the most profoundly in terms of the internal scholarship of another nation, by the Germans. There, the older generation of historians had been guilty of compliance with Hitler's actions or at least with atavistic German nationalism. By the later 1950s or early 1960s an interpretive vacuum became obvious. The Marxism of East German intellectuals, rigid in its familiar delineation of ruling-class manipulators and oppressed masses, could not fill the gap. Younger scholars, some of whom had studied in the U.S. and even in Madison, drew upon Williams for a fresh perspective on Empire. Others looked to Williams through the lenses of his devoted friend George Mosse, who had personally rewritten the cultural history of modern Europe.

Hans-Ulrich Wehler, who trained in part with German scholars in the U.S., might be considered the most prominent of the new generation. No more a Marxist than Williams (but perhaps also no less influenced by Marx's ideas), Wehler sketched out in *Bismarck und der Imperialismus* (1969) and in *Das Deutsche Kaisserreich 1871-1918* (1973) a view of Bismarck's rise to power and the consequences for the new German nation. Like Williams, whose influence he readily acknowledged, Wehler saw divided ruling groups and domestic conflicts unified and resolved through expansionism and the German version of the Open Door. The Bismarckian clique, like Williams's Progressive-era rulers, could be admired for the intelligence of their overview, their acuity in planning reforms and social welfare to preserve the system—even when their successes led to national disaster. Particularly noteworthy, from a different standpoint in Williams's work (and the complimentary influence of Hans Rosenberg, a German exile historian who remained in the U.S.), was Wehler's attempt to see the workings of the system in its entirety.[16]

Wehler and a handful of other German scholars also had a more direct lineage to Williams's view of imperialism and foreign policy. Werner Link's *Die Amerikanische Stabilisierungspolitik in Deutschland 1921-32* (1970) owed a reading of several manuscript chapters (in English) to Williams and although heavily archival, also owed its overview of American leaders' intentions to Williams's insights. Ekkehart Krippendorf's *Die Amerikanische Strategie: Entscheidungsprozess und Instrumentarium der Amerikanische aussenpolitik* (1970) acknowledged Williams only indirectly, but clearly followed the line taken by the diplomatic revisionists. Wehler's more general anthology, *Imperialismus* (1970), refined terms and offered analyses somewhere beyond Marxism, but intimately close to Williams's interpretations.[17]

British radical historians, like the Germans, had internal divisions which shaped Williams's significance for them. The older group had graduated from the Communist Party with a passion for lower-class social history and a firm grasp of historical materialism. Their luminaries, including Christopher Hill, E. P. Thompson, V. G. Kiernan, and Eric Hobsbawm, were often taken as models for New Left scholars in the U.S. A younger group, by contrast, had evolved through the political New Left via Louis Althusser and the journal *New Left Review*, defining itself less through social history than in terms of ideologies and the capitalist system as seen from above. Despite Williams's early stay in Britain and his attachment to Guild Socialism, he had surprisingly little contact with the first circle. But Kiernan, an enyclopedic scholar, penned *America: The Newer Imperialism* (1978) within an unmistakable Williams framework. Seeking to comprehend the nature of economic control and political overlordship without the formality of a Colonial Office, he popularized American perspectives thirty years in the making.[18]

The *New Left Review* circle, which naturally tended to place Empire alongside class as a central historical category, cast Williams in terms that New Left Marxists the world over would recognize. On the one hand, Williams had deftly grasped the changing contours of Empire and its powers to lull the masses. On the other hand, Williams seemed in European Marxist terms a naif, the all too typical American Socialist who viewed the world in his own parochial terms.[19] Not surprisingly, when *Review* editor Perry Anderson selected a dozen intellectuals as his chosen subjects of a book-length essay on Western Marxism, Williams did not make the list (neither, it is fair to say, did E. P. Thompson, W. E. B. DuBois, or indeed any other historian). If British scholars of U.S. history leaned more and more heavily upon Williams to explain how the successor to their own nation's Empire had both built and destroyed, the more prestigeous Marxist intellectuals took too little account of him as an important international writer and theorist.[20]

Something of the same might be said for academic life in Holland, Sweden, France, and most other European countries in terms of Williams's early usefulness and the ultimate difficulty of incorporating his work. If during the Vietnam years Williams helped explain the American Empire, he stood too far outside Marxist and other currents to fit the study of the societies at hand. Italy marked an exception, because here American Studies was influenced early and heavily by American antiwar and New Left cultural perspectives. *Contours of American History* was translated and published in 1968 by Laterza, a liberal publishing house long associated with the works of Benedetto Croce. As *Storia degli Stati Uniti*, it replaced the translation of the familiar and conservative Morison and Commager textbook for a handful of mostly youngish professors. *Contours*, whose cadence defied translation, proved daunting to average young Italians who had little or no background in U.S. history. The book also proved difficult to assimilate in its own terms, as an auto-critique of American civilization. But for teachers and graduate students who had plunged themselves into American culture, it opened eyes and made for especially exciting dialogues over the logic of imperialism and the meaning and direction of ongoing Italian "Americanization."

During the 1970s and after, Williams's Italian impact took more unexpected turns. His influence on a budding school of Italian "corporate" theorists had hardly consolidated before it was subjected to a sharp criticism by Americanists inspired instead by the social history of Herbert Gutman's and David Montgomery's labor-based scholarship. The subsequent rise of post-revisionist diplomatic history in the mainstream of

American studies—and the rightward drift of Italian society itself—tended to push Williams to the side, but never entirely. For former New Leftists now greying at the temples but reaching their stride in writing and teaching, Williams remained with a few others the lasting guide to the immanent critique which they sought, in their own ways, to apply to Italian as well as American history and life.[21]

Since the 1960s, Williams's works had also reached Japan and the People's Republic of China. For Asian scholars, the U.S. Open Door to the Pacific in the nineteenth and twentieth centuries was naturally of enormous interest. To the Japanese, Williams offered not only a somewhat mitigating look at Japanese expansionism, but also a parallel or contrasting view (as in the German case) of how Empire becomes a mechanism to quell internal contradictions. The Marxist traditions in Japanese scholarship, and the handful of graduate students who actually studied in Madison, made the academic New Left especially receptive of his work. As Williams devotee Yui Daizaburo put it, "studies of American diplomatic history have inevitably been influenced by the dominance of ideas that underlay specific policies," a perspective wide open to a leftish or Williamsesque interpretation. Shimizu Tomohisa's *Amerika teiloku* (The American Empire), written very much under Williams's influence, likewise defined Empire as a "system of capitalistic control and domination," a system as old as the American republic. Expansionism is for Shimizu and other Japanese scholars influenced by Williams the consistent and inevitable theme of U.S. history—in part because it helped explain Japanese history *sans* illusions as well.[22]

Yet other Asian studies in a variety of areas of U.S. diplomatic history, shaped in part by the interest in ethnicity, increasingly adopted topics of the immigration question and its relation with the logic of race and Empire. Beyond all this, Williams has a continuing appeal for those scholars across the world drawn to what the Germans called *Staatswissenschaft*, the ways in which the State mechanism operated through the political economy and social-cultural life of the nation. To the Chinese, opening at last to a wide world of scholarship, Williams was recently "discovered" for the first time.

In China and elsewhere, a growing debate about the history and meaning of the Open Door was bound to prompt discussion over the value of Williams's (and more generally, the revisionist) approach. Regardless of the direction taken by particular societies, and regardless of the scholars' political credentials, the work he had done would prove heuristic into the foreseeable future. Almost certainly, for at least some of the scholars from Europe to Africa and Asia to the Pacific archipelago, it would be inspiring as well.[23]

## 3

Williams entered his year as President of the Organization of American Historians on strong ground, with a real mandate from vigorous sectors of the membership. He had, at the time of his election, great hopes for the coming generations of scholars, and he made real progress along certain lines. His expectations were undercut, however, by an underlying pessimism and by the inevitable organizational inertia.

Writing an open memo to department colleagues in 1976 based on a version of the program intended for the OAH presidency, Williams concerned himself mainly with the consequences of academic specialization. Historians more and more tended to address each other (and graduate students) rather than undergraduates and the public. "As a historian and a citizen, " he reflected,

> I see a strong probability, if we do not rapidly and drastically change our ways, that the next generation will be masters of particulars that have little or no bearing on the general state of mankind—East or West, or North or South.[24]

Looking ahead to his presidency of the OAH, he envisioned addressing this problem with exhortation and personal example, meanwhile revolutionizing the inner life of the organization. In his official statement for election, he argued that "the immediate health, creativity and welfare of our profession is dependent upon the imaginative regeneration of the undergraduate history major in close alliance with young political theorists, political economists, teachers of literature and young scientists." Revitalization demanded the capacity to pose the question "What If," so as to ask Americans to consider breaking free of their collective past.[25] On the practical side, he planned to raise three quarters of a million dollars for an organization that (unlike its sister American Historical Association) had never possessed a capital fund. In doing so, he would also raise up those categories of scholars, like women and minorities, who had the least resources and the least opportunity to benefit from the traditional grants.

He had a most pleasing base of initial operations. At the behest of his student Ed Crapol, the College of William and Mary (whose *Quarterly* had published him during the dark 1950s) invited him to be the James Pinckney Harris Chair in the Spring semester of 1980. One of precious few honors accorded Williams, it was also a joy, according to his private letters, for the aging and insular radical to meet new people, to explore the vicinity of Williamsburg, Virginia, and to play fierce rounds of bridge with Wendy as his partner against friendly adversaries Ed and Jeanne Crapol.[26] Here, he spent the first months of his term as OAH president and hatched his plans for its transformation.

A few months earlier, he had written to a National Endowment for the Humanities officer pleading assistance to help resolve a "major problem involving the intellectual health of our society and culture" and the situation of historians in particular. Unable to find work as professors, large numbers of talented youngsters and especially women and minorities were in the process of drifting away, depriving the profession of its future resources. Meanwhile, the government had set about to destroy large numbers of important documents, effectively narrowing the historical record. Against these associated threats, he sought the basis for a capital fund and major grants for two programs: an oral history of citizen "experiences and responses" to the atomic bomb, Korea and Vietnam; and "a documentary foundation for a history of the culture coming to terms with a drastically new reality."

In effect, Williams wanted a historians' version of the New Deal's Works Progress Administration, an idea often discussed informally in those days as a solution to the employment crisis but rarely addressed formally.[27] He put the same proposition to Senator Mark Hatfield, pleading for the documentation of the atomic bomb's implications on ordinary American lives and suggesting that if the federal government began the funding, state historical societies and legislators would feel compelled to add enough to get the job done.[28]

"If we can save Lockheed and Chrysler, we can save history! Or am I naive?" Williams probed and asked his favorite politician, recalling the recent taxpayer bailout of corporations.[29] He was indeed naive, for most leaders of a society lurching toward Reaganism proved eager to literally bury the radioactive past in favor of the pleasant movie-style myths of happily government-free yesterdays.

By the time he had returned to Corvallis, just about everything seemed to go wrong with his plans. A small flood of memos aimed at the OSU administration placed claims upon stamps, long-distance phone use, travel and half-time salary. He received less than he had hoped (the OAH actually provided most of the traveling expenses), but he managed. More galling by far to him was the indifferent response of fellow historians, either to assist him in obtaining a National Endowment for the Humanities matching grant or corporate funding. By the spring of 1981 he wrote bitterly that he had "attempted over the better part of two years to engage the members of the OAH, various agencies of the government, and sundry corporations and foundations, in various programs and projects to re-energize historians to revitalize the place of History in our culture."[30] He had invested a great deal of time, thought, mundane labor, and even money of his own that he could not easily spare.

Williams concluded in a low moment that the organization was nothing more than a "white middle class gentlemen's club that is long on rhetoric about the importance of history but unwilling to act on the rhetoric." If historians would not "put their money or their backs to work in support of their rhetoric," they could guarantee that "neither the government, the corporations, or the public takes us seriously." As far as Williams could see, historians did not take themselves seriously enough to care.[31]

He had exaggerated the indifference, or taken the widespread uncertainty toward his plans as blanket refusal. He announced to the OAH governing council early on that he would approach corporate heads directly and through fellow scholarly volunteers. Such volunteers proved indeed few, but Williams's own approach to a regional giant, the lumber corporation Weyerhauser, produced no model for others to follow. Plans for contacting some one hundred and fifty other major corporations evaporated. He seized the only available alternative source for funds, the members themselves, writing personal letters to one hundred well-off members asking them each to equal his own five-thousand-dollar contribution. The total he raised by this method did not come to five thousand dollars altogether. He had expected that scholars with the two-income family that he had never been fortunate enough to experience (and had at some points admittedly resisted) would see their savings as excess. Not even his old-time Madison mentors agreed.

The failure to raise a capital fund and to create a historians' WPA was only, as it turned out, a small part of his legacy. Isolated among his own generational cohort of historians, Williams in office ironically found his readiest allies among women's history enthusiasts and above all the OAH president-elect, distinguished women's historian Gerda Lerner. Herself a veteran of political wars—widow of a prominent Hollywood blacklistee—and an adept organizational activist, Lerner made plans to push harder for some of the key programs that Williams wanted but by the less direct method of asking prestigious historians to devote their lecture fees. In the end, his initiative had been most valuable as a call from an unusual activist president for worthy goals achievable down the road.

In one other extremely important respect, he succeeded quickly and admirably. He established two ad hoc committees on the issue of government control of information: one to grasp the implications of the Freedom of Information Act on record preservation and release, the other to target the State Department's policies towards foreign relations documents. Now at last, historians would act in a collective, public manner to anticipate and to prevent the destruction of records—something which the Reagan administration clearly intended.

The first committee, headed by distinguished civil libertarians William Preston (a Madison PhD from the early 1950s and the nephew of famed ACLU founder Roger Baldwin) and Blanche Cook, had an immediate impact on publicizing the FBI plan to destroy its massive field office and headquarters files. A personal deposition in *AFSC v. Webster* noted Williams's own discoveries that the Wilson administration had misused its authority to seek the destruction of Senator William Borah; and that the State Department during the 1930s had begun determinedly "redlining" (destroying) revealing documents. Based on these discoveries, he condemned the "self-interested destruction of documents [as] a subversive act in the truest meaning of that much abused term."[32] Historians also joined as plaintiffs, filing an eloquent amicus brief. Drafted partly by Williams, the Brief challenged on behalf of the OAH the notion "that government documents have no other purpose than to serve the needs of the agency creating them." Nor, it went on,

> does the OAH believe that the law gives no recourse to private parties to challenge the destruction of documents that constitute this country's historical past. Such acts of self-inflicted amnesia cannot have been intended by a people that have revered the documents of their heritage and erected a magnificent archival system for their preservation and appraisal . . . . Should the government motion prevail, Washington will indeed have discovered a new way of fouling its own nest . . . . Historians and their many doctoral candidates working in 20th century history could no longer describe unique aspects of dissent, the civil rights movement, radicalism, and antiwar and student protests, and other activities that the FBI deemed worthy of investigation. This vision of an historical future in an environment without a documented past is surely not one that can escape challenge and rejection.[33]

The historians had not merely made a scholarly intervention or plea. Their action marked a complete rejection of the cold-war patronage in which certain prominent historians had argued for executive privilege free from public scrutiny or had cooperated quietly with CIA subterfuge operations conducted beyond the reach of reasonable documentation. The case was won on freedom of information grounds, even if future violations could hardly be precluded. An East European writer with a similarly bitter taste of state authority described "the struggle of man against power [as] the struggle of memory against forgetting," and that was surely the framework for Williams's most successful OAH committee.[34]

At the State Department, where the in-house Historical Office grew increasingly protective of secrets, the other OAH committee (and a sister committee from the Society of Historians of American Foreign Relations) failed to prevent the parallel drift toward secrecy. Indeed, a new classification system stopped publication of State's own Foreign Relations Series and it further classified documents that had been earlier available. More than a decade later and with a Democrat in the White House, many records dating from the 1950s still awaited declassification. As a new Russian government allowed *its* files to be examined and scholars rushed to look for the evidence of charges made decades earlier, many Americans (and not only historians) continued to wonder when similar U.S. archives would be open. Only then could the real story of covert U.S. policies from Europe and Africa to Asia, the Philippines, Central and South America, and the Caribbean regions, and the participation of Americans in those programs, be opened for discussion and debate.

The two committees, in their three years of life, could hardly manage to lay open the books of highly guarded state secrets. They nevertheless accomplished much and boldly attempted more: they testified at congressional hearings against legislative amendments and executive guidelines limiting openness, worked to see that the FBI met criteria of the court on record preservation, opposed budget cuts intended to limit the National Archives' ability to respond to requests, convened OAH panels on issues of access, and supported the idea of a politically independent National Archives.[35]

Williams and committee members also anticipated, in important ways, the dangerous burst of illegal behavior late in the cold war and the gaps in the curtain of secrecy which prompted the Iran-Contra hearings. Stunned by the crude manipulations of fact by Reagan's State Department team (most notably Jeane Kirkpatrick and Elliott Abrams) toward Latin American events, senior liberal historians probably came closer than at any previous time to endorsing Williams's sentiments. Tragically, neither they nor other scholars and investigators could prevent Congress from limiting its probes and the media from loosening their pressure on the President at a time when the evidence became too damning and too revealing of the Democrats' all-too-willing participation in deceptive procedures. With a little more political courage or the simple abandonment of cold-war traditions, the efforts of the freedom of information activists might possibly have prepared the way to shatter the administration's authority and bring an early end to the era of unprecedented waste and plunder.[36]

In the emerging context of Reagan-style neoconservativism, Williams lacked the patience to look ahead to possible vindications, and to consolidate or simply enjoy the real victories he had won. His manner, more than his properly ambitious programs, alienated him unnecessarily. Historians, he now complained bitterly, were "cub scouts without a den mother." The same attitude had made him, a decade earlier, eager for the insularity of Oregon. If he blamed himself on occasion for helping to create a specialized professoriate less accessible to the public, he blamed others far more severely. He seemed to rage at the gentlemanly sensibility that he had once considered the *sine qua non* of educated citizenry in professional life, meanwhile expecting yesterday's rebels to haul out their wallets. Once again, the fact that so many younger historians held him in enormously high esteem scarcely altered his view favorably, as if he considered their failings more egregious because they should have known better. A different Williams would surely have pursued and cultivated them as a political base from which to build the needed support for his programs after he had left office.

The conflict of sensibilities had long since turned explosive when Williams addressed the largest of the handful of emerging radical and public history groups, the Mid-Atlantic Radical Historians Organization (and sponsor of the *Radical History Review*) in New York City in 1978. Inebriated and upset by rude challenges from the floor, he went on for nearly an hour, mortifying a mostly adulatory audience. Some years after the confrontationist campus New Left had disappeared, he plainly still felt uncomfortable with this generation of radicals—even when they pointedly shared his concerns for the classroom. He probably felt uneasy with this new breed of *Eastern* intellectuals. He could not have understood that more than a few in the New York audience remembered their own Madison days as the best of their lives.

He also felt plainly uncomfortable, he often wrote in letters, at being a highly lauded figure. The OAH spotlight sometimes seemed to make him especially queasy. Faced with the prospect of major audiences listening to him as president-elect, and with his back problems making travel uncomfortable, he turned to the cocktail glass for relief. His introductory remarks—normally a glowing tribute to the predecessor in office—were only two sentences long. His presidential address the next year was, however, an intellectual triumph of typical Williamsesque vintage.[37] After the OAH experience, at any rate, he had reached a point from which retreat to Waldport and his public or private life as an Oregon citizen was paramount and nearly absolute.

4

Since his return, Williams had been vitally concerned with the Oregon scene. Here he found some degree of real satisfaction. By the 1980s, with his triumphs and disappointments well behind him, the elderly Williams poured his energies into matters that the young Williams would have recognized as a contribution to public life.

One strain passed through the sciences and their relation to Liberal Arts at OSU. Williams had never entirely left behind his fascination with science and technology, and could often be found in the university library at Madison or Corvallis looking at technical journals. Very late in life, he became deeply interested in the construction of a new bridge near his home, photographing it in process and exhibiting the photos on an easel at a Waldport store. At OSU, he repeatedly emphasized the importance of finding ways to draw scientists into a dialogue, a small but important contribution to that discussion necessary "if we are to survive and create a humane new world." He asked scientists to consider anew the ends as well as means, and liberal arts scholars to make themselves aware of the scientific developments which did so much to reshape the world.

Williams argued, in venues as distant as the *Nation* and the shortlived but highly esteemed quarterly journal, *democracy*, that such regionalism held the promise of a democratic and radical future. He premised his 1981 call in the *Nation* for "Backyard Autonomy" on the seemingly unlikely appeal, by the president of the Mormon Church, for elimination of the MX missile system. The inability of radicals to grasp the importance of such religious and regional resistance pointed to their inability to "imagine a *different* America," their lack of staying power in the "rudimentary work of people-to-people politics," and their reluctance to commit themselves "to changing conditions in the places in which we live." They needed to look at democracy afresh, to drop an all-or-nothing perspective and instead set themselves to "fragmenting centralized power" via a variety of means. Radicals, Williams concluded, must "develop a different conception and practice of America and then persuade our neighbors that we are honoring the true spirit of America. That we together are the bearers of the torch. That *We* rather than *They* decide our common future."[38]

This was a bit vague, but he claimed (during an exchange of views in the Letters Column of the *Nation*) to have received many letters and phone calls urging him on. As one of the letter-writers noted, Williams aimed in fact at piecemeal disarmament in the frame set forth across the Atlantic by END (European Nuclear Disarmament) led by Englishman and fellow historian E. P. Thompson. A particularly brilliant pamphleteer, Thompson had recently penned *Protest and Survive*, a bestseller in the U.K., and become a major international peace spokesman through ceaseless public engagements. Williams lacked the European setting in which even radical intellectuals could become public heroes, and above all he lacked the personality for this kind of political work.[39]

He felt more at home, anyway, linking present-day perspectives with historical experience. Thus writing in *democracy*, he insisted that after the Civil War and during a situation of severe national flux, Americans *could* have developed a different view of the world including an acceptance of a regionalized socialism. "But in the end," he concluded sadly, "we crab-scuttled away from the challenge." No one sounded the alarm (he had forgotten, again, to treat aspects of Populism at variance with his own interpretation). The Marxist acceptance of the population megalopolis and over-centralized industries only reflected the subsequent muddle of radical thought. The "friendly and erotic fascism" of technocratic fantasy as well as capitalist reality had repeatedly swept aside the quieter dreams of subsequent regionalism, most notably the decentralist spirit of the early Tennessee Valley Authority (TVA) project, leaving behind fewer and fewer real community resources. If "twentieth century radicals followed Marx in becoming victims of his fascinating combination of capitalist assumptions and socialist utopianism," they needed at long last to unburden themselves of these illusions.

He also echoed the somber tone of late-life considerations so vividly expressed in *Empire as a Way of Life*. We "twentieth century radicals are aging. Realistically we are old. Candidly we are dying." In the time remaining, space had to be won to create time for this generation's children to "refine our thoughts" and set them right. "If we fail," above all in halting the drift toward nuclear war, "we destroy time." To halt the drift, radicals needed to look at community and at religion, "another word for community." Rather than saving the world, American radicals should turn to saving their own communities, the space around them. They needed to create something like the Federalist Papers, through discussions with a lot of nonacademics. Was it a utopian conception? Yes, if "the purpose of a radical utopia is to create a tension in our souls." To evoke a widespread feeling that the nation was not doing well enough demanded the effort by intellectuals to imagine something better, something which "defines us as people who offer our fellow citizens a meaningful choice about how we can define and live our lives."[40] If *The Great Evasion* had been Williams's version of *Looking Backward*, he urged radicals and intelligent conservatives to dream again, and better than he had done.

These were bold strokes and thoughtful ones, in tune with the early moment of mass disillusionment and radical hope, Washington protest parades, and Latin American radical insurgencies during Reagan's first two years in office. The political turnaround, with Truman-style heavy military expenditures boosting economic growth, ensured the former actor's popularity; the successful conspiracy to finance the Contras secretly meanwhile buried hopes for a peaceful adjustment to hemispheric inequalities. Localism seemed either like the last gasp of a dated 1960s counterculture vision, or an expression of the narrowness of the emerging NIMBY (Not In My Back Yard) movements. Even the journal *democracy*, off to an intellectually promising beginning, folded after a few years. For that matter, so did Eugene D. Genovese's own journal, *Marxist Perspectives*, which had also invited contributors from Left and Right seeking dialogue but which foundered on its editor's rocky personal temperament.

Williams had meanwhile already taken his own advice and turned to the state and regional scene. From 1981 to 1986, he wrote semi-weekly (sometimes weekly or monthly) columns for the *Capitol Journal* and the *Statesman Journal*, working hard to attain a regional sensibility. The West, he often emphasized, was a different place, with a relatively small population controlled or directed from the East (and more recently, the South). The West had a "different attitude, a different psychology, a different hierarchy of values," some involving escapism but others set in the aspiration for a human scale of life and politics. Westerners learned to say "No" to becoming a mere natural raw material center for the rest of the nation, a "surplus of land and resources" that others could exploit at will. But if they did not learn to say no to central government and to find their own way forward, "the West is dead. And so is America."[41]

Williams specialized as a regional columnist in developing extended examples such as water policy. He exposed how such a purportedly water-conscious political leader as Washington's Senator Henry "Scoop" Jackson (an undaunted Democratic hawk on Vietnam, best known in the Northwest and the nation's capitol as the "Senator from Boeing") actually supported the vast wastage of resources while claiming to protect regional supplies from incursions by Californians. Jackson was barely more than a vulgar lobbyist for military spending, despite a vigorous campaign of foreign-policy hard-liners for his nomination in 1972. But the ordinary adopted Oregonian who "built a retirement home with two full bathrooms, including water-jet toothbrushes, a hot tub, a sauna, a jacuzzi, an automatic dishwasher, a five-cycle washing machine and a sprinkling system" for the lawn and flowers represented a popular constituency which shared large parts of Jackson's worldview.[42] Unfortunately, although Williams neglected to say so, this retiree was a member of the fastest growing population on Williams's own coastal territory, which during the 1980s began to blossom with strip malls and garish housing complexes.

Williams's rapier thrusts at Truman and Kennedy also probably earned him more hostility than admiration. Oregonians did not like any more than other Americans to admit that, as Williams put it, in the struggle to conquer the planet, "success is failure," and the "truth about power is defined by its limits."[43] Likewise, if peace demonstrations in Europe inspired him (and especially Wendy, who shared moments of enthusiasm for her fellow Britons), his appeals to join the anti-nuke crusade almost certainly struck home to the peacenik constituencies of Oregon Public Radio more than to the "ordinary folks" of the pool halls and fishing docks.[44]

Perhaps, however, Williams had earned the satisfaction of writing about himself and his interests, saying whatever he chose for whoever would listen. One week he might address the foolish funding of college athletics, complaining that organized sports wasted precious university funds, encouraged vicarious pleasure-taking, and discouraged real play. He had early on discovered, he recalled, that even the scholarship given him to attend Kemper for basketball would have been better awarded to more worthy but less athletic kids. Another week he might ruminate on history as art, his views of the Middle East (where he believed that Israelis badly needed to rethink their occupation policies if they hoped for future accord), or anything else that struck his attention.[45]

His public talks increasingly had a similar let-it-all-hang-out tone, heavily flavored with personal experiences. For instance, he addressed journalism students recalling (perhaps from high school days) that he had nearly joined the Fifth Estate fraternity of newspapermen himself. He had learned in the subsequent decades that the mass audience was "assumed to be largely uninterested . . . in serious and sustained information and analysis about their natural and human environment." Information was therefore presented them at random, while a tiny minority was treated "as honorary members of the information and opinion elite."

He had found, especially in regard to Vietnam and Central America (even after Watergate and Contragate) that the *New York Times* for instance rarely encouraged a "fundamental debate about the nature, necessary limits, or consequences of Empire, and similarly with nuclear weapons, poverty, racism, sexism, unemployment or education." For that reason, the journalism of the elite "misleads the elite" by defining "what is fit to take seriously." Falsely defined by their exercise of power, Henry Kissinger and even Ronald Reagan were made somehow to look like intellectuals, while intelligent ordinary citizens were treated as dummies and responded by tuning out. If "history is thoughtful reflection upon critically evaluated human experience," and so little of it was available in intelligent form, "I hope but I also weep."[46]

He urged, as in his newspaper columns, that the Constitution be used to attack the oppressive national state through diminishing its power of taxation. He urged the state legislature be used to return authority to the citizen, and take it away from the corporation. He likewise urged regional public enterprises "not so much [because] small is good, as that small is human" even if sometimes less efficient. He saw no other way out of the morass of distant authority and citizen apathy.[47]

In that melancholy tone, he repeatedly treated what he often described as the crisis of American democracy, seeing the nation's "Weary and Nostalgic Culture" as the heart of the problem. The non-perception of a crisis during the massively destructive 1980s was the most certain evidence that the crisis had reached epic proportions. Reagan's promise to start the world over with "morning in America" was at once crazed and unworkable "short of having the Lord on hold on the Hot Line." The Reagan plan to free corporate or individual philanthropy to care for the poor until the economy gave them all jobs reminded Williams of the capitalist John D. Rockefeller giving away dimes on the streetcorner.

Anguished by the sheer banality of it all, Williams reached his eloquent apex as Cassandra:

> There is no community and no commonwealth in contemporary America. Instead there is a Superpower within which there is not even a dream of the common welfare. As for shared values, there are two: first, get it while you can; second, anybody who gets in the way is a Communist. On four days a week the Superpower asserts its meaningless military power by subverting the Constitution. It uses the other three days to offer various excuses about why it can neither help improve the quality of life of its citizens nor allow them to change the society.
>
> America is indeed weary. Only a handful of its citizens seek seriously to create a community and a commonwealth. There are no strikes, as there were within memory (say the 1930s) to define and sustain the essence of being an artisan or a yeoman.
>
> The heroes of the moment, not just today but for long years past, are people who lie. Most of our leaders admit that they lie, and nobody gives a damn. It is taken as a given. So? Granted his serious competition in those sweepstakes, Colonel Oliver North captured the affection of the American public with his candid remark to a Congressman: "I lied to you in good faith."
>
> Yes, America is weary when it takes that as honest. It is a dreary and scary epitaph for the idea, or the ideal, of community and commonwealth.

Somehow—and now Williams could no longer quite imagine how—America had to move beyond its now-ancient vision of itself as the City on the Hill ready to instruct or bulldoze everyone who saw things differently. As Williams turned repeatedly to the historic wars waged upon Vietnam, Mexico, and the Philippines, the message came back again and again. Once "the dream and the magic of Arcadia, of Walden Pond, no longer had a basis in reality," America would logically be compelled to join the human race like everyone else. But its leaders refused. For that reason, they had to try to style history in their own image, preserving half-truths as to render "a once vibrant people frightened of human beings who are trying to realize the ideal of community and commonwealth."[48]

It would have been impossible for Williams to miss not only an echo of the "low intensity" brushfire wars ongoing, but also the ill effects of current unconstitutional conduct by highly-placed former Naval officers on the *élan* of the U.S. military. He took great pride in Oregonians' demonstrations against U.S. interventionism here and there. But he evinced still more interest in the uproar around Oliver North and the Contragate scandal. He corresponded with career Navy men who readily agreed with Williams's view of the demoralization brought by civilian misleadership. And from Williams's testimony, so did the rising star and future Joint Chiefs commander Colin Powell.

Williams therefore enthused when his Naval Academy alma mater invited him back to lecture the midshipmen. He gave his audience a dramatic picture of Alfred Mahan's importance both in devising a global-imperial overview and elaborating the *noblesse oblige* mission "to be honorable and generous." Every midshipman, he recalled, was assigned the "Pocket Bible," a handbook stressing that the oath of service was taken neither to persons nor offices but to the Constitution. Williams read that as the "crucial right and responsibility" to "challenge an order that violates his oath to the Constitution and his tradition," a promise demanding "courage beyond combat." Colonel North and those other fellow Annapolis graduates John Poindexter, Robert McFarland, and James Webb could have said "no" to illegal orders. Instead they lied or pretended not to remember. (Williams claimed that many in North's class returned their rings in disgust.)[49]

The enduring naval connection also excited Williams's last (and mostly unrecorded) scholarly passion: for the sea and everything connected with it. From the middle 1970s, he had urged Oregon State to take up its potential for an original and outstanding program in which, by no accident, he could play a central role. Maritime Studies never achieved the solidity that Williams hoped for, but it drew upon some outstanding younger scholars, such as Michael Sprinker—an English teacher and a personal bridge between Williams and Edward Said.[50] Bringing scientists into the program as equal partners also fulfilled a long-term ambition of Williams, who continued to scan a variety of scientific journals, recalling his undergraduate training and discussions with some of his closest Madison academic friends.

Classroom discussions inspired his own research and rumination in a number of related areas. He sought more information on the Chinese explorer Cheng Ho, who had halted his historic journeys of fleets to Africa before da Gama rather than draw China into a sea empire (fulfilling Williams's notion of saying "no"—certainly a strange interpretation, as friends noted, of a land dynasty).[51] He urged the study of pirates as a proto-community which sought in the Renaissance era and afterward to create its own rules, and prompted widespread fear in the existing empires.[52] And he set out to learn more about a very particular wreck famous on the Oregon shore, the grounding of a British ship in October 1913. Its captain was Captain Owen Williams from Wales, a not-so-far-fetched possible relative to the family. The more Williams probed, the more he was hooked. He recounted, in an exceptionally lively tone, the results in the *American Neptune*, a noted maritime journal.

"Walking along the fist-sized basalt rocks and looking out to sea," he recalled his view of the wreck's sight exactly sixty years afterward:

> One could see the curtain of water vapor rolling upward from the water. One felt that awe of forces beyond control . . . . Today it remains hazardous despite electronic navigational aids . . .
>
> Several reasons had prompted me to come north from my home on the beach just north of Waldport to seek an understanding of what it was like at that place at that time. Like everyone else who has seen the photographs taken by Charles Wood (and others), I had been initially baffled and intrigued. But I was drawn into it further because I had sailed the sea aboard a wishbone-staysail-rigged ketch, and had later navigated the Caribbean and much of the Pacific as the executive officer of a ship that could be as tricky and as difficult to handle under some conditions as the *Glenesslin*.
>
> Those experiences evoked in me a sense of awe and mystery about the sea—not the sea as romantic myth or metaphor, just the sea as a very necessary and demanding friend. And so, when I much later became a historian, I thought of the sea . . .
>
> Facts are not simply discrete entities proceeding on their individual way. Facts are interacting parts of a whole. Hence I have always thought of the historian as one who tries to discover and explain those interrelationships. There are many guides: from Spinoza to Henry Adams, from Adam Smith to Karl Marx; but also oceanography and geology—disciplines that deal with particulars as part of a whole.[53]

Here, Williams expressed almost a whole life's interests together. He condemned the corporate planners who described the sea as the "next frontier," not only because of the brute treatment given to other frontiers but because the sea had obviously been *the* frontier that had led to the industrial revolution. Sailing was integral to human development, probably beginning before writing. It expressed for Williams the development of a community, in the complexity of shipbuilding and of navigation. The three-masted bark (like the *Glenesslin*) he could see as at once an imperial instrument and a "poem to man's creativity." It was finally, from a military angle, the "first inter-continental missile" aimed by one part of the world at another far away.[54]

He sought to explain the wreck in detail and with great empathy for the victims. The crews of such ships had been reduced, since the emergence of steamships, to a skeleton of often inexperienced and nutritionally deprived men little able to handle themselves or even to see properly at night. As water rushed over the deck, the sailor faced many sudden jerks which could easily throw him overboard. Standard histories of the incident had from the first blamed the captain, suggesting the influence of alcohol. Williams drew out of himself the memories of aching tiredness and the inevitable reliance upon mates who often did not entirely know their job. Tragedy could have struck quite without any notable blundering human assistance, in Williams's estimation. Now, as he looked at rubble from a highway construction project covering the "bones of the *Glenesslin*," he mused:

> The sea will have its way. Slowly, but certainly, the sea will free *Glenesslin*. And perhaps someday we will recover the essence of *Glenesslin*: that awareness of common purpose; that knowing that being a sail master rather than a master does not demean a person; and that commitment to behaving like a captain even if one is an apprentice seaman.
> Once we did all those things in the name of Empire. Perhaps now we can do it to create a different and more human kind of community.[55]

The subject had touched his inner being; Williams was not likely in any scholarly effort to become more eloquent and intimate. It was also an observation of a man who at sixty seemed to have seen as much of life as he wanted.

In the same spirit, he turned to a past that he had never previously written about, perhaps as a way to tie up loose ends. During the later 1970s he had refused a five thousand dollar offer made on the basis of an outline about his life's story. A few years later, he used some of the research materials for a family memoir, "A Good Life and a Good Death: A Memoir of An Independent Lady," ostensibly to leave a record of his mother's life as a kind of gift to his children. He sent an outline to a press or two, but without any serious hope of publication. The result was a family self-justification, often charming in its details and revealing of a way of life he had left far behind. It was also, transparently, about the making of William Appleman Williams.

The eighty-page essay undoubtedly captured the positive side of prosperous Iowa commercial and small-town society, and offered particularly incisive glimpses of the family's two strong-minded women. It spoke honestly to the trials of Mildrede Williams, interpreting with extraordinary empathy her stresses and her decisions. The Iowa and the family scenes he depicted were mainly Williams's imagined human-scale society struggling through a difficult but in some ways hopeful period, chiseled in outline against the darker, militarized and bureaucratic future of the post–World War II era. This vignette might have been better projected fictionally onto Iowa's genuinely isolationist districts (as Atlantic was not) or to the Farmer-Labor and Progressive Party voting counties of Minnesota or Wisconsin.

But he portrayed what he chose to see about the only home town and the only family that he could call his own.[56]

During his final years, he set out on a very different project, a fictional treatment of his own Civil Rights days. A lifelong reader of novels, he had for decades been convinced that he could turn out a novel with an effective story line and well-developed characters. Once he claimed to have written a novel before any of his historical works, and burned it. However that might be, he resolved now to bring 1945-46 back to life, recalling fictionally "the effort to make the victory against The Axis in World War II into a better and more equitable culture and society . . . and the frustration of that effort through prejudice, violence and indifference."[57]

His current friends had difficulty telling him how far he was from the stylistic mark. His dialogue—nearly always the most difficult element for the amateur fiction writer to master—never lost its artificiality. His characters all seemed underdeveloped except the protagonist "Cat," i.e., Williams himself. At that, he could hardly imagine the human frailties required to fill out his narrative realistically. Not that Cat lacked human desires or vices, especially sex (with his wife) and liquor. But he and his mates—to say nothing of the African American locals courageously throwing their weight against armed racism—were too good, too narrow. Encouraged by his new friend Gore Vidal, who had spent days with Williams in Corvallis and struck up a correspondence afterward, he nevertheless pressed ahead. He was crestfallen although hardly surprised at various publishers' indifference.

## 5

Williams's status as a scholarly giant and historiographical influence had risen to an apex, ironically, a decade after his authorial success seemed to hit bottom. Part of this was generational. The younger historians shaped by the Vietnam War experience were now moving into senior positions, and the Schlesinger, Jr., generation of liberal cold warriors looked toward retirement. The New Deal had obviously ceased to be at the center of the twentieth-century experience, and even the Second World War grew further and further away. Yet a good number of older historians, mostly those beyond the range of the East Coast notables, had also seen their views of U.S. foreign relations significantly changed. Even when they rejected Williams's political suggestions and declined to credit him with influencing them, they nonetheless appropriated portions of his analyses of foreign policy and imperial overreach. Williams had, in short, by this time gained a kind of almost unimpeachable integrity within a history profession prone to personal rifts and intellectual vendettas.

From another and more practical standpoint, Williams certainly did not provide the particular cutting edge that social historians sought in treating women, labor, and minorities. But at the classroom level, it was his perspective (often retailed and refurbished through books by Walter LaFeber and Lloyd Gardner, among a growing multitude of others) that informed lectures not only on foreign policy but also, increasingly, on various other aspects of the eighteenth- and nineteenth-century experience. Seeking a fresh synthesis of U.S. history not yet nearly in sight, scholars and teachers began to incorporate the themes of Empire and imperial consensus along with African American history, Indian people's history, and women's history.

Outside the profession, the thin slice of the public which read popular history books might not even have noticed the trend, so much did Civil War history and the flattering mode of "insider" histories like Arthur Schlesinger, Jr., on the Kennedys and David McCullough on Harry Truman continue to dominate limited shelf space. Yet Williams's classics, especially *The Tragedy of American Diplomacy*, remained in the hearts of now-experienced teachers and at hand on the scholar's shelf, trustworthy conceptual guides to the movement of large trends.

After the Maddox flap had almost passed from memory, historical meetings on foreign policy no longer elicited what John Lewis Gaddis described as "torrents of impassioned prose . . . provoking calls for the suppression of unpopular points of view, or threats of lawsuits."[58] As Lloyd Gardner put it at the 1983 meeting of the Organization of American Historians, neither side felt capable any more of convincing the other. Many scholars opted out of the conflict entirely, citing "irreconcilable differences."[59] Middle-of-the-roaders sought an elusive compromise.

Harvard Europeanist Stanley Hoffman thus observed characteristically that in their assessment of Soviet diplomatic behavior, the revisionists were probably closer to the truth, whereas in their assessment of American diplomatic behavior the traditionalists were more accurate. The Soviets had acted defensively as nationalists; no monolithic worldwide Communist conspiracy had existed. But the revisionists had failed to take into account the inconsistencies within U.S. policies.[60]

A new school, labelled "post-revisionist," quickly emerged. Many historians considered it tepid, but it offered a roundabout vindication of liberal-skeptical positions and mainly for that reason succeeded cold-war liberalism at the prestigious ramparts of influence. Hence, for example, the "post-revisionists" conceded that the U.S. was an Empire, that it did bear a heavy responsibility for the cold war, and that economic factors did heavily influence American policies. Yet, while the Soviet Union reacted defensively and cautiously, Stalin's Russia represented one of the most repressive regimes in world history. If mistakes were inevitably made on both sides, the U.S.—constrained by bureaucratic considerations and the force of public opinion—never followed a clear or consistent policy. The leading exponent of post-revisionism was none other than John Lewis Gaddis.[61]

The great weakness of this position was its too-evident attempt at adjustment *sans* synthesis. Traditionalist Warren F. Kimball called Gaddis's position "orthodoxy plus archives." Bruce R. Kuniholm added that the questioning of fundamental assumptions "is what revisionism was all about," and without which nothing had been seriously revised.[62] Noted left-liberal Barton J. Bernstein admiringly observed that unlike many anti-revisionists, Gaddis was "never angry or polemical, never sharp-tongued or snide . . . [but] polite, modest and even disarming."[63] Yet he fundamentally missed "the subtle formulation of Williams's conception of the 'Open Door' ideology" of which the economic component was only a part. Gaddis treated the concerns of American policy-makers with economic expansion, self-determination, and collective security as independent variables, "not as integrated parts of an ideology" in Williams's understanding.[64] Williams himself, who mostly stayed largely out of the debate, was also unimpressed with the recent nuances.[65]

In a notable address to diplomatic historians in December 1992, Gaddis revealed the extent to which and ways in which post-revisionism could be used to reinforce the interpretations of traditional orthodox historians. He began by praising *The Tragedy of America Diplomacy* as "one of the most influential books ever written about the history of United States foreign relations." But he fretted that Williams's views, shared by many scholars, now risked becoming a new orthodoxy, presumably the last thing Williams would have wanted. Presenting his own perspective as if it represented a new twist, Gaddis reiterated Schlesinger's familiar argument that the United States during the early cold war was dealing not "with a normal, everyday, run-of-the-mill, statesmanlike head of government" but rather with "a psychologically disturbed but fully functional and highly intelligent dictator." Throughout the twentieth century the U.S. had played a central role in resisting authoritarianism, whether that of Lenin, Stalin, Hitler, Mao, Ho Chi Minh or Fidel Castro. The "American Tragedy," reread as the distance between its aspirations and accomplishments, therefore faded in comparison with the tragedies of other great powers.[66] As Bruce Cumings quipped memorably in response,

> Bill Williams gets flogged whether he is a pro-Communist, a revisionist, a reductionist, an American Exceptionalist, the author of the new orthodoxy in diplomatic history, or, by implication, a dishonest historian who ignored the millions who died at the hands of world-historical monsters. And we still wait, through two decades of writing,

for John Lewis Gaddis to take one of his arguments seriously and try to refute it.[67]

Not only had Gaddis come to honor Williams in order to bury him. In linking Ho and Castro to Hitler and Stalin (conveniently ignoring the bundle of authoritarian governments that the U.S. had propped up with cash and intelligence or direct military assistance), Gaddis seemed to be justifying the Vietnam War, as well as past and future interventions into Latin America. No wonder Gaddis felt dismayed that so many historians still subscribed to Williams's views. Indeed, at the time of Williams's death and after, many conservative and liberal historians—often those who still smarted from perceived personal slights during the Vietnam campus protests or who resented the career advances of New Left and feminist historians and scholars of minority cultures—treated the fall of communism as a long-awaited vindication of America's cold-war policies and of themselves personally as well. Or, from more detached perspective, they saw the opportunity to take a slap at Williams for his decades-old support of foreign revolutions and revolutionaries.[68]

Williams would not have found it difficult to formulate responses to their arguments. Obviously, as he had long suggested, if the U.S. had accommodated and cooperated with revolutionary movements at an earlier date, many of the helpful changes at the end of the cold war would have come more peacefully without bringing the world to the brink of nuclear war and devastating large parts of the civilian population and planet itself with militarization and environmental poisoning. We could have learned something humanly invaluable from the societies that our government and its clients proceeded to destabilize and overthrow.

His critics almost invariably overlooked the enormous tragedy endured by American society precisely because of its counterrevolutionary posture. "If everyone elsewhere *does* deny us the chance to realize ourselves by changing them," Williams wrote half-ironically in the preface to *History as a Way of Learning*, "we nevertheless have a magnificent fall-back position: we can finally confront the question of what we are going to make of America."[69] That dialogue had now been postponed so long since the unresolved social dilemmas of the 1960s had burst into crises, it seemed almost beyond recollection. Political leaders of both parties, as Williams might have observed, had abandoned anything like a vision of a better or more democratic society. They offered nothing more meaningful than the universal panaceas of growth and economic expansion; all else was calculated spin control.

And of course, it remained to be seen how well the capitalist world would survive the legacies of the cold war, especially when capitalism had nothing more to absorb. As frequent mainstream commentators noted gloomily, the early post-Communist prediction of democracy as world destiny was swiftly and rudely shaken by events in Afghanistan, Somalia, Haiti, the former Soviet Union, and the former Yugoslavia, to name only a very few locations. As the rainforests toppled, the cities of the world grew more ugly and crime-scored and the ozone layer thinned, happy endings were indeed scarce. George Frost Kennan, the last surviving formulator of Containment, observed that the cold war, with its enormous costs, really had no victors at all.[70]

Williams's theses remained at the center of other debates over U.S. history as well. An aging Schlesinger, Jr., clearly disturbed by the concerns of younger generations of scholars and nervously looking over his shoulder for his old foe's shadow, compulsively lashed out again and again. Schlesinger's effort to rewrite his own synthesis so thoroughly revolved around Williams and the New Left that his late scholarly effort can be regarded as a sort of mirror-image or *doppelgänger* to Williams's texts, its author possessed by the notion of expunging the dissident voices and reestablishing the canon unchanged at its essence.[71]

The Open Door theorists were not open-minded like himself, Schlesinger, Jr., insisted in *The Cycles of American History* (1986), and they felt compelled to commit "historical malpractice," to "distort evidence in order to bolster their thesis." The Open Door argument was "evidently not falsifiable. Because it explains everything, it explains very little. It is not a testable historical hypothesis at all. It is a theological dogma." Schlesinger, Jr., unwilling to respond to the variety of criticisms rained down on him by younger historians for especially dark moments of his own political past and for his sometimes doubtful scholarly ethics, wrapped up the collective critic into Williams and found it "difficult to understand why any thesis so intellectually parochial, so thinly documented, and so poorly argued . . . should cast a spell on a generation of American historians."[72]

Much of the rest of *The Cycles of American History* was cast in light of Reaganism, which Schlesinger, Jr., thoroughly disliked but adamantly refused to see in any way as emblematic of American society and politics. Where Williams perceived the wastefulness and self-destructive shortsightedness of the 1980s as all too typical of a way of life, Schlesinger Jr., cheerfully insisted that, at worst, the excesses of the period merely encouraged the swing of the pendulum back from the Right, preparing another phase centerward or slightly beyond.[73] No permanent harm had been done. Williams privately described this pendulum theory as the "birth control method of history," pointing instead to the 1980s as one disaster after another in a compounding and culmination of past conservative and liberal mistakes. The predecessor of Reagan as military budget-buster, world policeman, and domestic political smear artist had not after all been

Eisenhower or Hoover but Harry Truman.

Schlesinger, Jr., also implicitly assailed Williams's views on larger trends. If Williams's *The Great Evasion* described a society which could not face up to its limits, Schlesinger, Jr., insisted that Marx had precisely failed to anticipate the power of the democratic citizenship which outstripped class theories of structural inequality by encouraging social responsibility (and, he might have added, by outreaching all possible limits). If many of Williams's works had insisted that imperial policy corrupted what was best in America, Schlesinger, Jr., simply wished that policy out of existence. Certainly, he admitted, conflicts existed between policies of human rights and national interest, but after all, "a nation's supreme interest is self-preservation." Conquest of the Third World by force had in any case always been exaggerated, since at least some portion of natives in each conquered society had collaborated with the colonialists and used imperialism for their own purposes. The American Empire, as anything like an oppressive force, had scarcely ever existed at all and certainly not in recent decades. Vietnam was a judgment error. Lyndon Johnson's other misadventures of Gunboat Diplomacy and the CIA-backed coups following the 1954 overthrow of the Guatemalan government—including those Latin American activities of the early 1960s in which Schlesinger, Jr., himself had a hand—dropped from sight. Because public opinion no longer tolerated such CIA moves, they had, Schlesinger, Jr., suggested, finally been abandoned.[74] What policies did Schlesinger imagine the Reagan administration practiced in Central America?

Williams and his favorite social critics had, for many generations, deplored the centralization of power as a loss of democratic possibility. For Schlesinger, Jr., however, national "leadership is really what makes the world go round . . . . Numerical majorities are no substitute" for leaderly action, and democratic decentralization of the type Williams favored was obviously undesirable as well. Centralization of power had grown not from overweening ambition, Schlesinger, Jr., insisted, but from the complexity of society and the "psychology of mass democracy." Kennedy had obviously been a model leader, Nixon a bad leader, Reagan evidently a dreadful leader. But the excesses of presidential power, even Watergate and Contragate, cast no doubt for Schlesinger, Jr., on the underlying mechanisms themselves. Presidents needed to be strongmen at home and abroad.[75]

The oddest touch in *Cycles of American History*, and the one most clearly related to his struggle with Williams, was Schlesinger, Jr.'s confidence that Kennedy's guiding influence had "touched and formed a generation of young men and women in the 1960s . . . moved by his aspirations and shaped by his ideals." But those must surely have been the anti-Vietnam protestors and erstwhile civil rights activists who fell under Williams's influence and whose university protests Schlesinger, Jr., had cursed in the

*New York Times* and elsewhere. "Their day is still to come," he promised.[76] But would he welcome it then?

Schlesinger, Jr., devoted his next volume to a blistering polemic against the epicenter of this very generation's influence on the universities, seen in the rise of multiculturalism. *The Disuniting of America* made no mention of William Appleman Williams (nor of Empire, nor imperialism) in the text. But it might be said to have moved toward a triumphal defense of Schlesinger's views of thirty years earlier, just as Williams had sought in his last few books to move beyond the limits of his own older work toward an egalitarian, tragic, and multiracial view of the American saga.[77]

Because Williams did not live to comment on this book, the dialogue (or rather, the exchange of criticisms) between the two historians ended here— or at least one side of it did, because Schlesinger, Jr., has continued to defend himself against a ghost, filing charges against those younger historians seen as proxies of Williams. Observers expected another large dose in his memoirs. Would the exchange finally end with the demise of Schlesinger, Jr.? Presumably not, because just as he had long since assumed the archetype of the Cold War Democrat, Williams had been the archetypal anti-imperial democrat, big "D" against little "d" in an intellectual set piece of the half century after World War II. Others would continue these positions, with or without the names of the original debaters.

In a field ostensibly far from foreign affairs, Williams's side meanwhile received a vindication and extension that neither he nor Schlesinger, Jr., had probably ever imagined. A decade or so after the last U.S. withdrawal from Vietnam, a fresh generation of scholars in Western history, confronted with a virtual absence of acceptable interpretations, found in Williams a guide to a new and drastically revised view of national experience. Yale professor John Mack Faragher, the award-winning biographer of Daniel Boone, notes that in graduate school during the Vietnam days he was struck in reading *Contours* by Williams's view of continental expansion as a substitution of Manifest Destiny for the earlier vision of the Christian Commonwealth. *Roots of the Modern American Empire* made the connection between continental and overseas expansion explicit. The problem of expansion and its implications for community, as described and analyzed by Williams, neatly became, in Faragher's considered view, the catchspring for some of the most influential and radical scholarship of the emerging scholarly generation.[78]

Williams certainly did not set the course for this field, as he did in diplomacy. But his provocation came at just the right moment to prompt young scholars in the direction that already called them, and to give them what their own predecessors in Western history could not: a view at once personally sympathetic and realistically (even harshly) critical of the consequences. Without placing any particular stress upon the fate of Mexican Americans, Indians, or of the land—at least until his last books—Wiliams had also made it possible for the next generation of scholars to pursue the inner logic and the various meanings of expansionism from the viewpoint of victor and victim.

Williams's own intellectual lineage can be interrogated one last time in this regard. His classmate David W. Noble has suggested that Williams's true importance on this matter can be understood best through re-examining the problems for U.S. history which Frederick Jackson Turner earlier articulated: if the frontier were the key to American specialness and success, what would happen when the frontier closed? Warren Susman, Williams's intimate friend, saw the continual scholarly reevaluation of Turner as the clearest symptom of changing attitudes about American life, and how these attitudes tended nevertheless to return to the same, almost obsessive questions of expansion.[79] Williams discerned in Turner less the master scholar than the essayist looking for a grand metaphor; perhaps Williams understood this best because it so matched his own temperment. Williams offered the freshest insights of any historian for generations on that continuing controversy about the frontier.

How, Noble asks provocatively, can we explain the enormous impact of a youngish scholar like Patricia Limerick, whose *Legacy of Conquest* (1987) may be said to have precipitated more than any other work the change in the way the history of the American West is taught? Limerick's innovation was, foremost, in periodization: the history of the West does not begin in the eighteenth century and end in 1890, but must instead be seen as a continuous history of contest and conquest. The study of contestation, in Limerick's work, becomes a reconceptualizing of that history as a continuing saga where a seemingly fragmented and discontinuous past gains coherence at last.[80]

Limerick does not invoke Williams directly and has no need to do so. Williams shaped the background against which subsequent scholarship's patterns now move. The next generation also demonstrated, in passing, many of the smaller points that Williams struggled to make against an unwilling profession. For instance, Richard White has pinpointed Woodrow Wilson as the first massive betrayer of evolving conservation policy toward the West, stripping millions of acres of proposed national parkland for exploitation.[81] The fighting idealist of Arthur Link and Arthur Schlesinger, Jr., is extraordinarily difficult to find in this Wilson, precursor of Reagan and Bush's woodlands sell-off policies.

Noble elaborates what Faragher affirms: that by drawing domestic conclusions from diplomatic history, and by perceiving the limits of earlier progressive history, Williams cut the famous nexus of 1890 (or thereabout) which bedeviled Beard with conflicting contemporary impulses of democracy and Empire. Already in *American-Russian Relations* and *Tragedy*, Williams assumed the kind of community of interests or *Weltanchauung* which unified America. *Empire as a Way of Life*, most fittingly, drove home the lesson again and finally. He thereby placed a capstone on his lifetime of work by reminding readers of the consequence of market choices: the wages of conquest which deprive the conquered and conqueror alike of the possibility for a higher purpose.

6

The future impact of Williams's works can hardly be foreseen. Much depended, of course, upon the shape of scholarship, even more perhaps on the shape of politics. One scholarly direction obvious long before the end of the cold war predicted, however, a large body of work reflecting the current sense of political stasis. Several of the older revisionists, notably Thomas McCormick and to some extent Walter LaFeber and Gabriel Kolko, as well as a few younger neorealists such as Michael J. Hogan, adroitly moved revisionism in the direction of corporatism. Merging the influence of Williams into a larger pool of resources including recent European and Latin American studies, they moved beyond the study of business corporations to make room for corporate-minded labor and the increasingly vital role of the State.

Closely examined, corporatist functional groups had worked in voluntary but often intimate association to shape national policies. Basic to their shared belief has been the concept of "productivism," the determination to increase the size of the overall pie in order both to avoid a redistribution of wealth and to forestall revolutionary threats. Corporatist theories have been applied particularly to the U.S. foreign policies of the Progressive era (sometimes defined as 1913-33) and the early cold-war period, 1945-53.[82] Martin J. Sklar, for some years a very Williamsesque editorial writer of the Socialist weekly *In These Times*, applied his own corporatist perspective to a close study of turn-of-the-century America and, in his collected essays, to a somewhat larger time frame.[83]

The political implications are yet more difficult to see. Hugh De Santis perceptively analyzes this corporatism as a hybrid of Beardian Progressivism and Marxism, resurrecting from the top of society the dichotomy of the Establishment versus the people.[84] A methodologically similar tendency from seemingly opposite sources has a surprising consequence: the addition of "world systems" theory to corporatism, embracing the entire Western world. This view, largely inspired by Immanuel Wallerstein's work, is in some ways a sharp departure from Americo-centric approaches, because New

York and Washington become only two of the rotating centers of the "informal Empire" on a wide-wide scale. Even before the end of the Second World War, American foreign policy, although still largely shaped by domestic needs, had been increasingly influenced by "an international marketplace and a culture created by a new technology," as Walter LaFeber puts it. In truth, "later twentieth century capitalism . . . has little respect for national borders," perhaps the most significant implication of all.[85]

If the national framework increasingly falls away—even with Washington firmly at the strategic center of the New World Order—does Williams's immanent critique of Empire lose its meaning or value? Only in the sense, one could argue, that the modes established by Americans tend to become a world norm. Business and political elites from impoverished African nations to rising Asian "Tigers," and from Latin America to the former Soviet Union, look to the U.S. for behavioral norms. From business suits to the proliferation of golf courses, the respective middle classes likewise copy the American style of consumption. No matter that nationalism rises sharply and competition adds to the already dangerous effects of world trade arrangements on the living standards of ordinary people. The world's winners, jettisoning concerns for growing class disparities or ecological degradation, adopt neoliberal strategies of rapid development and capital accumulation. Neoliberalism, already the kernal of corporate intellectual reflection in Woodrow Wilson's day, becomes a grim, final ideology of liberalism, worthy successor to the rampant individualism of the eighteenth and nineteenth-century American "great barbecue" frontier-style. This time more than ever, the planet is on the spit, revolving just above the flame.

This is the future Williams perceived from another angle, the apparent collapse of Socialist hopes, in one of his last pieces of sustained correspondence. Responding in the summer of 1989 to the question of whether he still considered himself a Marxist, he had "no apologies and no denying of the problems inherent." Marx had viewed nature as a resource to be exploited at will, and Williams readily admitted that as a young man he had shared that view. By now, he had learned better. Ecological crisis more and more frighteningly raised the right question: what is the purpose of economic growth?

Capitalism had its own answer, as Williams had detailed at great length. But efforts to create socialism had, at least at points, been on another track. Contrary to popular belief, Williams insisted, Lenin had urged a sort of decentralization in the New Economic Policy period just before his death. If centralization had won out in Stalin's version of Elizabethan mercantilism ("with that kind of romantic personalized violence institutionalized in the Gulag"), it was a distorted mirror reflection of capitalism's world project.[86] Centralization, Williams continued, had served Stalin's purpose for primitive accumulation just as Queen Elizabeth had sent Sir Francis Drake off to piracy against the Spanish and Portuguese expropriation of the New World. The newly rebellious colonies of Europe, after the Second World War, attempted a similar strategy, adopting centralized mercantilism as the only way to become modern. All this had been finally swept away in the world market and the recuperation of capitalism's hegemony, without acknowledgment that the underlying premises of socialism had barely been glimpsed. The humane purpose of economic planning, to satisfy human and now more obviously, planetary needs, had been lost in the shuffle and needed to be found again.[87]

Williams's characteristic contribution to this future discussion remained what it had always been, his ability to see far beyond the ideologies and assorted claims of the moment to the operation of the system over centuries' time. No doubt his frequently repeated revelation that Marxism had shown "the interplay of ideas and reality" and "made my work as useful as it is," reflected both the Marxist-influenced content and the unique quality of his achievement.[88]

Then again, it would be as mistake to forget the underlying moral element of his life's effort. A keen-eyed British observer, writing in 1987, noted that Williams's importance had often been attributed to the Vietnam War's effect on Americans and to the rise of the New Left. Yet many of his closest and most sympathetic readers were not particularly radical, nor even Americans. His widespread and continuing influence might just as well be traced to "his own remarkable qualities," above all

> his striking intellectual integrity, manifested not so much in his treatment of historical evidence (which has sometimes raised scholarly eyebrows) as in his unswerving allegiance to the logic of his own thoughts and values.[89]

This, almost certainly, was the way that Williams would have chosen to be remembered. A self-made intellectual in many ways, he had risen out of his insular Iowa background, his Navy experiences, and his civil rights activities into a dialogue with professors and fellow graduate students which allowed him to shape his narrative according to conclusions he had reached very much independently. Whatever the limitations of his two great works, the *Tragedy of American Diplomacy* and *Contours of American History*, the ideas in them had the unmistakable marks of originality. He lived out the rest of his life, less as a scholar and more as a public citizen, likewise according to his own credo.

Had he failed, and does the rebel—the intellectual and political loner who bucks the system—ever really succeed? The socialistic-minded science fiction writer Philip K. Dick, who rose from similar obscurity to a mass 1960s-70s following and a late-life spiritual commitment, observed in his penultimate work that one fundamental postulate survives through the ages: "the empire has never ended." Empire, the very codification of derangement, imposed its madness upon everyone through the violence which is endemic to the phenomenon. The ancient destruction of community, according to Dick, left its victims "idiots" (a word drawn from the Greek for "private"), unable in their aloneness to make sense of what their eyes told them.[90]

The LSD-dropping Dick from the postmodernist hometown of Berkeley, a college ROTC-resister to boot, was as far from Williams's personal mentality as one could imagine. And yet the two, both astonishingly keen observers of Empire and its various manifestations, had moved through very different paths of the 1950s toward similar ends. Indeed, as Dick became a late-life Gnostic before his death in 1974, Williams reconciled himself to the Episcopalian Church (Wendy, for her part, was a Unitarian) in Waldport. Perhaps he sought solace, and with spreading cancer he had every reason to do so. But Christianity heavy with symbolism also signified his mental return to the premodern era where, in *Contours of American History*, he had placed the origins of the modern historical imagination. There, whatever the enormity of society's flaws, a sense of community had persisted, perhaps as remnant of a distant age.

Williams sometimes remarked comically that he remained determined to stay alive if only to give Arthur Schlesinger, Jr., more restless nights. But the real point was of course to move ahead, to develop an overview which worked by explaining or helping to explain events and ideas. Williams frequently said, especially in later years, that to do so made arguments with the likes of Schlesinger, Jr., irrelevant, because their constant pursuit of ideologies showed that they simply had no idea of how the system actually worked. Perhaps they did not wish to know. A valid explanatory framework, at any rate, would serve a hundred times better than debating those who wished to lay Williams low.

And so he passed, in March of 1990, after repeated surgery, never finished but still struggling for understanding and expression.

An intimate friend speaking at the memorial service imagined William Appleman Williams at the service himself, saying,

> Well, this is all getting a bit much, a little dreary. After all, I haven't really gone, I just got bored and terribly tired, and finally found the time to be constructively lazy. If you want to find me, don't look in the lecture halls or the library. Come to the top of Cape Perpetua and watch the sun set, and the moon rise to claim the sky and dance its path across the water. Look at the beach at Seal Rock, or south near Waldport or Yachats. I'll be there with you poking around the tidepools, and sizing up the surf fishing, and taking photographs of the

cormorants and the sea anemones. Take my hand and climb the dunes at Florence; taste the salt wind and watch the gathering of a winter storm—and wonder at the hard beauty and the eerie power of the ocean and the interconnectedness of it all.[91]

This neatly-done picture offers us Williams at his happiest, near the end of a remarkable life often connected with the ocean and more often with solitude. It tells us little about the content of his ruminations, if he had any, as he walked, looked, fished, and photographed the spectacular scene. Perhaps Oregon, the last frontier of the small businessman and reputedly also of the farmer more interested in leisure than profits, was Bill Williams's natural last frontier as well. When he reached it, he stayed until crossing over to an Unknown that his self-styled Christian Socialism had never delineated.

But he could satisfy himself, if he needed the consolation, that of all his remarkably creative work, his own most marvelous creation had been himself. Neither U.S. history, nor the writing of any kind of history from the world's dominant power, would see his like soon again.

# NOTES

## INTRODUCTION

1 Quoted by Howard Schonberger, "In Memoriam: William Appleman Williams, 1921–1990," *Radical Historians Newletter*, May, 1990.

2 Bruce Cumings, "Global Realm with No Limit, Global Realm with No Name" *Radical History Review*, 57 (Fall, 1993), 55.

3 William Appleman Williams, "Thoughts on the Fun and Purpose of Being an American Historian," *Organization of American Historians Newslette*, February, 1985.

4 Interview with Merle Curti by Edward Rice-Maximin, May, 1993.

5 Edward Said, *Culture and Imperialism* (New York, 1993), 64–65.

6 Amy Kaplan, "'Left Alone in America': the Absence of Empire in the Study of American Culture," introduction to *Cultures of American Imperialism*, ed. Amy Kaplan and Donald E. Pease (Durham, 1993), 14.

7 Sylvia Wynter, "The Counterdoctrine of Jamesian Poiesis," in *C.L.R. James's Caribbean*, edited by Paget Henry and Paul Buhle (Durham, 1992), 66–67.

8 Amy Kaplan, "'Left Alone with America,'" 13–14.

9 Amy Kaplan, "'Left Alone with America,'" 14.

10 George F. Kennan, "The Failure of Our Success," *New York Times*, Mar. 14, 1994.

11 A public opinion poll reported in the *New York Times* that seventy-five percent of Americans agreed when asked the question "Don't you think Americans over-consume?"; most of the same people insisted that overconsumption was one of the best things about being American. Wade Greene, "Overconspicuous Consumption," *New York Times*, Aug. 28, 1994.

## CHAPTER 1

1 This insightful suggestion was made by W. A. Williams's daughter, Kyenne Williams, in an interview with Paul Buhle, June 10, 1993, and confirmed by Jeannie Williams in an interview with Paul Buhle, Oct. 20, 1993. In writing the memoir, Williams had the advantage of detailed correspondence and other records that his grandmother had saved. We are not so fortunate. He disposed of the raw material when he finished the memoir, a decision that may have been a matter of convenience as he cleaned out his grandparents' effects. But as Kyenne Williams suggests, it may well speak also to his determination to have the final word.

2 "A Good Life and a Good Death: A Memoir of an Independent Lady," n.d., William Appleman Williams Papers, Oregon State University; and "Ninety Days Inside the Empire," by "Billy Apple," an unarchived manuscript very kindly made available to us by Karla Robbins. See Chapter 7, on Williams's attempts at straightforward autobiography.

3 Only the use of the word "visceral" probably exceeded "honored" in Williams's published and unpublished prose. He sought to convey a physical sensibility, a more than cerebral way of seeing and engaging the world, but without neglecting those traditions which made life and sensibility possible.

4 "'New Left' Historian Williams, Iowa native, dies of cancer at 68," *Des Moines Register*, n.d., clipping in Williams Papers.

5 Interview with Lloyd Gardner by Edward Rice-Maximin, June 10, 1994; interview with William Robbins by Paul Buhle, Oct. 12, 1993.

6 For his father's side of the family, see the *Compendium of History and Biography of Cass County, Iowa* (Chicago, 1906), 557–58. Williams's great aunt Katie Williams, his paternal grandfather's twin, was a schoolteacher "and a student in an advanced course at the State Normal School, Cedar Falls." Thanks to Neil Basen for supplying this reference. Williams, "A Good Life and a Good Death," II, 6 (manuscript not paged consecutively).

7 Williams, "A Good Life and a Good Death," II, 10.

8 William J. Peterson, *Iowa: The Rivers of Her Valleys* (Iowa City, 1941), 280–91.

9 Alan Bogue, *From Prairie to Corn Belt: Farming on the Illinois and Iowa Prairies in the Nineteenth Century* (Chicago, 1963), Ch. 6-9.

10 Williams, *Roots of the Modern American Empire: A Study of the Growth and Shaping of Social Consciousness in Marketplace Society* (New York, 1969), xxi.

11  Bogue, *From Prairie to Corn Belt*, 205.

12  "A Good Life and a Good Death," II, 11.

13  We wish to thank Neil Basen for supplying this information.

14  *Iowa: A Guide to the Hawkeye State, Compiled and Written by the Federal Writers Project of the Works Progress Administration for the State of Iowa* (New York, 1940), 495–96.

15  Williams, "MacCormick Reports on Russia: A Study of News and Opinion on Russia in the Chicago Tribune from 1917–1921," unpublished master's thesis, University of Wisconsin-Madison, 1948, 159–62. William J. Peterson, *Iowa*, 291.

16  Bogue, *From Prairie to Corn Belt*, 184–86.

17  "A Good Life and a Good Death," II, 18–19.

18  "A Good Life and a Good Death," I, 3-II,1.

19  "A Good Life and a Good Death," II, 17.

20  Williams, *Americans in a Changing World: A History of the United States in the Twentieth Century* (New York: 1977), 179.

21  Outline for "A Historian Reflects Upon his Memories," Williams Papers.

22  Telephone interview with Corrinne Williams by Paul Buhle, July 10, 1994.

23  "A Historian Reflects Upon his Memories."

24  "A Good Life and a Good Death," V, 22.

25  See, e.g., Colin Wilson, *New Pathways in Psychology: Maslow and the Post-Freudian Revolution* (New York: 1972), Ch. 3-4.

26  Williams, *Roots*, xxii.

27  Williams, *Americans in a Changing World*, 267.

28  "A Good Life and a Good Death," VI, 1-2.

29  Lloyd Gardner to William Robbins, Mar. 19, 1985, lent to the writers by William Robbins.

30  Certificate from Secondary School, in, William W. Jeffries Memorial Archives, Naval Academy, Annapolis.

31  See his comments in Williams, *Americans in a Changing World*, 198.

32  Williams, *Americans in a Changing World*, 184–85.

33  Williams, *Americans in a Changing World*, 64–65.

34  "A Good Life and a Good Death," VIII, 12.

35  Interview with Jeannie Williams.

36  "A Good Life and a Good Death," VIII, 21.

37  See Paul Buhle's biography of James: *C. L. R James, the Artist as Revolutionary* (London, 1988), Ch. 5.

38  Grade transcript, 1941, Kemper Military School, in Naval Academy Archives.

39  Interview with Williams by Michael Wallace, in Henry Abelove et.al., eds., *Visions of History* (New York, 1983), 126.

40  Interview with Jeannie Williams; "A Good Life and a Good Death," VIII, 13.

41  Williams, "Notes on the Death of a Ship and the End of a World: The Grounding of the British Bark *Glenesslin* at Mount Neahkahnie on 1 October 1913," *American Neptune*, 41 (1981), 131.

42 Transcripts, 1944, United States Naval Academy, William W. Jeffries Memorial Archives.

43 Telephone interview with former classmate John Piro, Nov. 17, 1993; "William Appleman Williams," *Lucky Bag* (Annapolis yearbook). n.p., 1944.

44 "William A. Williams, '45," "The Flame of Faith," *The Trident Magazine* (Spring, 1944), 12, 38–41. Copies of the magazine were kindly made available by the Nimitz Library of the U.S. Naval Academy.

45 "William A. Williams '45," "Today is Russia," *The Trident Magazine* (Winter, 1944), 12–13, 39–44. While this essay reveals a characteristic naïveté of the time about the leadership of Stalin and the success of the Five Year Plans, it has a keen interpretation of the Soviet appeals for Western alliance against the Nazis and the indifference of the future Allies. (Williams carefully also excluded the U.S. and American leadership from any complaints).

46 Williams interview, *Visions of History*, 126; "William A. Williams," *Lucky Bag*, 1944.

47 Fred Harvey Harrington, interview with Edward Rice-Maximin, June 12, 1992. See also Williams interview, *Visions of History*, 126–27; Henry W. Berger, "The Revisionist Historian and His Community," introduction to Berger, ed., *A William Appleman Williams Reader* (Chicago, 1992), 13–14; William Robbins, "William Appleman Williams: 'Doing History is Best of All. No Regrets,'" in Lloyd Gardner, ed., *Redefining the Past: Essays in Diplomatic History in Honor of William Appleman Williams* (Corvallis, Oregon, 1986), 4–5. Berger has the text of Williams's speech on his return to Annapolis in 1987. See Chapter 7 for an analysis of it.

48 Williams, *Americans in a Changing World*, 322.

49 Williams, *Lucky Bag*, 1944.

50 "Dear Jim," July 22/23, 1989, Williams Papers.

51 Williams, *Americans in a Changing World*, 332.

52 "Billy Apple," "Ninety Days Inside the Empire," 430.

53 Williams, *Americans in a Changing World*, 334.

54 Williams, "Notes on the Death of a Ship," 137.

55 Interview with Williams by David Shetzline, Williams Papers.

56 Interview with Williams by David Shetzline, Williams Papers.

57 Williams interview, *Visions of History*, 127.

58 "Ninety Days Inside the Empire," 66. It is interesting to note that the director of *The House I Live In* was to become a prominent Hollywood Blacklistee. The lyricist for Sinatra's tune, Abel Meeropol, later adopted the sons of "atom spy" victims Julius and Ethyl Rosenberg. One of the two sons, Michael, took classes with Williams and became one of his admiring interpreters.

59 Charlotte Gilmor, letter to Paul Buhle, Nov. 17, 1993.

60 *CORPUS CRISIS*, May 9, 1946. NAACP Papers, Group II, Box C 189, Branch File, Corpus Christi , Library of Congress. Typical headlines read "WILLIE FRANCIS FIGHTS FOR LIFE" and "NEGRO MOTHER HONORED FOR 1946."

61 Teresa Grace Herold to H. Boyd Hall, May 15, 1946; and Rt. Rev. Monsignor John F. Basso to H. Boyd Hall, May 15, 1946, NAACP Papers.

62 "Minimum Wage Bill Fighting Hard," and "Normal Contracts Needed," *CORPUS CRISIS*, May 9, 1946; "Local Chapter Sends Wire," and "Fight Inflation," ibid., May 17, 1946.

63 Williams, "My Life in Madison," in *History and the New Left: Madison, Wisconsin, 1950–1970*, edited by Paul Buhle (Philadelphia 1990), 266.

64 Interview with Williams by David Shetzline, Williams Papers.

65 Paul D. Meyer, "Book Review," *CORPUS CRISIS* May 17, 1946. Interestingly, Williams later claimed to have read W. E. B. DuBois's *Black Reconstruction* around this time. James S. Allen's book which stressed biracial action for justice, was seen at the time of its publication as a kind of antidote to *Black Reconstruction*, which portrayed Southern racism as a totalistic force.

66 Williams interview, *Visions of History*, 128. NAACP correspondence reveals a somewhat different story. See Boyd Hall to Walter White, May 19, 1946. Seeking guidance about how to act within a controversy-ridden situation, Hall was advised, via an internal memo to White, that the Corpus Christi chapter would do well simply to let the whole controversy pass. "Memorandum, To: Mr White, From: Miss Black. Re: Letter from H. Boyd Hall," May 27, 1945, NAACP Papers.

67 Williams interview, *Visions of History*, 134.

68 Williams interview, *Visions of History*, 128.

69 At first many veteran New Dealers resisted this divisive course, insisting that it aided the Right, but ADA spokesmen like Arthur Schlesinger, Jr., pressed ahead. See Steven M. Gillon, *Politics and Vision: The ADA and American Liberalism, 1947–1985* (New York, 1987), 21–32.

70 "Life Inside the Frontier," tentatively titled one-page outline for an autobiographical novel, Williams Papers.

71 Williams wrote to the national NAACP headquarters mentioning his Corpus Christi activity and noting he had "never received my official notification of membership or card" despite being "desirous of being active in all localities for many years to come." Williams to "The Executive Secretary, the NAACP" from Atlantic, Iowa, Aug. 13, 1946, NAACP Papers. Perhaps alerted to controversy, the organization simply "overlooked" his application, embittering Williams from another side.

72 In one of his published interviews, Williams insists that he had an earlier experience, teaching YMCA summer camp while at Kemper, learning the love of teaching. This cannot be confirmed, and Jeannie Williams insists that he imagined or at least greatly exaggerated this experience. No independent confirmation has been found.

73 "Billy Apple," "Ninety Days Inside the Empire," 437.

74 Outline, "Life Inside the Frontier."

75 Williams interview, *Visions of History*, 129; the insight into Williams's career belongs to Wendy Williams, in an interview given June 10, 1993.

## Chapter 2

1 This anecdote was reported by Williams to Mitzi Goheen, and was relayed in a telephone conversation, June 12, 1993.

2 This cannot be independently confirmed, and Jeannie Williams casts doubt upon the memory.

3 Telephone interview with Mitzi Goheen by Paul Buhle.

4 Williams to William Robbins, n.d. [1985], made available by William Robbins.

5 Fred Harvey Harrington to William Robbins, Feb. 22, 1985, letter made available by William Robbins.

6 According to an interview with Merle Curti, Turner was intrigued by Simons's interpretations. Interview with Merle Curti by Paul Buhle, Nov. 17, 1993.

7 See, e.g., Bernard C. Borning, *The Political and Social Thought of Charles A. Beard* (Seattle, 1962), parts 2–3.

8 See John D. Hicks, *My Life With History: An Autobiography* (Lincoln, 1968), ch. 3. 9, 11; Warren Susman, in *History and the New Left*, 275–84; See also Howard K. Beale, ed., *Charles A. Beard: An Appraisal* (Lexington, 1954), discussed below in Chapter 3.

9 Fred Harvey Harrington, *God, Mammon and the Japanese: Dr. Horace N. Allen and Korean-American Relations, 1884–1905* (Madison, 1944); Harrington, *Fighting Politician: Major General N.P. Banks* (Philadelphia, 1948).

10 File Notes, William Hesseltine Collection, State Historical Society of Wisconsin.

11 Warren Susman, "The Smoking Room School of History," in *History and the New Left*, 44.

12 Williams to Walter LaFeber, Jan. 15, 1985, Williams Papers; and interviews with Fred Harvey Harrington.

13 Williams to Walter LaFeber, Jan. 15, 1985, Williams Papers; communication from David W. Noble to Paul Buhle, May 7, 1993.

14 Williams, "My Life in Madison," in *History and the New Left*, 267, n.1.

15 Williams to William Robbins.

16 Ibid.

17 Ibid. See also Evan Stark, "In Exile," in *History and the New Left*, 173–74.

18 Harrington to William Robbins.

19 See George Catephores, "The Imperious Austrian: Schumpeter as Bourgeois Marxist," *New Left Review* #205 (May-June, 1994), 3–15. We might expect Madison graduate students to have read an essay by Schumpeter, "The 'Communist Manifesto' in Sociology and Economics," in the *Journal of Political Economy*, 1949. Cited in Catephores, 8, n. 9. In an interview with David Shetzline, n.d. [1976], Williams suggested that he had read Schumpeter (without giving a specific volume) at the proper moment, in Madison of the 1940s. Williams Papers.

20 See Maurice Glasman, "The Great Deformation: Polyani, Poland and the Terrors of Planned Spontaneity," *New Left Review*, #205 (May-June 1994), 59–69.

21 Interview with Susman by Paul Buhle, September, 1982; these observations were confirmed by Curti in the interview noted above.

22 Harrington to William Robbins.

23 Not to romanticize this brief retrospect: during World War I, faculty members, by a large majority, demeaned themselves by signing a public document repudiating LaFollette's courageous stand. See Paul Buhle, introduction to *History and the New Left*, 10–17.

24 See a slightly later account of the *Cardinal* milieu in Richard Schickel, "A Journalist Among Historians," in *History and the New Left*, 85–100. Schickel joined the *Cardinal* staff in 1950, en route to life as a film reviewer and critic at *Time* and elsewhere.

25 Harrington to William Robbins.

26 "Marzani Case . . . the Editor's Mailbag," *Daily Cardinal*, Dec. 16, 1947; and "Filling Out the Picture of Campus Politics," *Daily Cardinal*, Sept. 23, 1949.

27 "University Society News—Marxists Convene," *Daily Cardinal*, Dec. 16, 1947; "Portrait of a Woman" (advertisement), *Daily Cardinal*, Dec. 12, 1947; "Golden Boy," *Daily Cardinal*, Dec 17, 1947.

28 "Thomas Blasts Foes in Madison Address," *Daily Cardinal*, Sept. 15, 1948; "Gerth Stresses German Needs," *Daily Cardinal*, Feb. 26, 1949; "Full House Hears Taylor," *Daily Cardinal*, Sept. 21, 1948.

29 Harrington to William Robbins.

30 An anonymous observer insists that Williams appeared at a civil rights meeting in Chicago around this time, attended by a wide range of the Left, including members of the Communist-oriented Civil Rights Congress. This memory cannot be verified.

31 See for example, "Badger Village Houses 78 New Families, Married Veterans continue to Occupy Apartments," *Daily Cardinal*, Sept. 23, 1948; Williams's own reflection on the GIs-turned-students of that day are in Williams interview by Michael Wallace, *Visions of History*, 129.

32 David W. Noble to Paul Buhle, May 7, 1993.

33 Williams, "McCormick Reports on Russia: A Study of News and Opinion on Russia in the *Chicago Tribune* from 1917–1921," MA Thesis, University of Wisconsin, 1948, 29, 75.

34 Williams, "McCormick Reports," ibid., 147–48, 199.

35 The fullest version of Robins's life is told in Neil V. Salzman, *Reform and Revolution: The Life and Times of Raymond Robins* (Kent, Ohio, 1991). Salzman interviewed Williams, used materials uncovered by him, and credited him with important archival discoveries.

36 Williams, "Raymond Robins and Russian American Relations," PhD Dissertation, University of Wisconsin, 1950, 126.

37 Quoted, from an unpublished manuscript, in L. P. Carpenter, *G.D.H. Cole, An Intellectual Biography* (Cambridge, 1973), 47.

38 Justus Doenecke letter to Paul Buhle, Sept. 19, 1993.

39 Charles S. Maier, "Marking Time: The Historiography of International Relations" in Michael Kammen, ed., *The Past Before Us: Contemporary Historical Writing in the United States* (Ithaca, 1980), 364–66; interview with Harrington by Edward Rice-Maximin, June 12, 1992.

40 See Ralph Miliband, *Parliamentary Socialism: A Study in the Politics of Labour* (New York, 1964), Ch. 9 for an overview of Labour's timidity, both on foreign policy and in regard to the possibilities of worker-controlled factories. Centralization of power dominated the few nationalizations of industry carried out.

41 Quoted and discussed in Peter Novick, *That Noble Dream: The "Objectivity Question" and the American Historical Profession* (Cambridge, U.K., 1988), 318.

42 See Michael Meeropol, "Cold War Revisionism," in *Encyclopedia of the American Left* (New York, 1990), 144–46.

43 Williams, *American-Russian Relations, 1781–1947* (New York, 1952).

44 Hugh Seton-Watson, *International Affairs* (London), 30 (October, 1954), 514–15.

45 Bradford Perkins, "A Matter of Interpretation," *New York Times Book Review*, Nov. 9, 1952, 20.

46 O. T. Barck, Jr., *American History Review*, 59 (January-March, 1953), 83–85; William A. Brandenburg, *Mississippi Valley Historical Review*, 40 (June, 1953), 169–70; Ruhl Bartlett, *Pacific Historical Review*, 22 (May, 1953), 422–23; Alfred A. Skerpan, *Indiana Magazine of History*, 49 (June, 1953), 225–28.

47 Harold C. Hinton, *Catholic Historical Review*, 39 (Fall, 1954); Paul A. Fitzgerald, *Catholic Historical Review*, 41 (Fall, 1956); and William A. Nolan, *American Catholic Sociological Review*, 14 (October, 1953), 198–99.

48 Richard Van Alstyne, *Far Eastern Quarterly*, 12 (May, 1953), 311–12; E. H. Carr, *American Slavic and East European Review*, 12 (1953), 392–94. Another, more predictably favorable review was by the American Socialist intellectual exiled to Paris, Samuel Bernstein, in *Science & Society*, 17 (Summer, 1953), 276–77.

49 Robert Friedman, "Crisis Laid to Anti-Soviet Policy by Oregon University Professor's Book," *Daily Worker*, Dec. 22, 1942.

50 Ernest B. Haas, *Journal of Political Economy*, 62 (June, 1954), 137–38.

51 Letter from David Noble.

52 Williams to William Robbins.

53 William Appleman Williams, "Brooks Adams and Expansion," *New England Quarterly*, XXV (June, 1952), 82–85.

54 Interview with Merle Curti by Paul Buhle, Nov. 20, 1993.

55 Interview with Thomas McCormick by Edward Rice-Maximin, June 11, 1992.

56 Telephone conversation with Charles Vevier, Jan. 7, 1994.

## Chapter 3

1 Memo to William and Karla Robbins, Mar. 17,1985, Williams Papers.

2 Together with Raymond Robins's personal papers, these constituted a vital nugget of materials about those who strove to bridge the gaps between the U.S. and the early Soviet governments. While working on the recovered documents for his first book, Williams declined to make them available to cold war scholars, touching off Schlesinger, Jr.'s first recorded attack on Williams as "pro-Communist." Ironically, Schlesinger, Jr., would later bear the brunt of professional complaints that he had used Kennedy family sources available to no one else, and Williams as president of the OAH would lead the struggle against the destruction of State Department and FBI documents. See Arthur Schlesinger, Jr., to Boyd Shafer, July 1, 1954, American Historical Association Papers; Williams explained with frustration to Warren Susman that the Robins Papers had been uncollected in Florida for a quarter century and none of the pro-State Department scholars showed any interest until Williams's use of them. Williams to Warren Susman, n.d. [1960], letter made available by Bea Susman. See also Williams to Clifford Lord, June 4, 1955, State Historical Society of Wisconsin General Administrative Collection, and Lord to Williams, Aug. 20, 1952, General Administrative Collection. Special thanks to Scott McLemee for making the full set of documents related to Schlesinger, Jr.'s charges against Williams available to us.

3 Ron McCrea and Dave Wagner, "Harvey Goldberg," in *History and the New Left*, 244.

4 Interview with Peter Weiss, Nov. 20, 1993; and telephone conversation with Corrinne Williams, July 25, 1994. Therapist, musician, and former undergraduate student of Fred Harvey Harrington, Weiss was one of the closest social friends of the couple during the 1960s.

5 Williams, "Harvey Goldberg and the Virtue of History," Harvey Goldberg Memorial Lecture, Oct. 22, 1987, Williams Papers.

6 Quoted in McCrea and Wagner, "Harvey Goldberg," 244.

7 Memo to William and Karla Robbins [1985], Williams Papers; Interview with Jeannie Williams, Oct. 9, 1993. This episode is only briefly discussed in various interviews. See for example the Williams interview in *Visions of History* (New York, 1983), 132.

8 Telephone conversation with Corrinne Williams, July 11, 1994.

9 William A. Williams to Warren Susman, n.d. [1957], letter made available by Bea Susman.

10 Memo to William and Karla Robbins [1985], Williams Papers. Williams to Warren Susman, March, 1957, and undated [1957]. Letters made available by Bea Susman. In an explanation to Walter LaFeber, Williams added, "You know as well as I do: hell, I read so many damn Russian documents in the archives of the

American Embassy in Moscow that it would drive anybody out of their mind . . . we are so bloody good as imperialists that you get the other side's position in our documents as to make wandering-off to their archives a kind of exercise in funded vacations!!" Nov. 10, 1983, Williams Papers.

11 Jonathan M. Wiener, "Radical Historians and the Crisis in American History, 1959–1980," *Journal of American History*, 76 (September, 1989), 402; Peter Novick, *That Noble Dream: The "Objectivity Question" and the American Historical Profession* (Cambridge, 1988), 300. Novick quotes Arthur Schlesinger, Jr., as saying a few years later that the very words "capitalism" and "socialism" belonged "to the vocabulary of demagoguery, not . . . analysis." From "Epilogue: The One Against the Many," in *Paths of American Thought* (Boston, 1963), edited by Arthur Schlesinger, Jr., and Morton White, 536. The following owes much to Warren Susman, "The Historian's Task," a seminar paper written in 1952 for fellow Madison graduate students and published as "Appendix One" to *History and the New Left*, 275–84. Special thanks to William Preston for making this document available for publication.

12 Peter Novick says that historians' attacks on "moral relativism" were not systematic, but later offers evidence of Morison, Nevins, Schlesinger, Jr., and Handlin sharply attacking relativists and relativism. Novick, *That Noble Dream*, 286–87, 342–43. Susman was far closer to the mark in his comments, "The Historian's Task," 278.

13 Susman, "The Historian's Task," 281.

14 Quoted in Jesse Lemisch, *On Active Service in Peace and War: Politics and Ideology in the American Historical Profession* (Toronto, 1975), 69. In the *Harvard Guide to American History*, Morison with unconscious hilarity urged colleagues to offer their services chivalrously to such noted right-wing (and especially at that time, notably racist) ladies' organizations as the Daughters of the American Revolution and the Daughters of the Confederacy for patriotic festivals. Challenged on the racial politics of his own noted textbook, he suggested "some essential docility in their character" that made blacks a race ideally suited for slavery. Novick, *The Noble Dream*, 350, n.46.

15 Cited in Novick, *That Noble Dream*, 342; see also Lemisch, *On Active Service In Peace and War*, 70–71.

16 Lemisch, *On Active Service*, 74–78.

17 Sigmund Diamond, *Compromised Campus: The Collaboration of Universities with the Intelligence Community, 1945–1955* (New York, 1992), 151–66 and 139–45. According to Diamond, Buckley was a regular campus informant, and young Henry Kissinger, a particular protégé of Arthur Schlesinger, Jr., opened the mail of fellow graduate students and sent the contents to federal authorities.

18 Novick, *That Noble Dream*, 326.

19 Novick, *That Noble Dream* , 325–332.

20 Jon Wiener, "Radical Historians and the Crisis in American History, 1959–1980," *Journal of American History*, 76 (September, 1989), 411–12, n. 29. Wiener's sketch of the repressive atmosphere faced by future leading historians is also illuminating.

21 Interview with Fred Harvey Harrington, Nov. 19,1993, about his own experiences as a department head in 1957.

22 Novick, *That Noble Dream*, 308.

23 Quoted in Lemisch, *On Active Service*, 88–89.

24 Richard Wightman Fox, *Reinhold Niebuhr: A Biography* (San Francisco, 1985), 244–47, 272, 274–75. He also notes that Niebuhr's editorial, "The Evil of the Communist Idea," was published and widely broadcast a short time before the execution of Ethel and Julius Rosenberg. Niebuhr earnestly believed that they deserved execution, although he later recanted this conviction. Ibid., 254–55.

25 See Richard Reinitz, *Irony and Consciousness: American Historiography and Reinhold Niebuhr's Vision* (New York, 1980), 99.

26 Quoted in Lemisch, *On Active Service*, 53–54.

27 Quoted in Gary Dorrien, *The Neo-Conservative Mind: Politics, Culture and the War of Ideology* (Philadelphia, 1993), 362.

28 Susman, "The Historian's Task," 282.

29 Susman, "The Historian's Task," 282.

30 Michael Wreszin, "Arthur Schlesinger, Jr., Scholar-Activist in Cold War America: 1946–1956," *Salmagundi*, 63-64 (Spring-Summer, 1984), 255–285.

31 Arthur Schlesinger, Jr., "The Future of Socialism, III," *Partisan Review*, 14 (May-June, 1947), 229–241.

32 Schlesinger, Jr., "The Future of Socialism," 236–37.

33 Schlesinger, Jr., "The Future of Socialism," 241.

34 This tendency in Schlesinger's work was keenly identified by Elaine May, in her *Homeward Bound: American Families in the Cold War Era* (New York, 1988), 98.

35 A few years later, Niebuhr attacked Eisenhower as the "Chamberlain of our day," and "decent but soft." Still later, he developed the distinction between "authoritarian" allies and "totalitarian" enemies widely used by Jeane Kirkpatrick during the Reagan years. Fox, *Reinhold Niebuhr*, 265, 272, 274–75.

36 Susman, "The Historian's Task," 284.

37 See for instance, John Bellamy Foster, *The Theory of Monopoly Capitalism* (New York, 1986) and Paul Sweezy, "Interview," *Monthly Review*, 38 (April, 1987), for a basic sense of *MR* theory and history. We are grateful to Paul Sweezy and Harry Magdoff for letters of reminiscence about Williams.

38 Interview with Saul Landau by Paul Buhle, May, 1982. A part of the interview, but not this part, was excerpted into Landau, "From the Labor Youth League to the Cuban Revolution," in *History and the New Left*, 107–112. Landau and others were Left activists on the Madison campus of the 1950s.

39 Thanks to Alan Wald for pointing out Williams's status on the *American Socialist*, which merged into *Monthly Review* in 1960.

40 See David Goldway, "Science & Society," in *Encyclopedia of the American Left* (New York, 1990), edited by Mari Jo Buhle, Paul Buhle, and Dan Georgakas, 679–80; and Goldway, "Fifty Years of Science & Society," *Science & Society*, 50 (Fall, 1986). Williams also offered around the same time to contribute an essay on Big

Band jazz to *Mainstream*, a leftish cultural journal thought to represent former Communist intellectuals distancing themselves from the Party. Among the *American Socialist* pieces, his 1958 essay, "The Large Corporation and American Foreign Policy" was reprinted into his essay collection, *History as a Way of Learning* (New York, 1974). On the connection with *Mainstream*, we have benefitted from Alan Wald making available several of Williams's letters to Charles Humboldt, its editor, in 1959. See also Annette Rubinstein, "Mainstream," *Encyclopedia of the American Left*, 445–46.

41 See Margaret Morley, "Freda Kirchwey: Cold War Critic," in Lloyd Gardner, ed., *Redefining the Past: Essays in Diplomatic History in Honor of William Appleman Williams* (Corvallis, 1986), 157–68. Morley was one of Williams's final graduate students and his only female PhD; Interview with Margaret Morley, Nov. 15, 1993. The *Reporter* was known for its concocted revelations, such as an essay by a defecting Russian colonel on how the Russians had trained the North Korean Army. The colonel had been an invention of the CIA. See the American Social History Project, *Who Built America* (New York, 1992), 489. The *New Leader* was the leading publication of an intellectual milieu around the social-democratic wing of the garments trade whose foremost figures had established the CIA-funded international agencies of the AFL and later AFL-CIO. See Paul Buhle, "Lovestoneites," *Encyclopedia of the American Left*, 437; and Daniel Cantor and Julia Schor, *Tunnel Vision: Labor, the World Economy and Central America* (Boston, 1987), 34–48. See Chapter 4, on the Central American and Caribbean matters in which Williams dealt.

42 Williams, "Moscow Peace Drive: Victory for Containment?" *Nation*, 177 (July ll, 1953), 28–30.

43 Williams, "Irony of Containment: A Policy of Boomerangs," *Nation*, 182 (Apr. 5, 1956), 376–79.

44 Williams, "Babbit's New Fables: Economic Myths," *Nation*, 182 (Jan. 7, 1956), 3–6.

45 Williams, "Needed: Production for Peace," in "If We Want Peace: Barriers and Prospects," special issue of the *Nation*, 188 (Feb. 21,1959), 149–53.

46 William Appleman Williams, "The American Century: 1941–1957," *Nation*, 185 (Nov. 2, 1957), 297–301.

47 William Appleman Williams, "The 'Logic' of Imperialism," *Nation*, 185 (July 6, 1957), 14–15.

48 Williams, "The Tribune," 5.

49 Williams, "Cold War Perspectives: A Historical Fable," *Nation*, 180 (May 28, 1955), 458–61.

50 The term "public intellectuals" and the following description owes much to Russell Jacoby, *The Last Intellectuals* (New York, 1982), notwithstanding Jacoby's own narrow and eccentric views of which writers could be considered "public" or important (mostly authors for New York highbrow magazines) and which disregard not only widely-read public intellectuals such as Williams but film and television writers, popular critical poets and novelists, etc., as well as writers for the large sec-

tions of the leftish press, e.g., *Nation* and *Village Voice* to *Ramparts* and *Mother Jones* magazines.

51 Williams, preface to *Roots of the Modern American Empire*, xv–xvi.

52 Interview with Fred Harvey Harrington by Paul Buhle, Madison, Nov. 20, 1993. See also comments by William G. Robbins, "William Appleman Williams," in *Redefining the Past*, 9; William Marina, "William Appleman Williams," in *Dictionary of Literary Biography*, 17; *Twentieth Century American Historians*, ed. Clyde N. Wilson (Detroit, 1983), 17.

53 Preface to *Shaping of American Diplomacy I* (Cleveland, 1956), xiv. A. T. Volwiler, "Harrison, Blaine, and American Foreign Policy, 1889–1993," and Nelson M. Blake, "Cleveland's Venezuela Policy," in *Shaping of American Diplomacy*, 356–64 and 364–73, respectively.

54 Williams, *Shaping of American Diplomacy I*, xii–xiii.

55 Charles A. Madison, "Reviews," *Science & Society*, 21 (Fall, 1957), 372–73; Rufus G. Hall, Jr., *Southeastern Social Science Quarterly*, 37 (March, 1957), 380.

56 Paul A. Varg, *World Affairs Quarterly*, 28 (July, 1957), 1292–95. See also Alan Conway, *International Affairs*, 33 (April, 1957), 259.

57 James P. O'Brien, "Comment," *Radical America*, IV (August, 1970), 50.

58 William Appleman Williams, "Charles Austin Beard: The Intellectual as Tory-Radical," in *American Radicals: Some Problems and Personalities* (New York, 1957), 304, 305, 299.

59 Harvey Goldberg and Williams, "Introduction: Thoughts about American Radicalism," in *American Radicals*, 3, 4.

60 *American Radicals*, 8.

61 *American Radicals*, 12.

62 *American Radicals*, 6, 15.

63 Williams, preface to *Roots of the Modern American Empire*, xv–xvi.

64 This discussion is based on Williams, "Open Door Interpretation," in *Encyclopedia of American Foreign Policy, Vol.II, Studies of the Principal Movements and Ideas*, edited by Alexander DeConde (New York, 1978), 703–10; and "Confessions of an Intransigent Revisionist," in *A William Appleman Williams Reader: Selections from His Major Historical Writings*, edited by Henry W. Berger (Chicago, 1993), 342–44.

65 *The Accumulation of Capital—An Anti-Critique by Rosa Luxemburg/Imperialism and the Accumulation of Capital by Nikolai Bukharin* (New York, 1972), translated by Rudolf Wichmann. See especially Kenneth Tarbuck's Introduction which sets out the issues clearly. When Michael Harrington in 1971 accused Williams of being a "Leninist" because of his critique of imperialism, Williams could rightly point to the far greater importance of Luxemburg and Hobson on his views. See Chapter 6.

66 Williams to William Robbins, n.d. [1985], Williams Papers.

67 Williams to William Robbins.

68 Williams, "A Note on Charles Austin Beard's Search for a General Theory of Causation," *American Historical Review*, 62 (October, 1956), 59–80. This was the first of Williams's contributions accepted by the *AHR*.

69 William Appleman Williams, "Brooks Adams and American Expansion," *New England Quarterly*, 25 (June, 1952), 217–32; and "Communication: On the Restoration of Brooks Adams," *Science & Society*, 20 (Summer, 1956), 376–79. Williams also showed how the "frontier thesis" could still inspire a 1956 election in Oregon with all the heroes and villains of frontier imagery and the foreign policy of the classic frontiersman: "get more markets for raw materials and agricultural surpluses, and settle disputes by organizing a committee of vigilantes and arming oneself with more and bigger guns." See Williams, "Historical Romance of Senator [Richard] Neuberger's Election," *Oregon Historical Quarterly*, Vol. 56 (June, 1956), 101–5. See also his "Neuberger Ducked the Basic Issues," *Frontier*, 6 (October, 1955), 5–6.

70 William Appleman Williams, "The Frontier Thesis and American Foreign Policy," *Pacific Historical Review*, 24 (Nov., 1955), 379–95.

71 William Appleman Williams, review of Arthur S. Link, *Woodrow Wilson and the Progressive Era, 1910–1917* (New York, 1954), in *Science & Society*, 18 (1954), 348–51.

72 William Appleman Williams, "The Convenience of History," review of George F. Kennan, *Russia Leaves the War, Vol. I: Soviet-American Relations, 1917–1920* (Princeton, 1956), *Nation*, 183 (Sept. 15, 1956), 222–24. Williams took the opportunity here to reveal his inveterate hostility to "infantile leftism," affirming his sympathy for Lenin and Trotsky's reluctant signing of the Treaty of Brest-Litovsk "rather than go out in a blaze of romantic revolutionary pyro-technics."

73 Williams, "A note on American Foreign Policy in Europe in the Nineteen Twenties," *Science & Society*, 22 (1958); Williams, "The Loss of Debate," review of Herbert Hoover, *The Ordeal of Woodrow Wilson* (New York, 1958), *Nation*, 186 (May 17, 1958), 452–53. Williams found his favorite protagonists among those long ridiculed by the liberal historians, William Borah and the "Sons of the Jackass" from the West who (in Borah's words) considered "futile and unAmerican" any effort "to run the world by establishing an American system comparable to the British empire." Borah's vision of the U.S. supporting "movements of reform and colonial nationalism" could not be realized, but remained a monument to clear-headedness. See William Appleman Williams, "The Legend of Isolationism in the 1920s," *Science & Society*," 18 (Winter, 1954), 1–20, reprinted in *A William Appleman Williams Reader*, 75–88; and Williams, "Latin America: Laboratory of American Foreign Policy of the Nineteen Twenties," *Inter-American Economic Affairs*, 1 (Autumn, 1957), 3–4.

74 Williams, "The Legend of Isolationism," 129.

75 William Appleman Williams, "Schlesinger: Right Crisis—Wrong Order," review of *The Age of Roosevelt: The Crisis of the Old Order* (New York, 1956), *Nation*, 184 (Mar. 23, 1957), 257–60.

76 See Susman's important essay, "The 1930s," in *Culture As History* (New York, 1987). Little has been written about Susman's own scholarly legacy. The pamphlet-length collective tribute, *In Memory of Warren Susman, 1927–1985* (New Brunswick, 1985), unfortunately does not touch upon his intimate connection with Williams.

77 Novick, *That Noble Dream*, 450. A decade later, Schlesinger, Jr., admitted that "the fact that in some aspects the revisionist thesis [of Williams] parallels the official Soviet argument must not, of course prevent consideration of the case on its merits, nor raise questions about the motives of the writers, all of whom, as far as I know, are independent minded scholars," in "Origins of the Cold War," *Foreign Affairs* 46 (1967), 24. Novick rightly suggests that the phrase "as far as I know" left open the possibility that Williams and his colleagues might be Soviet agents after all.

78 Williams, memo to William and Karla Robbins, 1985, made available by William Robbins.

79 Bernard Malamud, *A New Life* (New York, 1961).

80 Williams to Warren and Bea Susman, Aug. 3, 1955.

81 Interviews with Jeannie Williams and Kyenne Williams.

82 Norman Thomas, "The New American Imperialism," *Socialist Call*, XXXVI (July-August, 1958), 8. Only a few years earlier, Thomas had joined Reinhold Niebuhr and others in denying that any such thing as American imperialism could exist in the present. See "Open Letter to USA Socialists," *Socialist Commentary*, IV (Mar., 1951), 70–72. For his part, Niebuhr continued generally to compare independence unfavorably to colonialism. See, e.g., Reinhold Niebuhr, "The Army in the New Nation," *Christianity & Crisis*, 35 (May 2, 1966), 84, in which he refers to Kwame Nkrumah's efforts as "ridiculous." Although Niebuhr supported Martin Luther King, Jr., he likewise directed torrents of abuse at Malcolm X and others who rejected continued Western (i.e., white) control of world politics and economy.

83 Interview with Harrington, Nov. 19, 1993.

84 Interview with Harrington, Nov. 19, 1993. In a letter to William Robbins, Feb. 22, 1985, Harrington confessed his own uneasiness at drawing Williams to Madison when he was not sure of his own advancement into the administration. "But we did persuade him," and gave him tenure by 1958. Letter given to the authors by Robbins.

## CHAPTER 4

1 See for instance Arthur Hove, *The University of Wisconsin: A Pictorial History* (Madison, 1991). Fred Harvey Harrington, who assumed the reins in 1962, was quoted three years later as saying that in the last half dozen years there had been "more building in Madison than in the whole history of the campus," in ibid, 242.

2 See Paul Buhle, introduction to *History and the New Left*, 24–25; Saul Landau, "From Labor Youth League to the Cuban Revolution," in ibid., 107–112.

3 See Richard Schickel, "A Journalist Among Historians," 85–100; Warren Susman, "The Smoking Room School of History," 43–46; Herbert Gutman, "Learning about

History," 47–49; and William Preston, "WASP and Dissenter," 50–53, in *History and the New Left*. Preston would carry out Williams's program for an official Organization of American Historians committee to demand access to hidden government records; see Chapter 7.

4 See Jeffrey Kaplow, "Parenthesis: 1952–1956," in *History and the New Left*, 58–66. We wish to thank Larry Gara, a Madison graduate student of the early 1950s and later an activist for the War Resisters League, for offering his personal observations about pacifists' roles during this period. A small handful of Trotskyists had mainly an intellectual role, but figured interestingly in the later rise of social history. George Rawick, youth editor of a national Trotskyist tabloid while a graduate student at Madison, would become one of the most important scholars of slave history and a political disciple of C. L. R. James. See Rawick, "I Dissent," in *History and the New Left*, 54–57. Among the other radicals, Gabriel Kolko was a national leader of the small and scattered Student League for Industrial Democracy and in a decade or so, Williams's counterpart in the radical scholarship of diplomatic history.

5 Nina Serrano, "A Madison Bohemian," in *History and the New Left*, 67–84. Bertell Ollman, "From Liberal to Social Democrat to Marxist: My Political Itinerary Through Madison in the Late 1950s," in ibid., 101–6.

6 Interview with Saul Landau by Paul Buhle, Oct., 1980.

7 See Harvey J. Kaye, *The British Marxist Historians* (Oxford, 1984) and Harvey J. Kaye, *The Education of Desire: Marxists and the Writing of History* (New York, 1992). It is interesting, however, that the main journal that sought to coordinate such a New Left, the *American Socialist*, added Williams to its board of editorial advisors and that one of its major younger figures, David Herreshoff of Wayne State University, was a highly original scholar of American radicalism.

8 See Lee Baxandall, "New York Meets Oshkosh," *History and the New Left*, 127–33; and Appendix 2, by Lee Baxandall, Marshall Brickman and Danny Kalb, "The Boy Scouts in Cuba," *History and the New Left*, 285–90.

9 Telephone interview with Henry W. Berger, Nov. 20, 1993.

10 Karl Gutknecht, "Students Jam State Capitol for Joint HUAC Hearing," *Cardinal*, Feb. 22, 1961.

11 Sig Eisenscher, "Teaching to Think," *People's Daily World*, Apr. 20, 1990. A Wisconsin Communist, Eisenscher recalled the incidents decades later, shortly after Williams's death.

12 Jeff Greenfeld, "Legislator Rebuffs HUAC Foes," *Daily Cardinal*, Mar. 2, 1961 see also Mailbox, "Anti-Anti-Huac," *Daily Cardinal*, Mar. 10, 1961.

13 "Peace Center Pickets Heckled at Meeting," *Daily Cardinal*, Mar. 11, 1961.

14 Letter from George Mosse to Paul Buhle, October, 1992.

15 Interview with Thomas McCormick by Edward Rice-Maximin, June 11, 1992; and comments by McCormick in Dina M. Copelman and Barbara Clark Smith, editors, "Excerpts from a Conference to Honor William Appleman Williams," *Radical History Review*, 50 (Spring, 1991), 44–45. Based on a memorial colloquium

and roundtable convened by the Institute for Policy Studies, June 10, 1990. Referred to hereafter as Copelman/Clark Smith.

16 Interview with McCormick by Edward Rice-Maximin, June 11, 1992.

17 Interview with McCormick, June 11, 1992. In McCormick's case, an Irish-American who already had no love for the British Empire and felt admiration for Herbert Hoover mistrusted the idea of socialism, but was in some ways a natural convert to Williams's views.

18 Taped version of oral presentations by Lloyd Gardner, Thomas McCormick, and Martin J. Sklar at Williams Memorial Conference, Institute for Policy Studies; tapes kindly made available by Dina Copelman.

19 Taped oral presentations by Lloyd Gardner, et al.

20 Fred Harvey Harrington interview by Edward Rice-Maximin, June 12, 1992; and McCormick in Copelman/Clark Smith, 46–47.

21 McCormick in Copelman/Clark Smith, 46–47.

22 Gardner in Copelman/Clark Smith, 45.

23 Interview with McCormick; Letter from J. Quinn Brisbane, June 30, 1993. Brisbane was an undergraduate in Williams's 1959 foreign policy course, later a southern "Freedom School" teacher, and still later the 1992 candidate for President on the Socialist Party ticket.

24 Margaret Morley made this point especially in an interview with Paul Buhle, Oct. 20, 1993, and in Copelman/Clark Smith, 48–49. Morley was one of Williams's very last graduate students, and one of his few women students; interview with Alan Bogue, Apr. 30, 1993; relevant correspondence in the Fred Harvey Harrington Papers, State Historical Society of Wisconsin archives, includes Williams to Harrington, Nov. 7, 1961, complaining of placement procedures; and Harrington to Williams, Nov. 9, 1961, chiding Williams gently for his overeagerness.

25 See for example Williams, "Memorandum on Diplomatic History Jobs: 13 November 1961," in Fred Harvey Harrington Papers, State Historical Society of Wisconsin.

26 He also wrote Susman that he had been denied a leave by the Research Committee which deemed the manuscript for *Contours of American History* insufficiently important. Williams to Susman, Nov. 1, 1960, letter made available by Bea Susman.

27 Williams to Susman, July 22, 1961, letter made available by Bea Susman.

28 Williams Memo to William and Karla Robbins, n.d. [1985], made available by William Robbins.

29 The most lucid overview of *Tragedy* remains James Livingston's obituary and tribute, "Farewell to Intellectual Godfather William Appleman Williams," *In These Times*, Mar. 28-Apr. 3, 1990. This account owes much to him.

30 For more detailed summaries of *Tragedy*, see Berger's introduction to *A William Appleman Williams Reader*, 19–22, 116, 133, 156; and William Marina, "William Appleman Williams," *Dictionary of Literary Biography, Vol. 17, Twentieth-Century*

*American Historians* (Detroit, 1983), edited by Clyde N. Wilson, 452–54; A telephone interview with William Marina by Paul Buhle, Nov. 10,1993, did much to amplify the published discussion.

31 Williams, *The Tragedy of American Diplomacy* (Cleveland, 1959), 2–3.

32 Williams *Tragedy*, 292–93. This passage was also quoted in Anders Stephanson's unpublished paper, "The United States," prepared for the Conference on the Cold War, in honor of William Appleman Williams, University of Wisconsin, Madison, October, 1992.

33 Marilyn Young, in taped version of William Appleman Williams Memorial Conference, Institute for Policy Studies.

34 Williams, *Tragedy*, 13.

35 Williams, *Tragedy*, 305, 308–9.

36 William Appleman Williams," in *Visions of History*, 132–33.

37 Foster Rhea Dulles, *American Historical Review*, 44 (July, 1959), 1022–23.

38 Armin Rappaport, *Pacific Historical Review*, 28 (August, 1959), 288–90. Rappaport's appointment at Berkeley had been held up in 1949 by general suspicions. See Peter Novick, *That Noble Dream*, 330.

39 Gordon M. Craig, *International Journal*, 14 (Autumn, 1959), 317–18.

40 Adolf A. Berle, Jr., "A Few Questions for the Diplomatic Pouch," *New York Times Book Review*, Feb. 15, 1969.

41 Berle, Jr., "A Few Questions."

42 Bernard C. Borning, *The Political and Social Thought of Charles A. Beard* (Seattle, 1962), 228–35.

43 Lloyd Gardner, speech to symposium on Williams at the Institute for Policy Studies, April, 1990.

44 Telephone conversation with Henry W. Berger, Nov. 20, 1993; Berger set up this meeting on the spur of the moment.

45 Williams to Susman, Nov., 1959 and Mar. 22, 1959.

46 William Appleman Williams, *Visions of History*, 133.

47 Ibid.

48 Williams to Susman, Nov. 1, 1990, letter made available by Bea Susman.

49 Telephone interview with George Mosse by Paul Buhle, June 20, 1993.

50 These methods, adopted extensively in Central America toward the end of the 1960s, produced an ecological nightmare. See for instance, Daniel Farber, *Environment Under Fire: Imperialism and the Ecological Crisis in Central America* (New York, 1993), which indicates that Salvadorean and Nicaraguan peasants had twenty to thirty times the pesticide levels in their blood as North Americans, with cancer and other premature death rates racing upward, large "dead" zones disrupting wildlife migration, and a growing pattern of U.S. toxic dumping in these lands, ruled by U.S. client governments.

51 Sigmund Diamond reports that a high-ranking CIA officer, later a special assistant to Yale President Kingman Brewster and the organizer of a special "company" team to overthrow the elected Arbenz government of Guatemala, apparently

arranged a meeting with Schlesinger, Jr., to prepare the White Paper on the Bay of Pigs operation. Schlesinger, Jr., afterward sent a memorandum to President Kennedy praising the "skill and care" of the disguise so as to make the invasion appear "a spontaneous Cuban effort," and to deceive the public at home and elsewhere into believing "that the alleged CIA personnel were errant idealists or soldiers of fortune working on their own." Schlesinger, Jr., reportedly went on, "When lies must be told, they should be told by subordinate officials" in order to protect higher-ups from damaging revelations of past deceits. U.N. Ambassador Stevenson, who had believed himself a trusted and longstanding friend of Schlesinger, Jr.'s, was stunned to learn that he also had been deceived, duped into swearing U.S. innocence at a U.N. session. Diamond, *Compromised Campus: The Collaboration of Universities with the Intelligence Community, 1945–1955* (New York, 1992), n. 39, 335–36.

52 William Appleman Williams," *Visions of History*, 133.

53 Telephone interview with Corrinne Williams, July 9, 1994.

54 Williams to Lloyd Gardner, n.d., letter made available by Gardner.

55 William Appleman Williams, *Visions of History*, 133.

56 HUAC's harassment no doubt further encouraged certain Wisconsin state legislators to make noises about investigating Williams themselves. They backed down after the university took his side. Harrington had rightly guessed that Williams could take care of himself, and if not, Harrington would no doubt have thrown his full weight behind his student.

57 Henry W. Berger, introduction to *A William Appleman Williams Reader*, 23; William G. Robbins, "William Appleman Williams: 'Doing History is Best of All. No Regrets,'" in Lloyd Gardner, ed., *Redefining the Past: Essays in Diplomatic History in Honor of William Appleman Williams* (Corvallis, 1986), 13–14.

58 Quoted in James Weinstein and David Eakins, introduction to *For a New America: Essays in History and Politics from* Studies On the Left, *1959–1967* (New York, 1970), 8–9.

59 Weinstein and Eakins, introduction to *For a New America*, 10–11.

60 Interview with Saul Landau by Paul Buhle, Oct., 1980.

61 Williams to Susman, July 22, 1961, letter made available by Bea Susman. In 1961, the Socialist Club, evidently on a lark, invited Khrushchev and Castro to speak on campus. They were promptly slapped down by the Student Council for improper procedure.

62 Williams to Susman, July 22, 1961; James Weinstein, "Studies On the Left," and Saul Landau, "From the Labor Youth League to the Cuban Revolution," in *History and the New Left*, 113–117 and 107–112. See also Martin J. Sklar, *The United States as a Developing Country: Studies in U.S. History in the Progressive Era and the 1920s* (New York, 1992), especially 46, fn. 7 and 152, fn. 3, in which Sklar acknowledges Williams's influence and describes his contribution.

63 Andrew Hacker, "The Rebelling Young Scholars," *Commentary* 30 (November, 1960), 404, 407.

64 Hacker, "Rebelling Scholars," 408, 412.

65 C. Vann Woodward, "Comment on Genovese," *Studies On the Left* 6 (November-December, 1966), 36.

66 Peter Novick, *That Noble Dream*, 332.

67 Reinitz, *Irony and Consciousness*, 162–68.

68 Richard Collins, "The Originality Trap: Richard Hofstadter on Populism," *Journal of American History*, 76 (June, 1989), 150–67.

69 The most extreme attacks on Populism, however, were made at the hands of cold war militants like Oscar Handlin who treated Bryan's famed Cross of Gold speech as an anti-Semitic outburst, or Edward Shils's *The Torment of Secrecy*, a shallow polemic against Populism, as the source of McCarthyism from a writer himself notably close to McCarthyism's defenders at the CIA-sponsored *Encounter* magazine, co-edited by Irving Kristol. This was exactly the kind of case that raised questions about intellectual integrity and not only on the Left: intellectuals both eager to whip up hysteria for a clash of titans and simultaneously determined to attribute its least loveable qualities to ordinary Americans.

70 Interview with Merle Curti, Nov. 20, 1993. Curti was particularly sharp about the influence of the Trillings on Hofstadter. A sophisticated argument by Peter Novick attributes the anti-Populist shift in historiography to an ethnic variation: the Jewish scholars in Eastern schools had European ancestors and relatives threatened by uncontrolled crowds of gentiles. But this insight is not sophisticated enough. During the 1950s, a notably left-wing tradition of Jewish thought, communist and noncommunist, was under fierce attack from Jewish mainstream institutions and officials. A new Jewish radical generation had come through the war or grown up shortly afterward and would fill out radical historians' ranks, including many supporters and some severe critics of Williams. See the essays in *History and the New Left*, and see Howard Zinn, *You Can't Be Neutral On a Moving Train: A Personal History of Our Times* (Boston, 1994), Part Two. We also wish to thank Alfred Young for his own account of a young Jewish radical historian in this period.

71 This draws directly on the memory of U.S. history courses taught at the University of Illinois from 1962 to 1966 but is consistent with many undergraduates' experiences. Alfred Young has also been very helpful.

72 In a 1983 essay, "American Historians and the Democratic Idea," Irving Kristol makes this point clear, even disparaging his unreflective fellow neoconservative Boorstin for misunderstanding the conservatism of Edmund Burke. See Kristol, *Reflections of a Neo-Conservative* (New York, 1983), 105.

73 The evidence for this thick pattern of friendship and collaboration is seen best in the Richard Hofstadter Papers, Special Collections, Columbia University. Here, for instance, Kristol, Lipset, and Riesman, among others, exchange ideas clearly previewing the corporate-funded neoconservatism that Kristol would personally champion. See e.g., Riesman's railing at C. Wright Mills and insisting as late as 1964 that "Big Business" could not possibly be the enemy of freedom because intelligent corporations allowed ample room for individuality. Riesman to Hofstadter,

Dec. 7, 1964. This account also owes a great deal to the interpretations by Reinitz, *Irony and Consciousness*; and to David W. Noble, "William Appleman Williams and the Crisis of Public History," in *Redefining the Past*, 45–62.

74 Robert M. Collins, "The Originality Trap," 166. The later Hofstadter should thus be contrasted with the later S. M. Lipset, Irving Kristol, or Daniel Boorstin. Interestingly, Williams was later a casual friend of the writer Harvey Swados, in turn brother-in-law of Hofstadter. Had the latter lived, it is more than possible that a dialogue between Williams and Hofstadter would have illuminated large territories.

75 William Appleman Williams, "The Age of Reforming History," *Nation*, 182 (June 30, 1956), 552–54.

76 See Alan Wald, *The New York Intellectuals* (New York, 1986), Part III, Ch. 9–11.

77 A most remarkable text in this regard from a non-historian influential on historians is Riesman, *Individualism Reconsidered and Other Essays* (Glencoe, 1954). The much admired author of *The Lonely Crowd* considered himself a pacifist and in that sense a dissident from the arms race, but his description of dissenters and radicals as alienated outsiders was anything but complimentary. More than anyone else except perhaps his associates Daniel Bell and Nathan Glazer, his mixture of psychological, anthropological, and sociological influences nearly reversed the emphasis of liberal writers from the New Deal and World War II years. See also Thomas L. Hartshorn, *The Distorted Image: Changing Conceptions of the American Character Since Turner* (Cleveland, 1968).

78 See Mari Jo Buhle and Paul Buhle, "The New Labor History at the Cultural Crossroads," *Journal of American History*, 75 (June, 1988), 137–41.

79 Walter P. Webb, *The Great Frontier* (Lincoln, 1952). See also Necah Stewart Furman, *Walter Prescott Webb: His Life and Impact* (Albuquerque, 1976), especially Ch. 10–12.

80 These phenomena were not entirely unrelated. Arthur Schlesinger, Jr., was easily the most unremitting liberal critic of the Hollywood Blacklistees, those writers, directors, actors, and technicians driven out of the movie business. See Dalton Trumbo's witty response to Schlesinger, Jr.'s *Look* magazine attacks on the Blacklistees, in Trumbo, *Additional Dialogue* (New York, 1971), 124.

81 Riesman, *Individualism Reconsidered*, 476–77.

82 Phone interview with Carl Marzani by Paul Buhle, Oct. 1, 1994. Marzani, a founder of the little Prometheus Books, noted that he had also offered to publish any of Williams's works which could not be published elsewhere.

83 See James Livingston, "Farewell."

84 Livingston, "Farewell."

85 Martin J. Sklar, "Dear Board Members," Nov. 19, 1960. Studies On the Left Papers, State Historical Society of Wisconsin.

86 Williams previewed this section of *Contours* with "The Age of Mercantilism: An Interpretation of the American Political Economy, 1763 to 1828," *William*

*and Mary Quarterly*, 15 (October, 1958), 419–37; and with "Samuel Adams: Calvinist, Mercantilist, Revolutionary," *Studies On the Left*, I (Winter, 1960), 47–57.

87 See Henry W. Berger's comments on *Contours* in his various introductions to *A William Appleman Williams Reader*, 24–26, 162, 221, 239.

88 Apart from the parallel impulse of British historian E. P. Thompson to recuperate William Morris through an expansive biography, a handful of Socialist writers sought to reinterpret the legacy of the Middle Ages. Among them, C. L. R. James's essay, "Dialectical Materialism and the Fate of Humanity," published obscurely in the later 1940s, reprinted by *Radical America* as a pamphlet in 1971 and finally in James, *Spheres of Existence: Selected Writings* (London, 1980), 70–105, is closest to Williams's intent.

89 Williams to Warren Susman, Mar. 10, 1958. Letter made available by Bea Susman.

90 William Appleman Williams, *Contours of American History* (Cleveland, 1961), 95–96.

91 See Paul Buhle, "Marxist Historiography, 1900–1940," *Radical America*, IV (December, 1970), 5–36; this argument is simplified and refined in Buhle's "Marxism and Its Critics," in Mary Kupiec Cayton, Elliott J. Gorn and Peter W. Williams, eds., *Encyclopedia of Social History* I (New York, 1993), 371–86.

92 Williams, *Contours*, 137.

93 Williams, *Contours*, 136–48.

94 A telling comparison on questions of Indian policy and slaves can be made between Schlesinger, Jr.'s Pulitzer Prize–winning *The Age of Jackson* (Boston, 1945), and a recent authoritative textbook, *Out of Many* (Engelwood Cliffs, 1994), by John Mack Faragher, Mari Jo Buhle, Daniel Czitrom, and Susan H. Armitage, especially 281–84.

95 Wilson's role in gutting parklands was little discussed by historians until a major reevaluation of Western history. Under Wilson, the Olympic Natural Monument lost half its land and the Rocky Mountain National Park was robbed of two-thirds of its original planned territory. Happily, Stephen Mather, an early Sierra Club member, created the National Park Service, lobbying for better care of national parks and using his own money to buy lands and pay staff. Without Mather's determination, Wilson's misrule would have been far more destructive. See Richard White, *"It's Your Misfortune and None of My Own": A New History of the American West* (Norman, 1991), 413–15. White's book was dedicated to Vernon Carstensen, collaborator of Merle Curti's in the multi-volume history of the University of Wisconsin and yet another favorite Madisonian scholar.

96 Williams had set out the outlines of "corporatism" in several of the essays he had written for the *Nation*, but even in *Contours*, never fully elaborated his conceptualization. Thomas McCormick, whose wife was typing the manuscript, says that Williams was "running out of steam" at this point in the book. Interview with McCormick by Edward Rice-Maximin, June 11, 1992.

97 The most important socialist theorists were William English Walling and Louis C. Fraina. See Walling, *Progressivism and After* (New York, 1914), the most cogent of his volumes, and Louis C. Fraina, *Revolutionary Socialism* (New York, 1918), for the two best primary sources; See also Paul Buhle, *A Dreamer's Paradise Lost: Louis C. Fraina/Lewis Corey, 1892–1953* (Atlantic Highlands, N.J., 1995) for a summary and discussion of the dialogue during the 1910s.

98 Anders Stephanson, "The United States," unpublished paper delivered at a Madison, Wisconsin, conference on the cold war, October, 1991. Thanks to Stephanson for lending us a copy of this address.

99 Ronald Radosh, "The Corporate Ideology of American Labor Leaders from Gompers to Hillman," *Studies On the left*, reprinted in *For a New America* (New York, 1970), 125–52.

100 James Weinstein, "Gompers and the New Liberalism, 1900–1909," *For a New America*, 101–14.

101 Martin J. Sklar, "Woodrow Wilson and the Political Economy of Modern United States Liberalism," *For a New America*, 46–100. This essay, the longest essay published in *Studies* and in *For a New America*, was a chapter from Sklar's MA thesis.

102 See Chapter 7.

103 Michael Meeropol and Gerald Markowitz, "Neighborhood Politics," in *History and the New Left*, 211.

104 See Casey M. Blake, *Beloved Community: The Cultural Criticism of Randolph Bourne, Van Wyck Brooks, Waldo Frank and Lewis Mumford* (Chapel Hill, 1990).

105 Williams, *Contours*, 472–73.

106 Williams, *Contours*, 491. As noted by Herbert Aptheker, "American Development and Ruling-Class Ideology," *Studies On the Left*, III (1962), 97.

107 *Selected Correspondence of Karl Marx and Frederick Engels,* (Moscow, 1955), 300. Thanks to Timothy Messer-Kruse for pointing out this passage. A section of the *Communist Manifesto* entitled "Reactionary Socialism—Feudal Socialism," indeed attributes to the anachronistic aristocrats a resistance which is "half lamentation, half lampoon," containing a "bitter, witty, and incisive criticism," striking the bourgeoisie "to the very heart's core." Karl Marx and Frederick Engels, *The Communist Manifesto* (New York, 1961), 49.

108 Ian Tyrrell, *The Absent Marx: Class Analysis and Liberal History in Twentieth-Century America* (Westport, 1986), 138–39. Unfortunately, Tyrrell's own understanding is severely limited by a certain prejudice but even more by an extremely vague notion of "New Left history" and a remarkable underuse of sources in which young historians sought to overcome Williams's weaknesses. See Chapters 5 and 6, and Jon Wiener's more reliable if brief account, "Radical Historians and the Crisis in American History, 1959–1980," *Journal of American History*, 76 (September, 1989), 399–434.

109 See for instance the "Introduction" by Lawrence Krader to *The Ethnological Notebooks of Karl Marx* (Assan, Netherlands, 1972), edited by Lawrence Krader.

110 William A. Williams to Lloyd Gardner, n.d. [1986].

111 Handlin, *Mississippi Valley Historical Review*, 68 (Mar., 1962), 743–45.

112 John Higham, "Communications," *Mississippi Valley Historical Review*, 49 (September, 1962), 407–08.

113 John Higham, "The Contours of William A. Williams," *Studies On the Left I* (Spring, 1960), 74–75.

114 John Higham, "Communications," 408.

115 John Braeman, *American Political Science Review*, 56 (December, 1963), 1005–06.

116 John C. Malin, *South Atlantic Quarterly*, 61 (Winter, 1962), 123–24. In an interview with Paul Buhle, Oct. 20, 1993, Alan Bogue described the conference in Kansas (in which Bogue first encountered Williams), hosted by a conservative foundation close to Malin, but featuring a Williams paper.

117 Letter from David Noble to Paul Buhle, May, 1992.

118 Aptheker, "American Development," 97.

119 Ibid. 97–105.

120 Conversation from c.1986 reported by Jim Murray to Paul Buhle, June 1994.

121 "E. P. Thompson," in MARHO, *Visions of History* (New York, 1983), 22. Fortunately for Thompson, the conversation was held at close range, with people he could see regularly.

122 Manning Marable, Thomas McCormick, and Lloyd Gardner, in Copelman/Clark Smith, 59–61.

123 James Weinstein, "The Need for a Socialist Party," *Studies On the Left*, VII (Jan-Feb., 1967), reprinted in *For a New America* (New York, 1970), 338. See the parallel comments on Williams's importance in Eugene Genovese, "Legacy of Slavery and Roots of Black Nationalism," *Studies On the Left*, VI (Nov.-Dec., 1966), reprinted in *For a New America*, 419.

124 Maurice Isserman, *If I Had a Hammer: The Death of the Old Left and the Birth of the New Left* (New York, 1987), 109.

125 James Weinstein, "Studies On the Left," in *History and the New Left*, 117.

126 William Appleman Williams, *The United States, Castro and Cuba* (New York, 1962), 1.

127 Williams noted that Draper's anti-Castro thesis was quickly borrowed by cold war strategists and its perspectives adopted as the "central theme" of the State Department's White Paper of April, 1961. Many believed that the counter-strategy encouraged massive repression, not excluding ethnocide of troublesome indigenous peoples. Williams, *The United States, Castro and Cuba*, 70, 71.

128 Quoted in Williams, *The United States, Cuba, and Castro*, 15.

129 A communication from Alan Wald to Theodore Draper, July 9, 1987, made available to Paul Buhle, cites numerous interviews with former Communists recalling Draper as "the Commissar" of the literary left in the later 1930s, demanding loyal support of American intellectuals to Stalin's view on the Moscow Trials, attacking critics of those trials in the pages of the *New Masses* and slurring them as Nazi-like in their attack upon the Soviet Union. We are grateful to Wald for mak-

ing this document available. See Alan Wald, "Search for a Method: Recent Histories of American Communism," *Radical History Review,* 61 (Winter, 1995), n. 11.

130 Theodore Draper, "The Strange Case of Professor Williams," *New Leader,* 46 (Apr. 29, 1963), 13–19. Draper's earlier attacks on the Cuban Revolution had appeared in the British-based *Encounter,* for much of the 1950s a tainted outlet of CIA funds. The *New Leader* had its own Latin American story. Daniel James, a *New Leader* editor, had written in 1954 a cold war propaganda tract, *Red Design on the Americas,* and gone on a promotional tour for it. Responsible historians later confirmed the devastating U.S. role and the dissimulation involved in the press cover-up. See Walter LaFeber, *Inevitable Revolutions: The United States in Central America* (New York, 1983 edition), 113–27; and Van Gosse, *Where the Boys Are: Cuba, Cold War America and the Making of a New Left* (London, 1993), Ch. 2. Under restored U.S. hegemony and with American military training for officers, subsequent Guatemalan governments became notorious for human rights abuses in general and the premeditated slaughter of Indians in particular.

131 Williams's response finally appeared in *Studies On the Left* despite the private misgivings of some editors that Williams had missed the chance to meet Draper flatly and to quash his disingenuity. See William A. Williams, "Historiography and Revolution: The Case of Cuba, A Commentary on a Polemic by Theodore Draper," *Studies On the Left,* 3 (Summer, 1963), 78–102. See Williams's letters to Myron Kolatch, Executive Editor of the *New Leader,* May 6, 18, 1963, *Studies On the Left* Papers, State Historical Society of Wisconsin.

132 Eleanor Hakim to Martin Sklar, Oct. 4, 1960. *Studies On the Left* Papers, State Historical Society of Wisconsin.

133 See "Stanley" [Aronowitz] to Board Members, n.d. [1965], ibid. Aronowitz scribbled at the bottom of his letter, "either we move in these directions or I'm afraid the magazine will continue to decline in prestige and readership." See also Eleanor Hakim's retrospective essay "The Tragedy of Hans Gerth," in Buhle, ed., *History and the New Left,* 252–63, on the general decline of interest in theory after the early *Studies* days.

134 Williams to Lloyd Gardner and Warren Susman, Nov., 1964. Around the same time, he described family problems as "so damn enervating that I feel some times as though I would like just to go quietly to sleep[,] I am so weary." Williams to Gardner, n.d. These letters kindly loaned by Lloyd Gardner.

135 Interview with Kyenne Williams, June 9, 1993.

## CHAPTER 5

1 One of the few written accounts of Goldberg, in Tom Bates, *Rads* (New York, 1992), is a travesty, treating him as a radical pied piper corrupting naive midwestern youth. For a partial antidote, see Ron McCrea and Dave Wagner, "Harvey Goldberg," in *History and the New Left,* 241–45.

2 Williams, Harvey Goldberg Lecture, Madison, 1989, Williams Papers. Goldberg destroyed his personal papers, but the Goldberg Center in Madison continues to keep his memory alive. We wish to acknowledge their sponsorship of a lecture by Paul Buhle on the late historian E. P. Thompson, in November 1993, during which research and interviews on Williams could be conducted.

3 See, e.g., Paul Breines, "The Mosse Milieu," and McCrea and Wagner, "Harvey Goldberg," *History and the New Left*, 246–51 and 241–45, respectively.

4 Letter from George Mosse to Paul Buhle, Sept. 20, 1993, stressed the signal importance of two volumes loaned to Williams in 1962, *The Church and the Working Classes* and *Through the Lord's Body*, both conveying a British "incarnational theoogy" with a heavy emphasis on a highly structured symbolic religious service. See also George Mosse, "New Left Intellectuals," in *History and the New Left*, 234.

5 Williams to Merle Curti, Oct. 5, 1964, Curti Papers, State Historical Society of Wisconsin.

6 Memo to William and Karla Robbins, n.d. [1985], Williams Papers.

7 For readings of Bellamy, see e.g., Daphne Patai, ed., *Looking Backward, 1988–1888: Essays on Edward Bellamy* (Amherst, 1988); Csaba Toth, "Utopianism as Americanism," *American Quarterly*, 45 (December, 1993), 649–58; and Franklin Rosemont, "Edward Bellamy," in *Surrealism and its Popular Accomplices* (San Francisco, 1982), edited by Franklin Rosemont, 6–16.

8 Williams, *The Great Evasion* (Chicago, 1963), 12, 20.

9 Williams, *Great Evasion*, 132.

10 Staughton Lynd, *Intellectual Origins of American Radicalism* (New York, 1968).

11 Williams, *Great Evasion*, 167.

12 Williams, *Great Evasion*, back cover.

13 Williams, *Great Evasion*, 142.

14 Williams, *Great Evasion*, 175–76.

15 Williams, *Great Evasion*, 111–13.

16 See Susman's "'Personality' and the Making of Twentieth-Century Culture," in Warren Susman, *Culture as History: The Transformation of American Society in the Twentieth Century* (New York, 1982), 271–86.

17 Max Horkheimer, "Authority and the Family," in *The Family: Its Function and Destiny* (New York, 1949), Ruth Nanda Anshen, ed., 367.

18 There was one vitally important exception: theories of Black poverty, attributed by Daniel Patrick Moynihan among many others to the African American matriarchy, gained new popularity among liberals and conservatives toward the end of the 1960s. Later, of course, Christopher Lasch would revive and restate the Horkheimer critique in a sustained polemic against feminism. See Chapter 6.

19 Robert Heilbroner, "Marx and the American Economy," *New York Review of Books*, 3 (Jan. 14, 1965), 21–22.

20 Floyd A. Cave, *American Political Science Review*, 60 (Jan., 1966), 127.

21 Milton Cantor, "Inheritors of the Faith, "*Nation*, 120 (Apr. 5, 1965), 366–68.

22 Eugene D. Genovese, "William Appleman Williams on Marx and America," *Studies on the Left*, 6 (Jan-Feb., 1966), 70–89. Among other sympathetic views of the book, perhaps the most insightful was written by a libertarian conservative: William Marina's "William Appleman Williams."

23 George Mosse, "New Left Intellectuals," 234.

24 Susman, "'Personality,'" 284–85.

25 See Christopher Lasch, *Haven in a Heartless World* (New York, 1977), Ch. 7.

26 Kirkpatrick Sale, *SDS* (New York, 1973), 188–89; Carl Oglesby, *Containment and Change* (New York, 1967).

27 Indeed, another Madison graduate student of the time, Ellis Hawley, would produce the most impressive theoretical analysis of consensual corporatism. At a panel of the Organization of American Historians in 1994, Hawley and Sklar shared the platform, arguing that contemporary corporatism as the governing system of the nation had evolved into something close to a merger of traditional Socialist and capitalist ideals. Hawley had always held beliefs close to what might be described as a traditional democratic-liberal pluralism; Sklar had evolved toward it, while continuing to insist upon the value of Williams's ideas. See his later essays *The United States as a Developing Country* (Cambridge, 1992), especially "The Corporate Reconstruction of American Capitalism: A Note on the Capitalism-Socialism Mix in U.S. and World Development," 209–18. See also Ellis Hawley, "The Discovery and Study of a 'Corporate Liberalism,'" *Business History Review*, 52 (Autumn, 1978), and Hawley, *The Great War and the Search for a Modern Order: A History of the American People and Their Institutions, 1917–1933* (New York, 1979), 91–105.

28 Williams, "Our Leaders are following the Wrong Rainbow," Apr. 1, 1965, reprinted in Louis Menashe and Ronald Radosh, editors, *Teach-Ins, USA: Reports, Opinions, Documents* (New York, 1967), 45–53.

29 "Williams on Policy for U.S. Radicals," *National Guardian*, Nov. 27, 1965. He claimed, in private correspondence, that the response in mail to him had been overwhelmingly positive.

30 The first Socialist Scholars Conference meeting was held in September 1965, with a steering committee which included Eugene Genovese, *Monthly Review*'s Paul Sweezy, and two *Studies on the Left* editors, James Weinstein and James O'Connor. See "1,000 Attend Socialist Scholars Meeting in New York," *National Guardian*, Sept. 18, 1965.

31 See Stuart Ewen, "The Intellectual New Left," in *History and the New Left*, 178–82.

32 Researchers pointed especially to the Land Tenure Center and to the School for Workers, apart from the various projects funded by military sources directly or indirectly.

33 An extremely misleading account has been offered of the day's events by *Rads*, evidently for the purpose of discrediting war protesters by crediting the club-swinging police as hardworking proletarians. Fire fighters, soon drawn to the side of the campus and community progressives by a mutual hostility toward the thuggish spe-

cial squad which was called out against demonstrators, were remarkably slow a few years later to answer a call to quell an accidentally exploded gas grenade in the basement of the police department. With major changes in city government instituted by the administration of a former peace demonstrator, Paul Soglin, a new, liberal élan and professionalization entered the police force and the hardliners were marginalized. See "Introduction" to *History and the New Left* for a more accurate version of the Dow events.

34 This article was reprinted in many places but see Nan Robertson, "Students Angry, but Frustrated," *Sunday Oregonian*, Nov. 26, 1967.

35 This recollection is a collective one, but depends primarily upon the memory of Paul Buhle, one of those who handed out the bananas in Williams's class. It may be worthwhile to add that this technique or theatrical stroke was entirely spontaneous on the part of several graduate students, none knowing the others would do the same. There was not a hint of resentment in it, nor did Williams take it as such.

36 Letter from Michael Meeropol, June 20, 1994.

37 We wish to thank Michael Hirsch, who attended the Alternative University in New York, for these recollections.

38 This recounts a conversation between Williams and Paul Buhle, the editor of *Radical America*, in November 1967, scarcely a month after the Dow Demonstration, in which Madison SDSers had played a prominent if by no means leadership role. *Radical America* went on, in later years, to emerge as a major voice of Socialist feminism and a Socialist version of gay liberation. Its leading editor of the 1970s, historian Linda Gordon, returned to Madison and became Vilas Professor. In some sense, then, the sceptre had almost literally been passed from hand to hand.

39 Our gratitude to Alfred Young for making this suggestion.

40 Williams to Lloyd Gardner, January, 1966, letter donated by Lloyd Gardner.

41 Williams to Gardner; and telephone interview with Corrinne Williams, July 11, 1994.

42 Interview with Phyllis Weiss by Paul Buhle, November 18, 1992.

43 Memo to William and Karla Robbins, 1985.

44 Williams, "An American Socialist Community?", *Liberation*, June, 1969, reprinted in William Appleman Williams, *History as a Way of Learning* (New York, 1972), 383–90.

45 Williams, *History as a Way*, 388.

46 Williams, *History as a Way*, 389.

47 The attempt to pass a ballot measure in Madison against the war in Vietnam brought just this hostility. See Michael Meeropol and Gerald Markowitz, "Neighborhood Politics," in *History and the New Left*, 214–15.

48 Tom Bates makes the very serious and unfounded suggestion, in *Reds*, that Harvey Goldberg in some way incited this traumatic event, resulting in the death of a researcher. Williams never thought so. And those who knew the youngsters personally, as Paul Buhle did Leo F. Burt in a discussion section for a U.S. History course, dismiss the charge out of hand.

49 Kevin Phillips, *The Emerging Republican Majority* (New York, 1969). Decades later, Phillips would offer real wisdom which sounded very much like echos of Williams's own views.

50 This account owes considerable to Michael Meeropol, "W. A. Williams's Historiography," *Radical America*, IV (Aug. 1970), 29–49.

51 This point is made best by James Livingston, "Farewell to Intellectual Godfather William Appleman Williams," *In These Times*, Mar. 28-Apr. 3, 1990.

52 Other devotees of LaFollette would answer plausibly that he had undergone a radicalization on questions of Empire. See for instance R. David Myers, "Robert M. La Follette," in Mari Jo Buhle, Paul Buhle and Harvey J. Kaye, eds., *The American Radical* (New York, 1994), 159–66.

53 Peter Novick has pointed out that Williams long believed the real truth and not just a relativistic truth could be told through a sufficiently determined personal effort. See *That Noble Dream*, 423.

54 Williams, *Roots of the Modern American Empire*, 452.

55 Irving Howe, "The New 'Confrontation Politics' is a Dangerous Game, "*New York Times Magazine*, Oct. 20, 1968, 27–29, 133–39; and "Political Terrorism: Hysteria on the Left," *New York Times Magazine*, Apr. 12, 1970, 25–27, 124–28. Alan Wald incisively describes this aspect of Howe's work and the drift of the New York Intellectuals toward neoconservativsm in Ch. 10–11 of his *The New York Intellectuals: The Rise and Decline of the Anti-Stalinist Left From the 1930s to the 1980s* (Chapel Hill, 1987).

56 Christopher Lehmann-Haupt, "Down on the Farm," *New York Times*, Nov. 24, 1969; John William Ward, "Does the Study of the Past Have a Future?" *New York Times Book Review*, Feb. 22, 1970, 10, 12, 14.

57 Carl Degler, *American Historical Review*, 75 (October, 1970), 172–74. Writing almost twenty years later on the influence of radical history on the profession, Degler warned against "celebratory" discussions, insisted that evidence and not opinion convinced true historians, and described only a small handful of radical scholars as worthy of mention; Williams was not among them, proving once more that old grudges die hard. He also freely admitted that he had advised against the publication of the essay by Jon Wiener describing the rise of the Williams-influenced trend. See Carl Degler, "What Crisis, Jon?" *Journal of American History*, 76 (Sept., 1989), 467–70.

58 Gretchen Kreuter, *Minnesota History*, 42 (Summer, 1971), 235–36; David M. Pletcher, *Journal of American History*, 57 (June, 1970), 172–74.

59 J. R. T. Hughes, *Business History Review*, 44 (Winter, 1970), 567–68. The more progressive Lewis E. Hill found *Roots* a "bold new approach to the interpretation of American economic development and growth," written with both creativity and courage.

60 Michael Harrington, "America, II," *Partisan Review*, 37 (1970), 498–505. Harrington himself later described his opposition to the New Left in terms strikingly like those used by Williams, while insisting upon supporting Hubert

Humphrey and while regretting the dramatic shift of his political mentors and long-term labor allies away from George McGovern into the Nixon camp. Breaking off from this political tendency, he went on to head the Democratic Socialists Organizing Committee (DSOC) and later Democratic Socialists of America (DSA), which vehemently opposed U.S. guidance and funding of the "dirty wars" in Central America and Africa. See Michael Harrington, *Fragments of the Century* (New York, 1973), 223–25, and Robert Gorman, "Michael Harrington," in *The American Radical*, 337–44.

61 Williams, Letters column, "Loose Lips," *In These Times*, Oct. 18-24, 1989.

62 Ironically, former Williams student Ronald Radosh had become by the 1990s a frequent contributor to *Partisan Review*, still run by the now elderly cold warrior William Phillips.

63 Howard Zinn, "America, II," 519–27.

64 Howard Zinn, *You Can't Be Neutral on a Moving Train: A Personal History of Our Times* (Boston, 1994), Ch. 1-2.

65 Arthur Schlesinger, Jr., "America II," 505–19.

66 Williams, "America II," *Partisan Review*, 38 (1971), 67–78. Schlesinger, Jr., and Harrington offered brief rejoinders, 78–83.

67 Richard Leopold, Reviews, *Pacific Historical Review*, 39 (August, 1970), 307–8.

68 Lawrence Goodwyn, *Democratic Promise: The Populist Movement in America* (New York, 1976), xi, xiii, xv. For a potpourri of various scholarly views on Populism, see William F. Holmes, ed., *American Populism* (Lexington, 1994). This edition does not excerpt from Williams's writing, and includes only a passage from Hofstadter among the 1950s "School" of anti-Populists. The rest of the essays take up Populism from various aspects, but none recycles the old charges of anti-Semitism and irrationalism. The discussion had simply moved onward.

69 Goodwin, *Democratic Promise*, 532.

70 Williams, *Roots*, xvii.

71 Richard W. Van Alstyne, "Beyond the Last Frontier," *Nation*, 210, Feb. 23, 1970, 214–15; Michael Meeropol, "William A. Williams's Historiography,"and James P. O'Brien,"Comment," in *Radical America*, 4 (Aug., 1970), 29–49 and 50–53. James O'Brien, et. al., "New Left Historians of the 1960s," *Radical America*, IV, (Nov.-Dec., 1970), 82–83.

72 Telephone interview with Corrinne Williams, July 11, 1994.

73 Williams, *Americans in a Changing World*, 3.


## CHAPTER 6

1 Outline for "A Historian Reflects Upon His Memories," n.d., Williams Papers.

2 Clifford Solway, "Turning History Upside Down," *Saturday Review*, June 20, 1970, 62.

3 "Eugene Genovese: The Uncommon Marxist," *Intellectual Digest* (October, 1970), 79.

4 Williams, *Some Presidents: Wilson to Nixon* (New York, 1970), 26.

5 Williams, *Some Presidents*, 30, 31. Italics added.

6 Williams, *Some Presidents*, 39.

7 Williams, *Some Presidents*, 72.

8 Williams, *Some Presidents*, 77.

9 Williams, *Some Presidents*, 80–81.

10 Howard Zinn, a bombadier, came close but rarely wrote about his experiences in his historical studies. At a guess, most other World War II veterans-turned-historians remained Truman or Kennedy Democrats.

11 Williams, *Some Presidents*, 83.

12 Williams, *Some Presidents*, 84.

13 Williams, *Some Presidents*, 102.

14 Williams, *Some Presidents*, 103.

15 Williams, *Some Presidents*, 87.

16 Indeed, he urges the reader to "try to be a historian. Or if you (like me) prefer the idiom of Thucydides, try to be a citizen." Williams, *Some Presidents*, 84.

17 Richard Hofstadter, *The Progressive Historians: Turner, Beard, Parrington* (New York, 1968), 453. Quoted from Jonathan Wiener, "Radical Historians and the Crisis in American History," *Journal of American History*, 76 (September, 1989), 429.

18 Wiener, "Radical Historians," 430–31.

19 Peter Novick, *That Noble Dream* (Cambridge, 1988), 447–49.

20 Arthur M. Schlesinger, Jr., *New York Review of Books*, 7 (October 20, 1966), 37.

21 John Leo, "Some Scholars, Reassessing Cold War, Blame U.S.," *New York Times*, Sept. 24, 1967, 33.

22 Arthur M. Schlesinger, Jr., "Origins of the Cold War," *Foreign Affairs*, 46 (October, 1967), 22–52, especially 22–23 and 45–52. In grudging praise, Schlesinger, Jr., found Williams the "most subtle and ingenious" of the revisionists.

23 Christopher Lasch, "The Cold War Revisited and Re-Visioned," *New York Times Magazine*, Jan. 14, 1968, 26ff, especially 27, 51, 59.

24 H. Stuart Hughes, "The Second Year of the Cold War: A Memoir and an Anticipation," *Commentary*, 48 (August, 1969), 27–32. Hughes characteristically hardened his positions as well in the post–Vietnam War era, insisting only a few years later that one could never possibly trust a Stalin, who was "only a few degrees less loathsome than Hitler," in Hughes, "Cold War and Detente," *New York Review of Books*, 23 (Feb. 19, 1976), 3–6.

25 Martin Diamond devotes several illuminating chapters to the intelligence agencies' influence, secret and open, upon Harvard and Yale, and the quiet collaboration of such figures as Talcott Parsons in the process. See *Compromised Campus: The Collaboration of Universities with the Intelligence Community, 1945–1955* (New York, 1992).

26 Noted by a hostile critic in a heavily funded conservative magazine for under-graduates: Edward S. Shapiro, "Responsibility for the Cold War: A Bibliographical Review," *Intercollegiate Review*, 23 (Winter 1976-77), 113–20, especially 113–14.

27 A. Kent MacDougall, "Looking Back: Radical Historians Get Growing Following, Despite 'Myths' of Past," *Wall Street Journal*, Oct. 20, 1971.

28 *Hearings Before the Subcommittee on Europe of the Committee on Foreign Affairs, House of Representatives, Ninety Second Congress, First Session* (Washington, 1971), 9–10.

29 *Hearings Before Subcommittee*, 18–19. Williams added that Henry Wallace's experience was "classic." He was "disparaged as a mind and . . . labeled as a tool of the communists. He didn't happen to be guilty on either count," 18. Of course, Schlesinger, Jr., had been guilty of the labeling. Foreign relations (and Vietnam War) hardliner Adam Ulam disparaged Williams's views on the early cold war, warning against "this compulsive guilt feeling which we seem to have been experiencing in our national life," 22.

30 *Hearings Before Subcommittee*, 28, 44.

31 Daniel M. Smith, "The New Left and the Cold War," *Denver Quarterly*, 4 (Winter, 1970), 788; Charles S. Maier, "Revisionism and the Interpretation of Cold War Origins," *Perspectives in American History*, 4 (1970), 313–47, especially 338–39, 345–47.

32 Fred Warner Nal and Bruce D. Hamlet, "The Never-Never Land of International Relations," *International Studies Quarterly*, 13 (Sept, 1969), 281–305, especially 304–5. See also Willard L. Hogeboom, "The Cold War and Revisionist Historiography," *Social Studies*, 61 (December, 1970), 314–18.

33 Lloyd C. Gardner, Arthur M. Schlesinger, Jr., and Hans J. Morgenthau, *The Origins of the Cold War* (Waltham, Mass, 1970), 105–9, 115–16.

34 Quoted in Steve Gillon, *Politics and Vision: The ADA and American Liberalism, 1947–1985* (New York, 1987), 196. Ironically for Williams's personal sympathies, as Gillon notes, the ADA cold war hardliners around the AFL-CIO, like Gus Tyler, were more sympathetic to Johnson, while the "Dump Johnson" faction of the ADA, including Schlesinger Jr., hailed back to the Kennedy years. As usual, no branch of liberalism held much for Williams.

35 Oscar Handlin, "'Revision' Perverts 27-Year U.S. Policy," *Freedom At Issue*, 15 (Sept.-Oct., 1972), 2. This was a publication of the New Right.

36 Walter Laqueur, "Rewriting History," *Commentary*, 55 (March, 1974), 53–63.

37 Arthur M. Schlesinger, Jr., "Was the Cold War Really Necessary?" *Wall Street Journal*, Nov. 30, 1972. See also his effort to redefine terms and defend what the 1940s generation called "anti-Stalinism" in "Communication," *American Historical Review*, 78 (February, 1973), 190–91. This view was ironic or misleading in that Schlesinger, Jr., had in fact rarely used the phrase "Stalinists"—in those days large-ly a Trotskyist term to differentiate *real* Leninism from the current Russian vari-ety—preferring to attack Russian "Communists" and their American counterparts.

38 Interview with David Shetzline, n.d. [1976], Williams Papers. Thomas McCormick interview, June 11, 1992.

39 A synopsis of the book was published in a conservative journal (and warmly prefaced by Oscar Handlin), as "Cold War Revisionism: Abusing History," *Freedom at Issue*, 15 (Sept.-Oct., 1972), 3–6, 16–19. See also Maddox's follow-up, "Revisionism and the Liberal Historians," *Freedom at Issue*, 19 (May-June, 1973), 19–21.

40 Jack Chatfield, "Refuting Gauguinism," *National Review*, 17 (August, 1973), 904–5; Clare Z. Cafey, "Uncovering an Academic Watergate," *Intercollegiate Review*, 9 (Winter, 1973-74), 51–53; Francis Lowenheim, "Who Started It? You Did! Who says So? We do! Who Are You?" *New York Times Book Review*, June 17, 1973, 6–7.

41 Lowenheim, "Who Started It?" 8, 10.

42 Richard H. Miller, "A Verbal Mugging," *Commonweal*, 98 (August 24, 1973), 457–58. Miller also reviewed Maddox's book for *Science & Society*, 38 (Spring, 1974), 90–91. Ronald Radosh, one of Williams's most devoted students and later a hostile critic, lambasted Maddox in "Hot War with the 'New Left,'" *Nation*, 217 (July 2, 1973), 55–58.

43 Ronald Steel, "The Good Old Days," *New York Review of Books*, 20 (June 14, 1973), 33–36, a review of several volumes.

44 Norman A. Graebner, *Pacific Historical Review*, 43 (February, 1974), 183–89; Robert D. Schulzinger, "Moderation in Pursuit of Truth is No Virtue; Extremism in Defense of Moderation is a Vice," *American Quarterly*, 27 (May, 1975), 222–36, a review of several books. See also Thomas A. Krueger, "New Left Revisionists and Their Critics," *Reviews in American History* (December, 1973), 463–70; Richard W. Leopold, *Journal of American History*, 643 (March, 1974), 1183–85.

45 Warren F. Kimball, "The Cold War Warmed Over," *American Historical Review*, 79 (October, 1974), 1119–36, especially 1128–34.

46 Oscar Handlin, *Truth in History* (Cambridge, 1979), 156–57; Robert Maddox, "The Rise and Fall of Cold War Revisionism," *Historian*, 66 (May, 1984), especially 421–24; and Maddox, "Diplomatic Blunders," *Society*, 23 (March, 1986), 9–10.

47 Williams, "Confessions of an Intransigent Revisionist," reprinted from *Socialist Review*, 1973, into *A William Appleman Williams Reader* (Chicago, 1993), 337–39.

48 Williams, "Confessions," 339.

49 Williams, "Confessions," 344.

50 R. W. Fleming to Carson, May 29, 1967, Williams Papers.

51 Don McIlvenna, "William Appleman Williams, the Historian and His Community, the Oregon Years," Williams Papers. Special thanks also to McIlvenna for making himself available for an on-campus interview. Among correspondence on the subject of Williams's departure from Madison, see, e.g., Williams to McCauley, Oct. 17, 1966, about Williams's love for the coast; and recommendations to George Carson from Gordon Wright, May 25, 1967; Merle Curti, May 26, 1967;

Warren Susman, May 26, 1967; and see Thomas McClintock to Dean Gordan Ghillie, Feb., 1967. Williams Papers.

52 Merle Curti to George Carson, June 24, 1967, Williams Papers.

53 OSU *Barometer*, Feb. 5, 1973, Williams Papers. Williams's talk was entitled, "Adam Smith and Female Persons: A Different Approach to Women's Liberation."

54 See his letter to "Dear Frank and All," dated June 19, 1985, Williams Papers, in which he complains that "truly emancipated women" should not care about special courses in women's history.

55 Williams to Merle Curti, June 1, 1967, Williams Papers.

56 Interestingly, so did Christopher Lasch, who had attacked the New Left, its scholarly elements often as much as its campus activism, but wanted to be part of a group of Socialist historians. See "History as Social Criticism: Conversations with Christopher Lasch," interviews by Casey Blake and Christopher Phelps, in *Journal of American History*, 80 (March, 1994), 1326. Among the younger radical historians at the Chicago meeting, held at the apartment of historian Jesse Lemisch and feminist-scientist Naomi Weisstein, were Mari Jo and Paul Buhle. *Socialist Revolution*'s editorial group included former *Studies* editors David Eakins, Saul Landau, James O'Connor, Martin J. Sklar, and James Weinstein (who emerged as the strongest figure, until his departure to found the newspaper *In These Times* in 1976). Among the younger editors were intellectual historian Eli Zaretsky and a graduate student, John Judis, who as a columnist for *In These Times* and later a contributing editor of the *New Republic* sometimes sought to bridge the gap between the ideas of Williams and those of opponents who sought to banish Williams's influence entirely.

57 Williams to Merle Curti, June 1, 1967, Williams Papers.

58 Williams to McCauley, Oct. 10, 1973, Williams Papers.

59 Williams to "Mother and Father Tomlin," Apr. 27, 1985.

60 See William G. Robbins, "William Appleman Williams: 'Doing History is Best of All. No Regrets,'" in *Redefining the Past* (1986), ed. Lloyd Gardner, 3–20.

61 Mark O. Hatfield, letter to Donald Wax, Chair of History, OSU, Mar. 19, 1986, Williams Papers. Hatfield recalls Williams's "profound" influence on Hatfield's views from the time of the historian's appearance on the OSU faculty. Williams allowed an essay on Hoover to be reprinted into a volume that Hatfield prepared.

62 "Seven Americas on the Way to the Future: An Exploration of American History," outline-prospectus for a textbook, n.d. [1975?], Williams Papers.

63 "Seven Americas."

64 Williams to McCauley, May 29, 1979, Williams Papers.

65 Williams to McCauley, Apr. 27, 1981, Williams Papers.

66 McIlvenna, "William Appleman Williams."

67 Williams to McCauley, Mar. 4, 1978, Williams Papers.

68 Conversation with Kyenne Williams, June 15, 1993.

69 John Simon to McCauley, Jan. 31, 1967, Williams Papers.

70 Angus Cameron to McCauley, Jan. 18, 1967, Williams Papers. Eventually, a major survey history text was produced with the "community" theme central to it: John Mack Faragher, Mari Jo Buhle, Daniel Czitrom, and Susan H. Armitage, *Out of Many: A History of the American People* (Englewood Cliffs, 1994).

71 Theodore Solotaroff to Jerry McCauley, Aug. 26, 1968, Williams Papers.

72 McCauley, draft of speech to Washington, D.C., IPS memorial symposium, Williams Papers.

73 Quoted by McCauley in speech, Williams Papers.

74 See William A. Williams, *History as a Way of Learning*, xiii, for bitter remarks about the *New York Times*–owned Quadrangle for dumping the book after promising earlier to publish it.

75 Patricia Irving to McCauley, Dec. 7, 1976, Williams Papers.

76 "Seven Americas."

77 Interview with Gerda Lerner by Paul Buhle, May 10, 1993.

78 Williams to Henry Berger, June 30, 1976. We are grateful to Berger for making this letter available to us.

79 Williams to William Robbins, n.d. [October, 1985], in the private collection of William Robbins.

80 Interview with Warren Susman, May, 1982.

81 *Americans in a Changing World*, 471.

82 *Americans in a Changing World*, 97.

83 Anonymous critique, prepared for Wiley & Sons., n.d., Williams Papers.

84 We owe the frame of "what if" to a conversation with Williams's sometime Oregon student and longtime close friend Mitzi Goheen, whom he acknowledged generously in the book's preface. Phone conversation, June, 1993. He became close to her parents, an Old Left Jewish academic couple who lived in Corvallis, and stayed in touch as she went on to foreign study and to teach anthropology at Amherst College.

85 Robert M. Senkewicz, *America*, 136 (Jan. 8, 1977), 57–58.

86 Michael Zuckerman, "Recasting American Historical Consciousness," *Nation*, 223 (Sept. 11, 1976), 214–16.

87 Thomas G. Kennedy, *American Historical Review*, 82 (June, 1977), 724.

88 Gaddis Smith, "The United States as Villain," *New York Times Book Review*, Oct. 10, 1976, 25.

89 Edmund S. Morgan, "The American Revolution: Who Were 'The People,'" *New York Review of Books*, 23 (Aug. 5, 1976), 29.

90 Clip of *Christian Science Monitor*, n.d., Williams Papers.

91 Notes from Noel Pugach phone conversation with Williams, Jan. 13, 1974, Williams Papers. In less than a decade, Williams's defender Horowitz—always given to caricature of complex arguments—had swung from far Left to far Right, arguing in *Soldier of Fortune* magazine and other conservative outlets for a bullying U.S. posture abroad. Even more remarkably, he played a starring role in a high-pro-

file Washington "Second Thoughts" conference of Reagan-leaning former New Leftists and others.

92 Special thanks go to Martin Sherwin for making available extensive correspondence and papers from this meeting.

93 Christopher Lasch, "William Appleman Williams on American History," *Marxist Perspectives*, 2 (Fall, 1978), 118.

94 Jon Wiener, "Radical Historians and the Crisis in American History, 1949–1980," *Journal of American History*, 76 (September, 1989), 399–434. The *Radical History Review* was by the later 1970s a main symbol of this activity, succeeding *Radical America* and *Studies On the Left*; but beneath and behind the literary production lay networks of former campus political activists who entered public history in many different venues, from documentary film to extra-academic conferences to historical exhibits and theater. In one thin sense, Lasch was correct: this activity more and more ceased to be called "New Left." But in the more meaningful sense of shared and continuous political commitments, it continues today among New Left veterans from the pages of the *Journal of American History*, *American Historical Review*, and the *Nation* to prestigious documentary film production companies, the Smithsonian Institution's museums, and the labor/social history exhibits, not to mention the libraries of notable scholarly volumes produced.

95 Lasch, "William Appleman Williams," 125–26.

96 Lasch's volume *The True and Only Heaven: Progress and Its Critics* (New York, 1991), a dense intellectual history, was finally (among a wide assortment of other things) an apotheosis of that cold-war master Reinhold Niebuhr.

97 Not until Eric Foner's election in 1993 did the sixties generation of historians take this symbolic position for themselves without an older generation intermediary. The 1994 annual meeting in Atlanta, featuring one major session devoted to re-examining U.S. foreign policy after the cold war (with Leonard Liggio and Marilyn Young, among others, presenting papers) and another devoted to the influence of the late E. P. Thompson, was in part an honoring of scholarly and personal influences from the older radical generation, now virtually all gone. A "Cold War Revisited" conference at the University of Wisconsin in 1992, dedicated to Williams, offered a smaller but more intense version of this apotheosis. A forthcoming volume of papers delivered at the conference discusses the Williams legacy extensively.

98 Edward Crapol, "William Appleman Williams: The Historian and His Community," Organization of American Historians meeting, 1991. Manuscript kindly supplied by Crapol.

## CHAPTER 7

1 Williams to Jeff and June Safford, Jan. 12, 1976, Williams Papers.

2 Howard Schonburger, "William Appleman Williams," *Radical History Newsletter*, 62 (May, 1990), 8.

3 William Appleman Williams, "Empire as a Way of Life," *Nation*, 231 (Aug. 2–9, 1980), 104–119. Respondents included Robert Lekachman, Walter Dean Burnham, Philip Green, Thomas Ferguson, Joel Rodgers, Alan Wolfe, Clair Clark, Marcus G. Raskin, and Sidney Morgenbesser, 120–27; A later issue of the *Nation*, 231 (Nov. 1, 1980), included an exchange of letters over the Williams essay with Carl N. Degler, Martin Green, Lewis Perry, and Virginia Held adding their comments and Williams replying, 426, 443–45.

4 William Appleman Williams, *Empire as a Way of Life* (New York, 1962), 102.

5 Williams, *Empire*, 157. Italics removed from quotation.

6 Williams, *Empire*, 213.

7 Williams, *Empire*, 226.

8 Advertising copy, Williams Papers.

9 Frank Unger, "History as a Way of Learning: On the Death of American Historian William A. Williams," *Initial: Zeitschrift für Politik und Gesellschaft*, 7 (1990), translation in manuscript, Williams Papers.

10 Unger, "History as a Way."

11 Lawrence S. Kaplan, *Journal of American History*, 68 (June, 1981), 96–97; Robert H. Farrell, *South Atlantic Quarterly*, 80 (Summer, 1981), 361–62; Rush Welter, *Annals of the American Academy of Political and Social Science*, 455 (May, 1981), 202–3; See also *Choice* (April, 1981), 1158; and Roger R. Trask, *History: Reviews of Books*, 9 (Oct., 1980), 67.

12 A. J. Beitzinger, " 'Old' and 'New' History," *The Review of Politics*, 43 (Oct., 1981), 611–13; Joseph M. Siracusa, *Business History Review*, 86 (Oct., 1981), 906–7.

13 John Lukacs, *New Republic*, 183 (Oct. 11, 1980), 31–33; Henry Pachter, *New Leader*, 63 (Oct. 20, 1980), 724–25.

14 Williams's last major scholarly contribution, *America in Vietnam: A Documentary History* (Garden City, 1985), was co- edited by Williams with Thomas McCormick, Lloyd Gardner, and Walter LaFeber. An eminently useable collection of documents and introductory essays, the book gained quick adoptions in U.S. foreign policy and Vietnam War history courses. Williams's direct contributions, however, were limited to the period before 1945 and an essay that reiterated familiar themes. Daniel Hémery, Vietnam specialist at the Sorbonne and the only major reviewer, found Williams's essay "excellent" and the overall collection "first-rate." Daniel Hémery, *Pacific Affairs*, 59 (Winter, 1986-87), 724–25.

15 John A. Thompson, "Changing the Outline of American Historiography," *Guardian*, n.d. [March, 1990?], in Williams Papers.

16 Hans-Ulrich Wehler, *Das Deutsche Kaiserreich 1871–1918* (Göttingen, 1973). Special thanks to Volker Berghahn for making German-language sources available to us, and for a discussion of their relevance.

17 Werner Link, *Die amerikanische Stabilisierungspolitik in Deutschland 1921-32* (Düsseldorff, 1970). See also Wehler's translated essay, "Industrial growth and Early German Imperialism," in *Studies in the Theory of Imperialism* (London, 1972), edited by Roger Owen and Bob Sutcliffe, 71–92.

18 V. G. Kiernan, *America: The New Imperialism* (London, 1978). We owe thanks to Harvey J. Kaye, editor of several volumes of Kiernan's writing, for pointing to Williams's influence on him. See also Harvey J. Kaye, ed., *Imperialism and Its Contradictions: Writings of V. G. Kiernan (Volume III)* (New York, 1995).

19 Gareth Stedman Jones, "The Specificity of U.S. Imperialism," *New Left Review*, 60 (Mar.-Apr., 1970), 59–86. Jones suggested that although Williams "had tried to break away from conventional patriotic fantasies," he "remained imprisoned in a moralistic problematic," and yet "shows expansionism to have been a consistent theme running throughout American history," allowing others to "raise more adequately the problem of the specificity of American imperialism," 61, 62.

20 Perry Anderson, *In the Tracks of Historical Materialism* (London, 1983).

21 Many thanks for helpful letters on this subject from Bruno Cartosio and Nando Fasce among others; see also the survey essay on Williams by a Wisconsin PhD, Malcolm Sylvers, "Storia Nazionale e Imperialismo nella Riflessione di Uno Storico Americano 'Revisionista,'" *Qualestorica* 8 (June, 1980), 16–23. Sylvers treats at length yet another translation, of *History as a Way of Learning*, as *Le frontiere dell'impero americano. La cultura dell' "espansione" nella politica statunitense* (Bari, 1978).

22 Yui Daizaburo, "History of American Foreign Relations," in *International Studies in Japan: A Bibliographical Guide* ed. Sadao Asada (Tokyo, 1988), 93–103. Special thanks to Masahiro Hosoya for making this document available to us, and to Charles Neu for assisting us in locating Japanese scholars familiar with Williams's influence. Bruce Cumings added some crucial insights to this perspective in a letter to Paul Buhle, Jan. 7, 1994.

23 Michael H. Hunt, "New Insights But No New Vistas: Recent Work on Nineteenth Century American–East Asian Relations," in *New Frontiers in American-East Asian Relations* (New York, 1983), edited by Warren Cohen, 7–43, especially 24.

24 "To: All members of the History Department," May, 1976, Williams Papers.

25 "Organization of American Historians, Biographical Data for 1979 Nominees," Williams Papers.

26 Ed Crapol, "William Appleman Williams: The Historian and His Community," Organization of American Historians, 1991, manuscript supplied by Ed Crapol.

27 "Wm. A. Williams, President Elect," to Stephen Goodell, Program Office, National Endowment for the Humanities, Sept. 14, 1979. Document made available by William Preston.

28 "Bill Williams: President Elect," to Senator Hatfield, Sept. 14, 1979. Williams Papers.

29 Williams to Hatfield.

30 "From: Bill Williams, To: The Department," Apr. 16, 1981, Williams Papers; Williams to "Bill" [William Preston], Jan. 29, 1980, letter supplied by William Preston.

31 "From: Bill Williams, To: The Department," Apr. 16, 1981, Williams Papers.

32 Affadavit of William Appleman Williams, AFSC v. William H. Webster. Supplied by William Preston.

33 "Amicus Brief: Opposing the Government's Motion to Dissolve Judge Greene's Preliminary Injunction," supplied by attorney Marshall Perlin, at the suggestion of Michael Meeropol.

34 Milan Kundera, quoted by Sigmund Diamond in *Compromised Campus: The Collaboration of Universities with the Intelligence Community, 1945–1955* (New York, 1992), 285.

35 This information was helpfully summarized by William Preston.

36 See Arthur Schlesinger, Jr.'s hand-wringing account of CIA activities in *The Cycles of American History* (Boston, 1986), 60–61.

37 Published as William Appleman Williams, "Thoughts on Reading Henry Adams," *Journal of American History*, 68 (June, 1981), 7–15.

38 Williams, "Beyond Resistance: Backyard Autonomy," *Nation*, 232 (Sept.5, 1981), 161, 179–80.

39 See Monty Wiley letter and Williams's response in "Letters: Backyard Autonomy," *Nation*, Oct. 31, 1981, inside front cover; on Thompson, see for example, Paul Buhle, "E. P. Thompson," *TIKKUN*, 8 (Nov.-Dec., 1993), 82–84. The two historians admired each others' work enormously, but never met.

40 Williams, "Radicals and Regionalism," *Democracy*, 1 (Oct. 1981), 87–98. This journal was established and edited by the distinguished political scientist Sheldon Wolin. Under different historical circumstances, it might have become the ideal vehicle for Williams's effort to establish a dialogue transcending the usual political lines.

41 "Keeping a Hold on the West," *Statesman Journal*, undated clipping, Williams Papers.

42 "A Waste-Our-Water Lifestyle," *Statesman Journal*, Aug. 5, 1981. Fulfilling one of Williams's earlier historical themes of corporatism and labor leaders, Jackson's other major support came from the AFL-CIO chiefs who deserted George McGovern in favor of a Truman-like candidate with promises of heavy military spending and a vitriolic hatred for the peace constituencies.

43 "The U.S. and Uses of Power," *Statesman Journal*, Mar. 17, 1982.

44 "Why They March in Europe," *Capitol Journal* (Portland), May 19, 1982, and "Time to Rehumanize War," *Capitol Journal*, May 5, 1982.

45 "On Funding College Athletics," *Statesman Journal*, July 22, 1981; "Learning to Forget History," *Statesman Journal*, July 29, 1981.

46 "One Historian's Challenge to Journalists," unpublished address, n.d., Williams Papers.

47 "The Crisis of American Democracy," unpublished address, n.d., Williams Papers.

48 "America as a Weary and Nostalgic Culture," unpublished address, n.d., Williams Papers.

49 Printed for the first time as "The Annapolis Crowd," in *A William Appleman Williams Reader,* 385–92.

50 See *Edward Said: A Critical Reader* (Oxford, 1992), edited by Michael Sprinker.

51 Williams, "The Comparative Uses of Power: China on the African Rim and the United States on the Pacific Rim," unpublished address, Williams Papers.

52 We are grateful to Marcus Rediker for making available several letters from Williams to him on this subject.

53 Williams, "Notes on the Death of a Ship and the End of a World: The Grounding of the British Bark *Glenesslin* at Mount Meahkahnie on 1 October 1913," *The American Neptune,* 41 (1981), 123–24.

54 Williams, "Notes on the Death of a Ship," 127–28.

55 Williams, "Notes on the Death of a Ship," 138.

56 "A Good Life and A Good Death: A Memoir of an Independent Lady," with the inscription on the second page, "By Her Son William Appleman Williams for Her Grandchildren," Williams Papers.

57 Summary-outline prospectus, Williams Papers, titled "Life Inside the Frontier," later retitled in manuscript "Ninety Days inside the Empire," Williams Papers. Williams continued to work on this project until the year before his death.

58 John Lewis Gaddis, "The Emerging Post-Revisionist Synthesis on the Origins of the Cold War," *Diplomatic History,* 7 (Summer, 1983), 171, originally presented to the meeting of the Organization of American Historians, April, 1983.

59 See Peter Novick, *That Noble Dream,* 454–57.

60 Stanley Hoffman, "Revisionism Revisited," in *Reflections on the Cold War: A Quarter Century of American Foreign Policy* (Philadelphia, 1974), 3–6, especially 10–15, edited by Lynn H. Miller and Ronald W. Pruessen; for a different and unrecalcitrantly conservative overview see Joseph M. Siracusa, "The New Left, the Cold War, and American Diplomacy: The Case for Historiography as Intellectual History," *World Review,* 14 (March, 1975), 37–52.

61 John Lewis Gaddis, "The Emerging Post-Revisionist Synthesis," 171–72, 180–83. Gaddis first formulated his views in *The United States and the Origins of the Cold War, 1941–1947* (New York, 1972). For his comments on the revisionists, see 357–58. Among other leading "post-revisionist" works were George C. Herring, *Aid to Russia, 1941–1946;* Lynn E. Davis, *The Cold War Begins;* Daniel Yergin, *Shattered Peace;* and Bruce R. Kuniholm, *The Origins of the Cold War in the Near East.* For a good discussion of the post-revisionists, see Richard A. Melanson, *Writing History and Making Policy: The Cold War, Vietnam and Revisionism* (Lanham, Maryland, 1983), 97–119.

62 Warren F. Kimball and Bruce R. Kuniholm, replies to John Lewis Gaddis, in "The Emerging Post-Revisionist Synthesis," 198–99, 201.

63 Barton J. Bernstein, "Cold War Orthodoxy Restated," *Reviews in American History,* 1 (December, 1973), 453–62. Bernstein spoke too early or simply about a young Gaddis, as Bruce Cumings observed; the later Gaddis was none too polite.

64 Bernstein, "Cold War Orthodoxy Revisited," 454; See also Bruce Cumings, "'Revising Postrevisionism,' or The Poverty of Theory in Diplomatic History," *Diplomatic History*, 17 (Fall, 1993), 539–69, considered further below.

65 Williams, "Demystifying Cold War Orthodoxy," *Science & Society*, 39 (1975), 346–51.

66 John Lewis Gaddis, "The Tragedy of Cold War History," *Diplomatic History*, 17 (Winter, 1993), 1–16.

67 Cumings, "'Revising Postrevisionism,'" 555.

68 "[N]ow we can see the absurdity of the recently fashionable view that for two centuries the United States has been struggling to preserve a sclerotic Present and fight off the Future, as represented by a regenerative revolutionary world," said David Brion Davis in a 1989 presidential address to the Organization of American Historians, footnoting in the printed text *America Confronts a Revolutionary World*. A distinguished scholar of race and racism, Davis insisted that the "America Triumphant" cold war liberal or neoliberal (or conservative) view had not been vindicated, either. But in singling out Williams, he seemed to be making a personal point, related perhaps to Niebuhr's enduring influence upon him. David Brion Davis, "American Equality and Foreign Revolutions," *Journal of American History*, 76 (December, 1989), 729ff, especially 730–31. In a letter to the editor of the *New York Review*, Feb. 5, 1986, in the Williams Papers, Williams hailed David Brion Davis as "an exceptionally accomplished, thoughtful and insightful historian who reads documents with a fine sense of nuance and an unusual feel for relationships," a more generous judgment by far than Davis's of Williams.

69 Williams, *History as a Way of Learning* (New York, 1974), xvi.

70 George F. Kennan, "The G.O.P. Won the Cold War? Ridiculous!" *New York Times*, Oct. 28, 1992; Kennan's volume, *Around the Cragged Hill: A Personal and Political Philosophy* (New York, 1993) offered another installment of sobering reflections. In contrast to many observers, including Arthur Schlesinger, Jr., Kennan was distinctly pessimistic about the consequences of the cold war and modern culture at large.

71 We are grateful to David Krikun for suggesting that Williams and Schlesinger, Jr., mirrored each other for decades.

72 Arthur M. Schlesinger, Jr., *The Cycles of American History* (Boston, 1986), 137, 141.

73 Schlesinger, Jr., *Cycles of American History* 248–55.

74 Schlesinger, Jr., *Cycles of American History*, 161, 282, 311.

75 Schlesinger, Jr., *Cycles of American History*, 419, 285.

76 Schlesinger, Jr., *Cycles of American History*, 418.

77 Arthur Schlesinger, Jr., *The Disuniting of America: Reflections on a Multicultural Society* (New York, 1991). Consistent with the growth and development of scholarship in the multiple sources of American culture, an Organization of American Historians president skewered *The Disuniting of America* in his 1993 presidential address and in a subsequent sharp exchange with Schlesinger, Jr. In a none-too-subtly race-tinged commentary on non-European and specifically African traditions,

Schlesinger, Jr., had perceived only sources of "despotism, superstition, tribalism and fanaticism," as usual reserving for the Europeans all the good political traits inherited by Americans. Schlesinger, Jr.'s response to Lawrence Levine's shattering commentary was notably weak and self-contradictory; See Levine, "Clio, Canons and Culture," *Journal of American History*, 80 (December, 1993), 865–66; and the exchange of the two in "Letters to the Editor," *Journal of American History*, 81 (June, 1994), 367–68.

78 Letter of John Mack Faragher to Paul Buhle, Dec. 25, 1993. For his part, an elderly Schlesinger, Jr., no longer accused the critics of Western dispossession of Mexicans and Indians as potential subversives serving the interests of communism (as he had in *The Vital Center*), but he insisted that internal expansion was entirely exaggerated because the U.S. had never conquered Canada or all of Mexico! *Cycles of American History*, 149–52.

79 David W. Noble, "The American Wests: Refuge from European Power or Frontiers of European Expansion," in *The American West as Seen by Europeans and Americans,* ed. Rob Kroes (Amsterdam, 1989), 19–36. See also the discussion by Warren Susman, "The Frontier Thesis and the American Intellectual," in Susman, *Culture as History: The Transformation of American Society in the Twentieth Century* (New York, 1985).

80 Noble, "The American Wests," 31. For Limerick's own account see "Introduction" to *Legacy of Conquest: The Unbroken Past of the New American West* (New York, 1987), 17–32.

81 Richard White, *"It's Your Misfortune and None of My Own": A New History of the American West* (Norman, 1991), 411–12.

82 Walter LaFeber, "Liberty and Power: U.S. Diplomatic History, 1750–1945," in *The New American History* ed. Eric Foner (Philadelphia, 1990), 275–76; Michael J. Hogan, "Corporatism," in "Explaining the History of American Foreign Relations," *Journal of American History*, 77 (June, 1990), 153ff; Hugh De Santis, "The Imperialist Impulse and American Innocence, 1865–1900," in *American Foreign Relations* ed. Gerald K. Haines and J. Samuel Walker (Westport, 1981), 74.

83 Martin J. Sklar, *The Corporate Reconstruction of American Capitalism, 1890–1916* (Cambridge, 1988) and Martin J. Sklar, *The United States as a Developing Country: Studies in U.S. History in the Progressive Era and the 1920s* (Cambridge, 1992). Mark Leff has a perceptive commentary on the latter volume and Sklar's own political trajectory in a review of *The United States as a Developing Country* in *Journal of American History*, 80 (December, 1993), 1117–18.

84 Hugh DeSantis, "The Imperialist Impulse," 74.

85 Walter LaFeber, "Liberty and Power," 276–77; and Thomas J. McCormick, "World Systems," 125ff.

86 This remains an extremely unpopular view, but one heavily endorsed in a careful analysis of Lenin's last years by C. L. R. James. See "Lenin and the Problem," in C. L. R. James, *Nkrumah and the Ghana Revolution* (London, 1977), 189–213. This essay was originally published in a special "C. L. R. James Anthology" issue of

*Radical America* in 1970 edited by Paul Buhle and may well have influenced Williams's views.

87 Williams to "Jim" [no last name given], July 22/23, 1989. Williams Papers.
88 Williams to "Jim."
89 John A. Thompson, "Reviews," in *International History Review*, 14 (August, 1987), 513.
90 Philip K. Dick, *VALIS* (New York, 1981), 220, 221, 224.
91 Mitzi Goheen, untitled, Williams Papers.

# BIBLIOGRAPHY

### MANUSCRIPT COLLECTIONS CITED

American Historical Association Papers, Washington, D.C.
Columbia University
  Richard Hofstadter Papers
Library of Congress
  National Association for the Advancement of Colored People Papers
New York University, Tamiment Library
  Oral History of the American Left
Oregon State University, Kerr Library
  William Appleman Williams Papers
State Historical Society of Wisconsin
  Merle E. Curti Papers
  Fred Harvey Harrington Papers
  William Best Hesseltine Papers
  *Radical America* Papers
  *Studies on the Left* Papers
United States Naval Academy
  William Appleman Williams File

## Works by William Appleman Williams

### Unpublished Manuscripts

"McCormick Reports on Russia: A Study of News and Opinion on Russia in the *Chicago Tribune* from 1917 to 1921," MA thesis, University of Wisconsin, 1948.

"Raymond Robins and Russian American Relations," PhD dissertation, University of Wisconsin, 1950.

"Ninety Days Inside the Empire," a novel.

"A Good Life and a Good Death: A Memoir of an Independent Lady, By Her Son . . . for Her Grandchildren," in William Appleman Williams Papers, Oregon State University.

### Books and Edited Works

*American-Russian Relations, 1781-1947*, New York, Rinehart, 1952.

*The Shaping of American Diplomacy, 1750-1955*, two volumes, Chicago, Rand McNally, 1956. Revised 1972.

*The Tragedy of American Diplomacy*, Cleveland, World Publishing Company, 1959. Revised 1962, 1972. Twenty-Fifth Anniversary Edition, New York, Norton, 1988. Also published in Spanish and Japanese translations.

*The Contours of American History*, Cleveland, World Publishing Company, 1961. New Edition, New York, Norton, 1989. Also published in British edition and Italian translation.

*The United States, Cuba, and Castro*, New York, Monthly Review Press, 1962. Also published in Spanish translation.

*The Great Evasion: An Essay on the Contemporary Relevance of Karl Marx and on the Wisdom of Admitting the Heretic into the Dialogue about America's Future*, Chicago, Quadrangle Books, 1964.

*The Roots of the Modern American Empire: A Study of the Growth and Shaping of Social Consciousness in a Marketplace Society*, New York, Random House, 1969. Also published in British edition.

*From Colony to Empire: Essays in the History of American Foreign Relations*, New York, John Wiley and Sons, 1972. Also published in Italian translation.

*Some Presidents: Wilson to Nixon*, New York, New York Review of Books, 1972.

*History as a Way of Learning*, New York, New Viewpoints, 1974. Also published in Spanish translation.

*America Confronts a Revolutionary World, 1776-1976*, New York, Morrow, 1976.

*Americans in a Changing World: A History of the United States in the Twentieth Century*, New York, Harper and Row, 1978.

*Empire as a Way of Life: An Essay on the Causes and Character of America's Present Predicament Along with a Few Thoughts about an Alternative*, New York, Oxford University Press, 1980. Also published in British edition and Spanish, German, and Japanese translations.

*America in Vietnam: A Documentary History*, edited with notes and introductions with Walter F. LaFeber, Thomas J. McCormick, and Lloyd Gardner, Garden City, New York, Anchor Press/Doubleday, 1985.

*A William Appleman Williams Reader: Selections from His Major Historical Writings*, edited with an introduction and notes by Henry W. Berger, Chicago, Ivan Dee, 1992.

## Selected Essays

"Today is Russia," *The Trident Magazine*, United States Naval Academy, (Winter 1944):12ff.

"The International Impact of National Economic Planning," University of Leeds, England, 1948.

"A Frontier Federalist and the War of 1812," *Pennsylvania Magazine of History and Biography*, 76 (January 1952):81-85.

"Brooks Adams and American Expansion," *New England Quarterly*, 25 (June 1952):217-232.

"A Second Look at Mr. X," *Monthly Review*, 4 (August 1952):123-128.

Review of Albert A. Woldman, *Lincoln and the Russians, Science & Society*, 17 (1953):363-364.

"Moscow Peace Drive: Victory for Containment?" *Nation*, 177 (11 July 1953):28-30.

"A Note on the Isolationism of Senator William E. Borah," *Pacific Historical Review*, 22(November 1953):391-392.

Review of Arthur S. Link, *Woodrow Wilson and the Progressive Era, 1910-1917, Science & Society*, 18(1954):348-351.

"Raymond Robins, Crusader—The Outdoor Mind," *The Nation*, 179 (30 October 1954):384-385.

"Collapse of the Grand Coalition," review of William H. McNeill, *America, Britain and Russia, Nation*, 179 (6 November 1954):408-409.

"The Legend of Isolationism in the 1920's," *Science & Society*, 18 (Winter 1954):1-20. Reprinted in Armin Rappaport, editor, *Essays in American Diplomacy*, New York, MacMillan, 1967, and in Henry W. Berger, editor, *A William Appleman Williams Reader*, Chicago, Ivan Dee, 1992.

Review of Michael Florinsky, *Russia: A History and an Interpretation, Science & Society*, 19 (1955):346-350.

"Cold War Perspectives—A Historical Fable," *Nation* 180 (28 May 1955): 458-461.

"The Historical Romance of Senator Neuberger's Election," *Oregon Historical Quarterly*, 56 (June 1955):101-105.

"The Frontier Thesis and American Foreign Policy," *Pacific Historical Review*, 24 (November 1955):379-395. Reprinted in Henry W. Berger, editor, *A William Appleman Williams Reader*, Chicago, Ivan Dee, 1992.

Review of Robert D. Warth, *The Allies and the Russian Revolution, Science & Society*, 20 (1956):84-86.

"Babbitt's New Fables," *Nation*, 182 (7 January 1956):3-6.

"Great Boomerang: The Irony of Containment," *Nation*, 182 (5 May 1956):376-379.

"On the Restoration of Brooks Adams," *Science & Society*, 20 (Summer 1956):247-253.

"Challenge to American Radicalism," *Frontier*, 7 (June 1956):3-6.

"The Age of Re-forming History," A review of Richard Hofstadter, *The Age of Reform, Nation*, 182 (30 June 1956):552-554.

"Reflections on the Historiography of American Entry into World War II," *Oregon Historical Quarterly*, 57 (September 1956):274-279.

"The Convenience of History," review of George F. Kennan, *Russia Leaves the War, Nation*, 183 (15 September 1956):222-224.

"A Note on Charles Austin Beard's Search for a General Theory of Causation," *American Historical Review*, 62 (October 1956):59-80.

"Introduction," with Harvey Goldberg, and "Charles Austin Beard: The Intellectual as Tory-Radical," in Harvey Goldberg, editor, *American Radicals: Some Problems and Personalities*, New York, Monthly Review Press, 1957. Essay on Beard reprinted in Henry W. Berger, editor, *A William Appleman Williams Reader*, Chicago, Ivan Dee, 1992.

"Taxing for Peace," *Nation*, 184 (19 January 1957):53.

"The Empire of Theodore Roosevelt," review of Foster Rhea Dulles, *The Imperial Years* and Howard K. Beale, *Theodore Roosevelt and the Rise of America to World Power, Nation*, 18(2 March 1957):191-192.

"Schlesinger: Right Crisis—Wrong Order," review of Arthur M. Schlesinger, Jr., *The Crisis of the Old Order, 1919-1933, Nation*, 18(23 March 1957):257-260.

"Go Left or Go Under," *Liberation*, (April 1957):14-17.

"The 'Logic' of Imperialism," review of Amaury de Riencourt, *The Coming Caesars, Nation*, 18(6 July 1957):14-15.

"The Nature of Peace," *Monthly Review*, 9 (July-August 1957):112-114.

"China and Japan: A Challenge and a Choice of the Nineteen Twenties," *Pacific Historical Review*, 26 (August 1957):259-279.

"Latin America: Laboratory of American Foreign Policy of the Nineteen Twenties," *Inter-American Economic Affairs*, 11 (Autumn 1957):3-30.

"The American Century, 1941-1957," *Nation*, 185 (2 November 1957): 297-301.

*America and the Middle East: Open Door Imperialism or Enlightened Leadership?* (pamphlet), New York, Rinehart, 1958.

*Source Problems in World Civilization* (pamphlet), New York, 1958.

"Loss of Debate," review of Herbert Hoover, *The Ordeal of Woodrow Wilson, Nation*, 18(17 May 1958):452-453.

"The Age of Mercantilism: An Interpretation of the American Political Economy, 1763-1828," *William and Mary Quarterly*, 15 (October 1958): 419-437. Reprinted in Armin Rappaport, editor, *Essays in American Diplomacy*, New York, MacMillan, 1967.

"A Note on American Foreign Policy in Europe in the 1920's," *Science & Society*, 22 (Winter 1958):1-20.

"Needed: Production for Peace," *Nation*, 188 (21 February 1959): 149-153.

"Take A New Look at Russia," *Foreign Policy Bulletin*, 38 (15 April 1959):118-119.

"Samuel Adams: Calvinist, Mercantilist, Revolutionary," *Studies on the Left*, 1 (Winter 1960):47-57.

"On the Origins of the Cold War: An Exchange," *Commentary*, 31 (February 1961):142-159.

"Protecting Overseas Investors," *Nation*, 193 (26 August 1961): 100-101.

"The Irony of the Bomb," *Centennial Review*, 5 (Fall 1961):373-384.

"Foreign Policy and the American Mind: An Alternate View," *Commentary*, 33 (February 1962):155-159.

"A Proposal to Put *American* Back into American Socialism," in "American Socialism and Thermonuclear War: A Symposium," *New Politics*, 1(Spring 1962):40-45.

"Fire in the Ashes of Scientific History" (review article), *William and Mary Quarterly*, 19 (April 1962):274-287.

"Cuba: The President and His Critics," *Nation*, 196 (16 March 1963):226, 236.

"Historiography and Revolution: The Case of Cuba," *Studies on the Left*, 3 (Summer 1963):78-102.

"American Intervention in Russia, 1917-1920," *Studies on the Left*,3 (Fall 1963):24-48; 4 (Winter 1964):39-57.

"The Acquitting Judge," review of Ernest R. May, *Imperial Democracy: The Emergence of America as a Great Power, Studies on the Left*, 3 (Winter 1963):94-99.

"Cuba: Issues and Alternatives," *Annals of the American Academy of Political and Social Sciences,* 351 (January 1964):72-80.

"The Vicious Circle of American Imperialism," *New Politics,* 4 (Fall 1965):48-55. Reprinted in K. T. Fann and Donald Hodges, editors, *Readings in U.S. Imperialism,* Boston, F. Porter Sargent, 1971.

"Last Chance for Democracy," review of John Bartlow Martin, *Overtaken by Events: The Dominican Crisis from the Fall of Trujillo to the Civil War, Nation,* 204 (January 29 1967):23-25.

Review of Tristam Coffin, *Senator Fulbright: Portrait of a Public Philosopher, Ramparts,* 5 (March 1967):57-59.

"A Natural History of the American Empire," *Canadian Dimension,* 4 (March-April 1967):12-17.

"The Cold War Revisionists," *Nation,* 205 (13 November 1967):492-495.

"The Rise of an American World Power Complex," in Neal D. Houghton, editor, *Struggle Against History: U.S. Foreign Policy in an Age of Revolution,* New York, Washington Square Press, 1968.

"The Large Corporation and American Foreign Policy," in David Horowitz, editor, *Corporations and the Cold War,* New York, Monthly Review Press, 1969.

"An American Socialist Community?" *Liberation,* 14 (June 1969):8-11.

"How Can the Left Be Relevant?" *Current,* 109 (August 1969):20-24.

"The Crown on Clio's Head," review of J. H. Plumb, *The Death of the Past, Nation,* 210 (9March 1970):279-280.

"What This Country Needs. . . ." Review of Gene Smith, *The Shattered Dream: Herbert Hoover and the Great Depression, New York Review of Books,* 15 (5 November 1970):7-11.

"Notes for a Dialogue with Messrs. Harrington, Schlesinger, and Zinn," *Partisan Review,* 38 (January 1971):67-78.

"Officers and Gentlemen," review of nine books on military history, *New York Review of Books,* 16 (6 May 1971):3-8.

"Wilson," review of five books on Woodrow Wilson, *New York Review of Books,* 17 (2 December 1971):3-6.

"Ol' Lyndon," review of Lyndon Baines Johnson, *The Vantage Point: Perspectives of the Presidency, 1963-1969, New York Review of Books,* 17 (16 December 1971):3-6.

"Excelsior!" Review of Rowland Evans, Jr., and Robert D. Novak, *Nixon in the White House* and John Osborne, *The First Two Years of the Nixon Watch, New York Review of Books,* 18 (24 February 1972):7-12.

"Confessions of an Intransigent Revisionist," *Socialist Review,* 17 (September-October 1973):89-98. Reprinted in Henry W. Berger, editor, *A William Appleman Williams Reader,* Chicago, Ivan Dee, 1992.

"A Historian's Perspective," *Prologue: The Journal of the National Archives,* 6 (Fall 1974):200-203.

"Demystifying Cold War Orthodoxy," review of George C. Herring, *Aid to Russia, 1941-1946* and Thomas G. Paterson, *Soviet-American Confrontation: Postwar Reconstruction and the Origins of the Cold War*, Science and Society, 39 (1975):346-351.

"Schurman's Logic of World Power," review of Franz Schurman, *The Logic of World Power, Bulletin of Concerned Asian Scholars*, 84 (October-December 1976):47-48.

"Raymond Robins," *Dictionary of American Biography*, Supplement 5, 1951-1955, New York, Charles Scribner's Sons, 1977.

"Social Protest in Three American Cities: Is Radicalism an Urban Phenomenon?" 48th Australian/New Zealand Association for the Advancement of Science (August 1977).

"Open Door Interpretation," in *Encyclopedia of American Foreign Policy: Studies of the Principal Movements and Ideas*, volume II, New York, Charles Scribner's Sons, 1978.

"Amerikas 'idealistischer' Imperialismus, 1900-1917," in Hans-Ulrich Wehler, editor, *Imperialismus*, Konigstein, Althenaum, 1979.

Review of David Burner, *Herbert Hoover, New Republic*, 180 (10 March 1979):35-36.

"You Aren't Lost Until You Don't Know Where You've Been," review of Frances FitzGerald, *History Schoolbooks in the Twentieth Century*, Nation, 229 (27 October 1979):405-407.

"An Interview with William Appleman Williams," by Mike Wallace, *Radical History Review*, 22 (Winter 1979-1980):65-91. Reprinted in Henry Abelove et al., editors, *Visions of History*, New York, Pantheon, 1984.

"Is the Idea and Reality of America Possible Without Empire?" *Nation*, 231 (2-9 August 1980):104-119, 120-127.

"America and Empire: An Exchange," *Nation*, 231 (1 November 1980): 426, 443-445.

"Notes on the Death of a Ship and the End of a World: The Grounding of the British Bark *Glenesslin* at Mount Neahkahnie on 1 October 1913," *The American Neptune*, 41 (1981):122-138.

"Thoughts on Rereading Henry Adams," *Journal of American History*, 68 (June 1981):7-15.

"The Whole World in Its Hands," review of Holly Sklar, editor, *Trilateralism: The Trilateral Commission and Elite Planning in World Management, Mother Jones*, 6 (June 1981):53-54.

"Regional Resistance: Backyard Autonomy," *Nation*, 233 (5 September 1981):161, 179-180.

"Radicals and Regionalism," *Democracy*, 1 (October 1981):87-98.

"History as Redemption: Henry Adams and the Education of America," *Nation*, 234 (6 March 1982):266-269.

"Procedure Becomes Substance," *Democracy*, 2 (April 1982):100-102.

"Missile Ban in Washington: 1921," *Nation*, 237 (26 November 1983):530-533.

"The City on a Hill on an Errand into the Wilderness," in Harrison Salisbury, editor, *Vietnam Reconsidered: Lessons from a War*, New York, Harper and Row, 1984.

"Thoughts on the Fun and Purpose of Being an American Historian," *Organization of American Historians Newsletter*, 13 (February 1985):2-3.

"William Appleman Williams: 'Doing History is Best of All. No Regrets,'" interview with William G. Robbins, in Lloyd C. Gardner, editor, *Redefining the Past: Essays in Diplomatic History in Honor of William Appleman Williams*, Corvallis, Oregon State University Press, 1986.

"Thoughts on the Comparative Uses of Power," George Bancroft Lecture, United States Naval Academy (September 1986), in Henry W. Berger, editor, *A William Appleman Williams Reader*, Chicago, Ivan Dee, 1992.

"The Annapolis Crowd" (August 1987), in Henry W. Berger, editor, *A William Appleman Williams Reader*, Chicago, Ivan Dee, 1992.

"My Life in Madison," in Paul Buhle, editor, *History and the New Left: Madison, Wisconsin, 1950-1970*, Philadelphia, Temple University Press, 1990.

## Select Secondary Studies

Buhle, Paul, ed., *History and the New Left: Madison, Wisconsin, 1950-1970*, Philadelphia, Temple University Press, 1990.

Buhle, Paul, *Marxism in the United States: Remapping the History of the American Left, From 1870 to the Present Day*, London, Verso, 1987.

Buhle, Paul, "Marxism and Its Critics," in Mary Kupiec Cayton, Elliott J. Gorn, and Peter W. Williams, editors, *Encyclopedia of Social History*, volume I, New York, 1993.

Buhle, Paul and Edward Rice-Maximin, "War Without End: Why the U.S. Can't Stop," a review article considering Marilyn B. Young, *The Vietnam Wars, 1945-1990*, 1991; William Appleman Williams, *The Tragedy of American Diplomacy*, New Edition, 1988; and William Appleman Williams, *The Contours of American History*, New Edition, 1989 in *The Village Voice Literary Supplement*, 5 November 1991.

Copelman, Dina M. and Barbara Clark Smith, editors, "Excerpts from a Conference to Honor William Appleman Williams," *Radical History Review*, 50(Spring 1991):39-70.

Dee, Ivan R., "Revisionism Revisited," in Lloyd C. Gardner, editor, *Redefining the Past: Essays in Diplomatic History in Honor of William Appleman Williams*, Corvallis, Oregon State University Press, 1986.

Gardner, Lloyd, editor, *Redefining the Past: Essays in Diplomatic History in Honor of William Appleman Williams*, Corvallis, Oregon State University Press, 1986.

Genovese, Eugene, "William Appleman Williams on Marx and America," *Studies on the Left*, 6 (January-February 1966):70-86.

Hess, Gary R., "After the Tumult: The Wisconsin School's Tribute to William Appleman Williams," *Diplomatic History*, 12 (Fall 1988): 483-499.

Lasch, Christopher, "William Appleman Williams on American History," *Marxist Perspectives*, 2 (Fall 1978):118-126.

Livingston, James, "Farewell to Intellectual Godfather William Appleman Williams," *In These Times* (28 March–3 April 1990).

Marina, William, "William Appleman Williams," *Dictionary of Literary Biography*, vol. 17, *Twentieth Century Historians*, Detroit, Gale Research Company, 1983.

Meeropol, Michael, "Cold War Revisionism," in Mari Jo Buhle, Paul Buhle, and Dan Georgakas, editors, *Encyclopedia of the American Left*, New York, Garland, 1990.

Meeropol, Michael, "William Appleman Williams's Historiography," and Comments by James P. O'Brien, *Radical America*, 6 (August 1970):29-53.

Melanson, Richard A., "The Social and Political Thought of William Appleman Williams," *Western Political Quarterly*, 31(September 1978):392-409.

Melanson, Richard A., *Writing History and Making Policy: The Cold War, Vietnam and Revisionism*, Lanham, Maryland, University Presses of America, 1983.

Mommsen, Wolfgang J., *Theories of Imperialism*, translated by P. S. Falla, Chicago, University of Chicago Press, 1982.

Mosse, George, "New Left Intellectuals/New Left Politics," in Paul Buhle, editor, *History and the New Left: Madison, Wisconsin, 1950-1970*, Philadelphia, Temple University Press, 1990.

Noble, David W., *The End of American History*, Minneapolis, University of Minnesota Press, 1985.

Noble, David W., "William Appleman Williams and the Crisis of Public History," in Lloyd C. Gardner, editor, *Redefining the Past: Essays in Diplomatic History in Honor of William Appleman Williams*, Corvallis, Oregon State University Press, 1986.

Novick, Peter, *That Nobel Dream: The "Objectivity Question" and the American Historical Profession*, New York, Cambridge University Press, 1988.

Perkins, Bradford, "*The Tragedy of American Diplomacy*: Twenty-Five Years Later," *Reviews in American History*, 12 (March 1984):1-18. Reprinted in Lloyd C. Gardner, editor, *Redefining the Past: Essays in Diplomatic History in Honor of William Appleman Williams*, Corvallis, Oregon State University Press, 1986, and in *The Tragedy of American Diplomacy*, Twenty-Fifth Anniversary Edition, New York, Norton, 1988.

Rice-Maximin, Edward, "William Appleman Williams," in Mari Jo Buhle, Paul Buhle, and Harvey J. Kaye, editors, *The American Radical*, New York, Routledge, 1994.

Said, Edward, *Culture and Imperialism*, New York, Knopf, 1993.

Schonberger, Howard, "William Appleman Williams," *Radical History Newsletter*, 62 (May 1990):1, 7-8.

Theoharis, Athan G., "Revisionism," in *Encyclopedia of American Foreign Policy*, volume 3, *Studies of the Principal Movements and Ideas*, New York, Charles Scribner's Sons, 1978.

Thompson, J. A., "William Appleman Williams and the 'American Empire'," *Journal of American Studies* (United Kingdom), 7 (April 1973):91-104.

Tyrrell, Ian, *The Absent Marx: Class Analysis and Liberal History in Twentieth Century America*, Westport, Connecticut, Greenwood Press, 1986.

Weiner, Jon, "Radical Historians and the Crisis in American History, 1949-1980," *Journal of American History*, 76 (September 1989):399-434.

# INDEX

54, 81, 187-192, 216, 240-243;
impact in U.S., xiv, 27, 34, 37, 42-
47, 53, 57, 58, 65, 77, 111; liberal
intellectuals and, 57, 122-124, 132,
146, 155, 170, 194
Commager, Henry Steele, 37, 71,
135, 223
*Commentary*, 119, 189, 192
Commons, John R., 43
*Commonweal*, 175, 194
Communists (American), 29-30, 56,
74-75, 88, 96, 102, 130, 142, 157,
167, 257n.66, 263n.40; (British),
22, 103, 222; Communist Party
USA, 79, 139, 142; anti-
Communists, 29-30, 71-72, 194;
Labor Youth League, 102; *Daily
Worker*, 56; *Political Affairs*, 142
Community (in Williams's thought),
xii-xiii, 2, 17, 23, 129, 155, 182,
232, 235, 238, 287n.70;
CIO-PAC (Political Action
Committee), 29, 257n.66
Congress of Racial Equality (CORE),
149-150
Conservatives: enlightened, 111, 180,
205, 209; Hamiltonian, 84, 182;
neo-, 107, 121, 186, 195, 207, 229,
272n.73; libertarian, xi, 72, 107;
New Right, xiv-xv, 72-73, 180; *See
also* Historians; Wisconsin,
University of.
Constitution, United States, 129-132,
234-236
Containment, 76, 80-82
Cook, Blanche, 227-228
Corporatism, 82, 94, 100, 118, 124,
126, 133-134, 137, 141, 223, 247,
274n.96, 279n.27; corporate capi-
talism, 57-58, 62, 95, 112, 126, 128;
corporate community, 129; corporate liberalism, 100, 138, 139, 158,
185; corporate socialism, 153; cor-
porative commonwealth, 175
Coser, Louis 140
Craig, Gordon M., 112
Crane, Walter, 127
Crapol, Edward, 213, 225
Croly, Herbert, 133
Cuba, 110, 118, 149; Bay of Pigs,

110, 115, 185, 271n.51; Cuban
Missile Crisis, 185; Cuban
Revolution, 140-143
Cumings, Bruce, xii, 241
Curti, Merle, 36-37, 45, 46, 52, 59,
72, 102, 105, 120, 128, 148, 151,
197, 213; *Growth of American
Thought*, 37
Daizaburo, Yui, 224
Daughters of the American
Revolution (essay contest), 15
Davis, David Brion, 293nn.68,69
De Santis, Hugh, 247
Debs, Eugene V., 58, 88, 206, 219
Declaration of Independence, 39, 132
Dee, Ivan, 151
Degler, Carl, 171-172, 281n.57
Democratic Party, 131, 139, 148, 158,
165, 180, 217, 220; convention
(1980), 217; Democrats, 67, 229
*Democracy*, 231, 232
Dewey, John, 46
Dick, Philip K., 249-250
Dilthey, William, 40, 109, 196
*Dissent*, 140, 172, 221
Dollard, John, 122
Donald, David, 131, 187, 209
Dos Passos, John, *U.S.A.*, 83
Douglas, Congresswoman Helen
Gehagen, 219
Draper, Theodore, 141-143,
276n.129, 277n.130, 131; *Castro's
Revolutions*, 141
Drummond, Roscoe, 211
DuBois, William Edward Burghardt,
79, 85, 137, 138, 219, 223; and the
"American Assumption," 88, 130;
*Black Reconstruction*, 209, 257n.65
Dulles, Foster Rhea, 112
Dulles, John Foster, 81-83, 188, 189

Easum, Chester, 35
Eisenhower, Dwight David, general,
182-183; president, 62, 91, 107,
185, 207, 209, 263n.35
Ely, Richard T., 43
Empire, xi-xv, 2, 5, 17, 24, 39, 90, 97,
106, 109, 113, 128-130, 134, 169-
170, 174, 188, 208, 209, 212, 216,
219, 223, 224, 234, 240, 244, 248-

INDEX

317

Wisconsin, State Historical Society
of, 43, 65, 100-102
Wisconsin, University of, 34-47, 101-
108, 118-119, 148-150, 157-162,
166-167, 199, 259n.23, 280n.32;
Anti-Military Ball, 103; anti-war
protests, 157-161, 279n.33; Army
Mathematical Research Building,
166-167, 281n.48; *Connections*
(underground paper), 159; conservatives, 104, 107,147; *Daily
Cardinal*, 44-45, 103; Dow
Chemical protests, 159-160; Robin
A. Fleming (chancellor), 197;
Glenn Frank (president), 43;
Friends of SNCC, 149-150;
History Department, 34-40, 42-43,
92, 97, 105-107, 148-149, 163, 164,
192, 197; Jewish students, 43, 102,
104, 173; liberals, 150; Marxists,
34, 45, 119; radicals, 43, 149-150,
157-161, 165; ROTC, 46, 102-103;
"Smoking Room School of
History," 101-102; Socialist Club,
103, 117, 118, 271n.62; Teaching

Assistants Association, 163; Teach-
Ins, 158-159; Williams's graduate
students, 106-108, 116-117, 163;
"Wisconsin School of Diplomatic
History," 116-117, 197, 209; Young
Democrats, 104
Wolin, Sheldon, 291n.40
Women's Movement (feminism), 2,
13, 150, 154-157, 167, 170, 177-
178, 180, 198, 206; anti-feminism,
157
World War II, 182, 207, 218; atomic
bomb, 24
Woodward, C. Vann, 119
"World Systems," 247

Youth, 154; Counter Culture, 150,
167, 170, 232; Youth Culture, 161-
162, 164

Zeidler, Frank, Mayor of Milwaukee,
45
Zinn, Howard, 147, 173-174,
283n.10
Zuckerman, Michael, 210

# Effective Listening
## Key to Your Success

# Effective Listening
## Key to Your Success

**Lyman K. Steil**
University of Minnesota and
Communication Development, Inc.

**Larry L. Barker**
Auburn University and
SPECTRA Communication Associates

**Kittie W. Watson**
Tulane University and
SPECTRA Communication Associates

**ADDISON-WESLEY PUBLISHING COMPANY**
Reading, Massachusetts • Menlo Park, California
London • Amsterdam • Don Mills, Ontario • Sydney

**Library of Congress Cataloging in Publication Data**

Steil, Lyman K.
  Effective listening.

  Includes index.
  1. Communication in management.    2. Listening.
I. Barker, Larry Lee, 1941–        .    II. Watson, Kittie W.
III. Title.
HD30.3.S75 1983        658.4'52        82-11512
ISBN 0-201-16425-6

# Preface

This volume is intended to serve as a guide for listening improvement for professionals in business and industry as well as a textbook for use in listening and communication courses in colleges and universities. Each of the authors conducts training seminars in listening for government, business, and industry, education, and the military. This book serves to complement these seminars. Other trainers and organizational communication consultants should find the volume useful in their training seminars, short courses, and workshops. As a textbook, this book has been written with practical applications in mind. Although many reference sources, and studies are alluded to, the text is primarily concerned with building awareness, understanding, and appreciation of listening excellence by the reader. We hope that "students" at all levels will find this book useful toward those ends.

This book owes its origins not only to the combined efforts of the authors, but also to several pioneers in listening research. Dr. Ralph Nichols, the "Father of Listening," of necessity influenced the authors' development and theories of listening. The Sperry Corporation, the "corporate leader in listening enhancement," both directly and indirectly provided an impetus to this volume. Sperry represents *the* corporate model of listening theory applied in the modern organization.

In addition to Dr. Ralph Nichols and the Sperry Corporation, the authors gratefully acknowledge the contributions of many other people who made the final product possible. First, we owe much to friends and colleagues who contributed to Larry Barker's text *Listening Behavior*. Secondly, to

Telstar Productions and Bob Miller, we express sincere appreciation for helping develop the "first" educational video program focusing on listening. Thirdly, to Brian Walker, our thanks for seeing the potential of our project and for helping to get the ball rolling. Fourth, to our many professional colleagues and associates in the International Listening Association, we owe a multinational debt of gratitude. Fifth, we recognize the significant and continuing contributions of our innumerable "clients" in their many "real worlds." Sixth, to a variety of friends, students, and colleagues, our thanks for providing encouragement, examples, and refinement of the manuscript. Finally, but by no means least importantly, our joint appreciation to Dee Steil for her countless contributions to this book.

We hope that you will enjoy the text and profit from its content. If you feel like responding to us by letter or phone concerning the ideas, examples, or illustrations used in the text, please do so—our addresses are listed on page 151.

**L.K.S.**
**L.L.B.**
**K.W.W.**

# Contents

# Listening Quiz

Before you begin reading this text, answer the following true–false questions regarding the listening process. The answers follow the quiz on the next page.

T \_\_\_ F \_\_\_ 1. Speaking is a more important part of the communication process than listening.

T \_\_\_ F \_\_\_ 2. Since listening requires little energy, it is very easy.

T \_\_\_ F \_\_\_ 3. Listening is an automatic, involuntary reflex.

T \_\_\_ F \_\_\_ 4. Speakers can command listening to occur in an audience.

T \_\_\_ F \_\_\_ 5. Hearing ability and listening ability can be used interchangeably.

T \_\_\_ F \_\_\_ 6. When they need to, people can force themselves to listen well.

T \_\_\_ F \_\_\_ 7. The speaker is primarily responsible for the success of communication.

T \_\_\_ F \_\_\_ 8. People listen every day. This daily practice eliminates the need for listening training.

T \_\_\_ F \_\_\_ 9. Competence in listening develops naturally.

T ___ F ___ 10. When you learned to read, you simultaneously learned to listen.

T ___ F ___ 11. Listening is only a matter of understanding the words of the speaker.

T ___ F ___ 12. People remember most of what they hear.

T ___ F ___ 13. Although you may not listen well all the time, when you need to or want to, you can turn your listening ability on and listen well.

T ___ F ___ 14. Your listening cannot be improved.

T ___ F ___ 15. Attitudes are unrelated to listening.

T ___ F ___ 16. Memory and listening are the same thing.

T ___ F ___ 17. You listen as well as you will ever be able to.

T ___ F ___ 18. Listening is primarily impacted by intelligence.

T ___ F ___ 19. Your listening and reading vocabularies are identical.

T ___ F ___ 20. Listening habits cannot be changed.

## ANSWERS TO THE LISTENING QUIZ

All of the statements were false. If you marked one or more true, this text should be extremely valuable in helping you gain a deeper understanding about the listening process, and particularly, about the role of active listeners during communication. If you marked all of the statements false, congratulations! You already are aware of some basic principles concerning listening which many people do not recognize. This book should reinforce your ideas regarding listening and help you channel your listening energy more effectively by providing guidelines for isolating listening problems and improving your listening skills.

# 1

# Listening: A 3000 Year Oversight

*We have been given two ears and but a single mouth in order that we may hear more and talk less.*

**Zeno of Citium**

Communication has played an essential role in shaping our civilization. Throughout history, communication skills have helped us meet our basic needs in family, work, and social relationships. In everyday life, communication skills allow us to use modern conveniences such as television, radios, or cars, to play poker or bridge, to know if our spouse left dinner in the oven, and to learn how to read this book.

Visualize, if you will, the following communication situations:

(1) You look through an open door of a corporate training seminar where the instructor is delivering his lecture in an extremely entertaining and animated fashion. As you glance around the room, you note that there are no company employees present—just the instructor giving his lecture.

(2) There is an open-air rally at your local courthouse concerning gubernatorial elections. A political candidate is standing on the courthouse steps eloquently outlining his campaign platform to rows and rows of empty chairs.

(3) You walk into a radio station and see one of the latest popular records revolving on a turntable inside the studio. However, as you look around, you find that the station's transmitter is turned off.

It doesn't take a critical observer to note that the basic element missing in each of these situations is an audience or listener. Even with listeners present, there is no assurance that communication is taking place. Communication requires active participation and shared meanings. Communication comes from the Latin word *communis* which means commonness or sharing of meaning. Communication cannot take place without speakers and listeners; even so, many people think of communication as primarily the spoken or written word, and devote little or no time to improving listening skills.

Historically, listening failures have cost lives, time and money. Think about how different life might be if: during the Civil War, the southern army had followed General Lee's order to attack at the Battle of Gettysburg (failure to attack may have altered the course of the war); the captain of the *Titanic* had heeded warnings of approaching icebergs; or Stalin had listened to his intelligence staff's reports regarding Hitler's buildup along the Russian frontier during World War II. These are only a few examples of how poor listening has affected history. Without listening, communication cannot exist; yet, it was not until the early 1900's that listening began to be studied and analyzed independently of speaking.

## HOW MUCH TIME DO YOU SPEND COMMUNICATING?

If you stopped to think about how much time you spend communicating, you would probably be surprised. Responding to sounds from alarms, turning on radios, reading morning papers, answering phones, stopping at traffic lights, buying gas from local dealers, getting messages and giving instructions to assistants, writing memos, ordering coffee, and so on—within a few hours you have sent and received thousands of communication messages.

If we communicate this often during a morning, think about the time you spend communicating each day. In 1926, Dr. Paul Rankin first attempted to find out how much time we spend communicating and discovered that adults spend 70% of their waking day in some form of communication. A closer examination of Rankin's study (1929) broke verbal communication into four basic categories.

| Type of Communication | Percentage of Time |
|---|---|
| Writing | 9% |
| Reading | 16% |
| Speaking | 30% |
| Listening | 45% |

Even in 1926, nearly half of an adult's communication day was spent listening. Other studies conducted since confirm these findings and reveal that, since Rankin's day, mass communication sources such as television and radio have increased the time spent in listening situations (Bird, 1953; Klemmer and Snyder, 1972). For example, in business settings, research indicates that executives spend 63% of their days listening (Keefe, 1971). Moreover, a recent study found that college students spend about 53% of their communication time listening. Another change is that 21% of our listening time is devoted to mass communication sources. The following chart (Barker, et al., 1981) shows other changes:

| Type of Communication | Percentage of Time |
|---|---|
| Writing | 14% |
| Reading | 17% |
| Speaking | 16% |
| Listening | 53% |
| (Other than mass communication, i.e., classrooms, formal, interpersonal) | 32% |
| (Mass communication, i.e., radio, television, music) | 21% |

As the time spent in different types of communication changes, so does the amount of time we spend communicating. Studies show that, on average, adults now spend 80% of their waking days communicating. If you were to keep a record of your own communication activities during the next 24 hours, how much time do you think you would devote to writing? reading? speaking? listening? Occupational responsibilities have a lot to do with the types of communication you use. Computer programmers spend more time writing and reading, while organizational trainers and developers spend more time speaking. However, if you're typical, over half of your communication time is spent in listening and that percentage increases as people rise in positions of responsibility and authority.

Since so much of your time is devoted to listening, no one can afford the numerous costs associated with even the simplest listening mistakes. Daily activities require you to listen to numerous people in a variety of situations and poor listening can cost you valuable information. We all like to think of ourselves as good listeners; yet how often have you had to reorder supplies, repeat instructions, or explain mistakes caused by listening errors. Off-the-cuff comments such as "He never listens," "I wish someone would teach her to listen," "Why didn't you hear it the first time?" "Didn't you understand?" are common enough.

It is difficult to understand why people do not take listening more seriously when it is so important to job success. However, there seems to be a logical explanation—people have never been trained to listen. That is, there has been a gap in our education. Although we were trained in reading and writing and may have taken courses in speaking, very few of us have received or are receiving training in listening. It is time to close the gaps in our education and learn to listen more effectively. Fortunately, change is now afoot!

## LISTENING TRAINING

How did you acquire the ability to listen? Did you take a course in listening techniques? Has your company or organization instituted a listening development program? Probably not. Our listening habits are not the result of training, but rather the result of a lack of training. Listening is a communications skill that we rarely receive formal training in; yet listening is the skill we develop first and use most often. Instead of training, our listening behaviors are developed by watching and listening to others. Infants begin to develop listening behaviors from birth which are observable at 3 to 9 months, speaking skills at 18 to 24 months, and reading and writing skills at 4 to 6 years of age. More importantly, theorists believe that listening and learning go hand in hand (Wood, 1976).

Since we learn listening skills first and use listening skills more than any other communications skill, we might think that there would be formal training in listening during the educational process. Right? *Wrong!* As the "Father of Listening," Dr. Ralph G. Nichols noted in the mid-1950's that "Our schools are upside down." Our educational system spends the most time training students in the skills they use the least (Nichols, 1957). Thirty years later, little has changed. Americans concentrate most on improving our two least used communication skills, writing and reading. Writing and reading are important, of course, but a breakdown of our educational skills training clarifies the challenge (Steil, 1978).

**Communication Activities and Training**

|  | Listening | Speaking | Reading | Writing |
|---|---|---|---|---|
| Learned | 1st | 2nd | 3rd | 4th |
| Used | Most | Next to most | Next to least | Least |
|  | (45%) | (30%) | (16%) | (9%) |
| Taught | Least | Next to least | Next to most | Most |

In a systematic, overt, and directed fashion, our educational system has focused its attention on writing and reading. Approximately 12 years is devoted to writing and 8 years to reading, while little attention is given to speaking and almost none to listening. The relationship between learning and listening is most evident in classroom situations in which as much as 66% of the time is devoted to listening! Professionals who attend special training seminars receive over half their information through listening.

Much of our listening training comes from people who are unaware of their influence. As parents we say, "Listen when I'm speaking to you" or "Don't you know how to listen?" but don't listen when the child talks. Teachers and professionals adapt to poor listener habits by giving key words and phrases such as "This is important to remember," "Pay close attention," "Listen to this" and "Let me repeat." Obviously, indirect methods of learning to listen are not as effective as they could be.

Educators and business executives are concerned with the problems created by ineffective listening. Although, by comparison, there has been little systematic training in listening, we know that listening attitudes and behaviors are learned and since they are learned, they can be improved (Devine, 1967; Steil, 1977; Smeltzer and Watson, 1982). In schools where listening is taught, listening comprehension has as much as doubled in a few months. It is time for us to devote time to listening training.

While improving our listening behavior, there are several points we should keep in mind. First, many adults serve as poor listening models for children. Ineffective role models impact greatly on children's poor listening habits. Second, adult listening behaviors become habitual. Our listening behaviors have been acquired and reinforced over a long period of time. As adults we rarely think about how we listen or consider that it takes time to change old habits. We listen the way we do because we have learned to listen that way. Third, punishing listening behavior tends to produce negative effects which usually causes more serious listening problems. Fourth, people tend to generalize with regard to all types of listening situations and have difficulty in discerning types of listening most appropriate for different situations.

Awareness of these principles should help you understand some of the listening obstacles we face. When listening training is incorporated into our school systems and organizational development programs, we will have more effective communication. Until that time, if we want to be more successful listeners, we need to fill in the gaps in our listening education. This book is designed to fill some of our educational listening gaps by:

(1) explaining the causes, nature, and costs of poor listening;

(2) fostering self-insight into your listening strengths and weaknesses; and

(3) initiating a method of training to improve your listening behavior.

## REFERENCES

Barker, L., Edwards, R., Gaines, C., Gladney, K., and Holley, F. An investigation of proportional time spent in various communication activities by college students. *Journal of Applied Communication Research*, **8**, 1980, 101–109.

Bird, D. Teaching listening comprehension. *Journal of Communication*. November 1953, **3**, 127–130.

Devine, T. Listening. *Review of Educational Research*, April 1967, **37**, 152–158.

Keefe, W. F. *Listen Management*. New York: McGraw-Hill, 1971.

Klemmer, E., and Snyder, F., Measurement of time spent communicating. *Journal of Communication*, June 1972, **22**, 142–158.

Nichols, R. and Stevens, L. *Are you Listening?* New York: McGraw-Hill, 1957.

Rankin, P. Listening ability. *Proceedings of the Ohio State Educational Conference's Ninth Annual Session*, 1929.

Smeltzer, L., and Watson, K. W. Improving listening skills used in business: An empirical comparison of discussion length, modeling, and level of incentive. Presented to the International Listening Association Convention, Washington, D.C., 1982.

Steil, L. K. Listen My Students. . . And You Shall Learn. *Towards Better Teaching*, Fall 1978, Vol. 11, No. 12.

Steil, L. K. *A Longitudinal Analysis of Listening Pedagogy in Minnesota Secondary Public Schools.* Unpublished doctoral dissertation, Wayne State University, Detroit, Michigan, 1977.

# 2
# Listening: An Essential Element of Communication

*I know that you believe you understand what you think I said, but I am not sure you realize that what you heard is not what I meant.*

**Anonymous**

All organizational problems have at one time or another been characterized by a breakdown in communication. Paradoxically, the panacea or cure-all for these operational weaknesses has typically been more effective communication. Concern over potential communication failures has led to a spate of training seminars and workshops devoted to improving communication skills. In numerous organizations, in-house training seminars on effective speaking, management techniques, selling tips, interpersonal effectiveness, or writing skills have been conducted. While the above skills are essential and should not be minimized, we note that speakers or sources do not operate independently during communication. Successful communication also depends on listeners as receivers of messages.

Concern in recent years about basic communication skills' effectiveness has led to studies designed to identify the most important communication needs. In 1978, Dr. Harold T. Smith undertook a survey of 457 members of the Academy of Certified Administrative Managers who identified "active listening" (hearing how the speaker feels as well as showing concern for the speaker as an individual), as the most critical managerial competency (*Training*, 1978). A similar survey by Professor Jerald Carstens of the University of Wisconsin (River Falls) in 1979 of 45 companies with more than 1000 employees rated listening as the most important communication skill (Mundale, 1980). Even so, of the 45 companies, only nine provided listening skills training for their employees. In 1980, Dr. Aubrey Sanford of the Atlanta Consulting Group undertook a survey of "Fortune 1000" corporation presidents and found poor subordinate listening habits were related to work situations that were most anxiety-producing for top management (Mundale, 1980). The tendency to listen poorly has also been rated as the number-one communication barrier in accountant–accountant relationships and for first-line supervisors (Golen, 1979; Smeltzer, 1979).

Until recently, listeners have been seen as passive participants in communication. Now, however, large numbers of success-oriented people are assuming more active roles and attempting to improve their communications skills by increasing their listening effectiveness. Listening errors are costly and many organizations are now stressing the importance of listening improvement. One corporate leader that has carried the importance of listening to all of its organizational levels is the Sperry Corporation. Paul Lyet, former chief executive of Sperry, says "Effective listening has been an important part of our success, it pays dividends . . ." (Storm, 1980). Listening is so important to Sperry that the company mounted a promotional campaign around the slogan "We understand how important it is to listen." (Courtesy of Sperry Corporation). Central to the success of Sperry's effort was top management's commitment to listening as a corporate philosophy and their revolutionary internal listening training effort. In the initial years of their listening development program, Sperry trained more than 20,000 employees (from top management on down) from more than 30 countries.

The time, money, and talent that Sperry invested resulted in improved employee and customer relations. Similarly,
the time and effort you invest in improving your listening
skills can work benefits for you. Since all elements of the
communication process are important, you need to understand their roles and relationships to become a successful
communicator.

## COMMUNICATION IN ACTION

Professionals spend nearly 80% of their working days communicating. When communicating you attempt to share a
common meaning with another person. Obviously for communication to take place, there must be a sender or source of
communication. The sender initiates interactions with a specific purpose in mind. Sources send ideas in the form of verbal (words) or nonverbal (gestures, facial expressions, etc.)
*messages.* Each message has unique content (concepts, ideas,
words, meaning, etc.) and treatment (delivery, arrangement,
etc.). *Channels* of communication carry the messages to their
final destination—*listeners* or receivers. Receivers may act
upon a message by *sensing* what has been said, *interpreting*
what has been heard, *evaluating* what has been sensed and
interpreted, and *responding.* When the message is *sensed* in a
relatively complete fashion, correctly *interpreted,* and effectively *evaluated,* productive and positive *response* or feedback
will hopefully result. Negative or ambiguous feedback will
result when the message is not completely sensed, or is misunderstood, or is not effectively evaluated. As feedback is
given, the communication process continues over again with
the source in the listener or the receiver role. Communication
is a dynamic and continuous process that is not, in essence,
intermittent. Even "silent treatments" relay messages. No response is a response! In other words, we cannot not communicate!
Communication is influenced by the *context* or situations. You communicate in particular environments, at special times, in unique ways. You make choices about how

messages are sent, what channels are used and types of feedback given. Couples avoid arguing in front of friends, company mergers are negotiated behind closed doors, and election results are shared with large crowds of anxious campaign supporters. The quality of communication can be affected at any time. *Noise* or barriers such as telephones ringing, static over radios, babies crying, machinery operating, internal physical or psychological pain cause communication distortion or breakdown.

Among the most influential operating factors during communication are the *filtering agents* of senders and receivers. Similar to filters used with a camera lens, filtering agents allow the passage or blockage or coloring of other elements. Consider how professional photographers use filters designed to let in some rays of light while screening out other rays that may ruin or distort a picture. While a filter is in use, it becomes a part of the camera and affects the final outcome of the picture. Camera filters are changed to get desired results. Similar to a camera lens, filtering agents affect communication with others. Filtering agents such as past work experiences, educational training, opinions, emotions, attitudes, feelings, and language abilities influence how you send and receive messages. Understanding your personal filtering agents puts you in a position to maximize your communication and listening success.

It is critically important for listeners to identify the sender's purpose, because communication breakdowns occur when senders and receivers have different purposes. If you take time off from your busy schedule to attend a paid seminar or a professional conference, you expect to gain information or learn something. If the seminar or conference leader spent the bulk of his or her time on something other than the expected purpose, you would feel frustrated.

The "communication purpose model" shown in Fig. 1.1 identifies *four primary purposes* of human communication. These purposes are contributory to each other and skilled listeners identify and adapt their listening behavior to specific communication purposes. Skilled listeners recognize the im-

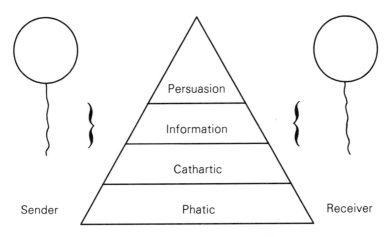

**Fig. 1.1** Communication Purpose Model

portance of achieving congruence of purpose. They work hard at correlating sender and receiver purposes. The four communication purposes of *phatic, cathartic, information,* and *persuasion* are primary to professional and personal success.

## Phatic

Whenever we engage in "small talk," "chit-chat," or conversation that helps us build personal relationships, we are engaging in phatic communication. Many of us may view small talk as unimportant and a waste of time; effective listeners, however, realize it is important and requires a special listening attitude and behavior. Casual chit-chat about the weather, the weekend, the news, the family, the vacation, the World Series, etc., allows a building of personal awareness and a sense of relationship.

Phatic communication helps develop binding relationships and is contributory to all higher-level communication purposes. We may tend to downplay the importance of phatic communication, but in reality, it plays a critical role in our total communication success. As a rule, we generally communicate better at higher levels with people who we're "bound up with" than others with whom we have not developed such relationships. In other words, when our phatic or binding communication diminishes or ceases, our other communication efforts will suffer.

## Cathartic

Catharsis is the process of releasing emotion, the ventilation of feelings, the sharing of problems or frustrations with an empathic listener. Without catharsis, when needed, senders' pent-up emotions and unreleased feelings will result in ulcers, anger, nervous breakdowns, and of course, strained communication. The listener's role is critical since cathartic communication *requires* a caring, empathic, nonjudgmental listener. Catharsis basically requires a *willing* and *able* listener who is observant to the cathartic need cues and clues of others. Individuals in need of catharsis often exude verbal and nonverbal cues, and effective listeners are sensitive to them. Unfortunately numerous individuals purposefully avoid cathartic or unloading communication, since they believe that listening to catharsis takes unwarranted time and energy. In addition, many don't understand the relevance of catharsis, or realize that when it is needed and not allowed, the other purposes of communication will suffer. Cathartic fulfillment is necessary for optimal success at all other levels of communication.

## Informational

A third purpose of communication is the sharing of information. The primary goal or purpose of information exchange is the mutual sharing of ideas and data with others. Of course, sharing information with others is one of the most frequent and important purposes of communication. New employees are given informational orientation sessions to learn about company benefits and policies; mechanics listen to automobile owners describe the strange sounds their cars make; students listen to hours of information day in and day out; our dentist shares the value of dental flossing. Politicians, parents, teachers, flight attendants, medical professionals, news and weather forecasters, friends, the clergy and all others engaged in social contact are heavily involved in informational communication, both as senders and receivers. Of course, the ultimate success of informational connection centers on whether or not specific data (information) has been thoroughly transmitted and received, correctly interpreted, effectively evaluated, and responded to. But remember, no one is assured of perfect understanding, accuracy, and response. Consider the following information exchange*:

> A new employee approached one of the women in our office with an important-looking paper in his hand, pointed to the paper-shredding machine and asked her to show him how to operate it. "Of course," she said. "You just turn the switch on here, put your sheet of paper in here, like this, and that's all there is to it."
>
> As the machine devoured his document, the new man thanked her for her help and then asked, "By the way, how many copies will this make?"

## Persuasive Communication

Door-to-door salespeople, antique auctioneers, car dealers, TV and radio pitchmen, or political candidates are the first people who come to mind when thinking about persuasive communication. Other persuasive appeals such as ball point pen advertisements, complimentary matches from your favorite restaurant, family portraits on office desks, or wearing three-piece suits go relatively unnoticed as forms of persuasion. Persuasive communication attempts to (1) reinforce existing attitudes and beliefs, (2) instil new attitudes and beliefs, or (3) affect behaviors and actions. All communication is essentially persuasive in that we want our ideas to be ac-

---

*Gary Seering and Durreshahwar Baig, *Reader's Digest*, June, 1980, p. 184. Reprinted by permission.

cepted and liked. However, the success of persuasive communication depends on a person's conscious or unconscious listening. Many commercials appeal to unconscious buyers who are unaware that persuasion took place even when they enter checkout lines with products in hand.

Communication purposes rarely operate independently of each other and are often difficult to isolate. Nevertheless, senders as well as receivers of messages usually have, at a given moment, a primary purpose or goal of communication. A civic group may think a speaker has come to discuss the dangers of inflation when actually his primary purpose may be to sell silver coins as investments. We tend to seek out situations and interactions that are consistent with our own purposes. Difficulties arise when speakers' and listeners' stated purposes and intended purposes do not coincide.

## CONGRUENCE OF PURPOSE

Effective and productive listeners distinguish among the different communication purposes, since each purpose calls for a different listening approach. Phatic communication requires time, patience, an other-orientedness, and a recognition of the larger value of relationship building. Cathartic communication requires caring, concerned, risk-taking and nonjudgmental listening. Truly empathic people suspend evaluation and criticism when they listen to others. Here the challenge is to enter into the private world of the speaker, to understand without judging actions or feelings. By contrast, the task of listening to a persuasive speaker eventually involves evaluating the speaker's case and deciding whether we agree or disagree, and then taking appropriate action.

Significant failures in listening result when the speaker and listener communicate at cross-purposes. We've all experienced individuals who attempt to persuade us before providing the necessary information needed to make a rational decision. By the same token, people who engage in catharsis when we desire hard data about a problem do not communicate well. As good listeners, we must consciously ask ourselves four questions: What is the speaker's purpose? What is my purpose for listening? How can I act to align those purposes? What special listening requirements does any given purpose call for?

It's important to note that, as Fig. 1.1 suggests, these four purposes are hierarchical in nature. Phatic communication provides the basis for the other three purposes of communication, often coming before and laying the ground work for catharsis, information, and persuasion. Similarly, a person desperately needing catharsis will not be able to effectively transmit information or persuade others until his or her emotional needs have been met. Finally, we know that persuasive communication must be based upon evidence and information before it can be truly successful.

## LEVELS OF COMMUNICATION

*One advantage of talking to yourself is that you know at least somebody's listening.*

**Franklin P. Jones**

Communication is often thought of as simply a matter of sending messages between two people; however, we participate in communication on several levels daily. Communication that takes place inside you is intrapersonal communication. You constantly communicate with yourself by planning the day's agenda, controlling your temper, or making decisions to get out of bed. Even in intrapersonal communication, we communicate at any given moment for a specific communication purpose. Socrates once said, "Know thyself." It is important for us to learn to listen to ourselves. As we communicate well with ourselves at the intrapersonal level, we will more likely communicate well with others at the interpersonal and public levels.

Job interviews, telephone conversations, marital and family interactions and business meetings are examples of interpersonal communication or person-to-person communication. Listening is essential since each person plays the role of speaker and listener simultaneously. Group communication occurs when three or more people get together. Successful group encounters provide all members with the opportunity to participate. Of course, active participation includes listening as part of the communication process.

Public communication, or one person addressing a group, usually places the primary focus for communication success on the speaker; however, without an audience composed of effective listeners, no productive communication would exist. Mass communication such as TV and radio is characterized by mechanical reproduction, rapid distribution, and delayed feedback. Listeners can usually cope with more distractions when tuned to mass communication. Receivers or listeners may, for instance, leave televisions on while talking on the phone, answering questions from others, or reading a newspaper.

Although the occasions, environments, situations, and participant relationships are different in the foregoing examples, and have an impact on the listening task, it is also obvious that there are numerous common listening elements in all contexts.

Organizations typically exhibit all levels of communication. Learning to listen well at lower communication levels (for example, phatic vs. persuasion) makes listening easier at other levels when necessary. As you begin to identify some of your filtering agents, types of interactions, potential distractions and communication strengths you will be in a better position to control your communication effectiveness.


## WHO HAS THE PRIMARY RESPONSIBILITY FOR COMMUNICATION?

Earlier we mentioned that communication responsibility has been historically placed on the speaker in this society. Should this necessarily be so? Senders and receivers both have the ability to control elements during the communication process, so who should accept primary responsibility for communication success, the speaker or the listener? In other words, if communication breakdowns occur, who is to blame? Of the thousands of people throughout the United States, who have been asked this question during our seminars, 70% believe the primary responsibility for communication success rests with the speaker, 25% with the listener, and 5% fail to respond. Those who believe that speakers hold the primary responsibility contend that:

1. Senders initially control the communication act.

2. Senders hold a vested interest in communication.

3. Senders determine the primary and secondary purposes of the specific communication.

4. Senders analyze filtering agents of receivers and develop messages for specific audiences.

5. Senders select the channels for communication.

6. Senders choose the context for communication.

7. Senders observe and receive feedback from which to evaluate.

Those that view receivers as primarily responsible have similar arguments, such as:

1. Receivers have the power to accept or reject the communication.

2. Receivers determine the meaning of the communication.

3. Receivers control the channel of the communication.

4. Receivers control the feedback factors of communication.

5. Receivers control the context of the communication.

Both sides have valid arguments, but either view places speakers and listeners in passive positions. Individuals agreeing with the 70% who give primary responsibility to speakers, in a sense say that listeners should participate from the standpoint of: "Ok, I'm here . . . now you'd better . . . make it interesting, keep my attention, have something valuable to say, and . . . ." Similarly, 25% of the general public give listeners the primary responsibility, by their response, for making sure that messages are ethical, well researched, organized and interesting. In either case, these viewpoints have one interesting characteristic in common: shifting the burden for success to others and thus letting others control their behavior or destinies. In work, home, social, church, and educational situations, there are millions of us who place the primary burden of communication success on others. Yet, who is in the best position to control your own future? You are of course and because you are, *you* need to be the more responsible co-municator.

As skilled listeners, we need to take a position different from others. Our challenge is to accept a "minimum 51% responsibility" for communication success no matter if we are in the role of sender or receiver. Your mission—"if you decide to accept it"—will positively affect your communication and listening behavior. In every communication situation, regardless of purpose, you play primary roles of senders and receivers of messages. Picture yourself as wearing two hats: one hat is your sender hat and one hat is your receiver hat. During communication, you constantly change these hats. Now imagine a third hat: a minimum 51% responsibility hat. See yourself as wearing it at all times. When used as the foundation for the other hats, this third hat will make you a more successful communicator. Using all three hats, regardless of your momentary role during communication, will move you from passive through responsible to active communication. Your acceptance, constant practice, and real commitment will aid you *both* as a sender and as a receiver. But due to our typical existing beliefs and consequent practices, this acceptance of the minimum 51% responsibility will serve you most as listener. Try it, you"ll buy it!

## THE SIER MODEL: THE FOUR STAGES OF LISTENING

The listening act really consists of four connected activities—sensing, interpreting, evaluating and responding. Taking the first letter from each of these terms, we arrive at the S–I–E–R Model represented in Fig. 2.1.

Listening is not synonymous with hearing, but good listening begins at the level of sensing the sender's message. Sensing is basic to the other three activities involved in listening—if the listener does not sense the message, he or she can do nothing further with it.

After the message is sensed, a second activity comes into play: accurate interpretation. Here we encounter semantic problems: the sensitive listener asks, "I heard the words used by the speaker, but am I assigning a comparable meaning to them?" Effective listeners remember that "words have no meaning—people have meaning." The assignment of meaning to a term is an internal process; meaning comes from inside us. And although our experiences, knowledge, and attitudes differ, we often misinterpret each other's messages while under the illusion that a common understanding has been achieved.

Active listeners go beyond sensing and interpretation to another act: evaluation. Here the listener decides whether or

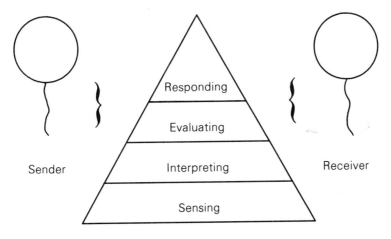

**Fig. 2.1** SIER: Communication Stages Model

not to agree with the speaker. The evidence is weighed, fact is sorted from opinion, and judgment is rendered. Poor listeners begin this activity too soon, often hearing something they disagree with and tuning out the speaker from that point on. When this occurs, sensing and interpretation stop —so does listening. Speakers have the right to be heard, and the best listeners delay judgment until the message is fully presented. Moreover, the best listeners work hard at developing their judgmental skills and abilities.

Finally, to be complete, the listening process must result in response. Responses can be of many kinds, ranging from nonverbal cues to the speaker showing that we've received the message (smiling, frowning), to giving the speaker feedback, asking questions, and requesting clarification. Ultimately the listener asks, "What's expected of me now? What action, if any, should result?"

Every effective executive realizes the critical importance of responding. Ultimately, the ability to respond is linked to a sense of responsibility. The meaning of responsibility when applied to listening was well expressed by Erich Fromm in *The Art of Loving*: "Today responsibility is often meant to denote duty, something imposed on one from the outside. But responsibility, in its true sense, is an entirely voluntary act. . . . To be responsible means to be ready and able to 'respond.'"

The response stage of listening is especially crucial for judging the success of the listening act as a whole. This is true because the first three stages—sensing, interpreting, and evaluating—are internal acts. They take place inside of us; no one can directly observe them. Until the listener makes a concrete response, it's often difficult to determine whether the speaker has been successful in getting the point across. The response stage (see Fig. 2.1) is the first to include behaviors we can see and measure. If there is a breakdown at any stage (S, I, E, or R), it will not be apparent until the response stage.

These four stages of listening are hierarchical, just as the purposes of communication. The message must be sensed before it can be interpreted or evaluated. And one cannot intelligently respond to a message until it's been properly evaluated, interpreted and sensed. Any failure at the sensing level will impede success at the "higher" levels. And the listener who evaluates a message before correctly understanding it does not understand the complete nature of the listening process.

When faced with communication breakdowns, we usually wonder what went wrong. The SIER model can be used as a *diagnostic* tool to determine at what level the observed communication breakdown started. Although we always see the *response* level results, the first point to remember when diagnosing a listening breakdown is to look for the lowest level where the breakdown could have started. In ascending order from S to I, I to E, and E to R, we need to check all levels of the listening process to determine the point of origin.

Of course when diagnosing a problem, there is no way to be absolutely certain about the level of error since we cannot see inside another person's head. However, by looking at external signs and indications we can make a good guess as to where the problem started. Again, we have to look to the lowest level at which the problem could have started. Otherwise, we may be diagnosing a symptom rather than a cause of the actual communication problem. See if you can identify the lowest-level errors in the following situations.

In 1938 Hitler's invasion of Czechoslovakia caused tension in the United States. On October 30, 1938, millions of Americans tuned their radios to CBS's "Mercury Theatre of the Air" to be entertained. That night Orson Welles introduced H. G. Well's *War of the Worlds* and attempted to control possible side effects by broadcasting repeated warnings that the radio play newscast was fictional and not to be taken seriously. However, the program set off a nation-wide panic with audiences believing aliens from Mars had invaded New Jersey. Thousands of calls were made to the news media, many people reported seeing aliens, there were huge traffic jams, and U.S. troops were alerted for action. Because of its impact, FCC passed regulations prohibiting future fictional news bulletins.

At first, this example might seem to be focused at the response level, but we have to look for the origin of the problem. For many, this situation was probably caused by a sensing error and we know that sensing problems cause errors with interpretation, evaluation and response. Many people who panicked did not sense the repeated warnings of a fictitious broadcast. Thus their ultimate processing and response was inappropriate. In this case, when segments of a message were missed, important information was lost.

As listeners, we need to think about ways to improve our ability to sense a message accurately. It may help to select a better place to sit, turn up the volume on the radio or television, eliminate overriding distractions, controlling emotions, taking notes, or asking for repetition. Repeating a message several times is often a useful device to help people hear a message, but as with the *War of the Worlds* broadcast, repeated warnings were not effective either. Our mind-set often causes us to hear what we expect to hear. Now let's look at a second illustration.

Saturday, March 1, 1980, was the first time the U. S. had supported a United Nations Security Council resolution sharply criticizing Israel. Two days later on March 3, 1980, the White House reported that a mistake had been made in their Security Council vote. According to *Time Magazine* here is what happened.

On February 28th, 14 members of the Security Council approved a draft of a resolution condemning settlement of the Arab populated West Bank by Israelis. A copy of the proposal was sent by U. S. Ambassador McHenry to Secretary of State Vance in hopes of presidential approval. The President had three reservations. Vance was directed to tell McHenry to abstain unless (1) the council deleted a paragraph implying that Israel did not guarantee religious freedom, (2) McHenry had reservations about the wording of a controversial paragraph demanding dismantling of all Israeli settlements, and (3) all references to Jerusalem were excised from the text.

Confusion surrounded Carter's third reservation. According to Vance's aide, he thought Carter was concerned only about the mentioning of Jerusalem in the controversial paragraph. Vance did not tell McHenry that every reference to Jerusalem had to be removed. McHenry met the President's requirements according to Vance. Vance telephoned the President on Saturday morning before the vote and Vance told Carter that the references to Jerusalem were removed, although Vance knew that was not literally true. The President did not ask for Vance to read the final proposal and gave his approval to vote yes.

Basically, Carter and Vance had an interpretation problem. Vance was instructed to remove *all* references to Jerusalem, but Vance did not take the president literally. If Carter had asked for the proposal to be read or had had a copy to read himself, maybe the United States would have avoided worldwide scorn and ridicule. You have probably experienced a situation in which messages were interpreted differently than you had intended, and have an understanding how easily interpretation errors occur. The next example is the result of a different type of listening error.

In 1972, Richard Grimshaw, 13, was riding with a neighbor on a road near San Bernardino, California when another automobile plowed into the rear of their car. Their gas tank ruptured and 90% of Richard's body was badly burned. Today, Richard is still receiving operations to help repair his body.

In court, the plaintiffs charged that the manufacturer's crash testing research had revealed weaknesses in their gas tanks which caused excessive gas leakage upon impact. However, the company chose not to spend the ten dollars per car it would have taken to correct the weaknesses. The result was a $128.5 million jury verdict in favor of the plaintiff.

In this situation, evidently someone had heard and interpreted the message correctly, but the appropriate response was not taken. So where did the problem occur? It appears that someone made a judgment that the gas leakage and weak tanks were not serious problems. However, this evaluation resulted in consequences that caused suffering for everyone concerned. This example could just as easily have been a success story if the message had been evaluated differently. Incorrect judgments ultimately create reaction or response problems and the potential for communication breakdowns.

Let's look at one last seemingly small example, although we know the resulting problems add to significant consequences.

> A company softball team ordered uniforms for all of its players. The captain of the team went to a local sporting goods store and ordered 18 uniforms. Each uniform was to have the player's name embroidered above the front shirt pocket and the company name Union Carboneers sewn on the back of the shirt in large letters visible to spectators. The salesperson took the order and repeated the information and agreed that the company name would be a good advertising device. Two weeks later when the uniforms arrived the uniforms had the company name above the front pocket and the players' names in large letters on the back of the shirts. The captain refused the shipment.

What happened? We know the salesperson heard the instructions, since he repeated exactly what was expected. It's possible that the salesperson did not understand the order. On the other hand, it may be that the salesperson made a poor judgment and did not think that the lettering mattered. Then what went wrong? It seems that the problem started at the response level. Somehow the sporting goods store responded differently than what they intended and lost money and future business. Perhaps the salesperson heard, understood, agreed, but simply forgot. We know he didn't respond appropriately. There have probably been situations in which you have responded differently than you had planned. When situations like this occur, it is not a sensing, interpreting, or evaluation problem; it is a response problem.

These few examples show that communication can be successful at one level and still fail at higher levels. By using the SIER model to diagnose problems that have occurred, applying communication principles to correct the problem, and planning ways to prevent communication breakdowns, you can improve your listening and communication effectiveness.

Communication is more complex than listening to an occasional message. Secretaries remind managers of appointments while they talk on the telephone, sign letters, and listen to employee complaints. Professionals are often bombarded by several messages and reach points of information overload. Communication situations change so quickly that many difficulties go undetected until days or weeks after the fact. Some time ago, for example, President Carter told his aides to call the military commander at Fort Chaffee, Arkansas. The order instructed the commander to use the force necessary to restrain Cuban refugees. That order never reached the commander and consequently on June 3, 1980, the Army backed down when Cubans awaiting relocation started running for the gates. The riot that ensued left 60 people injured and four buildings burned to the ground. Although Carter had issued an order, no one knew there was a breakdown in communication until it was too late.

## EXPANDED SIER MODEL

As we have considered the SIER model to this point, we have viewed the communication and listening process primarily with respect to a "frozen frame moment." To reflect the dynamics of the real world, the "expanded SIER model" (Fig. 3.1) clarifies the overlap of levels in the ongoing communication process. This sawtooth model illustrates the ascending-order requirement associated with the challenge of fulfilling your commitment as a listener.

Each person who takes part in the communication process brings unique filtering agents to the interaction. The expanded SIER model shows how our interactions progress through time. As we switch back and forth between sender and receiver roles, we sense, interpret, evaluate, and respond

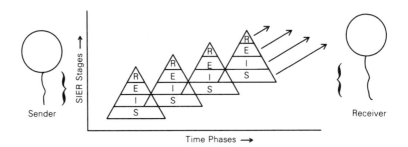

**Fig. 3.1** SIER Sawtooth Process Model

simultaneously. If a communication breakdown occurs, we usually think of one error as causing the problem. However, through the model, you can see that the potential for errors during communication is limitless. This model represents the interaction between two people, but think about the increased complexity as you add other people to the conversation.

As more people are added to conversations, the potential for misunderstandings multiplies. Errors occur at different communication levels, with senders and receivers, and at the beginning, middle, and end of interactions. Errors in initial meetings usually cause breakdowns in later meetings. We can all think of times we've failed to listen to an entire message because we felt that we already knew what a person was going to say. At times our expectations are accurate, but sometimes they are not. An example from *Reader's Digest\** highlights this point.

> When their son left for his freshman year at Duke University, his parents gave him a Bible, assuring him it would be a great help. Later, as he began sending them letters asking for money, they would write back telling him to read his Bible, citing chapter and verse. He would reply that he was reading the Bible—but he still needed money.

---

\*Contributed by John T. Spach *Reader's Digest*, March 1980, p. 197. Reprinted by permission.

When he came home for a semester break, his parents told him they knew he had not been reading his Bible. How? They had tucked $10 and $20 bills by the verses they had cited in their letters.

We need to learn to listen to the complete message so we won't miss out on important information later. Communicating with different purposes or errors is likely to cause serious communication failures. Whenever there are difficulties initially, think of a possibility of future misunderstanding.

A president of a large southern power company mentioned that his greatest frustration takes place with retiring employees. He has learned not to mention the possibility of work after retirement or even how much a person will be needed because he's often misinterpreted. Once he mentioned the possibility of future consulting with a retiring employee and later found the employee telling other employees that the company was making a policy exception in his case so that he could work past the age of 65. When the president confronted him again and repeated that he could not work past 65, the employee got angry and believed the president had gone back on his word.

Obviously, the president and employee had different communication purposes as well as at least one level of listening error. Avoiding the issue is not the best solution. In the example above, the president assumed that a listening error occurred. This is probably the case, since the employee seemed only to listen to what he wanted to hear. However, the president could also look at his own communication to see if there were any errors on his part. At the time of the first interaction, he could have asked the employee to repeat what he said to make sure that there were no sensing errors. Then he could have asked the employee to explain what he had said to check for interpretation errors. Again looking at the lowest level of interaction helps us to detect more than just a symptom in a communication breakdown.

## TYPES OF LISTENING

We mentioned earlier that many people have difficulty in adapting their level of listening to different situations. Most of us participate in two types of listening contexts: social and serious (Barker, 1971). We listen informally in social situations such as coffee breaks, concerts, or dinner table talk. We take part in serious listening in formal situations such as contract negotiations, loan requests, and jury duty.

Four types of social listening that may be associated with conversation or entertainment are: appreciative listening, conversational listening, courteous listening, and listening to indicate love or respect.

Appreciative listening involves recognizing aspects of a speaker's style, interpreting characters in a dialogue, listening for rhythm in music, or visualizing images from hearing a message. When we listen to a poem being read, a concert, a play, or a TV program, we listen appreciatively. With appreciative listening comes some sort of satisfaction or pleasure from active participation.

ʳConversational listening involves two-way communication. Conversational listening may also take place in serious situations, but generally, it is seen as social listening because of the informal settings in which it occurs. If you think about the conversations you've had in a typical day, you'll find that the best conversationalists are also good listeners. ˒Courteous listening includes conversation, but you are primarily involved as a listener. This is sometimes a difficult role to play because we usually enjoy talking. We use courteous listening when listening to employees complain about paperwork or try out their ideas for a new safety training program.

A type of listening that goes along with courteous listening is listening to indicate love or respect. Unfortunately, we often neglect the importance of listening with love and respect. When a parent listens to a child say something which may not be important to the parent but is extremely important to the child, or when a child listens to an elderly parent tell the same stories over and over again, he or she listens with love and respect.

Serious listening can be classified as either selective or concentrated listening. Selective listening involves listening only to segments of a message. Concentrated listening involves listening to the entire message and attempting to take in all aspects of what is said. At times we need to remember everything that has been said, while other times all the information may not need to be remembered. Unfortunately, some listeners do not realize that they are listening selectively. Selective listening may result from poor listening habits and if you find yourself missing important information, then maybe you have been using selective listening inappropriately.

Serious listening is divided into subcategories of critical and discriminative listening. Critical listening attempts to analyze information offered as evidence, and make critical judgments about the validity and quality of materials presented. We analyze politician platforms, architects' plans, and the ideas in advertising campaigns. Discriminative listening is intended for understanding and remembering. When you try to remember directions from a service station attendant in a new city, relay a message to a client, or listen to a question asked of you during a press interview, you take place in discriminative listening.

Although it is important to be aware of the types of listening, a situation can rarely be characterized by only one type of listening. For example, after you talk about your birdie putt, you might talk about the latest Supreme Court decision concerning tax deductions. Like communication itself, listening is a process and we need to keep in mind that in one situation we engage in a variety of types of listening.

## NONVERBAL LISTENING

*He that has eyes to see and ears to hear may convince himself that no mortal can keep a secret. If his lips are silent, he chatters with his*

*finger tips; betrayal oozes out of him at every
pore.*

**Freud**

One important type of listening that does not require the
ability to hear is nonverbal listening. The deaf "listen"—often very well—through alternative channels of sight, taste,
smell, and touch. Those of us who can hear are at a distinct
advantage over deaf listeners, yet we often fail to capitalize
on our advantage.

Many of our daily decisions are based on information
derived through channels other than hearing, although we
rarely stop to think about the importance of total sensory
listening. Think for a moment about what it would be like to
communicate only through sounds. Without all our senses,
many of the communication experiences such as tastes of
food, a lover's embrace, spectator sports, and familiar smells
would be lost. Of the senses we take for granted, one of the
most valuable besides hearing is sight.

Recently there has been increased interest in nonverbal
aspects of communication. Body language, facial expression,
eye contact, vocal characteristics, clothing, and spatial dis-
tances often substitute for verbal forms of communication.
We all know that information comes from what a person
*does* as well as what a person *says,* and we run the risk of
misinterpreting information when we fail to consider both.
Think about the importance of nonverbal behavior. Dressing
for employment interviews, employees who arrive late for
work, pats on the back from company presidents, shutting
doors to inner offices, and avoiding angry clients all communicate messages nonverbally. In fact, when verbal and nonverbal messages contradict each other, we have a tendency to
believe the nonverbal message (Mehrabian, 1972). Glancing
at your watch, putting on your jacket, and looking at the
door often signal that you need or want to leave even when
verbally you may say "Sure, I have time to look over your
new proposal."

We cannot avoid communicating, the clothes we wear, the way we sit, the arrangement of our offices, and even the cars we drive communicates information to ourselves and others. It is important to gain greater awareness of how we communicate nonverbally in order to reduce chances for sensing, interpreting, evaluating, and responding erroneously. Combined sensitivity concerning verbal and nonverbal messages will increase your probability of listening success in everyday relationships.

## SUMMARY

By now you should have a clearer understanding of elements in the communication process. The complexity of communication lies in the dual role played by listeners and senders of messages. Accepting the minimum 51% responsibility both as sender or receiver in all communication situations increases our chances for successful listening. Phatic, cathartic, informational, persuasive, and entertainment communication are stages of communication that apply to our communication relationships whether on the level of intrapersonal, interpersonal, groups, organization, public or mass.

Because of the complexity of communication, we often have breakdowns. The SIER formula helps us detect the lowest level in which errors occur. Analysis of sensing, interpreting, evaluating, and responding levels helps both senders and receivers detect communication breakdowns. The SIER model locates difficulties in social and serious listening situations when verbal communication breakdowns occur. We should also be aware of the role of nonverbal communication because nonverbal messages may relay as much information as verbal messages. Up to this point we have emphasized the complexity of communication and the importance of listening in the communication process. In the next chapter we will consider ways to help you identify your listening strengths and weaknesses.

## REFERENCES

Barker, L. *Listening Behavior.* Englewood Cliffs, NJ: Prentice-Hall, 1971.

Conigliaro, S. Listen your way to the top. *Graduating Engineer,* Winter 1980, 15–17.

Golen, S. An analysis of communication barriers in public accounting firms. *The Journal of Business Communication,* **17,** 1980, 39–49.

Mehrabian, A. *Nonverbal Communication.* Chicago: Aldine-Atherton, 1972.

Mundale, S. Why more CEO's are mandating listening and writing training. *Training,* October 1980, 37–41.

Smeltzer, L. Barriers to effective communication for the first line supervisor: Implications for the instructor of business communication. *Proceedings* American Business Communication National Convention, 1979, 173–178.

Storm, B. Sperry Corporation. *Madison Avenue,* February 1980, **22,** 50, 54.

The 20% activities that bring 80% payoff. *Training,* June 1978, 6.

# 3

# Are You Getting the Most From Your Listening?

*As friends, we don't see eye to eye, but then we don't hear ear to ear either.*

**Buster Keaton**

You hear thousands of messages each day. Listening is central to your professional and personal success. But skilled listening is more than just sensing what has been said; you also have to interpret, evaluate and respond to what is said. Listening is a major communication activity, yet 80% of people surveyed rated their listening ability as average or lower (Steil, 1980). Clearly that's not good enough for successful communication. As we have seen, many businesses have not established training programs to improve employee listening habits and poor listeners are apt to make more mistakes which translate into lost revenues. Marriage counselors claim that a major cause of divorce is poor communication. For this reason, before saying "I do" many churches require couples to attend communication training sessions that stress the importance of listening in relationships.

## WHY LEARN?

*The greatest problem in communication is the illusion that it has been accomplished.*

**Daniel W. Davenport**

In its landmark campaign to improve listening skills of its employees, Sperry Corporation came up with an advertisement headlined:

### KNOWING HOW TO LISTEN COULD DOUBLE THE EFFICIENCY OF AMERICAN BUSINESS. DID YOU HEAR THAT?
*(Courtesy of Sperry Corporation)*

The point was made:

> Business today is held together by its communication system.
>
> And listening is undoubtedly its weakest link.
>
> Most of us spend about half our business hours listening. Listening poorly. Research studies show that on the average we listen at a 25% level of efficiency.
>
> A statistic that is not only suprisingly low, but terribly costly.
>
> With more than 100 million workers in America, a simple ten dollar listening mistake by each of them would cost a billion dollars.
>
> Letters have to be retyped; appointments rescheduled; shipments reshipped.
>
> And when people in large corporations fail to listen to one another, the results are even costlier.

Unfortunately, many mistakes cost much, much more. When people fail to listen, the results can be devastating.

> A large engineering firm had a team of 24 engineers working on a major military project at a cost of about $1000 per man

per week, plus an independent engineering consultant whose fee was $4,000 per week. The team encountered a critical problem that threatened to delay the entire project and subject the firm to a heavy penalty for lateness under its contract. So the head of the project telephoned the consultant, assigned him to work out a solution to the problem, and specified that the company must absolutely have the solution in one week. Later the project head told one of our authors, "At the end of the week, I again telephoned the engineer and learned he had been working on an entirely different phase of the problem than the one for which we needed a solution. Obviously, I had failed to make clear to him what we needed. But in our original conversation, he had indicated that he understood what needed to be done. So I had to divert all our engineers on the project until we got the solution."

The cost of this breakdown:

| | |
|---|---|
| The consultant's fee for one week | $4,000 |
| Salaries and fringe benefits of company engineers | 24,000 |
| Penalty for lateness under the company's contract | 122,000 |
| Total: | $150,000 |

(Steil, 1979)

Ideas get distorted by as much as 80% as they travel through the chain of command. Even those distortions that do not cost money can affect employee relations. Employees feel more and more distant, and ultimately alienated from top management. Alienation hurts organizational morale and productivity. Employees need to feel that someone is listening.

Listening is critical to your success, and most listening skills are learned by chance. A recent survey of executives in 72 major corporations emphasizes that good listening skills don't come naturally (*Corporate Report*, 1979). Our hit-or-miss educational system is not working. Research shows that most of us are partially effective as listeners and need improvement. Much of what is heard is not remembered. Over

30 years of research clearly indicates that we listen at approximately 25% effectiveness and efficiency (Dietze and Jones, 1931, Steil, 1975). In other words, on average, we deal productively with about ¼ of what we listen to! Is that good enough? A buyer in a large retail clothing chain did not think so—especially after she received 800 pairs of a line of fall shoes after placing a phone order for 80. There are simply too many people who do not listen as well as they should or could.

Think for a moment about communication breakdowns you have experienced at work, at home, or socially. What resulted from the confusion? Did the misunderstanding cause the loss of an important business account, a divorce, arrival at a party on the wrong night, or failure on a driving examination? The most serious communication breakdowns are usually caused by poor listening. Listening mistakes cost time, money, human relationships, psychological and physical pain, lawsuits, and more.

## Costs of Poor Listening

With the demands of modern living, we value our time. It would be difficult for most of us to place a price tag on the value of a few hours alone with someone special, the latest best-selling novel, or sailing on a lake. Our time is precious, yet we frequently lose time through ineffective communication and listening errors. You make plans for a dinner date tonight; your guests planned to come tomorrow. You thought your partner said Columbus, Ohio, not Columbus, Georgia. Recently, while waiting at an airport a businessman was overheard telling his wife, "Honey, I CAN'T HELP IT! The secretary must have told me the wrong day. I'll fly home later tonight and come back next week! There's no use arguing about it now."

Lost time is an inconvenience and often places strains on relationships. People often get too busy to listen and relationships dissolve with notes saying "I need someone to listen, and he (she) does . . ." Children are crushed when parents forget little league games, birthday parties or family outings. You may hear what someone is telling you without really listening to the meaning.

Communication errors not only cost disrupted relationships; they also cause physical and psychological pain. Occasionally we hear reports of hospital patients receiving the wrong operation. One New Orleans patient (Mr. Johnston) reported that orderlies came in and told him it was time for his operation. Mr. Johnston was a little surprised since he checked in only two hours earlier. The orderlies assured him that the doctor requested him to be brought to the operating room. In the elevator, Mr. Johnston asked if knee operations were always conducted so quickly. The orderlies looked at each other and said "You're having an abdominal operation!" Sensing that Mr. Johnston was nervous about his operation, they failed to listen to his explanation. Eventually the doctor was called and the orderlies went to get another Mr. Johnston who was on the same floor.

Historically, poor listening has led to devastating consequences, as the following descriptions of military and aviation disasters indicate.

In 1940 Americans deciphered a Japanese secret code referred to as MAGIC. Breaking the code enabled the United States to detect Japanese war maneuvers. Throughout 1941 Washington issued warnings to military commanders in Hawaii to be prepared for war with Japan. Even though these warnings confirmed the commanders' expectations, they didn't think that Pearl Harbor was threatened. The commanders increased air reconnaissance in the Pacific, but not north of Hawaii. On November 27, 1941 a stronger warning was issued stating that aggressive action was expected from Japan in the next few days. Again, the commanders believed that the target could not be their own base.

On December 7, 1941, the Japanese destroyed the United States Pacific Fleet at Pearl Harbor. When Japanese planes arrived over Pearl Harbor, no alert was sounded until the Japanese bombs began to explode. The attack began at 8:00 on Sunday morning, when most of the naval officers and enlisted men were on leave or just getting up from their bunks. The Japanese bombed 96 anchored American ships. They sank or damaged all eight battleships, three cruisers, and four other vessels in the harbor. Over 2,000 men were killed and at least 2,000 more were listed as wounded or missing. Most of the Navy and Army buildings and aircraft installations were completely destroyed and many considered Pearl Harbor the worst military disaster in American history.

The military authorities at Pearl Harbor had been warned, yet not one really listened. Some probably didn't sense the warnings; some probably didn't correctly interpret them; some probably didn't effectively evaluate them and of course the response was not adequate.

In the worst aviation disaster in history, to date, we see communication and listening failure at the heart of tragedy.

On March 27, 1977, a KLM 747 with 248 passengers and a Pan American 747 with 380 vacationers prepared to take off from the fog-shrouded airport at Tenerife in the Canary Islands. The KLM pilot was directed by the control tower to taxi up the runway, make a 180 degree turn and "Standby for take-off clearance." Meanwhile the Pan American 747 was directed by the same control tower to taxi up the same foggy runway and turn off at the third off ramp. There were four exits from the runway to the taxi way. The Pan American crew, however, considered the first turn to be inactive because it was blocked by other aircraft. So the Pan Am crew headed for the fourth instead of third exit. Nevertheless, the tower made a request and Pan Am acknowledged that they would report when clear of the runway.

Both planes and the control tower were tuned to the same radio frequency and should have heard the various communication exchanges between all parties. Yet, according to a nine minute tape recording, no clearance was given to the KLM 747 to take off. Evidently, the KLM pilot misunderstood his instructions. The KLM 747 attempted to take off and when the pilot saw the other 747, he was approaching at 186 miles per hour and there was no way to avoid a collision that cost:

581 lives
$500 million in lawsuits (many still are in court)
2 Boeing 747's worth $63 million dollars

If both pilots and the control tower had fully sensed, properly interpreted and evaluated, and responded appropriately, the worst disaster in aviation history might have been avoided. Extreme examples like these emphasize the costs of poor listening and the need for improving listening effectiveness.

## Rewards of Effective Listening

Like any other skill, listening requires active commitment and effort. As mentioned earlier, active participation is necessary in serious and social situations. Serious listening during contract negotiations, loan requests, political speeches, training seminars, or jury duty requires one or more of the following abilities: comprehension, retention, understanding, criticism, and evaluation. Serious listening is either selective or concentrated. For someone who listens selectively, the segments of a message fade in and out, while a concentrated listener attends to the entire message. At times you do not need to remember everything that is said. Unfortunately, many listeners do not realize it when they tune out. If we get into a habit of listening half-way, we may find ourselves missing critical material and thus unable to respond effectively.

In social situations, such as parties, coffee breaks, watching television, rock concerts, dinner tables, or talking with friends, we often listen for pleasure and entertainment. Both types of listening are needed in the same conversations. Business associates, family members and friends constantly alter their discussion topics from birdie putts, to Supreme Court decisions about EEOC hiring guidelines to the latest vacation, to the President's new budget cuts. Preparing yourself for all types of listening situations makes you a better communicator.

As one adapts to various purposes of communication, several benefits from effective listening accrue (Barker, 1971).

Listening effectively increases your knowledge and experience. Much information in today's computers or data banks is inaccessible or very difficult to retrieve. By "picking other people's brains," we mean listening to gain a shortcut to knowledge. Asking questions and really listening to the answers gives you information that might take days, weeks, or years to learn by reading books or sitting in front of a computer terminal. Effective listening saves time which translates into saved dollars, time, energy, and productivity.

Recently, a frantic mother called police when her four-month-old daughter was choking. An ambulance was sent, but in the meantime, a police officer described the Heimlich maneuver (in which pressure is applied suddenly below the ribs, forcing air through the throat, dislodging obstructions) by phone. The mother listened well and it worked. Effective listening helped this mother save her child's life.

Time is money, and whereas poor listening is costly, effective listening can result in profits. Consider the numerous times you have benefited through listening. Alert listening helps you pick up hints in business and personal affairs. For example, you may own stock in a textile corporation. While waiting for your stockbroker, you hear her tell a client that the next few months look bad for the textile market. This may be the time for you to sell. Keeping your ears open for "freebies" can give you tips on how to save money as well as decrease your incidence of communication errors.

Better listening means improved work performance. You are in an advantageous position to make decisions when you have all the facts, instructions, and details. One employee complained: "My supervisor never listens to me. Last week, I told him that a big problem was developing. There was no reaction. Then, today, I told his boss the same thing. Even though my supervisor was praised for my being alert, he jumped all over me for not telling him first!" When we fail to listen, we are taking unnecessary chances and may be missing out on the best solutions to problems.

Careful listening helps you learn to hear between the lines. People in sales, for example, often jump to conclusions about what customers want or need. How many times have you had salespersons try to sell you something they wanted you to have rather than what you had come to buy? A business forms salesperson, who was a good listener, recently called on a major airline. He planned to sell ticketing forms, but while talking to the president, he realized he should not push the ticketing forms and sold them personnel forms instead. Three months later, the airline called him to order ticket forms worth nearly a million dollars.

Interpersonal problems can be prevented by listening effectively. Frequently, we talk and act before we really listen. We commit ourselves to decisions that "can't," "don't," or "won't" be carried out. Hasty decisions disappoint family members, associates and customers. Not too long ago, a young woman's car was vandalized while at a body shop. The damage was the responsibility of the body shop where she had left the car for repairs. Before leaving she specifically asked to have the car left inside for extra protection. Evidently, no one listened. The next day, the car's chrome wheels and tires were stolen. Now along with the repairs, the shop had the problem of replacing $800 worth of wheels and tires and soothing an angry customer. Similarly, effective listening helps eliminate communication problems at home. A spouse who "wouldn't mind" going on a company picnic might, from these words, seem noncommittal. However, by listening with all our senses, we would have detected the vocal cues that were saying just the opposite. Listening to both message *content* and *treatment* is critical. Listening with the whole self reduces chances for misunderstanding or later conflict.

## SUMMARY

In this chapter, we have stressed the problems caused by inefficient and ineffective listening and why effective listening is critical to communication and personal success. Your awareness of listening problems, their potential costs as well as the rewards, will heighten your overall effectiveness. Some of the benefits include increased knowledge, increased self-confidence, improved performance and productivity, increased enjoyment and decreased tension, and better use of our time.

## REFERENCES

Barker, L. L. *Listening Behavior.* Englewood Cliffs, NJ: Prentice-Hall, 1971.

Dietze, A., and Jones, G. Factual memory of secondary school pupils for a short article which they read a single time. *Journal of Educational Psychology,* 1931, 22, 586–98, 667–76.

Learning to Listen. *Corporate Report,* November 1979.

Steil, L. What is your ear-Q? *Cereal Foods World,* March 1975, 20, 136–138.

Steil, L. "What Did You Say?" *Executive's Personal Development Letter,* Alexander Hamilton Institute, Inc., Vol. 6, No. 1, November 1979.

Steil, L. *Your Personal Listening Profile,* Sperry Corporation, 1980.

# 4

# What's Your Ear-Q?

*I understand a fury in your words, but not the words.*

**Shakespeare, Othello, Act IV**

A few weeks ago a friend with car trouble called her husband and asked him to pick her up at the corner of Nicollet and Emerson. Half an hour later, she called again. Her daughter said, "Daddy left 30 minutes ago." Later she found that he had gone to Nicollet and Green Acres—not even close. He had recognized Nicollet immediately in her conversation and assumed he knew where she would be without listening to the rest of her instructions. Such daily situations continue to lead to dissatisfaction with our own and others' listening abilities. The first step we'll take in order to deal with this unsatisfactory condition is to develop a personal listening profile.

## HOW WELL DO YOU RATE AS A LISTENER?

*Listen to yourself and the voices of your world.*

The following set of exercises were developed by Lyman K. Steil and are designed to develop a Personal Listening Profile by rating attitudinal and behavioral aspects of your listening practices. The Personal Listening Profile has been completed by thousands of individuals and although there are no correct or incorrect answers, your responses will increase your understanding of yourself as a listener and highlight areas of strength and weakness. After you complete the profile, we'll compare your responses with the average profile of thousands of others.

## PERSONAL LISTENING PROFILE

### 1. Self Analysis

A. Circle the word which best describes you overall as a listener.
Superior    Excellent    Above average    Average
       Below average    Poor    Lousy

B. On a scale of 0–100 (100=highest), how would you rate yourself overall as a listener?

_____

(0–100)

C. In your opinion, what four words best describe you overall as a listener?

_____      _____

_____      _____

### 2. Project Other/Self Analysis

A. TARGET 25: List, by name and relationship, 25 individuals who are most important, or significant, in your life. Do not prioritize or rank-order them; simply list by name and relationship.

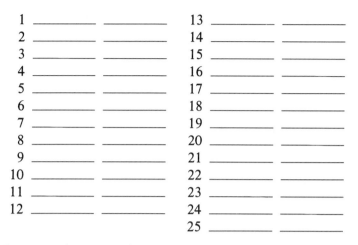

B. Once you have completed your identification of the individuals most significant to your life, place them on the
following target: five most significant in the bullseye,
next five in the next ring, etc.

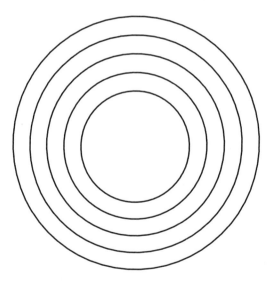

**Fig. 4.1** Target 25 Analysis

C. Now how do *you think they would rate you* overall as a listener? (Use the same scale of 0–100.)
Also list four words they would use to describe you as a listener.

(i.e.)

| | | |
|---|---|---|
| Your best friend | _____ | _____ |
| Your boss | _____ | _____ |
| A colleague | _____ | _____ |
| Job subordinate | _____ | _____ |
| Your spouse | _____ | _____ |
| Children | _____ | _____ |

## 3. Other/Self Analysis

A. Repeat your list of Target 25–your significant others.

B. Individually ask each to *rate* and *describe* you overall as a listener. (0–100) (Four Descriptive Words)

## 4. Self/Other Analysis:

A. Overall, how would you rate (0–100) (Descriptive Words) your significant others?

B. Best listener: Reflect on someone who you would consider to be representative of the *Best Listeners* you have ever known. Identify, rate and describe.
Who _____ 0–100 _____ 4 Descriptive Words
_____

C. Worst listener: Reflect on someone who you would consider to be representative of the *Worst Listeners* you have ever known. Identify, rate, and describe.
Who _____ 0–100 _____ 4 Descriptive Words
_____

Completing these exercises should help to heighten awareness of yourself as a listener and enable you to identify areas where your listening could be improved. (This profile is repeated in Appendix B if you would like to share it with others.) Analysis of part one of this exercise indicates that 90% of all people surveyed fall into the three-point range of above average, average, and below average on the Self-Analysis. We also find that 80% of all listeners rate themselves as average or less. Evaluating your listening behavior may have been difficult for you because of the absence of specific criteria on which to base your decisions. Yet, correctly or incorrectly, with or without criteria or definitions, most people have a perception of themselves as listeners. And the evaluative perception is definable and limited. When other abilities such as golf, black jack, or reading are evaluated, people tend to give a greater variety of answers. A superior golfer would probably break par whenever playing golf, while a terrible black jack player might take a hit on hard twenty (two tens).

It is especially difficult to rate your listening ability numerically. The numerical range for 1B for most people is from 35–85 with an average rating of 55. People rarely rate themselves below 10 or above 90. Typically, of course, scores of 55 on other tests such as driving tests, law boards, or certification exams are failures and have to be repeated.

In Self Analysis 1C the words you used to describe yourself may be positive, negative, or neutral listener characteristics. Of course, words are interpreted differently by different people in various situations. Thinking of yourself as a "critical" listener may have positive meanings for you and negative meanings to someone else. Nevertheless, careful consideration of how you would describe yourself overall as a listener will provide insight and direction for your listening enhancement.

Comparisons of self-rating and projected ratings find most respondents believing that best friends would rate them higher than they rate themselves. In fact, results indicate that best friends would rate you highest as a listener. Why? We can only guess that since best friends are in such intimate, special relationships that you must be a good listener to have this person as a best friend to begin with. People generally think that their bosses would rate them higher than they rated themselves. This may be wishful thinking, but in part is probably accurate. We do tend to listen better to those in authority positions. We listen better out of genuine respect, power need, fear of losing our jobs, or in hopes of promotions.

On average, ratings for colleagues and job subordinates work out almost the same as most people rate themselves or about 55. A dramatic change occurs when we compare our ratings with the projected ratings of spouses. On average, most people feel their spouse would rate them lowest of all. Unless the best friend and the spouse are the same person, the score here is usually significantly lower than the 55 average. Typically, the "projected other" score is 15 percentile points lower than the "self" score. What's particularly interesting is that the figure steadily goes downhill. While newlyweds tend to rate their spouse at the same high level as their best friend, as the marriage continues the ratings drop. So, in households where couples have been married for many years, there may be a lot of talk but no real listening. These descriptions should give you new insights into your listening behavior.


## COMMUNICATION CONNECTIONS

It would be difficult for you to remember all the people you've communicated with during the last month. Beyond our Target 25 List, we communicate with hundreds of people in all walks of life from store clerks to beauticians. With some people we communicate several times a day (primary encounters), others several times a month (secondary encounters), and others only occasionally (rare encounters). If you will, list by name the people with whom you have primary, secondary, and rare encounters. (Keep this list in a notebook for future reference.) After listing these people, think about the environment (a street corner, subway, bar, conference, telephone, etc.) in which you communicate. How important is what they have to say? Do they listen well? Do you listen well? Observations of continuing communication interactions often give the best indication of our listening effectiveness.

## CAN YOU MAKE YOURSELF LISTEN WELL?

You may be thinking that analyzing the ways we listen to others is fine and good, but it all depends on the situation. You say, "I may not listen well all the time, but when I need to, I do," or "Anybody can listen when they have to!" Most people tend to think that with more effort and concentration they can be effective listeners.

Even though this seems to make sense, in practice most people cannot compel themselves to listen well. Under pressure, many people tense up and are distracted by external factors. Then they blame their listening problems on such things as boring topics, cold rooms, fast speaking rates or a number of other outside distractions. Of course, listeners do face many obstacles, but one of the most influential is the pervasive assumption that effective listening can be willed or automatically turned on. We know listeners can turn listening off with ease, but it can only be turned on to the level to which we have developed our skills. Most important is the fact that with training, your Ear-Q can be improved.

## LISTENING EFFICIENCY AND INEFFICIENCY

Listening is not as simple as might be expected. As we noted earlier, most listeners operate on 25% efficiency. Tests show that after a ten-minute oral presentation, the average listener hears, receives, comprehends, and retains only about 50% of the message. After 48 hours, most listeners only remember about 25% of what they heard (Day, 1980; Rasberry, 1980).

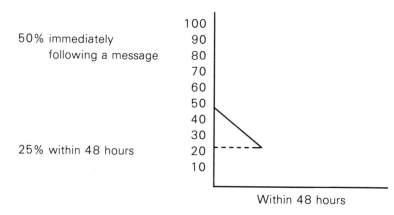

**Fig. 5.1** Listening Efficiency and Duration

Think about what you have listened to during the past 48 hours. Of what was said, what did you hear, understand, properly evaluate, remember and respond to appropriately? Probably not as much as you would like. Most people agree that their listening needs improvement and wonder where to begin. Awareness, self-assessment and training is the key. Effective runners begin with stretching exercises; they schedule programs to build strength; and finally after months of preparation reach distance goals of 2 miles, 5 miles, or even 25 miles. Listeners must develop their own individualized training programs.

Most people start each day willing and able to listen, but fail because of the lack of proper training. Before undertaking a listening training program, you first must identify your skills and shortcomings. An old proverb helps describe stages of training development.

> *"Some men know not, and*
> *Know not that they know not—*
> *They are fools . . . shun them;*

> *Some men know not, and*
> *Know that they know not—*
> *They are simple . . . teach them;*

*Some men know, and*
*Know not that they know—*
   *They are asleep . . . wake them;*

*Some men know, and*
*Know that they know—*
   *They are wise men . . . follow them."*

Awareness is of primary importance. Without an awareness of your personal skills and weaknesses, you can move no further. You are fortunate; you are already aware of the importance of listening effectiveness. Yet, awareness of the importance of listening is not enough. Thirty years of research shows that others have been aware, but have not changed their listening behavior. Your success depends on the combination of awareness and effort.

## SUMMARY

From the Personal Listening Profile, we can obtain a clearer picture of how our listening characteristics compare with others. We have learned that without proper training, we typically don't listen well. Our listening efficiency is approximately 50 percent immediately after a message and about 25 percent 48 hours later. This is one reason that listeners are often ineffective. However, we also know that with awareness and effort, listening can be improved. The next chapter explains typical listener strengths and weaknesses.

## REFERENCES

Day, C. How do you rate as a listener? *Industry Week.* April 1980.

Rasberry, R. W. Are Your Students Listening? A method for putting listening instruction into the business communication course. *Proceedings.* Southwest American Business Communication Association Spring Conference, 1980, 215.

# 5

# Identifying Your Personal Listening Strengths and Weaknesses

*I can't help hearing, but I don't always listen.*

**George Burns as God in *Oh God***

A supervisor in charge of a large group of clerical personnel held office meetings on Friday afternoons. Recently the supervisor began calling these meetings twice a week. A frustrated group of employees got together and wrote a memo complaining about wasted time in so many meetings. The next morning a memo was placed on each of their desks, "Poor listening causes MEETINGS!"

With an understanding of the importance of listening to overall communication success, you now need to identify your individual listening strengths and weaknesses. Before you do, remember you listen the way you do (effectively or not) because of years of practice. Listening is a learned behavior. It is also habitual. Most important, you *can* learn to improve your listening effectiveness by building on your strengths and eliminating your weaknesses.

## CHARACTERISTICS OF EFFECTIVE AND INEFFECTIVE LISTENERS

In 1948, the "Father of Listening," Dr. Ralph Nichols, identified characteristics of effective and ineffective listeners (Nichols, 1948). Dr. Nichols's discoveries of 30 years ago have continued to be studied with no significant differences being found between the good and poor listeners of 30 years ago and those of today. Good listeners are typically categorized as:

| | |
|---|---|
| Alert | Caring |
| Responsive | Attending |
| Patient | Other-centered |
| Non-interrupting | Curious |
| Empathic | Effective Evaluator |
| Interested | Non-emotional |
| Understanding | Not Distracted |

Poor listeners on the other hand are often categorized as:

| | |
|---|---|
| Inattentive | Self-centered |
| Defensive | Uncaring |
| Impatient | Quick to judge |
| Interrupting | Distracted |
| Disinterested | Apathetic |
| Insensitive | Emotional |

Certainly there are numerous other ways to categorize good and poor listeners. As an interesting exercise, ask ten friends, family members, co-workers, or acquaintances to each think of 10 words that describe the best listener and 10 words that describe the worst listener they have ever known.

Make a collective list and you will have a productive compilation to compare yourself to.

You probably recognize characteristics of your listening behavior from the foregoing columns or compiled lists. For further individual analysis of your listening skills, complete the following exercise.

## HOW WELL DO YOU LISTEN?

*Analysis of Your Bad Listening Habits*

How often do you indulge in ten almost universal bad listening habits? Check yourself carefully on each one:

| HABIT | FREQUENCY | | | | | SCORE |
|---|---|---|---|---|---|---|
| | Almost always | Usually | Some-times | Seldom | Almost never | |
| 1. Calling the subject uninteresting | ____ | ____ | ____ | ____ | ____ | ____ |
| 2. Criticizing the speaker's delivery | ____ | ____ | ____ | ____ | ____ | ____ |
| 3. Getting *over* stimulated by some point within the speech | ____ | ____ | ____ | ____ | ____ | ____ |
| 4. Listening only for facts | ____ | ____ | ____ | ____ | ____ | ____ |
| 5. Trying to out-line everything | ____ | ____ | ____ | ____ | ____ | ____ |
| 6. Faking atten-tion to the speaker | ____ | ____ | ____ | ____ | ____ | ____ |

7. Tolerating or
   creating dis-
   tractions ___ ___ ___ ___ ___|___

8. Avoiding diffi-
   cult expository
   material ___ ___ ___ ___ ___|___

9. Letting emo-
   tion-laden
   words arouse
   personal an-
   tagonism ___ ___ ___ ___ ___|___

10. Wasting the
    advantage of
    thought speed ___ ___ ___ ___ ___|___

Total ___

TOTAL SCORE INTERPRETATION: Below 70—
You need training.
From 79–90—You listen well. Above 90—You are ex-
traordinarily good.

| | |
|---|---|
| For every "Almost always" checked, give yourself a score of | 2 |
| For every "Usually" checked, give yourself a score of | 4 |
| For every "Sometimes" checked, give yourself a score of | 6 |
| For every "Seldom" checked, give yourself a score of | 8 |
| For every "Almost never" checked, give yourself a score of | 10 |

How does your score compare with your earlier rating
from 0 to 100 (Chapter 4:1. Self Analysis)? The average
score on this latest exercise is 62 compared to an average of
55 in 1. Self Analysis. It should have helped to break listening into specific areas of competence. Before examining each

of these listening problems in detail, we need to look at factors which may influence your listening effectiveness.

## FACTORS THAT INHIBIT LISTENING SUCCESS

How would you feel knowing that a jury would forget 75 percent of the information presented in your behalf? As we stated earlier, most people listen at rates of 25 percent effectiveness. Listening can be improved, but listening problems are different from other types of problems because you may not be aware that the problem exists. Four factors which inhibit listening are related to your mental state.

First, it is difficult to focus on what is being said when we have personal and or professional problems. Having an argument with your spouse before leaving for work takes much of your energy, and distracts analyzing what went wrong. Inner conflicts such as this make it difficult to concentrate when listening.

A second factor which inhibits listening is general anxiety. Inner conflict usually stimulates or increases your general anxiety. If you are concerned about an IRS audit, for example, or a shipment reaching its destination on time, or if you're being considered for promotion, you may find it difficult to listen to others. Regardless of the cause, anxiety causes you to lose attention and energy necessary to listen effectively.

A third inhibiting factor is a closed mind. It is difficult to tell whether or not we have closed minds because of our "filtering agents," which influence our perceptions. It is easy to be open-minded on issues we agree with, but controversial issues are more difficult. Look at your attitudes, opinions and beliefs to see if you have tendencies to turn people off by not seeing another side of the issue.

One of the most serious inhibitors of effective listening is trying to do too many things at once. Effective listening requires full-time attention. It is frustrating to you and to others if during a conversation, you talk on the phone, sign letters, wave to secretaries, or doodle on a notepad. Setting aside other tasks while in conversation will improve your ability to listen. The last portion of this chapter is devoted to analyzing poor listening habits. As you read, try to ask yourself "Am I guilty of this?"

## INFLUENTIAL LISTENING CHARACTERISTICS

*"There is no such thing as an uninteresting subject. There are only uninterested people."*

G. K. Chesterton

While examining your lists of good and poor listener characteristics, you may begin to see characteristics in yourself, other speakers, messages and environments which affect your listening ability and comprehension. Research has helped to identify internal and external variables which may influence your listening behavior. Many of these variables operate as distractions and will be discussed in greater detail later. We need to keep in mind that research data, when interpreted, is subject to human inadequacies and biases.

### Listener Characteristics

Our personal characteristics and prior experiences affect our ability to listen. Many observers question the listening differences between males and females. Numerous investigations (Brandon, 1956; Farrow, 1963; Lundsteen, 1963; Nichols, 1951; Caffrey, 1955) have resulted in conflicting conclusions regarding the impact of physical gender on listening. Weaver (1972) suggests that scores on listening tests may only reflect *differences* between sexes and not the *quality* of listening. Simply put, we note that males and females score differently as listeners, and that such differences should not lead to interpretations of superiority/inferiority. With societal changes impacting on both males and females, listening attitudes and behaviors could be expected to show subtle shifts over time.

Research has also attempted to find out if there are relationships between age and listening ability. Age of listener research indicates a relationship between the listener's age and listening comprehension which is slight to moderate in degree (Steil, 1977). It has however been reported that younger children "have considerably shorter attention spans than young adults. Similarly, when a person reaches old age and senility, . . . listening may be affected negatively" (Barker, 1971).

*Personality* has also been found to affect listening ability (Stromer, 1955). Ego involvement tends to reduce listener comprehension, while objectivity tends to increase listener comprehension. In addition, listeners who have personal worries or feelings of insecurity, or feel they are "doomed to failure" also tend to be poorer listeners than those who are optimistic and free from worry.

A characteristic that is related to personality is *listener apprehension*. People with high levels of listener apprehension have a tendency to respond to listening situations with anxiety. This anxiety reduces comprehension and retention of information. A few years ago the Receiver Apprehension Test (RAT) was introduced to measure trait listening anxiety (Wheeless, 1975). Recent results using the RAT suggest that receiver apprehension is related to inadequate information processing and cognitive complexity. The degree to which individuals are afraid of misinterpreting, inadequately processing, or adjusting to information affects how they listen (Scott and Wheeless, 1977). Listening failures in the past seem to compound the problem. Additional research has found relationships between cognitive complexity and receiver apprehension. People who process information more efficiently have less listener apprehension (Beatty and Payne, 1981).

*Intelligence* factors and their impact on listening have been investigated by many researchers. To summarize the relationship, it has been noted that it is obvious that any mental activity—including listening—depends to a certain extent on intelligence. Yet such research indicates a positive, but not high, relationship (Barker, 1971).

## Speaker Characteristics

Besides variables you have as a listener, your listening ability is also influenced by speaker variables. For a short period of time a knowledgeable individual can comprehend a technical report on nuclear power reactors delivered at a rapid speaking rate (perhaps 400 words per minute), but for longer time periods it is difficult to listen at a rate above normal (165 wpm) without training (Goodman-Malamuth II, 1956). The best speaking rate is dependent on the message content, knowledge level of the audience, length of message, and conditions under which listening is to occur. Along with the rate, research also suggests that it is easier for audiences to listen to more fluent (using fewer vocal pauses: uh, and um) speakers (Barker, Watson, and Kibler, 1982).

The visibility of a speaker also seems to improve listening ability (Gauger, 1951). As mentioned earlier, many meanings are transmitted through nonverbal cues. Through facial expressions speakers not only add interest to their messages, but also change the meanings of their words. Research also indicates that gestures are another form of nonverbal behavior which serves to influence listening (Haiman, 1949). The more gestures speakers use, the more information that listeners comprehend. Other speaker qualities that affect listening include: the speaker's reputation, how well a speaker is liked, and whether or not the speaker can be heard adequately.

## Message Characteristics

What we hear a speaker say also affects our ability to listen (Berlo and Gulley, 1957). Our personal values may influence our ability to understand a message without our even being aware of it. Research suggests that we comprehend more information when our values are in agreement with what is being discussed. However, there is a tendency for us to listen more carefully to a message that we strongly disagree with than to those messages we don't feel as strongly about. One reason for this may be that we often attempt to find points of weakness. Yet if we do find and focus on a weakness, our ability to listen to the rest of the message decreases.

## Environmental Characteristics

Listening ability is affected by variables in the listener, the speaker, the message, and the environment. Sometimes we fail to adjust for environmental factors that may interfere with our listening (Nichols, 1948). Rooms that are well ventilated and that have comfortable temperature settings are more conducive to effective listening. Can you remember what it was like listening to a commencement speaker on a hot day in June? Where you sit can also affect your listening effectiveness. The closer people sit to each other the more likely they are to listen carefully; whereas the people who sit further away tend to listen less effectively.

Other environmental factors that influence listening behavior include family circumstances. Research indicates that children raised without brothers or sisters tend to comprehend better than children from large families. An only child is used to being listened to and also to listening with little external interference, while children in large families are bombarded by large numbers of messages and learn to (and need to) screen out some messages. Children that are raised in homes where more than one language is spoken often listen less effectively than children in one-language homes. The use of two languages causes confusion and it takes time for a child to understand and use both languages properly. In addition to factors which influence our listening ability, we need to look at ways in which listening is inhibited.

## THE TEN WORST LISTENING PROBLEMS

It is often easier to identify undesirable listening traits in others than to see them in oneself. While examining the following poor listening habits, try to recall situations in which another person is engaged in the habit. If you recognize the behavior in someone else, next take a critical look at your own listening behavior.

## Viewing a Topic as Uninteresting

Most of us have been forced to attend meetings that were either mandatory or "strongly recommended." It may have been a stockholders' meeting, a training seminar, your boss's "state of the office" report, or a speech by your spouse's favorite author. Do you remember how you behaved as a listener? Chances are if you forced yourself to listen through the first part, your interest increased (at least minimally) and you learned more than you would have thought. There is a tendency for us to prejudge topics and situations as boring, unimportant, dull or dry. We develop a "who cares" attitude and quickly turn off the speaker or only half listen. When we tune out messages, we will not readily follow, effectively evaluate, or retain much of what was presented. In addition, we tend to reinforce our negative attitudes about the topic.

Skilled listeners search for areas of interest. At first they too may want to turn off the speaker, but good listeners quickly adjust their listening mode to match the situation. Time is a precious commodity and if you are forced by circumstances beyond your control to spend time in a communication situation where you can listen actively or passively, it seems reasonable that you would try to make the best use of your time. You may believe that mentally "blocking out" a message so that you can think about more important matters is a better use of time. At times however, a communication situation has potential for providing something you can use in the future.

Effective listeners know how to pick out the critical moments in listening situations which offer the most value. In particular, good listeners know how to spot the important aspects of meetings and lectures. When forced to attend meetings, it sometimes is a good idea to creatively make the best use of your time by working on other projects (mentally) until the information critical to you is discussed. Part of you must act as a monitoring device so that you do not miss valuable information.

It is important to point out that selectively listening for the most valuable moment is not appropriate for all situations. Half listening to a spouse or boss can get you into difficulty, especially if you fail to listen to all of a message because you felt that you already knew what was going to be said. Sometimes we must force ourselves to listen actively when interpersonal relationships may be affected.

Good listeners have a constructively selfish attitude. They look for valuable uses and possibilities that can be derived from each topic and situation. Remember even though critical value moments have a place in listening we still must be wary of dismissing situations prematurely by calling the subject uninteresting.

## Criticizing the Speaker's Delivery

Think for a moment about meetings you've attended. What speakers stood out in your mind? We often remember some aspect of their delivery or appearance rather than what was actually said. Our attention is quickly diverted by speakers who look at the floor while talking, speak in a monotone, play with objects, or wear clothes that do not match. Speakers need to be aware that visual aspects of their delivery negatively and positively affect untrained listeners. Good listeners however try to overlook or repress negative aspects of a speaker's delivery which may interfere with the message.

Since there is a tendency to remember the delivery rather than the message, effective listening requires us to focus on the content of what is said. Generally, the value of what we listen to is in the content, not in the delivery. We don't need to remember what the speaker's clothing, gestures, posture, or facial expressions were. As effective listeners, we must disregard negative or novel elements in a speaker's delivery or physical appearance that might divert our attention.

## Getting Overstimulated by Some Point in the Speech

When we are ego-involved with subjects that are being discussed, we usually let our emotions take control. When we disagree with a speaker's view, there is a tendency for us to make internal refutations or rehearse a response while the speaker is delivering the message. For example, a delegate from the school bus driver's association tells the board of education that the drivers will strike unless they receive pay increases. Unless the members of the board are good listeners, they will have a tendency to react emotionally to the remainder of the speaker's message. This emotional involvement may distort or interfere with their acquisition of important information which follows.

In Chapter 7, we will discuss ways to control the tendency to create emotional "deaf" spots with respect to what the speaker says. For now, we point out the need for witholding judgment until the entire message has been heard. We need to fully receive and understand first so that our judgment and responses will be appropriate later.

## Listening Only for Facts

Our educational careers have conditioned us to take notes in order to pass examinations. In addition, our work and daily lives have conditioned us to be preoccupied with "facts." This conditioning process creates a type of listener who listens primarily for factual information that can be recorded on paper (to be reviewed and used later). Obviously, there are times when it is important to listen just for facts (e.g., time to pick up payroll checks, the number of copies needed, the due date of the paper, or the list of errands that need to be completed before the office picnic). At other times, listening only for facts can be disadvantageous. The major problem promoted by this practice of listening only for facts is a tendency to avoid critical analysis and evaluation of the message while listening. If the message is full of symbolism or multiple interpretations, the practice of listening primarily for facts may produce a distorted version of the message. We get into the habit of Joe Friday, of "Dragnet" fame who said, "Just the facts, Ma'am the facts!"

Good listeners try to analyze the communication setting, the purpose, intent, structure, and the nature of the message. If facts are important, we listen for them, but if it is more important to interpret and analyze the message, we do not listen just for facts. When you evaluate the message, you increase your chances of remembering the facts too, because you have a better understanding of how all the parts fit into the complete message.

## Trying to Outline Everything

Another habit we have acquired, primarily from our educational experiences, is trying to outline everything we hear as we would in notetaking. This tendency to organize using an outline is sometimes effective, unless the speaker has a different organizational pattern, or no organizational pattern at all. As listeners we should be careful not to impose our own organizational pattern on the speaker. If we superimpose an outline on the speaker's message, it is possible that our notes will be misleading and cause problems for us later on. Other problems occur when you try to take down everything you hear or don't review what you've written down later. (Chapter 8 presents hints on notetaking.)

Rather than attempting to outline the message point by point, good listeners listen for a few minutes and then jot down key ideas and concepts. Search the message mentally for important points, and then try to avoid getting caught up in extended examples. The best listeners: take notes; adapt to the organizational structure of the speaker; and use the notes later on.

## Faking Attention to the Speaker

When was the last time you pretended to listen when your mind was actually miles away? At times certain thoughts race through your mind which are so interesting or important that you cannot force yourself to listen to a speaker. In these cases, we often pretend to listen because of embarrassment or fear of punishment from superiors. We use fake facial expressions, eye contact, and head nods to signal others that we are listening even if we are not interested in what they have to say. A failure to show interest may cause problems. We hope that the speaker is not aware that we're not listening to what he or she says. At other times, we take "mental trips" without realizing we've gone anywhere. A word or phrase gets our mind thinking about food, summer vacations, or an appointment. We snap back to reality, usually after only a few seconds, but a lot of information can be lost.

During World War II Hitler became aware of the "mental trip" listening problem. Since he wanted all German people to listen and respond to his radio broadcasts, marshalls were set up in neighborhoods to make sure that the masses tuned in. He still had no assurance that people were listening so in order to insure attention his marshalls quizzed the public periodically. If they failed to answer the questions correctly or unfavorably, they were reported and punished. Most speakers want us to listen to and not just hear what is said. Faking attention usually serves to reinforce the speaker, but you as the listener are not being sincere. Problems arise when faking becomes a *real* habit. When you are habituated to faking attention you may not be aware of what you are doing. If you often find yourself not remembering what the speaker has said, check yourself to see if you have been practicing this habit subconsciously. Remember, for communication success, we each need to pass the 51% minimum responsibility test.

## Tolerating or Creating Distractions

When we think of communication distractions, we may think of elementary children disrupting classes by throwing spitballs or shooting rubber bands. However, we all cause and/or tolerate distractions in all our communication activities. At home we leave the television on while talking at the dinner table, at work we turn our desks to be able to see what is happening in the hallway or outer offices, and at parties we try to greet everyone while talking to a long lost friend.

Some distractions such as soft music being played in the background, outside noise, movement around us, or similar physical distractions cannot be controlled in our environments. The new modular open office spaces are a prime example of an environment in which numerous distractions are always present. Employees have to deal with the sound of typewriters, telephones, conversations, normal traffic in and out, etc. Failure to adjust to, or compensate for, such distractions is a common listening problem. If you cannot modify the external environment conditions, you must modify your own internal listening behavior in order to take in messages directed toward you. Remember the first step to minimize your personal distractions is to identify them. Specific methods to help you control them will be discussed in Chapter 6.

## Avoiding Difficult Material

Listeners often tend to avoid messages that are difficult to understand. This tendency is similar to the habit of calling a subject uninteresting prematurely. Again, because of demands on your mental energy, you may tend to ignore or avoid what a speaker has to say. Especially in business, instead of listening to what has been said, there is a tendency to wait for a written report. Many people would rather avoid listening to "Meet the Press" or presidential speeches and buy a newspaper or weekly magazine with a condensed version or synopsis of an issue.

There are times when we need to listen to relaxing material (soap operas, television comedies, etc.), but our ears need practice for more difficult listening situations. The tendency to tune out difficult material may cause problems at work, since it is necessary to listen even when you are not strongly motivated. If you find yourself frequently avoiding difficult listening, try to modify your behavior. A key question is: What do you listen to? Good listeners seek out difficult and complex listening situations.

## Letting Emotionally Laden Words Arouse Personal Antagonism

This poor listening habit is similar to overreacting to some idea presented by the speaker; however, in this particular instance, listeners react to specific words rather than the broader concept expressed in the message. Poor listeners are generally unaware of these hot spots or "emotional triggers" that arouse their emotions. Words such as "Gun Control," "Abortion," "Right Wing," or "Left Wing," and "profanity" tend to have emotional connotations built into them. Regardless of their context, such words often trigger what are called "signal reactions." In other words, we react to the words and not their intended meanings. Ways to avoid reactions to emotionally laden words are discussed in Chapter 7. Skilled listeners come to know themselves well enough so that they can overcome the spontaneous response to their "trigger" words. They focus on what the speaker says and withold judgment while the speaker continues. By knowing the speakers, words, and subjects that trigger your emotions, you will be in a better position to control your communication situations and their results.

## Wasting the Advantage of Thought Speed

For some time, it has been known that we can think at a rate of over 400 words a minute, but speakers rarely talk at a rate of over 175 words a minute. This thought–speed/ speech–speed differential must be taken into consideration, otherwise the listener's mind may run ahead of the speaker. Because of this extra time, we often prepare to answer questions or points before fully understanding them. We think we know what the speaker is going to say and begin formulating mental or oral questions with regard to the message, or perhaps a "great comeback." This habit can make listeners appear rude, foolish, or not very bright. Be careful that you do not mentally jump so far ahead of the speaker, and begin to answer questions you think he is going to ask, that you miss part of his message.

The same problem relates to other areas of listening. Sometimes we develop listening habits that distract us from what the speaker is saying. Many listeners go off on so-called "mental trips." Constructive or destructive use of the time-rate differential often makes the difference between good and bad listeners. Good listeners use the time advantageously to evaluate, anticipate, review, and summarize what has been said.

In addition, there are other methods for enhancing your thought/speech speed advantage. You have, at times, listened to lectures or conversations, or news programs in which you thought the speaker was running on "slow." You may have wanted to push the person's speech–speed button to "fast;" to pull the words from his or her mouth; or, to say "Get to the point!" Unfortunately in most situations, we have little control over the speaker's speech speed.

In recent years, educators and researchers have focused on finding methods of enhancing the available thought-speed advantage through the use of *compressed speech*. Compressed speech shortens the time required by increasing the number of words spoken per minute (Weaver, 1972). The results have been encouraging. Normal speech has been compressed by 50 percent (282 wpm) without loss of comprehension (Fairbanks, Guttman, and Miron, 1957; Reid, 1968; Steil, 1976). Thus, with compression and listener development, oral messages can be listened to in substantially less time without significant loss of comprehension. Some people question the use of compressed speech, but researchers have found that most people actually prefer faster speaking rates. In fact, many blind people had been using a form of compressed speech for years, by increasing the speed at which their records are played. With the advanced state-of-the-art technology for speech compression developed by VSC (Variable Speech Control) company of San Francisco, listeners who choose to listen more efficiently are able to save time and increase their retention.

Of course, the listening problems we have been discussing are not exhaustive and many overlap each other. However, these are among the more persistent listening problems, since they were identified by Dr. Nichols nearly 35 years ago. If you recognize habits similar to these which hinder your listening effectiveness, first try to become sensitive to them. Awareness of the problems will assist you toward avoiding them in the future. The following chart provides a partial summary of the points and suggests some "checks" to help you analyze your own listening problems and strengths.

## TEN KEYS TO EFFECTIVE LISTENING

Following is a list of guidelines to better listening. These practices are in fact, a program for developing better listening habits that could last a lifetime.

| Ten Keys to Effective Listening | The Bad Listener | The Good Listener |
| --- | --- | --- |
| 1. Find areas of interest. | Tunes out dry subjects. | Looks for benefits and opportunities; asks "What's in it for me?" |
| 2. Judge content, not delivery. | Tunes out if delivery is poor. | Judges content; skips over delivery errors. |
| 3. Hold your fire. | Tends to enter into argument. | Doesn't judge until message is complete. |
| 4. Listen for ideas. | Listens for facts. | Listens for central themes. |

| 5. Be flexible. | Takes intensive notes using only one system. | Takes fewer notes; uses several different systems, depending on speaker. |
|---|---|---|
| 6. Work at listening. | Shows no energy output. Attention is faked. | Works hard, exhibits active body state. |
| 7. Resist distractions. | Distracted easily. | Fights or avoids distractions; tolerates bad habits; knows how to concentrate. |
| 8. Exercise your mind. | Resists difficult, expository material; seeks light, recreational material. | Uses heavier material as exercise for the mind. |
| 9. Keep your mind open. | Reacts to emotional words. | Interprets color words; does not get hung up on them. |
| 10. Capitalize on the fact that *thought* is faster than *speech.* | Tends to daydream with slow speakers. | Challenges, anticipates, mentally summarizes; weighs the evidence; listens between the lines to tone of voice. |

Identifying your listening strengths and weaknesses is the first step toward improving your listening success. The next three chapters are the "how to do it" chapters on improving your listening. Many of the ideas are "common sense" suggestions, which you may have thought of before, yet they are included because we often forget or neglect to use them in our listening. These suggestions should stimulate your thinking and help you to find additional common sense suggestions which directly relate to your personal listening behavior during family, work, and social interactions.

Remember, active listening takes energy and work. For you to gain the most from reading the next few chapters, you must *apply* the principles. It is relatively easy to identify a variety of solutions to a problem. However, implementing the best solution is a more difficult matter. How often have you come up with a great idea that failed because it was not carried out? Just as ideas cannot work until all the steps have been completed, listening improvement cannot occur until the suggestions are practiced in actual listening situations.

Before looking at specific suggestions for listening improvement, there are two general points that need to be stressed. The first is the need to constantly remind yourself that listening is vital to communication and your personal communication success. Second, you should periodically refer back to the poor listening habits in this chapter (see page 57) to modify or correct those habits that have appeared in your listening behavior.

## SPECIFIC SUGGESTIONS FOR LISTENING IMPROVEMENT

The following suggestions can be applied to all types of listening situations. While reading the rest of this book, try to keep these in mind as tips and techniques are given for dealing with distractions, emotions, message structures, and message evaluations and responses. First, *prepare* and *commit yourself to active listening.* Effective listening includes the matter of "psyching up" yourself to a state of psychological and physical readiness. As professional athletes prepare their minds and bodies for competition in sports, we need to train and condition for effective listening.

Second, *try to think about the topic and situation in advance.* Remember, you need to be a "selfish listener." Find ways to make the topic vital and rewarding to you. Look for the "value moments." When you are somewhat familiar with a topic, later learning is more efficient and longer lasting. When you think about topics, words, or people that distract you, you will be able to anticipate and overcome them.

Third, *concentrate and try not to let your thoughts wander.* Each of us takes "mental trips" while listening. A speaker mentions how oil prices have affected airline travel and before you even realize it, you may be thinking about your last business trip, a vacation to Hawaii, or that you'd like to take flying lessons. It sometimes takes effort to stay with the speaker throughout the entire message.

Fourth, *plan to report the general essence of what you are listening to to someone else later.* A commitment to report to another person will force you to change your listening behavior. You can't report what you haven't listened to earlier. At first, this is difficult, but eventually you will be able to condense a 20–30 minute message into a 3 or 4 minute overview.

Fifth, *take notes, but adapt your notetaking to the speaker, topic, organizational structure, and situation.* Of course, review your notes later and add to them for maximum development. Practice your notetaking in controlled situations (i.e., classes, church, news broadcasts, business meetings, conferences, and conventions.)

## SUMMARY

This chapter is designed to help you pinpoint some of your personal listening strengths and weaknesses. Completing the "How Well Do You Listen" exercise gives you a checklist of areas in which you can begin to improve your listening habits. Listener, speaker, message, and environmental variables may influence our ability to listen. Sometimes we fail to understand how mental states such as inner conflict, general anxiety, closed-mindedness, and trying to do too many things at once affect listening effectiveness. Our listening habits are learned, as we saw in our discussion of ten of the most frequent listening problems. To help you deal with them more effectively, we considered ten keys to effective listening. In the next chapter we will discuss specific factors which influence your listening sucess.

# REFERENCES

Barker, L. L. *Listening Behavior.* Englewood Cliffs, NJ: Prentice-Hall, 1971.

Barker, L. L., Watson, K. W., and the late Kibler, R. J. An investigation of the effect of presentations by effective and ineffective speakers on listening. Paper presented to the International Listening Association Convention, Washington, D.C., 1982.

Beatty, M. J. and Payne S. K. Receiver apprehension and cognitive complexity *Western Journal of Speech Communication,* 1981, **45**, 363–69.

Berlo, D. and Gulley, H. Some determinants of the effect of and communication in producing attitude change and learning. *Speech Monographs,* 1957, **24**, 14–18.

Brendon, J. An experimental TV study: the relative effectiveness of presenting factual information by the lecture, interviews, and discussion methods. *Speech Monographs,* 1956, **22**, 272–83.

Brown C. Studies in Listening Comprehension. *Speech Monographs,* 1959, **25**, 288–94.

Caffrey J. A. *Review of Educational Research,* April 1955, **25**, 121–38.

Erickson, A. An analysis of several factors in an experimental study of listening at the college level. Unpublished doctoral dissertation, University of Oregon, Eugene, Oregon, 1954.

Fairbanks, G., Guttman, N., and Miron, M. S. Auditory comprehension in relation to listening rate and selective verbal redundancy. *Journal of Speech and Hearing Disorders,* 1957, **22**, 23.

Gauger, P. The effect of gesture and the presence or absence of the speaker on the listening comprehension of 11th and 12th grade high school pupils. Unpublished doctoral dissertation, University of Wisconsin, Madison, Wisconsin, 1951.

Goodman-Malamuth II, L. An experimental study of the effects of rate of speaking upon listenability. Unpublished doctoral dissertation, University of Southern California, Los Angeles, 1956.

Haiman, F. An experimental study of the effect of ethos on public speaking. *Speech Monographs,* September 1949, **16**, 190–202.

Nichols, R. Factors accounting for differences in comprehension of materials presented orally in the classroom. Unpublished doctoral dissertation, State University of Iowa, Iowa City, 1948.

Reid, R. Grammatical complexity and comprehension of compressed speech. *Journal of Communication,* 1968, **18**, 236.

Scott, M. D. and Wheeless, L. R. The relationship of three types of communication apprehension to classroom achievement, *Southern Speech Communication Journal*, 1977, **42**, 246–55.

Steil, L. K. Compressed Speech — Another Educational Tool: Boon or Bane? *Toward Better Teaching*, Fall 1975, Vol. 9, No. 1.

Steil, L. K. A Longitudinal Analysis of Listening Pedagogy in Minnesota Secondary Public Schools. Unpublished doctoral dissertation, Wayne State University, Detroit, Michigan, 1977.

Stromer, W. Listening and personality. *Education*, January 1955, **75**, 322–26.

Weaver, C. H. *Human Listening: Process and Behavior.* Indianapolis: Bobbs-Merrill, 1972.

Wheeless, L. R. An investigation of receiver apprehension and social context dimensions of communication apprehension. *The Speech Teacher*, 1975, **24**, 258–68.

# 6

# Identifying and Dealing with Distractions

*Listening is a rare happening among human beings. You cannot listen to the word another is speaking if you are preoccupied with your appearance, or with impressing the other, or are trying to decide what you are going to say when the other stops talking, or are debating about whether what is being said is true or relevant or agreeable. Such matters have their place, but only after listening to the word as the word is being uttered.*

*Listening is a primitive act of love in which a person gives himself to another's word, making himself accessible and vulnerable to that word.*

**William Stringfellow** *Friend's Journal*

We live in a world of disruptive influences that block effective and accurate communication. Most interferences go relatively unnoticed and people generally are not aware that their listening is adversely affected. Distractions occur and affect us at all levels and in every situation. We are constantly interrupted by telephone calls, appointment schedules, employee traffic, correspondence, meetings and deadlines. Many secretaries minimize distractions for bosses by screening calls, sending sales personnel to other departments, and controlling the day's agenda. Unless you become aware of and skilled at combatting interfering forces, distractions can destroy your ability to listen.

## SHORT-TERM AND LONG-TERM MEMORY

Think about the number of times you have driven to the grocery store and had to call home to ask what you were to buy, or forgotten a joke until someone started telling it, or remembered a message you were to give someone too late after seeing them. Our memory, like our listening, is affected by internal and external distractions. For this reason, many people think of listening and memory interchangeably. At times, however, we may listen very carefully and still not remember something a few minutes later. By considering some of the differences between short-term and long-term memory, we may see the relationship between listening and memory.

Short-term memory operates when information is used immediately. Research suggests that information is forgotten in 30 seconds without some type of rehearsal such as repeating what was said or read (Shiffrin and Atkinson, 1969). Thirty seconds is not unduly long for us to retain information. Yet, think about situations in which you have forgotten a phone number after looking it up in the directory, a person's name shortly after being introduced, a phone message after hanging up, or instructions immediately after receiving them.

Short-term memory is associated with a rapid forgetting rate; moreover, it is also easily disrupted. Questions and/or comments made during conversations that are not relevant to the important information often causes people to forget the main points. The amount of information retained is limited in short-term memory. After hearing a series of numbers, list of items, or list of names, we have a limited capacity with regard to how much of the given information we can repeat later (Lefrancois, 1975).

Long-term memory, on the other hand, is what we rely on most heavily. Information learned in school, special vacations, activities you participated in while growing up, and songs, are types of information that are stored in long-term memory. Long-term memory is relatively unaffected by activity before and after an event.

Think about how good you feel when a one-time acquaintance remembers your name. Our names are very important to us, but how often have we forgotten a name after just being introduced or avoided someone whose name slipped our mind. Probably more often than we would like to admit. Even though remembering a person's name is a way of acknowledging their importance and individuality, many listeners get distracted during introductions to others.

It would seem to be very simple to catch at least a first or last name during an introduction, but so much happens during that first few minutes of an encounter that many of us don't. As mentioned earlier, our short-term memory forgets in about 30 seconds without a rehearsal. Most of us don't give ourselves time to rehearse during introductions because we are too busy thinking about what we are going to say, how we look, if we will come across well, how the other person looks, or some other aspect of the situation. Thinking about yourself often works to your disadvantage during introductions, especially when you make a negative impression by forgetting the person's name later.

Since our names are so important, the following keys to remembering names should help you with future introductions (Lorayne, 1975).

1. Be sure you hear the name.

2. Try to spell the name.

3. Make a remark about the name.

4. Use the name during the initial conversation.

5. Use the name when you leave.

A special occasion such as a first date may be anticipated and the memories retained indefinitely by deliberate effort.

Long-term memory is not limited like short-term memory. People easily remember information that goes back to their early childhood. Although recalling particular dates, names or cities may be slower and more difficult in later years, the information is often still "on the tip of our tongue."

## IMPROVING SHORT-TERM MEMORY

As we have seen, we ordinarily have the most difficulty with short-term memory. Before messages are stored in our memories, we first have to listen to the information. The following suggestions should help you improve your short-term memory (Lefrancois, 1975).

1. Pay attention to the information received. (Make sure that you can hear and see well.)

2. Repeat the information. (If necessary, take written notes.)

3. Reduce interference by using the information immediately. (Dial the number before doing anything else.)

Of course, our memory, both short- and long-term, is irrelevant if we do not first *sense,* or get the speaker's message. Although we can, and often do, forget what we have heard, it is of course obvious that we cannot remember that which we have never heard. Thus, let's examine the negative impact of distractions on listening.

## DISTRACTIONS

Let's consider two types of distractions: internal and external. Internal distracitons are influenced by your inner psychological states. Tension about a company merger, eating too much at lunch, having a head cold, getting only four hours of sleep, or the death of a close friend influences how you listen. External distractions are all around us and are usually not under our conscious control. Outside noises such as traffic or lawn mowers, interruptions by phone or personal visits, the physical environment, visual stimuli such as low cut dresses or hairy chests, physical mannerisms, or vocal characteristics such as dialects and professional jargon may adversely influence your listening behavior.

Internal and external distractions can function independently or in combination with each other. For example, let's say your daughter's teacher made an appointment to see you at 4:30 on a Friday afternoon. You arrive in a lousy mood after fighting traffic, not eating lunch, and losing a major account. On top of all your internal frustrations, the school's air conditioning system is broken, workers are hammering, children are playing in the room and a bell rings. Situations like this will understandably hinder your listening effectiveness. Some of these distractions may seem insurmountable, but with conscious effort and practice, you will develop the skill needed to overcome these and other distractions you face every day.

In Chapter 4, we considered the difficulty of willing yourself to listen. As we have seen, if you are listening effectively, you should hear what is said (sensing), correctly understand it (interpreting), determine whether it is important to remember (evaluating), and be able to retrieve it for later use (responding). If you did have trouble with listening, it is probably because you were distracted. You could have been interrupted, you may have felt that it wasn't important, or perhaps you said to yourself, "I give up, there are too many facts." Many of our distractions are self-induced and we fail to sense the message at all. If you never sense a message, you won't be able to deal with it at each higher level.

An analogy can be made between missing information when listening, and going fishing. If while fishing in a stream, you miss the first fish that go by, what do you do? Do you wade downstream after them? Of course not—you try for the next fish to come along. If you stand there thinking about the fish that got away, you'll probably miss the next fish, too. The same is true with listening. If you sit there thinking about the information that you missed, you will probably miss the next bit of information too. You need to come back later and deal with what you missed. Don't let it become another interference and because of it let all the information (fish) get away.

## Are You Tested on Distractions?

Occasionally we tell ourselves that some distractions are important, but are they? If they are, can you remember a time that you had to recall or report on distractions, on interference? Clearly, no. You are seldom, if ever, required to supply information on distractions that interfere with listening. We are, however, held accountable for the content of what is said, in spite of internal and/or external distractions which can destroy our listening effectiveness. Distractions, then, are a continuing problem that you face as a listener. But who is in the best position to overcome these interferences? You are, of course. If you are committed to the 51% minimum responsibility in communication, your effort to overcome distractions in listening is critical.

## Dealing with Distractions

There are techniques you can use to combat internal and or external interferences. First, *identify the potential forces of distraction in all of your listening situations.* Second, *actively work* to reduce the distractions. To begin with, you need to look at your personal environment, and in particular at those conditions that relate to your listening activities. Make a list of the significant factors, especially those that are predictable. Start with your home life. List the people with whom you communicate and distractions that have interfered with communication in the past. Try to find ways to minimize or avoid the distractions in the future. Next, look at your work environment and finally, look at your social environment. Analysis should focus on location, time, people, subjects, and communication situations. Try to set aside time to think through these situations. Analysis on paper will advance your understanding immensely. Remember, to improve, you first need to identify where the problems are located (see Appendix C).

Whenever you have the opportunity to test and practice your ability to overcome listening distractions remember to: (1) prepare yourself to listen; (2) identify any distracting forces; (3) take steps to overcome or minimize the distractions; and (4) try to report the information later. To get information, you must first sense it and to make sure that you are sensing a message you must learn to overcome distractions that block your sensing. With all the pressures and demands of daily life, we normally find it difficult to overcome the myriad of distractions. As an example, Sara was busy working on her annual report when Dan came in to ask about plans for a technical writing seminar. At first Sara was listening, then she began to focus on her annual report and next the telephone rang. Luckily, at that moment, Sara realized that she was being distracted. Realizing her distraction she apologized to Dan, cleared her desk and asked her secretary to hold all calls until she and Dan were finished. Sara had regained control of the situation and was fully prepared to listen.

Some distractions occur spontaneously and can't be anticipated. In the same interaction, Dan mentioned Larry Nichols who was working on the project. The name Larry prompted thoughts of her husband Larry, whom she had just married, and momentarily she was off on a tangent. Again, Sara had to get back into the conversation with Dan. If her trip had been longer than a few seconds, it would have been best for Sara to ask Dan to repeat what was said so that nothing important would be missed (sensing).

Interruptions and distractions from our listening efforts are difficult to overcome because we are never sure exactly when they will occur. That's why you need to make a plan to reduce their likelihood of occurrence and to deal with them when they do arise. Internal distractions are the most difficult to control because they are triggered by factors such as external conditions, overloaded agendas, physical maladies, something a speaker says, or mental tangents. With such distractions, we are seldom forewarned and often fail to recognize them immediately. The key is to focus on the message content; look for value moments; plan to report; and develop a mental/summary of the message.

## Overcoming Specific Distractions

You can overcome interferences by evaluating, anticipating, reviewing, and summarizing what the speaker is saying. Yet, any one of these techniques (evaluating, anticipating, reviewing or summarizing) can become a distraction in and of itself, and must be kept in bounds. You need to be careful, when asking yourself questions such as: How does this speaker know that? What evidence is being presented? What are the speaker's biases? If raised too frequently during a speech or conversation, such questions can become a distraction.

It is a difficult task, but you will profit if you evaluate, anticipate, review, and summarize while listening to messages. Using these techniques will help you to utilize the available time between your thought speed and the speaker's speech speed. Remember, wasting the thought speed–speech time differential can be dangerous because we are likely to go off on mental tangents.

The first step toward overcoming interferences is recognizing what your personal distractions are. See if you can separate your internal from your external interferences. Then, you can begin planning ways of mastering those interferences so that you will be in control of your own situation. (see Appendix C). As you read the next several examples, try to identify distractions that hinder you from listening to your best ability. Suggestions are given, but try to come up with your own personal strategy for helping to solve your listening distraction problems.

## Clock-Watching

Many people are clock-watchers. As soon as we sit down to hear a lecture, sermon, report, or conversation, we automatically look at our watches. At times, of course, we may need to know the time because of scheduled appointments or a dinner date; however, many of us look at our watches for other reasons. Some people enter listening situations and then frequently check how much time they have before lunch, or position themselves in view of a clock so they can judge when a speaker will finish, and continue to keep a close eye on the time. As these people watch their watches and clocks, they fail to hear much of what is being said. If you're a clock-watcher and it interferes with your listening, what can you do about this distraction?

First, understand that your focus on time is itself a tremendous waste of time. Second, accept the minimum 51% responsibility challenge, and resolve to listen responsively. Third, plan to report to some specific person within 8 hours. Fourth, take purposeful notes, as appropriate. If you are involved in notetaking, you won't be as busy focusing on the time. Physically you have several other options. Stop wearing your watch, reverse it, or put it in your pocket or purse until after your meetings are over. It would also be a good idea not to sit where you could see a clock easily. You need to try to avoid temptations that function as distractions. The ultimate key is to remember the sage advice posted beneath many schoolroom clocks; "Time will pass! —— Will you?"

## Telephones

Another distraction that many face at work and at home is the telephone. You may love to talk on the phone and appreciate its convenience, but telephones have the habit of ringing at times chosen by others. We have all found ourselves busy working on a project when we had to answer the phone. For this reason, we often miss vital information at the beginning of telephone conversations. Afterwards, we may wonder about the name of the person at the other end of the line, the name of their company, or what they wanted. In short, the telephone can serve as a distractor from our other listening situations, and of course we can be distracted while we listen on the telephone.

Where necessary, we should establish a system for dealing with the telephone in a manner that reduces its distractive impact. We seem to have a compulsion to get to the ringing phone. In fact, most of us will stop whatever we're doing to answer the phone. A personal review of options as to how a ringing phone should be handled can be profitable. Consider the use of answering machines, intermediaries (such as secretaries or assistants), transfer systems, and silencing switches.

We can also reduce our distractions when we are involved in telephone communication. Look at your office or home environment. Where is your phone located on your desk? Are you right-or left-handed? If your phone is on the right side of your desk and you are right-handed, then you probably pick up the phone with your right hand. If you do, you're distracted. As an alternative, place your phone on the left-hand side of your desk or answering space. Next, insure you have paper and pencil adjacent to every phone. Instead of picking up the phone when it first rings, always pick up your pencil first with your writing hand and get ready to listen. Now, as you answer the phone with your left hand, you have a pencil in hand and can write the vital information that comes at the beginning of the phone conversation. If you're left-handed, reverse the procedure.

### Multiple Agendas

See if you can relate to the next interference problem: the multiple agenda. A woman makes plans to meet her husband for lunch. She wishes that she could have planned it for the next day since she has to pick up her airline ticket, meet with her accountant, and call on three customers. As this woman sits down to lunch with her husband, her multiple commitments—her internal interferences—begin working against her as a listener. She loves her husband and he said that their lunch date was important, but. . . . Before she realizes it, she is off on a mental tangent involving her multiple tasks. Not only will she not listen well, she also will not resolve her other obligations. She will lose on both ends. How can she overcome her distractions? First of all, she needs to prepare herself to listen, and plan to report what she's listening to right here. She must utilize the differential between her thought speed and speech speed to keep concentrating on the conversation she is involved in with her husband. Every time another agenda item enters her consciousness, she must make note to deal with it *later*. If they are seated, and the restaurant has a lot of external interferences such as noise from the kitchen, a disruptive party, or the cash register, she might be advised to ask for another table with fewer distractions.

## Identify Interruptions

As we have seen, listening is interrupted in each of the above situations. When there is an interruption, it will have less of an effect if you have prepared yourself in advance (taken off your watch, moved your telephone, or chosen the best location to sit). To control the impact of interruptions, try to identify the interruption at the moment it occurs and say to yourself "Interruption! What did they just say? What are they saying? What are they going to say?" In this way you begin to acquire a reinforcement behavior to emphasize the importance of what was just said. Remember, the value lies in content!

## Ask Questions

After identifying internal and external interruptions, you can also apply another technique to improve listening success: Ask questions. For example, when possible after you recognize that you have been interrupted, you should ask for the message to be repeated. As listeners, we need to understand that our task of reception as a listener is different from our task as a reader. In reading, you control the pace. In listening, the speaker controls the pace along with the environment, redundancy, repetition, and clarification. You can decide if you want to read this book in one day or read only a chapter now and continue later. If something is unclear you can look up a word in the dictionary or reread the passage to gain a better understanding of it. If you get tired of reading, you can take a nap; but what happens if you take a nap while listening? Often, you'll lose information. In some situations, if you're interrupted, the message flow stops while you deal with the interruption. In other cases, if you allow it, the message flow continues during the interruption. The aware, inquisitive listener can, at times, stop the flow temporarily.

Even though speakers control the flow of information, there are various ways in which you can affect the flow. At times, you can ask for repetition. In some situations, you can ask speakers to explain what they mean or ask the person to slow down. In many cases, we are captive listeners; yet, there are times when you can monitor what is being communicated by interjecting questions or comments.

If you are not in a position to ask what a word or phrase means, then you have to continue listening. If you don't, you will miss something else. There are times when you may not understand the vocabulary and professional jargon of speakers, and won't be able to ask a listener to explain. In these situations, you must control the distraction by not worrying about it. Make notes and strive for understanding with questions afterwards. Poor listeners get flustered when confronted with unfamiliar language or too much data and give up. To become good listeners, we need to learn to go beyond what we may have missed. It is better to lose one bit of information than to miss everything else while worrying about what you missed earlier.

## LISTENING TO QUESTIONS

The suggestions presented in this chapter are designed to help you gain information more effectively when listening. Although most of our communication time is spent in receiving information, there are times such as when speaking to civic groups, press conferences, or board meetings when you are responsible for giving information to others. After these presentations, members of the audience often ask questions. If you have not prepared yourself to listen carefully, you may make mistakes which could affect your speaking success.

Before thinking about specific suggestions for ways to listen to questions, you should first think about why a person asks a question. Listeners ask questions for four basic reasons. They want: (1) to clarify points to improve their understanding; (2) to get more information or further support; (3) to satisfy their curiosity; or (4) to challenge the speaker. While listening, and before responding to a question, it helps to decide what the questioner's purpose or motive might be. Identifying a person's primary purpose for asking a question, enables you to answer the question with greater control and tact. Some speakers lose credibility by responding defensively when the questioner is not attacking them, but is merely confused or curious. Other speakers lose credibility by answering the wrong question or getting into side issues that are irrelevant.

The following guidelines should help you improve your question-answering ability.

1. *Listen carefully to the question.* Use all techniques appropriate to other listening situations.

2. If there is any confusion about what is being asked, paraphrase or repeat the question for the questioner.

3. Refer to the section of information that is pertinent to the question.

4. When clarification is necessary, explain the concept in different terms and provide different examples.

5. When further information is required, provide specific sources.

6. When a questioner challenges your position, provide further evidence to support your position.

7. Check back with the questioner to make sure that you answered the question satisfactorily.

## SUMMARY

The effects of internal and external distractions combine in numerous ways to adversely influence our listening behavior. Distractions rob you of the ability to receive, process, and use information. Sensitivity in your personal listening habits is the first step toward improving listening. Second, try to think about the topic and situation in advance. Third, concentrate and try not to let your thoughts wander. Fourth, plan to report the general essence of what you are listening to to someone else.

With a positive listening attitude, it is easier to learn to ignore momentary distractions. To overcome recurring distractions, we must first identify interferences in our home, work, and social environments. Next, we need to actively work to reduce those distractions that hinder effective listening. Identifying and controlling distractions is a continuing challenge.

The next chapter discusses ways in which our emotions affect our listening behavior.

## REFERENCES

Lefrancois, G. R. *Psychology.* Belmont, CA: Wadsworth, 1975.

Lorayne, H. *Remembering People: The Key to Success.* New York: Stein and Day, 1975.

Shiffrin, R. M., and Atkinson, R. C. Storage and retrieval processes in long-term memory. *Psychological Review*, 1969, **76**, 179.

# 7
# Identifying and Dealing with Emotions

*Congress is so strange. A man gets up to speak and says nothing, nobody listens and then everybody disagrees.*

**Will Rogers**

In the last chapter we considered the effects of internal and external distractions. This chapter focuses on an internal factor that is usually triggered by external stimuli—our emotions.

In listening, identification and control of our emotions is one of the most important and most difficult skills to acquire. Emotional listeners have a tendency to be poor listeners because of their spontaneous reactions to people, topics and language. To be able to control your emotions during listening, you first need to develop methods of controlling your emotions during communication. As we have noted, you need to: (1) prepare and commit yourself to listen actively; (2) try to think about the topic and situation in advance; (3) concentrate and try not to let your thoughts wander; (4) look for useful material or information; (5) plan to report the gist of what was said to someone else; and, (6) withhold your judgment and reaction until you have fully received and understood the speaker's position.

## EMOTIONAL TRIGGERS

Poor listeners lose emotional control. Three areas wherein our emotions are affected during listening are: the speakers, the topics, and the words. Something about speakers, topics, and or language often triggers an emotional response that hinders the listening process. Try to think of a situation in which you lost your temper because of what someone said. Did you listen to anything after that? Probably not. Sometimes we also fail to listen to people just because of who they are. You may disagree with the political views of a well-known celebrity and immediately turn the channel to another station or you may fake attention to a supervisor with whom you just had an argument. These responses (signal reactions) are a function of listening habits and conditioning. When you lose emotional control, your filtering agents cause you to evaluate and respond prematurely. Subsequently, further sensing and interpreting of messages is also affected.

Four key points should give you a better understanding about the relationship between emotions and listening. First, *we all have emotional triggers.* All listening situations are affected by our emotions. Think about the last decision-making discussion you took part in. Did someone turn off or argue against something that they did not want to hear? On the other hand, we also have a tendency to not listen as carefully to topics with which we strongly agree. As your subjective and emotional reactions increase, your logical and rational abilities decrease. This is especially important in personal situations and is probably one reason that many doctors refrain from diagnosing or treating members of their immediate families. Their emotional involvement could affect their ability to make the best possible decisions in times of an emergency. In home, work and social situations, when emotionality goes up, rationality goes down.

The second key point to remember is that *our emotional reactions to speakers, topics and/or words are directly related to our filtering agents.* Just as the filter on a camera affects the final photograph, our past experiences, knowledge, beliefs, attitudes and opinions likewise affect our emotional responses. Our filtering agents are in a constant state of change and therefore we must continually work to identify and analyze our emotional triggers.

A third point to remember about emotional triggers is that *they affect our communication and listening effectiveness.* By referring to the SIER model (page 21), you can see that our emotional triggers primarily affect us at the evaluation level. When emotions or feelings are triggered, we make judgments which affect our responses. Emotional evaluations lead to emotional responses, but what makes the listening problem more difficult is that emotional evaluation also short-circuits our ability to listen at the lower but crucial levels of sensing and interpreting. If you tune out a speaker that advocates the passage of the Equal Rights Amendment, for example, then you cannot sense accurately, interpret correctly, make sound judgments or respond properly later to the complete message. Any response will be an emotional and usually inadequate one.

A fourth key point is that our *emotions may be triggered positively, neutrally, or negatively.* We usually don't think of positive emotions as causing listening problems, but if positive emotions are triggered, you tend to relax your listening effort. Since you like what you hear (or think you like what you hear), you may tend to relax and become passive. Consequently, you are susceptible to accepting half-truths, inconsistent data, opinions, etc. Often we agree and applaud before listening to the full message. However, just because of positive emotional responses, we shouldn't lose sight of our responsibility as listeners.

We usually link neutrality with objectivity, but a precaution needs to be given. When you are emotionally neutral, many listeners say "This doesn't matter to me," and tune out because of emotional disinterest. Allowing disinterest to control your behavior can lead to poor listening habits. On the other hand, emotional neutrality can lead to "objective" listening. Negative emotions trigger predictable behaviors. Such listeners usually stop listening, tune out, or become argumentative. If, for example, someone wants to cancel your favorite advertising campaign, if an automobile executive is required to attend a Ralph Nadar lecture, or if a speaker tells a joke about your ethnic origin, then you may have a tendency to respond emotionally. We quickly move to evaluation and response. Nevertheless, our goal is to never respond before we've fully comprehended, rationally interpreted, and appropriately evaluated a message.

A fifth key point, related to our pressing need to identify and control our emotional triggers, is that *this world is filled with individuals and organizations that are well trained, skilled, highly motivated, and well paid to discover the emotional triggers of others.*

Successful listeners know what causes them to respond emotionally and develop skill in controlling their emotional reactions. Your goal as an effective listener is to sense and interpret a message thoroughly and correctly, prior to your final evaluation and response.

## WHO CONTROLS YOUR EMOTIONAL TRIGGERS?

How would you respond if you were asked, "Who controls your emotional triggers?" If typical, you would probably say "I do" or at least "I should." Yes, you should, but most people unconsciously allow others to play with their emotions. Without question, ineffective listeners don't control their listening emotionality. In fact, Hitler once said, "I know that one is able to win people far more by the spoken word, and that every great movement on this globe owes its rise to the great speakers and not to the great writers." Hitler and his associates were experts at controlling the emotional triggers of others. Currently, thousands of others throughout our universe are trained to control and manipulate our emotions. In all walks, advertising, education, politics, business, the clergy and the media, we see the skillful appeal to emotion.

While examining emotions that affect listening, there is one fact that we should keep in mind: You have emotional triggers and anyone who knows more about what triggers your emotions than you do is in a position to control you. Most important, we are not suggesting the elimination of our emotions. Even if we could, we shouldn't, as our emotions make us "alive"; however, in our quest for enhancing our listening skills, we need to recognize and control our emotional triggers, or others will. Think about it. You consume thousands of messages each day and behind those messages are people and organizations who are highly trained, skilled, motivated and financed to determine what affects your emotions. Millions of dollars worth of time and effort are spent to develop and send messages designed to trigger your emotions and reduce your ability to think rationally. Try to remind yourself as often as possible about the conscious effort given to messages designed to affect your emotional responses. Remember, *anyone who is in a position to know more about your emotional triggers than you do, is in a position to control you.*

The news headlines of the past few years provide numerous examples of such emotional influences. Were they rational when 913 people listened to the twisted Rev. James Jones's instructions to swallow the lethal grape drink at Jonestown? Were people responding logically when they stampeded supermarkets after Johnny Carson mentioned a rumor that there was a toilet paper shortage? Was Harry R. Truman logical when he refused to leave his home on the side of Mount St. Helens before it erupted? Were investors emotionally controlled when Joe Granville said "sell" and the market plummeted? Try to think of a time when you have spontaneously responded positively, neutrally, or negatively to a message and later wondered why? What triggered your response? If you want to be in control of your listening behavior, then you need to identify what affects your emotional triggers.

## IDENTIFYING EMOTIONAL TRIGGERS

Let's begin by considering possible responses to situations in which others are involved. After examining these situations, we'll look at your own emotional responses.

1. Ronald Reagan discussing his proposal to eliminate federal loans for college students.

2. President of a major oil company proposing the deregulation of oil prices.

Identifying emotional triggers is an ongoing project that needs constant effort. You need to discover the *people, topics,* and *words* that influence your emotional responses. Remember, reading these examples can affect you positively, negatively or neutrally. In any communication situation, you need to first identify your emotional position and response tendencies. Let's start our analysis by looking at how certain people trigger our emotions.

*People.* We come in contact with all types of individuals each day. Without even realizing it, we respond to them. For practice, read the sample list of famous names. Beside the name, indicate how you would respond emotionally to each person by checking along the continuum.

|  | *Positive* | *Neutral* | *Negative* |
|---|---|---|---|
| 1. Menachem Begin | _____ | _____ | _____ |
| 2. Johnny Carson | _____ | _____ | _____ |
| 3. Billie Jean King | _____ | _____ | _____ |
| 4. Mohammed Ali | _____ | _____ | _____ |
| 5. Jane Fonda | _____ | _____ | _____ |
| 6. Richard Nixon | _____ | _____ | _____ |
| 7. Jessie Jackson | _____ | _____ | _____ |
| 8. Jack Nicklaus | _____ | _____ | _____ |
| 9. Billy Graham | _____ | _____ | _____ |

|  | *Positive* | *Neutral* | *Negative* |
|---|---|---|---|
| 10. Ronald Reagan | _____ | _____ | _____ |
| 11. A. Khomeini | _____ | _____ | _____ |
| 12. Mother Teresa | _____ | _____ | _____ |
| 13. Mike Wallace | _____ | _____ | _____ |
| 14. Reggie Jackson | _____ | _____ | _____ |
| 15. Ann Landers | _____ | _____ | _____ |

After completing the exercise, try to think of reasons for your responses. Our responses often prevent us from listening completely. These people are generally well known, but our emotional responses are not limited to famous people. Complete this analysis on your Target 25 list in the Personal Listening Profile (Chapter 4). Emotional response also occurs

**Fig. 6.1** Visual Appearance Can Affect Listening

from visual stimuli. Look at the examples of clothing styles in Fig. 6.1 and again give your responses on the scale.

What characteristics of these clothing styles produced a response? Some of these outfits would be appropriate at home but not at work. Whenever we come in contact with others, we make judgments based on first impressions, but frequently these impressions are inaccurate. As you look at the people in your home, work, and social environments, try to think of the factors that influence you to respond positively, negatively, or neutrally. Try to minimize these factors that interrupt and distract your listening. Most important, analyze how your *emotional position* with respect to each person impacts on your listening to that person. How well do you listen to those to whose trigger you react positively? Neutrally? Negatively?

Identifying and analyzing people is an ongoing task. As our filtering agents change so do our emotional responses to people. It should be interesting to note where your emotional responses are consistent and inconsistent over a period of time. Right now, in fact, you can probably think of some people to whom you react differently today than you did a few months ago. On the other hand, our emotional response to certain others seems to never change. Keeping an updated notebook of how you are emotionally affected by the numerous people you listen to will yield significant benefits as you gain new insight into your own situation.

## Topics

Now let's look at how you respond emotionally to selected topics. Below we have a sample list of items. Check your emotional responses as you did with the people exercises. As you do, think about the ways you listen when someone discusses these sample topics.

|  | *Positive* | *Neutral* | *Negative* |
|---|---|---|---|
| 1. Gun control (Pro) | _____ | _____ | _____ |
| 2. Women in combat (Pro) | _____ | _____ | _____ |

|  | Positive | Neutral | Negative |
|---|---|---|---|
| 3. Computerized dating (Pro) | _____ | _____ | _____ |
| 4. Equal rights Amendment (Neg) | _____ | _____ | _____ |
| 5. Space exploration (Pro) | _____ | _____ | _____ |
| 6. Capital punishment (Pro) | _____ | _____ | _____ |
| 7. Socialized medicine (Neg) | _____ | _____ | _____ |
| 8. Airline deregulation (Pro) | _____ | _____ | _____ |
| 9. Organized religion (Neg) | _____ | _____ | _____ |
| 10. Labor unions (Neg) | _____ | _____ | _____ |

For some, such topics tend to generate extreme emotional reactions. Think about what triggers your emotions with these topics. How about other topics? Identify other topics that affect your emotional triggers on the positive, neutral and negative scale. What affect do you note on your listening? Remember, the more diligent you are in your identification and analysis, the better you will be at controlling your emotions in listening situations.

## Language

Some words cause immediate emotional responses. Buzzwords, labels, jargon, cliches, and profanity have a tendency to trigger our emotions. Again, to get you thinking about how words affect you emotionally, complete the following sample exercise by checking your emotional responses.

|  | Positive | Neutral | Negative |
|---|---|---|---|
| 1. Republican | _____ | _____ | _____ |
| 2. Pig | _____ | _____ | _____ |
| 3. Jock | _____ | _____ | _____ |
| 4. Sex | _____ | _____ | _____ |
| 5. Intellectual | _____ | _____ | _____ |
| 6. Money saved is $ earned | _____ | _____ | _____ |
| 7. Honkie | _____ | _____ | _____ |
| 8. Bastard | _____ | _____ | _____ |
| 9. Strike | _____ | _____ | _____ |
| 10. Discrimination | _____ | _____ | _____ |
| 11. Democrat | _____ | _____ | _____ |
| 12. Kike | _____ | _____ | _____ |
| 13. Bitch | _____ | _____ | _____ |
| 14. Management | _____ | _____ | _____ |
| 15. Labor | _____ | _____ | _____ |

Think about how these words would affect you if used during a conversation or speech. You may feel that words don't strongly affect you, but they do. When we hear certain words during a conversation, we often evaluate and respond before we realize it.

Now that you have *started* a personal analysis of your emotional "hot spots," we need to observe that: (1) your success is directly related to your effort; (2) there are no right or wrong answers; and (3) your identification effort will work, but it should be a private task. (Be careful where you leave your notebooks, as you would any personal item.)

## DEALING WITH EMOTIONS

Without question, emotions influence our ability to listen. The foregoing efforts toward identifying your emotional triggers is only a start. You now need to develop specific methods of *controlling* your emotions while listening. Emotional control is developed with *practice*. One of the best ways to practice is to consciously listen to the people, topics, and language that produce emotional responses and inhibit rationality. Again, you can use the SIER model as a guide. You first need to sense or hear what is being said and then fully understand what is meant. Then, and only then, are you in a position to effectively and rationally judge and respond to what has been said. A good method of learning control is to plan to report or make a commitment to report the essence of what you've heard to someone else.

Obviously it is difficult to conquer emotional responses with respect to people, topics, and language. It takes time and substantial effort. However, the following suggestions should help you. First, in every listening situation, identify prior to listening, those people, topics, and words that affect you emotionally. This practice will make you aware of the specific people, topics, and words that stimulate your reactions. Thus you are one step toward greater control. Next, attempt to analyze why these people, topics and words affect you the way they do. Think about your past experiences, or encounters that have influenced your emotional evaluation and reaction. Finally, try to reduce the impact of people, topics, and words on you by using a "defense" mechanism. One which is popularly suggested to help avoid emotional reactions is called "rationalization." Rationalization involves attempting to convince yourself that the person, topic, or word is not as bad or good as you think. No matter what defense mechanism you use, try to eliminate your emotionally conditioned response to people, topics, or words. Three additional suggestions which should help you compensate for an initial bias (positive or negative) are: (1) *Defer judgment.* As we have mentioned, you need to listen to an entire message before responding. (2) *Empathize.* Try to take the speaker's point of view while you listen. Search for reasons for the speaker's views and arguments, even if they are different from your own. (3) *Place your personal feelings in perspective.* Remember that your past experiences, including your cultural and educational background, have molded you into a unique person. If you critically evaluate your own views, then you should be better able to relate to the ideas of others.

The suggestions that have been presented throughout this chapter should help your emotional control during listening, but for the techniques to be useful, you must incorporate and practice them. You've first got to know what triggers your emotions and then you have to develop control through practice.

## SUMMARY

Controlling emotional response is one of the most important and difficult listening skills to develop. Any aspect associated with people, topics, or language may trigger or encourage emotional reactions while listening. Five key points help explain the relationship between emotions and listening. (1) All people have emotional triggers. (2) Emotions are directly related to filtering agents. (3) Emotional triggers affect communication and listening effectiveness. (4) Emotions may be affected positively, negatively, and or neutrally. (5) Some professionals are trained to understand what affects emotional responses in others. For this reason it is important to know what influences our emotions. Anyone who is in a position to know more about what triggers your emotions than you do is in a position to control you. It is possible to deal with emotions if they are identified prior to listening, if there is an attempt to analyze what people, topics, and language affect emotions and if attempts are made to reduce the impact of aroused emotions. Such control must be practiced and incorporated into everyday listening situations to be effective. The next chapter deals with messages; we will consider methods for identifying message structures, explaining how to evaluate and respond to messages, and discuss techniques of notetaking.

# 8
# Identifying Message Structures and Notetaking

*The reason you don't understand me, Edith, is because I'm talking to you in English and you're listening in dingbat!*

**Archie Bunker**

The last two chapters offered suggestions to help identify distractions and emotional triggers that hinder your listening effectiveness. By keeping these principles in mind, you should be able to control your internal and external interferences and emotional responses to people, topics, and language. This chapter should help you receive and remember more of the oral messages you hear by explaining how to identify message structures and providing directions for taking better, more productive, notes.

## IDENTIFYING MESSAGE STRUCTURES: UNIVERSAL PROBLEMS

As listeners, we face three universal problems: (1) we listen faster than average speakers speak; (2) we often fail to use the thought/speech–speed time differential productively; and

(3) we usually do not take effective mental and/or written notes. Poor listeners generally have difficulty in all three of these areas. Fortunately, you may have already begun to deal with the first two problems after reading and doing the exercises in earlier chapters. One way to approach the third problem is by learning to listen for organizational arrangement patterns that speakers use. The following list emphasizes, once again, differences between poor and good listeners that relate to message structure. Poor listeners do not:

1. Plan to report what they hear later to someone else.
2. Use the thought/speech speed differential to their advantage.
3. First look for the central idea and organizational pattern.
4. Take mental or written notes.
5. Adapt their listening to the organizational pattern of the speaker.
6. Anticipate the organizational pattern of the speaker.
7. Control diversion onto mental tangents that waste listening time.

Good listeners do:

1. Plan to report what they hear later.
2. Use the thought/speech speed differential to their advantage.
3. First look for the central idea and organizational pattern.
4. Take mental and/or written notes.
5. Adapt their listening to the organizational pattern of the speaker.
6. Anticipate the organizational pattern of the speaker.

7. Not waste time on mental tangents.

As listeners, we have to learn to adapt to a speaker's organization. A speaker's presentation is ordinarily somewhere between being carefully organized and completely disorganized. Whether a speaker's primary purpose is, phatic (small-talk binding), catharsis (venting), information, or persuasion; whether the situation is formal or informal; whether the speaker is prepared or unprepared; or whether the oral message is presented one to one or one to many, speakers fall on an organizational continuum. Try if you will to recall the last speaker you heard. You may have heard the president's "state of the union address," a sermon, a seminar lecture, a telephone chat, a community service meeting, or discussion around the fire. What do you remember about the speaker's message? Using this organizational continuum, where would you place the speaker?

| Very<br>Organized | | | | Very<br>Unorganized |
|---|---|---|---|---|
| | Moderately<br>Organized | N | Moderately<br>Unorganized | |

Why? You may not remember anything about the speaker's organization. If you don't, you need to start a plan for remembering the speaker's organizational habits and behaviors in order to make them work for you. You can get the speaker to work for you by first identifying whether or not the speaker is organized. If the speaker is organized, you need to find out how, and then adjust your listening to that structure. If the speaker is not organized, you need to find a method of organizing the unorganized message.

The key is to identify and adapt your listening to a speaker's organizational pattern. This is one way of using the advantage of your thought speed which is faster than the speaker's speech speed. Later in this chapter, typical organizational patterns will be explained. If you can tune in to the speaker's organizational pattern, you will have a clearer picture of the entire message. By seeing a message structure, you have a skeleton framework for the message. This skeleton gives you a pattern with which to attach the supporting data which helps you remember the message. Even with disorganized speakers, using a pattern will help you make sense out of a speaker's disorganized confusion. One final note: most speakers are habitual, and thus predictable, in the degree and nature of organizing material they use. By listening to "cue" and "clue" language you can determine if and how speakers are structured.

## MESSAGE STRUCTURES

The first step toward identifying an organizational pattern is to see if there is a message structure. Speakers can be seen to organize their ideas either climactically or anticlimactically. A climactic structure builds to a final conclusion. Mystery writers characteristically build their plots climactically. Readers are never sure of "who done it" until the final page of the book. In an anticlimactic structure, the conclusion is known from the beginning of the message.

Speakers who arrange their material by giving general information first and work to more specific information later use climactic structures. One example of a climactic presentation would be:

> *It's a pleasure to warn you*
> *Of the thief of life.*
> *This thief shortens your breath!*
> *This thief befouls your nest!*
> *This thief diminishes your savings!*
> *This thief reduces your friends!*
> *This thief ruins your clothing!*
> *This thief blackens your lungs!*
> *This thief steals your life!*
> *Smoking is a thief of life.*

From this example, you see that the speaker was well organized. The speaker moved from general information to specific conclusions. You may not agree with the speaker's conclusion, but this type of organizational structure usually gets attention. Listeners stay tuned in until the end so that they can find out "what happens." Effective listeners would recognize this climactical pattern immediately and listen to the detailed information because it supports the conclusion drawn in the end. If you fail to listen well to the details, it is impossible for you to adequately understand and evaluate what you've heard. In other words, you stand the chance of making interpretive, evaluative, and responding errors.

The same message could also be developed anticlimactically. The speaker's organization moves from a specific idea to a general conclusion. For example:

*Smoking is a thief of life.*
*Smoking is harmful to your health,*
*Your finances, your personal*
*Relationships, and your longevity!*
*Smoking is indeed a thief and I've got proof!*

*Smoking shortens your breath!*
*Smoking befouls your nest!*
*Smoking costs you money!*
*It ruins your clothing!*
*It costs you friends!*
*It blackens your lungs!*
*It steals your life!*

An anticlimactic organizational structure can affect the quality of your listening in several ways. If you agree (positive trigger) with the issue, then you might relax your listening and miss a point. In contrast, if you disagree (negative trigger), you may critically build a refutation and again miss something important. We see that one disadvantage of the anticlimactic organizational structure is that it does not serve to hold attention like a climactic structure does. Be sure as you identify these structures that you continue to listen by planning to report what you've heard to someone else afterwards. Again, if you practice withholding judgments, listening to the entire message, and plan to report later, you will listen better and retain more. Your notetaking should be adapted to the speaker's structure or organizational pattern, which we discuss next.

## ORGANIZATIONAL PATTERNS

There are numerous organizational patterns available to speakers. These patterns are used in combination with the climactic and anticlimactic structures. We'll look at four of the most typical organizational patterns: enumeration, problem/solution, time-sequence (chronological), and spatial. There are of course others, as you will discover.

The first of these common patterns is *enumeration*. As the word suggests, speakers organize their message around a given number of points. You have heard speakers use this pattern on numerous occasions: "My first four points are . . .", "The topic can be divided into three areas", or "There are six steps you should follow." Following is a more detailed example:

> I'm happy that you could join me this morning to discuss our fund-raising campaign. There are four points we need to cover.
>
> *First*, is setting our goal. We need to establish a realistic figure and subdivide it into targets for each department.
>
> *Second*, we need to identify our potential population.
>
> *Third*, outline our strategy.
>
> *Fourth*, setting completion dates for each strategy.

The enumeration pattern is extremely clear, since the speaker's cue language is direct; if you adapt to the speaker's structure, you should end up remembering substantially more information. (Even though enumeration is easy to follow, you will find that there are some drawbacks.) Speakers tend to use enumeration when they want to explain. Pure explanation can be boring when there is too much information to remember. If you find a speaker outlining more than three or four main points, try to take notes. Picking out the main points numerically should help you take better notes and thus retain more.

Another commonly used organizational pattern is the *problem/solution* pattern. When using this pattern, speakers usually focus on either the nature of the problem, its causes, effects, and solutions, or a combination of the four components. The following examples will help to illustrate.

> Ladies and gentlemen, we face a grievous *problem. We are the only major city in the entire state that does not have fluoridated water.* And this problem has been recognized by the dental association. . . .

Or the speaker may primarily develop the *cause* of a problem:

> Ladies and gentlemen, for months we have recognized the problem of our nonfluoridated water supply. Tonight I want to discuss the *cause* of our problem. As you well know, *our city engineer and city council have taken the position that.* . . .

Or the speaker may primarily develop the *effect* of a problem:

> Ladies and gentlemen, we must examine the *effect* of this fluoridation problem on our youthful population. The *primary effect of our nonfluoridated water will show up in our children's teeth. The effect will be increased cavities, increased dental bills, increased.* . . .

Or the speaker may primarily develop the *solution* of a problem:

> Ladies and gentlemen, the *solution* is complex but necessary. If we are to reduce this problem, we *must obtain the support of the majority of this community*—the solution will require . . . .

As we listen, we should be able to ascertain whether or not the speaker is zeroing in on the problem, its causes, effects, or solution, or a combination (i.e., problem and cause, or problem and solution). When trying to identify the organization pattern, the key is to listen to the speaker's "cue" language. After you have identified the speaker's central purpose and developed a structural skeleton, and adapted your notetaking (mental or written) to this structure, you will find yourself remembering more of the total message.

Using a *time-sequence* or chronological pattern is a third scheme of message organization. A speaker can trace a topic by looking at the past and building to the present and or future, or by looking at the present and digressing through the past. This pattern helps listeners with recall by pointing out relationships through the chronological progressions. Consider this example:

> If we analyze the widespread use of drugs in our society, we see a clear-cut *change over the years. Historically,* we can track the relative non-use by young persons of any drugs in the United States *up to the mid-1960's.* Without question, the widespread use of illegal drugs was nonexistent until the "beat generation" of the *1950's and 60's.* But the generation gap: the Vietnam War, the social revolution, and the political reaction of the mid-*1960's* corresponds with the growth and widespread use of numerous drugs, and this growth continued into the mid-*1970's.* However, by the latter part of the 1970's, we can see an interesting trend. In this time period, a general decline in the widespread use of illegal drugs is noted.
>
> And as we *look to the future* experts are predicting further change. . . .

In this situation, the speaker develops the message around a clear-cut time sequence pattern. Again, cue words that speakers use will help you identify the chronological pattern: "Let's look back to our beginnings . . .", or "An analysis of the past twelve years should show. . . ." Your listening will improve as you learn to adjust to a speaker's organizational pattern.

The fourth pattern that we will discuss is the *spatial, graphic,* or *pictorial technique.* This device is an interesting one for listeners because the speaker typically draws a picture to help explain the points being made. By tuning in to the speaker's cue language you will be able to determine whether or not the spatial pattern is being used. Take the following example:

> I heard an interesting speaker at our professional meeting today. Mr. Strand, a renowned financial investment expert, was explaining what it took to be financially successful in this country today. He suggested that we *needed to picture in our minds eye, the ladder of financial success.* He said that we have to climb four rungs on this ladder if we want to be financially successful. The first rung he talked about was a solid, thorough, liberal education. He said education was critical because. . . . The second rung he talked about was our contacts. He said the family we were born into, the people we went to school with, the people we worked with, lived with, and socialized with, all had an important impact on our financial success. The third rung he talked about was our long-term motivation. He said that every study of financially successful people showed high motivation. And finally, the fourth rung on his ladder of success was the most important of all. And you know as long as I saw that picture of his ladder of success with its four rungs, I can easily remember his key points. I carried more information out of that presentation than any I can remember for a long time.

This speaker used graphic examples to add emphasis to the presentation. If you begin to picture what the speaker is describing in your mind's eye, you will get more of the message. By also drawing upon your visual senses, you will perceive the organizational skeleton more readily. Remember, the speaker's cue words and language will help show which pattern is being used. Finally, your notes should reflect the graphic structure.

Speakers often use these four patterns in combination, or they may use altogether different patterns. The key for listeners is to pick out one arrangement as the primary pattern and another as a secondary pattern where evident. Using these patterns of arrangement will help you overcome the problems of wasting the speech–thought differential, poor notetaking, and listening primarily for facts rather than concepts. If the speaker is organized, listen for the central ideas and try to develop a skeleton to attach the facts. Use the speaker's structural system. If the speaker is unorganized, you need to recognize the lack of organization. Next you need to use any one of the four arrangement patterns to organize the material for your own use. Effective listeners have their favorite organization systems that they can quickly turn to when needed. These patterns have been used in the past to help speakers; you can use the same principles to help improve your ability to listen.

## SOME HINTS FOR NOTETAKING

Closely related to the listening process is the process of taking notes. You have frequently employed notetaking in classroom situations or meetings, but it is also appropriate in other public speaking or semiformal listening situations. Below are several suggestions designed to help you improve your notetaking ability (Barker, 1971).

(1) *Decide whether or not to take notes.* Notes may be useful in some settings, but unnecessary, and even distracting in others. Your purpose for listening should determine whether or not you need to take notes. If you feel you may need to refer to the information at a future time, the notes probably are necessary. However, if the information is for immediate use (e.g., announcements about the day's schedule at a summer workshop), it may be more effective simply to listen carefully without taking notes. Your own ability to comprehend and retain information is a variable which also must be taken into account. If you have high concentration and retention

abilities, you probably will need to take relatively few notes. However, if you have difficulty remembering information the day after it is presented, you probably should get out a notepad.

(2) *Decide what types of notes are necessary.* There are at least three different types of notes which people may elect to take. They differ in purpose and specificity. These three common types are key words, partial outline, and complete outline.

    (a) *Key words.* When you primarily want to remember some specific points in the message, key word notes are probably the most efficient. For example, if you wanted to remember an entertaining story about a member of the Democratic party who attended a meeting of the John Birch Society by mistake, so you could retell it later, you might elect to write the key words, "DP at Birch meeting," on your notepad. Key words are used to help provide cues for ideas which were presented during the listening setting. However, unless you can positively associate the meaning with the key words, they are not useful.

    (b) *Partial outline.* If you decide that there are several important elements you should remember in a message, it probably is desirable to take notes in partial outline form. The points in the message which seem important to you are noted rather completely, and other points which you do not deem important are not recorded. For example, suppose you are auditing a night class on statistics; your professor illustrates how to compute a mean, median, and mode, but you may decide that you want to remember only how to compute the mode. Consequently, you record in your notes only that portion of the lecture that relates to your specific interest. The notes you take are complete, but they do not represent all of the material that was presented.

(c) *Complete outline.* In many listening situations, it is important to record most of what is presented. In meetings and in other settings where you may need to have a complete record of what was said, a complete set of notes in outline form is necessary, because you often will be expected to provide specific information at a later time. Of course, the outline form should be adapted to the speaker's format.

The key is to determine in advance what type of notes you will need to take in a given listening setting, and then adapt your notetaking accordingly. If you modify your notetaking according to the demands of the situation and the speaker's system, you will make most efficient and effective use of your efforts.

(3) *Keep notes clear.* This involves not only using brief sentences and statements of ideas which are understandable after you have written them, but also includes such details as not cluttering the page, not scribbling, and not writing side comments. Use the paper efficiently; avoid crowding words together.

(4) *Keep notes brief.* This suggestion speaks for itself. The briefer your notes, the less time you will be spending writing, and the less likely you will be to miss what the speaker says.

(5) *Recognize as quickly as possible the organizational pattern (or lack of pattern) of the speaker.* First, as mentioned earlier, be aware of the fact that many speakers have no discernible orgainzational pattern. There is a tendency for some notetakers to try to organize notes on the basis of their own preferred patterns rather than the speaker's. For example, you may normally outline beginning with roman numeral I, followed by A and B, 1 and 2, a and b, and so forth. However, if the speaker is simply talking in random fashion without much formal organization, then artificially imposing an organizational pat-

tern on the message may distort its meaning. Therefore, it is important to determine quickly if the speaker is employing a formal organizational pattern and adapt your own notetaking to this pattern.

(6) *Review your notes soon afterwards.* This suggestion is extremely important in a learning situation because by reviewing information frequently we retain it longer. Ideas that we hear once tend to be forgotten within 24 hours. Without some review they may be lost to us forever. Another reason for reviewing your notes soon after taking them is that you may remember some details at that point which you might not remember when reading your notes at some future time.

## SUMMARY

Messages range on a continuum from very unorganized to very well organized and we need to adapt our listening to a speaker's pattern. This chapter described how message structures are organized either climactically or anticlimactically. There are numerous organizational patterns available to speakers. The four used most often are: enumeration, problem/solution, time-sequence (chronological), and spatial. Several hints for notetaking were given. Listeners should: (1) Decide whether or not to take notes; (2) Decide what type of notes are necessary; (3) Keep notes clear; (4) Keep notes brief; (5) Find the organizational pattern (or recognize the lack of pattern) as quickly as possible; and (6) Review the notes later. The next chapter suggests techniques for message evaluation and response.

## REFERENCE

Barker, L.L. *Listening Behavior.* Englewood Cliffs, NJ: Prentice-Hall, 1971.

# 9

# Message Evaluation and Response

*The greatest compliment that was ever paid me was when one asked me what I thought, and attended to my answer.*

**Henry David Thoreau**

Overcoming distractions and emotions enables you to sense and interpret messages more accurately, but your ultimate listening goal is to make appropriate evaluations and responses. The skilled listener is an evaluating and responsive listener. Successful listening requires accurate evaluations and judgments about what you have heard and understood. You cannot effectively evaluate what you do not completely sense or properly interpret. On the other hand, even messages that you sense and interpret accurately can nevertheless be misevaluated, as we shall explain.

## TYPES OF EVALUATION

Message evaluation is either immediate or delayed. Immediate evaluation is appropriate when messages are short, noncontroversial, or uncomplicated. Delayed evaluation is best for long, controversial, or complex messages. When a fellow employee asks if you'd like to go on a coffee break it's easy for you to make a decision without too much thought, but if the same employee asked you if some planned price increases would be sufficient to meet rising costs, you would probably need time to look at all the issues involved before answering.

As listeners we need to guard against premature evaluation, especially for complex issues. Premature evaluations are caused by uncontrolled emotional responses. Evaluation should take place only after you have considered whether or not the message is factual or opinionated, the content development is sound, the evidence supports the message, and the reasoning based on the evidence is valid. If one of your friends were to encourage you to buy a house in his or her neighborhood, you would expect your friend's viewpoint to be somewhat biased. Your friend would even have a stronger bias if he or she were also a real estate broker.

It is a good idea when listening for you to keep in mind whether or not the information is based on fact or opinion. Obviously, a friend who lives in the neighborhood is probably pleased with the school system, road maintenance, and neighbors, but he or she may subconsciously fail to mention some factors that are undesirable (floods during the spring, or no dog leash laws). This is not to say that decisions should not be based on opinion. We accept opinions daily; yet, in subsequent evaluation, we should attempt to determine the degree of objectivity a person has.

After a speaker makes a statement you need to look at the content. If a real estate broker were to tell you that the neighborhood is crime-free, the house is energy-efficient, and there is an assumable mortgage, you might be ready to buy. However, you need to stop and think about what you may not have been told. Is the house near a railroad track, is the basement waterproof, or are there problems with appliances? We need to listen for details of the total picture before responding and making a decision. Important information may be missing even though you have heard and understood everything that has been said.

Next in evaluating the content of the message, you need to weigh how the information was supported. Did your friend's opinions come from others in the area, statistics from local newspapers on housing costs, or facts from meter readings? For example, if you are told that a house is energy-efficient, you need to know who says so and how do they know. Did the information come from the previous owner, the contractor, or someone else? Is the information from recent reports or was it given several years ago? It could make a big difference in the cost of heating oil if costs were from 1975 instead of today.

Finally, after determining whether the information is based on fact or opinion, and after evaluating the content and evidence used, you need to look at the speaker's reasoning. You want to know if the conclusions reached by the speaker are logical, and based on the evidence given. If your friend says that the house is in a good location because the windows are shaded in the summer and hit by the sun in the winter, then that should help to cut energy costs. However, if your friend were to say that the shade trees help keep energy costs low but they do not shade the house's windows in the summer or let sunlight in during the winter, the reasoning would be questionable. It is important to remember to evaluate all sides when listening to messages. If you do you will be in a better position when making your decisions.

So far we have stressed the importance of waiting to hear the complete message before evaluating it. Along with avoiding premature evaluation, you also need to learn to identify biased communication. Two types of biased communication that listeners should be especially aware of are rumors and propaganda.

## Rumors

Rumors may or may not be started deliberately, whereas propaganda is carefully developed. Of course, all communication is biased to a certain extent. Examples of rumors are numerous. If you think about your interpersonal communication activities during the past week, it is likely that you can remember several rumors which you either heard or were instrumental in sending to others. Rumors range from personal rumors about yourself or your friends to large-scale rumors about governmental policy and international affairs.

Rumors have characteristics that can help you identify them: (1) Rumors are usually temporary in nature; (2) Rumors tend to run in cycles; (3) The content of most rumors deals with people or events; (4) Verification of a rumor is usually difficult or impossible; (5) Initiators of rumors generally are not experts regarding the subject of the rumor. Because few people are experts on a variety of different subjects, the possibility of rumor is high. People are often so busy that they do not have or want to take the time to verify rumors which therefore tend to escalate. A few years ago, it was rumored that a major fast food chain was using red worms to increase the protein rate in their hamburgers. This rumor ended up costing the company millions of dollars, since the chain had to develop an extensive advertising campaign to refute and reassure their customers.

There are several things listeners can do to avoid being deceived or misinformed by rumors. First, you must identify a message as a rumor. Five checks will help you determine whether or not the information is valid.

1. Check the source.

2. Check with the sender of the rumor to determine the basis of the information contained in the rumor.

3. Determine the consequences of the rumor for you and other people concerned.

4. Try to assess what motives might have contributed to the rumor.

5. Attempt to investigate systematically to uncover evidence which will prove or disprove the critical elements of the rumor.

The suggestions listed above are also useful in assessing propaganda. The following section describes the nature of propaganda and gives several additional suggestions to help us identify and deal with propaganda.

## Propaganda

*If you can't do anything to improve on the silence, don't disturb it.*

**Anonymous**

Most people associate negative connotations with the term propaganda. Propaganda is usually thought of in connection with subversive elements in society such as communists, "moonies," or fascists. However, common connotation is often misleading. In fact, propaganda exists in most newspapers and magazines that you read every day. There is nothing inherently bad about propaganda. It is simply a form of communication with built-in biases. Propaganda involves a conscious attempt to influence others. Its purpose may be either good or bad. Propaganda that attacks unequal employment opportunities, disease, monopolies, organized crime, or governmental bureaucracy is generally considered desirable. The desirability is not reduced because the appeals are primarily emotional rather than intellectual. In fact, most messages that use excessively emotional appeals are a form of propaganda. Propaganda exists in all communication media and we need to be able to recognize and analyze these types of biased messages.

One characteristic of propaganda campaigns is an increase in the number and intensity of rumors circulated. Rumors and propaganda are interrelated because rumors and propaganda thrive on each other. When examining the purpose of a message, the most important test is to determine whether the communicator or the general public will benefit from the ideas presented. If the suggested plan benefits the originators of the message and their interests primarily, the message may be seen as propaganda. Keep in mind that the fact that a message does happen to be biased does not necessarily mean that the results would be bad. Propaganda may benefit the originator as well as members of society. For example, with increasing crime rates numerous security systems have been marketed using emotional appeals. Yet, buying a security system for your home is beneficial to you and the promoter.

Following are some of the devices or signals which help us to identify propaganda in messages. *Half truths* involve telling only part of the story deliberately when the full story is known. *Card stacking* is a type of lie presenting only one side of an argument, and withholding information which might refute the position being advocated. *Hasty generalization* refers to distorting or carelessly misquoting the findings of a study or misrepresenting the findings by generalizing to a larger population than is justifiable. *Name-calling* is a device used to attack or degrade the personality of an opponent or opposing group. *Plain folks* devices attempt to make the speaker appear humble and one of the crowd by using such things as middle-or lower-class language, dressing conservatively or specifically for the situation. Finally, the *bandwagon* device is employed to show that "everyone else is doing it." These are only some of the devices used, but now we need to identify some methods of analysis.

Propaganda assessment is more difficult than rumor analysis because the source of the message is often unknown, and the full evidence is usually not available for examination. However, in trying to determine whether the message is a form of propaganda, first you need to carefully analyze what is being said. Then you should look at the evidence and try to determine who will benefit most from what is suggested. Again remember to use these principles along with the suggestions for analyzing rumors. The importance of active critical listening in the analysis of rumors and propaganda cannot be overemphasized. As a critical listener you can help repress unfounded rumors and minimize the negative effects of propaganda on yourself and others.

## MESSAGE RESPONSE (FEEDBACK)

*The spoken word belongs half to him who
speaks, and half to him who hears.*

**French Proverb**

As a listener, one of your final tasks is to develop the ability
to respond appropriately to messages. Until a listener responds, there is no way to know if he or she has sensed,
interpreted and evaluated the message fully and effectively. A
necessary element of the completed communication process is
feedback or response. A successful listener will not neglect
the responsibility to respond. As mentioned earlier, feedback
helps speakers to know if they have been understood, and if
they are interesting, etc. Feedback also helps you personally.
The feedback you receive when you listen to yourself can
help you correct mistakes in the future. For example, if you
mispronounce a person's name, it is important to hear that
so you will pronounce it correctly later. Responding to communication helps you to control some aspects of your own
and other speakers' behavior.

Earlier, we explained the differences between positive,
negative, and ambiguous feedback. There are also four classes of feedback response: verbal feedback, nonverbal feedback, combined verbal and nonverbal feedback, and the
absence of verbal and nonverbal feedback (silence). Think of
all the times you have sent feedback verbally today. You
probably answered questions and also gave spontaneous remarks such as commenting on someone's clothing, absence,
or punctuality. Nonverbal feedback is sent continually. Nonverbal feedback takes the form of body motions or vocal in-
tonations and provides a significant amount of information
in face-to-face interactions. Listeners usually respond verbally and nonverbally to messages. We tend to respond verbally
and nonverbally without thinking about it. Think about a
time when you gave directions to someone. It was probably
natural for you to explain verbally while using your arms
and hands to point and indicate directions. The last class of
feedback is silence. We often neglect silence as a pattern of

responding to messages. We are all familiar with the "silent treatment," yet silence can also be used positively to communicate concentration or sympathy.

We use feedback for different purposes. Feedback can be rewarding or punishing. Perceptions of reward and punishment differ from person to person. What is rewarding to one person may be punishing to another. For example, some employees accept negative criticism positively as a method to improve, but others feel as though they are being attacked. Another purpose of feedback that managers use very often is nondirective or directive feedback. Nondirective feedback is an attempt to replicate what has been said in an effort to encourage further discussion. Directive feedback places a value judgment on what has been said and is concerned with reward and punishment. Managers listen to employees explain why a project is delayed, giving nondirective feedback. After the employee's explanation the manager often responds with directive feedback about what should be done in the future. Effective listeners don't rely on one purpose for giving feedback, but try to adjust their feedback to meet the demands of the situation.

As listeners we are concerned with communicating our responses accurately to others. Listeners have the duty to respond to a message in order to complete the communication process. The following guidelines should help you increase your feedback effectiveness.

1. Send feedback that is appropriate to the speaker, message, and context.
2. Send the feedback promptly.
3. Make certain the feedback is clear in meaning.
4. Be certain the speaker perceived the feedback.
5. Beware of overloading the system.
6. Delay in performing any activity that might create an unintentional effect.

7. Keep feedback to the message separate from personal evaluation.

8. Use nondirective feedback until the speaker invites evaluation of the message.

9. Be sure that you understand the message before you send directive feedback.

10. Realize that early attempts at giving more effective feedback may seem unnatural but will improve with practice.

## SUMMARY

Total listening involves evaluation and response. In this chapter we discussed differences between immediate and delayed evaluation. Evaluation should take place only after you have considered whether or not the message content is factual or opinionated, the reasoning is sound, and the evidence is timely, supportive, and valid. We considered the characteristics of rumor and propaganda, and finally, the types of response or feedback were discussed.

# Epilogue

*It seems that we shall eventually come to believe that the responsibility for effective oral communication must be equally shared by speakers and listeners. When this transpires, we shall have taken a long stride toward greater economy in learning, accelerated personal growth, and significantly deepened human understanding.*

**Ralph C. Nichols and Leonard A. Stevens** *Are You Listening?*
(McGraw Hill, 1957, p. 221-22)

# Appendix A

The exercises in this appendix are designed to help you extend your understanding of the various communication purposes and stages. Specifically, you will have an opportunity to analyze your communication relationships and practices—past, present, and future. Exercise 1 focuses on identifying "primary" and "secondary" communicators with whom you relate. Exercise 2 examines the nature of your "phatic," "cathartic," "informational," and "persuasive" communication. Exercise 3 will help you utilize the SIER formula to understand and maximize your listening practices.

## EXERCISE 1

Periodically identify (by name) your communication connections. Who do you spend measurable time listening to?

*Primary Communicators*: List by name individuals with whom you communicate regularly (i.e., everyday or several times a day).

<table>
<tr><th>Name</th><th>Relationship</th></tr>
<tr><td>_____</td><td>_____</td></tr>
<tr><td>_____</td><td>_____</td></tr>
<tr><td>_____</td><td>_____</td></tr>
<tr><td>_____</td><td>_____</td></tr>
<tr><td>_____</td><td>_____</td></tr>
<tr><td>_____</td><td>_____</td></tr>
<tr><td>_____</td><td>_____</td></tr>
<tr><td>_____</td><td>_____</td></tr>
<tr><td>_____</td><td>_____</td></tr>
<tr><td>_____</td><td>_____</td></tr>
<tr><td>_____</td><td>_____</td></tr>
<tr><td>_____</td><td>_____</td></tr>
<tr><td>_____</td><td>_____</td></tr>
<tr><td>_____</td><td>_____</td></tr>
</table>

*Secondary Communicators*: List by name individuals with whom you communicate periodically (i.e., a few times per week).

<table>
<tr><th>Name</th><th>Relationship</th></tr>
<tr><td>_____</td><td>_____</td></tr>
<tr><td>_____</td><td>_____</td></tr>
<tr><td>_____</td><td>_____</td></tr>
</table>

_____    _____
_____    _____
_____    _____
_____    _____
_____    _____
_____    _____
_____    _____
_____    _____
_____    _____
_____    _____
_____    _____

## EXERCISE 2

Analyze _why_ (purposes) and _how well_ you communicate with specific individuals and how you can _improve_.

- Phatic (Binding) Communication

Name ten individuals with whom you experience productive phatic communication:

| Name | Relationship | Why |
|------|--------------|-----|
| _____ | _____ | _____ |
| _____ | _____ | _____ |
| _____ | _____ | _____ |
| _____ | _____ | _____ |

| | | |
|---|---|---|
| _____ | _____ | _____ |
| _____ | _____ | _____ |
| _____ | _____ | _____ |
| _____ | _____ | _____ |
| _____ | _____ | _____ |
| _____ | _____ | _____ |

In the "Why" column, briefly, indicate why you believe you experience productive phatic communication with each of the foregoing individuals.

Name ten individuals with whom you should, but _do not_ experience productive phatic communication.

| Name | Relationship | Why Not |
|---|---|---|
| _____ | _____ | _____ |
| _____ | _____ | _____ |
| _____ | _____ | _____ |
| _____ | _____ | _____ |
| _____ | _____ | _____ |
| _____ | _____ | _____ |
| _____ | _____ | _____ |
| _____ | _____ | _____ |
| _____ | _____ | _____ |
| _____ | _____ | _____ |

In the "Why Not" column, briefly identify why you believe you do not experience productive phatic communication with each of the foregoing individuals.

In each case, what can you _do_ specifically to improve the existing or desired phatic communication?

• Cathartic (Venting) Communication

Name ten individuals who serve your cathartic needs.

| Name | Relationship |
|------|-------------|
| _____ | _____ |
| _____ | _____ |
| _____ | _____ |
| _____ | _____ |
| _____ | _____ |
| _____ | _____ |
| _____ | _____ |
| _____ | _____ |
| _____ | _____ |
| _____ | _____ |

Generally speaking, how important is their listening to your catharsis and what are their observable characteristics?

Name ten individuals who should, but *do not* serve your cathartic needs.

| Name | Relationship |
|------|-------------|
| _____ | _____ |
| _____ | _____ |
| _____ | _____ |
| _____ | _____ |
| _____ | _____ |
| _____ | _____ |

_____     _____

_____     _____

_____     _____

In your opinion, why do these individuals not serve your cathartic needs? What are their observable characteristics? What is the impact of this cathartic neglect?

Name ten individuals whose cathartic communication needs _you serve_ as a listener.

| <u>Name</u> | <u>Relationship</u> |
| --- | --- |
| _____ | _____ |
| _____ | _____ |
| _____ | _____ |
| _____ | _____ |
| _____ | _____ |
| _____ | _____ |
| _____ | _____ |
| _____ | _____ |
| _____ | _____ |
| _____ | _____ |

Why?

What is the impact?

Name ten individuals whom _you can serve better_ as a cathartic listener.

Name                          Relationship

_____            _____

_____            _____

_____            _____

_____            _____

_____            _____

_____            _____

_____            _____

_____            _____

_____            _____

_____            _____


How? Outline your strategy on paper.


• Informational Communication

Name ten key individuals whom you communicate with for informational purposes.

Name                          Relationship

_____            _____

_____            _____

_____            _____

_____            _____

_____            _____

_____            _____

_____            _____

_____     _____

_____     _____

_____     _____

Outline three ways that your informational listening could be improved with each individual.

Name ten individuals that you should, but _do not_, communicate with well for informational purposes.

| Name | Relationship |
| --- | --- |
| _____ | _____ |
| _____ | _____ |
| _____ | _____ |
| _____ | _____ |
| _____ | _____ |
| _____ | _____ |
| _____ | _____ |
| _____ | _____ |
| _____ | _____ |
| _____ | _____ |

Why not?

Specifically, what can you do to enhance your listening for information with each individual?

• Persuasive Communication

Name ten key individuals that you communicate with well for purposes of persuasion.

| Name | Relationship |
| --- | --- |
| _____ | _____ |
| _____ | _____ |
| _____ | _____ |
| _____ | _____ |
| _____ | _____ |
| _____ | _____ |
| _____ | _____ |
| _____ | _____ |
| _____ | _____ |
| _____ | _____ |

Outline three ways that your listening to persuasion could be improved with each individual.

Name ten key individuals that you should, but *do not* communicate with well for persuasion purposes.

| Name | Relationship |
| --- | --- |
| _____ | _____ |
| _____ | _____ |
| _____ | _____ |
| _____ | _____ |
| _____ | _____ |

_____    _____

_____    _____

_____    _____

_____    _____

_____    _____

Why not?

Specifically, what can you do to enhance your listening for persuasion with each individual?

For maximum value, the foregoing set of exercises should be repeated every three to four months.

## EXERCISE 3

The SIER model can be utilized in a past tense (diagnostic), or present tense (application), or a future tense (planning) mode. At each level, consider the following:

- Past Tense (Diagnostic)

1. Sensing:

   A. Identify and outline a significant *past tense* break-down of communication that *started* at the *sensing* level.

   B. *What caused* the sensing problem?

   C. *How* could the sensing failure have been avoided?

   D. How did the sensing failure affect the ensuing I, E, and R levels of communication?

2. Interpretation:

   A. Identify and outline a significant *past tense* breakdown of communication that *started* at the *interpretation* level.

   B. *What caused* the interpretation problem?

   C. *How* could the *interpretation* failure have been avoided?

   D. How did the interpretation failure affect the ensuing E and R levels of communication?

3. Evaluation:

   A. Identify and outline a significant *past tense* breakdown of communication that *started* at the *evaluation* level.

   B. *What caused* the evaluation failure?

   C. *How* could the evaluation failure have been avoided?

   D. How did the evaluation failure affect the ensuing R (and possibly S and I) levels of communication?

4. Responding:

   A. Identify and outline a significant *past tense* breakdown of communication that *started* at the *responding* level.

   B. *What caused* the *responding* failure?

   C. *How* could the *responding* failure have been avoided?

   D. How did the responding failure affect the ensuing S, I, E, and R levels of communication?

• Present Tense (Application)

In critical concrete *present tense listening situations*, identify and outline how you can specifically enhance your:

1. Sensing success

2. Interpreting success

3. Evaluating success

4. Responding success

- Future Tense (Planning)

In significant and specific *future tense listening situations,* outline a concrete plan to ensure your:

1. Sensing success

2. Interpreting success

3. Evaluating success

4. Responding success

# Appendix B

## SELF ANALYSIS

Circle the word which best describes you overall as a listener.

Superior　　　Excellent　　　Above average

Average　　　Below average　　　Poor　　　Lousy

On a scale of 0–100 (100 = highest), how would you rate yourself overall as a listener?　　_____

(0–100)

In your opinion, what words describe you best overall as a listener?

_____　　　_____　　　_____

_____　　　_____　　　_____

_____　　　_____　　　_____

_____　　　_____　　　_____

_____　　　_____　　　_____

## PROJECTED SELF/OTHER ANALYSIS

Target 25: List, by name and relationship, 25 individuals who are most important, or significant, in your life. Do not prioritize or rank order them; simply list by name and relationship.

| | Name | Relationship |
|----|------|--------------|
| 1 | _____ | _____ |
| 2 | _____ | _____ |
| 3 | _____ | _____ |
| 4 | _____ | _____ |
| 5 | _____ | _____ |
| 6 | _____ | _____ |
| 7 | _____ | _____ |
| 8 | _____ | _____ |
| 9 | _____ | _____ |
| 10 | _____ | _____ |
| 11 | _____ | _____ |
| 12 | _____ | _____ |
| 13 | _____ | _____ |
| 14 | _____ | _____ |
| 15 | _____ | _____ |
| 16 | _____ | _____ |
| 17 | _____ | _____ |
| 18 | _____ | _____ |
| 19 | _____ | _____ |
| 20 | _____ | _____ |
| 21 | _____ | _____ |
| 22 | _____ | _____ |
| 22 | _____ | _____ |
| 23 | _____ | _____ |
| 24 | _____ | _____ |
| 25 | _____ | _____ |

Once you have completed your identification of the individuals most significant to your life, place them on the following target: five most significant in the bullseye, next five in the next ring, etc.

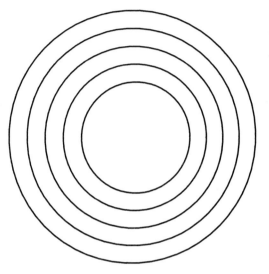

**Fig. 7.1** Target 25 Analysis

Now how do *you think they would rate you* overall as a listener? (Use the same scale of 0–100). Also list words they would use to describe you as a listener.

| (i.e.) | 0–100 | Adjectives | | |
|---|---|---|---|---|
| Your best friend | ____ | _____ | _____ | _____ |
| Your boss | ____ | _____ | _____ | _____ |
| A colleague | ____ | _____ | _____ | _____ |
| Job subordinate | ____ | _____ | _____ | _____ |
| Your spouse | ____ | _____ | _____ | _____ |
| Children | ____ | _____ | _____ | _____ |
| Parent | ____ | _____ | _____ | _____ |
| Teacher | ____ | _____ | _____ | _____ |

|  (i.e.) | 0–100 | Adjectives | | |
|---------|-------|-----------|---|---|
| Roommate | ____ | _____ | _____ | _____ |
| Club associate | ____ | _____ | _____ | _____ |

## OTHER/SELF ANALYSIS

Repeat your list of Target 25—your significant others. Individually ask each to *rate* and *describe* you overall as a listener.

| | Name | Relationship | 0–100 | Adjectives | | |
|---|------|-------------|-------|-----------|---|---|
| 1 | ____ | _____ | ____ | ____ | ____ | ____ |
| 2 | ____ | _____ | ____ | ____ | ____ | ____ |
| 3 | ____ | _____ | ____ | ____ | ____ | ____ |
| 4 | ____ | _____ | ____ | ____ | ____ | ____ |
| 5 | ____ | _____ | ____ | ____ | ____ | ____ |
| 6 | ____ | _____ | ____ | ____ | ____ | ____ |
| 7 | ____ | _____ | ____ | ____ | ____ | ____ |
| 8 | ____ | _____ | ____ | ____ | ____ | ____ |
| 9 | ____ | _____ | ____ | ____ | ____ | ____ |
| 10 | ____ | _____ | ____ | ____ | ____ | ____ |
| 11 | ____ | _____ | ____ | ____ | ____ | ____ |
| 12 | ____ | _____ | ____ | ____ | ____ | ____ |
| 13 | ____ | _____ | ____ | ____ | ____ | ____ |
| 14 | ____ | _____ | ____ | ____ | ____ | ____ |
| 15 | ____ | _____ | ____ | ____ | ____ | ____ |
| 16 | ____ | _____ | ____ | ____ | ____ | ____ |
| 17 | ____ | _____ | ____ | ____ | ____ | ____ |
| 18 | ____ | _____ | ____ | ____ | ____ | ____ |
| 19 | ____ | _____ | ____ | ____ | ____ | ____ |

|   | Name | Relationship | 0–100 | Adjectives | | |
|---|------|--------------|-------|------------|---|---|
| 20 | ___ | _____ | ____ | _____ | _____ | _____ |
| 21 | ___ | _____ | ____ | _____ | _____ | _____ |
| 22 | ___ | _____ | ____ | _____ | _____ | _____ |
| 23 | ___ | _____ | ____ | _____ | _____ | _____ |
| 24 | ___ | _____ | ____ | _____ | _____ | _____ |
| 25 | ___ | _____ | ____ | _____ | _____ | _____ |

## OTHER ANALYSIS

Overall, how would you rate (0–100) (descriptive words) your significant others?

|   | Name | Relationship | 0–100 | Adjectives | | |
|---|------|--------------|-------|------------|---|---|
| 1 | ___ | _____ | ____ | _____ | _____ | _____ |
| 2 | ___ | _____ | ____ | _____ | _____ | _____ |
| 3 | ___ | _____ | ____ | _____ | _____ | _____ |
| 4 | ___ | _____ | ____ | _____ | _____ | _____ |
| 5 | ___ | _____ | ____ | _____ | _____ | _____ |
| 6 | ___ | _____ | ____ | _____ | _____ | _____ |
| 7 | ___ | _____ | ____ | _____ | _____ | _____ |
| 8 | ___ | _____ | ____ | _____ | _____ | _____ |
| 9 | ___ | _____ | ____ | _____ | _____ | _____ |
| 10 | ___ | _____ | ____ | _____ | _____ | _____ |
| 11 | ___ | _____ | ____ | _____ | _____ | _____ |
| 12 | ___ | _____ | ____ | _____ | _____ | _____ |
| 13 | ___ | _____ | ____ | _____ | _____ | _____ |
| 14 | ___ | _____ | ____ | _____ | _____ | _____ |
| 15 | ___ | _____ | ____ | _____ | _____ | _____ |

| | Name | Relationship | 0–100 | | Adjectives | |
|---|---|---|---|---|---|---|
| 16 | ___ | _____ | ___ | ___ | _____ | ___ |
| 17 | ___ | _____ | ___ | ___ | _____ | ___ |
| 18 | ___ | _____ | ___ | ___ | _____ | ___ |
| 19 | ___ | _____ | ___ | ___ | _____ | ___ |
| 20 | ___ | _____ | ___ | ___ | _____ | ___ |
| 21 | ___ | _____ | ___ | ___ | _____ | ___ |
| 22 | ___ | _____ | ___ | ___ | _____ | ___ |
| 23 | ___ | _____ | ___ | ___ | _____ | ___ |
| 24 | ___ | _____ | ___ | ___ | _____ | ___ |
| 25 | ___ | _____ | ___ | ___ | _____ | ___ |

Best listener: Reflect on someone who you would consider to be representative of the *best listeners* you have ever known. Identify, rate and describe.

Name _____     Relationship _____     0–100

_____          _____          ___

Adjectives _____

_____          _____          ___

_____          _____          ___


Worst listener: Reflect on someone who you would consider to be representative of the *worst listeners* you have ever known. Identify, rate, and describe.

Name _____     Relationship _____     0–100

_____          _____          ___

Adjectives _____

_____          _____          ___

_____          _____          ___

# Appendix C

## ENVIRONMENTAL DISTRACTIONS

You need to be aware of distractions in your environment. Identifying potential and existing distractions is important; and since many go unnoticed until it is too late, the following exercise should help you. Draw a diagram of your primary office and/or work space (we say primary because many people have several places where they work). Locate objects such as chairs, cabinets, pictures, windows and doors. After you have finished your drawing, identify:

1. Negative space or factors (place an X on areas that cause some negativity, XX on areas that cause more negativity and XXX on areas that cause the greatest negativity).

2. Positive space or factors (place an O on the areas that

are somewhat positive, OO on areas that are positive, and OOO on areas that are most positive).

3. Shared space (place a square over areas that are shared with others).

4. Other's space (place a square with lines over other people's space that is not shared).

The attitudes and feelings that you have about your office affect your ability to listen in that environment. Now that you have labeled areas of your work space, think about the reasons why you feel positively or negatively. The first question to ask yourself is "What do I have the power to change?" Maybe you dislike a table in the corner. Why? Maybe it's always cluttered with piles of papers and books. Whenever someone enters your office, there is a tendency for you to think about the clutter rather than to listen. You may like your table or desk, but you may not like the colors of a picture on your wall. There are usually steps you can take to change what you do not like, but if not, forget it. You must find a way to overcome the distraction. Let's say that you do not like your doorway because there is so much noise from office traffic. You may not be able to limit the traffic, but you could shut your door or play soft music to muffle the sounds.

Now look at your work space in terms of potential listening distractions during conversations. As someone enters your office and sits down, is there a doorway or window behind them? If so, the movement of people walking by or other activity outside could tend to draw your attention away from what is being said. Think of a way to minimize these distractions. You could rearrange your office, make an effort to close the door behind the person, or draw the blinds. Look at your office carefully. Remember you want to identify any interference or distractions that could hinder your listening effectiveness. (This exercise can also easily be used in other communication situations such as your home.) For further information about inhouse training in listening, contact:

       SPECTRA Communication Associates
           Dr. Kittie W. Watson
           Dr. Larry L. Barker
           Post Office Box 5031
           Contract Station 20
           New Orleans, LA 70118
           (504) 831-4440

       Communication Development Inc.
           Dr. Lyman K. Steil
           25 Robb Farm Road
           St. Paul, MN 55110
           (612) 483-3597

# Index

# EXPLORER'S GUIDE

# MINNESOTA

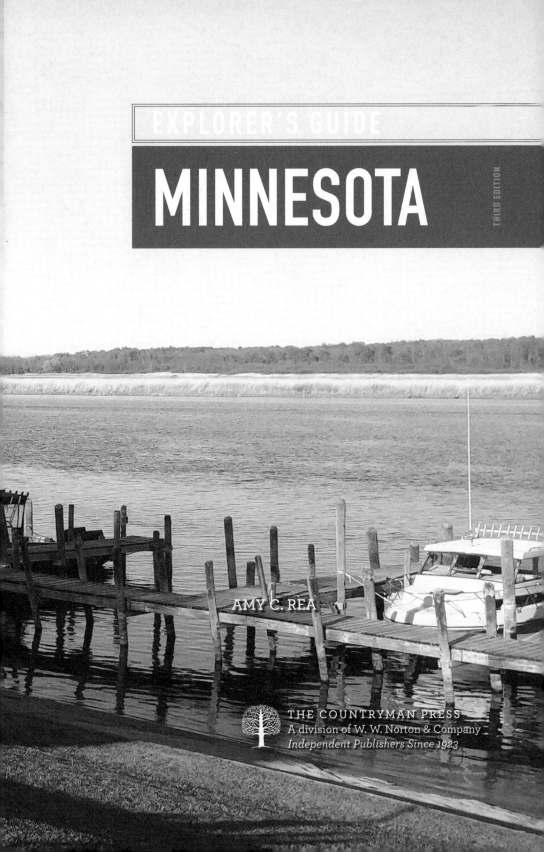

EXPLORER'S GUIDE

# MINNESOTA

THIRD EDITION

AMY C. REA

THE COUNTRYMAN PRESS
A division of W. W. Norton & Company
*Independent Publishers Since 1923*

For information about permission to reproduce selections from this book, write to
Permissions, The Countryman Press, 500 Fifth Avenue, New York, NY 10110

For information about special discounts for bulk purchases, please contact
W. W. Norton Special Sales at specialsales@wwnorton.com or 800-233-4830

Manufacturing by Versa Press
Book series design by Chris Welch
Production manager: Gwen Cullen

The Countryman Press
www.countrymanpress.com

A division of W. W. Norton & Company, Inc.
500 Fifth Avenue, New York, NY 10110
www.wwnorton.com

978-1-68268-467-2 (pbk.)

10 9 8 7 6 5 4 3 2 1

In memory of my father, Ernie Crippen, who helped build roads all over Minnesota during his career with MNDOT, and then enjoyed exploring the state for fun. This one's for you, Dad.

# EXPLORE WITH US!

**WHAT'S WHERE** In the beginning of the book, you'll find an alphabetical listing of special highlights, with important information and advice on everything from antiques to weather reports.

**LODGING** The prices range from low off-season rates to higher summer and holiday/event weekend rates, double occupancy.

| | |
|---|---|
| Inexpensive | Up to $100 per night |
| Moderate | $100–175 |
| Expensive | $175–250 |
| Very Expensive | More than $250 |

## KEY TO SYMBOLS

✎ The crayon symbol appears next to lodgings, restaurants, activities, and shops of special appeal to youngsters.

🐝 The extra-value symbol appears next to lodgings and restaurants that combine high quality and moderate prices.

♂ The wedding rings symbol appears beside facilities that frequently serve as venues for weddings and civil unions.

🐾 The dog paw symbol appears next to lodgings that accept pets (usually with a reservation and deposit) as of press time.

♿ The wheelchair symbol appears next to lodging, restaurants, and attractions that are partially or fully handicapped accessible.

🍸 The martini glass symbol appears next to establishments that have bars and/or nightclubs on the premises.

❄ The snowflake symbol appears next to establishments that are open during the off-season, which in Minnesota is generally October through April.

(((•))) The tower symbol appears next to businesses that have Internet/Wi-Fi access.

✪ The author's pick symbol appears next to establishments, historical landmarks, or must-sees that the author especially recommends.

☂ The umbrella symbol appears next to establishments that are good for rainy day activities.

▼ The triangle symbol appears next to establishments that cater to gay clientele.

❚❙ The fork-and-knife symbol appears next to lodging that have restaurants on site.

🍂 The leaf symbol appears next to establishments that are eco-friendly.

⚐ The beach umbrella symbol appears next to lodging that have swimming pools on site.

♨ The sink symbol appears next to lodging that have hot water.

DINING The dining listings are broken into two categories: Dining Out, which is more formal (and pricier), and Eating Out, which is more casual (and less expensive). Average prices refer to a dinner consisting of an entrée, appetizer or dessert, and glass of wine or beer (tax and gratuities not included).

| | |
|---|---|
| Inexpensive | Up to $20 |
| Moderate | $20–35 |
| Expensive | $35–50 |
| Very Expensive | $50 or more |

A NOTE ON PRICES Please don't hold us or the respective innkeepers/restaurant owners responsible for the rates listed as of press time in 2020. Some changes are inevitable.

Minnesota has a general sales tax of 6.875 percent, although local government units are able (with state approval) to levy additional sales taxes for various reasons; in Hennepin County (home to Minneapolis), for example, the sales tax is 7.275 percent, part of which funded the Minnesota Twins Target Field stadium, and in Minneapolis itself, the sales tax is 8.025 percent.

Please send any comments or corrections to:

Explorer's Guide Editor
The Countryman Press
500 Fifth Avenue
New York, NY 10110

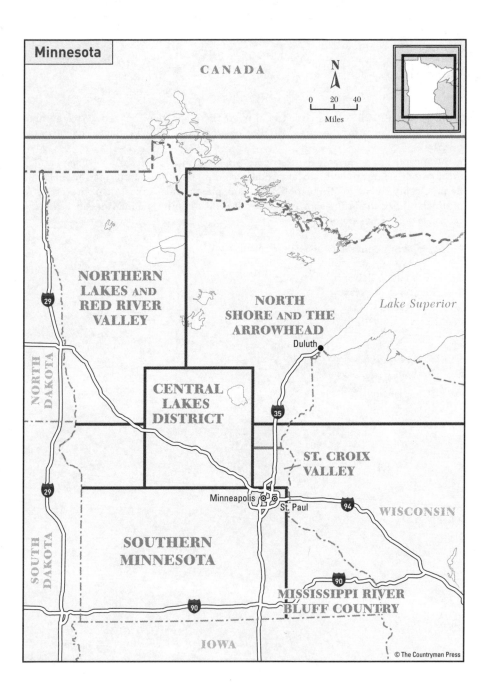

# CONTENTS

# MAPS

# INTRODUCTION

Minnesota is a land frequently misunderstood. For those who get their knowledge from popular media, Minnesota appears to be a land inhabited by those wacky gals from the *Mary Tyler Moore Show*, except for the one corner of Minnesota populated by rock stars as glamorized by the late, lamented Prince in *Purple Rain*. The rest of the state? Garrison Keillor's former *Prairie Home Companion* (now Chris Thile's *Live From Here*) and the Coen brothers' classic *Fargo* tell the rest of the story: funny accents, hats with ear flaps, church suppers, fish soaked in lye and served at Christmas dinner, a whole lot of snow, and backyard woodchippers. As usual, the truth is that the stereotyped images are somewhat true, but not the whole picture. Are there still people in small towns in Minnesota who talk like those people in Fargo? Sure. And while Mary Tyler Moore no longer throws her hat on Nicollet Mall, there is a sculpture immortalizing that very action. Prince? Still a Minnesota music icon, but far from the only one in what has become a booming local music scene.

Personally, I love these images. They do represent certain facets of Minnesota. Perhaps what they best represent is the diversity inherent in the state, where a vibrant metro area provides excellent access to the arts, pop culture, major league sports, dining, and shopping. For those who want more of an outdoor experience, the state has not 10,000 lakes, but more than 15,000, all with opportunities for swimming, fishing

GOOSEBERRY FALLS

THE WOOD-FIRED ROTISSERIE AT RED WING'S THE SMOKIN' OAK

(year-round; ice fishing is nearly as popular as open-water fishing in summer), boating, and water sports. Campgrounds abound throughout the state, as do resorts of all types and prices, from small, rustic mom-and-pops to historic bed-and-breakfasts to hotels and resorts that represent the height of luxury.

In a region where the seasons are clearly different, Minnesotans have turned each season into a reason for celebration, with each offering its own activities and festivals. If ice fishing isn't your cuppa, perhaps a visit to St. Paul's Winter Carnival would be more enjoyable. Or a getaway to one of Minnesota's thousands of cabin resorts. Once there, it's your choice: Enjoy hearty winter outdoor activities—snowshoeing or skijoring, anyone?—or curl up with a good book in front of the fireplace or woodstove and listen to the peace and quiet of a snowy day.

As a Minnesotan born and raised, I've lived in both environments, the urban metro and the rural far north. One of the joys of this state is in its ability to offer something for everyone to enjoy. There are visitors to Minnesota who are primarily interested in the Mall of America and base their multiple trips on that. Some visitors come into the Twin Cities from smaller towns, happy to experience the metro life for a few days, while city dwellers set out to find a small town or rural area for a change of scenery. Others use the Twin Cities as a jumping-off point for all kinds of ventures: historical sight-seeing throughout the state (including pioneer sites and villages, literary landmarks memorializing F. Scott Fitzgerald and Sinclair Lewis, a Jesse James reenactment, sobering reminders of the bloody Dakota Conflict, and a comprehensive and fun interactive history of the state at the Minnesota History Center), bike tours around the lakes of Minneapolis or along the Mississippi River to the Headwaters in northern Minnesota, foliage hunting in the fall, every imaginable outdoor activity along the North Shore, river explorations south of the metro, and rest and relaxation far from the maddening crowd.

In many national livability surveys, Minnesota tends to rank very high, and the factors that contribute to those rankings—high quality of life, diverse leisure time activities, wide variety of cultures and habitats—make Minnesota a leading choice for people of all ages, activity levels, and interests. Throughout the following chapters, I lead you through a wide variety of places to visit, from art museums to giant balls of twine to the deepest recesses of nature to the SPAM

HOUSEBOAT IN WINONA

Museum. It's all here, and it's yours to pick and choose. This guide will help you learn what the options are and what some of the best choices are in terms of types of attraction, lodging, and dining. There are options of all types: deluxe hotels and resorts, small family-owned cabins, bed-and-breakfasts; five-star dining, small-town cafés, and quirky little restaurants with just about every cuisine imaginable. Minnesota may be known for its Scandinavian heritage, but the current state residents come from all over the world, with growing Somali, Asian, and Hispanic populations, which have served to greatly improve the state's dining experiences. Shopping? The possibilities are nearly endless, from the massive Mall of America to the chic Galleria, to the antiques stores in Stillwater to the artist's galleries in Grand Marais. The brewery scene exploded in recent years, and the distilleries weren't far behind. It could take months to see and experience everything Minnesota has to offer, but with this guide, you can plan for the time you have available, maximizing whatever experience you want to have—active or relaxed, urban or rural.

As I mentioned, I grew up and have lived in this state most of my life. But while traveling its highways and byways doing research for the third edition of this book, I still found countless things that were new to me and learned that there's more out there to discover. It sounds corny, but I came away from writing this book with a sense that Minnesota is, indeed, a highly worthwhile place to visit, and one of the best things about it is how many different interests can be accommodated in one way or another. Besides that, the pride many Minnesotans take in their hometowns can be very infectious; stop in any of the small regional historic museums listed in this guidebook, and you are likely to meet people who are enthusiastic and well versed in their area's history, and they might very well have some interesting and little-known stories to share with you. Friendliness and helpfulness are in full supply; it's hard to beat the graciousness offered by lakeside resort owners and bed-and-breakfast proprietors.

Minnesota is part of what's often referred to as "flyover land." For those not familiar with the term flyover land, it's a derogatory term implying that only destinations on the East or West Coast are worth visiting. I hope this book will convince you otherwise, and that you will follow me on Instagram (@writerrea), where I continue to cover my travels and discoveries around the state.

# WHAT'S WHERE IN MINNESOTA

**AREA CODE** There are seven area codes in Minnesota. In the Twin Cities area, 612 denotes Minneapolis and immediate surroundings; 651 is St. Paul and suburbs, including much of the St. Croix Valley; 763 is the northern Minneapolis suburbs; and 952 is the southern and southwestern Minneapolis suburbs. Northern Minnesota is 218, central Minnesota (outside the Twin Cities metro and suburban area) is 320, and southern Minnesota is 507.

**AIRPORTS AND AIRLINES Minneapolis–St. Paul International Airport** (612-726-5555; mspairport.com) is the state's largest airport and is served primarily by Delta Air Lines (1-800-221-1212; delta.com), but there are several other carriers who serve the area as well. Flights depart to and arrive from all over the United States, as well as various international destinations, including Canada, Europe, the Caribbean, Mexico, and Asia. The following airlines serve Terminal 1–Lindbergh: Aer Lingus (1-800-474-7424; aerlingus.com), Air Canada (1-888-247-2262; aircanada.com), Air Choice One (1-866-435-9847; airchoiceone.com), Air France (1-800-237-2747; airfrance.us), Alaska Airlines (1-800-426-0333; airalaska.com), American Airlines (1-800-433-7300; aa.com), Boutique Air (1-855-268-8478; boutiqueair.com),

THE VIEW FROM GREAT RIVER BLUFFS STATE PARK

Frontier Airlines (1-801-401-9000; frontierairlines.com), KLM (1-866-434-0320; klm.com), Spirit Airlines (1-801-401-2222; spirit.com),and United Airlines (1-800-241-6522; united.com). At Terminal 2-Humphrey, Condor (1-866-960-7915; airtran.com), Icelandair (1-800-223-5500; icelandair.com), JetBlue (1-800-538-2583; jetblue.com), Southwest Airlines (1-800-435-9792; southwest.com), and Sun Country Airlines (1-800-359-6786; suncountry.com) offer a mixture of commercial and charter services.

**Bemidji Regional Airport** (bemidjiairport.org) and **Brainerd Lakes Regional Airport** (218-825-2166; brainerdairport.com) are served by Delta Air Lines; **Duluth International Airport** (218-727-2968; duluthairport.com) is served by American Airlines, Delta Airlines, and United Airlines; **International Falls International Airport** (1-800-221-1212; internationalfallsairport

.com) is served by Delta and SkyWest Airlines (434-634-3000; skywest.com); **Range Regional Airport** (218-262-3451; rangeregionalairport.com) is served by Delta; **Rochester International Airport** (507-282-2328; flyrst.com) is served by American Airlines, Delta Air Lines, and United Airlines; **St. Cloud Regional Airport** (320-255-7292; stcloudairport.com) is served by Sun Country Airlines and Allegiant Air (allegiantair.com); and **Thief River Falls Regional Airport** (218-681-7680) is served by Boutique Air.

AMTRAK  There is limited service in Minnesota by rail; **AMTRAK** (1-800-872-7245; amtrak.com) runs a train from the northwest corner, near North Dakota, through Minneapolis–St. Paul and onto Wisconsin and Chicago, once daily in each direction. The train is used more to transport people either east to Chicago or west to the Pacific Coast than to travel within Minnesota.

AMUSEMENT PARKS  **Valleyfair** (952-445-7600; valleyfair.com) in Shakopee is Minnesota's biggest amusement park, with rides for little kids and big ones, too, a water park, mini golf, bumper boats, go-carts, an IMAX theater, and live music. **Nickelodeon Universe** (1-952-883-8800; nickelodeonuniverse.com), Bloomington, is an indoor theme park at the Mall of America with a more limited selection of rides, but at least it's open year-round and is a Certified Autism Center.

ANTIQUARIAN BOOKS  The Twin Cities has several good options, including **Magers & Quinn** (612-822-4611; magersandquinn.com), **Rulon-Miller Books** (651-290-0700; 1-800-441-0076; rulon.com), and **James & Mary Laurie Booksellers** (612-338-1114; lauriebooks.com).

ANTIQUES  Antiques shops abound in Minnesota, especially in the Twin Cities and many of the historic towns along the St. Croix, Mississippi, and Minnesota

MISSISSIPPI RIVER HEADWATERS AT ITASCA STATE PARK

rivers. For detailed listings throughout the state, check with the **Minnesota Antiques Dealers Association** (651-430-0095; mnantiquesdealers.com).

AQUARIUMS **The Sea Life Minnesota Aquarium** (visitsealife.com/minnesota) exhibit at the Mall of America in Bloomington has more than 10,000 exotic sea creatures on display in 30 tanks, viewed by a 300-foot "ocean tunnel." In Duluth, the **Great Lakes Aquarium** (218-740-3474; glaquarium.org) has extensive tanks of fish, but as most of them are freshwater and native to the region, they may not be as interesting as the tropical sea life.

ARTISTS AND ART GALLERIES The Twin Cities has a large, healthy arts community, and the visual arts are no exception. Galleries abound throughout the metro area. Farther north, the artist community in Grand Marais keeps several galleries busy, and the scenic drives through the southeast portion of the state (Stillwater, Lanesboro) will also yield several art galleries to visit. And don't forget about the outdoor sculpture garden in Franconia. There are also art scenes developing in some of the state's smaller towns across the board.

BALLOONING Hot-air ballooning is popular in Stillwater, where the scenic St. Croix makes for a perfect bird's-eye trip. Contact **Aamodt's Hot Air Balloons** (651-351-0101; aamodtsballoons.com) or **Stillwater Balloons** (651-439-1800; stillwaterballoons.com).

BEACHES In the land of 10,000 (and more) lakes, it's a given that there's a beach around just about every corner. In many cases, the beaches are attached to resorts that reserve those beaches for paying guests. However, most lake communities have at least one good-sized public beach, and some have several. The central lakes district, including Brainerd, Willmar, and Mille Lacs, and Alexandria,

have hundreds of lakes with beaches public and private. Farther north, the lake areas around Bemidji and Detroit Lakes and up to the Canadian border, along Voyageurs National Park, have beaches, too, although the swimming season may be shorter. In the Twin Cities, Lake Harriet, Lake Nokomis, and Bde Maka Ska all have public swimming beaches. Many of the surrounding suburbs have city and county parks that have public beaches.

BED-AND-BREAKFASTS Especially down the eastern side of Minnesota, bed-and-breakfasts have become tremendously popular as a lodging option, especially given the number of historic homes that exist in those areas. Many are housed in grand 19th-century homes, some of which have prominent local citizens as the original owners. Today's owners take great pride in their properties, lovingly maintaining the historic feel, in many cases with period antiques or original furnishings and décor. The proprietors of these homes are generally well connected with their local community as well, with valuable insights into

THE LIGHTHOUSE BED & BREAKFAST, TWO HARBORS

THE BEACH AT ZIPPEL BAY RESORT

the history and the best places to go for entertainment and food, and they're more than happy to help. Rates run anywhere from $80 to over $300 per night, depending on location and amenities. There's also a state association for them:

BERWOOD HILL INN

**The Minnesota Bed & Breakfast Association** (952-303-2325; minnesotabedand breakfasts.org).

BICYCLING  All types of biking terrain are present in the state. If you like a relatively flat ride with both lakes and urban vistas, it's hard to beat the Grand Rounds in the Twin Cities, which cover 50 miles of trails winding around some of Minneapolis's popular lakes, along the Mississippi River, and near Minnehaha Falls. In greater Minnesota (collectively, the area of Minnesota beyond the Twin Cities metro area), there are literally thousands of miles of trails, ranging from paved or not, hilly or flat railway grade, wooded or riverside, located in the extensive systems of county and state parks, especially in the Brainerd lakes area and the river bluffs along the Mississippi, Minnesota, and St. Croix rivers. **The Minnesota Department of Transportation** (1-800-657-3774; dot.state.mn.us/bike) has detailed bike maps available on request, broken down by geographic region. **Explore Minnesota** (1-888-847-4866; exploreminnesota.com), the state tourism board, also produces bike trail brochures and maps, and many of the larger regional tourist boards have materials related to their area (regional tourist offices are listed at the beginning of each section).

BIRD-WATCHING  Given the number of wildlife preserves and state parks, it's no surprise that Minnesota has numerous areas with excellent birding opportunities. The Minnesota chapter of the **Audubon Society** (651-739-9332; mn.audubon .org) has detailed lists and maps, showing some of the best places to observe birds, among them the North Shore in the northeast, Big Bog and Lake of the Woods in the north, Itasca State Park and Lac Qui Parle–Big Stone in the central and central-northwest parts of the state, the St. Croix and Mississippi rivers along the eastern border, and the Minnesota River Valley in southwest Minnesota.

BOOKS  It's intimidating to try and list even a fraction of the literature based in Minnesota or written by Minnesotans, or both. The literary arts community in Minnesota is thriving and has been for decades; Minneapolis's **Open Book** (openbookmn.org) is a central stopping place for writing classes and author appearances, and there's a strong network of independent bookstores throughout the state, as well as the ubiquitous Barnes & Noble. But if you'd like to get a sense of the literary landscape, consider reading some of the following books.

F. Scott Fitzgerald, of course, produced classics *The Great Gatsby* and *Tender Is the Night*, among other works; he lived in St. Paul with Zelda. Sinclair Lewis, author of *Babbitt* and *Elmer Gantry*, lived in Sauk Center in his youth, and in spite of his skewering the town in the fictional *Main Street*, the community still honors his memory. Charles M. Schulz of *Peanuts* fame was from Minnesota. Ole Rolvaag, author of the classic pioneer tale *Giants in the Earth*, emigrated to the United States from Norway in 1896 and

THE FALLS AT MINNEOPA STATE PARK

lived the last half of his life in Minnesota. J. F. Powers, National Book Award winner, was a longtime professor and writer in residence at St. John's University and the College of St. Benedict. His books include *Morte d'Urban* and *Wheat That Springeth Green*. Naturalist Sigurd Olson memorably chronicled the beauty of Minnesota wilderness in books like *Reflections from the North Country* and *The Singing Wilderness*. Much-beloved children's authors also have roots in Minnesota, from Laura Ingalls Wilder's *Little House* series to Maud Hart Lovelace's *Betsy-Tacy* series and Wanda Gág's *Millions of Cats*.

Contemporary writers who are from or write about Minnesota include Garrison Keillor, the former host of *Prairie Home Companion*, who has penned several books, including *Lake Wobegon Days* and *Happy to Be Here*. Tim O'Brien, who won the National Book Award for *Going After Cacciato* and was a finalist for the Pulitzer for *The Things They Carried*, was born in Austin and grew up in Worthington. *Time* named his novel *In the Lake of the Woods* best book of the year in 1994. John Sandford, a pseudonym for John Roswell Camp, is the Minnesota author of the best-selling *Rules of Prey* series. Robert Treuer had a wide-ranging career path, from teacher to Native American tribal organizer, before settling down as a tree farmer in northern Minnesota. His books *Voyageur Country: A Park in the Wilderness* and *The Tree Farm* are lyrical nonfiction explorations about life and issues in the northern reaches. David Mura, author of *Turning Japanese* and *Song for Uncle Tom, Tonto & Mr. Moto: Poetry & Identity*, is a Minnesota resident, as is memoirist Patricia Hampl, who gracefully writes about growing up in St. Paul in books such as *The Florist's Daughter*. Brian Malloy's novels have detailed life for young gays in the Twin Cities, including *The Year of Ice* and *Brendan Wolf*. Anne Ursu's fictional Minnesota small town facing an emotional crisis in *Spilling Clarence* is for adults, while her trilogy, the *Cronus Chronicles*

(starting with *The Shadow Thieves*), get its start at the Mall of America. Shannon Olson gives us a Minnesotan Bridget Jones with *Welcome to My Planet: Where English Is Sometimes Spoken*. Lorna Landvik congenially covers all manner of small-town foibles and romantic mishaps in her books *The View from Mount Joy*, *The Tall Pine Polka*, and *Patty Jane's House of Curl*.

**BOUNDARY WATERS CANOE AREA WILDERNESS** Part of Superior National Forest is more than a million acres of pristine wilderness area, including 1,000 lakes, some of which are restricted to nonmotorized boats, known as the Boundary Waters Canoe Area Wilderness (BWCAW). The BWCAW is one of the state's top draws. The concept of an untouched, undeveloped, protected wilderness was conceived back in 1919, when the US Forest Service began developing management plans for what would eventually become the BWCAW. Beginning in 1926, roads and development were prohibited in the area, and by the late 1940s the federal government began buying out homeowners and resort owners who still had property in the protected zone. The only exception was Dorothy Molter, a longtime resident known as the Root Beer Lady, who moved into the wilderness in 1934. After locals protested her removal and the Forest Service recognized both the value of her nursing skills and her almost legendary status among the population, she was granted permission to remain in the BWCAW until her death in 1986.

The creation of this quiet, natural preserve was not without controversy. Recreationists who wanted access to the area via airplanes, snowmobiles, and motorboats fought hard in court to preserve the right to bring engines into the area. When the BWCA Wilderness Act was finally passed in 1978, it allowed motorboats on about a quarter of the area's lakes. This remains controversial to this day, as those who want motorboat access continue to push for more access, saying the small amount of water available to them is not enough, while those who have fought for restricting access to motorboats continue their fight, wishing to reclaim that last quarter. It isn't likely that the contentious stances will abate anytime soon, and when visiting the BWCAW, be sure to respect each side's territory.

One thing both sides agree on is the impressive nature of the area. The lakes, tributaries, and forests all combine together to give visitors an unforgettable wilderness experience. There's something for every level of traveler—easy day trips for beginners, and long portages deep into the wilderness for more experienced canoers and campers. Several outfitting companies, particularly in Grand Marais and Ely, can set up permits and equipment rentals, and can also custom design guided trips.

During the most popular season (May 1–September 30), permits are required for day visitors and campers. Also note that although camping reservations are not required, they are definitely recommended, because the area operates under a quota system during that season, and you could find yourself with no place to stay. For permits and reservations, contact **Reserve America** (1-877-444-6777; recreation.gov).

One final recommendation: Seriously consider purchasing the Superior National Forest Visitor Map. Published by the USDA in conjunction with Superior National Forest, this is an incredibly detailed map of the BWCAW. It wouldn't hurt to buy a magnifying glass with which to read it. The BWCAW is full of back roads, often barely more than gravel strips, that don't appear on most state maps. It's easy to get lost unless you're very familiar with the area. The map is available in a sturdy, waterproof plastic version for about $10. Many local gas stations and convenience stores sell it, or contact the Superior National

Forest headquarters in Duluth (218-626-4300) for information on ordering one.

BUS SERVICE **Greyhound Bus Lines** (1-800-231-2222; greyhound.com) is the primary source of public transit, serving more than 70 communities around the state, including several university locations.

CAMPING It almost seems as if the entire state is one giant campground. From the farthest northern corners of the state right down to the southern borders, state and county parks provide countless opportunities for camping, some with fairly modern campsites with electricity and facilities, others bare-bones in nature. Some require reservations and/or permits, some don't. Many of the major parks and forests, including Voyageurs National Park and the Boundary Waters Canoe Area Wilderness, are covered in this book. Minnesota's **Department of Natural Resources** (dnr.state mn.us) has extensive information about campsites and policies in the state parks and state forests, as well as some online reservations capabilities. The **National Park Service** (nps.gov/voya) has camping and reservation information for Voyageurs National Park. **Reserve America** (recreation.gov) provides requirements for permits and camping in the Boundary Waters Canoe Area Wilderness, but note that if you're working through an outfitter, they are likely to handle those arrangements for you; be sure to ask.

Wherever you choose to camp, always check with local authorities ahead of time as to fire restrictions. Summer droughts have become increasingly common, and the risk of wildfire is very real; you may find that campfires are prohibited.

Speaking of campfires, it's important to note that when using a state or national campground or park (and many regional parks as well), bringing in non-local firewood is not permitted

DEER AT GOOSEBERRY FALLS STATE PARK

because of the increased spread of forest pests, especially the emerald ash borer. Where there's a park and a campground, there are places to buy wood locally. Just be sure to get a receipt in case you're asked to prove where it came from.

CANOEING AND KAYAKING Lake Superior; Lake of the Woods; the Boundary Waters; Lake Kabetogama; the Mississippi, Minnesota, and St. Croix rivers; the Chain of Lakes in Minneapolis—these are just a few of the options for those who like to explore by water. Rentals and outfitters abound; where there is water, there is a way to get onto the water. Arrangements can be as elaborate as guided canoeing or kayaking and camping tours, or they can be as simple as an afternoon's rental. Canoeing in the Boundary Waters, where there are entire waterways restricted to nonmotorized boats, needs at least a daily entry permit (or a more formal permit for multiple days and camping).

CHILDREN, ESPECIALLY FOR Minnesota is generally a child-friendly state, and throughout this guide are numerous activities, museums, festivals, and restaurants that have been marked with the crayon symbol: ✐.

CRAFTS Conventional wisdom would say it's the result of long winters, but love of crafts is alive and well in the North Star State. In the Twin Cities metro area alone, dozens of craft stores, many independently owned and operated, sell fabric, yarn, beads, woodworking supplies, and scrapbooking supplies. The diversity of crafts being produced is burgeoning as well, and indie craft shows such as **No Coast Craft-o-Rama** (nocoastcraft.com) and **Craftstravaganza** (craftstravaganza .com) showcase unusual and funky projects that definitely turn the notion of crafts as fuddy-duddy right on its head.

Which isn't to say traditional craftwork isn't valued. Most notably, the **North House Folk School** (218-387-9762 or 1-888-387-9762; northhouse.org) in Grand Marais offers year-round classes in everything from knitting to bread making to canoe building to how to construct your own yurt or outdoor brick oven.

DINING Foodies are sitting up and taking notice at what's happening in Minnesota. No longer a culinary backwater, the state's chefs are generating interest and intrigue for their innovative menus, as well as their increased commitment to using locally grown products for seasonal menus whenever possible. In the Twin Cities, most restaurants are open nightly or, at most, closed Monday. In greater Minnesota, you may find

THE CAROUSEL AT LARK TOYS

restaurants with more limited weekly or seasonal hours. Recent years have seen numerous chefs and food writers from Minnesota being nominated for—and sometimes winning—the prestigious James Beard Foundation Awards. Restaurants with strong reputations with the fine-dining crowd, such Bachelor Farmer or Meritage, don't require reservations, but they're strongly recommended. There's also been a rise in the number of multicultural restaurants; immigrants have introduced authentic Asian, African, and Hispanic foods to the state. For diners who prefer their food not to be too Americanized, there are numerous worthwhile options to choose from.

DRESS CODE  One thing out-of-towners sometimes comment on is the dress code, or lack thereof, at restaurants and events that would be considered at least semiformal elsewhere. It's not uncommon to see casual khakis and sweaters alongside suits and dresses at fine-dining venues and the theater. Whether or not this is a good thing is up for debate—but don't be surprised when you see it.

EMERGENCIES  Call 911 from anywhere in the state. In each section, regional hospitals are listed.

FACTORY OUTLETS  Albertville, which is a community north of Minneapolis, has the **Albertville Premium Outlets** (premiumoutlets.com), with 100 stores, and is by far the largest outlet center in the state. This is discussed in more detail in the "Minneapolis's Neighboring Communities" chapter.

FALL FOLIAGE  September and October can be variable in terms of weather, but when the days are crisp and clear, the fall colors in various parts of the state can be spectacular. Starting up north across the eastern half of the state (along

LAKE WINONA

Voyageurs National Park and the Canadian border); through the Boundary Waters, the Iron Range, and the North Shore; and down south through the Twin Cities and the St. Croix, Mississippi, and Minnesota rivers, large areas of forests set on rolling land along water make for prime foliage viewing. Most restaurants, hotels, and bed-and-breakfasts are open at least weekends during the fall for visitors seeking the turning of the leaves.

FARM STANDS AND FARMERS' MARKETS Whether they're popular as a result of a long agricultural history or because today's foodies are increasingly interested in local, sustainable foods, farmers' markets and farm stands can be found in pretty much every corner of the state. It may be something as simple as a teenager selling corn off the back of a pickup or as elaborate as the revered farmers' markets in Minneapolis and St. Paul, but there's something for everyone. For complete listings, check with the **Minnesota Farmers' Market Association** (mfma.org). Note: In the Minneapolis and St. Paul sections, information about some of the more prominent city markets is included.

FESTIVALS Minnesota is a state full of festivals. Some are cultural explorations, such as Kolacky Days and Scandinavian Midsommar Tag. Others celebrate local history or agriculture, such as Irish Fest and Barnesville's Potato Days (mashed potato wrestling, anyone?). Some sound just plain goofy (Eelpout Festival, St. Urhu Day) but are beloved local traditions. Some of the "best of" are listed at the end of each chapter. Additional information and listings can be found by visiting the tourist boards listed in the Guidance sections at the beginning of each section.

FIRE Wildfires are always a concern in wilderness areas, and Minnesota is no exception, especially since recent years have seen significant droughts in parts

PAUL BUNYAN'S "GRAVE"

of the state. When planning a camping trip, be sure to find out if there are campfire restrictions. As this can change from one day to the next, it's best to check upon arrival to make sure you're not violating any new restrictions.

FISHING Fishing is a summer and winter sport in Minnesota, with options of open-water fishing to dropping your line in a hole cut in the ice, usually in an ice house. Many of the lake resorts have become year-round destinations due to the popularity of ice fishing, and it's possible in some areas to rent a sleep-ready ice house, complete with electricity and bathroom facilities. Fishing is a licensed activity, and licenses are generally easy to obtain, usually available from local DNR offices and convenience stores. For information on cost and restrictions, see dnr.state.mn.us.

GAMBLING Minnesota has 22 casinos scattered throughout the state, on 11 Indian reservations. All casinos offer slot machines and table games like blackjack and poker, and most offer bingo. Live entertainment is frequently scheduled at the larger casinos, like **Mystic Lake Casino** (mysticlake.com) in Prior Lake and **Grand Casino Hinckley** (grand casinomn.com) in Hinckley getting some well-known and current entertainers. In addition, **Canterbury Park** (canterbury park.com) in Shakopee offers card games 24/7, live horse racing during the summer, and simulcast horse racing from other tracks year-round.

GOLF  Minnesotans are passionate about golf, a fact demonstrated by the extreme weather golfers are willing to cope with in order to get out on the course. The state has nearly 600 courses, public and private, and the terrain varies from lush and meticulously maintained fairways to the northernmost golf course in the United States, the Northwest Angle Country Club. The **Minnesota Tourism Board** (exploreminnesota.com) can provide complimentary golf brochures on request, or check online at **exploreminnesotagolf.com** for a detailed directory.

HANDICAP ACCESS  Throughout this book, entries marked with the wheelchair symbol &#9855; indicate attractions, lodging, and restaurants that are handicapped accessible.

HIKING  Miles and miles of trails, paved and unpaved, flat and rolling, forest and prairie, await visitors statewide. The multitude of state parks offer just about every sort of terrain, wildlife viewing, and flora and fauna imaginable for the region. **The Minnesota Department of Natural Resources** (dnr.state.mn.us) has detailed information on each park on its website, and the department also offers two hiking clubs: The Hiking Club offers hikers graduated levels of awards for hiking preset mileage levels, with the ultimate awards coming in the form of free nights of camping. The Passport Club rewards travelers for visiting state parks. The regional tourism offices listed in each section can provide information and maps on that region's hiking opportunities, while the **Minnesota Tourism Board** (exploreminnesota.com) can provide complimentary hiking brochures on request.

HISTORY  Minnesota's history runs the full gamut from pioneers to fur traders to Native Americans to barons of industry; to famous politicians to contentious or well-beloved authors, actors, and musicians; to devastating natural tragedies to scandalous murders. Jesse James's epic arrival in Northfield, Hubert Humphrey's presidential campaign, John Dillinger's reign in St. Paul, former pro wrestler Jesse Ventura's reign as governor, the quintessential pioneer Laura Ingalls Wilder's travels through southern Minnesota, Bob Dylan's roots on the Iron Range, Bronko Nagurski's legendary football career getting its start in International Falls, musical icon Prince, and *A Prairie Home Companion*'s former host, Garrison Keillor, are just some of the legends past and present who are associated with Minnesota. And in one way or another, these people (and many more) and events throughout the state's history

THE VIEW FROM JOHN A. LATSCH STATE PARK

WINONA'S CARRIAGE HOUSE BED AND BREAKFAST

are commemorated in various displays, exhibits, and festivals.

HUNTING Hunting is a licensed activity in Minnesota. Among the game that's legal to hunt (with the proper license and in season) is bear, deer, pheasant, wild turkey, grouse, and waterfowl. Licenses are generally easy to obtain, usually available from local DNR offices (including some by phone or on the website) and convenience stores. For information on cost and restrictions, see dnr.state.mn.us.

INFORMATION ABOUT MINNESOTA, OFFICIAL **Explore Minnesota** (651-296-5029 or 1-888-868-7476; exploreminnesota.com) is the central state tourism organization. Visitors are welcome at the headquarters at 121 E. 7th Place in St. Paul, or at one of the travel information centers located in Albert Lea, Beaver Creek, Dresbach, Bloomington (Mall of America), Fisher's Landing, Grand Portage Bay, Moorhead, St. Cloud, St. Croix, Duluth, and Worthington. Explore Minnesota also partners with various local tourist boards, chambers of commerce, and convention and visitor bureaus all over the state. A thorough listing of local and regional tourism groups is available on the Explore Minnesota website.

INTERNET Throughout this book, Internet websites for attractions, recreational sites, lodging, and restaurants have been given whenever they are available. The Internet has been embraced as a wonderful informational tool by smaller businesses, to the advantage of the traveling public, and it's likely that even more companies will have gone online by the time this book goes to press. Access to high-speed Internet and Wi-Fi, often free, is becoming more prevalent as well. Many hotels, restaurants, coffee shops, libraries, and university campuses can provide online access to visitors. The tower symbol ((ᵠ)) appears next to businesses that have Internet/Wi-Fi access.

LAKES The land of 10,000 lakes is a slight underestimation. There are actually more than 15,000 lakes across the state, nearly 12,000 of which are at least 10 acres in size. The Minnesota DNR says that Minnesota's lakes and rivers have more shoreline than California, Florida, and Hawaii combined. To the delight of visitors, those shorelines provide ample opportunities for enjoyment year-round: boating, fishing (including ice fishing in winter), swimming, waterskiing, and sightseeing. Several state parks have multiple lakes, as does the one national park (**Voyageurs National Park**; nps.gov/voya). The North Shore, riding along the coast of Lake Superior, provides an almost oceanic viewing experience, while the Brainerd Lakes District is among some of the best known in the state for vacationers. Accommodations varying from rustic campsites to deluxe resorts with every possible amenity can be found; the demand is particularly high in summer, so booking in advance is strongly recommended.

LANGUAGE CAMPS The northern region of Minnesota is home to **Concordia Language Villages** (218-299-4544 or 1-800-222-4750; concordialanguagevillages.org). The program's headquarters are in Moorhead, but most of the year-round villages are just outside Bemidji. The villages are self-contained cultural units, with different camps developed for Spanish, French, German, Russian, Norwegian, and Finnish. Each village is designed to look like a classic village from that country. Additional summer-only villages are offered elsewhere in the state, including camps for Chinese, Italian, Arabic, Korean, and Swedish. There are programs offered for adults and children, most of them on an immersion basis, but it's not just language that's offered; students will learn about customs, culture, and foods of their chosen regions.

Even if you aren't interested in registering for a camp, a visit to the villages is worth the side trip—the attention to detail is impressive, and the villages are nestled in stately forests, giving the visitor an otherworldly feel.

**LEFSE AND LUTEFISK** Minnesota has a strong Scandinavian heritage, and especially around the holidays or at seasonal festivals, it's inevitable that the classic Scandinavian foods, lefse and lutefisk, will make an appearance. Of the two, lefse is more widely enjoyed; it's a potato pastry, rolled out thin and briefly grilled. Some choose to add butter, sugar, cinnamon, or all three (I recommend the last). Lutefisk is a horse of a different color, falling right into the "love it or hate it" category, and it's the subject of many jokes. Essentially, lutefisk is fish soaked in lye. Although not everyone's first choice, lutefisk is still very popular for holiday church dinners, festivals, and at Christmas time.

**LITTER** Littering in Minnesota is punishable on the first offense by a misdemeanor charge that goes on the driving record; subsequent offenses are subject to fines of several hundred dollars.

**LODGING** Minnesota offers a highly diverse group of lodging choices: bed-and-breakfasts, resorts, cabins deluxe and primitive, motels, private homes, overnight ice fishing houses, upscale hotels, houseboats, even yurts. The rates

CABINS AT BURNTSIDE LODGE

quoted in this book reflect a per-night rate for two people, and keep in mind that rates are fluid; please don't hold us or the accommodations to the rates quoted, but instead view them as a guideline, not an absolute. In general, most bed-and-breakfasts don't accept children under 12 (but it's noted if they do), and many cabins or lake resorts have minimum-stay requirements (anywhere from three to seven nights) during peak periods. Pets are not accepted unless the pet symbol 🐾 is shown, and even then it's a good idea to confirm when reserving as to what size or types of pets may be restricted and if additional fees apply. Nearly all accept credit cards; hotels will accept a credit card as a guarantee for arrival, while bed-and-breakfasts or lake resorts may require a prepaid deposit, and some smaller resorts prefer checks or cash. Cancellation policies vary, so confirm the policy before committing any money.

MALL OF AMERICA The **Mall of America** (mallofamerica.com) is a shopper's paradise, with over 4 million square feet that includes not only more than 500 stores, but 30 fast-food restaurants, 20 sit-down restaurants, an underground aquarium, a convenience store, photo studios, a 14-screen movie theater complex, a wedding chapel, a comedy club, a flight simulator, and an indoor theme park. The retail anchors are Nordstrom and Macy's, and the surrounding stores include everything from clothing to electronics to jewelry to books to cosmetics, to Christmas decorations to crafts to Irish gifts to items made in Minnesota. Across the street from the mall is home furnishings superstore IKEA and a Radisson Hotel with the Waterpark of America, so there's something for everyone to do.

MAPS The Minnesota Department of Transportation produces a new Official State Highway Map every other year, and one free copy can be obtained by

contacting **Explore Minnesota** (651-296-5029 or 1-888-868-7476), collecting one in person at one of the state's many travel information centers (see "Information about Minnesota, Official"), or by visiting the DOT's website (dot.state .mn.us), where portions of the maps can be downloaded and printed.

For maps detailed with a significant amount of tourist information, Professor Pathfinder's Supermaps, published by **Hedberg Maps** (hedbergmaps.com), come in a full-state version as well as regional maps (Twin Cities, northern Minnesota, southern Minnesota, Brainerd lakes) and are clearly marked and easily read.

As noted earlier in Boundary Waters Canoe Area Wilderness, a trip to the BWCAW wouldn't be complete without acquiring the Superior National Forest Visitor Map (along with a magnifying glass with which to read it). This map, published by the USDA in conjunction with Superior National Forest, is an incredibly detailed map of the BWCAW and is available in a sturdy, waterproof plastic version for about $10. Many local gas stations and convenience stores sell it, or contact the **Superior National Forest headquarters in Duluth** (218-626-4300) for information on ordering one.

If you'd really like to explore off the beaten path, consider buying road maps by county, also offered by the Minnesota Department of Transportation. These maps are highly detailed and include all the minor county roads that don't show up on the full state map. While GPS is useful, it doesn't always keep up with the lesser-used roads; a good map comes in very handy.

MINNESOTA GROWN Among the Minnesota-produced items available for purchase throughout the state are maple syrup, cheese, meats, honey, candles, jams, and, in season, all kinds of fresh vegetables and fruits (some of the latter available from pick-your-own farms). The **Minnesota Department of Agriculture**

SHA SHA RESORT

(651-201-6000 or 1-800-967-2474; mda.state.mn.us) has online and print directories for finding locally made items.

MINNESOTA PUBLIC BROADCASTING Minnesota has both public radio (**Minnesota Public Radio**; mpr.org) and public television (**Twin Cities Public Television**; tpt.org). Both are headquartered in the Twin Cities, but satellite stations throughout the state carry the public programming. Visit each company's website for specific locations and channels. Also note that MPR has three radio options: MPR itself is a classical radio station, while KNOW is talk and news radio, and the Current plays a widely diverse, eclectic selection of indie, local, and alternative music.

MOVIES Popular movies are easily tracked down in most communities. For those looking for smaller, independent, foreign, or art house movies, good bets in the Twin Cities include the **Uptown Theatre** and **Lagoon Cinema** in Minneapolis and the **Edina Cinema** in Edina (landmarktheatres.com), as well as the venerable **Oak Street Cinema** (mnfilm arts.org/oakstreet) at the University of Minnesota. The annual **Minneapolis–St. Paul International Film Fest** (mspfilm fest.org) is a big event each year, with nearly 70 films.

MUSEUMS Minnesota must be given credit for being a state highly supportive of museums big and small. From the world-class **Minneapolis Institute of Art** (artsmia.org) and the **Walker Art Center** (walkerart.org), which together comprise significant collections of classic and contemporary art, to smaller museums like the **Museum of Russian Art** (tmora.org) and the **Minnesota Marine Art Museum** (507-474-6626 or 1-866-940-6626; minnesotamarineart.org), patrons of the arts have much to choose from.

The **Weisman Art Museum** (weisman .umn.edu) is a newer member of the arts community, housed in a Frank Gehry building at the University of Minnesota and newly expanded as of late 2011. Duluth has the **Tweed Museum** (d.umn .edu/tma) at the University of Minnesota's Duluth campus, while down south in Winona is the **Minnesota Marine Art Museum** (minnesotamarineart.org), devoted to nautical artwork, including works by O'Keeffe, Monet, Picasso, and Van Gogh. Add in options for families, such as the **Minnesota Children's Museum** (mcm.org), the Science Museum of Minnesota (smm.org), and the **Bakken Museum** (thebakken.org), as well as historical options including **Mill City Museum** (mill citymuseum.org), the **Minnesota History Center Museum** (mnhs .org), the **Hinckley Fire Museum** (seans .com/sunset web/hinckley), the **Bronko Nagurski Museum** (bronkonagurski .com/museum.htm), and the nearly countless city and county historical societies that provide invaluable insights into all aspects of Minnesota history, and there is plenty for any museum aficionado to do.

MUSIC Minnesotans are passionate about their music, whether it's classical, country, rock, alternative/indie, jazz,

BIG OLE IN ALEXANDRIA

bluegrass, or anything in between. Live venues of every size are open in the Twin Cities, from **Target Center** (targetcenter .com) and **Xcel Energy Center** (xcel energycenter.com) to **Orchestra Hall** (minnesotaorchestra.org) and the **Ordway** (ordway.org) to the **Fine Line** (finelinemusic.com), the **Dakota** (dakota cooks.com), and **First Avenue** (first -avenue.com). Those are just the best-known options, but there are literally dozens, if not hundreds, of other clubs, stages, and bars with live music.

Besides concerts, music festivals are wildly popular in Minnesota, particularly in the summer, when they can be held outdoors. Among the big shows are the annual **WE Fest** (wefest.com), **Moondance Jam** (moondancejam.com), **Sonshine Festival** (sonshinefestival.com), the **Minnesota Bluegrass & Old-Time Music Festival** (minnesotabluegrass .org), and the **Boundary Waters Blues Festival** (elyblues.com). More festivals and information are listed in each chapter.

NATURE PRESERVES Minnesota has thousands of acres maintained as nature preserves (also called Scientific & Natural Area, or SNA), and as such, they provide numerous opportunities for hiking and wildlife viewing, with the heaviest concentration of such preserves in the western and southwestern parts of the state. The **Minnesota Department of Natural Resources** (dnr.state.mn.us) and the **Nature Conservancy** (nature.org) both have comprehensive listings of locations and what you can expect to find. Areas like the Black Dog Nature Preserve, Burnside Islands SNA, Frenchman's Bluff SNA, Glacial Ridge National Wildlife Refuge, and Bluestem Prairie SNA are just a few of the more than 140 preserves across the state that give glimpses of now hard-to-find prairies and untouched forests, not to mention deer, prairie chickens, eagles, wolves, falcons, whooping cranes, pheasants, owls, and herons.

NEWSPAPERS AND PERIODICALS In the Twin Cities, there are two major daily papers: Minneapolis's *Star Tribune* (startribune.com) and St. Paul's *Pioneer Press* (twincities.com). There are also a number of independent papers that publish weekly or monthly, including *City Pages* (citypages.com), which is an excellent resource for local events of every kind and in-depth restaurant reviews.

In terms of periodicals, *Minneapolis–St. Paul Magazine* (mspmag.com) is a monthly publication, available at most bookstores, newsstands, and grocery stores, that has information on Twin Cities events and an extensive restaurant guide. *Minnesota Monthly* (minnesotamonthly.com), although much of its coverage focuses on the Twin Cities, does provide good resources for restaurants, lodging, and events outside the metro area. A third magazine, *Metro Magazine* (metromag.com), focuses specifically on the Twin Cities and picks up some of the edgier, younger events and venues. All magazines publish several "Best Of" issues each year, often by theme or blanketing several topics (dining, shopping, etc.).

Nearly every city of any size has at least a weekly newspaper, and several (Duluth, Bemidji, Brainerd, Rochester, Faribault, International Falls, to name a few) have newspapers published five to seven days a week and available for sale at local stores.

PARKS AND FORESTS, NATIONAL **Voyageurs National Park** (281-283-9821; nps.gov/voya) is the only national park in Minnesota. It borders Canada along the northern edge of Minnesota, nudging up to **Superior National Forest** (218-626-4300; fs.fed.us/r9/forests/superior), which in turn contains the **Boundary Waters Canoe Area Wilderness** on the US side. Voyageurs National Park and Superior National Forest together comprise some of the most beautiful and remote wilderness areas in the state. Together they account for millions of acres of forests, lakes, and streams; connect the region to Canada; and provide countless opportunities for camping, hiking, canoeing, kayaking, houseboating, fishing, and hunting.

The other national area is **Chippewa National Forest** (218-335-8600; fs.usda .gov), a 1.6-million acre preserve south and west of Voyageurs National Park and Superior National Forest. Together with the latter two, Chippewa National Forest provides year-round recreational opportunities. Minnesota's third- and fourth-largest lakes, Leech Lake and Lake Winnibigoshish (also known as Lake Winnie), are in the forest, along with another 1,300 lakes. Wildlife is abundant in the three national areas; wolves, bald eagles, deer, moose, bobcats, owls, and cougars are not uncommon.

PARKS AND FORESTS, STATE The **Minnesota Department of Natural Resources** (dnr.state.mn.us) is the go-to organization for information about Minnesota's state parks, which rival the national parks and forests for recreation and amenities. There are more than 70 parks spread out across the state, including popular visitor sites such as **Gooseberry Falls** and **Split Rock Lighthouse** on the North Shore and **Itasca** in northern Minnesota (home to the Mississippi River headwaters) to the more remote but equally beautiful **Zippel Bay** in the far north region on Lake of the Woods, and **Mystery Cave** in southern Minnesota.

In addition, Minnesota also has 58 state forests, also managed by the Minnesota State DNR. All but one of these forests is located in the central and northern regions of Minnesota, while the **Richard J. Doner Memorial Hardwood Forest** is in the far southeastern corner of the state. Like the national parks and forests, the state parks and forests offer year-round recreational opportunities, with access to a vast number of lakes and rivers.

THE HISTORIC FIRE TOWER AT GRAND RAPIDS' FOREST HISTORY CENTER

**PETS** Accommodations that accept pets are noted with the 🐾 symbol in each chapter. But be sure to call ahead; most lodgings that take pets have restrictions regarding the types and sizes of pets, and there may be advance reservations and fee requirements.

**POPULATION** Per the US Census Bureau, the population of Minnesota is 5,266,214 (as of 2009).

**RAIL TRAVEL** See *AMTRAK*.

**SAILING** Even though winter puts a damper on the fun, the sheer number of Minnesota lakes makes sailing a popular warm-weather pastime. In the Twin Cities, sailboats can be seen on nearly all of the lakes, especially Bde Maka Ska, Lake Harriet, and Lake Minnetonka. But you can expect to see sailboats on just about any body of water or river throughout the state, and rentals can be arranged in every resort area.

**SKIING, CROSS-COUNTRY** State and national parks and forests, combined with county and city parks, provide thousands of miles of groomed and rough trails for cross-country enthusiasts. This is an activity that takes place in virtually every spot in the state, whether it's on flat prairie land with long-range views, through forests and challenging hills, or across lakes and along riverbanks. Rental equipment is available in most resort towns.

**SKIING, DOWNHILL** Mountains aren't the first things that come to mind when thinking about Minnesota, but the winter season combined with some larger-than-average hills do keep winter visitors busy. Among the biggest and most advanced ski resorts is **Lutsen** (218-663-7281; lutsen.com) on the North Shore, which comes complete with slope-side accommodations and all degree of runs (more information is in the "North Shore/Lutsen" chapter). Book ahead—winter weekends tend to be very popular.

**Afton Alps** (651-436-5245 or 1-800-328-1328; aftonalps.com), just outside of Hastings, is the biggest ski resort within easy range of the Twin Cities. There are no slope-side accommodations here, but there are several options in nearby Hastings.

Among the other downhill ski resorts around the state are **Buck Hill** (952-435-7174; buckhill.com) in Burnsville; **Spirit Mountain** (218-628-2891 or 1-800-642-6377; spiritmt.com) in Duluth; **Welch Village** (651-258-4567; welchvillage.com) in Welch; **Buena Vista** (218-243-2231; bvskiarea.com) in Bemidji; **Wild Mountain** (651-465-6315 or 1-800-447-4958; wildmountain.com) in Taylors Falls; and **Mt. Kato** (507-625-3363 or 1-800-668-5286; mountkato.com) in Mankato. Ski and snowboard lessons and rentals are available on-site, and several resorts have ski lodges and tubing hills as well.

BIG WINNIE STORE RV PARK & CAMPGROUND

SMOKING As of press time, smoking is banned in restaurants, bars, and other public establishments. Some counties and cities within Minnesota have enacted local legislation for stricter limitations. When in doubt, ask.

SNOWMOBILING Snowmobiling is a popular sport in Minnesota, used for both recreation and as a practical mode of transport, particularly in the western half of the state. However, that doesn't mean snowmobiles can go anywhere; parts of the Boundary Waters Canoe Area Wilderness are off-limits to motorized vehicles, including snowmobiles. Many state parks and forests have trails for snowmobilers, but be sure to stay on those trails, as wandering off-trail can interfere with the work being done in nature preserves throughout the park systems. The Twin Cities metro area has varying restrictions on snowmobiles, with some cities allowing them and others banning them. To get specific information on annual regulations and requirements, check with the **Minnesota Department of Natural Resources**

(dnr.state.mn.us/snowmobiling/index .html).

THEATER Minnesota's commitment to the arts community continues into the world of theater. Minneapolis has several world-renowned theatrical companies, including the **Guthrie Theater** (612-377-2224 or 1-877-447-8243; guthrietheater .org) and the **Children's Theatre Company** (612-874-0400; childrenstheatre .org). But theaters of all shapes, sizes, and theatrical genres thrive in communities large and small across the state. The Twin Cities is also home to the **Jungle Theater** (612-822-7063; jungletheater .com) and the **Chanhassen Dinner Theatres** (952-934-1525 or 1-800-362-3515; chanhassentheatres.com). In greater Minnesota, the **Paul Bunyan Playhouse** (218-751-7270; paulbunyanplayhouse .com) in Bemidji is one of the state's longest-running summer stock theaters. On the North Shore, the **Grand Marais Playhouse** (218-387-1284; arrowhead centerforthearts.org) offers productions year-round. **Commonweal** (507-467-2525 or 1-800-657-7025; commonwealtheatre

THE PAUL BUNYAN PLAYHOUSE

.org) in Lanesboro offers several productions each year—one of them is always by Norwegian playwright Henrik Ibsen—and also sponsors the annual **Ibsen Festival**. **The Great River Shakespeare Festival** (507-474-7900; grsf.org) in Winona takes place annually in the summer with highly professional Shakespearian productions. Other theaters are noted throughout the book.

TRAFFIC  Generally speaking, Minnesota roads are reasonably well maintained and well-marked. That said, there are always some trouble spots to plan around. The web of intertwining freeways around and through the Twin Cities metro area have routine rush hour slowdowns each weekday, especially during rainy or snowy weather. Friday and Sunday afternoons in the spring and summer find another kind of gridlock—the "going to the cabin" slowdown. Highways leading north from the Twin Cities, particularly I-94, I-494, and I-694, can crawl

along at an agonizingly slow pace each weekend, and even worse if it's a holiday weekend. Whenever possible, try to plan driving at other times; you'll get there faster with less aggravation.

Beyond the lakes traffic, be aware that many of the communities around the lakes and rivers have grown in popularity with vacationers faster than their road systems have been expanded. Driving through Brainerd or Stillwater or along MN 61 on the North Shore on a summer's day is almost guaranteed to be slow, with far more vehicles crowding the roads than usual, and bottlenecks occurring every block with stoplights or left-turning cars. Adding to the frustration is the increase in road construction and repair projects that take place in the summer. A good map can give you ideas of side roads to take, but it's not recommended to do that on a whim; a 5-mile paved road detour might turn into a 35-mile gravel road detour if your choice of side road is also undergoing construction. When planning driving routes, always check with the **Minnesota Department of Transportation** (651-296-3000 or 1-800-657-3774; dot.state.mn.us), which publishes frequent or real-time updates on road conditions and traffic problems all over the state.

WEATHER Minnesota definitely has a winter season; although it's more pronounced the farther north you go, it's not as wicked as legends would have it. That said, if you're traveling in the winter, be absolutely sure to keep an eye on local weather forecasts (local radio and TV stations carry forecasts from the National Weather Service, or the website weather.com provides up-to-the-minute information), especially if you're headed north. Snow is one concern, but for those heading to the western part of the state, wind and cold can be as big, if not a bigger, concern; the long flat plains and prairies have no way to break the wind, which can push snow into conditions of whiteout, and following a road can be close to impossible. When there is a travel advisory listed for a specific region, pay heed, and consider staying put. The snowflake symbol ❄ appears next to establishments that are open during the off-season, which in Minnesota is generally October through April.

WEBSITES Wherever available, website addresses have been included for accommodations, restaurants, attractions, tourist boards and chambers of commerce, and hospitals. When one isn't listed, that's only because none was offered at time of publication.

WINERIES Several entrepreneurial and hardy souls have attacked the notion that wine cannot be produced in a wintry seasonal climate. Wineries have begun to appear in all regions of Minnesota, some using specially cultivated grapes that are better able to withstand winter, and others using

EXHIBITS AT GRAND PORTAGE NATIONAL MONUMENT

fruits besides grapes (blueberries, rhubarb) to create unusual and fun wines. **Alexis Bailly Vineyard** (651-437-1413; abvwines.com) in Hastings was one of the first to work with grapes in Minnesota, producing its first vintage in 1978. Today there's even a **"Wine Trail"** (threeriverswinetrail.com)—a group of five wineries in the St. Croix, Mississippi, and Cannon river valleys in southeast Minnesota, all producing wines that are increasingly enjoying acclaim and success. At this point, most are still in the southern half of the state, where the climate is a bit more temperate, but not far from Bemidji is **Forestedge Winery** (forestedgewinery.com), which works with local fruits (chokecherries, raspberries, Honeycrisp apples) to create some flavorful wines.

# MINNEAPOLIS AND NEIGHBORING COMMUNITIES

■

## MINNEAPOLIS

## MINNEAPOLIS'S NEIGHBORING COMMUNITIES

# MINNEAPOLIS

I t's called the City of Lakes, and for a reason: The city of Minneapolis is home to seven lakes, five of which (Harriet, Lake of the Isles, Bde Maka Ska, Cedar, and Brownie) are connected by trails through the Grand Rounds National Scenic Byway. The lakes serve as a present-day memento from glacier movement centuries ago, and today they are a center of social and recreational activity. But it's not so much the lakes that brought Minneapolis into prominence as its location on the Mississippi River. The Mississippi was a necessary thoroughfare for the development of the logging and milling industries that set Minneapolis on the path from sleepy river town to a thriving economic and cultural force.

The land surrounding Minneapolis was originally settled by Dakota Indians, who turned over that parcel to the US government in 1805. It's thought that the first white man to explore the area was Father Louis Hennepin, a French missionary. Whether or not he was the first, his name was bestowed to the county and one of the major avenues through the city. Originally the area had two towns: St. Anthony (named for the St. Anthony Falls on the Mississippi) and Minneapolis, but in 1872 the two merged. What followed was an economic boom as Minneapolis became the leading lumber and flour milling center in the United States.

MINNEAPOLIS SKYLINE

Those glory days were done by 1930, as northern forests were becoming deforested and logging mills shut down. Flour milling began to take hold in other parts of the country, reducing Minneapolis's lock on the market. Today flour milling is still an important industry, as General Mills is headquartered here. Other agricultural and industrial companies related to the food industry began here and remain powerful today, including Cargill and Super Valu. Other industry giants that either were or are still headquartered in the City of Lakes include Honeywell, Medtronic, Best Buy, and Target. The University of Minnesota's Minneapolis campus grew exponentially during this time, particularly its medical and research departments, which have been leading innovators in medical procedures, including the first open heart surgery.

With major companies bringing in people and money, Minneapolis began to see growth of cultural institutions. The Guthrie Theater, now a world-renowned company, opened in 1960; the Minneapolis Institute of Art began receiving

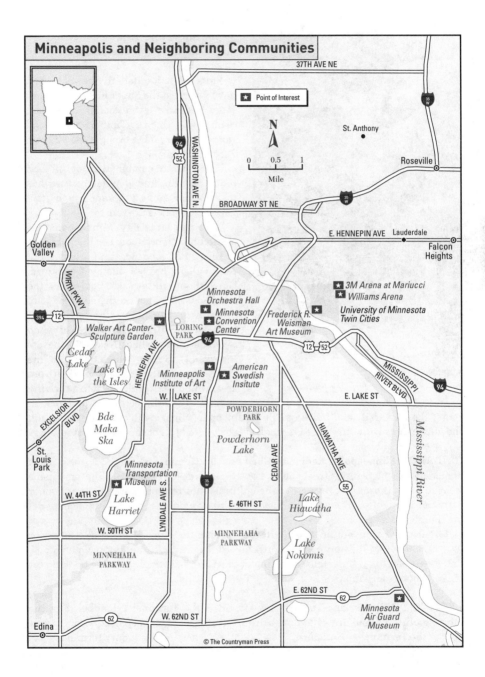

# Minneapolis and Neighboring Communities

37TH AVE NE

Point of Interest

N

0    0.5    1
Mile

St. Anthony

Roseville

BROADWAY ST NE

E. HENNEPIN AVE    Lauderdale

Golden Valley

Falcon Heights

WIRTH PKWY

394  12

Walker Art Center-
Sculpture Garden

LORING PARK

Minnesota
Orchestra Hall

Minnesota
Convention
Center

Frederick R.
Weisman
Art Museum

3M Arena at Mariucci
Williams Arena

University of Minnesota
Twin Cities

12  52

Cedar Lake

Lake of the Isles

HENNEPIN AVE

Minneapolis
Institute of Art

American
Swedish
Insitute

W. LAKE ST

E. LAKE ST

MISSISSIPPI
RIVER BLVD

94

Mississippi River

St. Louis Park

EXCELSIOR BLVD

Bde Maka Ska

POWDERHORN
PARK

Powderhorn
Lake

CEDAR AVE

HIAWATHA AVE

Minnesota
Transportation
Museum

W. 44TH ST

Lake Harriet

LYNDALE AVE S.

E. 46TH ST

55

Lake
Hiawatha

W. 50TH ST

MINNEHAHA
PARKWAY

Lake
Nokomis

MINNEHAHA
PARKWAY

E. 62ND ST

62

Edina

62

W. 62ND ST

© The Countryman Press

Minnesota
Air Guard
Museum

WASHINGTON AVE N.

94
52

DOWNTOWN EXCELSIOR

visitors in 1915; and the Walker Art Center began focusing on contemporary art in 1940s. Sports fans were given something to cheer about when the major league Minnesota Twins debuted in 1960 and went on to win the World Series in 1987 and 1991. The Minnesota Vikings brought NFL football to the state and have played in the Super Bowl four times. More recently, professional basketball teams (the men's Timberwolves and women's Lynx) have brought crowds into Target Center.

A dynamic combination of history, industry, arts, and popular culture has made Minneapolis a vibrant city to visit. Oh, and the lakes are fun, too.

Like any large city, Minneapolis has myriad neighborhoods. For the purposes of this book, lodging, dining and shopping will be broken out by Downtown, North Loop (otherwise known as the Warehouse District on the north edge of downtown), Northeast (across the river from downtown, the nearest area of which is sometimes called Near Northeast/ Riverfront), South (which includes the Uptown area), the Mississippi riverfront area (which has developed into a thriving community with recreation and restaurants), the University of Minnesota's East Bank area (which is full of fun eateries), and the university's Dinkytown area (a small corner packed full of shops and restaurants).

GUIDANCE **Minneapolis Regional Chamber of Commerce** (612-370-9100; mpls chamber.org), 81 S. 9th Street, Suite 200. Open weekdays 8–4:30. The chamber's website has a thorough overview of the cultural, entertainment, sports, and outdoor activities available in the city, and they offer links and order forms for informational brochures and maps.

**Minneapolis Convention and Visitors Association** (Meet Minneapolis; 612-397-9275 or 888-676-MPLS; minneapolis.org), 505 Nicollet Avenue, Suite 100. Open Mon.–Fri., 10–6 , Sat. 10–5. An extensive listing of tourist info, including online booking for air and hotel reservations.

GETTING THERE **By air:** The primary airport is the **Terminal 1–Lindbergh** at the **Minneapolis–St. Paul International Airport** (612-726-5555; mspairport.com); next door is the **Terminal 2–Humphrey** (612-726-5555), a smaller secondary terminal serving mostly no-frills and charter airlines. Both airports are in Bloomington, a western suburb. Taxis, limos, rental cars, and light rail service is available from the airports into the city.

**By bus: Greyhound** has a terminal downtown (612-371-3325; greyhound.com).

**By car:** I-94, I-394, I-35W, and MN 55 all lead into downtown Minneapolis.

# MINNESOTA'S "FIFTH SEASON"

Like any northern clime, Minnesota struggles to get as much road construction and repair done during the warm months as possible. Consequently, the old phrase "you can't get there from here" seems to hold an unfortunate truth at various points during the summer construction season. Spring, summer, and fall can present other inconveniences, such as rare but not unheard-of-flooding that closes roads. The bottom line is when planning your travel, particularly if you're traveling by car, check out current road conditions by visiting the Minnesota Department of Transportation's road and traffic conditions website (511mn.org) or call 511 (or 1-800-657-3774) for updated information.

**By rail: AMTRAK** (1-800-872-7245; amtrak.com) has a rail station in the restored Union Depot in Lowertown, St. Paul (240 E. Kellogg Boulevard, #70).

GETTING AROUND For travel within the city, **Metro Transit** (612-373-3333; metrotransit.org) provides extensive service via bus and light rail throughout the Minneapolis area. Currently, light rail service runs from downtown Minneapolis to US Bank Stadium, Historic Ft. Snelling, the Mall of America, and the airport, with a commuter line (the Northstar) that travels north to Big Lake, mostly for commuters. Ride-sharing services such as **Uber** and **Lyft** have become ubiquitous as well, making it easy to get around without a car. But if you're traveling outside the metro, or plan on taking many excursions that require transportation, a car rental can be helpful.

WHEN TO COME  The warmer months of spring, summer, and fall are always popular in the Twin Cities, but even the colder months can be an attractive time to visit. If staying in a downtown hotel, visitors may have access to the city's extensive system of skyways, allowing people to travel across the heart of the city without setting foot outdoors. And while the temperatures may be cold, the city's theater season, nightclub scene, and basketball/ football seasons are going strong. For those who like winter, outdoor events and sports are in full bloom January through March, including cross-country and downhill skiing, ice skating, snowshoeing, and ice fishing.

MEDICAL EMERGENCY Call 911. In the downtown area, the closest hospital is **Hennepin County Medical Center** (612-873-3000; hennepinhealthcare.org), 701 Park Avenue. Elsewhere in Minneapolis are the following hospitals: **University of Minnesota Medical Center—East Bank Hospital**, located at the University of Minnesota (612-273-8383; mhealth.org),

THE MILL CITY MUSEUM

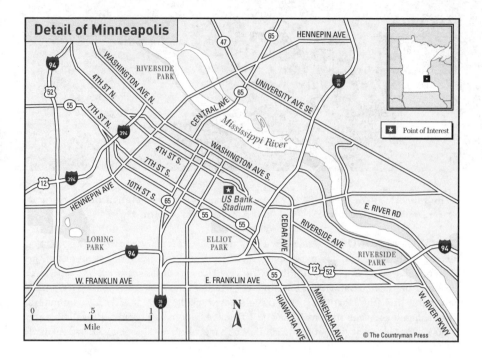

at 500 Harvard Street; **Abbott Northwestern** (612-863-4000; allinahealth.org/abbott -northwestern-hospital), 800 E. 28th Street; and **Children's Hospital**, located next to Abbott Northwestern (612-813-6000; childrensmn.org), 2530 Chicago Avenue S.

# ✳ To See and Do

MUSEUMS ✪ ♿ 🌐 🐾 ⚲ 📶 ☂ ❄ ⫴ **Minneapolis Institute of Art** (1-888-642-2787; artsmia .org), 244 S. 3rd Avenue. Open Tues.–Sat. 10–5 (Thurs. and Fri. until 9) and Sun. 11–5. General admission is free, but special traveling exhibits may require paid tickets, varying in price. Exhibits are varied and lively, including an impressionist gallery, an extensive collection of American photography, a gallery showcasing local artists, a display of Frank Lloyd Wright architectural pieces, and a wide array of ancient Asian and African artifacts. The institute has proven itself willing to take risks with its visiting exhibitions, which in recent years have included such diverse offerings as an Egyptian exhibit; a Villa America exhibit, featuring such contemporary American artists as Georgia O'Keeffe, Grant Wood, and Arthur Dove; an exhibit of treasures from the Louvre; and an exhibit of treasures from Egypt's sunken series. The institute offers a variety of programs, including Family Sundays, docent-led tours, lecture series, and the annual Art in Bloom fundraiser. The vast majority of exhibits are free admission, while visiting exhibitions are usually fee-based. The institute has a café, Agra Culture, for lunch, a lobby-level coffee shop, and an extensive gift shop with a wide variety of art-related gifts. Parking is free on the adjacent streets, but only if you get there early— there are few spots, and competition is fierce from the Children's Theatre and the Minneapolis College of Art and Design, which are all part of the institute complex. (Note: At the time of this writing, the city of Minneapolis was extending parking meters into previously free areas, so this may change in the foreseeable future.) There are also a pay parking ramp and pay parking lot within one block.

⊙ ♿ ✎ ⚲ (((ᵖ))) ⬆ ❋ ❚❚ **Walker Art Center** (612-375-7600; walkerart.org), 1750 Hennepin Avenue. Open Tues.–Sun. 11–5 (Thurs. until 9, Fri.–Sat. until 6). Adults $15, seniors 62 and older $13, students with student IDs $10, active military members $7.50. Free for Walker Center members, children under 18 and under, for visitors with a same-day event ticket, and on Thurs. nights after 5 and the first Sat. of each month. As the Art Institute is known as the traditional museum, the Walker is solely focused on contemporary artwork in a wider variety of mediums: painting, sculpture, video, performance art, and Internet art. The Walker offers special events tailored for families, LGBTQ individuals, singles, and film buffs; traveling

THE ORPHEUM THEATRE

exhibitions include the famed Diane Arbus retrospective, an examination of Picasso and his influences, an exhibit curated by John Waters, and a rare Frida Kahlo exhibit. Diners can enjoy a meal at Esker Grove, headed by acclaimed local chef Doug Flicker. The **Minneapolis Sculpture Garden** (see *Green Space and Outdoor Activities*) is free. Parking is available in a ramp beneath the museum or a pay lot across the street. Some street parking is available, but it can be difficult to get.

THE MINNEAPOLIS INSTITUTE OF ART

❂ ♿ ✏ 🐾 ⚲ ((•)) ⚐ ❄ **Frederick R. Weisman Art Museum** (612-625-9494; wam.umn
.edu), 333 E. River Road (on the East Bank of the University of Minnesota). Open Tues.–
Fri. 10–5 (Wed. until 8) and Sat. and Sun. 11–5. Admission is free. Looming over Washington Avenue on the University of Minnesota's East Bank is a large modern structure
designed by Frank Gehry. A building both loved and hated, the Weisman Art Museum
is visually hard to miss, and inside is a collection of 20th- and 21st-century art masters, including Georgia O'Keeffe and Alfred Maurer, as well as a large collection of
Korean furniture and international ceramics. An expansion project completed in late
2011 added five new galleries to showcase even more of the Weisman's permanent collection as well as collaborations with local artists and art students. While the Weisman
doesn't have a restaurant on-site, there are several small but good restaurants in the
nearby **Stadium Village** (walking distance). The museum offers a parking ramp for a
fee; free parking is pretty much nonexistent on this end of the university.

♿ ✏ ⚐ ❄ **The Museum of Russian Art** (612-821-9045; tmora.org), 5500 S. Stevens
Avenue. Open Mon.–Fri. 10–5, Sat. 10–4, and Sun. 1–5. Adults $10, seniors age 65 and
older $8, young adults 14 and older and university students with ID $5, and 13 and
under free. Located in a small building reminiscent of Spanish architecture in south
Minneapolis, the Museum of Russian Art is the only permanent museum of Russian
art and artifacts in North America. The building itself is worth a visit; originally a
church, it eventually was used as a funeral home before providing its current occupant
with an unexpectedly perfect venue for Russian art. Galleries range in size from small,
low rooms in the basement to a two-story chapel-esque gallery on the main floor. The
museum has a frequently rotating exhibition calendar covering all aspects of Russian
life, from Soviet propaganda art to matryoshka dolls and samovars to contemporary
Russian art. Be sure to visit the gift shop on the second floor, behind the main gallery; it's full of Russian treasures, including a fine collection of hand-painted lacquered
boxes.

❂ ♿ ✏ ⚲ ((•)) ⚐ ❄ 🍴 **The American Swedish Institute** (612-871-4907; asimn.org),
2600 S. Park Avenue. Open Tues.–Sat. 10–5 (Wed. until 8) and Sun. 12–5. Adults $12,
seniors 62 and older $8, children 6–18 and full-time students with ID $6, ASI members
and children under 6 free. Housed in the opulent Turnblad mansion (which is on the
National Register of Historic Places), the institute houses an extensive collection of
artwork and craft pieces from Sweden, as well as a permanent exhibition examining
the relationship between Sweden and Swedish immigrants to Minnesota. This may
sound subdued, but make no mistake, the institute is entirely child friendly, with special events for children and even babies and caregivers. Folk-song fests, mid-summer
celebrations, a packed holiday season, craft and cocktail nights, and quarterly Swedish
smorgasbords are just a few of the events on the museum's busy calendar.

❂ ♿ ✏ ((•)) ⚐ ❄ 🍴 **The Mill City Museum** (612-341-7555; mnhs.org/millcity), 704 S.
2nd Street. Open Tues.–Sat. 10–5 and Sun. 12–5. Holiday hours may apply. Adults $12,
senior citizens, veterans and active military members, and college students $10, chil-
dren 5–17 $6, Minnesota Historical Society members and children 6 and under free.
Mill City, built along the Mississippi River in downtown Minneapolis, gives visitors
a vivid glimpse of Minneapolis's role in the history of grain production and milling.
The museum has several interactive exhibits; groups that book ahead can participate
in a baking session in the kitchen. A partially demolished remnant of the original mill
exists and can be explored, or enjoyed as the venue for occasional outdoor concerts
sponsored by the museum.

♿ ✏ ((•)) ⚐ ❄ **The Bakken Museum** (612-926-3878; thebakken.org), 3537 S. Zenith Avenue. Open Tues.–Fri. 10–4, Sat. 11–5, Sun. 12–5. Adults $10, senior citizens and young
adults 13–24 $8, children 4–12 $5, and museum members and children 3 and under free.

THE AMERICAN SWEDISH INSTITUTE

The Bakken is a family-friendly museum that offers kids a chance to do some hands-on experiments involving electricity and magnetism. Not as dry as it sounds, the Bakken keeps things lively, although their science research is scholarly and impressive. The surroundings are worth a visit, too; the museum is in a Tudor mansion near Bde Maka Ska.

❊ **The Carl W. Kroening Interpretive Center** (612-370-4844; facebook.com/kroening interpretativecntr), 4900 Mississippi Court. Open Tues. and Thurs. 9–4; Wed., Fri., and Sat. 10–4; and Sun. 12–4. This center is a small but informative resource on anything you ever wanted to know about the heritage of the proud Mississippi. Call ahead to find out which organized programs are being offered; events vary seasonally.

## ❊ Green Space and Outdoor Activities

BICYCLING Minneapolis is called the City of Lakes for good reason, and one of the best aspects of the city's chain of lakes is the 50-mile bike trail that connects the Four Lakes Loop (Lake Harriet, Bde Maka Ska, Lake of the Isles, and Lake Nokomis). Well maintained and clearly marked, the trails around the lakes offer vistas of the best the city has to offer: blue waters, wildlife, houses of the rich and famous, and excellent people watching. Trails are available in other parts of the city as well, including along the Mississippi River, a route that takes riders into Minnehaha Park. **Perennial Cycle** (612-827-8000; perennialcycle.com; 3342 S. Hennepin Avenue) is located near Bde Maka Ska, rents bikes and in-line skates.

**Nice Ride MN** (niceridemn.com). Nice Ride is a bike rental system, where riders can rent a bike (during the non-snow months) for anywhere from an hour to days. Bikes can

THE MINNESOTA RIVER FROM SHAKOPEE'S THE LANDING

be returned to the location where they were originally rented or to any Nice Ride location (400 locations across the Twin Cities metro at the time of this writing).

E-SCOOTERS Minneapolis has authorized several e-scooter vendors to bring 2,000 scooters into the city limits starting in 2019, on a trial basis. At the time of this writing, the vendors include **JUMP** (jump.com), **Lyft** (lyft.com/scooters), **Spin** (spin.app), and **Lime** (li.me).

BOATING Those who would rather be on the lake than biking by it can bring their own watercraft or stop by Bde Maka Ska's boat rental station to rent canoes, kayaks, or paddleboats. Motorboats are not allowed. Depending on weather, rentals are available seasonally 11–7 daily. Sailboats and windsurfers are also allowed on the chain of lakes, and the **Minneapolis Sailing Center** offers classes for adults and children (612-470-7245; sailmpls.org).

PARKS AND OUTDOOR SPACES Minneapolis might be known as the City of Lakes, but it could also be known as the City of Green Spaces. Nearly every community and neighborhood has some kind of park, with facilities varying from playground equipment to basketball courts to tennis courts to swimming pools. For full details about the range of park offerings in the city, check with the **Minneapolis Park & Recreation Board** (minneapolisparks.org) for full details. What follows is a selected list of outdoor spaces to enjoy.

**Minneapolis Sculpture Garden** (612-375-7600; walkerart.org/visit/garden), 726 Vineland Place. The garden is open daily 6–midnight; the Cowles Conservatory is open Tues.–Sat. 10–8 and Sun. 10–5. Admission is free. The sculpture garden is a joint exhibit created and managed by the Minneapolis Park & Recreation Board and the Walker Art Center. There are 11 beautifully manicured acres, with both an indoor and outdoor floral garden and more than 40 sculptures, including the iconic Spoonbridge and Cherry fountain. Although most of the exhibits are permanent, some temporary sculptures have also appeared, including a mini golf course in which each hole was designed by a different contemporary artist. Parking is easiest in an adjoining pay lot. Some free or metered street parking is available, but it goes quickly.

**Loring Park** (minneapolisparks.org), 1382 Willow Street. Across Hennepin Avenue from the Minneapolis Sculpture Garden, Loring Park is an oasis in the city. The small but charming park offers a community pool, a basketball court, and a boat dock for the small lake at its heart. Bike and walking trails through the park are connected to trails leading to other parts of the city. Annual festivals, such as the **Pride Festival** (see *Special Events*) and the Loring Park Art Festival, are held here each year. And if you're hungry after enjoying nature, **Café Lurcat** (see *Where to Eat*) and **4 Bells** are right across the street.

**Minnehaha Park** (minneapolisparks.org), 4801 S. Minnehaha Avenue. Perhaps one of the most beautiful spaces in Minneapolis, Minnehaha (which means "laughing waters") is a 193-acre park that encompasses Minnehaha Falls, limestone bluffs, and views of the river. A small rail museum pays homage to the park's history as a railway station, two historical homes are open for visitors, and Longfellow Gardens and Pergola Garden showcase both formal gardens and wildflower displays. Hiking trails wind through the park, including near the waterfall. Picnic tables and a bandstand combine for relaxed weekend outings. **Wheel Fun Rentals** (wheelfunrentals.com) rents bicycles, and **Sea Salt Eatery** (see *Where to Eat*), open Apr.–Oct., serves fresh seafood, wine, and beer for your dining pleasure.

**Lake Harriet** (minneapolisparks.org), W. 43rd Street and E. Lake Harriet Parkway. Located near the charming Linden Hills neighborhood, Lake Harriet has a public beach, a boat launch (it's a popular sail boating lake), a beautiful rose garden, and a bandshell that features live music during the summer. Nearby is **Bread and Pickle** (breadandpickle.com), a walk-up eatery. The walking and biking trails around the lake give you the chance to enjoy the view, both of the lake and of the historic mansions that surround it.

**Bde Maka Ska** (3000 Calhoun Parkway) and **Lake of the Isles** (2500 Lake Isles Parkway). These neighboring lakes give you the best of both lake worlds; Bde Maka Ska is another boater's favorite, not to mention sunbathers and people watchers. **Lola's on the Lake** (see *Where to Eat*) gives you a quick and tasty meal before you strap on your blades and go for a ride. When you cross over to Lake of the Isles, you'll find a quieter, more scenic lake, with elegant historic homes lining the way. For more information, get in touch with **Minneapolis Park & Recreation Board** (minneapolisparks.org).

**Theodore Wirth Parkway** (minneapolisparks.org), 1339 Theodore Wirth Parkway. Theodore Wirth, at 759 acres, is the largest regional park in the Minneapolis park system. It's technically in adjacent Golden Valley, but Minneapolis is proud to claim this park, which has something for everyone: a lake, fishing pond, sledding hill, golf, hiking/biking trails, tennis courts, soccer fields, prairie, forest, children's garden, bird sanctuary, and a winding parkway to explore it all.

# ✳ Lodging

## HOTELS

### DOWNTOWN

✪ ♿ ✎ ⚙ (•) ☿ ❄ ▼ ⅋ **The Nicollet Island Inn** (612-331-1800; nicolletislandinn.com), 95 Merriam Street. Visitors looking for historic charm and ambience will be most successful at this small (24 rooms) but upscale hotel on Nicollet Island. Built in 1893, this limestone building with its timber-and-beam interior was originally a door manufacturer, then a men's shelter run by the Salvation Army, before the Minneapolis Park & Recreation Board bought it and turned it into an inn. All rooms have views of the Mississippi River and the Minneapolis skyline. Rooms include plasma TVs, plush robes, and 400-thread-count Egyptian cotton bedding. The inn has its own highly regarded dining room, but many other Minneapolis dining and entertainment spots are within walking distance or a few minutes' drive. Rates start at $139, with the higher rates on corner rooms, which are larger and have more views; the Deluxe Corner Room has a four-poster bed. Packages and specials available.

♿ ✎ 🐾 ⚙ (•) ☿ ❄ ▼ ⅋ **The Grand Hotel** (612-288-8888; grandhotelminneapolis .com), 615 S. 2nd Avenue. Housed in the former Minneapolis Athletic Club is a hotel that matches its predecessor in quiet elegance. This boutique hotel has 140 rooms, many of which offer four-poster beds and marble soaking tubs in the bath. Ideally located for visitors staying downtown, the Grand Hotel also offers a sizable fitness area and the SIX15 Lounge restaurant. Rates start at $348, with some specials and packages offered.

♿ ✎ 🐾 ⚙ (•) ☿ ❄ ▼ ⅋ **Loews Minneapolis Hotel** (612-677-1100 or 1-877-880-8918; loewshotels.com/ minneapolis-hotel), 601 N. 1st Avenue. This high-fashion, high-tech hotel with tasteful, comfortable rooms and suites is by far the best thing to come to the Block E entertainment complex, with its stylish and spacious public spaces and the well-regarded **Cosmos** restaurant (see *Where to Eat*), as well as multiple bar spots. For a price, visitors can book the Skybox Suite, a luxury pent-house overlooking the Minnesota Twins' Target Field. Room rates start at $159, with special packages available.

♿ ✎ 🐾 🐾 ⚙ (•) ☿ ❄ ▼ ⅋ **Le Méridien Chambers Hotel** (612-767-6900; marriott.com/hotels/travel/mspmd-le -méridien-chambers-minneapolis), 901 Hennepin Avenue. This is a hotel with its own brand of trendy charm. Chambers is housed in a restored building near the Orpheum and State theaters and has its own art gallery. The hotel offers only 60 rooms and suites, but they are designed for luxury and comfort. The hotel has a restaurant and bar, but is also steps away from several downtown Minneapolis restaurants. Rates start at $107 with deeper discounts for prepayment. Packages are available.

✪ ♿ ✎ ⚙ (•) ☿ ❄ ▼ ⅋ **W Minneapolis— The Foshay** (612-215-3700; marriott.com /hotels/travel/mspwh-w-minneapolis -the-foshay), 821 Marquette Avenue. Located within the historic Foshay Tower is this luxury hotel, which plays off its art deco beginnings and cheekily names its room categories things like Wonderful, Fantastic, and Spectacular (with the highest level reserved for the Extreme Wow Suite). Try dinner at the popular **Manny's** steakhouse (see "Steakhouses" on page 55), and follow that with a trip to the Prohibition Bar. Spa services can be arranged. Rates start at $189, with packages, prepayment, and weekend discounts offered.

♿ ✎ 🐾 ⚙ (•) ❄ ☿ ▼ ⅋ **Radisson Blu Minneapolis Downtown** (612-339-4900; radissonblu.com/en/hotel-minneapolis), 35 S. 7th Street. Small but comfortable rooms and a well-regarded restaurant (the **FireLake Grill House & Cocktail Bar**; see *Where to Eat*), make this a good choice both for businesspeople and tourists in for a weekend of major league sports or theater and shopping. Rates start at $105, with weekend discounts and packages available.

♿ 🐾 ⚲ 📶 ❄ ☂ ▼ 🍴 **Minneapolis Marriott City Center** (612-349-4000; marriott.com), 30 S. 7th Street. The Marriott has, besides its standard hotel rooms, suites and a private concierge level. The hotel also has the Northern Shores Grille, which serves standard American fare, but for guests with more adventurous tastes, there are numerous restaurants in easy walking distance that would be recommended. Rates start at $119, with packages and weekend discounts offered.

♿ 🐾 ⚲ ❄ ☂ ▼ 🍴 **The Westin Minneapolis Hotel** (612-333-4006; marriott.com), 88 S. 6th Street. The Westin should be a case study in how to renovate a historic building. The company took Farmers & Mechanics Bank Building and created a luxury hotel with a highly touted bar and restaurant (appropriately named **BANK**; see *Where to Eat*), but they kept the bank's vintage accoutrements. Rates start at $341, with packages and weekend discounts offered.

♿ 🐾 ⚲ 📶 ❄ ☂ 🍴 ▼ **The Hyatt** (612-370-1234; hyatt.com), 1300 Nicollet Mall. On Nicollet Avenue, where downtown Minneapolis begins to segue into neighborhoods, resides this active conference hotel. The Hyatt is close enough to walk to several downtown attractions and restaurants, and also has the Prairie Kitchen and Bar on-site. Rates start at $159, with packages and weekend discounts offered.

♿ 🐾 ⚲ 📶 ❄ ☂ ▼ 🍴 **Elliot Park Hotel** (612-389-2300; elliotparkhotel.com), 823 5th Avenue S. This boutique hotel is a newer entrant from Marriott. Each of the 155 rooms and 13 suites comes equipped with Amazon Alexa. Décor has been designed along the popular Scandinavian hygge theme, with simple, streamlined, yet tasteful appointments. Large windows provide appealing views of the city's skylines. The hotel's restaurant, Tavola Kitchen and Bar, serves Italian-themed foods and hearty breakfasts in a warm, inviting setting with a candles and wood-fired oven, and the hotel is located steps away from other restaurants as well. Rates start at $165, with packages available.

♿ 🐾 ⚲ 📶 ❄ ☂ ▼ 🍴 **Emery Hotel** (612-340-2000; hotelemery.com), 215 S. 4th Street. This boutique hotel is part of Marriott's Autograph Collection and offers upscale rooms and suites. It also has a Spyhouse Coffee (well-regarded local coffee chain) and Giulia Restaurant & Bar, a high-end Italian restaurant run by James Beard Award–finalist Steven Brown and Food Network's Josh Hedquist. The décor is a striking mid-century modern feel with high-end appointments. The fitness center includes Peloton bikes. Rates start at $150, with packages available.

♿ 🐾 ⚲ 📶 ❄ ☂ ▼ 🍴 **Hotel Ivy** (612-746-4600; marriott.com), 201 S. 11th Street. Hotel Ivy is ensconced in the historic Ivy Tower, which is on the National Register of Historic Places. The building itself was constructed in the Ziggurate style of a terraced pyramid of receding tiers. Its location within walking distance to Orchestra Hall and the Minneapolis Convention Center is desirable, as are the hotel's amenities. There are 127 rooms and nine suites with 10-foot floating ceilings, upscale linens, original artwork, soaking tubs and glassed-in showers in the bathrooms. The crown jewel is the Penthouse Suite, a two-story accommodation with private rooftop balcony and panoramic windows surrounding the suite. Guests in the penthouse also receive a complimentary bottle of Dom Perignon. Options for dining on-site include Monello, which serves Italian; The Bar, with a sizable champagne list and shared plate; and Constantine, a bar with craft cocktails and lounge food. Rates start at $215 for guest rooms and $1,680 for suits, and packages are available.

♿ 🐾 📶 ❄ ☂ ▼ **luMINN Hotel Minneapolis** (612-338-3500; luminnhotel minneapolis.com), 219 S. 4th Street. A newer boutique hotel built into the Historic Federal Plaza Building, luMINN has a gorgeous lobby bar (but no restaurant, although it's close to several). The 55 suites have kitchenettes, upgraded bedding and robes, and ambient lighting that allows guests to change the colors at will. Rates start at $159, with packages offered.

♿ ✆ ❄ ⏚ ▼ ‖ **The Millennium Hotel** (612-332-6000; millenniumhotels.com), 1313 Nicollet Mall. Across the street from the Hyatt, the Millennium is a comfortable hotel that caters to the business crowd and is connected by skyway through to the convention center. Rates start at $118, with packages and weekend discounts offered.

♿ ✆ ♂ ((•)) ❄ ⏚ ▼ ‖ ⸙ **The Hilton Minneapolis** (612-376-1000; 3.hilton.com), 1001 Marquette Avenue. The Hilton is in a prime location for convention visitors, as it's connected by skyway to the convention center. The Hilton offers standard hotel rooms and suites, and a set of executive rooms, which feature upscale furnishings and amenities. The hotel offers a number of dining options that span three meals a day, but for variety's sake, many options are within blocks of the hotel. Rates start at $143, with packages and weekend discounts offered.

## NORTH LOOP AND THE MILL DISTRICT

✪ ♿ ✆ ☙ ((•)) ❄ ⏚ ▼ ‖ **Canopy by Hilton Minneapolis Mill District** (612-332-0696; canopy3.hilton.com), 708 S. 3rd Street. This renovated 1900s manufacturing building has been updated with care and respect to its history. Rooms and public spaces have plenty of exposed wood and brick tastefully contrasted with contemporary furnishings. Suites have separate bedrooms, some with views of US Bank Stadium. There's a bar in the hotel along with the Canopy Central Café, which serves breakfast as well as snacks throughout the day. For evening meals,

there are several good eateries within easy walking or driving distance. Rates begin at $379, with packages available.

♿ ✆ ☙ ♂ ((•)) ❄ ⏚ ▼ ‖ ⸙ **The Depot Minneapolis** (thedepotminneapolis .com), 225 S. 3rd Avenue. There are two lodging options at the old Milwaukee Road railway depot. The first, the **Depot Renaissance** (612-375-1700), while still historic in nature, is geared more toward businesspeople, with smaller rooms and extensive technological amenities. The deluxe historic suites section of the Renaissance lives up to its name with generous suites decorated in early-20th-century style, with large windows overlooking the city. Rates begin at $165, with packages and weekend discounts offered. The second, the **Residence Inn** (612-340-1300) is an extended-stay format, with each unit containing a full kitchen. Rates begin at $157, with packages and weekend discounts offered. Both hotels have access to the Milwaukee Road Restaurant & Bar, but are also close to many of the Mill District/North Loop eateries, as well as the Mill City Museum and the Guthrie Theater.

♿ ✆ ☙ ((•)) ❄ ⏚ ▼ ⸙ **Aloft Minneapolis Hotel** (612-455-8400; marriott.com), 900 S. Washington Avenue. Cheerful rooms and suites with high ceilings and high-tech amenities combined with family-friendly kids' accommodations and a willingness to accept pets makes this a good choice for family travelers who like a touch of contemporary upscale. No sit-down dining available on-site, but there are several excellent restaurants within walking or short cab/Uber/Lyft distance. Rates start from $1,298; packages and weekend discounts available.

✪ ♿ ✆ ☙ ((•)) ❄ ⏚ ▼ ‖ ⸙ **Hewing Hotel** (651-468-0400; hewinghotel.com), 300 N. Washington Avenue. A recent addition to the hotel scene in Minneapolis, the Hewing is a rebuilt warehouse turned luxury hotel. The hotel's interior still has artful traces of its history, including original pine timber beams, complemented by local artwork of Minnesota artists and

# FINE DINING, FINE LODGING

Food and lodging have gone together since time immemorial, but there's a unique blend of fine dining and bed-and-breakfast in northeast Minneapolis. Beloved local food star, **Restaurant Alma** (see *Where to Eat*), expanded its upscale restaurant to include a well-received bakery, which in turn provides breakfast for the building's seven unique rooms. Each room has custom, locally made white oak furniture, eco-friendly mattresses and all-cotton linens, walk-in showers, and vintage and locally made rugs, baskets, and decorative fabrics. Rates start at $155.

photographers. On-site massage can be arranged, and there is a rooftop sauna and spa pool. The hotel's restaurant, **Tullibee** (see *Where to Eat*), is a worthy destination on its own. Rates start from $199.

## UNIVERSITY OF MINNESOTA— EAST BANK

🛏️ 🐾 ☕ 🅿️ (((•))) ❄️ 🍸 ▼ 🍴 **Graduate Minneapolis** (612-379-8888; graduatehotels .com/minneapolis), 615 SE Washington Avenue. This hotel is an attractive option on the East Bank of the university, close to restaurants and easy walking distance to Northrop Auditorium and the Weisman Museum. It has a mix of rooms and suites, as well as the Topgolf Swing Suite, an event room that provides virtual golf experiences. Complimentary bike rentals are included in the room fees. The hotel has an on-site restaurant, the Beacon, that serves three meals a day, and the hotel's Stadium Village location puts it in easy walking distance to several cafés and restaurants. Rates start at $97.

🛏️ 🐾 ☕ (((•))) ❄️ ▼ **The Days Hotel by Wyndham University Ave. SE** (612-623-3999; daysinn.com), 2407 SE University Avenue. The Days Hotel is on the edge of the East Bank adjacent to TCF Stadium and on the Green Line light rail, but still within walking distance to many university locations. Hot breakfast is included daily, as well as free shuttle service to locations within 3 miles. Rates start at $100, with packages and weekend discounts offered.

## ✳ Where to Eat

The Minneapolis restaurant scene continues to expand, both in quality and in types of foods offered. Visitors who think of Minnesota as the land of white food—Swedish meatballs, mashed potatoes, lutefisk, and lefse—will be in for a tasty surprise. Some of the upper-end restaurants have gained national attention (Spoon and Stable, Restaurant Alma, 112 Eatery) and several James Beard Award nominations (with 112 Eatery's Alex Roberts taking home awards), while numerous small independent and multicultural cafés have changed the city's culinary landscape to reflect the growing diversity. A caveat: The restaurant industry is always a volatile one, and the Twin Cities are not immune to the rapid turnover that can occur. Use the contact info to check the current status before arrival.

DINING OUT  Minneapolis has gone from being a culinary backwater to a foodie destination. But one thing that might surprise visitors to the area is the general casual approach to dining out. For better or for worse, Minnesota diners tend to be more on the informal side when it comes to dressing up for dinner. That's not to say that you won't see suits and ties, but it's not uncommon to see people in business casual—or even completely informal—at some of the leading restaurants.

## DOWNTOWN

&#9855; ♈ ❄ **4 Bells** (612-904-1163; 4bells.com), 1610 Harmon Place. Open Tues.–Sat. for dinner, Sun. for brunch. This restaurant was developed by the same team behind **Butcher & The Boar** (see below), but the emphasis at 4 Bells is on seafood. Depending on what's fresh and available, you might find a striped bass ceviche, buttermilk fried smelt, an oyster flight or oysters Rockefeller, or shrimp and grits. For diners not in the mood for seafood, remember that this team has a deft hand with meat and feel confident ordering the wagyu rib eye or Southern fried chicken. Expensive/very expensive.

&#9855; ♈ ❄ **BANK** (612-656-3255; bank mpls.com), 88 S. 6th Street. Open daily for all three meals. Located at the **Westin Minneapolis Hotel** (see *Lodging*) in the old Farmers & Merchant's Bank, BANK's developers wisely took the banking theme and ran with it, creating an unusual but lovely tribute to the olden days of banking. The food plays up the opulent setting. Very expensive.

&#9855; ♈ ❄ **Butcher & The Boar** (612-238-8888; butcherandtheboar.com), 1121 Hennepin Avenue. Open daily for dinner. Although meat is king in several Twin Cities restaurants, Butcher & The Boar smoke their own meats and make their own sausages in-house, using wild boar, turkey, veal, beef, and duck breast. You could just go light and take the charcuterie platter, but it would be sad to miss the entrées, such as the wagyu rib eye or double-cut smoked pork chop. This eatery also has one of the best downtown patios, a perfect place to while away a summer evening while enjoying the extensive cocktail list concocted by the bar. Expensive/very expensive.

&#9855; ♈ ❄ **Cosmos** (612-312-1168; cosmosrestaurant.com), 601 S. 1st Avenue, in the **Loews Minneapolis Hotel** (see *Lodging*). Open daily for all three meals. Quite possibly one of the most beautiful restaurants in the Twin Cities, Cosmos offers world-class cuisine that rises above standard hotel-restaurant food and a stellar wine list. Chef's tasting menus and kitchen table service available by reservation. The restaurant sources locally extensively, including using the Herbivorous Butcher's vegan foods, Baker's Field bread, and Red Lake Farm wild rice, among other local purveyors. Very expensive.

&#9855; ✐ ❄ ♈ **FireLake Grill House & Cocktail Bar** (612-216-3473; firelakerestaurant .com), 31 S. 6th Street, in the **Radisson Plaza Hotel** (see *Lodging*). Open daily for all three meals. The restaurant has won considerable acclaim for being an early adopter of sourcing from local produce, cheese, and meat producers, and artisanal-quality fare. A seasonal menu offers the chef the ability to tailor dishes to what's in season, such as locally fished walleye during the summer, prepared over a real fire and seasoned to perfection. Very expensive.

&#9855; ✐ ❄ ♈ **Giulia** (612-215-5450; dine giulia.com), 215 S. 4th Street. Open daily for all three meals. Located in Hotel Emery, Giulia is a highly regarded Italian restaurant run by local well-known chefs Josh Hedquist and Steven Brown. The menu is small but intriguing, including clam pizza, veal Milanese, and prawn cavatelli. Don't pass up the hand-drawn mozzarella, done tableside and served warm.

&#9855; ♈ ❄ **Oceanaire Seafood Room** (612-333-2277; theoceanaire.com), 50 S. 6th Street. Open daily at 5 p.m. for dinner. This eatery fast became a local favorite for its extensive fresh seafood menu. The chefs have kept the fresh fish, including varieties not often found locally, and added an extensive raw bar. Very expensive.

✐ &#9855; ♈ ❄ **CRAVE** (612-332-1133; crave america.com), 825 Hennepin Avenue. Open Mon.–Fri. for lunch, daily for dinner. Located across the street from the Orpheum and down the street from the State Theatre, CRAVE offers well-executed casual American fare, as well as an extensive sushi menu, and it's a good choice for

# BREWERY BOOM

Recent years have seen a veritable explosion in breweries across the metro. Here's a sampling of what's happening in the ale and beer market, and all these purveyors have taprooms. Check brewery websites for open hours and events. Some sell growlers, but current laws restrict which breweries can sell them, so call ahead if you want to purchase one.

**Surly Brewing** (763-999-4040; surlybrewing.com), 520 Malcolm Avenue SE. Surly was an early entrant into the craft brew scene. It was also hugely influential in fighting to overturn archaic Minnesota laws that didn't allow breweries to serve their products on-site. Thanks to Surly (and the Surly Bill, as it's known), myriad possibilities have since opened for Minnesota brewers. Surly hasn't rested on its legal laurels, but continues creating new brews while maintaining a roster of year-round favorites that includes its Furious and Hell ales. They also opened a large beer hall and beer garden, with an excellent beer hall menu to go with its exemplary ales.

**Fulton Brewery** (612-333-3208; fultonbeer.com), 414 N. 6th Avenue. Fulton was quick to follow Surly's leads and currently has two breweries in Minneapolis, although this location is the only one with a taproom. They keep a wide range of products on tap, including trademark brews Lonely Blonde and Sweet Child of Vine, along with changing offerings that might feature wheat beer, sour bear, and hard seltzer. A limited sandwich and snack menu is available, and live music is scheduled every Sunday.

**Dangerous Man Brewing** (612-236-4087; dangerousmanbrewing.com), 1300 NE 2nd Street. Focused on small-batch production, Dangerous Man has a frequently changing lineup in its taproom, which might have anything from peanut butter porter to cream ale to tri-hop sour. In other words, something to please every beer drinker. There's no kitchen on site, but visitors are welcome to bring their own food, and food trucks show up Thurs.–Sat. in the warmer months.

**Inbound BrewCo** (612-615-8243; inboundbrew.co), 701 N. 5th Street. This 12,000-square-foot taproom is dog-friendly and has 30 craft beers tapped at all times, along with craft sodas and kombucha. Beers are broken out by funky flavors, easy drinkers, hop heads, dark beers, and limited infusions. Inbound doesn't have food service, but allows visitors to bring in food, and frequently schedules food trucks outside.

**Indeed Brewing** (612-843-5090; indeedbrewing.com), 711 NE 15th Avenue. Pilsners, hoppy ales, sours, honey beers—they're all here in rotation, along with nonalcoholic root beer. Indeed is another supporter of the local food truck scene, bringing in trucks Wed.–Sun. in warmer months, and allowing people to bring their own food if they wish.

those looking for convenient pre-theater dining. It's something of a local chain with additional locations in Edina, Eden Prairie, and at the Mall of America (see *Minneapolis's Neighboring Communities* section on page 73). Expensive.

  &#9855; **Sea Change** (612-225-6499; seachangempls.com), 806 S. 2nd Street. Open daily for lunch and dinner. This is the place for dining at the **Guthrie Theater** (see *Entertainment*), not just because it's located in the same building, but because both its culinary offerings and dramatic interior satisfy all senses. It's a fitting design for a fine arts building, with eye-popping, futuristic décor. The architecture was designed with an eye to the environment, involving reclaimed raw materials. James Beard Award–winner Tim McKee designed the thoughtful, seafood-based menu that emphasizes sustainability as much as it does flavor. The raw bar is open for dinner. Very expensive.

## NORTHEAST

⚓ ♿ 🍸 ❄ **Red Stag Supperclub** (612-767-7766; redstagsupperclub.com), 509 1st Avenue NE. Open daily for lunch and dinner, Sat. and Sun. for breakfast. Red Stag made a name for itself by being the first LEED-CI certified restaurant to open in Minnesota, but it's the food that made it a success. Chef Jason Blair gave the menu a contemporary supper club feel, using local and organic ingredients to create twists on supper club standards, such as the popular smelt fries and truffled kettle corn. Expensive.

♿ 🍸 ❄ **Masu Sushi & Robata** (612-332-6278; masusushiandrobata.com), 330 E. Hennepin Avenue. Open Mon.–Fri. for lunch, daily for dinner. Another Tim McKee success story, Masu brought a new generation of Japanese dining to the Twin Cities with not only top-notch sushi, but with ramen dishes that have no resemblance to the little grocery-store packets, and robata, the ancient Japanese technique of charcoal cooking. Several other ramen and robata restaurants have since taken root, but this was the first. There's also a location at the Mall of America (see *Minneapolis's Neighboring Communities* section on page 73). Expensive.

♿ 🍸 ❄ **Restaurant Alma** (612-379-4909; restaurantalma.com), 528 SE University Avenue. Open daily for dinner. Local, seasonal, organic—that's been Restaurant Alma's mantra since opening, and consequently the menu changes frequently, but always to great acclaim. At the time of this writing, fixed-price dinners were on the menu, offering choices of warm egg custard and caviar, marinated mushroom and duck confit, mung bean pancakes, and crispy pan seared trout or duck two ways. The restaurant has been nominated for James Beard Awards numerous times and brought home the Best Chef Midwest. A recent addition includes a bakery open in the morning with delectable house-made pastries, smoothies and a limited but thoughtful breakfast menu including toasted oatmeal, yogurt and almond crème, and roasted poultry bone broth. Guests in the restaurant's hotel (see *Lodging*) receive breakfast from the café as part of their stay. Very expensive.

♿ 🍸 ❄ **Erté & the Peacock Lounge** (612-623-4211; ertedining.com), 323 NE 13th Avenue. Open Mon.–Sat. for dinner. This gorgeous restaurant and adjacent Peacock Lounge serves contemporary supper club food (including items like cauliflower steak, veal shank, and a wide range of steaks), lushly prepared in generous portions. Very expensive.

## NORTH LOOP/MILL DISTRICT

In the Warehouse District, a number of small restaurants and bistros have built niches as destination dining for fine-cuisine aficionados.

♿ 🍸 ❄ **112 Eatery** (612-343-7696; 112eatery.com), 112 N. 3rd Street. Open daily for dinner. Under the sure guidance of 112 Eatery's chef and owner, James

THE EDINA CINEMA

# STEAKHOUSES

**M**innesotans love their fish and seafood, and vegetarians and vegans are finding an ever-growing selection of dining options, but there are still many Minnesotans who wouldn't dream of turning their back on a prime piece of beef. Downtown Minneapolis is home to several outstanding steakhouses, which all seem to coexist peacefully; apparently there are plenty of steak lovers to keep them busy.

**Murray's** (612-339-0909; murraysrestaurant.com), 26 S. 6th Street. Open Mon.–Fri. for lunch, daily for dinner. This is the original Minneapolis steakhouse, famous for its "silver butter knife" tender steaks. Its reputation as a hometown favorite, as well as its tremendous steaks, keep it a serious contender. Groups of two or three can order strip sirloin to be carved tableside. Diners willing to arrive early can take advantage of early dinner specials, and Twins fans can get their burgers and beer on before games. Very expensive. ♿ 🍸 ❄

**Ruth's Chris** (612-672-9000; ruthschris.com), 920 S. 2nd Avenue. Open daily for dinner. This is one of the more economical offerings in the often-expensive steakhouse category, but the restaurant doesn't spare quality for price. Very expensive. ♿ 🍸 ❄

**Manny's** (612-339-9900; mannyssteakhouse.com), 821 Marquette Avenue (in the W Minneapolis at the Foshay; see *Lodging*). Open daily for all three meals. Manny's reinvigorated itself with a move into the heart of downtown, in the historic Foshay Tower. This is the steakhouse that provides a predinner show in the form of a meat cart and well-trained servers. Groups of up to 14 can reserve the Hideaway, a lavish private dining area. Very expensive. ♿ 🍸 ❄

**Capital Grille** (612-692-9000; thecapitalgrille.com), 801 Hennepin Avenue. Open Mon.–Fri. for lunch, daily for dinner. This is where local people of prominence go for steaks, as well as to store their personal wine selections in the cellar. Its location is convenient for theater goers. Very expensive. ♿ 🍸 ❄

**P.S. Steak** (612-886-1620; psmpls.com), 510 Groveland Avenue. Open daily for dinner. This elegant restaurant, across from the Walker Art Center, offers opulent steak options with an extensive list of steak cuts, as well as rack of lamb, pork chops, and bison. The restaurant also offers seafood towers with oysters, shrimp, mussels, langoustines, and tuna poke. There are several other dinner options, including seafood and smoked chicken, and the bar has an inventive cocktail list. Reservations for the dining room are strongly recommended, but there's also a lounge with a more limited menu that's available for walk-ins. Here you'll find the seafood towers as well as casual food times, such as a steak or lamb burger or scallop crudo. Expensive/very expensive. ♿ 🍸 ❄

**Fogo de Chao** (612-338-1344; fogodechao.com), 645 Hennepin Avenue. Open daily for lunch and dinner. This is a carnivore's fantasy swathed in Brazilian traditions. Rather than ordering from a menu, diners are served by gauchos who sidle through the restaurant, cutting meat to order off sizzling skewers. Sides are served family style, and all of this is presented as a fixed-price option. The sumptuously decorated interior, lined with murals of Brazilian ranch life, dark woods, and endless bottles of wine, inspires a true feeling of decadence. Very expensive. 🐾 ♿ 🍸 ❄

Beard Award–winning Isaac Becker, 112 Eatery continues to be a star in the local dining scene. The restaurant is small (only 48 seats), so reserve ahead and be willing to be flexible with your dining time. You'll be rewarded with choices of entrées like tagliatelle with foie gras meatballs, pan-fried skate wing with prosciutto crust, or nori-encrusted sirloin with ponzu. Expensive.

♿ 🍸 ❄ **Bar La Grassa** (612-333-3837; barlagrassa.com), 800 N. Washington Avenue. Open daily for dinner. Isaac Becker may have won the James Beard Award for his work with 112 Eatery, but he's equally admired for his work at this

# DISTILLERIES

Just as with breweries, there's been a strong surge in the growth of local distilleries in Minneapolis in recent years. Here's a selection of distilleries with public cocktail rooms. None of these distilleries has a kitchen, but most welcome outside food and often have food trucks parked outside.

**Tattersall Distilling** (612-584-4152; tattersalldistilling.com), 1620 Central Avenue NE. This popular distillery is a little tricky to find, with an entrance tucked back into an alley, but it's worth the effort. This highly creative distillery produces whiskey, gin, vodka, rum, and aquavit, along with several specialty liqueurs, such as the Bootlegger—a vodka blended with lemon, lime, and mint.

**Norseman Distillery** (612-568-6299; norsemandistillery.com), 451 Taft Street NE. Norseman was the first legal distillery in Minneapolis since Prohibition and today produces vodka, gin, whiskey, and aquavit, and a variety of specialty items as well, including coffee liqueur and pineapple chipotle gin. Bring your dog.

**Du Nord Craft Spirits** (612-799-9166; dunordcraftspirits.com), 2610 E. 32nd Street. Makers of award-winning gin and vodka, Du Nord also offers specialty items that include a blended whiskey and a Framboise.

**Twin Spirits Distillery** (612-353-5274; twinspirits.us), 2931 Central Avenue NE. Twin Spirits is the first one-woman-owned distillery in town. The distillery produces vodka, gin, whiskey, rum, and Mamma's Moonshine, a honey-based moonshine distilled once a month on the full moon.

**Brother Justus Whiskey Company** (612-886-1658; brotherjustus.com), 451 Taft Street NE. Single malt whiskey, from an underground distillery named after Brother Justus, a historical folk hero monk who supposedly helped farmers survive by building whiskey stills during Prohibition and giving them to farmers who were in dire straits.

nearby restaurant. Bar La Grassa has an extensive and innovative Italian menu, with choices including soft eggs and lobster bruschetta, pasta negra with sea urchin, chili, and mussels or 'nduja egg raviolo. Some dishes are made with dry pastas, others with fresh; the pasta dishes are all available in half portions. Expensive.

&#9831; &#9826; &#10048; **Spoon and Stable** (612-224-9850; spoonandstable.com), 211 N. 1st Street. Open daily for dinner, Sun. for brunch. Chef/owner Gavin Kaysen opened this restaurant to great acclaim, with cuisine rooted in local culture and seasonal ingredients, but prepared with Kaysen's French cuisine training. The restaurant was listed as one of *Food & Wine*'s 40 Most Important Restaurants of the Past 40 Years, and Kaysen took home the Best Midwest Chef James Beard Award in 2018. The menu changes regularly, but sample

items include rabbit pate, foie gras pavlova, ravioli verde with braised guinea hen, and a spice-crusted duck breast. Reservations are hard to get and should be planned in advance. Expensive/very expensive.

&#9831; &#9826; &#10048; **Tullibee** (651-468-0600; hewinghotel.com/tullibee-restaurant), 300 N. Washington Avenue. Open daily for all three meals. The highly regarded Tullibee is part of the **Hewing Hotel** (see *Where to Stay*), and is far more than the average hotel restaurant. Big draws are the wood-fired grill and the rooftop patio, giving views into Target Field. Tullibee focuses on local sourcing and seasonal offerings, and the menu could include heritage breed pork with rhubarb and green garlic, duck breast with morel mushrooms, or slow-braised rabbit. The restaurant's bar has a lounge menu including duck fat French fries and a hot-fried chicken sandwich, as well as an impressive list of stellar cocktails. Expensive/very expensive.

## SOUTH

& ⅋ ❀ **Chino Latino** (612-824-7878; chinolatino.com), 2916 Hennepin Avenue S. Open daily for dinner. Chino Latino pulls off a melding of Asian and Hispanic cuisine while maintaining its cutting-edge social reputation. Expect crowds and a noisy atmosphere, but also expect to have an exciting culinary experience. Go with a group and order one of the many bigger dishes to share, including Point Steak Bibimbap or the Swingers Party Platter. Expensive.

& ✐ ⅋ ❀ **Fuji Ya** (612-871-4055; fujiya sushi.com), 600 W. Lake Street. Open Tues.–Sun. for dinner. Fuji Ya has been around the Twin Cities for more than 50 years and is still considered an essential part of the Japanese food scene there. One major draw is the Japanese tearooms (reservations are a must), in which diners can enjoy their dinner quietly in a small, enclosed room, sitting on the floor in the traditional Japanese way. But tearoom or no tearoom, Fuji Ya serves some of the best Japanese food in the state. Their sushi is top quality, freshly made to order, and beautifully presented. But beyond sushi, Fuji Ya also shines, with a wide variety of Japanese salads, noodle and poke bowls, bulgogi, and meat and seafood entrées. Possibly because so much care is taken with preparation, service is slow; be prepared to relax and enjoy. Expensive.

& ⅋ ❀ **Tenant** (612-827-8111; tenant mpls.com), 4300 Bryant Avenue S. Open for dinner Tues.–Sat. This small restaurant offers a six-course, fixed-price menu that at time of publication was $50 per person with optional drink pairings. The menu changes with the seasons, especially with availability of summer vegetables. Very expensive.

**EATING OUT** There are almost countless options for more casual, less expensive quality dining throughout Minneapolis. What follows should be viewed as great suggestions rather than a fully comprehensive list.

## DINKYTOWN

✐ & ❀ **Al's Breakfast** (612-331-9991; alsbreakfastmpls.com), 413 14th Avenue SE. Open daily for breakfast. A miniscule venue with just 14 seats, Al's nearly always has a wait, but the fare is worth it. However, service can be less than friendly. Don't miss the pancakes. Inexpensive.

✐ & ⅋ ❀ **Loring Bar & Restaurant** (612-378-4849; loringbarrestaurant.com), 327 14th Avenue S. Open daily for dinner; Sat.–Sun. for brunch. Tucked into the Dinkytown/University of Minnesota area, the Loring serves global food and pastas in a sumptuous interior. Sunday nights feature a live flamenco band, and Tuesday is Date Night, with a $30 dinner for two. Moderate.

✐ ❀ **Annie's Parlour** (612-379-0744; annies-parlour-minneapolis.sites.table hero.com), 313 14th Avenue SE. Open daily for lunch and dinner. This friendly café has been a Dinkytown/University of Minnesota fixture for decades, and for good reason; the burgers and fries are close to perfect (especially the Plaza Burger, with sour cream, chives, and onions), but save room for the hot fudge sundaes—the hot fudge is so delicious, you won't need the ice cream. Inexpensive.

## DOWNTOWN

✐ & ⅋ ❀ **Hell's Kitchen** (612-332-4700; hellskitcheninc.com), 89 S. 9th Street. Open daily for all three meals. Hell's Kitchen is a Gothic haunt in downtown Minneapolis. The signature "damn good" breakfast foods can't be beat, and weekend servers might show up for work in their PJs. Live music is frequently offered in the spacious bar. If you can only go once, go for breakfast and try the lemon-ricotta hotcakes or the huevos

# OUTDOOR EATING

Whether it's because Minnesota is a state rich in the bounty of the natural world or because the winter months make everyone long to be outside, Minnesotans are very fond of eating outdoors. The good news is that many restaurants have options for doing just that; the bad news is often the outdoor venues are as dismal as seating on a sidewalk adjacent to a busy road with heavy bus traffic or overlooking vast asphalt parking lots. Here's a quick list of places where excellent food—and excellent outdoor views—have come together perfectly.

**Brit's Pub** (612-332-3908; britspub.com), 1110 Nicollet Mall. Open daily for lunch and dinner. A casual British pub with exemplary British dishes (fish-and-chips, ploughman's lunch), Brit's also has a rooftop bowling green surrounded by tables and umbrellas. The bowling green isn't just for looks—there are leagues that play throughout the summer. It's a bit of British refinement above the city. Moderate. ✍ ᕕ ♈ ✸

**Black Forest Inn** (612-872-0812; blackforestinnmpls.com), 1 E. 26th Street. Open daily for lunch and dinner. This neighborhood standby, serving up great German food since 1965, has an unexpectedly charming garden hidden behind the main restaurant. Moderate. ✍ ᕕ ♈ ✸

**Psycho Suzi's Motor Lounge and Tiki Garden** (612-788-9069; psychosuzis.com), 1900 Marshall Street NE. Open daily for lunch and dinner. Psycho Suzi's has a wonderful tiki bar patio overlooking the Mississippi River, along with cheerfully excessive food and tropical drinks. Moderate. ✍ ᕕ ♈ ✸

**Sea Salt Eatery** (612-721-8990; seasalteatery.com), 4825 Minnehaha Avenue. Open daily for lunch and dinner, roughly Apr.–Oct., depending on weather. Sea Salt is perfectly placed in the lovely Minnehaha Park overlooking Minnehaha Falls. Try a po'boy sandwich, large enough for two, but go early—the lines start forming before it opens on sunny days. Moderate. ✍ ᕕ ♈

rancheros; in either case, get a side of toasted sausage bread with house-made peanut butter. Moderate.

ᕕ ♈ ✸ **Barrio Tequila Bar** (612-333-9953; barriotequila.com), 925 Nicollet Avenue (with locations in St. Paul and Edina, as well as the Minneapolis–St. Paul International Airport and Target Field). Open daily for lunch and dinner. An enormous tequila list (and well-versed servers who can explain the different kinds) is well matched to its small plates menu of reasonably priced (and tasty) tacos and enchiladas. Moderate.

ᕕ ✍ ✸ ♈ **Pizza Lucé** (612-333-7359, 119 N. 4th Street; 612-827-5978, 3200 S. Lyndale Avenue; 612-332-2525, 2200 E. Franklin Avenue; with other locations in Hopkins, St. Paul, and Duluth; pizzaluce.com). Open daily for lunch and dinner. From lunch to late night, Pizza Lucé serves some of the best pizza the Twin Cities offers, along with substantive

hoagies and pastas. Whether you prefer traditional pizzas or feel adventurous, Pizza Lucé has something for you. This is also a good spot for vegans, with several non-animal-product offerings. Inexpensive.

## NORTHEAST

ᕕ ✍ ✸ ♈ **The Sample Room** (612-789-0333; the-sample-room.com), 2124 Marshall Street NE. Open daily for lunch and dinner. A casual noshing spot located in a historic building in the Northeast area. The eclectic menu includes one of the best meat loaf dinners ever. Inexpensive.

ᕕ ✍ ✸ ♈ **Gorkha Palace** (612-886-3451; gorkhapalace.com), 23 4th Street NE. Open Mon.–Sat. for lunch, daily for dinner. Nepali, Indian, and Tibetan foods cooked with no MSG and full of lively combinations. Don't miss the momos, a Nepali version of a pot sticker. Moderate.

&#x267F; &#x2702; &#x2698; **Kramarczuk Sausage Company** (612-379-3018; kramarczuks.com), 215 E. Hennepin Avenue. Open daily for lunch and dinner. This cafeteria-style restaurant specializes in eastern European foods, often made with the adjoining food store's top-notch sausages and meats. Inexpensive.

&#x267F; &#x2702; &#x2698; **Brasa Rotisserie** (612-379-3030; brasa.us), 600 E. Hennepin Avenue (with another location in St. Paul). Open daily for lunch and dinner. Meat eaters can't go wrong here with the succulent, Caribbean-flavored rotisserie offerings. But vegetarians will find plenty to eat from the hearty sides, including yams, yucca, and plantains. Moderate.

&#x267F; &#x2702; &#x2698; &#x1F374; **The Anchor Fish and Chips** (612-676-1300; theanchorfishandchips.com), 302 13th Avenue NE. Open Tues.–Sun. for dinner, Sat. and Sun. for lunch. Fish and chips, perfectly done, are the draw here, but other pub items—curry or gravy chips, pasties, shepherd's pie—are also well worth trying. This popular restaurant usually involves a wait to be seated. Moderate.

&#x267F; &#x2702; &#x2698; &#x1F374; **Gardens of Salonica** (612-378-0611; gardensofsalonica.com), 19 5th Street NE. Open Tues.–Sat. for lunch and dinner. Traditional and contemporary Greek food, with standard favorites like gyros and more unusual offerings like bougatsa and tarama. Moderate.

&#x267F; &#x2698; &#x1F374; **Young Joni** (612-345-5719; youngjoni.com), 165 13th Avenue NE. Open daily for dinner, Sat.–Sun. for lunch. Helmed by James Beard Award–winning Ann Kim (also of **Pizzeria Lola**, see *South*), Young Joni offers a robust roster of gourmet pizzas (broccolini, lamb, and La Parisienne, which includes prosciutto, gruyere, brown butter, arugula, and pickled mustard seeds) as well as entrées such as Thai sausage skewers and pork belly ssam. The Back Bar has a drink menu full of cheeky drinks: Goldendoodle Puppies, Birk's Tanning Salon Liquidation Sale, and I Love New York T-Shirt. Reservations

## FOOD TRUCKS

Food trucks are a relatively new development in the metro, but once they gained a foothold, they became hugely popular. Today you can find trucks serving high-quality sausage, tacos, pasties, soup, sushi, coffee, vegan entrées, all manner of Asian and Indian foods, fish and chips, ice cream, donuts, pizza—you name it, you can probably find it on a truck. An easy way to see what's available is to visit downtown Minneapolis, especially around Marquette Avenue and 2nd Street during weekday lunch hours—you'll find a flock them then. They can also frequently be found around breweries and distilleries and at several metro farm markets.

recommended for this local hot spot. Moderate.

### NORTH LOOP

&#x267F; &#x2702; &#x2698; &#x1F374; **Black Sheep Coal-Fired Pizza** (612-342-2625; blacksheeppizza.com), 600 N. Washington Avenue (with locations on Eat Street and in St. Paul). Open daily for lunch and dinner. Black Sheep's top-notch coal-fired pizzas come with creative topping choices, such as chicken and pickled peppers, oyster mushrooms, harissa, and Persian beef. The Farmers' Market Salad is always worth asking about, since it changes with the season and market availability. Moderate.

&#x267F; &#x2702; &#x1F374; &#x2698; **Red Rabbit** (612-767-8855; redrabbitmn.com), 201 N. Washington Avenue (another location in St. Paul). Open daily for lunch and dinner. Italian foods done with panache. The wood-grilled oysters and pizzas are both worth a visit. Moderate.

&#x267F; &#x2702; &#x1F374; &#x2698; **Smack Shack** (612-259-7288; smack-shack.com), 603 N. Washington Avenue. Open daily for lunch and dinner. Smack Shack got its start as a food truck and pop-up eatery, doing lobster boils at a dive bar in Northeast Minneapolis.

# MULTICULTURAL FOOD

Going deeper into Northeast, away from downtown, you'll come across a strip of diverse and exciting restaurants that draw visitors from all over the metro, for good reason.

**Holy Land Deli** (612-781-2627; holylandbrand.com), 2513 Central Avenue NE (with another outlet at the Midtown Global Market). Open daily for all three meals. Half restaurant, half grocery store, and wholly worth the drive, Holy Land Deli doesn't look like much from the outside, but drop by for the hearty and flavorful lunch and dinner options (the traditional dishes of gyros, souvlaki, and shawarma are all delicious, but don't overlook the stellar rotisserie chicken), then pop into the grocery side for Middle Eastern staples not found elsewhere. Inexpensive. ♿ ✎ ❄

**Sen Yai Sen Lek** (612-781-3046; senyai-senlek.com), 2422 Central Avenue NE. Open Mon.–Sat. for lunch and dinner. The restaurant's name means "big noodle, little noodle," which is apt: On the menu are Thai noodles and sticky rice dishes, flavorful and authentic, served at reasonable prices. There are plenty of vegetarian options. Moderate. ♿ ✎ ❄ Y

**El Taco Riendo** (612-781-3000; eltaco-riendo.com), 2412 Central Avenue NE. Open daily for lunch and dinner. An extensive and inexpensively priced menu will please diners who want their Mexican food to be authentic as well as those who prefer it Americanized. Portions are enormous. Inexpensive. ♿ ✎ ❄ Y

**Chimborazo** (612-788-1328; chimborazorestaurant.com), 2851 Central Avenue NE. Open daily for lunch and dinner, Sat. and Sun. for breakfast. Ecuadorean foods, served in hearty portions, from a menu created by the Ecuadorean owner. Inexpensive. ♿ ✎ ❄ Y

**Kieran's Kitchen Northeast** (612-354-5093; kieranskitchen.com), 117 14th Avenue NE. Open daily for all three meals. Located in the Food Building, this eatery uses the products of the building's other occupants (Baker's Field Flour & Bread, Red Table Meats, Alemar Cheese Company) to create delectable items including breakfast poutine, pancetta meatballs, and stellar sandwiches and pastas (try the NE Italian sandwich). Moderate. ♿ ✎ ❄ Y

Once in its own space, the culinary team went whole-heartedly into coastal seafood concepts, offering ceviche, poke, lobster poutine, and its famous and loved lobster roll. Moderate/expensive.

♿ ✎ Y ❄ **Borough** (612-354-3135; boroughmpls.com), 730 N. Washington Avenue. Open Mon.–Sat. for dinner, Mon.–Fri. for lunch, and Sat.–Sun. for brunch. A restaurant focused on local and whole-animal butchery (and a menu that changes frequently), Borough offers a number of small plates to allow diners a wider array of exploration. Guests might find sea urchin with chorizo, braised radishes with taggiasca and pesto, or duck breast with celeriac. On Friday and Saturday evenings, a trolley is brought into the dining room by a chef with additional small-plate offerings. Moderate/expensive.

♿ ✎ Y ❄ **Snack Bar** (612-383-2848; snackbarmpls.com), 800 N. Washington Avenue. Open daily for dinner. Simple foods done beautifully at reasonable prices. Try the Arctic char carpaccio or pressed game hen, or a myriad of pizzas by the slice or whole. Moderate.

## SOUTH

♿ ✎ ❄ Y **Pizza Lucé** (612-827-5978; pizza luce.com), 3200 S. Lyndale Avenue. Open daily for lunch and dinner. See the listing in Downtown for details.

♿ ✎ ❄ Y **Pizzeria Lola** (612-424-8338; pizzerialola.com), 5557 Xerxes Avenue S. Open daily for lunch and dinner. This highly regarded pizza spot is run by James Beard Award–winner Ann Kim, also of **Young Joni** (see page 59). Quirky, delicious pizzas, including a Korean pizza with house-made kimchi and the Sunnyside—served with soft eggs. Moderate.

  ♿ ✎ ☥ ❄ **El Burrito Mercado** (612-286-8089; elburritompls.com), 4820 Chicago Avenue. Open daily for dinner, Thurs.–Sun. for lunch. The Minneapolis outpost of the long-time West St. Paul stalwart (see "District del Sol Dining" on page 99), El Burrito Mercado has some Americanized Mexican options, but what you really want is the more authentic dishes: pozole, sopes, and tortas. Don't forget to add a margarita or one of the Mexican cocktails. Moderate.

  ♿ ☥ ❄ **Hammer & Sickle** (612-367-4035; hammerandsicklempls.com), 1300 Lagoon Avenue. Open daily for dinner. Upscale Russian food, with the traditional foods given contemporary updates. Try the assorted meat or fish platters, along with the shashlik (Russian BBQ skewers). Be sure to peruse the lengthy vodka menu, which includes offerings from Russia, America, Europe, and Asia. Several vodka flights are offered as well. Moderate/expensive.

  ♿ ✎ ☥ ❄ **Revival** (612-345-4516; revivalrestaurants.com), 4257 Nicollet Avenue (second location in St. Paul). Open daily for lunch and dinner. This local favorite was the first to drop serious southern-fried chicken into the Twin Cities market, including the aptly named Poultrygeist Hot (you can ask for a taste of the spice mix before ordering the chicken—it's powerful). The chicken is revelatory, but the starters and sides sold with them aren't something to ignore either. Get the fried oysters, pimento cheese and meat plate, grits, and cheddar drop biscuits. Moderate.

  ♿ ✎ ❄ ☥ **Tilia** (612-354-2806; tiliampls.com), 2726 W. 43rd Street. Open daily for lunch and dinner, Sat. and Sun. for breakfast. This neighborhood gem in the Linden Hills area opened to long lines and great acclaim. Its sophisticated menu with thoughtful preparation goes

## MIDTOWN GLOBAL MARKET

**M**idtown Global Market (midtownglobalmarket.org), Lake Street and Chicago Avenue. Open daily for all three meals (restaurants open for meals vary). The Midtown Global Market represents a major effort on the part of the city to not only revitalize a faltering neighborhood and restore a long-vacant Sears tower, but also to pay tribute to the ever-growing multicultural and culinary diversity in the area. Most of the food outlets here are quick-service, but they have surprisingly good quality and reasonable prices. This is an excellent place to wander on a weekend afternoon, trying different cuisines while taking in the live music or dancing in the central plaza. Places to try include Holy Land Deli, Salsa a La Salsa, Jakeeno's Trattoria, and Manny's Tortas, all of which have restaurants in other parts of the Twin Cities; also worthy of a stop are La Loma Tamales, Safari Express, Taqueria Los Ocampo, Pham's Rice Bowl, Hot Indian Foods, Moroccan Flavors, and Taco Cat. New arrival La Michoacana Purepecha brings its 50-plus homemade paletas and 30-plus flavors of ice cream, yogurt, chicharrones, and more. Whatever you choose, finish it off with dessert from Grand Italian Ice. ♿ ✎ ❄ ☥

hand in hand with a kids' menu that allows for family meals without choosing the lowest common denominator. Moderate.

  ♿ ✎ ☥ ❄ **Victor's 1959 Café** (612-827-8948; victors1959cafe.com), 3756 Grand Avenue S. Open daily for lunch and breakfast. If you've got a hankering for Cuban and Latin American food, Victor's is the place to go. It's tiny—you can expect to wait when it's busy—but it also has a small but attractive patio. Bonus: Kids are encouraged to draw on the walls. Get the Bistec Criollo or sweet plantain omelette along with a side of Cuban toast. Inexpensive.

# EAT STREET

**N**one of these restaurants clustered together over several blocks on Nicollet Avenue just outside of downtown are formal. But they do make up a broad multicultural swath, mostly at reasonable prices and of excellent quality. You could spend days exploring the world in just a few blocks.

**Bad Waitress** (612-872-7575; thebadwaitress.com), 2 E. 26th Street (with another location in Northeast Minneapolis). Open daily for all three meals. The name might seem like a warning, but actually it's a tease: Diners fill out their own order sheets at their tables and turn them in to the cashier to get their choice of delectable pancakes and sandwiches. Inexpensive. ♿ ✆ ❋ ⅄

**Peninsula Malaysian Cuisine** (612-871-8282; peninsulamalaysiancuisine.com), 2608 Nicollet Avenue. Open daily for lunch and dinner. Offers a broad and fascinating overview of Malaysian food. Prices are surprisingly low, given the range of food options. The soups and noodle dishes are especially recommended. Moderate. ♿ ✆ ❋ ⅄

**Christos** (612-871-2111; christos.com), 2632 Nicollet Avenue S. (with another location in Minnetonka). Open daily for lunch and dinner. Serves a solid Greek menu, from the traditional gyros and hummus to lamb, chicken, and pork dishes as well as a lengthy vegetarian menu. Moderate. ♿ ✆ ❋ ⅄

**Quang** (612-870-4739; quang-restaurant.com), 2719 Nicollet Avenue S. Open Wed.–Mon. for lunch and dinner. Provides banh mi sandwiches and jumbo Vietnamese noodle bowls, delicious and inexpensive, although the service is not always friendly. Friday is a popular day, as it's the only day the sea bass soup is offered. Inexpensive. ♿ ✆ ❋ ⅄

**Rainbow Chinese** (612-870-7084; rainbowrestaurant.com), 2739 Nicollet Avenue. Open Tues.–Sun. for dinner, Sat.–Sun. for lunch. The prices are quite reasonable for top-notch food at this casual but nice Chinese restaurant, a longtime Eat Street staple. Moderate. ♿ ✆ ❋ ⅄

**Pho 79** (612-871-4602), 2529 Nicollet Avenue. Open daily for lunch and dinner. Serves heaping bowls of Vietnamese pho, perfectly seasoned. Wear easy-wash clothing, as slurping your soup can get messy, but it's worth it. Inexpensive. ♿ ✆ ❋ ⅄

EAT STREET

&#9855; &#9998; &#10042; &#9884; **Broder's Pasta Bar and Deli** (612-925-9202; broders.com), 5000 Penn Avenue S. Open daily for dinner. Broder's is a reasonably priced neighborhood pasta bistro with far-above-average offerings. Each pasta dish is cooked to order with freshly made pasta and imaginative sauces. Across the street is Broder's Deli, open for lunch and take-out daily. Stop by for some lunch to take to Lake Harriet for a perfect afternoon picnic. Moderate.

&#9855; &#9998; &#10042; **The Zumbro** (612-920-3606; zumbrocafe.com) 2803 W. 43rd Street. Open Tues.–Sun. for breakfast and lunch. This small café in the Linden Hills neighborhood near Lake Harriet is something of a local tradition that's been around more than 20 years. The specialty is breakfast (the huevos and eggs Benedict are both popular, and the pancakes are a local favorite), and a limited breakfast menu is available over the lunch hour as well, but you'd miss out on the gourmet sandwiches, soups, and salads. Moderate.

&#9855; &#9998; &#9884; &#10042; **Geek Love Cafe** (612-642-1267; moonpalacebooks.com), 3032 Minnehaha Avenue. Open daily for all three meals. Tucked away in the back of Moon Palace Books, Geek Love Cafe has a surprisingly large and excellent food menu, along with beer and wine. Vegans and vegetarians will also find plenty of choices here, although carnivores won't suffer. Breakfasts are enormous and delicious, and the café's pizzas are stellar as well. Moderate.

&#9855; &#9998; &#10042; **The Egg and I** (612-872-7282; eggandimn.com), 2828 Lyndale Avenue S. (with another location in St. Paul). Open daily for breakfast and lunch. The Egg and I knows a thing or two about breakfasts. Their pancakes are huge and fluffy; their egg dishes are perfectly cooked in generous portions. Lunch is served, but breakfast is what you'll want. Inexpensive.

&#9855; &#9998; &#10042; **Jinx Tea** (612-367-4797; jinxtea.com), 4503 France Avenue S. Open daily from lunchtime through dinnertime. As has happened often in the metro area,

BREAKFAST AT GEEK LOVE CAFE

this venue began life as a food truck and morphed into a brick-and-mortar location. The tearoom offers a line of innovative tea drinks, including bubble teas and teas flavored like popular cocktails. Inexpensive.

&#9855; &#9998; &#9884; &#10042; **Prieto Taquerio Bar** (612-428-7231; prietotaqueria.com), 701 W. Lake Street. Open daily for lunch, Mon.–Thurs. for dinner. Authentic Mexican dishes, all made from scratch. The lengua tacos and brisket empanadas are especially recommended. Moderate.

## &#10042; Entertainment

**LIVE PERFORMANCES** Minneapolis is a theater- and music-lover's town. From large, internationally renowned companies like the Guthrie Theater and the Children's Theatre Company, arena rock at the Target Center and US Bank Stadium, and the theaters that host Broadway tours to smaller inventive and experimental groups like the Jungle Theater and the intimate jazz space of the Dakota Jazz Club, there's something for every taste.

♿ ✎ ❄ ♀ ¶ **The Guthrie Theater** (612-377-2224 or 1-877-447-8243; guthrie theater.org), 818 S. 2nd Street. This internationally renowned theater company has three separate stage areas, as well as what is considered to be some of the city's top-end dining with **Sea Change** (see *Where to Eat*). The Wurtele Thrust Stage hosts large-scale productions, such as classics and musicals, while the McGuire Proscenium Stage hosts more contemporary works, as well as productions from touring companies. The Dowling Studio acts as a training ground for University of Minnesota and Guthrie Theater acting students. Even if you don't want to see a particular play, a visit to the building itself is worth the time; the dramatic Endless Bridge, a cantilevered lobby with spectacular views of the Mississippi River falls, is a perfect place to start, followed by a stop at one of the building's restaurants or bars. Most of the public spaces are open to the public every day except Monday, even when no play is in production.

♿ ✎ ❄ **The Children's Theatre Company** (612-874-0400; childrenstheatre .org), 2400 S. 3rd Avenue. The CTC has an international reputation for its outstanding and innovative productions. The theater itself is adjacent to the **Minneapolis Institute of Art** (see *To See and Do*). Appropriately family friendly, the stage area has comfortable stadium seating with extra spacing between rows—helpful when transporting young children to the bathrooms during productions with minimal discomfort to other theatergoers. Snacks and coffee are sold in the lobby during intermission and after the show. Each season includes a variety of productions geared toward different age groups. Some of the classics that appear periodically include *The 500 Hats of Bartholomew Cubbins* (which leaves both kids and adults wondering, "How did they do that?"), *How the Grinch Stole Christmas*, and *A Year With Frog and Toad*. Parking is available in a ramp next to the theater, but arrive early; the spaces are limited, and on busy museum

THE CHILDREN'S THEATRE COMPANY

days, the competition for those spots is heavy. Street parking is also available.

 ♿ ⚲ ❄ **The Cowles Center for Dance** (612-206-3600; thecowlescenter.org), 528 Hennepin Avenue. This performing arts venue in town is the realization of a decades-long effort to rehabilitate two run-down historic buildings in downtown Minneapolis and join them with a third building as an education center. The Cowles is home to the Minnesota Dance Theater, James Sewell Ballet, Illusion Theater, and Zenon Dancy Company & School. Besides showcasing the works of those groups, the Cowles Center also hosts touring dance troupes and other performing arts groups.

♿ ⚲ ❄ 🍸 **The Hennepin Theatre District** (612-339-7007; hennepintheatredistrict.org). The district is made up of a series renovated theaters in downtown Minneapolis: the **State**, the **Orpheum**, and the **Pantages**, all located between 7th and 10th streets on Hennepin Avenue. The Orpheum and the State are Minneapolis's home base for Broadway touring productions as well as headlining music, magic, and comedy acts. Pantages is home to an intimate concert venue for touring musicians.

♿ ❄ **The Jungle Theater** (612-822-7063; jungletheater.com), 2951 Lyndale Avenue S. A small (150 seats), award-winning theater focused on intimate productions, mainly of a contemporary nature, and occasional musical performances. The Jungle is also known for commissioning and producing new works.

♿ ⚲ ❄ 🍸 **Northrop Auditorium** (612-624-2345; northrop.umn.edu), 84 Church Street SE. Situated at the top of Northrop Mall on the University of Minnesota's East Bank, Northrop's stately architecture gives access to a wide variety of performances: musicians of nearly every genre, comedians, and the annual Northrop Dance Series, which features a diverse selection of touring and local dance troupes.

♿ ⚲ ❄ 🍸 **Target Center** (612-673-0900; targetcenter.com), 600 N. 1st Avenue. Home to the Minnesota Timberwolves and the Minnesota Lynx (see *Sporting Events*) as well as many touring musical acts. There are two large parking ramps connected by skyway, and Target Center also offers a "parent's room" for adults who bring their offspring to concerts that the parent doesn't necessarily want to attend. Some of the music industry's most popular performers stop here, but it's not because of the great acoustics; St. Paul's Xcel Centre is a much better musical setting. But when that certain band comes to town, Target Center may be where they end up playing, even if the acoustics aren't ideal.

♿ ❄ 🍸 **Brave New Workshop** (612-332-6620; bravenewworkshop.com), 824 Hennepin Avenue. The long-standing home of improvisational and sketch comedy on Hennepin Avenue near Uptown. The company develops and produces original shows made up of several short pieces built around one theme, usually societal or political, with scathing humor. Weekend shows often have improv after the official performances. Beer, wine, and snacks available for purchase at the theater.

♿ ❄ 🍸 **Fine Line Music Café** (612-338-8388; finelinemusic.com), 318 N. 1st Avenue. Located in the Consortium Building, a historic site near the North Loop, the Fine Line quickly established itself as a first-rate music club, showcasing both local and national performers. This is not so much a dance club as an actual music club; Lady Gaga, the Pixies, the Cowboy Junkies, the Avett Brothers, and the Neville Brothers have all performed here. Acoustics are great, and the ambience is calmer than at nearby First Avenue (listing follows).

♿ ❄ 🍸 **Dakota Jazz Club & Restaurant** (612-332-5299; dakotacooks.com), 1010 Nicollet Avenue. Located right in the heart of downtown Minneapolis. Truly a jazz and blues lover's haven, the Dakota has a packed schedule of musicians in its intimate performance space, and it offers excellent food as well. Notable performers include Bettye LaVette, Nachito Herrera, Michael Feinstein, and Jearlyn Steele.

& ☀ ☥ **First Avenue** (612-332-1775; first-avenue.com), 701 N. 1st Avenue. The granddaddy of rock venues. Still operating at its original location, the nationally acclaimed First Avenue continues to serve the rock and alternative scene with both major players and up-and-coming musicians, including a wide range of local groups. And, of course, it's where Prince filmed the *Purple Rain* concert scenes. This bar is truly about the music—the environment does not lend itself well to comfort, and the smell of stale beer permeates the air. If ambience is what you want, this isn't the place. But for a true rock music experience, it can't be beat.

& ☀ **The Varsity Theater** (612-217-7701; varsitytheater.org), 1308 4th Street SE. Located in the University of Minnesota's Dinkytown neighborhood, the Varsity is rapidly becoming another popular destination for local and smaller touring bands. Although heavily frequented by U of MN students, the Varsity is by no means college only; the theater has been lauded for its sound and light systems and for its comfortable interior, as well as its willingness to book a wide variety of acts.

& ☀ ☥ **Part Wolf** (612-338-6424; partwolfmpls.com), 501 Cedar Avenue. Part Wolf is a neighborhood venue determined to provide a wide range of cultural activities, including live music ranging from rap to bluegrass, LGBTQIA dance parties, and bocce leagues.

& ☀ ☥ **The Cedar Cultural Center** (612-338-2674; thecedar.org), 416 Cedar Avenue S. The Cedar has had a lasting impact on the Twin Cities live-music scene, presenting musicians from all over the world.

& ☀ ☥ ⅋ **El Nuevo Rodeo** (612-728-0101; elnuevorodeo.com), 2709 E. Lake Street. An example of the growing Hispanic influence on the Twin Cities, restaurant and nightclub El Nuevo Rodeo

provides live Latin music and a lively Mexican menu.

& ⌀ ☀ ☥ ⅋ **Bryant-Lake Bowl** (612-825-3737; bryantlakebowl.com), 810 W. Lake Street. Yes, it's a bowling alley. But it's a bowling alley with a cabaret theater that hosts musicians, comics, writer's readings, and dance. Note: Many performances are not appropriate for children.

SPORTING EVENTS & ⌀ ☥ ⅋ **Target Field** (612-659-3400), 1 Twins Way. The Minnesota Twins baseball team is headquartered in this outdoor stadium, a beauty on the north edge of downtown and within easy reach of light rail and buses. Target Field is not only an attractive venue, it's popular—plan ahead to get tickets for specific games. Once inside, you'll be well fed; several local food purveyors were tapped to come up with better-than-average stadium-food offerings.

& ⌀ ☀ ☥ **Target Center** (612-673-1600; targetcenter.com), 600 N. 1st Avenue. Home to the Minnesota Timberwolves men's basketball team and the Minnesota Lynx women's basketball team. The Wolves and Lynx both have loyal fan bases; call ahead for tickets. Target Center also hosts touring sports exhibitions, such as figure skating and the timeless Harlem Globetrotters.

& ⌀ ☀ ☥ **US Bank Stadium** (612-777-8700; usbankstadium.com), 401 Chicago Avenue. Opened in 2016, US Bank Stadium is home to the Minnesota Vikings and has hosted the Super Bowl and the Final Four. It's also hosted a wide range of musical performers, from Metallica to Kanye West to Garth Brooks.

& ⌀ ☀ **The Minnesota Gophers** (gophersports.com). The official sports teams of the University of Minnesota are spread out across several athletic facilities, including US Bank Stadium and the university-sited Mariucci Arena, Williams Arena, and the TCF Bank Stadium.

& ⌀ **North Star Roller Derby** (northstarrollerderby.com), Minneapolis

# THE NORTHEAST MINNEAPOLIS ARTS DISTRICT

Arts are alive and well across the Twin Cities (and the rest of the state), but one area where they're really flourishing is in northeast Minneapolis, where a number of artist's studios have sprung up in historic buildings, many of which were built 100-plus years ago. Each of the following has multiple artists actively working. Hours of exhibit depend on the artist; see the websites or call for specific open information.

**Northrup King Building** (northrupkingbuilding.com), 1500 Jackson Street NE. This large complex originally belonged to the Northrup King seed company and is home to more than 300 artists as well as several nonprofits and entrepreneurs. Artists set their own hours; see the website for info.

**California Building** (californiabuilding.com), 2205 California Street NE. Housed in a former grain mill, the California is home to more than 80 artists and offers monthly open studios and other events.

**Casket Arts Building** (casketarts.com), 681 17th Avenue NE. Former home of the Northwestern Casket Company, Casket Arts provides studios for more than 140 artists and offers several public events.

**Van Buren Building**, 1400 Van Buren Street NE. Van Buren has a smaller number of artists coexisting with several companies, but the lovingly restored building itself is worth a visit.

**Grain Belt Studios** (612-401-4506; artspace.org/grain-belt), 77 13th Avenue NE. It used to be the Grain Belt bottling house and warehouse; now it's home to 30 artists who exhibit periodically, as well as a theater company called Dark & Stormy Productions.

Convention Center. They're wild and fierce, and they love their sport. The current teams operating under the North Star name include the Banger Sisters, Kilmore Girls, Violent Femmes, and Delta Delta Di.

## ✳ Selective Shopping

### DOWNTOWN

The downtown area of Minneapolis is home to some large chain stores like the Saks Fifth Avenue outlet store and Target (which has its corporate headquarters downtown as well), but retail has not been a strength of the downtown area in recent years. The city's extensive network of second-floor skyways that connect many of the buildings in the center of town (very handy for inclement weather) are home to numerous small retailers, usually gift shops or small clothing boutiques. To find more of the unique little shops, heading out of downtown is the best bet.

### NORTHEAST

✳ **I Like You!** (612-208-0249; i-like-you -minneapolis.myshopify.com), 501 1st Avenue NE (another location is in St. Paul). Open daily. The tagline is "Small things for a prettier life," and the shop is full of them, from jewelry to gifts to small pieces of art. The store offers a wide variety of classes, from book binding to copper enameling to knitting and sewing simple projects. The store has a large selection of locally produced items.

✳ **Knit & Bolt** (612-788-1180; knit andbolt.com), 2833 Johnson Street NE. Open Tues.–Sun. Sewing and yarn supplies, with a definite twist of the unexpected. This is not your mother's supply shop.

✳ **Architectural Antiques** (612-332-8344; archantiques.com), 1330 Quincy Street NE. Open Mon.–Sat. Exactly what it says—antique fireplace surrounds and mantels, doors, entryways, and ecclesiastical artifacts. A fascinating place to wander through.

**❄ Key North** (612-455-6666; key
northboutique.com), 515 1st Avenue NE.
Open Mon.–Sat. Women's clothing and
accessories, with an emphasis on fair
trade, organic materials, and responsible
manufacturing.

**❄ Lightworks** (612-724-8311;
lightworkslighting.com), 1325 Winter
Street NE. Open Mon.–Sat. Even if you
don't think you're in the market for lighting, give this place a visit—it's a huge
collection of restored vintage and historically accurate redesigned lighting.

**❄ Indigo** (612-333-2151; indigompls
.com), 1400 4th Street NE. Open Tues.–
Fri. A treasure trove of Asian and Native
American arts.

## NORTH LOOP

Right on the edge of downtown are several interesting and sometimes-quirky
independent retailers. ❄ **Mitrebox
Framing Studio** (612-676-0696; mitre
boxframing.com), 213 N. Washington
Avenue. Open daily. Ostensibly a framing
shop, Mitrebox is much more than that,
with all kinds of quirky gifts, one-of-a-
kind pieces of costume jewelry, and cards.

♿ ❄ **Cooks of Crocus Hill** (612-223-
8167; cooksofcrocushill.com), 210 N. 1st
Street (other locations in St. Paul and
Stillwater). Open daily. Anything anyone
could want or need regarding cooking
and baking, along with a full slate of
classes and events.

♿ ❄ **D.NOLO** (612-584-3244; dnolo
.com), 211 N. 3rd Avenue. Open daily. A
somewhat unusual fashion store, a cooperative that houses Bluebird Boutique,
Bumbershute, Kindred, Requisite, and
Rosegold. It also offers complimentary
valet parking at the nearby Monte Carlo
restaurant.

♿ ❄ **Phenom** (612-355-2250; phenom
global.com), 115 N. Washington Avenue.
Open Mon.–Sat. Men's clothing and
shoes, focused on streetwear and offering brands such as BBC, Diamond Supply, and Crooks & Castles.

♿ ❄ **The Statement Boutique** (651-
808-7663; thestatementboutique.com),
212 3rd Avenue N. Open daily. Women's
clothing and accessories, including Sta-
cey Johnson Jewelry, Raven Stoneworks,
Kind Lips, AG Jeans, and Karen Kane.

**❄ Form + Content Gallery** (612-436-
1151; formandcontent.org), 210 N. 2nd
Street. Open Thurs.–Sat. Eclectic contemporary art.

**❄ Antiques Riverwalk** (612-339-9352),
210 N. 3rd Avenue. Open Tues.–Sun. A
multi-dealer antiques shop.

## SOUTH

🔖 ❄ **Kitchen Window** (612-824-4417;
888-824-4417; kitchenwindow.com),
3001 Hennepin Avenue. Open daily. A
longtime stalwart in Uptown's Calhoun
Square, Kitchen Window has just about
every possible kitchen gadget you need,
and a full roster of classes and events to
boot.

🔖 ❄ **Patina** (612-872-0880; patina
stores.com), 1009 W. Franklin Avenue
(with location at 5001 S. Bryant Avenue
and in Northeast Minneapolis, as well as
St. Paul and several suburbs). Open daily.
Loads of fun and quirky gifts, jewelry,
and home accessories.

**❄ The Smitten Kitten** (612-721-6088;
smittenkittenonline.com); 3010 Lyndale
Avenue S. Open daily. A sex-toy shop
with the philosophy that its wares are like
any other life-enhancing products—not
something to be ashamed of. Unlike other
shops selling such items, this one isn't
seedy, it's in a reasonably good neighborhood, and it's owned and run by women.

♿ 🔖 ❄ **Electric Fetus** (612-870-9300;
electricfetus.com), 2000 S. 4th Avenue
(with another location in Duluth). Open
daily. This longtime Minneapolis music
retailer is much loved by locals, and it
carries a wide variety of music on vinyl
and CD, new and used. It also carries a
diverse array of clothing, accessories,
and gift items. Check the store's website
for frequent in-store performances.

# INDEPENDENT BOOKSTORES

Barnes & Noble has several locations across the Twin Cities metro area, but there is a group of sturdy independent stores that are holding steady in the competitive retail book field.

**Magers & Quinn** (612-822-4611; magersandquinn.com), 3038 Hennepin Avenue. Open daily. One of the premier independents in the Twin Cities, and also one of the largest, Magers & Quinn, located in the Uptown area, sells new and used books, including collectible items. ✐ ✻

**Birchbark Books** (612-374-4023; birchbarkbooks.com), 2115 W. 21st Street. Open daily. A small, cozy, family-friendly bookstore owned by novelist Louise Erdrich. The store specializes in Native American items but also carries a good selection of fiction, nonfiction, poetry, and has a children's area with a "tree house." ✐ ✻

**Uncle Edgar's Mystery** (612-824-9984; unclehugo.com) and **Uncle Hugo's Science Fiction** (612-824-6347; unclehugo.com) Bookstores, 2864 Chicago Avenue S. Open daily. Next door to each other, Uncle Edgar's and Uncle Hugo's have developed strong followings with their extensive selections of mystery and sci-fi books. ✻

**Once Upon a Crime** (612-870-3785; onceuponacrimebooks.com), 604 W. 26th Street. Open daily. All mysteries, all the time, and a knowledgeable staff earned this store a Raven Award from the Mystery Writers of America. ✻

**Dreamhaven Books** (612-823-6161; dreamhavenbooks.com), 2301 E. 38th Street. Open Tues.–Sat. A sci-fi/fantasy/comic book shop with a busy schedule of readings and author visits from prominent writers, and they also publish a line of books.

**The Irreverent Bookworm** (612-500-4339; irrevbooks.com), 5163 Bloomington Avenue S. Open Tues.–Sun. Purveyor of new and used books and gift items, along with numerous special events. ✐ ✻

**Milkweed Books** (612-215-2540; milkweed.org/bookstore), 1011 S. Washington Avenue. Open daily. Helmed by local independent publisher Milkweed Editions, this bookstore is tucked into the ground floor of the literary outpost Open Book and offers a thoughtful variety of books from small and independent publishers, including offerings not always seen at other bookstores.

**Moon Palace Books** (612-454-0455; moonpalacebooks.com), 3032 Minnehaha Avenue. Open daily. A sizable and well-curated collection of new and used books, Moon Palace is also home to the **Geek Love Cafe** (see *Where to Eat*).

**Wild Rumpus**. See "Linden Hills Shopping" on page 70.

## ✻ Special Events

*April:* ♿ ✐ ⬆ **Minneapolis–St. Paul International Film Festival** (612-331-7563; mspfilm.org/festivals/mspiff), various locations. More than 250 films, from local filmmakers and worldwide documentarians, are presented across several venues in late April. Several events and galas are also scheduled, and discussions with film directors are offered.

*April to November:* ♿ ✐ ⬆ **Minneapolis Farmers' Markets** (612-333-1718; mplsfarmersmarket.com), 312 E. Lyndale Avenue N. Open daily 6–1, mid-Apr. to mid-Nov. While there are several offshoots around the city, this is the granddaddy of the Minneapolis farmers' market scene. It can take some patience to get there—the signature red shed roofs that are visible from the freeway don't necessarily mean it's easy to find. But a huge selection of local produce and crafts that vary throughout the season

# LINDEN HILLS SHOPPING

**T**his small neighborhood in south Minneapolis, near Lake Harriet, has several fun shops all in one place. Some of these shops have additional locations, which are noted in the description.

**Bibelot GoodThings** (612-886-3615, 4301 S. Upton Avenue; also in St. Paul; shopgoodthings .com). Open daily. Featuring gifts and novelties, Bibelot GoodThings is not just another tacky souvenir shop; it carries all kinds of guilty pleasures, from locally made jewelry to unique women's clothing to off-the-wall kitchen and bath items. Their greeting card selection is good for more than a few giggles, and there is a well-chosen line of toys for the kids. ♿ ✎ ❄

**GoodStyle** (612-925-3175, 4315 S. Upton Avenue; also in White Bear Lake; shopgood things.com). Open daily. A sister store to Bibelot GoodThings, GoodStyle offers a wide range of women's clothing and accessories. ♿ ✎ ❄

**Copilot Dog Outfitters** (612-353-4045; copilotdogoutfitters.com), 4280 Sheridan Avenue S. Open daily. Every kind of gear you could possibly need for your dog, and grooming by appointment. ♿ ✎ 🐾 ❄

**Everett & Charlie** (612-444-8706; everettandcharlie.com), 2720 W. 43rd Street. Open Wed.–Sun. or by appointment. Gallery owner Suzie Marty is a painter and supporter of art of all kinds, which she showcases in this eclectic gallery. She also offers an extensive calendar of events, including artist talks and workshops, demonstrations, trunk shows, live music, and even an occasional dinner with an artist. ♿ ❄

**Grace & Co** (952-649-8449; graceco.business.site), 4317 S. Upton Avenue. Open Wed.–Sun. An eclectic (and sometimes cheeky) collection of home wares, gifts, and accessories. ♿ ❄

**Heart of Tibet & Sky Door** (612-926-8723; heartoftibet.com), 4303 S. Upton Avenue. Open daily. This import shop carries Tibetan textiles, clothing, jewelry, musical instruments, artifacts, crystals and beads, silks, cushions, and a diverse set of classes and events. ♿ ✎ ❄

**Heartfelt** (612-877-8090; heartfeltonline.com), 4306 S. Upton Avenue. Open daily. A great place to encourage hands-on creativity in children, Heartfelt offers a full array of crafting opportunities (not just for children), as well the supplies needed to make them. Especially attractive for the young ones is the large tree house in the back of the store. ♿ ✎ 🐾 ❄

**Jimmy Wilson Gallery** (612-201-0701; jimmypicture.com), 4304 S. Upton Avenue. Open Wed.–Sun. or by appointment. A fine art gallery focused on Jimmy Wilson prints and a variety of other artists. ♿ ❄

**Coffee & Tea Ltd.** (612-920-6344; coffeeandtealtd.com), 2730 W. 43rd Street. Open daily. Don't be deceived by its hole-in-the-wall size and ambience; this little shop has an excellent variety of coffee and tea products, and the staff is passionate on the topic. ❄

**Wild Rumpus** (612-920-5005; wildrumpusbooks.com), 2720 W. 43rd Street. Open daily. One of the best children's bookstores ever, it comes complete with its own pets, including a tail-less cat and a chicken; the front door has a small-fry door as well. Whatever you need to know, just ask; the staff seems to know everything worth knowing about children's literature. ✎ ❄

make it a worthwhile visit, if nothing else than to munch on samples for bread, nuts, cheese, and syrup, as well as seasonal fruits and vegetables. While officially open mid-April to late November, there are Christmas trees and greenery available in December, and a select number of vendors sell every Saturday during the winter.

*May:* ♿ ✎ 🍷 🍸 **Art-a-Whirl** (612-788-1679; nemaa.org/art-a-whirl). This annual event, which takes place the third weekend of May, serves to highlight the growing and active Northeast Minneapolis arts community. Local and national artists exhibit their work, while visitors get to see a rich variety of art while enjoying the artistic ambience of this corner of Northeast. Numerous local breweries and bars and restaurants offer specials and live music in conjunction with the art exhibits.

*June*: ♿ ☂ ♟ 🍸 **Pride Festival and Parade** (612-255-3260; tcpride.org). This is one of the nation's largest LGBTQ pride events, occurring every year in June. The raucous parade is a centerpiece of the festival, which also includes an art show, boat cruise, picnics, and Grand Marshall's Ball. An outdoor component of the festival is held at Loring Park, with booths and tents set up with informational, retail, and food vendors.

*June*: ♿ ☂ ♟ 🍸 **Rock the Garden** (rock thegardenfestival.com). A collaboration between indie public radio station The Current and the Walker Art Center, Rock the Garden takes place at the Walker's Sculpture Garden and includes a broad mix of local and national indie musicians.

*July*: 🍸 **Basilica Block Party** (basilica blockparty.org), Hennepin Avenue and 17th Street. Who says Minnesotans can't be tolerant? This annual event, a two-day rock/pop concert sponsored in part by local radio station Cities 97, takes place on the grounds of the Basilica of St. Mary. Besides nationally prominent acts, the block party also features a fiercely competitive battle of the bands for local acts. As it takes place each year in early July, the weather is often ideal, but if not, its location on the edge of downtown is convenient to other venues if being outside becomes too much.

♿ ☂ 🍸 **Aquatennial** (612-376-7669; aquatennial.com). The Aquatennial is spread across various venues in Minneapolis. Events include a water ski show, 5K races, a Caribbean-themed fest, a torchlight parade, and extensive fireworks.

*August*: ♿ ☂ 🍸 **The Metris Uptown Art Fair** (612-823-4581; uptownartfair.com). The Twin Cities are home to several annual art fairs, but this is the biggest, busiest, and perhaps best located—within easy walking distance to Bde Maka Ska. Taking place each year in August, the three-day juried art event allows 450 artists to take their highly coveted spot near the Uptown area. Besides artists of all sorts, food and beverage vendors also set up shop. This event attracts upward of 350,000 visitors each year, so parking can be a problem; either plan to arrive early and park locally, or consult bus maps for routes from downtown. In a nice twist, recent years have seen the Uptown Art Fair join forces with two other local art fairs, the Powderhorn Park Art Fair and the Loring Park Art Fair, and complimentary city bus service is available to transport visitors among the three.

♿ ☂ 🍸 **Minnesota Fringe Festival** (612-872-1212; fringefestival.org). A growing and popular event, the Fringe Festival takes place over roughly 11 days in early Aug (and a few of those days are designated as Family Fringe, with child-friendly productions). During that time, more than 20 venues present 700 performances of 130-plus shows, some live, some recorded, nearly all an hour or less in length. Quality and themes vary wildly, but enthusiasm is universal.

*August–September*: ♿ ☂ 🐾 ♟ 🍸 **Minnesota Renaissance Festival** (952-445-7361 or 1-800-966-8215; renaissancefest.com), S. US 169, Shakopee. Open weekends and Labor Day 9–7, mid-Aug.–Sept. Adults $24.95, seniors $22.95, children 5–12 $15.95, children 4 and under free. Discount tickets available on the website. Dogs (on leashes) welcome at $10 per pet, per day, through the Pet Gate (proof of rabies immunizations required). At this rowdy, sometimes bawdy re-creation of the Renaissance era, live music, jugglers, comedians, craft demonstrations and sales, and endless amounts of food (the turkey legs and sweet corn are not to be missed) are featured. Most weekends have a theme, such as Irish Heritage or Highland Fling. Note: A good time to go is the weekend before and the weekend of Labor Day, when crowds are smaller

than normal due to the **Minnesota State Fair** (see "The Minnesota State Fair" on page 104).

*October*: ☕ ⚷ ⛱ **Medtronic Twin Cities Marathon** (651-289-7700; tcmevents .org). Taking place the first weekend in October, the Twin Cities Marathon begins near US Bank Stadium in Minneapolis and finishes 26.2 miles later at the State Capitol in St. Paul. For those not willing to go the distance, the event also offers a 10-mile, 10K and 5K run/walks, and family events including a Diaper Dash and a Toddler Trot. Note: All events require preregistration; see the website for details. Some of the events end up in a lottery situation, so register early.

*November to December*: ☕ ⚷ ⛄ **Holidazzle** (612-376-7669; holidazzle.com). A long-time annual holiday event that has morphed from a giant parade into a holiday village in Loring Park. Running weekends between Thanksgiving and the weekend before Christmas, with live music, a kids zone, ice skating, games and singing, food, outdoor movies (yes, in December—bundle up!), and, of course, Santa.

# MINNEAPOLIS'S NEIGHBORING COMMUNITIES

There are several tiers of communities surrounding Minneapolis. The dreaded *s* word—suburb—technically defines them, but many started out as small towns in their own right before the sprawl of the city reached out and made them part of the metro area. Nevertheless, many of these communities have attractions, dining, and shopping that make them worth stepping out of the Minneapolis city limits.

## *Edina*

Edina is in an older suburb, but it's lost none of its cachet as a well-heeled destination with upscale shops and some far-better-than-average suburban dining spots.

    &#9855; &#9733; **Southdale** (952-925-7874; simon.com/mall/southdale-center), 66th Street and France Avenue. Open daily. Edina is the city that gave the rest of the United States enclosed shopping malls. Southdale, which opened in 1956, was the first to offer the indoor shopping mall experience, and as decades have passed, the mall has renovated and remodeled in order to keep up with changing tastes and clientele. It's still a bustling, busy mall, anchored by primary tenants Macy's department store and AMC Theatres. A robust mix of smaller stores includes the Apple Store, Gap, Ann Taylor, Banana Republic, Coach, and Restoration Hardware. Food options include a few fast-food outlets in the food court, or sit-down dining at P.F. Chang's, Dave & Buster's, Buffalo Wild Wings, or the Cheesecake Factory. While parking is ample on all sides of the mall, this is a very popular shopping destination—plan ahead and arrive early to avoid parking in the outfield.

    &#9855; &#9733; **The Galleria** (952-925-4321; galleriaedina.com), 69th Street and France Avenue. Open daily. Right across the street from Southdale is this smaller, more upscale shopping center. The Galleria offers more boutiques than large-scale stores. Shops include brand boutiques Cole Haan, Coach, David Yurman, Louis Vuitton, Lululemon, Peloton, and L'Occitane. Other shops include home accessories stores Crate and Barrel, Pottery Barn, and Ampersand. There is no food court, but there are seven restaurants to visit, all popular and busy at main meal times: Barnes & Noble Kitchen, serving upscale entrées in the bookstore; the Good Earth, serving healthy, hearty meals; Big Bowl, a fast-paced Asian restaurant with a "pick your own" stir-fry bar; Pittsburgh Blue, a steakhouse; People's Organic Coffee and Wine Café, a casual eatery; CōV Edina, a Nantucket-themed restaurant with extensive seafood options (and other items for non-seafood lovers); and Crave, an American cuisine restaurant with a sushi bar.

    &#9855; &#9733; **50th and France** (952-922-1524; 50thandfrance.com), 50th Street and France Avenue. Open daily. A small neighborhood collection of upscale shops and restaurants, this is not an enclosed shopping mall, but it's in a compact area that's very walkable. Clothing stores include Bumbershute, Belleson's, Equation, and Bluebird Boutique; gifts and home accessory shops include Burlap & Brass and Gather; and gourmet

THE MINNESOTA LANDSCAPE ARBORETUM

kitchen items can be found at Sur La Table. In the midst of the retail is the Landmark Edina Cinema, which has four screens showing a mix of popular and arthouse movies.

50th and France is not short of places to eat, and a variety of cuisines are represented. Cocina del Barrio offers new takes on Mexican food (and a considerable tequila menu). Beaujo's is a wine bar with a limited but thoughtful menu of salads, small plates, and entrées. The Edina Grill bills itself as an urban diner, and that's exactly what you can expect, but with a larger selection (beer-battered green beans, eggplant Parmesan) and better quality than you might expect. The casual Italian restaurant Arezzo Ristorante can seem pricey, but the food redeems the cost. Coalition is an upscale eatery focused on sourcing locally, and they make great cocktails (with another location in Excelsior).

Complimentary parking ramps are available on each side of 50th, but watch the signs—some parking areas are reserved for local grocer Lunds Foods. Also pay attention to the maximum parking times allowed on the lower levels of the ramps—the parking police do closely monitor these ramps, and tickets will be issued if you overstay the time allotted.

## Shakopee

This small town, southwest of Minneapolis along the Minnesota River, is home to four popular attractions, all very different in nature.

    &#9855; &#9998; &#9743; **Valleyfair** (952-445-6500; valleyfair.com), 1 Valleyfair Drive. Open daily Memorial Day to Labor Day, weekends only in early May and late Sept. Base ticket

# BLOOMINGTON

It may be located near Edina and its chic shopping areas, but Bloomington has a claim to fame that no other suburb can match: one of the world's largest shopping malls.

The Mall of America (952-883-8800; mallofamerica.com), 60 E. Broadway. This behemoth of retail and entertainment options opened in 1992 and encompasses more than 4 million square feet, which includes not only more than 500 stores, but dozens of sit-down and quick-service eateries, an underground aquarium, a nine-screen movie theater complex, a wedding chapel, a Crayola Experience center, and the Nickelodeon Universe indoor theme park. It's an intensely popular place, with more than 40 million visitors each year.

So what can you do at the mall? For starters, you can stay there: two hotels adjoin the mall, the JW Marriott and the Radisson Blu. You can walk; there are more than 4,000 registered participants in the mall's mall-walking club (walking around one level is slightly over 0.5 mile). You can visit the retail anchors, Nordstrom and Macy's, or the adjacent IKEA. You can browse through any of the more than 500 stores in just about every conceivable category; there are clothing stores for men, women, and kids; video game, electronics, and computer stores; jewelry, art, book, gift, athletic wear, Christmas decoration, bathing suit, and craft stores; cosmetics and body products stores; shops selling toys, Irish gifts, and made in Minnesota items; photo studios; and even a convenience store. ✐ ♻ (ⁱ) ❋ ⸙ ⵘ ¶ ᕼ

Great Wolf Lodge (greatwolf.com/minnesota), I-494 and Cedar Avenue. For the members of your traveling party who are not as inclined to spend hours at the Mall of America, book a stay at the Great Wolf Lodge at the park. The hotel has more than 400 rooms, and the water park comes complete with slides, a mile-long family raft ride, a wave pool, and a Flow Rider. Not interested in water activities? There's also a huge arcade and a spa. The water park is not available without a hotel stay. ᕼ ♻ ⸙ ❋ ¶ ✐

prices: Visitors 48 inches tall and up pay $41; kids under 48 inches tall, as well as senior citizens, pay $35. There are numerous discount programs and multiday ticket offers as well. There is no discount admission for nonriding chaperones. Parking starts at $12 per day. A permanent outdoor amusement park, Valleyfair has something for almost everyone, including a wide variety of gentle rides, including a miniature roller coaster, for younger park adventurers, and more intense rides and coasters for thrill seekers, including 13 thrill rides, some of which are daring roller coasters, some are high-speed swings, and one is a rip cord. Soak City Waterpark, included in admission, offers respite from hot summer days (swimsuits are available for sale, and a changing area is provided).

✪ ᕼ ✐ ❋ **The Landing** (763-694-7784; threeriversparks.org), 2187 E. County Route 101. Open daily from Memorial Day–Oct.; Mon. from Apr.–Memorial Day and Nov. Year-round special events and private tours available. Park admission is $8 for ages 18–64, $5 for ages 2–17 and over 65, and children under 2 are free. Right down the road from Valleyfair is this historical site, a pioneer village comprising 40 buildings set up to demonstrate life for Minnesota pioneers in the late 1800s. Visiting on the weekends during summer will find the addition of a living-history component, with guides dressed in clothing specific to that period, explaining how life was lived in those days. The Pioneer Kids Play House is exactly what it says—a house set up to be hands-on for kids, who can try on pioneer costumes, do laundry in a washtub, use printing blocks to make a newspaper, and simulate cooking.

ᕼ ⵘ ❋ **Canterbury Park** (952-445-7223; canterburypark.com), 1100 Canterbury Road. Live horse racing is offered from early May until Labor Day; simulcast racing is available year-round. The Card Club allows you to indulge your whims for blackjack and poker all year.

    🎣 **Sever's Fall Festival** (952-270-6293; seversfallfestival.com), 1100 Canterbury Road. Open Fri.–Sun. early Sept. to late Oct.; also open the Thurs. of MEA (Minnesota Education Association) weekend, usually the third weekend in Oct. Admission is $15 for ages four and up; children under four free. Local farm stand company Sever's opens this cornfield annually, but every year the field is laid out in a different design (past years have included the Titanic, the United States, and an Egyptian sphinx). Participants are given a map with clues to find their way through. A smaller hay bale maze is set up for younger kids, along with a petting zoo and camel rides. There are numerous other activities available, including a corn pit, obstacle course, straw sculptures, zip lines, a kiddie train, and live music and events. Concessions available. Be sure to wear sturdy shoes or boots, and be sure you don't mind if they get dirty—if there's been rain, the field will be muddy.

## Prior Lake

A western suburb, Prior Lake is home to the Shakopee Mdewakanton Sioux Community, which is the largest employer in the city.

    ♿ ⛾ ↑ ❄ ⑪ **Mystic Lake Casino** (952-445-9000 or 1-800-262-7799; mysticlake.com), 2400 Mystic Lake Boulevard. Open 24 hours. Casinos are popular attractions throughout the state, but the sheer size of Mystic Lake is astonishing. Slots are big business here, with more than 4,000 machines, and sprawling displays of table games and bingo as well. The sheer mass of Mystic Lake can be intimidating, but inside the casino is kept in sparkling condition, with ample nonsmoking areas. Food is available at several cafés and restaurants nearly 24/7. An attached theater is a fine venue for one of the many live performances the complex books, which in the past have included such venerable performers as Tony Bennett and Carrie Underwood. The property also has an 18-hole golf course with pro shop and outdoor patio and grill, as well as a spa offering massages, facials, and other body treatments. The Mystic Lake Casino Hotel recently expanded and has nearly 800 rooms and suites, making it one of the largest hotels in the metro area. If you're staying elsewhere, the casino offers complimentary bus service around the Twin Cities.

## Chanhassen

North of Bloomington is the small town of Chanhassen. It's a busy and rapidly growing community, and for visitors there is a notable place to visit.

    ♿ 🎣 ⛾ ⑪ ❄ **The Chanhassen Dinner Theatres** (952-934-1525; chanhassendt.com), 501 W. 78th Street. This long-standing Chanhassen venue serves full dinner and drinks with each production in its three theaters. Primarily musical in nature, the Chanhassen Dinner Theatres companies are definitely of professional stature, and while the food may not be on par with many of the Twin Cities top restaurants, it's reasonably good and completes the experience.

    ✪ ♿ 🎣 ↑ ❄ **Paisley Park** (officialpaisleypark.com), 7801 Audubon Road. When Prince died in 2016, he'd been in the process of converting his long-time home and studio into a museum reflecting his work and achievements. Today, visitors can see where he (and many other musical luminaries) worked and played, as well as the spaces where he frequently held last-minute concerts and parties.

THE CHANHASSEN DINNER THEATRE

## Chaska

Bordering Chanhassen, Chaska offers one of the loveliest green spaces in the suburbs.

♿ 🖍 ❄ 🍴 **Minnesota Landscape Arboretum** (952-443-1400; arboretum.umn.edu), 3675 Arboretum Drive. Open daily 8–8 (or sunset, whichever comes first), year-round; closed Thanksgiving and Christmas. Adults 16 and older $16, Arboretum members and children 15 and under free. The University of Minnesota is the proprietor of these 1,000-plus acres of gardens, landscaping, woodlands, wetlands, and trails, including a Japanese garden and sculpture garden. The Arboretum has a 3-mile paved road that is used by motorists and people on foot, and there are several off-road trails, including cross-country ski and snowshoe trails, that wind throughout the grounds. The Oswald Visitor Center has a large gift shop and cafeteria; picnic lunches are available with pre-order. Seasonal programs and events include annual and perennial exhibits, demonstrations about making maple syrup, an annual holiday decoration sale and Christmas tea, and fall foliage walks.

## Excelsior

Just down the road from Chanhassen, the small town on the southern shores of Lake Minnetonka is a visitor's dream, especially in the summer. Small shops, intimate restaurants, and parks and trails make for an inviting place to relax and unwind—once you've found a place to park.

### ✻ To See and Do

🖍 **The Excelsior Streetcar** (952-922-1096; trolleyride.org). Available early May through Sept. Reservations are not necessary; just arrive early at the Water Street

Station, at the intersection of Water and George streets. The Minnesota Streetcar Museum offers a ride through Excelsior's past with a summer service of vintage streetcar riding.

✐ ⅋ **The Steamboat Minnehaha** (952-474-2115; steamboatminnehaha.org), Water Street. Open Sat., Sun., and holidays, Memorial Day weekend–early Oct. Basic lake cruises are $15 for adults, $5 for children 4–12, free for under 4. If you'd like your history on water, take a ride on the little yellow steamboat with the colorful history. Part of a fleet of steamboats that were workhorses in the early 1900s, the Minnehaha was scuttled and sank to the bottom of Lake Minnetonka, where it remained until rediscovered 50 years later. Brought up to the surface and refurbished, the Minnehaha now provides visitors with a scenic tour of the lake.

# ❋ Where to Eat

DINING OUT ⅋ ❋ Ⴑ **Coalition** (952-283-1952; coalitionrestaurant.com), 227 Water Street (with a second location in Edina). Open daily for lunch and dinner. This sumptuous restaurant provides top-notch American cuisine, fairly meat-focused with an emphasis on local sourcing, with an admirable wine list. Expensive.

Ⴑ ✐ Ⴑ ❋ **Maynards** (952-470-1800; maynards-excelsior.com), 685 Excelsior Boulevard. Maynards is popular due in no small part to its prime location right on Lake Minnetonka, but the food makes it worth a visit too. It's a restaurant trying to fill a variety of tastes (sandwiches, pasta, burgers, salads), but where it really shines is the meat and seafood entrées. Some are offered in half portions and served with plentiful sides, too. Moderate.

Ⴑ ✐ Ⴑ ❋ **Olive's Fresh Pizza and Bar** (952-474-4440; olivesfresh.com), 287 Water Street. Open Tues.–Sun. for dinner, Thurs.–Sun. for lunch. Wood-fired pizza made from homemade dough with a range of choices from the standard (pepperoni) to the more adventurous (pizzas with salmon and cream cheese, or prosciutto, Gorgonzola and fig). Moderate.

Ⴑ ✐ Ⴑ ❋ **Red Sauce Rebellion** (952-234-4646; redsaucerebellion.com), 205 Water Street. A far better than average Italian restaurant, with house-made pizza and pastas, as well as a handful of meat- and fish-based entrées. You can't go wrong with any of the pastas (especially the Strozzapreti with butternut squash, spinach, brown butter, walnut, and pecorino), and the starters are meals unto themselves. Moderate.

Ⴑ ✐ Ⴑ ❋ **318 Café** (952-401-7902; three-eighteen.com), 318 Water Street. Open daily for all three meals. Located in the historic **Excelsior Mill** (see *Selective Shopping*), 318 is a small, cozy establishment with a fireplace, rough-hewn wood floors, an outdoor patio, and delectable soups, salads, flatbread pizzas, tacos, sandwiches, and baked goods. A wine bar by night, 318 also offers live music on a regular basis. Moderate.

EATING OUT ✐ **Adele's Frozen Custard** (952-470-0035; adelescustard.com), 800 Excelsior Boulevard. Open daily Feb.–Christmas Eve. A tiny café near MN 7 coming into Excelsior, Adele's doesn't look like much on the outside—just a rundown little house with a deck. But inside, along with a limited sandwich menu, is homemade frozen custard, available in cones, sundaes, and malts. Flavors vary daily. Forget about counting calories and indulge (and don't ignore the pulled pork sandwich). Inexpensive.

Ⴑ ✐ ❋ Ⴑ **Lago Tacos** (952-300-8495; lagotacos.com/excelsior), 30 Water Street (also in Uptown Minneapolis). Open daily for lunch and breakfast. Mexican-Asian fusion tacos and burritos with a robust set of fillings, including seafood and veggie. Moderate.

## ❋ Selective Shopping

⊤ ❋ **Provisions** (952-474-6953; provisionsmn.com), 320 Water Street. Home and kitchen goods and gifts.

⊤ ❋ **BE at Lakeside** (952-401-7501; be-atlakeside.com), 347 Water Street. A cozy yarn shop with a wide variety of materials and tools, as well as classes and events, for fiber enthusiasts.

✐ ⊤ ❋ **Capers** (952-474-1715; facebook.com/Capers-392959030736412), 207 Water Street. A gift shop with a solid line of humor-filled gifts, as well as inexpensive jewelry and kids' items.

⊤ ❋ **Brightwater Clothing & Gear** (952-474-0256; brightwaterclothing.com), 256 Water Street. Men's and women's clothing and accessories focused on lake life and the outdoors.

⊤ ❋ **The House of Amore & Fede** (952-401-3392; amorefede.com), 226 Water Street. Chic women's clothing and accessories.

⊤ ❋ **Down the Rabbit Hole** (952-484-3886; downtherabbitholemn.com), 351 2nd Street, Lower Level. Upscale women's clothing and accessories, including pieces by Stella McCartney, Chloe, Prada, and Chanel.

✐ ⊤ ❋ **Excelsior Bay Books** (952-401-0932; excelsiorbaybooks.indielite.org), 36 Water Street. Small bookstore with a good variety of reading materials for kids and adults alike, as well as games, puzzles, and gifts. Check the store's website for its packed event calendar.

⊤ ❋ **The Maker's Studio** (612-865-7335; themakerstudio-mn.com), 400 2nd Street. Artisan home goods from local artists.

⊤ ❋ **Ooh La La** (952-474-1743; oohlalaboutqiuemn.com), 274 Water Street. Trendy, reasonably priced women's clothing and accessories. Private shopping appointments available.

# *Wayzata*

Like Excelsior, Wayzata (pronounced *why-ZET-ta*) has the good fortune to be situated on Lake Minnetonka, and it counts as its residents and visitors many well-heeled lake lovers. The city is busy during the summer months, but don't discount a visit during the winter, when the shops and restaurants are not quite as busy.

## ❋ To See and Do

♿ ✐ ▽ **Al & Alma's Lake Cruises** (952-472-3098; al-almas.com/public), 5201 Piper Road, Mound. This long-time purveyor of lake entertainment offers both public and private cruises, most tied to a meal (brunch, picnic lunch, dinner) and drinks. It's a great way to see one of the most popular Minnesota lakes. Specialty cruises are often offered, including wine tastings and "Martini & Manicure" outings.

♿ ✐ ⊤ ❋ **Minnetonka Center for the Arts** (952-473-7361; minnetonkaarts.org), 2240 N. Shore Drive. Open Mon.–Sat. Just outside the town, the Minnetonka Center for the Arts has become a thriving school and gallery for local artists, budding and professional. The center is open year-round and offers a variety of events (check the website or call for specifics).

## ❋ Lodging

📞 ♿ 🍸 ♂ (📶) ❄ 🍷 🍽 **The Hotel Landing** (952-777-7900; thehotellanding.com), 925 Lake Street. Beautifully located close to Lake Minnetonka, this newer hotel has 92 rooms and suites presented in a sleek, minimalist décor. A full-service spa is on-site as well as the well-regarded **ninetwentyfive** restaurant (see *Where to Eat*). Rooms come with upscale bedding, 55-inch LCD HD smart TVs, and the Presidential Suite has separate dining and sitting areas with a fireplace. Rates begin at $199, with packages and specials available.

## ❋ Where To Eat

DINING OUT 📞 ♿ 🍷 ❄ **6Smith** (952-698-7900; 6smith.com), 294 Grove Lane E. Open daily for lunch and dinner. 6Smith's desirable location on Lake Minnetonka comes complete with a gorgeous rooftop dining area and patio. While the main menu is focused on meat and seafood, locally sourced and humanely/environmentally raised, the restaurant also offers a thoughtful vegan menu. Even the children's menu has a touch of sophistication to it. Expensive/very expensive.

📞 ♿ 🍷 ❄ **Al & Alma's Supper Club** (952-472-3098; al-almas.com/supper-club), 5201 Piper Road, Mound. Open daily Memorial Day–Labor Day for dinner; call for off-season hours. This long-time nautically themed supper club (and dinner cruise operator, see *To See and Do*) has current takes on classic supper club food, including a variety of steak cuts and preparations as well as BBQ ribs and walleye. Located on Lake Minnetonka, Al & Alma's offers dockside to-go options for boaters. Expensive/very expensive.

♿ 🍷 ❄ **Bellecour** (952-444-5200; bellecourrestaurant.com), 739 Lake Street E. Open daily for dinner, Sat.–Sun. for brunch. Owned and run by James Beard Award–winning chef Gavin Kaysen, Bellecour is a French bistro and bakery that garnered rave reviews from the moment it opened. The limited but diverse menu includes Escargots de Bourgogne, Tournedos Rossini, Canard a l'Orange, and Poulet Roti. There's a delightful bakery adjacent (see *Eating Out*). Expensive/very expensive.

♿ 🍷 ❄ **CōV Wayzata** (952-473-5253; covwayzata.com), 700 Lake Street E. Open daily for lunch and dinner, Sat.–Sun. for brunch. This Nantucket-themed restaurant with extensive seafood options (and other items for non-seafood lovers) has an enviable location right on Lake Minnetonka, and it takes advantage of the view with extensive windows and a lovely patio. Very expensive.

📞 ♿ 🍸 🍷 ❄ **Gianni's Steakhouse** (952-404-1100; giannis-steakhouse.com), 635 Lake Street E. Open daily for dinner. Gianni's is a congenial steakhouse with a traditional menu full of steaks, ribs, and fish. Very expensive.

📞 ♿ 🍸 🍷 ❄ **ninetwentyfive** (612-356-5330; ninetwentyfive.com), 925 Lake Street E. Open daily for breakfast, lunch, and dinner. Located in **The Hotel Landing** (see *Lodging*), ninetwentyfive offers modern Midwestern cuisine with an emphasis on fresh and local. Menu items include an upscale take on beef pot roast with charred carrots and potato puree, as well as updated versions of classic steakhouse dishes, such as Steak Forestiere. The restaurant's bar offers regular live music and other events. Expensive/very expensive.

📞 ♿ 🍸 🍷 ❄ **Lord Fletcher's** (952-471-8513; lordfletchers.com), 3746 Sunset Drive, Spring Park. Dining room open daily for dinner, Sun. for brunch; the Oar House and Wharf open daily for lunch and dinner. This popular long-time restaurant is also right on Lake Minnetonka and is situated to accept boat-in guests as well as those in vehicles. There are three dining venues on-site: the main dining room, the Oar House (sports bar), and the Wharf (bar and grill). The dining room menu is meat-forward, with ample seafood as well, and includes enormous steaks and pork chops along with elk and seabass, and the house specialty: walleye. Very expensive.

    ᕯ ✆ ❋ ♈ **Vann** (952-381-9042; vann restaurant.com), 4016 Shoreline Drive, Spring Park. Upscale, Scandinavian-focused restaurant with an emphasis on seafood. Offerings include octopus, caviar, scallops, and Icelandic cod; dessert might be a steamed sweet potato cake with baker's yeast ice cream or a Gjetost tartlet. Expensive.

EATING OUT ✆ ᕯ ♈ ❋ **Bellecour Bakery** (952-444-5200; bellecourrestaurant .com/bakery), 739 Lake Street E. Open daily for breakfast and lunch. The bakery part of the highly regarded Bellecour Restaurant (see *Dining Out*) offers a full spread of gourmet pastries and breads, as well as sandwiches, coffee, and tea. There's an adjacent patio that's perfect for enjoying a treat on summer days. Inexpensive.

    ✆ ᕯ ♈ ❋ **Benedict's** (952-923-1903; benedictswayzata.com), 845 Lake Street E. Open daily for breakfast and lunch. Hearty breakfast and lunch offerings, including eight iterations of Eggs Benedict (fried chicken and Cubano versions, among others), as well as classic lunch sandwiches like the Monte Cristo and crab grilled cheese. Inexpensive/moderate.

    ✆ ᕯ ♈ ❋ **Wayzata Bar and Grill** (952-473-5286; wayzatabarandgrill.com), 747 Mill Street. Open daily for lunch and dinner. A Wayzata staple since opening in 1947, the Wayzata Bar and Grill (known locally as "the Muni") has an extensive menu of bar food items, including sandwiches and burgers. The dinner hour offers walleye and sirloin nightly, with

pot roast, prime rib, and BBQ rib dinners offered once weekly. Inexpensive/moderate.

    ✆ ᕯ ♈ ❋ **McCormick's Pub & Restaurant** (952-767-2417; mccormicks.pub), 331 Broadway Avenue S. Open daily for lunch and dinner, Sat.–Sun. for brunch. McCormick's has two distinct dining areas, one an Irish pub and the other a more formal restaurant. The menu has several nods towards the owner's Irish ancestry, but it also has several upscale supper club-type items, including steak tartare, lobster rolls, and a Diane burger. Moderate.

## ❋ Selective Shopping

ᕯ ❋ **44 North Boutique** (952-473-0440; 44northboutique.com), 823 Lake Street E. Open Mon.–Sat. Upscale women's clothing and accessories.

    ᕯ ❋ **Five Swans** (952-473-4685; five swans.com), 309 Lake Street E. Open Mon.–Sat. Housed in a century-old building, Five Swans offers upscale gifts and home accessories.

    ᕯ ❋ **Highcroft Fine Linens** (952-746-5826; highcrofthome.com), 770 Lake Street E. Open Mon.–Sat. and by appointment. High-end home linens, accessories, and bath items.

    ᕯ ❋ **J. Hilburn** (612-991-5327; jena marxer.jhilburn.com), 170 Spur Circle. Call for appointment. Custom-made men's clothing.

    ✆ ᕯ ❋ **Modern Roots** (952-923-1450; modernroots.org), 1131B Wayzata Boulevard. Open daily. Organic body care products, with more than half of the ingredients grown on a local farm.

    ✆ ᕯ ❋ **The Owl and the Octopus** (952-473-1727; owlandoctopustoys.com), 1151 Wayzata Boulevard. Open daily. A toy store with an eclectic, wide-ranging selection.

# Maple Grove

Maple Grove was an early adopter of the suburban "walkable downtown," something other communities are emulating. But be warned—the main shopping area in Maple Grove can be slow going for motorists. There are countless stoplights, and lines can form.

    ᵔ ♪ ↑ ❋ ⅄ **The Shoppes at Arbor Lakes** (763-424-0504; shoppesatarborlakes.com), I-94/I-694 and Hemlock Lane. Open daily. Despite the rather prissy name, Arbor Lakes has made progress in reducing the concept of "soulless suburb" by providing a mix of retail and dining in actual city blocks with sidewalks to give it a small-town-center feel. While many of the usual chain-store suspects are present (Gap, H&M, Victoria's Secret, J.Jill, Pottery Barn), the strolling-friendly layout over four city blocks makes the shopping experience feel less suburban mall and more charming village. Dining options are pretty much casual, with a mix of quick-service eateries (Patrick's Bakery and Café, Potbelly Sandwiches) and sit-down dining (Biaggi's Ristorante Italiano, P.F. Chang's, Pittsburgh Blue, Granite City Food & Brewery).

# Albertville

On the far north end of the Minneapolis area is the town of Albertville, which is home to a massive outlet mall.

    ᵔ ♪ ↑ ❋ **Albertville Premium Outlets** (763-497-1911; premiumoutlets.com), 6415 Labeaux Avenue NE. Open daily. A sprawling collection of 100 outlet stores, including Polo Ralph Lauren, Lululemon, Banana Republic, Nike, Coach, Claire's Accessories, Kate Spade, Michael Kors, and Bath & Body Works. The outlet center offers occasional live concerts outdoors during the summer months, and the website lists events and promotions offered by the individual retailers. There's also a children's play area open daily.

# ST. PAUL AND NEIGHBORING COMMUNITIES

ST. PAUL

ST. PAUL'S NEIGHBORING
COMMUNITIES

# ST. PAUL

St. Paul serves as the capital for the state; it also at times suffers from being neglected in favor of its twin across the river. Take in a concert at the Xcel Energy Center and see what happens if the performer onstage makes the mistake of thanking the Minneapolis audience; it's a frequent and unfortunate occurrence.

But St. Paul holds its own for sheer beauty in its neighborhoods and downtown area. The ornate buildings downtown and grand mansions along many of the city's prominent streets (Summit Avenue being the most noticeable) reflect the city's historical roots. Named by a French priest who felt that the city's original name, Pig's Eye Landing, was not grand enough, St. Paul became the state's capital in 1849, an event that caused a population explosion of sorts, doubling in size in just three weeks. But the expansion didn't come without criticism; in the late 1800s, a New York newspaper cast aspersion on the local climate, saying it wasn't fit for human habitation. City officials disagreed, and thus was born one of the city's most cherished annual events, the **St. Paul Winter Carnival** (see *Special Events*).

The 20th century brought highs and lows to the city on the river. The 1920s saw increased crime and the presence of gangsters, due to the tolerance of the local police department. But when the US government determined that the favored hiding spot of John Dillinger needed attention, police began to crack down on crime and make St. Paul a safer place to be.

Regardless of safety, St. Paul lagged behind Minneapolis in terms of cultural growth, at least until the 1990s. As St. Paul became more aggressive toward drawing visitors,

THE COVINGTON INN

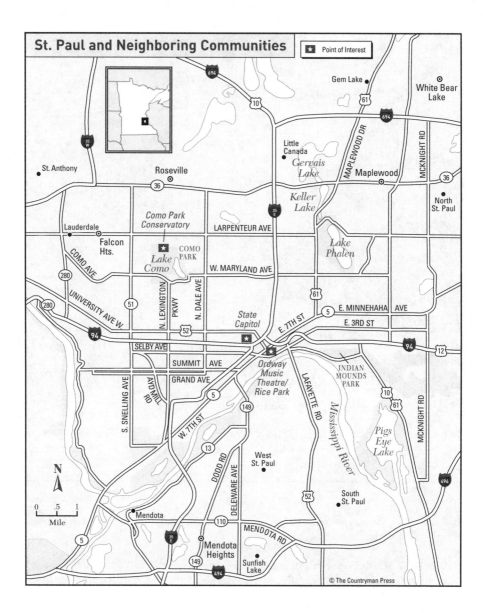

**St. Paul and Neighboring Communities**

★ Point of Interest

© The Countryman Press

development funds were given to projects like the **Ordway Center for the Performing Arts**, a popular and beautiful live performance venue (see *Entertainment*), and **River-Centre**, a convention center that is also home to the **Xcel Energy Center**, the acoustically superior counterpart to Minneapolis's Target Center. The **Science Museum of Minnesota** (see *To See and Do*) is one of the premier science museums in the country.

Today St. Paul continues to grow, adding new entertainment and dining options to the city. One note for visitors: Former governor and pro-wrestler Jesse Ventura once commented, to the consternation of loyal St. Paulites, that the city's streets had apparently been designed by a "drunken Irishman." Whoever designed them, Ventura had a point; the winding one-ways and dead-ends can be confusing, especially during

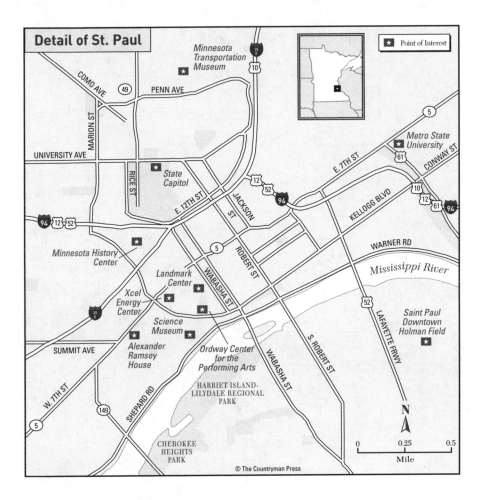

**Detail of St. Paul**

Point of Interest

Minnesota Transportation Museum

COMO AVE
PENN AVE
49
MARION ST
UNIVERSITY AVE
RICE ST
State Capitol
E. 12TH ST
JACKSON ST
12
52
94

E. 7TH ST
Metro State University
61
CONWAY ST
5
10
12
61
94
KELLOGG BLVD

94 12 52

Minnesota History Center

Landmark Center
Xcel Energy Center
Science Museum
Alexander Ramsey House
Ordway Center for the Performing Arts
WABASHA ST
ROBERT ST
5
WARNER RD

*Mississippi River*

52
LAFAYETTE FRWY
Saint Paul Downtown Holman Field

S. ROBERT ST
WABASHA ST

SUMMIT AVE
W. 7TH ST
SHEPARD RD
149
5

HARRIET ISLAND-LILYDALE REGIONAL PARK

CHEROKEE HEIGHTS PARK

N

0    0.25    0.5
Mile

© The Countryman Press

rush-hour. A good downtown city map is crucial for finding your way, and don't hesitate to ask for help.

GUIDANCE **St. Paul Convention and Visitors Authority** (651-265-4900 or 1-800-627-6101; visitsaintpaul.com), 175 W. Kellogg Boulevard, Suite 502. Offers extensive lodging and activity information for St. Paul.

GETTING THERE **By air:** The primary airport is the **Terminal 1–Lindbergh Terminal** at the **Minneapolis–St. Paul International Airport** (612-726-5555; mspairport.com); next door is **Terminal 2–Hubert** (612-726-5555), a smaller secondary airport serving mostly no-frills and charter airlines. Both airports are in Bloomington, a western suburb. Taxis, limos, rental cars, ride-sharing services, and light rail service are available from the airports into the city.

**By bus: Greyhound** has a terminal (612-371-3325; greyhound.com) a few blocks from the capitol.

**By car:** I-94, I-35E, US 12, US 61, and US 10 all lead into downtown St. Paul.

**By rail: AMTRAK** (1-800-872-7245; amtrak.com) has a rail station in the restored Union Depot in Lowertown St. Paul (240 E. Kellogg Boulevard, #70).

GETTING AROUND For travel within the city, **Metro Transit** (612-373-3333; metrotransit.org) provides extensive service with both buses and light rail throughout St. Paul. Ride-sharing services such as **Uber** and **Lyft** have become ubiquitous as well, making it easy to get around without a car. But if you're traveling outside the metro, or plan on taking many excursions that require transportation, a car rental can be helpful.

WHEN TO COME The summer months see an influx of tourists who come to enjoy the multitude of lakes and parks, but St. Paulites keep active in the winter, too, especially with the annual **St. Paul Winter Carnival** (see *Special Events*), which has myriad activities for visitors and residents alike.

MEDICAL EMERGENCY Call 911.

   **Regions Hospital** (651-254-3456; health partners.com/hospitals/regions), 640 Jackson Street.

THE PATIO AT MOSCOW ON THE HILL

ICE SCULPTURES AT RICE PARK

**Children's Hospital St. Paul** (651-220-6000; childrensmn.org), 345 Smith Avenue N.

**United Hospital** (651-241-8000; allinahealth.org/united-hospital), 333 Smith Avenue N.

**Health East St. Joseph's Hospital** (651-232-3000; fairview.org/locations/healtheast-st-josephs-hospital), 45 W. 10th Street.

# ✳ To See and Do

MUSEUMS AND HISTORIC SITES ♿ ✐ ⊤ ✳ ‖ **Minnesota History Center** (651-259-3000; mnhs.org), 345 W. Kellogg Boulevard. Open Tues. 10–8, Wed.–Sat. 10–5, Sun. 12–5. Adults $12; senior citizens, veterans and active military members, and college students $10; children 5–17 $6; children 4 and under and Minnesota Historical Society members free. Despite its rather dull name, the history center takes a lively, hands-on approach to history that makes it interesting and fun, even (and especially) for kids. Serious history buffs can find specialized research help; kids can crawl through a grain silo and explore the world of Minnesota music in a recording booth. An ongoing exhibit about Minnesota's weather extremes includes a tornado simulator that's scarily realistic. The gift shops are fun, and even the cafeteria is far above average.

♿ ✐ ⊤ ✳ **State Capitol** (651-296-2881; mnhs.org/statecapitol), University Avenue between Dr. Rev. Martin Luther King Jr. Boulevard and Cedar Street. Open Mon.–Fri. 8:30–5, Sat. 10–3, Sun. 1–4. General tours are free, although donations are recommended; special events may have varying admission fees. Groups of 10 or more should reserve tours two weeks in advance. Just down the street from the Minnesota History Center is another piece of Minnesota's past and present. Guided and self-guided tours are available through the venerable white marble building, which has undergone an extensive renovation and is beautiful to visit. Weather permitting, group tours explore the rooftop to visit the golden horses sculpture.

♿ ✐ ✳ **Minnesota Museum of American Art** (651-797-2571; mmaa.org), 350 N. Robert Street. Open Wed.–Sun. 11–5, Thurs. until 8. Admission is free. Located in the beautiful Pioneer Endicott building downtown, this museum focuses on American artists from the 19th century forward. Until late 2018, the museum struggled to find a permanent space, but now that it has one, it plans to have evolving exhibits of its thousands of collected artworks as well as special exhibits and events.

♿ ✐ ✳ **Capitol Mall** (mnhs.org). Stretched out below the State Capitol is the Capitol Mall, which has been developed into a large-scale memorial and park. A walking tour will take visitors past memorials representing Minnesota politicians and veterans of wars. The artwork is diverse and thoughtful, and it's well worth an afternoon's exploration.

♿ ✐ ⊤ ✳ **The Bell Museum of Natural History** (612-626-9660; bellmuseum.umn.edu), 2088 W. Larpenteur Avenue. Open Tues.–Sun. 10–5, also select evenings; call or check the website for details. Adults $12; seniors 65 and older $10; non–University of Minnesota students, and children 3–16 $9; children under 3 free. Admission is free for museum members; University of Minnesota staff, faculty, and students. The Bell Museum recently moved and is now located at the University of Minnesota–St. Paul campus, an apt location as it's both a working scientific facility and a center of nature in the heart of the city. The diorama halls introduce the natural world of Minnesota, while other galleries delve into nature and wildlife from around the world. The new planetarium is state of the art. The Touch & See Lab is ideal for kids, or anyone just curious as to what a live snake or the skull of a long-dead mammal looks and feels like. There are various programs and events, including a monthly Sensory-Friendly Saturday for people with sensory sensitivities.

🐾 ♿ 🛈 ⬆ ❄ **The James J. Hill House** (651-297-2555; mnhs.org/hillhouse), 240 Summit Avenue. Open Wed.–Sat. 10–4, Sun. 1–4. Adults $10; senior citizens 65 and older, veterans and active military members, and college students $8; children 5–17 $6; and children under 5 and Minnesota Historical Society members free. This was the residence of railroad impresario James J. Hill, and his prominence shows in the rich mansion. Inside, besides a piece of history, is a two-story art gallery with several pieces from Hill's own collection, focused primarily on French landscapes. Under the Minnesota Historical Society's innovative management, the Hill House has numerous events each year that are above and beyond the usual house tours, including Victorian Poetry Slams at Valentine's and a Nooks and Crannies tour in the summer that takes visitors into parts of the property not usually explored during regular tours.

🛈 ⬆ ❄ **The Wabasha Street Caves** (651-292-1220; wabashastreetcaves.com), 215 Wabasha Street S. Hours and admission fees vary depending on season and type of tour. The caves have a legendary history involving moonshiners and mobsters, and besides, they're caves. Tours are offered year-round, both with the caves as the primary attraction and as part of other tours (Gangster Tours in the summer, Ghosts and Caves in October).

♿ 🛈 ⬆ ❄ 🍴 **The Science Museum of Minnesota** (651-221-9444; smm.org), 120 W. Kellogg Boulevard. Open Sun.–Wed. 9:30–5, Thurs.–Sat. 9:30–9. Hours are sometimes extended in the summer and during special events. Admission for exhibits only is $20 for adults; $15 for children ages 4–12 and senior citizens 65 and older; free for children 3 and under and museum members. Admission to the 3D Cinema, the Omnitheater, and special exhibitions costs extra. The Science Museum has utilized its executive and marketing staffs to become one of the premier science museums in the United States.

THE SCIENCE MUSEUM OF MINNESOTA

A flexible management gives this staff the ability to make decisions more quickly than larger bureaucracies, enabling them to pounce on prime traveling exhibits. A large permanent collection covers all aspect of science, mostly from a hands-on perspective; visiting exhibits tend to be major events, with past visits including the Dead Sea Scrolls, the treasures of King Tut, technology behind video games, and the science involved in mental health. The Omnitheater has a giant surrounding movie screen with specially made movies (many by the Science Museum's staff) on view. When the weather's nice, stop by the mini-golf course behind the museum to learn some geology lessons while having fun with a golf club.

      ᕫ ✑ ⵢ ❋ ❙❙ **Minnesota Children's Museum** (651-225-6000; mcm.org), 10 W. 7th Street. Open Sun.–Thurs. 9–5, Fri. and Sat. 9–8, Sun. 9–5. Adults and children 1 year old and up $13; children under the age of 1 and museum members free. A rollicking three-story space for kids and adventurous parents. Displays are highly active and interactive; educational is an important part, but fun always rules.

      ᕫ ✑ **Historic Fort Snelling** (612-726-1171; mnhs.org/fortsnelling), 200 Tower Avenue, near the Minneapolis–St. Paul Airport. Open Tues.–Fri. 10–4 and Sat. and Sun. 10–5, Memorial Day–Labor Day; open Sat. 10–5, Sept.–Oct. Adults $12; senior citizens 65 and older and college students $10; children 5–17 $6; and children under 5, Native Americans, veterans, and Minnesota Historical Society members free. This fort, built in the early 1800s at the junction of the Minnesota and Mississippi rivers, was an army outpost to establish control of river traffic, but it quickly became a regional center for trade and social activities as well. The fort was used through World War II, when it was a processing and training camp, but it closed after the war's end. Today it's a living-history museum with costumed guides and hands-on activities during the summer, and home to several events each year, often focused on some aspect of fort life, whether it's cooking, the blacksmith's shop, or aspects of World War II military intelligence.

# ❋ Green Space and Outdoor Activities

      ᕫ ✑ ❋ **Rice Park**, 109 W. 4th Street. It's tiny, only one city block, but it has the Ordway Center on one side, the St. Paul Hotel across the way, and the St. Paul Public Library alongside, all of which are beautiful and, with the exception of the Ordway, decades-old buildings. The park itself has a walking path and a fountain; it's a prominent gathering place for visitors to the Ordway, and many of the city's festivals utilize the space for events and displays. Of special note is the annual **St. Paul Winter Carnival** (see *Special Events*), in which Rice Park is host to an ice sculpture competition that always has stunning pieces for visitors to see.

      ᕫ ✑ ✑ ⵢ ❋ ❙❙ **Como Park, Zoo, and Conservatory** (651-487-8200; comozoo conservatory.org), 1225 Estabrook Drive. Open daily 10–4 (until 6 p.m. in the summer). Admission is free, but a donation of $3 per adult and $2 per child is requested for the park's maintenance. It's like a city within a city: Como Park and Zoo comprise several acres with a lake, pool, mini golf, a vintage carousel, and golf course (the last three open summers only); walking trails; and even a mini amusement park. The Marjorie McNeely Conservatory has an extensive, lush indoor garden, a favorite for weddings and parties, as well as a great place to get a reprieve from the winter blahs.

      ✑ ❋ **Indian Mounds Park** (651-266-6400), 10 Mounds Boulevard. Open daily. Across the river from downtown St. Paul is this park, which serves both as a public park and a historical site with six Native American burial mounds. Some of the mounds date back 2,000 years and hold remains of the Hopewell tradition and the Dakota tribe. The park offers beautiful views of downtown St. Paul as well.

# HARRIET ISLAND

An island on the Mississippi across from downtown St. Paul, Harriet Island's public park has gained prominence in recent years. Amenities include a bandshell, stage, public boat launch, playground, river walk, and jumping-on points for a number of trails. The wide, flat space at the river's edge is ideal for setting up large-scale events, and the view of the St. Paul skyline makes a perfect backdrop.

But that's not all. Harriet Island is also home to the **Covington Inn Bed and Breakfast** (see *Lodging*), the St. Paul Yacht Club, and the **Paddleford Riverboats** (see *To See and Do*), which offers public river cruises.

Harriet Island has also become a venue for concerts and a central location for many of St. Paul's festivals, at least those of which can be held outdoors. Besides being easier logistically and in terms of security for the city, they've also made it pretty easy for visitors—many of the festivals offer patrons the option of parking in downtown St. Paul, then catching a free shuttle bus for the quick ride across the bridge to the island. There is some parking near the island, but it's limited. See Special Events for information about the St. Paul Winter Carnival and the Irish Fair, just two of the regular events held on Harriet Island.

✤ ❊ **Crosby Farm Regional Park** (651-632-5111), 2595 Crosby Farm Road. Open daily. A nature area with several miles of paved trails for hiking and biking, lakes for fishing, and a boat launch.

& ✤ ❊ **Fort Snelling State Park** (612-725-2389; dnr.state.mn.us/state_parks/fort_snelling), 101 Snelling Lake Road. Open daily 8 a.m.–10 p.m. Admission is $7 per car; free with a Minnesota State Park permit. Not far from the international airport is this state park, where the Mississippi and Minnesota rivers converge. The park offers 18 miles of hiking trails and 10 miles of mountain bike trails, as well as cross-country ski and snowshoe trails. Pike Island, located where the rivers meet, has 3 miles of hiking trails, too. The Thomas C. Savage Visitor Center has exhibits explaining the history and geographical significance of the area.

## ❊ Lodging

### BED-AND-BREAKFASTS

#### DOWNTOWN

(ᵂ) ❊ **Covington Inn Bed and Breakfast** (651-292-1411; covingtoninn.com), 100 Harriet Island Road. Four suites are available aboard the permanently moored towboat the Covington, which spent its first 30 years as a river towboat, moving cargo ships into place. Now it's a luxury guesthouse; all rooms have a private bath, fireplace, and air-conditioning. The décor reflects the glorious past days of river travel, and there are several salvaged fixtures and antiques. Rates begin at $145. Packages are available.

### HOTELS

#### DOWNTOWN

✪ & ✤ ✪ (ᵂ) ❊ ✗ ‖ **The St. Paul Hotel** (651-292-9292 or 1-800-292-9292; saintpaulhotel.com), 350 N. Market Street. This elegant old-world hotel, just over a century old, is situated on Rice Park, right across from the Ordway Center and just steps from **Xcel Energy Center** (see *Entertainment*), the **Science Museum** (see *To See and Do*), and several excellent restaurants (as well as having two top-notch restaurants in the hotel; see *Where to Eat*). Its 250-plus sumptuously appointed rooms are among the loveliest in the city, and if you're feeling posh, the Penthouse Suite has a dining room that seats 12, a fireplace, surround sound in

THE ST. PAUL HOTEL

the living room, a full kitchen, and two bedrooms and baths. The St. Paul Hotel has been host to numerous high-profile guests, including actors, politicians, and gangsters. Rates start at $150. Packages and specials are available.

♿ 🛎 📶 ✂ ❄ 🍸 **Hotel 340** (651-280-4120; hotel340.com), 340 Cedar Street. An upscale boutique hotel with suites and rooms in a 1907 building in the heart of downtown St. Paul. Cherrywood floors, high-quality furnishings, and TVs. Rates start at $109. Packages and specials are available.

♿ 🛎 📶 ❄ 🍸 **Celeste St. Paul** (651-222-0848; celestestpaul.com), 26 E. Exchange Street. St. Paul's newest hotel is adjacent to the Fitzgerald Theater and has a unique pedigree: It's at the site of a former convent and renowned music conservatory. The renovated rooms and suites are beautifully appointed and come with full breakfast. Suites include an honor bar credit, robes, and lounge areas. Rates start at $149.

♿ 🛎 ✂ 📶 ❄ 🍸 🍴 **InterContinental St. Paul Riverfront** (651-292-1900; intercontinentalstp.com), 11 E. Kellogg Boulevard. This popular conference hotel overlooks the river and is just blocks away from the Ordway Center and Xcel Energy Center. There are several room and suite configurations in this recently updated hotel. The hotel restaurant, **Citizen Modern American Cuisine and Bar** (see *Where to Eat*), offers better-than-expected hotel dining. Rates start at $165. Packages and specials are available.

♿ 🛎 ✂ 📶 🍸 ❄ 🍴 **Hyatt Place St. Paul/Downtown** (651-647-5000; hyatt.com), 180 E. Kellogg Boulevard. Located in the arts-oriented Lowertown part of St. Paul (and not far from the St. Paul Saints' home field), the Hyatt Place has 149 rooms and suites with sleekly minimalist décor. There's a pool on-site as well as 24/7 food options and a "coffee to cocktail" bar that opens at 6 a.m. Rates start at $135. Packages and specials are available.

# ST. PAUL BED AND BREAKFASTS

As befits a historic river city, there are beautiful homes that have been refurbished into luxurious bed-and-breakfasts.

Como Lake B&B (651-402-7930; comolakebnb.com), 1205 W. Como Boulevard. A beautiful Craftsman home in the Como Lake area, near the Como Zoo and Conservatory. The home has two bedrooms and two suites, all with private bath and full breakfast. One suite includes a heated sleeping porch, and the other occupies the entire third floor and includes a kitchenette and fireplace. Rates start at $95.

Corban Manor Inn (651-348-7239; corbanmanorinn.com), 96 Virginia Street. Located in Cathedral Hill, this recently renovated home has two rooms, a suite, and an apartment, all with private bath. All accommodations include refrigerators, tables and chairs, and off-street parking (one per reservation). The breakfast here is not on-site, but includes vouchers for a nearby breakfast café. Rates start at $160.

Historic District Bed and Breakfast (763-360-3717; hdbbsaintpaul.com), 483 Ashland Avenue. Built in 1896, this Cathedral Hill home was one of the first to be built with steel beam construction. It offers two rooms and a two-room suite, all with private bath and period-appropriate furnishings. Rates start at $150.

New Victorian Mansion Bed & Breakfast (651-321-8151; newvicbb.com), 325 Dayton Avenue. Built in 1881, this Cathedral Hill home has many restored Renaissance and Gothic architectural details. Four suites are offered, all with private bath. The Cathedral Suite has a turret overlooking the nearby Cathedral. Rates start at $175.

 

⚕ 🛗 (((•))) 🍸 ❄ 🍴 🐾 **Holiday Inn** (651-225-1515; histpaul.com), 175 W. 7th Street. Right across from Xcel Energy Center and an easy walk to the Ordway and Rice Park, the Holiday Inn offers the usual amenities and a reasonable price for a downtown location. The cheerful Irish pub **The Liffey** (see *Where to Eat*) is on-site. Rates start at $135. Packages and specials are available.

🛗 ⚕ (((•))) ❄ 🐾 **Drury Plaza Hotel** (651-222-3337; druryhotels.com), 175 10th Street E. This hotel is within easy walking distance or very short drives to downtown St. Paul attractions, dining, and entertainment options. There's an indoor pool, and daily cooked-to-order breakfast is included in the rates. Rates start at $150. Packages and specials are available.

🛗 ⚕ 🐕 (((•))) ❄ 🍸 🍴 🐾 **DoubleTree by Hilton** (651-291-8800; doubletree3.hilton .com), 411 Minnesota Street. This newer hotel has basic rooms and suites and offers convenient location to downtown sites and entertainment. Dining options include a daily breakfast spot and a bar and grill with pizza and snacks. The

hotel also has a fitness center and indoor pool. Rates start at $134. Packages and specials are available.

🛗 ⚕ 🐕 (((•))) ❄ 🍸 🍴 🐾 **Best Western Plus Capitol Ridge** (651-227-8711; bestwestern .com), 161 St. Anthony Avenue. Located near the State Capitol, this Best Western offers less-expensive accommodations. The hotel has an indoor pool and restaurant. Rates start at $105. Packages and specials are available.

## ✳ Where to Eat

### DINING OUT

#### CATHEDRAL HILL

✪ 🛗 (((•))) ❄ 🍸 **W. A. Frost** (651-224-5715; wafrost.com), 374 Selby Avenue. Open daily for lunch and dinner. One of the most romantic restaurants in the area, W. A. Frost has excellent food, much of it identified as to its local sourcing. The interior, dark but not gloomy, with high copper ceilings, speaks to intimacy, while the outdoor patio garden is a gem, one of the best in the metro. Dinner entrées could include rabbit pate, duck cassoulet, or yellow curry vegetables. W. A. Frost is also known for its meticulous paired cheese plates. Expensive/very expensive.

✪ ♿ ((•)) ❄ ♈ **Moscow on the Hill** (651-291-1236; moscowonthehill.com), 371 Selby Avenue. Open daily for lunch and dinner. Hearty Russian food served the Russian way—don't plan on eating in a hurry, but not in a bad way. Some pieces of the menu change with the seasons, and you can't go wrong with the ever-evolving Zukuski Platter, a Russian cheese and meat plate. This upscale bistro also has an excellent array of vodka (available in tasting flights). Don't miss the patio in the summer. Expensive.

## DOWNTOWN/LOWERTOWN

♿ ❄ ♈ **Citizen** (651-605-0190; citizen saintpaul.com), 11 E. Kellogg Boulevard. Open daily for all three meals. Adjacent to the InterContinental Hotel, Citizen has an upscale American menu, offering traditional items such as cedar-planked salmon, lamb chops, and chicken and dumplings as large plates. The more extensive small plates menu offers seared lemonfish and cacio e pepe. There are several gluten-free entrées, and cheese curds supplied by local Redhead Creamery. Expensive.

✪ ♿ ((•)) ❄ ♈ **St. Paul Grill** (651-224-7455; stpaulgrill.com), 350 Market Street. Open daily for lunch and dinner. Located in the **St. Paul Hotel** (see *Lodging*), the St. Paul Grill is right across Rice Park from the Ordway Theater. It's definitely a special-occasion restaurant, with an upscale American menu including steaks, lobster, and lamb chops. The bar is a great stop for a before-dinner or after-theater visit, with extensive wine and Scotch lists. Expensive/very expensive.

♿ ❄ ♈ **Meritage** (651-222-5670; meritage-stp.com), 410 St. Peter Street. Open Tues.–Sun. for lunch and dinner.

Chef Russell Klein built his menu from traditional French foods, then played off that by drawing on seasonally available ingredients. The result is a highly regarded restaurant that also offers an oyster bar (and an annual oyster fest), patio (in season), and crêpe stand on special occasions. Tasting courses, varying from five to nine courses, are offered along with wine pairings. Available only with reservation (and they need to be made well in advance) is the showy, delicious Duck a la Presse experience. Expensive/very expensive.

♿ ✎ ❄ ♈ **Pazzaluna** (651-223-7000; pazzaluna.com), 360 St. Peter Street. Open daily for dinner. Chef's table available; reserve in advance. This informal but upscale Italian restaurant offers a menu that changes seasonally but is always tasteful. It's a popular spot, especially pre-theater, but if you don't have a reservation and there's a long wait, consider eating in the bar, which is quick and attractive. Expensive.

♿ ✎ ❄ ♈ **Kincaid's Fish, Chop, and Steak House** (651-602-9000; kincaids .com), 380 St. Peter Street (with another location in Bloomington). Open Mon.–Fri. for lunch, daily for dinner. Kincaid's offers all the usual steakhouse suspects, beautifully prepared, and with the occasional fun twist; try the American Wagyu Meatloaf Wellington. Expensive/very expensive.

♿ ✎ ❄ ♈ **Sakura Restaurant and Sushi Bar** (651-224-0185; sakurastpaul.com), 350 St. Peter Street. Open daily for lunch and dinner. Sakura has come a long way from its humble, tiny beginnings. Now the restaurant is two stories, has a sushi bar, and has private tearooms. Best of all is the sushi, splendidly fresh and beautifully prepared. Expensive.

✎ ♿ ♈ ❄ **Market House Collaborative** (651-202-3415; facebook .com/Market-House-Collaborative -1468359279885648), 289 5th Street E. Open daily; hours vary by purveyor. This unique food-based collaboration was the brainchild of local restaurant

THE LANDMARK CENTER ON RICE PARK

star Tim McKee, who created a kind of eatery–farm market hybrid. Venues include the OCTO fishbar, which offers mainstream and less frequently seen seafood items, as well as seafood towers named after iconic singers and songs; Birch's Lowertown Tap Room & Barrel House, a brewpub with menu items sourced from the following vendors: Peterson Craftsman Meats and Almanac Fish, a butcher shop and fish shop. Prices vary.

⬠ ✎ ⍟ ❄ **Herbie's on the Park** (651-726-1700; herbiesonthepark.com), 317 Washington Street. Open Tues.–Sun. for lunch and dinner, Mon. only on event and game days at Xcel Energy Center. Housed in the lovely former Minnesota Club, Herbie's was founded by the Minnesota Wild hockey team owner, who named the eatery after legendary local hockey coach Herb Brooks. The menu is protein-heavy, with pork chops and shank, multiple steak cuts, and Minnesota walleye. Expensive/very expensive.

## WEST 7TH STREET

 &#9855; ✿ ☇ Ⴕ **Mancini's Char House & Lounge** (651-224-7345; mancinis.com), 531 7th Street W. Open daily for dinner. This venerable family-run steakhouse has been serving charbroiled steaks and lobster, along with generous martinis, for more than 70 years. Live music is offered in the lounge four nights a week. Expensive/very expensive.

&#9855; ✿ ☇ Ⴕ **Bennett's Chop & Railhouse** (651-228-1408; bennettschopand railhouse.com), 1305 7th Street W. Open daily for lunch and dinner, Sat.–Sun. for breakfast. A family-friendly supper club restaurant with old standbys including Chicken Kiev, numerous steak cuts, and liver and onions. The restaurant offers a shuttle to Minnesota Wild, Vikings, United FC, and Gopher football home games, and the shuttle is free for parties of 20 or more that make reservations in advance. Expensive.

&#9855; ☇ Ⴕ **In Bloom** (651-237-9630; inbloomstp.com), 928 7th Street W. Open daily for dinner, Sat.–Sun. for brunch. Located in the Keg and Case Market, In Bloom focuses on seasonal and local fine dining. The thoughtful menu offers both a la carte entrées along with plates with sides included, with options including a 2-pound porterhouse steak, an Asian pork belly, and venison ragu gnudi. Expensive/very expensive.

&#9855; ✿ ☇ Ⴕ **Downtowner Woodfire Grill** (651-228-9500; downtownerwoodfire.com), 253 7th Street W. Open daily for all three meals. Formerly the Woodfire Café, this eatery transitioned its dinner service into more of a fine dining experience at lunch and dinner. It still relies on its open wood-fired grill to produce its delicious meat dishes. The restaurant also offers pizzas and pastas, with several vegan options. Expensive.

## EATING OUT

### CATHEDRAL HILL

&#9855; ☇ ✿ **Nina's Coffee Cafe** (651-292-9816; ninascoffeecafe.com), 165 Western Avenue N. Open daily for all three meals. With a limited but quality menu of pastries, sandwiches, and soups, Nina's is a congenial neighborhood hangout in an attractive historic building. Free Wi-Fi is available to patrons. Inexpensive.

&#9855; ☇ ✿ Ⴕ **The Fitz** (651-219-4013; thefitzstpaul.com), 173 Western Avenue N. Open daily for dinner. Sandwiches, salads, and creative wood-fired pizzas, the last of which are named after various international locales (the Paris pizza has Dijon cream, gruyere, ham and egg, while the Osaka has Spam, pineapple chutney, and Japanese mayo). Inexpensive/moderate.

### DOWNTOWN/LOWERTOWN

&#9855; ☇ ✿ Ⴕ **Black Sheep Coal-Fired Pizza** (651-227-4337; blacksheeppizza.com), 512 Robert Street N. (with two locations in Minneapolis). Open daily for lunch and dinner. Black Sheep's delightful coal-fired pizzas come with creative topping choices, such as fennel sausage, hot salami, onion, and cracked green olive. Moderate.

&#9855; ☇ ✿ Ⴕ **M ST. Café** (651-228-3855; saintpaulhotel.com/m-st-cafe), 350 Market Street. Open daily for breakfast and lunch. Located in the lower level of the **St. Paul Hotel** (see *Lodging*), the M ST. Café offers breakfast classics and soups, salads, and sandwiches. Moderate.

&#9855; ☇ ✿ Ⴕ **Saint Dinette** (651-800-1415; saintdinette.com), 261 5th Street E. Open Tues.–Sun. for dinner, Sat.–Sun. for brunch. A deceptively casual-looking neighborhood eatery that has sophisticated takes on traditional comfort foods. Bologna plates, Midwestern caviar,

# ASIAN FOOD

While Minneapolis has Eat Street and the Midtown Global Market, St. Paul has its own neighborhoods filled with immigrants and authentic and delicious home cooking. University Avenue is home to dozens of small, casual Asian restaurants that don't always rely on Americanization to sell their foods. University Avenue also has a light rail line running down it, making it easier to use public transit.

**Hoa Bien** (651-647-1011; hoa-bien.com), 1105 University Avenue. Open daily for lunch and dinner. Excellent Vietnamese food, especially the seafood dishes. Inexpensive. ♿ ✍ ❄

**Ngon Vietnamese Bistro** (651-222-3301; ngonbistro.com), 799 University Avenue. Open daily for lunch and dinner. An unexpectedly elegant entry into the city's Asian restaurants, Ngon has extensive wine and beer lists and fusion food—and some of the best pho around. There's also a sharp focus on French-Vietnamese food. Moderate. ♿ ✍ ❄ ⏣

**Pho by Saigon Restaurant** (651-225-8751; facebook.com/saigon-restaurant-saint-paul -129743374913), 704 University Avenue. Open Tues.–Sun. for lunch and dinner. Counter service eatery providing excellent cooking and low prices. Best bets are the banh mi and any version of the numerous soups. Inexpensive. ♿ ✍ ❄ ⏣

**Cheng Heng** (651-222-5577; chengheng448.com), 448 University Avenue. Open daily for lunch and dinner. An extensive menu of Cambodian food, varied and tasty. Inexpensive. ♿ ✍ ❄

**Little Szechuan** (651-222-1333; littleszechuan.com), 422 University Avenue. (another location in Minneapolis). Open daily for lunch and dinner. With a casual but attractive interior, Little Szechuan differentiates itself by specializing in Szechuan hot pot, making for a fun and delicious way to enjoy a meal. Moderate. ✍ ♿ ⏣ ❄

lobster and grits, and fried chicken with nuoc cham are just a few of the excellent choices. Vegetarians have several options as well. Moderate.

♿ ✍ ❄ ⏣ **The Nook** (651-698-4347; crnook.com), 492 Hamline Avenue S. Open daily for lunch and dinner. Sure, it's a dive bar—but a dive bar with some of the best burgers in the state. The Nook has taken the local specialty known as the Juicy Lucy (burger stuffed with cheese and sometimes other ingredients) to heart with multiple iterations. Inexpensive.

♿ ✍ ❄ ⏣ **Cossetta Alimentari** (651-222-3476; cossettas.com), 211 7th Street W. Open daily for lunch and dinner. Cossetta's has been in St. Paul for almost a century, and there's a reason for that. A recent expansion led to the addition of a dinner-only restaurant (Louis Ristorante & Bar), while this casual Italian eatery cooks up seriously delicious pastas and pizzas, and the adjacent Italian market and Pasticceria have fresh ingredients and baked goods to take home. Inexpensive (eatery); moderate (Louis).

❄ ✍ **Mickey's Diner** (651-222-5633; mickeysdiningcar.com), 36 7th Street W. Open daily, 24 hours. This is truly a St. Paul institution, listed on the National Register of Historic Places. A rehabbed dining car with a tasty breakfast and burger grill menu, Mickey's is the classic quick-and-cheap eating spot. The waitresses are trained to deliver food, not make friends—and make sure you follow the posted rules regarding minimum dollars spent and maximum time allowed. Inexpensive.

♿ ✍ ❄ **Keys Café** (651-646-5756; keyscafe.com), 767 Raymond Avenue (several locations across the metro). Open daily for breakfast and lunch. Breakfast is served all day at this location, and you really don't need to look at the lunch menu (although it's good, too). Enormous cinnamon rolls and giant omelets (including a Loon omelet with wild rice and mushroom sauce) will take care of your appetite. Inexpensive.

  ♿ ✆ ⅄ ❀ **The Liffey** (651-556-1420; theliffey.com), 175 7th Street W. Open daily for all three meals. An Irish pub with an American and Irish menu, so you can have corned beef and cabbage or a burger. Moderate.

  ♿ ⅄ ❀ **Barrio Tequila Bar** (651-222-3250; barriotequila.com), 235 6th Street E. (with locations in Minneapolis and Edina). Open daily for lunch and dinner. Upscale, authentic Mexican food at reasonable prices—and an extensive tequila list. Moderate.

  ♿ ✆ ❀ ⅄ **The Bulldog Lowertown** (651-221-0750; thebulldogmn.com), 237 6th Street E. (two locations in Minneapolis). Open daily for lunch and dinner. Bulldog has a robust menu of sandwiches, burgers, and hot dogs, with an emphasis on quality. Try the Black Forest Elk Burger or the Capicola Cheese Melt. Moderate.

  ♿ ✆ ❀ ⅄ **Birch's Lowertown** (651-432-4677; birchslowertown.com), 289 5th Street E. Open daily for dinner, Sat. for early happy hour. A sizable taproom with an underground piano lounge. The food menu is limited, but worthy of a visit. Try the Brawt Burger with bacon jam or the smoked pork tacos. Moderate.

  ♿ ✆ ❀ ⅄ **Holman's Table** (612-800-5298; holmanstable.com), 644 Bayfield Street. Open daily for all three meals. Located at the St. Paul Downtown Airport's Holman Field, this restaurant not only serves far better-than-average "airport" food, it can also arrange helicopter rides. Dinner offerings include hearty sandwiches as well as steaks, scallops, pork chops, grilled sturgeon, and pasta. Moderate.

## WEST 7TH STREET

  ♿ ✆ ⅄ ❀ **Keg and Case** (kegandcase .com), 928 7th Street W. Open daily for all three meals. This retail/restaurant/farm market concept opened in the iconic former Schmidt Brewery and offers local food retailers (Forest to Fork

mushrooms, Green Bee Juicery, and Wandering Kitchen heat-and-eat meals) as well as a variety of eateries, including **In Bloom** (see *Where to Eat*), Pimento Jamaican Kitchen, Revival Smoked Meats, and Rose Street Patisserie. Something for every appetite and budget. Moderate to expensive.

  ♿ ✆ ⅄ ❀ **Pajarito** (651-340-9545; pajaritostp.com), 605 7th Street W. Open daily for lunch and dinner. Inventive Mexican foods, including soft shell crab tacos, octopus and lamb albondigas plates, and several grilled meat entrées. Moderate.

## GRAND AVENUE

Parking on or near Grand Avenue can be difficult. There is a ramp at Grand and Victoria, but given that the retail and dining area stretches more than 30 blocks, the ramp may not be near where you're going, and the restaurants often don't have their own parking lots. When looking for side-street parking, pay close attention to road signs; many side streets are for residents with permits only, and violating that can lead to tickets and towing.

  ♿ ✆ ❀ ⅄ **Saji-Ya** (651-292-0444; sajiya .com), 695 Grand Avenue. Open Mon.–Sat. for lunch and dinner, Sun. for dinner. Japanese cuisine, including extensive sushi options and teppanyaki tables. Moderate.

  ♿ ✆ ❀ **Grand Ole Creamery and Pizzeria** (651-293-1655; grandolecreamery .com/site), 750 Grand Avenue (another location in Minneapolis). Open daily for lunch and dinner. Homemade ice cream, and a creative line of pizzas. Need I say more? Inexpensive/moderate.

  ♿ ✆ ❀ ⅄ **Red Rabbit** (651-444-5995; wild-onion.net), 788 Grand Avenue (another location in Minneapolis). Open daily for lunch and dinner. An extensive menu of traditional Italian dishes updated with contemporary ingredients. Moderate.

  ♿ ✆ ❀ ⅄ **Café Latte** (651-224-5687; cafelatte.com), 850 Grand Avenue. Open

# DISTRICT DEL SOL DINING

**A**cross the Mississippi from St. Paul, the **District del Sol** (districtdelsol.com) is a large Hispanic settlement with tempting food options. If you're in town for Cinco de Mayo, stop by for the festivities (see *Special Events*).

**El Burrito Mercado** (651-227-2192; elburritomercado.com), 175 Cesar Chavez Street (another restaurant location in Minneapolis). Open daily for all three meals. This longtime Mexican grocer has served the District del Sol for more than 25 years, offering Hispanic foods at low prices. Summer often finds a corn feed of sorts on the sidewalk outside, with ears of corn served with chile powder and sour cream. **El Café Restaurant**, in the back of the mercado, has both cafeteria and table service, but more importantly, excellent food at low prices. You can go for the Americanized versions or stick to the more authentic foods, such as steamed mussels or huarachote. Mexican beer, wine, and cocktails are offered. Inexpensive. ♿ 🐾 ❄ 🍸

**Don Panchos Bakery** (651-225-8744; facebook.com/Don-Panchos-Bakery), 140 Cesar Chavez Street. Open daily. In an unassuming white house is this little bakery. It may not look like much outside or in, but the aroma of fresh bakery goods wafting out the door will make you not care what the ambience is. Look for the guava-cheese turnovers. Inexpensive. 🐾 ❄

**Blue Cat Coffee & Tea** (651-291-7676), 151 Cesar Chavez Street. Open Mon.–Sat. 7–4. Across from the El Burrito Mercado is this neighborhood caffeine provider, a cozy bistro. Inexpensive. ♿ 🐾 ❄

**Boca Chica** (651-222-8499; bocachicarestaurant.com), 11 Cesar Chavez Street. Open daily for lunch and dinner. Mexican foods madefrom scratch on-site, including authentic offerings along with Americanized versions. Live mariachi music offered the fourth Saturday of every month. Moderate. ♿ 🐾 ❄ 🍸

EL BURRITO MERCADO

daily for lunch and dinner. It may be a cafeteria, but forget tasteless casseroles and limp iceberg salads. Latte serves up fresh, lively food, often taking advantage of seasonal produce for a changing daily menu of soups and salads. Whatever you choose, leave room for dessert—Café Latte has one of the most decadent bakeries in the Twin Cities. Tucked away in the back is a pizza and wine bar. Inexpensive.

    &#x267F; &#x270E; &#10052; &#x1F377; **Brasa Rotisserie** (651-224-1302; brasa.us), 777 Grand Avenue (with another location in Minneapolis). Open daily for lunch and dinner. Their lively menu features Southern- and Caribbean-flavored meats and sides. Moderate.

    &#x267F; &#x270E; &#10052; &#x1F377; **Bap and Chicken** (651-333-0929; bapandchicken.com), 1328 Grand Avenue. Impeccable Korean-American street food, including Korean fried chicken, several iterations of bibimbap, and Korean bar snacks. Moderate.

    &#x270E; &#x267F; &#10052; **Uptowner Café** (651-224-0406), 1100 Grand Avenue. Open daily for breakfast and lunch. This small but delicious café serves impeccable breakfast foods, including house-made breads and buns for the breakfasts and lunch sandwiches. Inexpensive.

    &#x267F; &#x270E; &#10052; &#x1F377; **Everest on Grand** (651-696-1666; everestongrand.com), 1278 Grand Avenue. Open Wed.–Mon. for lunch and dinner. Nepali food served in a friendly atmosphere. The momo are delicious, as are the many curries. Vegetarians have lots of choices. Inexpensive/moderate.

OTHER AREAS IN ST. PAUL

    &#x267F; &#x270E; &#10052; &#x1F377; **Luci Ancora** (651-698-6889; ristoranteluci.com), 2060 Randolph Avenue. Open Tues.–Fri. for lunch, daily for dinner. Italian specialties incorporating local food sources, with four-course tasting menus offered nightly and a twice-weekly date night. Moderate.

    &#x267F; &#x270E; &#10052; &#x1F377; **Rusty Taco** (651-699-1833; rustytacomn.com), 508 Lexington Parkway. Open daily for all three meals.

Breakfast tacos, lunch tacos, and dinner tacos. Inexpensive.

    &#x267F; &#x270E; &#10052; **Pho 79** (651-644-2327; pho79.net), 2233 Energy Park Drive (with another location in Minneapolis). Open Mon.–Sat. for lunch and dinner. If you need a heaping, hearty bowl of flavorful soup (Pho and Hu Tieu), look no further. Inexpensive.

    &#x267F; &#x270E; &#10052; &#x1F377; **Blue Door Pub** (651-493-1865; thebdp.com), 1811 Selby Avenue (three additional locations in Minneapolis). Open daily for lunch and dinner. Blue Door gives **The Nook** (see page 97) a run for its money in the burger department. Its most famous burger is the Juicy Blucy (featured on *Diners, Drive-Ins and Dives*), a half-pound of beef stuffed with blue cheese and garlic. Moderate.

## &#10052; Entertainment

LIVE PERFORMANCES &#x267F; &#x270E; &#10052; &#x1F377; **The Fitzgerald Theater** (651-370-2953; the fitzgeraldtheater.com), 10 E. Exchange Street. The Fitzgerald used to be the property of Minnesota Public Radio, but recently was purchased by First Avenue (see page 66), which at least initially seemed committed to continuing to provide the eclectic variety of performances MPR used to. The historic building in downtown St. Paul hosts a wide variety of programming, from classical music to indie rock darlings, book discussions, and comedy events.

    &#x267F; &#x270E; &#10052; &#x1F377; **Ordway Center for the Performing Arts** (651-224-4222; ordway.org), 345 Washington Street. The Ordway is a spectacular theater set on the edge of downtown St. Paul, on Rice Park and within easy walking distance to several prime St. Paul restaurants (Pazzaluna, Sakura, Meritage, St. Paul Grill; see *Where to Eat*). Home of the renowned Minnesota Opera, the Ordway also hosts touring musicians, dancers, and Broadway musicals, as well as presents several locally developed theatrical shows each year. Place your bar order ahead of time to have it ready and waiting during intermission.

♿ ✎ ❄ **Landmark Center** (651-292-3225; landmarkcenter.org), 75 W. 5th Street. Across the street from the Ordway is this impressive building, originally built in 1902 to serve as a federal courthouse and post office. Today it's a cultural center, with a variety of events—music, dance, theater, walking tours—taking place throughout the year. The building also houses several art galleries.

♿ **Minnesota Opera** (612-333-6669; mnopera.org), Ordway Center, 345 Washington Street. The Minnesota Opera formed in the 1970s, and in the mid-1980s it became one of the original tenants of the new Ordway Center. Today the company produces four or five full operas each year, using both local and international opera performers in innovative stagings. The primary focus is bel canto, and each season includes at least one bel canto masterpiece. The company

has also premiered several new works and brought back Bernard Herrmann's *Wuthering Heights*, a rarely performed piece. The opera is also developing programming aimed at young children, with special performances and opera camps.

♿ **Penumbra Theatre** (651-224-3180; penumbratheatre.org), 270 N. Kent Street. Penumbra is one of a few African-American theaters in the country to produce a full season each year. Creative director Lou Bellamy has led the company to national prominence with quality productions and high-profile theatrical premiers, including several August Wilson works. Programming includes socially relevant productions along with educational events to spur discussion in the community. The company's Black Nativity is one of the Twin Cities' most popular holiday events each year.

♿ ✎ **St. Paul Chamber Orchestra** (651-291-1144; thespco.org), 408 St. Peter Street, third floor. The SPCO is a

ORDWAY CENTER FOR THE PERFORMING ARTS

full-time professional chamber orchestra, and they are a busy group; besides performing in their own music hall on St. Peter Street, they also headline the Ordway Center and offer suburban venues, including in Wayzata and Eden Prairie. The company gives more than 150 performances each year, including a set of children's concerts and occasional international tours.

&⚹ ❋ ☂ ❙❙ **Xcel Energy Center** (651-726-8200; xcelenergycenter.com), 199 W. Kellogg Boulevard. Part of the larger RiverCentre entertainment and convention complex, the Xcel Energy Center is home to the Minnesota Wild NHL team (see *Sporting Events*) and plays host to a wide variety of touring performers. Like its counterpart across the river, the Target Center, Xcel brings in top-level entertainers and bands; unlike Target Center, Xcel was built with concert acoustics in mind. Locals rejoice when their favorites play here, because the sound is much better.

&⚹ **History Theatre** (651-292-4323; historytheatre.com), 30 10th Street E. A theater company devoted to original plays focused on the American experience, primarily Minnesotan, both historical and current. Recent productions have included plays about the infamous Glensheen murders and a world premier rock musical about the northern Minnesota Runestone controversy.

&⚹ **Circus Juventas** (651-699-8229; circusjuventas.org), 1270 Montreal Avenue. Circus Juventas is a performing-arts circus school for people ages 3 to 21. Besides offering workshops and camps, the Juventas troupes put on two shows annually. Call or check the website for a schedule.

SPORTING EVENTS &⚹ ☂ ❙❙ **St. Paul Saints** (651-644-6659; saintsbaseball .com), CHS Field, 360 Broadway Street. The Saints is the Twin Cities' minor league baseball team, owned in part by actor Bill Murray. Their move to a new stadium in Lowertown St. Paul provided them with a fantastic new venue that includes far more amenities, including bars and food areas, than their previous Midway Stadium did. In addition, there's a grassy hill area that visitors can get cheap tickets for and bring a blanket and a picnic. The Saints have also partnered with the Lowertown arts community to provide display space for many local artists. They may not have the name power of the Minnesota Twins, but the Saints do have goofy activities and displays between innings, including a live pig as mascot.

&⚹ ☂ ❙❙ **Minnesota Wild** (651-602-6000; nhl.com/wild), 175 W. Kellogg Boulevard. Minnesota's NHL hockey team plays its home games at the Xcel Energy Center.

&⚹ ☂ ❙❙ **Minnesota United** (763-476-2237; mnufc.com), Allianz Field, 400 Snelling Avenue N. Professional soccer got its own stadium in Minnesota in 2019 with Allianz Field and the Minnesota United Football Club. The stadium comes complete with a beer garden–type restaurant offering 96 taps and local foods.

&⚹ ☂ ❙❙ **Minnesota RollerGirls** (320-634-6674; mnrollergirls.com), Xcel Energy Center, 175 W. Kellogg Boulevard. The RollerGirls play their regular season at Xcel Energy Center's Roy Wilkins Auditorium and are founding members of the Women's Flat Track Derby Association. They were the first league in the United States to have a professional arena for practices and bouts, and the four home teams (Atomic Bombshells, Dagger Dolls, Garda Belts, and Rockits) play with spirit and athleticism.

## ❋ Selective Shopping

Stores are open year-round unless otherwise noted.

BOOKS &⚹ ❋ **Next Chapter Booksellers** (651-225-8989; nextchapterbooksellers .com), 38 S. Snelling Avenue. Open daily.

# GRAND AVENUE SHOPPING

**J**ust outside of downtown St. Paul is Grand Avenue, which runs parallel to Summit Avenue, home to many sumptuous St. Paul mansions (including the governor's mansion). Grand Avenue itself is a walker's paradise of restaurants and shops, many in rehabbed homes. The heart of the area is Victoria Crossings, the intersection of Grand Avenue and Victoria, where a public parking ramp and several restaurants are situated. An annual festival, Grand Old Day, showcases the neighborhood (see *Special Events*). Following is an overview of some of the shops to visit (see grandave.com for details).

**GoodThings Bibelot** (651-222-0321; shopgoodthings.com), 1082 Grand Avenue, with another location in Minneapolis. Open daily. GoodThings Bibelot stores carry all kinds of guilty pleasures, from locally made jewelry to unique women's clothing to off-the-wall kitchen and bath items, greeting cards, and toys for kids. ♿ ✿ ❄

**Cooks of Crocus Hill** (651-228-1333; cooksofcrocushill.com), 877 Grand Avenue (with locations in Minneapolis and Stillwater). Open daily. All the fine cooking supplies you ever thought, or never knew, you needed. Cooks also offers an extensive class list. ✿ ❄

**Northern Brewer** (651-223-6114; northernbrewer.com), 1150 Grand Avenue. Open daily. Supplies for home-brew or winemaking beginners and aficionados, including many class offerings. ♿ ❄

**Treadle Yard Goods** (651-698-9690; treadleyardgoods.com), 1338 Grand Avenue. Open daily. Fabric and supplies for those interested in sewing, including some unusual and high-end items. ♿ ✿ ❄

**Golden Fig** (651-602-0144; goldenfig.com), 794 Grand Avenue. Open daily. This gem offers a large selection of (mostly local) gourmet foods, treats, spices, local artisanal cheese, and heavenly chocolates. ♿ ✿ ❄

This thoughtfully stocked bookstore, originally owned by Garrison Keillor, has a frequently updated set of offerings and a heavy roster of in-store events.

♿ ✿ ❄ **Red Balloon Bookshop** (651-224-8320; redballoonbookshop.com), 891 Grand Avenue. Open daily. This bookstore in a refurbished house focuses solely on children's books, and their expertise is considerable. The shop carries a wide range of books, and they host several events every month. The staff is knowledgeable and friendly.

♿ ✿ ❄ **Winding Trail Books** (651-414-9431; windingtrailbooks.com), 2230 Carter Avenue. Open Tues.–Sat. Books and gifts in the uber-charming St. Anthony neighborhood.

**YARN** Possibly because of the climate in the winter, or just because arts and creativity are prized in this community, the Twin Cities metro area has an unusually large selection of yarn shops. The following shops are in St. Paul unless otherwise noted.

♿ ✿ ❄ **The Yarnery** (651-222-5793; yarnery.com), 840 Grand Avenue. Open daily. A tiny cottage of a shop, but with a good selection and a small sales annex.

♿ ✿ ❄ **Three Kittens Needle Arts** (651-457-4969; 3kittensneedlearts.com), 750 Main Street, Mendota Heights. Open Tues.–Sun. A sizable yarn shop with a wide variety of products.

♿ ✿ ❄ **Sheepy Yarn Shoppe** (651-426-5463 or 1-800-480-5462; sheepyyarnmn.com), 2185 3rd Street, White Bear Lake. Open Mon.–Sat. A cozy shop, complete with fireplace, for yarn lovers to relax, shop, or pursue their favorite yarn activity.

♿ ✿ ❄ **Knitting From the Heart** (651-702-0880; heartknit.com), 1785 Radio Drive, Woodbury. Open Mon.–Sat. Carries a wide and changing variety of yarns, including new and unusual brands.

# THE MINNESOTA STATE FAIR

Minnesota State Fair (651-288-4400; mnstatefair.org), 1265 N. Snelling Avenue. Open for 10 days through Labor Day. Adults $11; senior citizens $9; children 5-12 $8; children under 5 free. Various discounts are offered; check the website for details. Billed as the "Great Minnesota Get-Together," the fair is the classic rite of passage from summer to fall. Attended by more than 2 million people each year, the state fair is held on permanent fairgrounds in St. Paul. Parking can be tricky and expensive; most public transit companies around the Twin Cities offer state fair buses that bypass the parking issue. The fair has something for everyone: animals (farm and pets); farm machinery; rides small and large; live entertainment all day (some included in the admission, some incurring extra costs, especially the grandstand shows that tend to have the name performers); exhibits with crafts and fine arts; games; a Miracle of Birth Center, where animals are on display during their birth process; parades; haunted house; hands-on exhibits from vendors; and food. The fair is well-known for its food, much of which lacks a healthy quality but makes up for it in taste and, in recent years, has seen some sharp increases in quality and creativity. Go early, go often.

## ✳ Special Events

*Spring and fall*: **St. Paul Art Crawl** (651-233-7233; saintpaulartcrawl.org), Downtown and Lowertown. Held in the spring and fall, and allows more than 200 local artists and galleries to open their studios to visitors and potential buyers.

*Year-round*: **Minnesota Historical Society** (mnhs.org/calendar). The historical society, which maintains sites all over the state, has numerous events, some annual, some one time only. Check their website for information on upcoming festivities at their St. Paul headquarters, as well as around St. Paul and the state, including **Historic Fort Snelling** (see *To See and Do*). Special events around various holidays, including haunted State Capitol tours for Halloween and multitudes of historical Christmas celebrations, are of special interest.

*January*: **Saint Paul Winter Carnival** (651-223-4700; wintercarnival.com), various sites. Legend has it that this festival began in response to comments about St. Paul made by a New York reporter who said winters were "unfit for human habitation." Hence, a carnival to prove that not only is the winter not uninhabitable, but it can be quite hospitable and even fun. For 12 days starting in late Jan., St. Paul hosts a wide variety of events, including a coronation of winter royalty, a torchlight parade, snow sculpting and ice carving contests, a medallion treasure hunt, numerous kids' activities, and a "Frozen" 5K and half marathon. Check the website for details of each year's events; some years have included the building of an ice palace.

*May*: **Festival of Nations** (651-647-0191; festivalofnations.com), River Centre, 175 W. Kellogg Boulevard. For nearly 90 years this festival has been held annually in early May, celebrating the melting-pot diversity of America and, increasingly, Minnesota. Nearly 100 different cultures are represented, with shops, cafés, musical and dance performances, craft demonstrations, and displays of cultural traditions.

**Cinco de Mayo** (651-223-7400; cinco demayosaintpaul.com), District del Sol. St. Paul's vibrant West Side, already the home to many Hispanic restaurants and shops (see *Where to Eat*), hosts this annual event. Two days of food, fun, live entertainment, a low-rider car show, parade, 5K and 1-mile races, salsa-tasting contests, and children's activities are all part of the celebration. Proceeds are reinvested into the neighborhood.

*June*: **Grand Old Day** (651-699-0029, grandave.com), Grand Avenue. Held the first Sunday in June. It's only one day, but what a day. Grand Old Day kicks off with races of varying lengths (8K, 5K, 0.5 mile, 0.25 mile), followed by food, parades, an art fair, kids' activities, live music, and a teen battle of the bands.

*August*: **Irish Fair** (952-645-0221; irishfair.com), Harriet Island. Just as summer is starting to wind down, Harriet Island hosts three days of everything Irish: options can include music, food, dance, drink, rugby matches, sheepherding, Gaelic football games, kids' activities, and a Best Legs in a Kilt contest.

*September*: **St. Paul Bike Classic Bike Tour** (952-882-3180; bikeclassic.org), University of St. Thomas. Not a race, but an actual tour; there are two routes, 15 and 30 miles, for bikers to choose from, which cycle along the Mississippi River and then on to either Summit Avenue or up to Indian Mounds Park and around Lake Phalen. Routes can change; check the website for details.

*November*: **Hmong American New Year** (651-207-8467; hmongamericaninc .org), Minnesota State Fairgrounds, 1265 N. Snelling Avenue. This annual holiday celebrates and educates visitors about the Hmong New Year with traditional foods, clothing, music, dance, and shopping. The Hmong population in the Twin Cities is one of the largest in the United States, and this celebration has taken place for more than 40 years.

# ST. PAUL'S NEIGHBORING COMMUNITIES

**M**any of the suburbs around St. Paul began life as small towns, becoming suburbs as the city spread out to meet them. Some of the older communities, like White Bear Lake, have grown while still retaining the small-town charm associated with tiny stores in old brick buildings along narrow streets, making for a most pleasant way to spend an afternoon.

## Apple Valley

Apple Valley in its present form has only existed since the mid-20th century, but for decades before that it was farmland—not surprising given its proximity to the rolling, fertile land along the Minnesota River.

    ᗢ ♪ ❀ ⑪ **Minnesota Zoo** (952-431-9200 or 1-800-366-7811; mnzoo.org), 13000 Zoo Boulevard. Open daily; hours vary by season. Adults $18; senior citizens and children 3–12 $12; children under 3 and zoo members free. Parking is additional. This is one of the two major zoos in the Twin Cities area. The other is **Como Park, Zoo, and Conservatory** in St. Paul (see page 90), in the heart of the city; the Minnesota Zoo is out in the country, and the two zoos are different enough to justify visiting both. The emphasis at the Minnesota Zoo is on natural habitat, so instead of regular cages, many of the larger animals have large parcels of land to call their own. Some of the traditional zoo animals, such as elephants and giraffes, aren't seen here, unless in a visiting exhibition. But there is plenty to see, including a wide variety of monkeys and large cats, and a new dolphin area has regular shows. There's a food court on the property, but it's OK to bring in your own picnic. The zoo offers numerous special events each year, including an indoor sandbox and beach day in February. Check the website for details.

THE SIBLEY HOUSE

## Mendota

The name Mendota comes from the Dakota word for "where the waters meet." It's a tiny town—the population is less than 200—but is known for its prominent historic site, the Sibley House.

    ♪ **Sibley House Historic Site** (651-452-1596; mnhs.org/sibley), 1357 Sibley Memorial Highway. Open Sat. 10–5 and Sun. 1–5, Memorial Day–Labor Day. Adults $7; senior citizens, active military and veterans, and college students $6; children 5–17 $5; children under 5 and Minnesota Historical Society members free. Some of the state's oldest remaining buildings are at this site, the former home of Henry Hastings Sibley, who worked at the trade center for the American Fur Company in the mid-1800s and eventually became governor. Guides are available to lead visitors through three buildings, including the residence and the fur company coldstore.

# White Bear Lake

This small town on a lake has risen above its suburban roots to become a destination for the dining and shopping crowd.

## ✳ Where to Eat

DINING OUT ♿ ♉ ✳ **Acqua Restaurant & Bar** (651-407-7317; ursulaswb.com), 4453 Lake Avenue S. Open daily for dinner. This cozy restaurant in a former home is located on White Bear Lake and has three dining rooms, two decks, and a patio. The Italian-focused menu offers less pasta and more meat and seafood dishes, along with a few options for vegetarians. A three-course tasting menu that changes frequently is also offered. Expensive.

♿ ♉ ✳ **Mizu Japanese** (651-653-4888; mizuwbl.com), 4475 Lake Avenue S. Open Tues.–Sun. for dinner. Upscale Japanese menu, including a lengthy sushi-sashimi area, but also offerings including roasted pork and kimchi and pork belly ramen. A five-course tasting menu for two is a good bargain at $55 per person. Moderate/expensive.

♿ ♉ ✳ **The Alchemist** (651-429-9286; thealchemistwbl.com), 2222 4th Street. Open Tues.–Sat. for dinner, Sun. for brunch. The Alchemist is primarily a cocktail bar, with an extensive menu of handcrafted cocktails. But the bar also has a limited but creative (and tasty) food menu to accompany those drinks, including charcuterie and cheese trays and a fig and truffle honey flatbread. Moderate/expensive.

♿ ✐ ♉ ✳ **Ingredients Cafe** (651-426-6611; ingredientscafe.com), 4725 US 61 N. Open Mon.–Sat. for lunch and dinner,

Sun. for dinner. A menu that changes monthly, focusing on fresh, locally available foods, and good wine and martini lists make this place worth a visit. Moderate/expensive.

♿ ✐ ♉ ✳ **Rudy's Redeye Grill** (651-653-6718; rudysredeye.com), 4940 US 61 N. Open daily for lunch and dinner. Upscale steakhouse with a wide variety of steaks, seafood, and pasta, plus a full bar. Expensive.

EATING OUT ♿ ✐ ♉ ✳ **Washington Square Bar & Grill** (651-407-7162; washingtonsquareonline.net), 4736 Washington Avenue. Open daily for all three meals. Neighborhood bar and grill with outstanding burgers. The outdoor patio is used three seasons and is a lovely spot. Moderate.

♿ ✐ ✳ **Ban Thai Restaurant** (651-407-8424), 2186 3rd Street. Open Tues.–Sun. for lunch and dinner. This little restaurant is often said to be one of the best, if not the best, Thai restaurant in the Twin Cities. Moderate.

♿ ✐ ✳ **Grandma's Bakery** (651-779-0707; grandmasbakery.com), 2184 4th Street. Open daily. A classic small-town bakery, full of enticing donuts, cakes, cookies, pastries and bars, pies, and breads. There is also soup available, different variety every day. Inexpensive.

♿ ✐ ✳ **Cobblestone Café** (651-429-6793; facebook.com/Cobblestone-Cafe -102219766487660), 4760 Washington Square. Open daily for breakfast and lunch. Enormous home-cooked breakfasts and lunch entrées. Inexpensive.

    ♿ ✎ ✳ **Pizzeria Pezzo** (651-778-7844; pizzeriapezzo.com), 2143 4th Street. Open Tues.–Sun. for dinner. Coal-fired pizza that's far better than chain offerings. Try the Rustica, with grilled eggplant and goat cheese, or the Cardinale, with prosciutto, goat cheese, and arugula. Moderate.

    ♿ ✎ ⛾ ✳ **CG Hooks BBQ Restaurant & Bar** (651-493-6763; cghooks.com/cg -hooks-restaurant-bar), 4441 Lake Avenue S. Open daily for lunch and dinner. CG Hooks is a bar and grill that's part of Tally's Dockside, a boat and water sports rental operation on the lake. As the name implies, barbecue is king here, with brisket, pulled chicken, and ribs, but there are salads, hot dogs, and tacos as well. Moderate.

## ✳ Selective Shopping

    ♿ ✳ **Truly** (651-426-8414; trulyonline .com), 2175 4th Street. Open daily. Shop specializing in handmade gifts by independent artists and artisans.

    ♿ ✎ ✳ **SweetLife Lane** (651-705-8600; sweetlifelane.com), 2180 3rd Street. Open daily; hours vary seasonally. Candy and sweet shop (and treats for visiting dogs).

    ♿ ✎ ✳ **The Farmer's Daughter** (651-653-6768; thefarmersdaughterwbl.com), 4905 Long Avenue. Open daily. Features handmade gift items from local artists and artisans.

    ♿ ✳ **Frank Murphy Fashions** (651-762-9200; frankmurphyfashions.com), 4750 MN 61 N. Open Tues.–Sat. High-end international fashion and accessories.

    ♿ ✳ **Primp** (651-340-4717; primp yourself.com/whitebearlake), 4766 Banning Avenue. Open daily. Inexpensive, fun women's fashions and accessories.

    ♿ ✎ ✳ **A Beautiful Pause** (651-456-8298; abeautifulpause.com), 2179 4th Street. Open Thurs.–Sat. or by appointment. Capitalizing on the interest in the Scandinavian concept of hygge, this store offers gifts meant to relax and refresh the buyer's (or recipient's) spirit.

    ♿ ✎ ✳ **Lake Country Booksellers** (651-426-0918; facebook.com/Lake -Country-Booksellers-191453436875), 4766 Washington Avenue. Open daily. Books and related gifts.

# Woodbury

Woodbury was first settled in the mid-19th century, primarily as a farming community for Scandinavian, Irish, and Scottish settlers. Today it's a growing suburb with an emphasis on shopping.

    ♿ ✎ ✳ ⛾ ⫱ **Woodbury Lakes** (651-251-9500; woodburylakes.com), 9020 Hudson Road. Open daily. Opened by the same company that handled the **Shoppes at Arbor Lakes** (see *Maple Grove* on page 82), Woodbury Lakes is designed to feel more like a small-town shopping center rather than a giant mall by providing a mix of retail and dining in actual city blocks with sidewalks. While many of the usual chain-store suspects are present (Gap, Banana Republic, Victoria's Secret, and J.Jill), the strolling-friendly layout over four city blocks makes the shopping experience feel less suburban mall and more charming village. It's also the site of the first Minnesota location of the Alamo Drafthouse movie theater chain, with full menus and bar. Dining options are much more limited than in Maple Grove, with only three sit-down restaurants and a bubble tea shop.

# NORTH SHORE AND THE ARROWHEAD

■

HINCKLEY

DULUTH

NORTH SHORE/LUTSEN

GRAND MARAIS/GRAND PORTAGE/
GUNFLINT TRAIL

BOUNDARY WATERS/ELY

INTERNATIONAL FALLS/
VOYAGEURS NATIONAL PARK

THE IRON RANGE

# NORTHSHORE AND THE ARROWHEAD

I n a state that has stately forests, lakes small and large, prairies, and rolling country-side, it's hard to pick one area as the most scenic. But the North Shore and the Arrow-head region (named after its shape) have arguably some of the loveliest vistas in the state, and the region is one of the state's most popular for visitors.

The eastern edge of the Arrowhead runs along the shores of Lake Superior, while the northern border runs along Canada, areas rich in geological and historical inter-est. Much of the Lake Superior area was inhabited by the Ojibwe before the arrival of the Europeans, who came searching for trade routes and posts. The French were prom-inent explorers and settlers in this area, looking for furs and other goods for trade, and their influence is seen in community names like Grand Marais and Grand Portage. Fur trading was a central activity until about 1840, when most of the traders and trappers moved elsewhere, including the Mississippi Headwaters area. However, the arrival of railroads in 1869, combined with increased ship traffic on Lake Superior, lead to a pop-ulation boom. The growth of commercial fishing as well as the development of the iron ore industry, combined with more sophisticated infrastructure and shipping methods, lead not only to established communities but to the beginning of the tourism industry.

While fishing and mining enjoyed their heydays, the lumber and agricultural indus-tries were booming as well, at least until the Depression years, when competition in other parts of the country reduced their prominence.

Today's North Shore and Arrowhead still sees considerable commercial fishing and mining activity, but tourism has come to play an ever-increasing role in the local economy. The establishment of the million-plus-acre Boundary Waters Canoe Area Wilderness within Superior National Forest, which keeps this wilderness preserved nearly as it was in the days of the voyageurs, brings thousands of visitors each sum-mer for camping, hiking, and boating. But whereas visitors used to come only in the summer for fishing and hiking, now they come year-round, taking advantage of the area's winter landscape for activities like skiing, snowmobiling, snowshoeing, and even dogsledding.

GUIDANCE **Hinckley Convention and Visitor Bureau** (320-384-0126 or 1-800-952-4282; hinckleymn.com), P.O. Box 197, Hinckley, MN 55037. Contact them via their web-site or phone number to order a visitor's guide to the area.

**Cloquet Area Tourism Office** (218-879-1551 or 1-800-554-4350; visitcloquet.com), 225 Sunnyside Drive, Cloquet.

**Duluth Convention and Visitor Bureau** (218-722-4011 or 1-800-438-5884; visitduluth .com), 225 W. Superior Street, Suite 110, Duluth. The Duluth CVB has extensive infor-mation about the city on the lake, but be aware that the website is packed full of text and images, and can be overwhelming.

**Visit Cook County** (218-387-2524 or 1-888-922-5000; visitcookcounty.com/community /lutsen-tofte-schroeder).

**Tofte Information Center,** 7136 W. MN 61, Tofte.

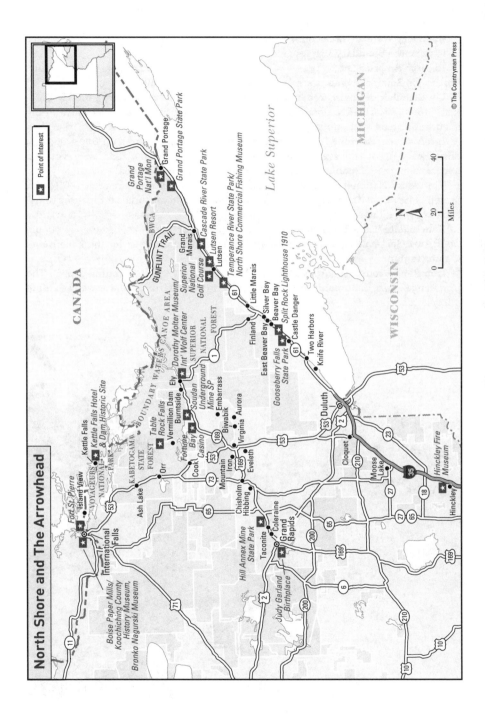

# North Shore and The Arrowhead

★ Point of Interest

© The Countryman Press

CANADA

Grand Portage Nat'l Mon.
Grand Portage
Grand Portage State Park

BWCA

GUNFLINT TRAIL

Cascade River State Park
Lutsen Resort
Grand Marais
Lutsen
Superior National Golf Course
Temperance River State Park/
North Shore Commercial Fishing Museum

SUPERIOR NATIONAL FOREST

Dorothy Molter Museum/
Int'l Wolf Center
Ely
Soudan Underground Mine SP

Embarrass
Aurora
Biwabik
Virginia

BOUNDARY WATERS CANOE AREA

Burntside
Vermillion Dam
Rock Falls
Table
Fortune Bay Casino

KABETOGAMA STATE FOREST

Orr

Kettle Falls
Kettle Falls Hotel
& Dam Historic Site

VOYAGEURS NATIONAL PARK

Island View
Fort St. Pierre
International Falls

Boise Paper Mills/
Koochiching County
History Museum,
Bronko Nagurski Museum

Ash Lake

Cook
Mountain Iron
Eveleth
Chisholm
Hibbing
Coleraine
Grand Rapids
Taconite
Hill Annex Mine State Park
Judy Garland Birthplace

Little Marais
Finland
East Beaver Bay
Silver Bay
Beaver Bay
Split Rock Lighthouse 1910
Castle Danger
Gooseberry Falls State Park
Two Harbors
Knife River

Lake Superior

Duluth
Cloquet
Moose Lake
Hinckley
Hinckley Fire Museum

WISCONSIN

MICHIGAN

N

Miles
0    20    40

**Grand Marais Information Center**, 116 W. MN 61, Grand Marais. Provides information for visitors to the popular ski resort of Lutsen as well as Grand Marais, Grand Portage, and the Gunflint Trail.

**Boundary Waters** (bwca.com). A website full of practical information and resources on visiting the Boundary Waters area.

**Reserve America** (1-877-444-6777; recreation.gov). A major national site where visitors to the Boundary Waters area can reserve sites and permits.

**Ely Chamber of Commerce** (218-365-6123 or 1-800-777-7281; ely.org), 1600 E. Sheridan Street, Ely. The Ely Chamber can provide help and information not just on Ely itself, but also on the Boundary Waters.

**International Falls and Rainy Lake Convention and Visitor Bureau** (1-800-325-5766; rainylake.org), 301 2nd Avenue, International Falls. A well-organized CVB devoted to tourism along the Canadian border and into the Voyageurs National Park area.

**Voyageurs National Park Association** (612-333-5424; voyageurs.org), 126 N. 3rd Street, Suite 400, Minneapolis. Provides information and resources for visitors to the state's only national park.

**Kabetogama Lake Tourism Bureau** (218-875-2621 or 1-800-525-3522; kabetogama .com), 907 Gamma Road, Lake Kabetogama. Tourist information for the Lake Kabetogama region.

**Iron Range Tourism Bureau** (218-749-8161 or 1-800-777-8497; ironrange.org). The Iron Range Tourism Bureau offers a free print guide to the Iron Range as well as online information.

TRAVELING THE GUNFLINT TRAIL

GETTING THERE  **By air:** The primary commercial airport in the region is the **Duluth International Airport** (218-727-2968; duluthairport.com), served by Delta, with flights to Minneapolis–St. Paul and Detroit; American and United Airlines, with flights to Chicago; and, on a charter-only basis, Sun Country. **International Falls** also has an airport (218-283-4461; internationalfallsairport.com) served by Delta Airlines and SkyWest Air Lines, both offering feeder routes from Minneapolis–St. Paul, as well as charter service via Sun Country. Many of the smaller cities have municipal airports that can handle smaller jets or prop planes. Taxis, limos, rental cars, and light rail service is available from the airports into Duluth and surrounding areas.

**By car:** From the Twin Cities, I-35W. will take you up to Duluth and scenic MN 61, which leads all the way up to the Canadian border. If you're heading to the eastern half of the Boundary Waters or the Gunflint Trail, this is the best route to take. If you're looking for the western parts of the Boundary Waters, you can take I-35W toward Duluth, then take MN 61 north of Silver Bay to MN 1, which takes you directly to Ely and parts west. An additional option between the Twin Cities and Duluth is the **Skyline Shuttle** (skylineshuttle.com), which operates out of the Minneapolis–St. Louis International Airport with daily round-trip bus service.

If you're driving toward Voyageurs National Park, you can take US 169 north out of the Twin Cities through the Iron Range to Chisholm, where you could pick up MN 73, which merges farther north with US 53, which continues to International Falls. An alternate route would be I-94 W. to St. Cloud, crossing over to US 10 to MN 371 through Brainerd and merging with US 71 south of Bemidji. US 71 then continues north to International Falls.

GETTING AROUND  Duluth has a public bus system that covers the metro area, with reduced service on weekends and holidays. The service is designed primarily to transport students and employees from outlying homes to work and school within the city. Contact **Duluth Transit Authority** (218-722-7283; duluthtransit.com) for more information. For maximum flexibility, a car is recommended and is a necessity if you're traveling outside of Duluth. If you're staying in the downtown Duluth area and can walk or take a brief taxi ride to other downtown destinations, you could survive without a car. The remaining regions of northeastern Minnesota require a vehicle.

WHEN TO COME  The summer months are a particularly popular time in the Duluth, greater North Shore, and Voyageurs National Park areas, where the cooler temperatures generated by Lake Superior keep the heat from rising to intolerable levels. The scenery is beautiful, and countless events and festivals up and down the shore take advantage of that. Autumn months draw foliage visitors to all parts of the North Shore and Arrowhead region, while winter draws sports enthusiasts, particularly skiers to Lutsen and snowmobilers, snowshoers, dog sledders, and ice fishers to the more remote areas. Be aware that the winter months can produce some bitterly cold temperatures, particularly in the far northern reaches, but local stores are well prepared to provide the necessary outerwear. And if you're not fond of cold weather, bundle up in one of the many bed-and-breakfasts or lodges with cozy fireplaces and enjoy the snowy scenery from the warmth of indoors.

MEDICAL EMERGENCY  Call 911.
  **St. Luke's Hospital** (218-249-5555; slhduluth.com), 915 E. 1st Street, Duluth.
  **Lake View Memorial Hospital** (218-834-7300; slhduluth.com/Find-a-Location/Lake -View-Hospital.aspx), 325 11th Avenue, Two Harbors.

**North Shore Health and Hospital** (218-387-3040; northshorehealthgm.org), 515 W. 5th Avenue, Grand Marais.

**Fairview Range Medical Center** (218-262-4881 or 1-888-870-8626; fairview.org), 750 E. 34th Street, Hibbing.

**Ely Bloomenson Community Hospital** (218-365-3271; ebch.org), 328 W. Conan Street, Ely.

**Grand Itasca Clinic & Hospital** (218-326-3401; granditasca.org), 1601 Golf Course Road, Grand Rapids.

**Rainy Lake Medical Center** (218-283-4481; rainylakemedical.com), 1400 US 71, International Falls.

# HINCKLEY

About halfway between the Twin Cities and Duluth on I-35W is the small community of Hinckley.

## ✳ To See and Do

GAMING ♿ ⚲ ⏱ ❋ ⏲ **Grand Casino Hinckley** (1-800-472-6321; grandcasinomn.com), 777 Lady Luck Drive. Open 24/7. Grand Casino offers extensive gaming opportunities for slots, blackjack, and bingo. Five restaurants are available for dining, and the on-site Kids Quest provides childcare for kids too young to be on the casino floor.

MUSEUMS ♿ ⚲ **Hinckley Fire Museum** (320-384-7338; hinckleyfiremuseum.com), 106 Old Highway 61 S. Open Tues.–Sun. 10–5, May–mid-Oct.; open daily Jul. and Aug. Admission is $5 for adults ages 18–61; $4 for 62 and older; $2 for age 7–17; 6 and under free. On September 1, 1894, a historic event occurred in the quiet logging town of Hinckley, just south of Duluth. A fire started, and while any fire that burns out of control in the wilderness can be considered a wildfire and therefore devastating, the fire that consumed Hinckley was worse. Its technical name is "firestorm"; flames shot up 4 miles into the air, and 20 square miles of land were destroyed in less than four hours. The firestorm evolved much like a natural disaster, with cyclones of fire advancing and wreaking havoc. The only other comparable firestorms in the 20th century were related to the launching of atomic bombs in Hiroshima. The Hinckley Fire Museum is housed in a small building that previously served as the town's railroad depot (the one built to replace the one destroyed by the firestorm). Though small, it has a sizable collection of fire artifacts, as well as a brief documentary movie and Native American items. The friendly staff knows the history of the firestorm well and is happy to answer questions or provide information on the individual artifacts.

## ✳ Lodging

BED-AND-BREAKFASTS ⚲ ♿ ❋
**Dakota Lodge** (320-384-6052; dakotalodge.com), 40497 MN 48. The Dakota offers a wide variety of accommodations: four bed-and-breakfast lodge rooms, all with private bath and fireplaces; cabins; and a two-bedroom guesthouse. The bed-and-breakfast rooms come with a full breakfast daily.

THE HINCKLEY FIRE MUSEUM

The property is a naturalist's haven, with easy access to nearby St. Croix State Park. Moderate/expensive.

  ✦ ❄ **Woodland Trails Bed & Breakfast** (320-655-3901; woodlandtrails .net), 40361 Grace Lake Road. Built in 2003, this country charmer is situated on 500 acres of woodland. The property includes 4 miles of trails for hiking as well as access to Grace Lake for bird-watching, paddleboating, or catch-and-release fishing. There are golf carts, snowshoes, and fat-tire bikes available for guests. The five guest rooms all have private baths and electric fireplaces; full breakfast is included. Expensive/very expensive.

HOTELS ✦ ✐ Y ❄ ¶ **Grand Casino Hinckley Hotel** (1-800-468-3517; grand casinomn.com), 777 Lady Luck Drive. This is the larger of the Grand Casino Hinckley hotels, with 281 rooms and suites. Inexpensive/moderate.

  ✦ ✐ ❄ **Grand Hinckley Inn** (1-800-468-3517; grandcasinomn.com), 777 Lady Luck Drive. The inn, operated by the Grand Casino Hinckley, has 154 rooms and suites, as well as an indoor pool. Inexpensive.

# DULUTH

**D**uluth is a wonderfully historic community right on the shores of Lake Superior. Originally settled by Sioux and Chippewa, its position on the lake made it a boom-town during the logging, shipping, and mining years, and at one point it was home to more residents per capita than anywhere else in the United States. Today it's home to a lively waterfront area with an extensive walkway and a host of historic lodgings.

## ✳ To See and Do

FOR FAMILIES ♿ ✎ ⚲ ✳ **Great Lakes Aquarium** (218-740-FISH; glaquarium.org), 353 Harbor Drive. Open daily 10–6; closed Christmas Day. Adults $17.99; age 62 and older $14.99; youth 13–17 $13.99; children 3–12 $11.99; children under 3 free. Located along the shore near Canal Park, the Great Lakes Aquarium specializes in freshwater fish and aquatic life. The offerings have expanded over the years to include everything from amphibians to reptiles to otters to invertebrates.

MUSEUMS AND HISTORIC SITES ♿ ✎ ✳ **The Tweed Museum of Art** (218-726-7823; d.umn.edu/tma), 1201 Ordean Court, University of Minnesota–Duluth. Open Tues.–Sun. Admission free. Named after art collectors George and Alice Tweed, the Tweed Museum focuses on early 20th-century American and European artwork as well as brings in exhibits from regional artists past and present.

♿ ✎ ✳ **The Lake Superior Railroad Museum** (218-727-8025; lsrm.org), 506 W. Michigan Street. Open daily; hours vary by season. Adults 14 and older $14; children 3–13 $6; children under 3 and museum members free. AA and AARP members receive a 10 percent discount. Admission includes entrance to Depot Square. This small museum is devoted to Duluth's locomotive history, including vintage wood-burning steam engines (including the largest one ever built), railroad snowplows, and an operating model train exhibit. Between Memorial Day and Labor Day, visitors can ride a vintage electric trolley around the museum

SUNSET AT GRAND MARAIS HARBOR

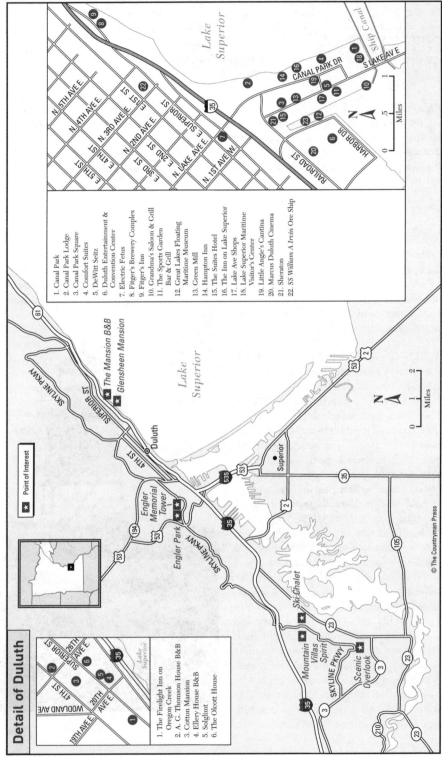

# Detail of Duluth

★ Point of Interest

1. The Firelight Inn on Oregon Creek
2. A. G. Thomson House B&B
3. Cotton Mansion
4. Ellery House B&B
5. Solglimt
6. The Olcott House

1. Canal Park
2. Canal Park Lodge
3. Canal Park Square
4. Comfort Suites
5. DeWitt Seitz
6. Duluth Entertainment & Convention Center
7. Electric Fetus
8. Fitger's Brewery Complex
9. Fitger's Inn
10. Grandma's Saloon & Grill
11. The Sports Garden Bar & Grill
12. Great Lakes Floating Maritime Museum
13. Green Mill
14. Hampton Inn
15. The Suites Hotel
16. The Inn on Lake Superior
17. Lake Ave Shops
18. Lake Superior Maritime Visitor's Center
19. Little Angie's Cantina
20. Marcus Duluth Cinema
21. Sheraton
22. SS William A Irvin Ore Ship

© The Countryman Press

or sign up to take a ride on the North Shore Scenic Railroad, which has a number of options. (Visitors who purchase a ride on the North Shore Scenic Railroad are eligible for discounts on museum admission.)

    ♿ ✎ ❄ **Depot Square** (218-727-8025; lsrm.org), 506 W. Michigan Street. Open daily; hours vary by season. Adults 14 and older $14; children 3–13 $6; children under 3 and museum members free. AA and AARP members receive a 10 percent discount. Admission includes entrance to the Lake Superior Railroad Museum. This historical complex is a re-creation of two Duluth streets set in 1910.

    ♿ ✎ ❄ **Duluth Children's Museum** (218-733-7543; duluthchildrensmuseum.org), 115 S. 29th Avenue W. Open Tues.–Sun. Admission $9 for everyone age 2 and older. Under 2 is free. There may be different rates for special events and exhibits. The Duluth Children's Museum exhibits are geared for kids 10 and younger, with events appealing to children older than 10. The museum is packed with hands-on activities that encourage imagination and exploration—and will tucker out the most energetic child.

    ♿ ✎ ❄ **Duluth Art Institute** (218-733-7560; duluthartinstitute.org), 506 W. Michigan Street. Open daily. Free admission. The DAI is focused on local and contemporary art, by both professional and emerging artists, in a wide variety of media.

    ♿ ✎ ⚥ ❄ **Glensheen** (218-726-8910; glensheen.org), 3300 London Road. Open daily. General admission is $18 for adults 16 and older; $16 for ages 62 and older and veterans; children ages 6–15 $7; patrons with limited mobility $5. Tours vary in price from $12–150. Just north of downtown Duluth, on a stretch of Lake Superior shoreline, is the 39-room mansion Glensheen. Built in the early 1900s by the prosperous Congdon family, Glensheen is now open as a historical site (maintained by the University of Minnesota). There are three levels of tours available: the home's exterior and grounds; the home's exterior, grounds, and first and second floors; or all of these plus the third floor, attic, and basement. The last tour takes the longest (and can be toasty in warmer weather—central air was not an available amenity when the mansion was built), but if you can, it's worth the extra time. The docents are well trained and full of interesting tidbits about the history and construction of the 39-room mansion, filled with mostly original furniture, decorations, and artwork. Ahead of their time, the Congdons incorporated electricity throughout (but maintained gaslights as well, as Chester Congdon was not convinced that electricity wasn't just a fad), as well an early version of a central vacuum system. The grounds, set on a wide expanse of shoreline, include a rocky beach, a boathouse, a carriage house, and a gardener's home, as well as extensive, lavish gardens. Among the myriad tour options is a tour starting with kayaking on Lake Superior.

    One thing that is not mentioned on the tour, but you can now ask about it at the end (in earlier years, docents were not allowed to talk about it), is the murder of Elisabeth Congdon and her nurse at Glensheen in 1977.

    For some, this is reason enough to visit, but even if you have no interest in the real-life murder and subsequent trials, visiting Glensheen provides an unusually detailed and carefully preserved view into a lost way of life.

    ✎ **S.S. *William A. Irvin*** (218-722-7876; decc.org/william-a-irvin), Duluth Entertainment Convention Center, 301 Harbor Drive. Open daily Memorial Day–mid-Sept.; hours vary by season. Adults $15; students 11 and older and seniors 60 and older $9; military with ID $6; children 10 and under free per paid adult ticket. Run by the Great Lakes Floating Maritime Museum, the S.S. *William A. Irvin* spent more than 40 years delivering coal and iron ore as well as transporting dignitaries around the Great Lakes region. During October, special Ship of Ghouls tours are available.

# ❋ Green Space and Outdoor Activities

**PARKS AND PARKWAYS** **Skyline Parkway.** A narrow road that winds through residential and rural areas, Skyline Parkway can be maddening to follow (it's not terribly well marked, especially on the northern end), but it's worth the effort if you want to catch some spectacular views of Lake Superior, the city of Duluth, and western Wisconsin. Take a detailed Duluth map with you, and be aware that parts of the road are closed during the winter months. And don't forget your camera.

**Enger Park.** Located along Skyline Parkway, Enger Park is a small but lush picnic area complete with its own stone tower. During the summer months, the floral display is breathtaking, and shaded picnic tables are spread generously throughout the grounds. Climb the tower for a wide-open view of Duluth and Lake Superior.

**Leif Ericson Park.** A large park set along Lake Superior, Leif Ericson Park has an open-air amphitheater that hosts live performances during the summer months, and a lovely and (in season) fragrant rose garden. It's a great place for strolls along the lakeside.

**RAFTING** **Minnesota Whitewater Rafting** (218-522-4446; minnesotawhitewater.com), 2023 W. Superior Street. Open daily May–Sept. Must be 12 years of age and older. Minnesota Whitewater Rafting offers rafting and sea kayaking on the St. Louis River. Kayaking can be done as a guided tour or as a rental only. Reserve early for Saturday excursions.

**SKIING** ✧ ❋ ⊘ **Spirit Mountain** (218-628-2891 or 1-800-642-6377; spiritmt.com), 9500 Spirit Mountain Place. While the word mountain might be overstating things a bit, the Spirit Mountain area is a popular stop for winter visitors to Duluth. Skiing is available daily, and while there aren't nearly as many runs or levels of difficulty as northern neighbor Lutsen-Tofte, for those who want to get a little skiing in without venturing farther north, Spirit Mountain works fine. During the summer, campsites with panoramic views of Lake Superior and the city are available for rental. Book lodging at the Mountain Villas Resort, a collection of 14 octagonal tree houses that make up the only lodging on the mountain.

**TOURS** ⛓ ✧ ⊘ ⍟ ⫴ **Vista Fleet Sightseeing and Dining Cruises** (218-722-6218 or 1-877-883-4002; vistafleet.com), 323 Harbor Drive. Available spring–fall. Rates vary. Vista offers several daily cruises during the season, some of which board in Duluth and some of which board across the lake in Superior. Sightseeing, natural history, brunch, lunch, and dinner cruises are offered.

# ❋ Lodging

## HOTELS

### CANAL PARK

There are several hotels in the compact Canal Park area, all offering convenient access to shops, dining, and strolling along the Lake Walk. Given the popularity of summer in Duluth, plan ahead—many of these hotels fill to capacity in advance, especially on weekends.

⛓ ✧ ⍥ ❋ ⚲ **Canal Park Lodge** (218-279-6000; canalparklodge.com), 250 Canal Park Drive. One of the newer properties in Canal Park, the lodge has 116 rooms with a pool, hot tub, and high-speed Internet and Wi-Fi access. Full breakfast included with accommodations. Rates start at $122. Specials and packages available.

# BED-AND-BREAKFASTS

**B**ed-and-breakfasts abound here, not surprising given the historic nature of the city and its early builders. Many of the beds-and-breakfasts are in an area just north of Duluth, most of which are not right on Lake Superior, but are nearby.

**The Firelight Inn on Oregon Creek** (218-724-0272 or 1-888-724-0273; firelightinn.com), 2211 E. 3rd Street. A luxurious entry in the bed-and-breakfast category, the 1910 home offers rooms with private baths, all with robes, fireplaces, and Jacuzzis. A full breakfast is served in the room. Rates start at $229. ✳

**The Olcott House** (218-728-1339; olcotthouse.com), 2316 E. 1st Street. This 1904 Georgian Colonial Revival mansion includes luxurious accommodations within the home—five suites with private baths—as well as a separate carriage house suite. Several of the suites have fireplaces and whirlpool tubs; all have air-conditioning, LCD TVs, and either four-poster or canopy beds. Hot breakfast is served each day. Rates start at $220. Some packages are available. ✳

**The Ellery House** (218-724-7639 or 1-800-355-3794; elleryhouse.com), 28 S. 21st Avenue. Ellery House's four elegant suites all have private baths, robes, and feather beds; one suite has a private sunporch, while another has a separate sitting area. Wi-Fi is available throughout the property. Breakfast can be served in the rooms if requested. Rates start at $159. Some packages are available. ((·)) ✳

**A.G. Thomson House** (218-724-3464; thomsonhouse.biz), 2617 E. 3rd Street. Built in 1909 by architect Edwin H. Hewitt, the A.G. Thomson House has four rooms with private bath in the main house as well as three rooms with private bath in the adjacent carriage house. With advance notice, elopements can be arranged in house. Full breakfast is available in the dining room or it can be served to the room. Rates start at $189. Some packages are available. ✳ ♂

**Cotton Mansion** (218-724-1775 or 1-800-228-1997; cottonmansion.com), 2309 E. 1st Street. This 16,000-square-foot 1908 Italianate mansion offers seven rooms and suites, all sumptuously appointed, many with fireplaces and whirlpools. With advance notice, elopements can be arranged in house. A full breakfast is served each morning by candlelight, and an afternoon wine and cheese service is provided on weekends. Rates start at $165. Some packages are available. ((·)) ✳ ♂

**Solglimt** (218-727-0596; solglimt.com), 828 S. Lake Avenue. This inn is located across the Aerial Lift Bridge from Canal Park and has 120 feet of frontage on Duluth's Park Point Reach. Rather than a mansion, Solglimt is more of a seaside cottage, with three suites with private baths. Amenities include full breakfast daily prepared with locally grown, organic foods, and Amazon Echo in every room. Rates start at $135. Some packages are available. ((·)) ✳ ⊹

& ♪ ((·)) ✳ ↖ **Comfort Suites Canal Park** (218-727-1378; choicehotels.com), 408 Canal Park Drive. One of the smaller Canal Park properties, this all-suite hotel has a pool and whirlpool, some in-room whirlpools, and high-speed Internet and Wi-Fi access. All rooms come with refrigerator, microwave, and coffeemaker. Full breakfast included with accommodations. Rates start at $114. Specials and packages available.

& ♪ ✳ ((·)) ↖ **Hampton Inn–Duluth** (218-720-3000; hamptoninn.com/hi/duluth), 310 Canal Park Drive. This Canal Park lodging has mostly hotel rooms, with a handful of Jacuzzi suites, and offers high-speed Internet and Wi-Fi access. The property has a pool and whirlpool, and daily full breakfast for guests. Rates start at $129. Specials and packages available.

& ♪ ✳ ♂ ((·)) ↖ **The Inn on Lake Superior** (218-726-1111 or 1-888-668-4352;

theinnonlake superior.com), 350 Canal Park Drive. The inn is one of the larger properties in Canal Park, offering both hotel rooms and suites. All rooms have refrigerator, microwave, and coffeemaker. Some rooms have fireplaces, whirlpools, and full kitchens. The property has two pools, one indoor and one outdoor, and in an unusual twist for this climate, the outdoor pool is open year-round; it's situated on the roof with a sheltering wall, and the water is kept luxuriously warm. Also offered year-round is the evening s'mores tradition, where kids of all ages can come out by the shoreline and toast marshmallows. Rates start at $135. Specials and packages available.

    & &#9835; &#10052; ((•)) &#102; **The Suites Hotel** (218-727-4663 or 1-800-794-1716; thesuitesduluth.com), 325 S. Lake Avenue. This all-suite hotel has an indoor pool, with full kitchens in each suite and a wide range of sizes and amenities, from a three-bedroom condo with fireplace and four-person whirlpool to smaller studio suites which are located in the center of the building and thus don't have windows (but are considerably less expensive). Rates start at $123. Specials and packages available.

## ✳ Lodging

### CITY OF DULUTH

& &#9835; ((•)) &#10052; &#102; **Beacon Pointe Resort** (877-462-3226; beaconpointeduluth.com), 2100 E. Water Street. Located between the popular Lakewalk and the shores of Lake Superior itself, Beacon Pointe has a mix of guest rooms and suites, the latter of which offer one to four bedrooms, full kitchens, fireplaces, and whirlpools. Penthouse suites have striking views of the lake. Continental breakfast is included, and bikes are on-site for the guests' use. Underground heated parking is a nice perk in winter. Lakeside accommodations come with balconies or patios.

Rates start at $215. Specials and packages are available.

    & &#9835; &#9855; ((•)) &#10052; &#8851; &#102; **Radisson** (218-727-8981; radisson.com/duluthmn), 505 W. Superior Street. The Radisson is the distinctly circular building in downtown Duluth, with views of Lake Superior from many of its rooms. The Radisson is a local landmark both because of its shape and because it was one of the first upscale hotels in the area. The property has a pool, sauna, hot tub, and whirlpool, and high-speed Internet and Wi-Fi access. The hotel's signature restaurant, **JJ Astor** (see *Where to Eat*), is open daily for breakfast, lunch, and dinner, in a revolving restaurant at the top of the hotel. Rates start at $108. Specials and packages available.

    & &#9835; ((•)) &#10052; &#8851; &#102; **Sheraton Duluth** (218-733-5660; marriott.com), 301 E. Superior Street. Opened in 2007, the Sheraton is just a few blocks from the Canal Park area in downtown Duluth. The hotel has an indoor pool, and rooms have flat-screen TVs. **Restaurant 301** (see *Where to Eat*) offers upscale American classic food in a sleek interior. The Sheraton Club level offers larger rooms with sitting areas, as well as access to the Club Lounge. Rates start at $155. Specials and packages available.

    & &#9835; &#9855; ((•)) &#10052; &#8851; &#9851; **Fitger's Inn** (218-722-8826; fitgers.com), 600 E. Superior Street. Fitger's started life as a beer brewery in 1881, and today the large complex (listed on the National Register of Historic Places) is a mix of hotel, retail, and restaurants. The inn is a small boutique hotel with views of both downtown Duluth and Lake Superior. A variety of room types is available, from a comfortable standard room to sumptuous whirlpool penthouse suites, which also include fireplaces, balconies, skylights, and large living areas. Rates start at $153. Specials and packages are available.

    &#9835; ((•)) &#10052; **Cottage on the Point** (218-727-3837; cottageonthepoint.com), 3332 Minnesota Avenue. This three-bedroom cottage built in the 1880s is located on Park Point, a 5-mile sand peninsula that separates Lake Superior from the Superior Bay. The home has a full kitchen, laundry, gas grill, gas fireplace, and heating and air conditioning. It also offers kayaks for guests. Rates start at $208.

## ✸ Where to Eat

DINING OUT &. ✂ ⊺ ✳ **Bellisio's** (218-727-4921; bellisios.com), 405 S. Lake Avenue. Open daily for lunch and dinner. This upscale offshoot from the Grandma's Restaurant group offers excellent Italian cuisine and a sizable wine list. Reservations recommended. Expensive.

&. ✂ ⊺ ✳ **JJ Astor** (218-722-8439; jjastorsrestaurant.com), 505 W. Superior Street (in the Radisson Hotel). Open Mon.–Sat. for breakfast, lunch, and dinner, Sun. for dinner. JJ Astor's major claim to fame is that it is a circular revolving restaurant providing generous views of Duluth and Lake Superior. But it has also updated its menu in recent years, giving it more of a fine dining approach, with hearty steaks and several seafood options (including local favorite walleye). Expensive/very expensive.

&. ✂ ✳ ⊺ **New Scenic Café** (218-525-6274; newsceniccafe.com), 5461 N. Shore Drive. Open daily for lunch and dinner. Just north of Duluth is this destination dining spot, a favorite of locals and visitors alike due to both its beautiful location near the lake and its well-deserved excellent reputation for its food. New Scenic Café serves a frequently changing menu of sophisticated, seasonal contemporary American cuisine, sourced locally whenever possible. Offerings may include lake trout with grapes and fennel or pork shank with chocolate mole. In the summer, allow time to enjoy the surrounding gardens. Expensive.

&. ✂ ✳ ⊺ **The Boat Club** (218-727-4880; boatclubrestaurant.com), 600 E. Superior Street. Open daily for all three meals. Located in the Fitger's complex, The Boat Club is a fine dining establishment offering upscale supper club options, including surf and turf, pasta, and Lake Superior trout. Expensive/very expensive.

&. ✂ ✳ ⊺ **Pickwick Restaurant & Pub** (218-623-7425; pickwickduluth.com), 508 E. Superior Street. Open daily for lunch and dinner. Pickwick has an indoor charcoal grill, allowing them to provide truly grilled meats, including a number of steak cuts and a Jack Daniels–glazed pork chop. But the restaurant also offers a number of seafood options, including walleye and lake trout, as well as vegetarian salads and a grilled vegetable kabob entrée. Expensive/very expensive.

EATING OUT &. ✂ ⊺ ✳ **At Sara's Table Chester Creek Café** (218-724-6811; astccc.net), 1902 E. 8th Street. Open daily for all three meals. Located near the University of Minnesota campus. Don't let the lengthy name intimidate you; this restaurant, casual and friendly, serves delicious meals, often using organically grown and local food sources in season, and even grows its own organic foods and herbs nearby. It also offers extensive gluten-free and vegan options. Breakfasts are hearty and plentiful; lunch and dinner can be simple or elaborate, depending on your mood. Moderate.

&. ✂ ✳ **New London Café** (218-525-0777; newlondoncafeduluth.com), 4721 E. Superior Street. Open daily for all three meals, Sun. for breakfast and lunch. This is where the locals gather. A tiny café on Duluth's busy E. Superior Street, it's not fancy, but it does prove that simple food prepared well can be outstanding. Be sure to have the New London Potatoes, or stop by on a Friday evening for the fish fry. Inexpensive.

✂ &. ✳ **Uncle Louie's Café** (218-727-4518), 520 E. 4th Street. Open daily for breakfast and lunch. Diner food, the

# NORTH SHORE BREWERIES

The brewery scene in the state has exploded in recent years, and not just in the Twin Cities metro. The North Shore is home to several highly regarded breweries.

**Fitger's Brewhouse** (218-625-8646; fitgersbrewhouse.com), 600 E. Superior Street, Duluth. In one form or another, Fitger's has been in the brewing business since 1857 (including the Prohibition years, when it produced pop and candy bars). Today Fitger's offers a wide range of beer styles, including a unique North Shore Pale Ale as well as the more traditional IPA, stout, Belgian, wheat beer, lager, ales, and sour beers. The brewery also has a bar and grill on-site.

**Castle Danger Brewery** (281-834-5800; castledangerbrewery.com), 17 7th Street, Two Harbors. Named after the small town where it started, Castle Danger has since expanded and moved to Two Harbors. Its current location offers a large patio overlooking Lake Superior. Rotating taps could include anything from their cream ale, stouts, honey raspberry wheat, black lager, or experimental IPA.

**Bent Paddle Brewing Co.** (218-279-2722; bentpaddlebrewing.com), 1832 W. Michigan Street, Duluth. Bent Paddle has a formidable list of beers, both flagship and specialty/seasonal, many offered in their taproom. Flagship flavors include the Venture Pilsener Lager, Cold Press Black Coffee Ale, and Extra Special Amber, while seasonal and specialty offerings range from an intensely hoppy Pordij to the Roof Rack Vienna Style Lager.

**Ursa Minor Brewing** (218-481-7886; ursaminorbrewing.com), 2415 W. Superior Street, Duluth. Ursa Minor has more than a dozen taps running at any time, including various styles of IPA, Belgian, stout, pilsner, German bock, and fruited and infused flavors. The taproom also has a limited but fun food menu with items that go well with beer: Pizza, pretzels, and meat sticks.

**Blacklist Brewing Co.** (2218-606-1610; blacklistbeer.com), 120 E. Superior Street, Duluth. Blacklist has a series of small-batch beers, with their Or de Belgique strong golden, Classic Wit Belgian wheat ale, and Finally American IPA their all-the-time selections. Seasonal offerings include an imperial Belgian stout, an imperial IPA with spruce tips, and a wheat ale with rhubarb, among others. Also: axe throwing.

way it's supposed to be. Hearty pancakes and Greek-influenced lunches. Inexpensive.

&. ✎ ⍭ ❋ **Fitger's Brewhouse and Grill** (218-279-2739; fitgersbrewhouse.com), 600 E. Superior Street. Open daily for lunch and dinner. Located in the historic Fitger's complex, Fitger's Brewhouse is a cheerful take on the "burger and beer" concept. Hearty sandwiches, burgers, and quesadillas all available with your choice of brew. Check out the wild rice burgers made with Minnesota wild rice, or the Lake Superior whitefish burger. Moderate.

&. ✎ ⍭ ❋ **Lake Avenue Restaurant & Bar** (218-722-2355; lakeaveduluth .com), 394 S. Lake Avenue. Open daily for brunch and dinner. This quiet and

tasteful restaurant in the **Dewitt-Seitz Marketplace** (see *Selective Shopping*) focuses on local and seasonal when possible, getting creative with grilled octopus, shrimp boil, and a housemade ramen noodle bowl. Moderate/expensive.

&. ✎ ⍭ ❋ **Mexico Lindo** (218-727-1978; fitgers.com/fitgers-shopping-mall /mexico-lindo-duluth), 600 E. Superior Street. Open daily for lunch and dinner. The menu may not be unique, but the cheerfully Americanized Mexican entrées are skillfully prepared in hearty portions and are especially tasty when combined with the house margarita. Moderate.

&. ✎ ⍭ ❋ **Grandma's Saloon & Grill** (218-727-4192; grandmasrestaurants

.com), 522 S. Lake Avenue. Open daily for lunch and dinner. This hometown favorite has a cheerfully American menu packed with steaks, sandwiches, chicken pot pie, and pasta. Summer is especially popular at Grandma's, as it has deck seating overlooking the Aerial Lift Bridge. Moderate.

    ♿ 🔌 ⅃ ❄ **Little Angie's Cantina** (218-727-6117; littleangies.com), 11 E. Buchanan Street. Open daily for lunch and dinner. Southwest and American foods served in jumbo portions, with an agreeable assortment of margaritas and cocktails. Try the mahi mahi tacos. In summer, enjoy Little Angie's outdoor deck while having a drink and watching the crowds on Canal Park. Moderate.

    ♿ 🔌 ⅃ ❄ **Burrito Union** (218-728-4414; burritounion.com), 1332 E. 4th Street. Open daily for lunch and dinner. A cheerful Mexican-themed casual eatery with burrito sold either "1-fisted" or "2-fisted." Choose from the Fat Capitalist (pork carnitas and jack cheese), Jamaican Jerk, or Rasputin (the last available only two-fisted). Fitger's beers are offered, along with creative margaritas and wine.

    ♿ 🔌 ⅃ ❄ **Valentini's Vicino Lago** (218-728-5900; valentinisduluth.com), 1400 London Road. Open Mon.–Sat. for all three meals. This Duluth outpost of the long-time Chisholm supper club has a great location with lake views and an extensive Italian menu at reasonable prices. The menu offers an extensive list of Italian sauces, all made in-house. The restaurant also offers a number of gluten-free pastas, breads, and sauces. Moderate.

    ♿ 🔌 ❄ **Zeitgeist Arts Café** (218-722-9100; zeitgeistarts.com/café), 222 E. Superior Street. Open Mon.–Sat. for lunch and dinner, Sun. for brunch. Located in the Zeitgeist Arts building, which offers a wide variety of arts programming, the café (like the arts organizations, a nonprofit) is a great place to have a reservation before a film or theater event. The menu is focused on sandwiches, salads,

and soups, with a limited entrée menu that includes Lake Superior Trout. Several menu items can be made gluten-free or vegan. Moderate/expensive.

    ♿ 🔌 ⅃ ❄ **OMC Smokehouse** (218-606-1611; omcsmokehouse.com), 1909 W. Superior Street. Open daily for lunch and dinner. High-quality barbecued meats and fish with nods both to the South and to Asia. Try the Korean BBQ Pork Belly Sandwich or the Pork 'n' Grits, and be sure to get the Beef Fat Fries for a side. Moderate.

    ♿ 🔌 ❄ **Amazing Grace Bakery & Cafe** (218-723-0075; amazinggracebakeryand cafe.com), 394 S. Lake Avenue. Open daily for breakfast and lunch (and early dinner). A friendly café focused on local sourcing and making foods from scratch, including breads and buns. The menu is sandwiches and salads, with creative offerings including a Turkey-Bacon-Brie Sandwich and a Spinach-Walnut Veggie Burger. Moderate.

## ❄ Entertainment

♿ 🔌 ❄ **Duluth Entertainment Convention Center** (218-722-5573; decc.org), 350 Harbor Drive. The DECC is home to touring concerts and productions that come through Duluth, as well as host to the Duluth-Superior Symphony Orchestra and the Minnesota Ballet. Besides the theater and convention center, the DECC is also home to the **S.S. *William A. Irvin*** (see *To See and Do*).

## ❄ Selective Shopping

The Canal Park area, geared as it is for tourists, has several enticing shops.

    ♿ 🔌 ❄ ⅃ ❙❙ **The Dewitt-Seitz Marketplace** (218-722-0816; dewittseitz .com), 394 S. Lake Avenue. Open daily. Located in the heart of Canal Park, the marketplace is housed in a century-old manufacturing and warehouse site that's now on the National Register of

Historic Places. Tourist shops worth a stop include Minnesota Gifts by Sandra Dee, full of north woods–themed apparel and souvenirs; J. Skylark, an engaging toy and game shop for kids; Blue Heron Trading Co., which has cooking items and gifts; and the Art Dock, which sells regional art and crafts. Hepzibah's Sweet Shoppe can easily take care of that chocolate craving, but if you'd rather have a quick bite to eat, stop by either the Amazing Grace Bakery & Cafe, which offers heavenly baked goods, or Lake Avenue Café, a small but surprisingly creative deli. Looking for tasty goodies to take home? Northern Waters Smokehaus has the finest smoked fish and meats and a diverse selection of cheeses.

🔥 ✎ ❄ 🍷 🍴 **Fitger's Brewery** (218-722-8826; fitgers.com), 600 E. Superior Street. Besides a hotel (see *Lodging*) and restaurants (including **Fitger's Brewhouse and Grill**; see *Where to Eat*), Fitger's also has a variety of retail to explore through its ambling hallways. Shops include Fitger's Wine Cellars, a small but carefully stocked wine and spirits shop; Whimsy, fun and trendy children's clothing, gifts, and décor; Trailfitters, a supplier of outdoor and active clothing, footwear, and gear; Snow Goose, which carries locally made crafts and gifts; and the Bookstore at Fitger's, a charming store with a mix of popular and literary books and gift items.

✎ ❄ **The Electric Fetus** (218-722-9970; electricfetus.com), 12 E. Superior Street. Open daily. Just steps away from the waterfront, the Electric Fetus has one of the largest music inventories in the state (along withits sister locations in the Twin Cities and St. Cloud), as well as gifts and jewelry.

✎ ❄ **Duluth Trading Company** (218-481-7580; duluthtrading.com), 300 E. Superior Street. Open daily. Hardy, well-made men's and women's clothing.

❄ **Flagship** (218-260-7948; flagship duluth.com), 345 S. Lake Avenue. Open daily. This unique tourist shop sells Duluth-related clothing, but done through the eyes of local artists. Screen printing is done to order.

❄ **Lake Superior Art Glass** (218-464-1799; lakesuperiorartglass.com), 357 Canal Park Drive. Open daily. This glass-blowing studio and gallery offers glass art from more than 60 artists, and it also offers glassblowing classes.

❄ **Waters of Superior** (218-786-0233; watersofsuperior.com), 395 S. Lake Avenue. Open daily. This thoughtful shop sells regional art, jewelry, clothing, and home furnishings.

## ❋ Special Events

*January*: **John Beargrease Sled Dog Marathon** (218-722-7631; beargrease.com). One of the most beloved events in this region, the Beargrease (as it's known), held annually since 1983, is the longest sled dog event in the Lower 48. The event draws dogsled teams and visitors from across the country and is a qualifier for Alaska's Iditarod race.

*May*: **Duluth Dylan Fest** (bobdylan way.com), Duluth. A full week of all things Bob Dylan has supplanted the festival previously held in Hibbing, Dylan's hometown. But this event has a considerable amount of live music, poetry readings, tour of Dylan-related sites, and a singer-songwriter contest, among other offerings.

*June*: **Grandma's Marathon** (218-727-0947; grandmasmarathon.com), Duluth. Grandma's Marathon is one of the premier marathon events in Minnesota. Taking place over the third weekend of June, the marathon has a variety of activities besides the marathon itself—a health and wellness expo, kids' races and a 5K run, live evening entertainment, and a spaghetti dinner. Plus, of course, the actual marathon.

*August*: **Bayfront Blues Festival** (715-817-6933; bayfrontblues.com), Bayfront Festival Park. This annual three-day celebration of the blues in early August is a popular and long-running event; ordering tickets early and making hotel or camping reservations well in advance is recommended.

**Glensheen's Festival of Fine Art and Craft** (218-726-8910; glensheen.org), Glensheen Mansion, 3300 London Road. Glensheen is itself worthy of a visit (see *To See and Do*), and in mid-August, it hosts a fine-art festival on its grounds that attracts thousands of people annually. It's hard to imagine a better setting than this opulent 19th-century mansion and its sumptuous gardens.

PALISADE HEAD

# NORTH SHORE/LUTSEN

O nce you leave Duluth, you will want a car, if for no other reason than to be able to stop on a whim and visit scenic overlooks, trails, shops, and cafés. Make sure you take Scenic Highway 61 (MN 61) out of Duluth; you'll miss the lake views if you take Superior Street instead.

## ❋ To See and Do

  ✿ ❋ **Gooseberry Falls State Park** (218-595-7100; dnr.state.mn.us/state_parks /index.html), 3206 E. MN 61, Two Harbors. Open daily 9–5. Admission is free. This waterfall area is by no means the largest waterfall in the United States, but it's visitor friendly, with a sizable visitor center and extensive trails and walkways. Pets are allowed, and there are "doggie bags" strategically placed to encourage owners to clean up after their pets. The park twists and turns around the base of the falls, allowing access to both sides. Be sure to wear sturdy shoes; crossing wet rocks is a tricky proposition in the best of footgear, and flip-flops could be downright dangerous.

  **Split Rock Lighthouse** (218-226-6372; mnhs.org/splitrock), 3713 Split Rock Lighthouse Road (in Split Rock Lighthouse State Park, dnr.state.mn.us/state_parks/index.html), Two Harbors. Open daily May 15–Oct. 31. Adults $10; senior citizens, college students with ID, and active military and veterans $8; children 5–17 $6; children under 5 and MNHS members free. North of Duluth on MN 61 is Split Rock Lighthouse. This small beacon for passing ships is not large in stature, but placed as it is on a dramatic, steep cliff, it has proved its worth for decades. Now it's open for tourists to visit, along with a large visitor center with gift shop and video presentation. If you're feeling fit, take the trail that leads down the side of the cliff to the beach below (171 steps each way) for amazing views of the lighthouse and the surrounding shorelines. The lighthouse grounds are connected to the **Gitchi-Gami State Trail** (see *Green Space and Outdoor Activities*), which can be used by bikers or inline skaters. Split Rock is open seasonally, with a special opening each November 10 (call for hours) to commemorate the sinking of the *Edmund Fitzgerald*.

HIKING TRAIL AT TETTEGOUCHE STATE PARK

# TWO HARBORS

**N**orth of Duluth is the iron ore and fishing port of Two Harbors. Turn off Scenic Highway 61 (MN 61) onto Waterfront Drive to visit the historic shore area, and to tour the *Edna G.*, the last coal-fired, steam-powered tugboat. Towering over the *Edna G.* is an enormous ore dock, still in use today. Nearby is the Duluth and Iron Range Depot, formerly the headquarters for that company and home to the Depot Museum. A short distance from the museum is the Two Harbors Light Station. First lit in 1892, the light station is still operational, although automation has replaced the lighthouse keeper. The site is a historic museum open seasonally, and part of the lighthouse serves as the Lighthouse Bed & Breakfast, for guests who enjoy a historic stay. The grounds have short but scenic hiking trails, including a breakwater out into Lake Superior that affords great views of the dock and the town.

THE *EDNA G.* TUGBOAT AND IRON ORE DOCKS AT TWO HARBORS

    ♿ ✒ ❄ **North Shore Commercial Fishing Museum** (218-663-7050; commercial fishingmuseum.org), 7136 MN 61, Tofte. Open Tues.–Sat. mid-May–mid-Oct., Fri.–Sat. mid-Oct.–mid-May. Adults $3; children 6–16 $1; children under 6 free. This museum is dedicated to preserving and giving insight into the long history of commercial fishing on Lake Superior.

## ❄ Green Space and Outdoor Activities

The North Shore is all about the outdoors, whether it's summer or winter.

DOGSLED RIDING **Stoney Creek Kennels** (218-663-0143; facebook.com/Stoney -Creek-Sled-Dogs/1688802601367184), 142 Sawbill Trail, Tofte. Open seasonally depending on snowfall, usually Dec.–Mar. Experience firsthand the thrill of riding behind a team of well-trained sled dogs. Excursions can run anywhere from 15 minutes to a full day.

HIKING **Superior Hiking Trail** (218-834-2700; superiorhiking.org), 731 7th Avenue, Two Harbors. Trail information center open Mon., Thurs., and Fri. Run by the Superior Hiking Trail Association (SHTA), this collection of hiking byways and trails covers more than 320 miles along the Lake Superior shoreline from the Minnesota-Wisconsin state borders southeast of Jay Cooke State Park to the Canadian border west of Grand Portage. Frequent campsites and parking lots allow visitors to choose between backpacking and taking short day hikes. Contact the SHTA for information on their lodge-to-lodge hiking programs.

**Gitchi-Gami State Trail** (ggta.org). Long-term plans show an ambitious 89 miles of nonmotorized trails extending from Two Harbors to Grand Marais. Nearly 30 miles have been completed and are open for visitors. A large section is open beginning at Gooseberry Falls through to Tofte.

**Palisade Head,** 4 miles northeast of Silver Bay. The road to Palisade Head is a short, narrow, gravel road that brings you to a parking lot and a scenic overlook off a 200-foot rock cliff formed by lava more than a billion years ago. It's a popular spot for rock climbers, but even if you

SPLIT ROCK LIGHTHOUSE

don't climb, you'll be rewarded with the panoramic views of Lake Superior and the shoreline for miles on a clear day—all the way to Split Rock Lighthouse to the south, the Sawtooth Mountains to the northeast, and Wisconsin's Apostle Islands directly east. Hang on to small children—there are no safety fences.

PARKS ✍ ❄ **Tettegouche State Park** (218-353-8800; dnr.state.mn.us/state_parks /index.html), 5702 MN 61, Silver Bay. Tettegouche has nearly every kind of natural feature—Lake Superior shoreline, waterfalls and rivers (including the 60-foot-tall High Falls), mountainous hiking terrain, six inland lakes, and dense forests. There are 23 miles of hiking trails; in winter, cross-country skiers have 15 miles of trails. Snowmobilers and ATV users have limited trail access as well.

✍ ❄ **Temperance River State Park** (218-663-7476; dnr.state.mn.us/state_parks /index.html), MN 61, Schroeder. A heavily wooded state park with waterfalls, rivers, hiking trails, camping, snowmobiling, cross-country skiing, and rock climbing. Hikers should be sure to take the trail that winds upstream from the parking lot until you reach the Temperance River gorge, incredibly narrow and leading to spectacular waterfalls.

SKIING **Lutsen Mountains** (218-663-7281; lutsen.com), Ski Hill Road (County Route 5), Lutsen. Lutsen is Minnesota's largest ski area, with 95 runs of varying difficulty across four mountains. Downhill skiers, snowboarders, and cross-country skiers have

## HISTORY AND SCENERY COMBINED

**N**ear Schroeder, you'll see a sign pointing the way to Father Baraga's Cross. Father Baraga was a Slovenian priest who took on the arduous task of ministering to a number of Ojibwe settlements in Minnesota, Wisconsin, and Michigan, often traveling by snowshoe or canoe. After surviving a devastating storm in his canoe when it was tossed by the wind into the mouth of the Cross River, Father Baraga erected a wooden cross in thanks, which was later replaced with the granite cross that stands there today. A visit to the site in inclement weather gives you some idea what Father Baraga faced and why he was so thankful to have survived.

FATHER BARAGA'S CROSS

1,000 acres of land at their disposal, along with an alpine slide and a mountain tram for prime sightseeing. There are also adaptive ski options. Horse-drawn sleigh rides are available during the winter. Lutsen is not just popular in the winter, although that's its prime season; hiking, horseback riding, mountain biking, rock climbing, and kayaking and canoeing are all offered in the summer, when the lush greenery attracts skiers and non-skiers alike.

TOURS **North Shore Scenic Cruises** (218-464-6162; northshoresceniccruises.com), MN 61, Beaver Bay at the Silver Bay Marina. North Shore Scenic Cruises offers Lake Superior sightseeing and history boat tours as well as private cruises and special event outings.

# ❋ Lodging

There is a seemingly endless supply of lodging along the North Shore from Duluth to Lutsen, from small mom-and-pop motels to bed-and-breakfasts to large, deluxe resorts. But in spite of the number of accommodations you see, they do book up during prime seasons (winter for the Lutsen area, summer along the North Shore in general), so plan ahead.

BED-AND-BREAKFASTS ❂ ✐ (((•))) ❋ **Northern Rail Traincar Inn** (218-834-0955 or 1-877-834-0955; northernrail .net), 1730 County Route 3, Two Harbors. It's not false advertising—this is a bed-and-breakfast built out of actual train cars. The cars have been developed into surprisingly tasteful and comfortable suites. Guests check in at the "depot" before arriving at one of the 18 suites (all are themed, including north woods, Victorian, and safari themes). The property provides guests with private baths,

continental breakfast, trail access, snow-shoe rental, and summer bonfires, all tucked into a quiet wooded area. Rates start at $109. Packages are available.

❂ ✐ ❋ **Lighthouse Bed & Breakfast** (218-834-4898 or 1-888-832-5606; lighthousebb.org), 1 Lighthouse Point, Two Harbors. Built in 1892, the Lighthouse is on the National Register of Historic Places; proceeds from guests contribute to the Lighthouse's ongoing restoration. There are four rooms with shared bath, all with views of Lake Superior. A full Scandinavian breakfast is served daily. Children accepted with prior arrangements. Rates start at $165.

❋ **Baptism River Inn** (218-353-0707 or 1-877-353-0707; baptismriverinn .com), 6125 MN 1, Silver Bay. Cozy doesn't do justice to this charming three-bedroom bed-and-breakfast. Each room has a private bath; all have the rustic qualities of a log cabin. As it's situated on the Baptism River, guests have easy access to hiking and skiing. Children ages 11 and older accepted. Rates start at $149.

NORTHERN RAIL TRAINCAR INN

CABINS ✿ ❋ **Temperance Landing** (1-877-723-6426; bluefinbay.com/temperance-landing), Temperance Trail, Schroeder. Comprised of 3,000-square-foot log cabins, Temperance Landing is a Lake Superior luxury option. Each cabin has at least three bedrooms and baths; all come with fireplaces (some gas, some wood burning), fully equipped kitchens, access to hiking trails and canoe/kayak launch areas, and a fully restored classic Finnish sauna. Rates start at $395.

RESORTS AND LODGES ♿ ✿ 🐾 ✿ ((ꞏ)) ❋ ☖ ¶ **Superior Shores Resort & Conference Center** (218-834-5671 or 1-800-242-1988; superiorshores.com), 1521 Superior Shores Drive, Two Harbors. This large resort complex has all the bells and whistles: pebbled beach on Lake Superior; lodge rooms or lakehomes; indoor and outdoor pools; easy access to hiking, cross-country skiing, and snowmobiling trails; and close proximity to an 18-hole golf course. Rates start at $89. Weekend discounts and packages are available.

♿ ✿ 🐾 ✿ ((ꞏ)) ❋ ☖ ¶ **Cascade Lodge** (218-387-1112 or 1-800-322-9543; cascade lodgemn.com), 3719 W. MN 61, Lutsen. The best of both worlds, Cascade Lodge is nestled into Cascade River State Park, with access to several trails and stellar views of Lake Superior. Accommodations vary from motel rooms and lodge rooms to cabins and two private homes. Stop at the restaurant for dinner (see *Where to Eat*). Rates start at $79. Specials and packages are available.

✿ 🐾 ((ꞏ)) **Solbakken Resort** (218-663-7566 or 1-800-435-3950; solbakkenresort .com), 4874 W. MN 61, Lutsen. Open mid-Apr.–Nov. A combination resort with motel rooms, lodge rooms, and lakeshore cabins and homes, Solbakken offers direct access to cross-country ski trails. Rates start at $95.

♿ ✿ 🐾 ((ꞏ)) ❋ ☖ ¶ **Bluefin Bay on Lake Superior** (218-663-3346 or 1-800-258-3346; bluefinbay.com), 7192 W. MN 61, Tofte. Studios and condominium units are available for rental at this resort right

on Lake Superior. The property boasts year-round indoor and outdoor pools, dining at the **Bluefin Grille** (see *Where to Eat*), and a full-service spa, Waves of Superior. Rates start at $79. Packages are available.

♿ ✿ 🐾 ❋ ☖ ¶ **Caribou Highlands Lodge** (218-663-7241 or 1-800-642-6036; caribouhighlands.com), 371 Ski Hill Road, Lutsen. A year-round resort nestled into Sawtooth Mountain in Lutsen, Caribou Highlands offers lodge rooms, town homes and condos, and Poplar Ridge homes, log cabins with multiple bedrooms and fireplaces. During the winter, the property offers ski-in, ski-out access to Lutsen Mountains. There is a restaurant and taproom at the lodge, as well as indoor and outdoor pools, saunas, and tennis courts. Other amenities include evening bonfires, massage, and Wi-Fi. During the summer, the Mountain Kids Camp offers half- or full-day themed camp programs for kids ages 5–12. Rates start at $92. Packages are available.

# ❋ Where to Eat

DINING OUT ♿ ✿ ☖ ❋ **Bluefin Grille** (218-663-6200; bluefinbay.com/dine/Bluefin-grille), 7192 W. MN 61, Tofte. Open daily for all three meals. Located at the **Bluefin Bay resort** (see *Lodging*), Bluefin Grille serves American food with an emphasis on local, particularly Lake Superior seafood when available. Expensive/very expensive.

♿ ✿ ☖ **Cascade Lodge** (218-387-1112 or 1-800-322-9543; cascadelodgemn.com), 3719 W. MN 61, Lutsen. Open daily for all three meals. The restaurant at Cascade Lodge (see *Lodging*) provides hearty American fare in a casual, North Shore-themed setting. Moderate.

EATING OUT ♿ ✿ ❋ **Betty's Pies** (218-834-3367 or 1-877-269-7494; bettyspies .com), 1633 MN 61, Two Harbors. Open daily for all three meals. Local legend

GOOSEBERRY FALLS

cheese bread, and mozzarella sticks. Moderate.

   **Judy's Cafe** (218-834-4802; facebook.com/judyscafemn), 623 7th Avenue, Two Harbors. Open daily for breakfast and lunch, Mon.–Sat. for early dinner. A classic small-town café, with plenty of sandwiches as well as patty melts and liver and onions. Inexpensive.

   **Rustic Inn Café** (218-834-2488; rusticinn.cafe), 2773 MN 61, Castle Danger. Open daily for all three meals. Breakfast is served all day, but there are separate lunch and dinner menus, which include burgers, sandwiches, and slow-roasted pork and beef. Moderate.

   **Vanilla Bean Restaurant** (218-834-3714; thevanillabean.com), 812 7th Avenue, Two Harbors. Open daily for breakfast and lunch. Updated diner food with an emphasis on local, including walleye eggs Benedict and cranberry wild rice pancakes for breakfast, and smoked fish spread and Iron Range pasties for lunch. Inexpensive/moderate.

## ✳ Selective Shopping

MN 61 has about as many small shops along the drive as it does small restaurants and cafés. As winter sports have picked up traffic farther north, many of these shops stay open year-round.

   ✳ **Playing with Yarn** (1-877-693-2221; playingwithyarn.com), 276 Scenic Drive, Knife River. Open Wed.–Mon. This small but packed yarn shop, located right on the shores of Lake Superior, offers everything needed for the fiber enthusiast. Even better if you're a dog lover—the owner's dogs reside in the house next door and can be introduced upon request.

   ✳ **Russ Kendall's Smoke House** (218-834-5995; facebook.com/RussKendalls), 149 Scenic Drive, Knife River. Open daily. As the name suggests, this is a great spot for smoked items, especially the fish—lake trout, herring, salmon. Gifts are also available.

Betty's Pies has everything, from attitude ("Pies just like Mom used to make, before she took up bingo, cigarettes & beer") to truly delectable pies. A limited short-order menu includes broasted chicken, pasties, burgers, sandwiches, salads, and "pie shakes." But it's the pies that will bring you back again and again. Inexpensive.

   **Blackwoods Bar & Grill** (218-834-3846; blackwoods.com), 612 7th Avenue, Two Harbors. Open daily for lunch and dinner. Hearty bar-and-grill/comfort food offerings, including a wild rice melt, pot roast, chicken pot pie, and build-your-own mac and cheese, as well as steak and ribs. Moderate.

   **Do North Pizza** (218-834-3555; donorthpizza.com), 15 Waterfront Drive, Two Harbors. Open Wed.–Sun. for dinner. Extensive pizza options, along with chicken drummies and strips, garlic

✳ **Northwoods Pioneer Gallery & Gifts** (218-834-4175; pioneercrafts.com), 2821 MN 61, Two Harbors. Open daily mid-May–mid-Oct.; Fri.–Sun. from mid-Oct.–Dec.; closed Jan.–Feb.; Sat. and Sun. from Mar.–mid-May. Art and crafts items made by local artisans.

✐ ✳ **Great! Lakes Candy Kitchen** (218-834-2121; greatlakescandy.com), 223 Scenic Drive. Open daily from Apr. 27–Dec. 23. Purveyors of handmade candies, produced in small batches using traditional techniques using high-quality chocolate, butter, and cream.

## ✳ Special Events

*March*: **St. Urho's Day** (218-353-0300; friendsoffinland.org/st-urhos-day), 7344 MN 1, Finland. Possibly one of the oddest historical festivals in Minnesota. Located in Finland, a tiny town just north of Silver Bay, St. Urho is celebrated each year in mid-March with a four-day festival. What's odd is that there is no St. Urho; the people of Finland (the city in Minnesota, not the country) created him to have something to celebrate. Ostensibly he drove the grasshoppers out of Finland (the country) in an act similar to St. Patrick driving the snakes out of Ireland. Regardless of veracity, the festival goes on; even in the country of Finland, St. Urho has a pub named after him.

*September*: **North Shore Inline Marathon/Half-Marathon** (218-723-1503; northshoreinline.com). Held in mid-September, the inline marathon begins in Two Harbors and flies 26.2 miles along Scenic Highway 61 (MN 61), ending at the Duluth Entertainment Convention Center. The half marathon begins at the 13.1-mile point, ending at the same destination. Participants must be 13 and older; there is a kids' sprint on Friday night.

*November*: **Annual Edmund Fitzgerald Memorial Beacon Lighting** (218-226-6372; mnhs.org/splitrock/activities/beacon-lighting), Split Rock Lighthouse, 3713 Split Rock Lighthouse Road, Two Harbors. On November 10, 1975, the freighter *Edmund Fitzgerald* sank in raging gales in Lake Superior; all 29 men onboard were lost. The somber anniversary, commemorated in the Gordon Lightfoot song "The Wreck of the Edmund Fitzgerald," is marked each year with a ceremony at Split Rock Lighthouse. If you plan to visit, please dress appropriately, as the weather can be cold and windy; the Minnesota Historical Society recommends bringing a flashlight.

**Master's Bluegrass Festival** (218-387-1272; northshoremusicassociation.com/bluegrass.php), Lutsen Resort. This annual festival takes place the first weekend in November, a perfect time to cozy up to the fireplace and listen to the masters of bluegrass.

# GRAND MARAIS/ GRAND PORTAGE/ GUNFLINT TRAIL

The farthest northeast corner of the state, running along the Canadian border through the Boundary Waters, is a nature lover's paradise. The opportunities for kayaking, canoeing, fishing, hunting, bird-watching, hiking, biking, and observing wildlife are countless. Which is not to say there are no other things to do in the area—but they act as accompaniments to the natural centerpiece.

A car is pretty much a necessity, and if you're planning on venturing into the Boundary Waters, it's strongly recommended to purchase the Superior National Forest Visitor Map. Published by the USDA in conjunction with Superior National Forest, this is an incredibly detailed map of the Boundary Waters Canoe Area Wilderness (BWCAW). It wouldn't hurt to buy a magnifying glass with which to read it. The BWCAW is full of trails that don't appear on most state maps, and it's easy to get lost unless you're very familiar with the area. The map is available in a sturdy, waterproof plastic version for about $10. Many local gas stations and convenience stores sell it, or contact the **Superior National Forest headquarters in Duluth** (218-626-4300) for information onordering one. Also be sure to check out *Green Space and Outdoor Activities* for some suggested outfitters.

## ✳ To See and Do

ARTS AND CRAFTS ♿ ✎ ✳ **North House Folk School** (218-387-9762 or 1-888-387-9762; northhouse.org), 500 W. MN 61, Grand Marais. North House is a nonprofit organization committed to rekindling interest in and developing abilities of old-style crafts and survival techniques. More than 200 courses are offered each year, some as short as a day, some taking several days. Courses include not only how to cook and bake in an outdoor brick oven, but how to build the oven; constructing kayaks and canoes; building yurts and a facsimile of Thoreau's cabin; knitting, papermaking, and jewelry making; and ancient Native American techniques for basket weaving.

♿ ✎ ✳ **Grand Marais Art Colony** (218-387-2737; grandmaraisartcolony.org), 120 W. 3rd Avenue, Grand Marais. The city itself is known as an art colony, a quiet seaside-like community with diverse seasons that attracts resident and visiting artists. It's no wonder then that the official Grand Marais Art Colony is a popular and active organization. The colony sponsors year-round artclasses, art events and competitions, and an annual arts festival (see *Special Events*).

GAMING ✳ **Grand Portage Casino** (1-800-543-1384; grandportage.com), 70 Casino Drive, Grand Portage. Open 24/7. This casino takes the north woods theme and runs with it, including a northern lights display in the carefully designed ceiling. The casino has a hotel (see *Lodging*) and offers a shuttle to Thunder Bay, Ontario (US citizens will need passports to cross the border).

MUSEUMS ♿ 🎣 **Chik-Wauk Museum and Nature Center** (218-388-9915; chikwauk
.com), 28 Moose Pond Drive, Grand Marais. Open daily 10–5, May–mid-Oct. Admission is $5 for adults, ages 5–18 $2; or free for children under 5 and Gunflint Trail Historical Society members. The Chik-Wauk is a new addition to the Gunflint Trail, located on the farthest end from Grand Marais, and well worth a visit. A small but packed nature center details the history and geography of the Trail, while five hiking trails crisscross through the site's 50 acres with varying levels of difficulty, including one ADA trail.

## ❄ Green Space and Outdoor Activities

BOUNDARY WATERS CANOE AREA WILDERNESS ADVENTURES Be aware that visitors to the BWCAW, except for day-only visitors, need to reserve a permit ahead of time. Your outfitter can do this for you, or you can contact **Reserve America** (1-877-444-6777; recreation.gov).

**Boundary Country Trekking** (218-388-4487 or 1-800-322-8327; boundarycountry .com), 11 Poplar Creek Drive, Gunflint Trail. Ted and Barbara Young, proprietors of the **Poplar Creek Guest House** (see *Lodging*), offer a variety of adventure arrangements in the Gunflint Trail/Boundary Waters area. They can organize lodge-to-lodge hiking and biking trips, canoe/biking trips, mountain biking trips, and canoeing trips.

**Clearwater BWCA Outfitters** (218-260-2253; clearwateroutfitters.com), 772 Clearwater Road, Grand Marais. Residing along Clearwater Lake in the Boundary Waters area, Clearwater offers both a lodge (see *Lodging*) and an outfitting company, the latter of which has operated for more than 100 years. The proprietors can assist you with canoeing, hiking, fishing, birding, and even wildlife photograph trips.

GRAND MARAIS HARBOR

# GRAND PORTAGE NATIONAL MONUMENT

**G**rand Portage National Monument and Heritage Center (218-475-0123; nps.gov/grpo), 170 Mile Creek Road, Grand Portage. The historic site itself is open daily, late May–mid-Oct., while the heritage center is open year-round. Admission is free. This monument is really a don't-miss for visitors to the area. An extensive re-creation of the life of traders and Native Americans before there was a United States and Canada, the national monument has a traditional Ojibwe village, a reconstruction of the Northwest Company's stockade (including a great hall and kitchen), a fur trade canoe under construction, and historic gardens that represent what the original trading villages grew. Kids' programs are offered in the summer, and costumed historical guides are available to answer questions. Trails outside the stockade take visitors deep into the northern wilderness, and there are snowshoe trails available during the winter. The national monument also serves as the departure point for the ferry to Isle Royale, which is the largest island in Lake Superior (and technically is part of Michigan). After visiting the monument, if you feel ambitious, cross the street and hike the Mount Rose Trail, a 0.5-mile, very steep trail that will reward you with panoramic views of the monument, Lake Superior, and the Sawtooth Mountains. ✎ ♿

GRAND PORTAGE NATIONAL MONUMENT, SEEN FROM THE MOUNT ROSE TRAIL

**Sawbill Canoe Outfitters** (218-663-7150; sawbill.com), 4620 Sawbill Trail, Tofte. Sawbill has been arranging BWCAW trips for more than 50 years, and they've got keen insight into navigating the wilderness. Sawbill offers full and partial outfitting, canoe touring, and even food-only arrangements.

PARKS AND PARKWAYS From Grand Marais north is an abundance of state parks and wildlife areas. Be sure to check local conditions before visiting—nearly annual droughts have brought severe fire restrictions in parks and campsites in recent years, and some park access is limited during wildfires. Check with individual parks for up-to-the-minute information.

**Judge C.R. Magney State Park** (218-387-6300; dnr.state.mn.us/state_parks), 4051 E. MN 61, Grand Marais. Open daily summer (call for winter hours). This park, located between Grand Marais and Grand Portage, is home to the Brule River. The Brule leads to Devil's Kettle, a unique 50-foot waterfall that is rumored to have a bottomless cauldron. Nine miles of hiking trails, including an ascent to Devil's

DEVIL'S KETTLE WATERFALL AT JUDGE C.R. MAGNEY STATE PARK

Kettle, are open during the season, as well as several fishing sites. Campsites are available; advance reservations are recommended.

❋ **Grand Portage State Park** (218-475-2360; dnr.state.mn.us/state_parks), 9393 E. MN 61, Grand Portage. Open daily. This park, the only Minnesota state park operated jointly with an Indian tribe, has naturalists on hand during the summer months who are tribe members that can speak about local Ojibwe history. The park also boasts Minnesota's highest waterfall, the 120-foot-tall High Falls. Camping is not available, but the falls are easily accessible for day visitors via a 0.5-mile trail and boardwalk.

**Gunflint Trail** (1-800-338-6932; visitcookcounty.com/community/gunflint-trail). A 57-mile paved road leading from Grand Marais to Saganaga Lake near the Canadian border, the Gunflint Trail is hands down one of the most beautiful drives in the region. Acres of forest uninterrupted by more than the occasional café or shop, the trail also has an extensive collection of lodging options (see *Lodging*) nestled within the trees, as well as a new historical center and hiking spot at **Chik-Wauk Museum** (see *To See and Do*). Watch your speed as you drive; it's not unusual to have a deer, wolf, or even a moose appear on the road, and all of these animals can do as much harm to you and your vehicle as you can do to them. The area has enjoyed a growth in year-round tourism, thanks to the increased popularity of winter sports joining the ranks of other favored pastimes, such as birding, mountain biking, fall foliage viewing, canoeing and kayaking, camping, fishing, and even mushroom and berry picking. In extreme weather the road may be closed, but since there are year-round residents, it is plowed whenever feasible.

# ✳ Lodging

## GLAMPING

### GRAND MARAIS

✐ ✳ **Wunderbar Eatery & Glampground** (218-877-7655; wunderbarmn.com), 1615 MN 61. Five vintage campers and two lotus belle tents, available year-round. The glampground's bar and grill will deliver food to the camper or tent. Interior décor varies, with options including lava lamps, hammocks, gnomes, and twinkle lights. Rates start at $50.

## BED-AND-BREAKFASTS

### GRAND MARAIS

✐ 🐾 ✳ **Art House B&B** (218-370-1625; arthousebb.com), 8 7th Avenue W. This 100-year-old home offers four rooms with private bath. Guests are welcome to use the kitchen, the barbecue grill, and the backyard fire pit. Children 8 and older and well-behaved dogs are welcome. Rates start at $95, with discounts offered for whole-house rentals.

✳ **Bally House Bed and Breakfast** (218-387-5099; ballyhousebnb.com), 121 E. 3rd Street. Built in 1913, this bed-and-breakfast is full of antiques and furnishings previously belonging to the Bally family, which owned the house for nearly 100 years. There are four rooms, each with private bath. Children 12 and over are welcome. Rates start at $125, with a two-night minimum stay.

✳ **Ella's Inn** (218-387-3131), 118 3rd W. Avenue. Four guest rooms with three baths, and guests have access to the kitchen, living room, and dining room as well. The inn is a short walk to the lake, just across the street from the Grand Marais Art Colony and a short walk to the North House Folk School. Students at either of those schools are eligible for a discount. Rates start at $79.

✳ **MacArthur House B&B** (218-260-6390; macarthurhouse.net), 520 W. 2nd Street. Four rooms and two suites, all with private bath. Some rooms have views of Lake Superior. Children ages 12 and older are welcome, and discounts are available for students at the North House Folk School and the Grand Marais Art Colony. Rates start at $84.

### GUNFLINT TRAIL

✐ ✳ **Poplar Creek Guesthouse B&B** (218-388-4487 or 1-800-322-8327; poplarcreekbnb.com), 11 Poplar Creek Drive. Tucked into a peaceful wooded area off the Gunflint Trail, the Poplar Creek Guest House has two guest rooms, each with private bath, and a suite. The rooms are graciously appointed, and they share a common room with kitchenette, fireplace, and private deck. The suite has a private kitchen area as well as deck. Hosts Barbara and Ted have run a bed-and-breakfast in the north woods for many years, and they know exactly how to do it right, especially when it comes to the full breakfast served in the cheerful, welcoming breakfast room. Poplar Creek can also arrange a variety of lodge-to-lodge arrangements (see *Green Space* and *Outdoor Activities*). Also available is a year-round yurt (see **Tall Pines and Croft Yurts** on page 150). Rates start at $135. Packages are available.

✳ **Pincushion Trails Inn Bed & Breakfast** (218-387-2009; pincushiontrailsinn .com), 968 Gunflint Trail. Pincushion Trails is on 43 acres just 3 miles from Grand Marais and, sitting on the Sawtooth Mountain ridgeline, has impressive views and on-site access to hiking trails. This peaceful inn has four rooms, all with private bath, and a common living area with fireplace. Full breakfast served daily. Children 12 and older are welcome. Rates start at $125.

## CABINS, VILLAS, AND TOWNHOUSES

### GRAND MARAIS

♿ ✐ 🛜 ✳ **Cobblestone Cove Villas** (218-387-2633 or 1-800-247-6020; cobblestonecove.com), 17 S. Broadway.

Located on the harbor, Cobblestone Cove Villas is a newer townhouse property with upscale accommodations within easy walking distance to shops and restaurants. Rates start at $109.

🔥 (📶) **Opel's Lakeside Cabins** (218-663-7971 or 1-800-950-4361; opelslakeside cabins.com), 1593 Croftville Road. Open mid-May–mid-Oct. Opel's has five cabins available, all directly on the Lake Superior shoreline. The cabins are charming and were recently remodeled, and the views and location are hard to beat. Rates start at $110.

## GUNFLINT TRAIL

🔥 🏕 **Cross River Lodge** (218-388-2233 or 1-866-203-8991; crossriverlodge .com), 196 N. Gunflint Lake Road. Open May–Oct. Cross River Lodge is situated on Gunflint Lake. The property offers two lovely bed-and-breakfast rooms and a suite, each with private bath, and five cabins near or on the lake, with fireplaces, complete kitchens, and decks with barbecues. Rates start at $100.

♿ 🔥 ❄ 🍸 🍽 **Bearskin Lodge** (218-388-2292 or 1-800-338-4170; bearskin.com), 124 E. Bearskin Road. Located almost 30 miles from Grand Marais on the Gunflint Trail, Bearskin Lodge is a model of peace and retreat. The resort has 11 cabins and four lodges with townhouse accommodations. There's a hot tub and sauna on-site, and massage can be arranged. During the summer, boats, canoes, and pontoons are available, as well as bikes; children's naturalist programs can be arranged. Rates start at $156. Specials and packages are available.

♿ 🔥 🏕 **Clearwater BWCA Outfitters** (218-260-2253; clearwateroutfitters.com), 772 Clearwater Road, Grand Marais. Open May–Oct. This lodge, which has an outfitter on-site (see *Green Space and Outdoor Activities*) has 12 rustic cabins, plus a suite and three bed-and-breakfast rooms and two suites in the lodge (breakfast served daily for lodge guests only) and five bunkhouses that sleep

BEARSKIN LODGE

between six to 10 people. Rates start at $66.

❂ ♿ 🔥 🏕 🔥 ❄ 🍸 🍽 **Gunflint Lodge** (218-388-2294 or 1-800-328-3325; gunflint.com), 143 S. Gunflint Lake. Gunflint Lodge has 23 cabins of varying amenities, from the more rustic Canoers Cabins (bunk beds, shared bath in a nearby building) to the Romantic Cottages (lakeview cabins with fireplace, hot tub, and full kitchen) to the Gunflint Lake Home (with two to four bedrooms, fireplace, hot tub, and sauna). Three dining rooms on-site offer an alternative to cooking in the cabin (see *Where to Eat*), and an extensive list of year-round activities includes winter and summer sports, outfitting, canopy tours, horse riding, and massage. Rates start at $150.

## HOTELS

### GRAND MARAIS

♿ 🔥 🏕 (📶) ❄ **Best Western Plus Superior Inn** (218-387-2240 or 1-800-780-7234; bestwestern.com), 104 1st Avenue E. A solid choice for mid-price travelers, the

THE PATIO AT GUNFLINT LODGE

Best Western offers microwaves and refrigerators, and upgraded rooms have fireplaces. Full breakfast is provided each day. There are winter vehicle plug-ins, plus parking for trailers and snow-mobiles. Rates start at $125.

✤ ⌂ ((ᵞ)) ❄ **East Bay Suites** (218-387-2800 or 1-800-414-2807; eastbaysuites.com), 21 Wisconsin Street. Located right on Lake Superior, close to restaurants and shops, Easy Bay Suites all have decks or patios overlooking the lake, as well as full kitchens, fireplaces, washers and dryers, and complimentary full breakfast, and complimentary full breakfast. Accommodations vary in size from studio to three-bedroom, with some suites offering bunk beds. Telescopes are available for guests, as well as passes for the YMCA pool and fitness center. Rates start at $107.

## GRAND PORTAGE

✪ ♿ ✤ ¶ **Naniboujou Lodge** (218-387-2688; naniboujou.com), 20 Naniboujou

Trail. Open daily from mid-May to late Oct. and specific weekends from Christmas–Mar. Call for specific dates. Naniboujou is listed on the National Register of Historic Places, and its colorful history matches its bright interior. Built in the 1920s as a private club for founding members that included Babe Ruth and Jack Dempsey, it never reached its potential as the country reached the Depression years. Eventually reborn as a hotel and lodge, Naniboujou has a beautifully decorated great hall, painted in designs reflective of the Cree Indians, that serves as the dining room (see *Where to Eat*). The rooms are tastefully and comfortably set up, and there are no TVs, telephones, or Wi-Fi in order to preserve the sense of getting away from it all. Rates start at $99.

♿ ✤ ((ᵞ)) ❄ ⍭ ¶ ⌁ **Grand Portage Lodge & Casino** (1-800-543-1384; grandportage.com), 70 Casino Drive. Located just south of the Canadian border, the Grand Portage Lodge has spacious rooms, cabins, a new lodge and a friendly staff ready to help with anything you need. The hotel offers an indoor pool and sauna, a full-service restaurant overlooking Lake Superior, and a seasonal (mid-May–mid-Oct.) RV Park. Rates start at $79. Specials and packages available.

## ✳ Where To Eat

### DINING OUT

#### GRAND MARAIS

⚜ ✳ **The Crooked Spoon** (218-387-2779; crookedspoon cafe.com), 17 W. Wisconsin Street. Open Wed.–Sat. for lunch and dinner. Contemporary American cuisine, presented as dress-up food in a casual atmosphere. Moderate/expensive.

⚜ **Naniboujou Lodge** (218-387-2688; naniboujou.com), 20 Naniboujou Trail. Open daily for all three meals, early May to late Oct. Miniconjou's major claim to fame—and it alone is worth the visit—is the resplendent public dining room, with its 20-foot domed ceiling, massive stone fireplace, and the vividly painted Cree-themed walls and ceilings. The menu is contemporary American cuisine, with plenty of local ingredients, along with wine and beer. Expensive.

#### GUNFLINT TRAIL

♿ ⚜ ✳ 🍸 **Justine's at Gunflint Lodge** (218-388-2294; gunflint.com), 143 S. Gunflint Lake. Open daily year-round for all three meals except for a week in Nov. and Apr. The Gunflint Lodge has a beautiful restaurant and bar open to the public, with a stone terrace overlooking the beach outdoors and a massive stone fireplace inside. The food is contemporary American cuisine, often with locally sourced, native ingredients. Expensive.

### EATING OUT

#### GRAND MARAIS

✳ ⚜ **My Sister's Place** (218-387-1915; mysistersplacerestaurant.com), 401 E.

THE DINING ROOM AT NANIBOUJOU LODGE

MN 61. Open daily for lunch and dinner. More charming on the inside than on the outside, My Sister's Place has friendly service and solid soups and sandwiches that will satisfy any taste and hunger (including some vegetarian options, such as The Fungi mushroom sandwich and the wild rice burger). Moderate.

✳ ⚜ **South of the Border Cafe** (218-387-1505; facebook.com/South-of-the -Border-Cafe-196159180440215), 4 W. MN 61. Open daily for breakfast and lunch. Don't be confused by the name—the "border" referred to is the Canadian border, not the US–Mexico border. Instead of Mexican food, you'll find hearty home cooking. Inexpensive.

⚜ **Dockside Fish Market & Deli** (218-387-2906; moreysmarket.com), 418 W. MN 61. Open daily for lunch and dinner, Apr.–Dec. This retail market also has a deli with a limited but delicious menu, including several varieties of fish caught locally. Moderate.

⚓ **World's Best Donuts** (218-387-1345; worldsbestdonutsmn.com), 10 Wisconsin Street. Open daily at 7 a.m. (the walk-up window opens at 4:30 a.m.), mid-May–mid-Oct. No matter that the name doesn't seem modest; the doughnuts are truly wonderful. Inexpensive.

♿ ❄ ⚓ **Sven & Ole's** (218-387-1713; svenandoles.com), 9 W. Wisconsin Street. Open daily for lunch and dinner. You can't have a northern Minnesota experience without the quintessential Sven and Ole's. Contrary to the name, this is no bland Scandinavian fare, but a local pizza haunt with hearty, flavorful pizzas. The menu does include an option for a lutefisk pizza, but unless you have the $1 million in cash that the pizza is priced at, it's better to order one of the other offerings. Inexpensive.

♿ ⚓ **Angry Trout Cafe** (218-387-1265; angrytroutcafe.com), 408 W. MN 61. Open daily for lunch and dinner, late Apr.–mid-Oct. The Angry Trout has indoor or outdoor dining, with a strong focus on local ingredients and sustainability. And be sure to check out the artsy bathrooms. Moderate/expensive.

♿ ⚓ ❄ **Gunflint Tavern** (218-387-1563; gunflinttavern.com), 111 W. Wisconsin Street. Open daily for lunch and dinner. This cheerful tavern serves up tasty food in enormous portions, a more-than-decent menu of microbrews on tap, including those brewed in the on-site brewery. Live music offered regularly. Many menu items are made with organic and/or local ingredients. Moderate.

### GUNFLINT TRAIL

⚓ **Trail's End Café** (218-388-2212), 12582 Gunflint Trail. Open daily for all three meals, mid-May–mid-Oct. Trail's End serves basic but hearty meals, including burgers, sandwiches, and pizzas. The knotty pine interior fits well with the wooded wonderland outside. Inexpensive.

## ❋ Entertainment

**Grand Marais Playhouse** (218-387-1284; grandmaraisplayhouse.com), 51 5th Street. The playhouse runs local theatrical productions periodically during the year, primarily in the summer and during the pre-Christmas season.

## ❋ Selective Shopping

⚓ ❄ **Drury Lane Books** (218-387-3370; drurylanebooks.indielite.org), 12 E. Wisconsin Street, Grand Marais. Open Mon.–Sat. This shop is small, but it has an excellent selection of books for all your North Shore needs, whether escapist fiction or local information. Authors frequently make appearances, and writing workshops are occasionally offered.

⚓ ❄ **Beth's Fudge & Gifts** (218-387-2081; facebook.com/BethsFudge), 11 S. Broadway, Grand Marais. Open daily. If the doughnuts and pie in Grand Marais haven't satisfied your sweets craving, Beth's Fudge will. Creamy, smooth, and very much a treat.

⚓ ❄ **Lake Superior Trading Post** (218-387-2020; lakesuperiortradingpost.com), 10 1st Avenue W., Grand Marais. Open daily. Part souvenir shop, part outfitter for rural experiences, the trading post is staffed with friendly people who know their stock. The log cabin construction gives it a northwoods feel, and Lake Superior is right outside the door.

⚓ ❄ **Gunflint Mercantile** (218-387-9228; gunflintmercantile.com), 12 1st Avenue W. Open daily. A food store for backpackers and general visitors alike. Come in for the free fudge sample, view the extensive supply of lightweight foods for the trail, and then stay for the coffee and soup.

❄ **Sivertson Gallery** (218-387-2491; sivertson.com), 14 W. Wisconsin Street. Open daily. A popular art gallery focused on regional artists, including Canadian First Nation and Native American art.

❄ **Yellow Bird Fine Art** (218-370-0476; yellowbirdfineart.com), 101 W. MN 61. Open daily in summer, Fri.–Sat. winters. Contemporary art in the forms of paintings, sculptures, and jewelry.

## ✳ Special Events

*July*: **Grand Marais Arts Festival** (218-387-2737; grandmaraisartcolony.org), Grand Marais. A juried art show held annually in mid-July.

North Shore Dragon Boat Festival, Grand Marais. This newer festival is a great excuse to hang out along Grand Marais's harbor and enjoy the sight of vividly painted dragon boats being rowed by ambitious oarsmen (and women) in a series of races.

*September–October*: **Art Along the Lake Fall Studio Tour** (facebook.com /artalongthelake). A tour of artist studios along Lake Superior's northern end, including stops in Lutsen, Grand Marais, Grand Portage, and Thunder Bay, Ontario. (Note: If you venture into Canada, you'll need to present your passport for reentry into the United States.)

*October:* **Moose Madness** (218-387-2524; visitcookcounty.com/event/moose -madness), Grand Marais. Always held the third weekend in Oct., the same weekend when schools are closed for the annual statewide teachers' convention, this festival has contests, moose tours, a treasure hunt, and moose essay- and poetry-writing contests.

# BOUNDARY WATERS/ELY

outh of Grand Marais, MN 61 connects with MN 1, a brief stretch of highway that moves inland from Lake Superior to Ely, a gateway city into the Boundary Waters. Ely is a tourist town, and one well prepared for the outdoors enthusiasts who flock through the area each year.

A car is pretty much a necessity, and if you're planning on venturing into the Boundary Waters, it's strongly recommended to purchase the Superior National Forest Visitor Map. Published by the USDA in conjunction with Superior National Forest, this is an incredibly detailed map of the Boundary Waters Canoe Area Wilderness (BWCAW). It wouldn't hurt to buy a magnifying glass with which to read it. The BWCAW is full of trails that don't appear on most state maps, and it's easy to get lost unless you're very familiar with the area. The map is available in a sturdy, waterproof plastic version for about $10. Many local gas stations and convenience stores sell it, or contact the **Superior National Forest headquarters in Duluth** (218-626-4300) for information on ordering one.

## ✳ To See and Do

✐ **Dorothy Molter Museum** (218-365-4451; rootbeerlady.com), 2002 E. Sheridan Street, Ely. Open daily May–Oct. Arrangements for winter tours can be made by calling the museum phone number. Adults $7; seniors $6.50; children 6–17 $4.50; children under 6, veterans and active military members, and museum members free. This is a loving tribute to the last living person in the Boundary Waters. Dorothy Molter lived a great deal of her adult life in a cabin in the BWCAW, and even when the US government evicted other tenants when declaring the area a wilderness, she was granted lifetime tenancy. During her many years in her rustic cabin, she brewed homemade root beer for boaters and anglers coming through her area, earning the nickname "the root beer lady." After her death, her log cabin was painstakingly disassembled and reassembled on the east edge of Ely and turned into a museum. The cabin is crammed full of Dorothy's things, and the adjacent gift shop sells books about her as well as cases of root beer (worth the purchase). The only downside is the noise of traffic from nearby MN 169, which can make visitors (this one, at least) wonder why they couldn't have sited the museum just a bit farther down the road in an effort to recapture something more similar to the peace of nature enjoyed by Molter.

TED THE BEAR, AT THE NORTH AMERICAN BEAR CENTER

DOROTHY MOLTER'S CABIN

 ♿ ✏ ❄ **The International Wolf Center** (218-365-4695; wolf.org), 1396 MN 169, Ely. Open daily mid-May–mid-Aug. and Fri.–Sun. from mid-Aug.–mid-May. Adults $14; senior citizens $12; children 4–12 $8; children under 4 and museum members free. Internationally renowned for wolf education and information, the center tries to address public fears and concerns about wolf behaviors through press relations and public visits. The center has hands-on exhibits and Wolf Cams allowing visitors to watch wolves from a great distance; they also coordinate learning vacations that bring visitors into the wilderness to meet "ambassador" wolves.

♿ ✏ ❄ **North American Bear Center** (218-365-7879 or 877-365-7879; bear.org), 1926 MN 169, Ely. Open daily May–Oct. (year-round for pre-reserved groups). Adults and teens $13; senior citizens 60 and older and military members $12; children 3–12 $8; children under 3 and members free. One mile west of Ely is this center, similar in intent to the International Wolf Center. Visitors can learn more about bears through videos and exhibits, then watch the bears in their 2-acre habitat from a viewing deck.

✏ **Soudan Underground Mine** (218-300-7000; dnr.state.mn.us/state_parks), 1302 McKinley Park Road, Soudan. Open daily Memorial Day–Labor Day. Admission to the grounds is free; guided tours are $15 for adults; $10 for children 5–12; and free for children under 5. The Soudan Mine gives visitors insight into the daily life of miners in this once-operational mine. Adventurous tourists can take the tour, which carries them 27 stories beneath the ground. (Note that extensive walking is required, including through confined areas.) Those who don't wish to go below can wander the grounds for free. The scenery from the hillside mine is breathtaking, particularly during fall foliage season.

## ✳ Green Space and Outdoor Activities

**BOUNDARY WATERS** The Boundary Waters is an amazing natural preserve within Superior National Forest, encompassing more than a million acres of woods and at least 2,500 of Minnesota's famed lakes, teeming with wildlife. It is largely meant to be explored as explorers of old traveled: by canoe, with backpack and tent. While a few areas have opened up to motorized vehicles, the beauty of this area is the peacefulness caused by the lack of motors, allowing visitors to hear the myriad bird calls, wolf howls, and the sound of water and wind.

It is possible to day trip in the Boundary Waters, or least along the edges, by starting from Ely or the Gunflint Trail (see page 139). More ambitious travelers may want to portage in with canoes and set up camp. Experienced canoers and campers can plot their routes, but if you're fairly new to this type of adventure, you might consider working with an outfitter. There are several in the Ely area, including **Piragis Northwoods Company** (see *Selective Shopping*).

Be aware that visitors to the Boundary Waters, except for day-only visitors, need to reserve a permit ahead of time. Your outfitter can do this for you, or you can contact **Reserve America** (1-877-444-6777; recreation.gov). Permits for camping visitors are required in order to limit the number of entrances each day into the BWCAW, an effort made to keep the wilderness, well, wild.

BOAT AT BURNTSIDE LAKE

LAKE VERMILION STATE PARK

**Lake Vermilion State Park** (dnr.state.mn .us/state_parks), Soudan. This is Minnesota's newest state park, and it was combined with the adjacent **Soudan Underground Mine** (see *To See and Do*). The 3,000-acre tract has 10 miles of shoreline along Lake Vermilion, along with areas of massive rocky areas that are billions of years old. Hiking trails to the highest point in the park will afford views for miles in every direction on a clear day.

DOGSLEDRIDING ✎ **Wintergreen Dogsled Lodge** (1-877-753-3386; dogsledding .com), 1101 Ring Rock Road, Ely. With more than 40 years of dogsled adventures under their belt, the proprietors of the Wintergreen Dogsled Lodge know a thing or two about taking visitors on a dogsled trip, whether it's first-timers or seasoned sledders. Trips can be arranged with stays at the lodge itself, just east of Ely, as lodge-to-lodge treks or as camping excursions. Multiple-night or one-day-only trips available. Special opportunities include parent-daughter trips and photography workshops.

## ✳ Lodging

Not surprisingly, the Boundary Waters area is surrounded by countless places to stay, everything from rustic mom-and-pop resorts to more elaborate, deluxe accommodations. What follows is a sample of recommended places, which also represents the diverse offerings available.

BED-AND-BREAKFASTS ✎ 🐾 ✳ **A Stay Inn Ely** (218-365-6010; jaspercompany .com/locations/jasper-inn), 112 W. Sheridan Street, Ely. This charming three-story bed-and-breakfast has newly remodeled rooms, all with private bath, and a large common area with full kitchen. Kids (and adults!) who like hideaways will particularly enjoy staying in the Indigo Room, an attic room tucked under a slanted roof. Each room is paneled with a different kind of locally harvested wood. Rates start at $80.

✳ **Blue Heron Bed & Breakfast** (218-365-3223; blueheronbnb.com), 827 Kawishiwi Trail, Ely. Five beautifully decorated rooms, some with exposed log walls, make up this charming bed-and-breakfast. Rooms come with private baths, lake views, full breakfast, use

THE GATHERING ROOM AT A STAY IN ELY

of canoes or snowshoes, and use of the sauna. Rates start at $148.

CABINS 🛶 🦌 ❄ **Timber Trail Lodge** (218-365-4879 or 1-800-777-7348; timbertrail.com), 629 Kawishiwi Trail, Ely. Timber Trail has 16 cabins ranging from one to six bedrooms as well as four motel units with kitchenettes. The resort can arrange boat rentals and guides, massage is offered on-site, and once-weekly float plane rides are offered to guests. Rates start at $95. Specials and packages are available.

🛶 🦌 ❄ **Tall Pines and Croft Yurts** (1-800-322-8327; poplarcreekbnb.com), 11 Poplar Creek Drive, Boundary Waters. For a true wilderness experience, the Tall Pines and Croft Yurts are open year-round for summer or winter adventures. Four people can sleep on bunk beds or a futon, although additional bedding can be provided for more guests. A fully equipped kitchen is included; an outhouse is steps away, as well as a complimentary canoe. Rates start at $95.

♿ 🛶 🦌 ❄ 🍷 🍴 **Silver Rapids Lodge** (218-365-4877 or 1-800-950-9425; silverrapidslodge.com), 459 Kawishiwi Trail. This hundred-year-old resort is located on a private peninsula with water on three side. It offers lakeside cabins, motel suites, and campgrounds. Some cabins have fireplaces, whirlpools, saunas, decks, and private fire pits. There are private hiking and cross-country ski trails on the grounds. A restaurant is open during the summer, and the lounge is open year-round. Rates start at $59. Packages and specials are available.

🛶 ❄ **Log Cabin Hideaways** (218-365-6045; logcabinhideaways.com), 1321 N. County Route 21, Ely. For those truly wanting the wilderness experience, Log Cabin Hideaways provides hand-hewn log cabins on the edge of the BWCAW. Each cabin comes with a canoe, but no electricity or indoor plumbing. Propane is provided for cooking; all units have a Finnish sauna. Some of the cabins are accessible by water only. None of the cabins have "neighbors"; each cabin is on its own secluded site. Rates start at $155.

🛶 📶 ❄ **Timber Bay Lodge & Houseboats** (218-827-3682; timberbay.com), 8347 Timber Bay Road, Babbitt. Located along Birch Lake, Timber Bay has log-sided cabins and houseboats for rental. Cabins are widely spaced for maximum privacy and include decks, fireplaces, and barbecue grills. Most cabins have two or three bedrooms, but there's also a six-bedroom unit available. There are several houseboats available for rental, ranging from 30- to 52-feet in size and holding two to 12 people. The resort offers children's and naturalist programs. Rates start at $305. Packages and specials are available.

♿ 🛶 🍷 🍴 **Burnside Lodge** (218-365-3894; burnside.com), 2755 Burnside Lodge Road, Ely. Open mid-May to late Sept. West of Ely, on Burnside Lake, Burnside Lodge has been offering gracious hospitality to guests for nearly a century, and it's arguably one of Minnesota's most famous accommodations. The resort offers several cabins in varying sizes, all tucked into the woods or near the lake; the peaceful ambience is assisted by the lack of TVs and telephones. The lodge itself is on the National Register of Historic Places, and its dining room (see *Where to Eat*) serves delicious food in a large, open room. The adjoining gift shop has several items of local interest. Rates start at $195.

🛶 📶 **River Point Resort** (1-800-456-5580; riverpointresort.com), 12007 River Point Road. Open mid-May–early Oct. A peaceful resort on a private peninsula along Birch Lake and the South Kawishiwi River. The resort offers several cabins, villas, and chalets that offer private sundecks and private entrances along with lake, river, and forest views. A sauna is on-site for guests, and boat rental is offered, as well as guided day and overnight BWCAW trips. Rates startat $150. Specials and packages are available.

BURNTSIDE LODGE

HOTELS 🚹 ⚡ 🐾 📶 🍸 ❄ 🍽 **Grand Ely Lodge** (218-365-6565 or 1-800-365-5070; grandelylodge.com), 400 N. Pioneer Road, Ely. Just outside of the city of Ely is this resort, the largest in Ely, with 61 rooms and suites (and ice-fishing houses for day occupancy in the winter). The resort is very family friendly, with kids under 10 staying and eating free with paid adults. There's an indoor pool and sauna, and lake activities are provided at the marina on Shagawa Lake. The Evergreen Restaurant is open all day; there's also a lounge. Mountain bikes are available to guests who want to use the Trezona Trail across the street, which connects to the **International Wolf Center** (see *To See and Do*). Rates start at $140. Specials and packages are available.

⚡ 🐾 📶 ❄ ↝ **Adventure Inn** (218-365-3140; adventureinn-ely.com), 1145 E. Sheridan Street, Ely. Right in the heart of downtown Ely, the Adventure Inn is a small but charming motel with economy and standard/deluxe rooms, which are clean and comfortable; several of the rooms boast handmade quilts. The hotel

is a member of Green America and the Green Hotels Association. Rates start at $105.

🚹 ⚡ 🍸 ❄ 🍽 🦴 **Fortune Bay Resort Casino** (218-753-6400 or 1-800-555-1714; fortunebay.com), 1430 Bois Forte Road, Tower. Seemingly in the middle of nowhere, this newer resort and casino is on Lake Vermilion and offers attractive rooms and suites, an indoor pool, dining room, 24-hour casino, RV park, and golf course. An on-site marina has fishing boats, pontoons, canoes, and paddleboats available for rent, or you can bring your own boat and dock it at the marina. Non-motorized rentals are free for hotel guests, including paddleboards, kayaks, hydro bikes, and mountain bikes. Rates start at $89. Specials and packages are available.

## ❉ Where to Eat

DINING OUT ⚡ ❄ 🍸 **The Ely Steak House** (218-365-7412; elysteakhouse .com), 216 E. Sheridan Street, Ely. Open daily for lunch and dinner. Steakhouse and bar with fresh fish specials, prime rib on weekends, and steak whenever you like. Expensive.

🦀 🍸 **Burntside Lodge** (218-365-3894; burntside.com), 2755 Burntside Lodge Road, Ely. Open Wed.–Mon. for dinner, mid-Apr. to late Sept. One of the nicest restaurants in the Ely area is in this historic lodge (see *Lodging*), just west of Ely. The dining room serves ambitious fare focused on seasonal specialties, while the adjacent bar has a more casual atmosphere and menu. Reservations required. Expensive.

&. 🦀 ❄ 🍸 **Evergreen Restaurant** (218-365-6565; grandelylodge.com/restaurant -bar/evergreen-restaurant), 400 N. Pioneer Road, Ely. Open daily for all three meals. Located within the Grand Ely Lodge, Evergreen offers upscale supper club food in both hearty and smaller portions. You can't go wrong with any of the steaks, or the Shore Lunch Bluegill Dinner. Moderate/expensive.

EATING OUT 🦀 ❄ 🍸 **Insula Restaurant** (218-365-4855; insularestaurant.com), 145 E. Sheridan Street, Ely. Open Tues.–Sat. for all three meals, Sun. for brunch. This eatery is heavily focused on local and sustainable, and its varied menu highlights Minnesota wild rice, berries, maple syrup, and locally grown meats and fish. The menu is creative and thoughtful, and while it's fairly meat-heavy, vegetarians aren't given short shrift: try the Forager Burger, made with smoked sweet potato, mushrooms, and a bean patty, or the Mock Duck Pot Pie. Moderate.

🦀 ❄ 🍸 **Rockwood Bar & Grill** (218-365-7772; rockwoodely.com), 302 E. Sheridan Street, Ely. Open daily for lunch and dinner. A northwoods-themed restaurant with enormous sandwiches and salads, as well as steak and walleye (combined, they're called Woods and Water). Moderate.

🦀 ❄ **Gator's Grilled Cheese Emporium** (218-365-7348; gatorsinely.com), 955 E. Sheridan Street, Ely. Open Mon.–Sat. for breakfast and lunch. Grilled cheese takes on a wider meaning in this amiable eatery with a huge menu of grilled sandwiches that involve cheese as well as a hearty breakfast menu. If you're up for a challenge, try The Mutt: pulled ham and chicken, smoked turkey, prime rib, bacon, mac and cheese, and a fried egg, all between two grilled cheese sandwiches. Besides winning a prize if you finish it by yourself, Gator's donates money to local animal shelters for each Mutt consumed. Inexpensive (except for The Mutt, which is moderate).

🦀 ❄ **Sir G's** (218-365-3688; sirgs.com), 520 E. Sheridan Street, Ely. Open daily for lunch and dinner. Italian food, including pasta made on-site. Inexpensive/ moderate.

🦀 ❄ **Front Porch Coffee and Tea** (218-365-2326; elysfrontporch.com), 343 E. Sheridan Street, Ely. Open daily for breakfast and lunch. A cozy, inviting coffeehouse with a limited but tasty menu of soups, sandwiches, burritos, and pastries. Inexpensive/moderate.

🦀 🍸 ❄ **Boathouse Brewpub and Restaurant** (218-365-4301; boathouse brewpub.com), 47 E. Sheridan Street, Ely. Open daily for lunch and dinner. A cheerful pub with an in-house brewery and typical bar food—burgers and sandwiches—and walleye (walleye grilled cheese, anybody?), the Minnesota staple. Moderate.

## ❄ Selective Shopping

Ely has several blocks of shops with a good variety of merchandise, from regular tourist things like shirts and mugs to specialty items and artwork.

❄ **Brandenburg Gallery** (218-365-6563 or 1-877-493-8017; jimbrandenburg.com), 11 E. Sheridan Street, Ely. Open daily. The gallery showcases the award-winning nature photography of Jim Brandenburg, who has traveled the world for National Geographic and who has a special love for the Boundary Waters area (he makes it his home part of the year).

❄ **Wintergreen Designs** (218-365-6602 or 1-844-359-6233; wintergreen northernwear.com), 205 E. Sheridan Street, Ely. Open daily. Specialists in high-quality and attractive outdoor apparel, Wintergreen produces its work in Ely and sells it at this local retail store (another store is open in Duluth).

❄ **Piragis Northwoods Company** (218-365-6745 or 1-800-223-6565; piragis.com), 105 N. Central Avenue, Ely. Open daily. This large outfitting shop sells and/or rents all manner of outdoor gear, including canoes and camping gear. Piragis also offers guided canoeing and camping trips in the BWCAW.

✐ ❄ **Steger Mukluks & Moccasins** (218-365-6634; mukluks.com), 33 E. Sheridan Street, Ely. Open daily. Inspired by Native American designs, these mukluks and moccasins are made in Ely from moose hide and are highly regarded for their comfort and winter protection.

✐ ❄ **Legacy Toys** (218-249-0263; legacytoys.com), 5 N. Central Avenue, Ely. Open Mon.–Sat. A cheerful toy store offering a wide variety of toys for all ages, as well as its own candy and a 400-gallon saltwater aquarium.

✐ ❄ **Mealey's Gift & Sauna Shop** (218-365-3639; mealeysinely.com), 124 N. Central Avenue, Ely. Open daily. Mealey's is exactly what its name describes: a one-stop shop with saunas and sauna accessories, but also high-quality gift and home décor items.

# ❋ Special Events

*February*: **Ely Winter Festival** (218-365-7669; elywinterfestival.com), Ely. It's never too cold for a festival, as this annual midwinter event shows. Snow-sculpting lessons and contests, Nordic ski racing, the Mukluk Ball, snowshoe tours, snowmobile races, and musical concerts are all part of the fun during the 10-day event.

*July*: **Blueberry Arts Festival** (218-365-6123 or 1-800-777-7281; ely.org), Ely. Annual three-day arts fair held in late July.

*September*: **Harvest Moon Festival** (218-365-6123 or 1-800-777-7281; ely.org), Ely. This annual September festival includes three days of art and craft exhibits, children's activities, live musical performances, and food.

# INTERNATIONAL FALLS/ VOYAGEURS NATIONAL PARK

The northern border of the state is an outdoorsman's paradise. Lake of the Woods and Rainy Lake are fine fishing lakes year-round, and there are ample opportunities for just about any other kind of outdoor activity you can imagine. Moreover, visitors can get a taste of what it must have been like for early pioneers as they navigated Chippewa National Forest or Voyageurs National Park, with acres of undeveloped lands to explore.

## ✳ To See and Do

⚓ ♿ ✳ **Koochiching County Historical Museum/Bronko Nagurski Museum** (218-283-4316; koochichingmuseums.org), 214 6th Avenue, International Falls. Open daily. Adults $4; students $2; children 6 and under free; admission gains entrance to both museums. Two museums share one building, each focused on history specific to the region. Bronko Nagurski is a local legend, a farm boy who became one of the best professional football players in the sport's history. His side of the museum details not only his life and sports career, but also the impact of the times (the Depression, World War II) on his life and that of others. The Koochiching County Historical Museum has a well-rounded collection of artifacts reflecting the area's history with Native Americans and French voyageurs, as well as its relationship to Canada. Museum volunteers and staff are well versed in the collections and can answer questions and offer insightful tales.

**Boise Cascade Paper Mill** (218-285-5011), 400 2nd Street, International Falls. Open Mon.–Fri., Jun.–Aug. No admission fee. Children under 10 not allowed; cameras prohibited. Boise Cascade, one of the world's largest paper-making companies, offers both mill tours and woodland tours. Call ahead for reservations—these tours are very popular.

## ✳ Green Space and Outdoor Activities

Not surprisingly, this area is full of activities in the great outdoors, some more rustic than others.

FISHING **Rainy Lake/Rainy River** (rainylake.org). Rainy Lake, which stretches north into Canada, has some of the best fishing in the state, particularly for walleye, and there are many resorts and houseboats offering accommodations and fishing guides (see *Lodging*). Rainy River connects Rainy Lake with Lake of the Woods to the west; its 80 miles of river provide not only excellent fishing opportunities (walleye, smallmouth bass), but also great canoeing and kayaking.

GOLF **The River Golf Course, Inc.** (218-283-4491; therivergolf.com), 4402 County Route 152. Designed by Joel Goldstrand, the Falls Country Club golf course is challenging and beautiful, and it's open to the public.

PARKS AND PARKWAYS **Waters of the Dancing Sky** (watersofdancingsky.com), MN 11. Named after the Northern Lights, this stretch of highway that travels more than 190 miles from the North Dakota border into Voyageurs National Park covers a full range of northern Minnesota scenery: rivers, lakes, prairies, farmland, and a host of small towns. Note: The western edge of the byway is completed when MN 11 connects with US 59, then MN 175.

**Voyageurs National Park** (218-283-6600; nps.gov/voya), 3131 US 53, International Falls. Centuries ago, French traders paddled these waters on their way to Canada, looking to trade animal pelts and goods with the natives. Today Voyageurs National Park is a haven for those who love to be on the water, whether by canoe, kayak, or houseboat. Hikers, snowshoers, and cross-country skiers

PIRAGIS NORTHWOODS COMPANY

travel the grounds year-round. A series of connected lakes and bays, as well as miles of untouched forest, provide an intimate north woods experience. Wildlife is abundant.

There are three visitor centers. The Rainy Lake Visitor Center (218-286-5258) is the primary source and the only one open year-round. Located 10 miles east of International Falls, it is open daily from late May–September, and Wed.–Sun. from October–Memorial Day. The Kabetogama Lake Visitor Center (218-875-2111) is open daily from late May–late September, and the Ash River Visitor Center (218-374-3221) is open Thurs.–Sun., late May–September.

Boat tours from the visitor centers are offered during the summer, as is a tour to Ellsworth Rock Gardens, a lush garden spot built over a period of 20 years by Jack Ellsworth and maintained today by the National Park Service.

There are campgrounds available on a first-come, first-served basis (groups can reserve ahead of time with one of the visitor centers), but note that the campgrounds within the park are only accessible by boat. A free permit is required for camping, which can be obtained at the visitor centers or at self-permit stations within the park. If you're interested in camping but would rather be able to drive up to your campsite, look into reserving a site at the **Woodenfrog State Campground** (218-365-2520), County Route 122, Ray. Located in Kabetogama State Forest, part of Voyageurs National Park, Woodenfrog has campsites available from mid-May to mid-Sept. that don't require boat access.

## ✳ Lodging

Within International Falls itself are several small motels or budget hotels, such as the Days Inn and Super 8 on US 53. Most accommodations that provide more of the "northern" experience are on the outskirts, or along MN 11 east to Voyageurs National Park.

CABINS

INTERNATIONAL FALLS

✐ 🏕 ✳ **Camp Idlewood** (218-286-5551; campidlewood.com), 3033 County Route 20, International Falls. Camp Idlewood has nine cabins with knotty pine interiors and full kitchens; the resort itself has a beach, and a canoe, paddleboat, inner tubes, and tow ropes available at no fee.

Boats and motors can be rented, or you can bring your own; each cabin has one dock space included, and additional spaces can be rented. Weekly rates start at $1120.

✂ 🏠 ❄ ⛾ ⅋ **Island View Lodge and Cabins** (218-286-3511 or 1-800-777-7856; gotorainylake.com), 1817 E. MN 11, International Falls. Located 12 miles east of International Falls, Island View sits on the edge of Rainy Lake with gorgeous views and direct lake access. There are 15 cabins available, as well as several lodge rooms. An adjacent spa has a hot tub and sauna, and the lodge has a dining room and lounge. Rates start at $130.

♻ ♿ ✂ ✂ ⛾ ⅋ **Sha Sha Resort on Rainy Lake** (218-286-3241 or 1-800-685-2776; shashaonrainylake.com), 1664 E. MN 11, International Falls. Open May–Sept. Literally at road's end, Sha Sha Resort is the final destination for MN 11 east from International Falls. The resort offers nine beautiful log cabins. Another of the resort's benefits is a sprawling, multilayered outdoor deck where diners and libation seekers can enjoy the view of Rainy Lake. Rates start at $280.

## LAKE KABETOGAMA

✂ 🏠 ❄ **Voyageur Park Lodge** (218-875-2131 or 1-800-331-5694; voyageurparklodge.com), 10436 Waltz Road, Kabetogama. Open mid-May–Sept. Ten cottages along Lake Kabetogama, along with a lodge suite, offer guests peaceful privacy. Full kitchen, barbecue grill, and campfire site are included with each cabin (campfires only when conditions allow). Use of canoes, kayaks, and paddleboats is free; fishing boats, pontoons, and motors can be rented on-site. In winter, overnight ice houses are available to rent. Rates start at $160.

✂ 🏠 ❄ **Herseth's Tomahawk Resort** (218-875-2352 or 1-888-834-7899; hersethstomahawkresort.com), 10078 Gappa Road, Ray. Herseth's offers nine cabins with lake views. The resort has a large sand beach with free canoes and

paddleboats. Motorized boats available for rent. The proprietor is a certified scuba diver and is happy to arrange diving excursions into Lake Kabetogama. Rates start at $173.

✂ 🏠 **Moosehorn Resort** (218-875-3491 or 1-800-777-7968; moosehornresort.com), 10434 Waltz Road, Kabetogama. Open late Apr.–mid-Oct. Moosehorn has nine cabins stretched along Lake Kabetogama with sandy beach. This is an especially family-friendly resort, located in a quiet bay that keeps the lake waters calmer than in other spots. Canoes, kid-sized kayaks, and a playground area are included for guests. Boats are available for rental. Weekly rates start at $825.

✂ 🏠 ❄ ⛾ **Kec's Kove Resort** (218-875-2841 or 1-800-777-8405; kecskove.com), 10428 Gamma Road, Kabetogama. Kec's has eight cabins and a lodge with whirlpool and sauna; a massage therapist is available for guests. If you go fishing and need some help afterward, Kec's can provide fish cleaning and freezing services. Motorized boats are available for rent; paddleboats, canoes, and kayaks are complimentary. Weekly rates start at $825; daily rates are offered in winter.

✂ 🏠 ❄ **Northern Lights Resort & Outfitting** (218-875-2591 or 1-800-318-7023; nlro.com), 10179 Bay Club Drive, Kabetogama. Northern Lights offers 13 cabins along Lake Kabetogama, as well as a number of activities for all interest levels. Guides can be arranged for fishing or other expeditions; a ladies' pontoon cruise is held weekly, with coffee and muffins; an adults social cruise is offered weekly in the evening. Rates start at $145.

## HOTELS

### INTERNATIONAL FALLS

♿ ✂ 🏠 ((◦)) ⛾ ❄ ⅋ ⚐ **AmericInn** (218-283-8000 or 1-800-331-4443; wyndhamhotels.com), 1500 MN 11, International Falls. A well-appointed hotel within International Falls, the AmericInn has an indoor pool, restaurant, and even a garden walk down to the river, where guests can fish. Rates start at $107.

🚣 ✼ **Bear Ridge Guest House** (218-340-4274; bearridgeguesthouse.net), 1841 MN 11, International Falls. Offering one-, two-, and three-bedroom suites, the Bear Ridge Guest House is a great choice for visitors to Rainy Lake. It's located on a hill overlooking the lake, with private decks to enjoy the view. Some suites have full kitchens and fireplaces. Rates start at $175.

🚣 ✼ ⛉ **Rainy Lake Inn & Suites at Tara's Wharf** (218-286-5699 or 1-877-724-6955; taraswharf.com), 2065 Spruce Street Landing, Ranier. Near Woody's, the Rainy Lake Inn offers four suite accommodations in a charming "seaside" setting. The ice cream shop will keep everyone happy. Rates include daily breakfast at one of two local cafes, as well as a free ice cream cone. Rates start at $95.

RANIER

## VOYAGEURS NATIONAL PARK

🚣 ⛉ ‖ **Kettle Falls Hotel** (218-240-1724 or 218-875-2070 [winter]; kettlefallshotel .com), 12977 Chippewa Trail, Kabetogama. Open early May to early Oct. While I have not visited this hotel personally, it's enough of a legend that it can't be ignored. Located on an odd geographical twist that allows you to stand on the Minnesota side and look south to Canada, this hotel is the only lodging within Voyageurs National Park, and it's accessible only by plane or by boat. Nearly a century old, Kettle Falls Hotel has a rich history that includes bootleggers selling whiskey during Prohibition. Today the hotel has 12 rooms with shared baths, a full-service restaurant, and a saloon that still bears the marks of wilder early years. Rates start at $70.

## ✼ Where to Eat

EATING OUT 🔌 🚣 ✼ **Sammy's Pizza Restaurant & Tavern** (218-373-0190;

sammyspizzaifalls.com), 301 3rd Avenue, International Falls. Open daily for lunch and dinner. A cheerful, family-friendly American-Italian restaurant with pizza, pasta, salads, and burgers. A buffet is available, as is an arcade area for kids. Moderate.

🔌 🚣 ✼ **Coffee Landing** (218-373-2233; facebook.com/coffeelandingcafe), 444 3rd Street, International Falls. Open daily for breakfast and lunch. A full-service coffee, espresso, and tea shop, along with an extensive food menu including breakfast items, sandwiches, pastries, soups, and salads. Inexpensive.

🔌 🚣 ✼ **Rose Garden Restaurant** (218-283-4551), 311 4th Avenue, International Falls. Open Mon.–Fri. for lunch and dinner, Sat. for dinner. Classic Chinese-American food, with large portions at reasonable prices. Moderate.

🔌 🚣 ✼ **Chocolate Moose Restaurant Company** (218-283-8888; chocolate mooserestaurant.com), 2501 2nd Avenue W., International Falls. Open daily for all three meals. The Chocolate Moose serves up platter-sized portions of

# HOUSEBOATS

An alternative to hotels and resorts is the houseboat experience. Rainy Lake has two companies that have several houseboats available for rental.

**Northernaire Houseboats** (218-286-5221; northernairehouseboats.com), 2690 County Route 94, International Falls. Open May–Sept., Northernaire offers 10 houseboats of varying sizes and levels of amenities, including some with open decks and some with screened-in decks. Rentals include a tow-behind boat, free delivery on the lake twice weekly (for groceries, etc.), and a guide service for the first 4 miles to orient you to the maps and buoy systems. Order ahead, and your boat's kitchen will be stocked with foods and beverages of your choice. Rates start at $285. Specials are available. ✎

**Rainy Lake Houseboats** (218-286-5391 or 1-800-554-9188; rainylakehouseboats.com), 2031 Town Road 488, International Falls. Open mid-May–mid-Oct. Rainy Lake's fully equipped houseboats have kitchens, a tow-behind boat, swim platforms and water slides, and deck table and chairs. Guide service is available with prearrangement, and groceries can be ordered ahead as well. Rates start at $285. ✎

pancakes, burgers, pasta, and dinner entrées including steak and shrimp. Inexpensive/moderate.

&. ✎ ❋ **Rainy Lake Grill** (218-540-1002), 2079 Spruce Street, Ranier. Open Wed.–Sun. for brunch and dinner. Enormous breakfast dishes, pizzas, sandwiches, salads, a build-your-own pasta option at dinner, and steak, walleye, and shrimp. Inexpensive/moderate.

&. ✎ ❋ ☂ **Almost Lindy's** (218-286-3364; almostlindys.com), 3003 County Route 20, International Falls. Open daily for dinner. BBQ, pizza, and chicken—broasted chicken, to be specific—as well as slow-smoked ribs, steak, walleye, and an impressive array of pizzas. Try the Perogi pizza: sour cream, potato, bacon, and onion. Moderate.

## ❋ Selective Shopping

&. ✎ **Border Bob's** (218-283-4414; borderbobs.com), 200 2nd Avenue, International Falls. Open daily Memorial Day–Labor Day. The quintessential souvenir shop, with local goods such as maple syrup, commemorative Minnesota/Canada items, T-shirts, and other tourist goods. Also a great place to stop for ice cream.

**Pine Ridge Gift Shop** (218-875-3313), 9903 Gamma Road, Lake Kabetogama. Open daily May–Sept. Pine Ridge is housed in a log cabin on Gamma Road, near CR 122; located near a cluster of resorts on Lake Kabetogama, the shop is easy to find. Its merchandise runs the gamut from touristy to collectible. Local arts, crafts, quilts, cabin amenities, Christmas decorations, candles, locally produced foods (including their own roasted coffee), and clothing make up the bulk of this shop, staffed by cheerful locals who know the area well.

## ❋ Special Events

*January*: **Icebox Days** (218-283-9400 or 1-800-325-5766; ifallschamber.com /icebox-days), International Falls. This annual festival includes such winter fun as frozen turkey bowling, smoosh races (four people on two skis), a human sled dog race, snowshoe races, an open ice golf tournament, toilet seat toss, chili feed, and the Freeze Yer Gizzard Blizzard Run. Occurs in mid-January.

# THE IRON RANGE

The Iron Range is the mini melting pot of Minnesota. Immigrants from more than 40 countries settled here in the 19th century, joining the population of Native Americans already in the region. Mining was a driving force here for many years. The Iron Range (or simply "the Range," as locals call it) is the birthplace of several notable people, not least of whom is Bob Dylan.

## ✳ To See and Do

✪ ♿ ✐ ⚲ ❄ **Minnesota Discovery Center** (218-254-7959 or 1-800-372-6437; mndiscoverycenter.com), 1005 Discovery Drive, Chisholm. Open Tues.–Sun. Adults $9; seniors 62 and older and military members $8; children 3–17 $5; children 2 and under free. Admission is free for everyone on Thurs. after 3 p.m. The Minnesota Discovery Center is a wonderful stop for visitors to the Iron Range. The grounds themselves are beautiful (and frequently used for weddings and receptions). An indoor museum details the Iron Range's extensive history and hosts traveling exhibits, while a trolley takes visitors to the Glen Location, a former mining town where people can explore the historical buildings. Heritage Park includes a series of re-created pioneer homes.

♿ ✐ **Greyhound Bus Museum** (218-263-5814; greyhoundbusmuseum.org), 1201 Greyhound Boulevard, Hibbing. Open daily mid-May–Sept.; open by request for groups in the off-season. Adults $5; senior citizens $4; students $2; children 6–12 $1; children under 6 free; $10 for families and $3 per person for tour groups. Documents the development of the US bus industry from its days as a single vehicle in Hibbing to the current national route.

♿ ✐ ❄ **US Hockey Hall of Fame** (218-744-5167 or 1-800-443-7825; ushockeyhall.com), 801 Hat Trick Avenue, Eveleth. Open daily Memorial Day–Labor Day; Fri.–Sun. Labor Day–Memorial Day. Adults $8; seniors 55 and older and students 13–17 $7; children 6–12 $6; children under 6 free. A must-see for hockey fans—and the Iron Range tends to have a lot of local hockey fans—the hall of fame includes memorabilia not just from local hockey teams, but also from national events, including the 1980 "Miracle on Ice" Olympic team and the 1998 women's gold-medal Olympic team.

✐ **Finnish Heritage Homestead Tours** (218-984-2084; embarrass.org), MN 135 and County Route 21, Embarrass. Open Thurs.–Sat. at 1 p.m., Memorial Day–Labor Day. Adults $6; $5 per person for large groups or senior citizens; children 12 and under free. This three-hour guided tour to the small town of Embarrass illustrates the Finnish part of Minnesota's history. Handcrafted log structures, antique farm and weaving machinery, and a gift shop are all part of the tour.

**Bob Dylan's Childhood Home,** 2425 Dylan Drive, Hibbing. While it's not open for tours, fans of Bob Dylan can drive by the childhood home on the renamed street.

♿ ✐ ❄ **Paulucci Space Theatre** (218-262-6720; facebook.com/paulicci), 1502 E. 23rd Street, Hibbing. Hours and admission vary. A 3D IMAX screen shows films about space and planets.

♿ ✐ ❄ **Forest History Center** (218-327-4482 or 1-888-727-8386; mnhs.org/foresthistory), 2609 County Route 76, Grand Rapids. Open Tues.–Sat. Jun.–early Sept.

THE JUDY GARLAND MUSEUM

Cross-country ski trails open daily in winter. Adults $10; seniors 65 and older, military members and veterans, and college students $8; children 5–17 $6; children under 5 free. The Forest History Center has a visitor center and a re-created turn-of-the-20th-century logging camp with costumed characters for guides. Visitors can board a floating cook shack, climb a 100-foot fire tower, and crawl through a decayed log while learning about Minnesota's logging history. A trail system takes visitors through the forest and along the Mississippi River.

♿ 🩹 ❄ **The Judy Garland Museum** (218-327-9276 or 1-800-664-5839; judygarlandmuseum.com), 2727 S. Pokegama Avenue, Grand Rapids. Open daily 10–5, Memorial Day–Sept. 30; Fri. and Sat. 10–5, Oct.–Mar.; Mon.–Sat. 10–5, Apr.–Memorial Day. Admission is $8 for those older than age one; under age one is free. Admission includes the Children's Discovery Museum. Judy Garland was born in Minnesota in 1922 and spent her first four years here. The home she lived in has been moved from its original street to a location on US 169, a busy highway across from Home Depot, which detracts slightly from the house's charm. The house has been lovingly restored with considerable attention to detail, and the curators have procured a wide variety of artifacts, including the carriage Dorothy rode in upon her arrival at Oz. The museum did have a pair of ruby slippers which were stolen in 2005. They were finally found in 2018, but since the investigation is ongoing, the shoes have not (at the time of this writing) been returned to the museum. The museum hosts an annual **Judy Garland Festival** (see *Special Events*), which draws visitors from all over the country.

♿ 🩹 ❄ **Children's Discovery Museum** (218-326-1900 or 1-866-236-5437; cdmkids.org), 2727 US 169 S., Grand Rapids. Open daily mid-May–Sept.; Fri. and Sat. 10–5, Oct.–mid-May, as well as selected "school's out" days. Admission is $10 for those 2 and older; under 2 is free. Admission includes the Judy Garland Museum. This hands-on children's museum includes a kid-sized town, a river forest with talking tree (but a friendlier tree than the ones encountered by Dorothy on her way to Oz), a "Dino Dig," and an art room.

## ✲ Green Space and Outdoor Activities

**Wellstone Memorial and Historic Site**, 7343 Bodas Road, Eveleth. A wooded 5-acre site is the memorial to Minnesota senator Paul Wellstone and the other travelers who died when their plane crashed near this site in 2002. Trails are lined with boulders naming the victims and interpretive signs explaining Wellstone's work and legacy.

✍ **Hill Annex Mine State Park** (218-247-7215 or 1-866-856-2757; dnr.state.mn.us/state_parks/hill_annex_mine/index.html), 880 Gary Street, Calumet. Open daily 9–5, year-round; tours given Wed.–Sun. and on holidays in summer. Tours are adults $10; children 5–12 $6; children under 5 free. This area was mined for 65 years, ending in 1978, and can now be explored during the summer months by taking one of three guided tours—a mine tour, a boat tour, and fossil hunt.

# ✳ Lodging

BED-AND-BREAKFASTS ✳ (ᵞ) **Mitchell-Tappan House** (218-288-4972; mitchell-tappanhouse.com), 2125 E. 4th Avenue, Hibbing. Built in 1897 for a mine superintendent, the Mitchell-Tappan House was moved, as many Hibbing houses were, in the early 1920s when it was discovered that ore ran right underneath it. Today this bed-and-breakfast has one room and one suite with private baths, plus cozy common areas. Full breakfast is included. Rates start at $110.

HOTELS ♿ ✍ 🐾 ✳ ∱ **AmericInn Lodge & Suites** (218-208-0230; americinn.com), 5480 Mountain Iron Drive, Virginia. This member of the AmericInn chain provides a solid, reliable choice, with hotel rooms and suites (some with fireplaces), an indoor pool, and daily continental breakfast. Rates start at $107.

♿ ✍ ✳ ∱ **Chisholm Inn & Suites** (218-254-2000 or 1-877-255-3156; chisholminn.com), 501 Iron Drive, Chisholm. Similar to the AmericInn, the Chisholm Inn offers hotel rooms and suites, and breakfast is included for guests. Larger rooms offer whirlpool baths. The hotel also has an indoor pool and sauna. Rates start at $95.

♿ ✍ 🐾 ✳ ♂ (ᵞ) ♨ **Quality Inn & Suites** (218-749-1000 or 1-866-430-2692; hotelsone.com), 502 Chestnut Street, Virginia. Located in downtown Virginia, the rooms all overlook the indoor pool area, which includes a whirlpool and sauna. A buffet breakfast is served each morning. Rates start at $99.

♿ ✍ ✳ ▾ ‖ ∱ **Hibbing Park Hotel and Suites** (218-262-3481 or 1-800-262-3481; hibbingparkhotel.com), 1402 E. Howard Street, Hibbing. One of Hibbing's nicest hotels, the Hibbing Park has 120 rooms and suites, as well as an indoor pool. The hotel was recently renovated, and the rooms have been updated. The hotel's restaurant, **Grandma's in the Park** (see *Where to Eat*), is similar to the Duluth-area Grandma's. Rates start at $79.

# ✳ Where to Eat

EATING OUT ♿ ✍ ▾ ✳ **Grandma's in the Park** (218-262-3047; hibbingparkhotel.com), 1402 E. Howard Street, Hibbing. Open daily for lunch and dinner. While not a direct branch of the Duluth Grandma's restaurants, this dining spot, in the **Hibbing Park Hotel** (see *Lodging*), is related and has a similar menu, complete with ribs, pasta, steak, and fish. Moderate/expensive.

♿ ✍ **A&W Drive In** (218-229-2240), 103 S. Main Street, Aurora. Open daily for lunch and dinner, mid-May–mid-Sept., weather permitting. An honest-to-goodness drive-in restaurant, A&W serves you your burgers and fries in your car so you can eat it on the spot. Be sure to order a big frosty mug of root beer. Inexpensive.

♿ ✍ ▾ ✳ **Adventures** (218-741-7151; adventuresrestaurants.com), 5475 Mountain Iron Drive, Virginia. Open daily for lunch and dinner. Typical entrées include burgers, sandwiches, salads, and pasta; walleye sandwiches and wild rice meat loaf are great choices. Moderate.

♿ ✍ ▾ ✳ **Grandma's Saloon & Grill** (218-749-1960; grandmasrestaurants.com), 1302 S. 12th Avenue, Virginia. Open daily for lunch and dinner. One of the Duluth Grandma's Restaurants family, this branch, like its Duluth siblings, provides reliablegrill food and a sturdy drink menu. Moderate.

## ✳ Special Events

*February*: **Laskianen Finnish Sliding Festival** (218-229-2813; ironrange.org), Aurora. The first weekend of February brings this annual celebration of Scandinavian—particularly Finnish—traditions. The two-day event includes a ball, sleigh and carriage ride, special dinners, and, of course, sliding.

*June*: **Land of the Loon Festival** (218-749-5555; landoftheloonfestival.com), Virginia. Taking place annually the third weekend of June, Land of the Loon bills itself as a multicultural arts and crafts festival. The two-day festival offers a parade, more than 300 vendors, live music, and a kid's area with a petting zoo and face painting. A variety of food (German, Finnish, Mexican, Greek, and Cuban, among others) is available for sale.

**Judy Garland Festival** (1-800-664-5839; judygarlandmuseum.com), Grand Rapids. The **Judy Garland Museum** (see *To See and Do*) sponsors this annual festival, which occurs in late June, after Garland's birth date (June 10). It's a popular event, attracting visitors from around the United States, so plan ahead if you'd like to attend. The festival has previously included speakers on Judy Garland, informal sing-alongs, screenings of popular Garland movies, a gala dinner and fundraiser, a collector's exchange, a seminar on the dangers of drug use, and occasional visits from the actors who portrayed some of the Munchkins. There's an adjacent Wizard of Oz Festival at the children's museum next door.

# NORTHERN LAKES AND RED RIVER VALLEY

■

PARK RAPIDS/WALKER

BEMIDJI AREA

BAUDETTE/ROSEAU/WARROAD

THIEF RIVER FALLS/RED RIVER
VALLEY/DETROIT LAKES

# NORTHERN LAKES AND RED RIVER VALLEY

The northern lakes region and the Red River Valley provide visitors with a range of geological vistas. The lakes area is made up of rolling and heavily forested land, while the valley, contradictory to its name, is flat agricultural plains, where you can drive for miles and see nothing but sunflowers, corn, and soybean crops. This is a region shaped by former glacial lakes and settled by Chippewa Indians, followed by French traders and eventually Scandinavians, looking for fertile farmland.

The lakes that punctuate the region are known for excellent fishing and boating, and not just in the summer. The fishing season has been extended to the winter by increased technology; today many northern lakes are dotted by buildings ranging from little more than shacks to "sleepers"—larger, heated buildings with attached portable potties. No matter the level of grandeur, all are considered ice houses. Ice fishing, combined with other winter sports such as cross-country skiing, snowmobiling, and snowshoeing, have made the northern region a year-round destination rather than a summer-only spot.

Rivers, as well as lakes, play an important role in this region. The Mississippi River has its starting point here in Itasca State Park, where the Headwaters, first accurately identified by explorer Henry Schoolcraft in 1832, can be crossed easily by foot, giving

THE *CHESTER CHARLES II* TOUR BOAT AT ITASCA STATE PARK

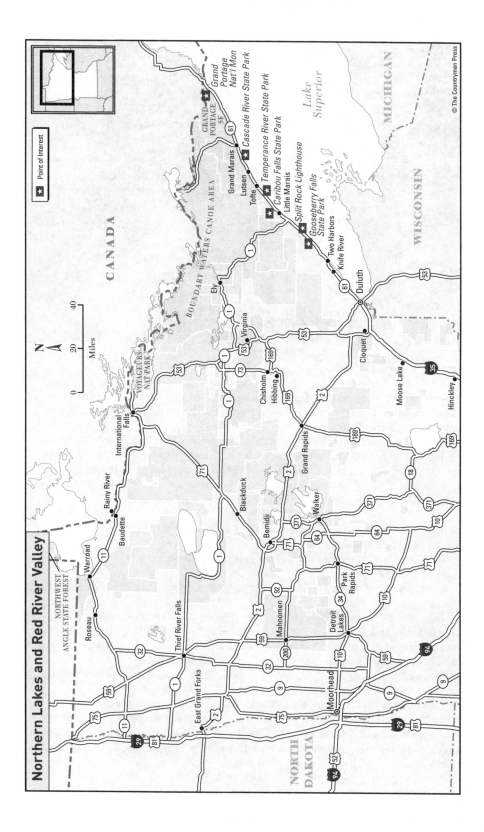

# Northern Lakes and Red River Valley

Point of Interest

CANADA

MICHIGAN

WISCONSIN

NORTH DAKOTA

Lake Superior

BOUNDARY WATERS CANOE AREA

VOYAGEURS NAT'L PARK

GRAND PORTAGE SF

NORTHWEST ANGLE STATE FOREST

Grand Portage Nat'l Mon
Cascade River State Park
Temperance River State Park
Caribou Falls State Park
Split Rock Lighthouse
Gooseberry Falls State Park

Grand Marais
Lutsen
Tofte
Little Marais
Two Harbors
Knife River
Duluth
Cloquet
Moose Lake
Hinckley

Ely
Virginia
Chisholm
Hibbing
Grand Rapids
Walker
Blackduck
Bemidji
International Falls
Rainy River
Baudette
Roseau
Warroad
Thief River Falls
East Grand Forks
Mahnomen
Detroit Lakes
Park Rapids
Moorhead

N

Miles
0    20    40

© The Countryman Press

PIONEER CEMETERY AT ITASCA STATE PARK

no sign of its becoming the Mighty Mississippi. The Red River on the northwestern side of the state is not the most scenic of rivers, but the flatlands surrounding it are an agricultural center for the state.

The plains give way to the lake-heavy region around Detroit Lakes, bodies of water carved by the glaciers that moved through centuries ago. Now the region is a popular tourist destination for lake lovers. Tourism plays a major role in this area's economy, and the annual WE Fest has become one of the country's largest country music festivals, attracting 50,000 people each year. (See "WE Fest" on page 193.)

GUIDANCE **Leech Lake Chamber of Commerce** (218-547-1313 or 1-800-833-1118; leech-lake.com), 205 Minnesota Avenue, Walker.

**Park Rapids Chamber of Commerce** (218-732-4111; parkrapids.com), 1204 S. Park Avenue, Park Rapids.

**Visit Bemidji** (218-759-0164 or 1-877-250-5959; visitbemidji.com), 300 Bemidji Avenue.

Lake of the Woods Tourism Bureau (1-800-382-3474; lakeofthewoodsmn.com), MN 11, Baudette. Open daily in the summer, Mon.–Fri. the rest of the year. Provides tourism information for the general Lake of the Woods area that runs along the Canadian border, including Baudette, Warroad, and the Northwest Angle.

**Roseau Tourism** (218-463-0009; goroseau.com). Provides information on lodging and events in the Roseau area.

**Thief River Falls Convention and Visitor Bureau** (218-686-9785; visittrf.org), 102 N. Main Avenue, Thief River Falls. A tourist board for all things Thief River Falls.

**Fargo Moorhead Tourism** (701-282-3653 or 1-800-235-7654), 2001 S. 44th Street, Fargo. Provides information for visitors to the twin cities of Moorhead and Fargo, North Dakota.

**Detroit Lakes Regional Chamber of Commerce** (218-847-9202 or 1-800-542-3992; visitdetroitlakes.com), 700 Summit Avenue, Detroit Lakes. Serves as the central tourist information center for the greater Detroit Lakes area.

GETTING THERE **By air:** Regional commercial airlines, primarily Delta and Mesaba, serve the cities of Bemidji, Thief River Falls, and Fargo (across the river from Moorhead). Taxis and rental cars are available from the airports: **Bemidji Regional Airport** (218-444-2438; bemidjiairport.org), 3824 NW Moberg Drive, Bemidji; **Thief River Falls Regional Airport** (218-681-7680; visittrf.com), 13722 Airport Drive, Thief River Falls; and **Hector International Airport** (701-241-8168; fargoairport.com), 2801 NW 32nd Avenue, Fargo, ND.

**By car:** Park Rapids is served by MN 34 and US 71. MN 34 ends at MN 200 in Walker; MN 200 and MN 371 are the primary routes through Walker. MN 371 ends at US 2, while MN 200 merges with US 71, both of which are the major highways through Bemidji. Follow US 71 north to MN 72 in order to head north to Baudette; from Baudette, MN 11 is the major road crossing west to Warroad and Roseau. The primary highway to East Grand Forks is US 2; to Moorhead (and Fargo, North Dakota), I-94 is the major freeway, while US 10 also serves Moorhead, as well as Detroit Lakes.

The Northwest Angle, a ridge of land bordering Canada, is the northernmost part of the contiguous United States, and it can be accessed by car through Canada (with US passport), or by seaplane or boat.

**By rail: AMTRAK**'s (1-800-872-7245; amtrak.com) Empire Builder route offers rail service between Minneapolis–St. Paul and Fargo/Moorhead. Local stations include Union Station, 240 E. Kellogg Boulevard in St. Paul, and Station Building, 420 N. 4th Street, in Fargo, North Dakota.

WOODENFROG REFECTORY, LAKE KABETOGAMA

GETTING AROUND  Having a vehicle is a necessity when traveling around the northern lakes region.

WHEN TO COME  The summer months see an influx of tourists who come to enjoy the multitude of lakes and beaches, but summer isn't the only popular time, especially for fishing enthusiasts who cast their poles in open water in summer and through holes in the ice in winter. Hunters and winter sports aficionados appreciate the fall and winter seasons as well.

MEDICAL EMERGENCY  Call 911.
 **CHI St. Joseph's Hospital** (218-732-3311 or 1-800-556-3311; chisjh.org), 600 S. Pleasant Avenue, Park Rapids.
 **Sanford Bemidji Medical Center** (218-751-5430; sanfordhealth.org), 1300 NW Anne Street, Bemidji.
 **LifeCare Medical Center** (218-463-2500; lifecaremedicalcenter.org), 715 Delmore Drive, Roseau.
 **Northwest Medical Center Hospital** (218-681-4240; sanfordhealth.org), 120 LaBree Avenue, Thief River Falls.
 **Sanford Medical Center** (701-417-2000; sanfordhealthcare.org), 801 N. Broadway, Fargo, ND.
 **Essentia Health St. Mary's** (218-844-2347; essentiahealth.org), 1027 Washington Avenue, Detroit Lakes.

HIGHWAY 1 SUNSET

# PARK RAPIDS/WALKER

The north-central part of the state has a number of worthy venues for visitors, including Walker and Leech Lake, a large lake popular for sailors and fishing enthusiasts (and also home to the annual Eelpout Festival; see *Special Events*), and Dorset, a food-minded village on the Heartland Trail. Dense forests and countless lakes make up the scenery here in a most Minnesotan way.

## ❋ To See and Do

& ⛾ ❋ **Northern Lights Casino and Hotel** (1-800-252-7529; northernlightscasino.com), 6800 Frontage Road NW, Walker. Open daily. Slots, poker, and blackjack are open 24/7. Two restaurants and a snack bar are in the casino, while the attached hotel has an indoor pool and sauna, and extensive arcade.

⛾ **Forestedge Winery** (218-224-3535; forestedgewinery.com), 35295 MN 64, LaPorte. Open Tues.–Sun. May–Dec. Northwest of Walker is this winery, which produces wines from hardy northern crops such as chokecherries, blueberries, raspberries, and plums. Forestedge's rhubarb wine has won several awards. Stop by for a sample, and enjoy the beautiful gardens. Tables are available if you'd like to enjoy a bottle right on the spot.

## ❋ Green Space And Outdoor Activities

❋ **Heartland Trail** (dnr.state.mn.us/state_trails/heartland/index.html), Park Rapids. This 49-mile trail uses old railroad grades to create a multiuse trail system. The trail is paved and can be used by hikers, bicyclists, and bladers (but be aware that the terrain is very steep in some areas and rough in others), and an adjacent grass trail can be used by horseback riders and mountain bikers. Snowmobile enthusiasts will find the trail is groomed all winter long.

❋ **Leech Lake** (leechlake.org). North of the popular Brainerd Lakes area is Leech Lake, a favored fishing lake surrounded by forests and opportunities for

GRAND RAPIDS TRAIL AT THE FOREST HISTORY CENTER

year-round outdoor activities. Hundreds of resorts flank the lake (see *Lodging* for some examples) and boaters, anglers (both summer and winter), skiers, snowmobilers, and hunters have all contributed to the growth of this area as a four-season destination.

## ✳ Lodging

BED-AND-BREAKFASTS ✐ ✳ ⟨⟨•⟩⟩ **Heartland Trail Bed and Breakfast** (218-732-3252; heartlandbb.com), Dorset. The **Restaurant Capital of the World** (see "Dorset—Restaurant Capital of the World" on page 172) is also home to this charming bed-and-breakfast, a renovated 1920s community school building. The inn has five spacious guest rooms, all with private baths and fireplaces; full breakfast is served daily. Located on the **Heartland Trail** (see *Green Space* and *Outdoor Activities*). Rates start at $75.

✳ 🍃 **Lady Slipper Inn B&B** (218-573-3353; ladyslipperinn.com), 51722 270th Street, Osage. A true nature retreat, this

HISTORIC FIRE TOWER AT THE FOREST HISTORY CENTER

bed-and-breakfast is in a farmhouse surrounded by 160 acres of forest, meadows, ponds, and streams. Five guest rooms, all with private bath and gas fireplaces. Some rooms have private decks and entrances. A separate lodge offers guests a full kitchen and common area with tables and chairs for games or crafts. A historic local Catholic Church building was moved onto the property and can be used for on-site weddings. Rates start at $135.

✳ ⟨⟨•⟩⟩ ⤳ **Embracing Pines Bed and Breakfast** (218-224-3519 or 218-731-5026; embracingpines.com), 32287 County Route 38, Walker. This quiet inn has two rooms with a shared bath and a suite with private bath. The rooms are decorated with a north woods theme, and the common area evokes a log cabin. Embracing Pines is an active participant in the Minnesota Bed & Breakfast Association's Green Journeys Program, implementing ecologically friendly practices and products throughout the home. Rates start at $79.

CABINS ✐ 🐾 ♿ ✳ **Breezy Point Resort** (218-573-3125 or 1-800-939-2630; breezy point.com), 54852 MN 34, Osage. Breezy Point has 10 log cabins with knotty pine interiors, spacious and comfortable. A new "tiny house" cabin is also available for people interested in trying out the tiny home concept. The resort offers boat and motor rental, and guided fishing trips can be arranged. There's a sandy beach with a variety of beach toys—paddleboats, hydro bikes, and kayaks—included in the rates. Pets accepted in the off-season. Rates start at $110.

♿ ✐ ⤳ **Crow Wing Crest Lodge** (218-652-3111; crowwing.com), 31159 County Route 23, Akeley. Open mid-May–Oct. Crow Wing's 19 cabins, set on a pristine lake, vary from rustic to upscale. The resort prides itself on its environmental stance; the proprietors recycle lake water, use no pesticides or herbicides, and use only all-natural cleaning products. The owners also have a holistic approach to vacations, and reflexology, aromatherapy, massage, and yoga are offered. Kids' activities are offered daily during the summer; that is, if they aren't entertained enough on the sandy beach with the beach toys, paddleboats, kayaks, or the playground, or the fishing dock. Rates start at $83.

♂ **Bailey's Resort on Leech Lake** (218-547-1464 or 1-800-458-7540; baileys resort.com), 33216 CR 38, Walker. Open mid-May–early Oct. Bailey's has nine cabins situated on 24 acres, making it an uncrowded retreat that focuses on families. There are water toys galore, bikes for rent, and a boat launch from a narrow harbor onto Leech Lake. Rates start at $122.

♂ ✳ **Brindley's Harbor Resort** (1-888-547-5477; brindleysharbor.com), 9530 NW Pine Point Road, Walker. This quiet resort on Leech Lake has 15 cottages, a lakehome, and five luxury log cabins. A huge sandy beach has four piers for fishing as well as a boat slip and marina. The use of canoes, kayaks, sailboats, bikes, and hammocks are all included; boats and ice houses are available for guest rental. The staff will clean and freeze your catch of fish. Rates start at $135.

✪ ♿ ♂ 🦴 ♂ ✳ ⛴ **Chase on the Lake** (218-547-7777 or 1-833-669-8820; chase onthelake.com), 502 Cleveland Boulevard, Walker. Chase on the Lake is a classic upscale resort with lovely hotel rooms and condos, the latter of which come equipped with full kitchens and laundry units. There's a full-service spa on-site, and golf packages at two nearby 18-hole courses are available. Chase has its own two-lane bowling alley, and a supervised kids program is offered during the summer. If you don't feel like cooking, fine dining is on-site, too (see *Where to Eat*). Rates start at $109. Specials and packages are available.

## ✳ Where to Eat

DINING OUT ♿ ♂ ✳ ⛴ **The Boulders** (218-547-1006; facebook.com/the bouldersrestaurant), 8363 NW Lake Land Trail, Walker. Open daily for dinner. An upscale restaurant with a casual atmosphere, the Boulders offers steak, salmon, lamb chops, and even paella, which is beautifully prepared and served. A good special-occasion choice. Expensive.

♿ ♂ ✳ ⛴ **Lucky Moose Bar and Grill** (218-547-0801; luckymoosebargrill.com), 441 Walker Bay Boulevard, Walker. Open daily for lunch and dinner, Sat.–Sun. for brunch. A casual bar and grill housed in a log building. The menu includes burgers and comfort-based entrées (think meat loaf, steak, and bangers and mash), as well as a house specialty of lavosh crackers treated like pizzas. Moderate/ expensive.

♿ ♂ ✳ ⛴ **The 502 at Chase on the Lake** (218-547-8502; chaseonthelake .com), 502 Cleveland Boulevard, Walker. Open daily for lunch and dinner, Sat. and Sun. for breakfast. The restaurant at the **Chase on the Lake** resort (see *Lodging*) is a special-occasion restaurant for locals and serves up sizable portions

THE EFFIE CAFÉ

## DORSET—RESTAURANT CAPITAL OF THE WORLD

This tiny town has, tongue firmly in cheek, billed itself as the Restaurant Capital of the World, and certainly it's hard to believe any other town has as many restaurants per capita as this one does. With just 22 residents, Dorset has four restaurants—that's one for every 5.5 villagers. (This is also a town that once elected a local 5-year-old as its mayor.) What's more surprising is that while the restaurants may not be profiled in *Food & Wine* anytime soon, they are worthy of a visit if you're in the neighborhood (which is east of Park Rapids on County Route 18, north of MN 34). Just follow the boardwalk down the main street (or take a detour from the Heartland Trail if you're out hiking or biking), and you'll find a good meal somewhere.

**Dorset General Store** (218-732-0275; dorset-general-store.business.site), 20470 MN 226. Open daily for dinner, Tues.–Sun. for all three meals, May–Sept. Breakfast features include the standard pancakes and omelets, along with stuffed French toast and potato pancakes; lunch offers a few pasta items, along with burgers and sandwiches; and dinner is a changing roster of Italian foods. Moderate. &⌀Y

**Dorset Chick'n Coop Restaurant and Bar** (218-732-4072; facebook.com/dorsetchicken), 20456 MN 226. Open Mon.–Fri. for dinner, Sat. for lunch and dinner, Sun. for all three meals year-round. Broasted chicken steak, lobster and shrimp, as well as burgers, salads, sandwiches, and daily specials that can include meat loaf, chicken pot pie, or a broasted chicken and wild rice bake. Moderate. &⌀❋Y

**Dorset House Restaurant and Soda Fountain** (218-732-5556; facebook.com/DorsetHouse Restaurant), 20414 Fajita Loop. Open daily for lunch and dinner in the summer. Pizza, sandwiches, and burgers, with homemade pies for dessert and, of course, ice cream. Inexpensive/moderate. &⌀Y

**Companeros** (218-732-7624; companerosofdorset.com), 20427 MN 226. Open daily for lunch and dinner, Jun.–Aug.; Thurs.–Sun. for dinner and Sun. for brunch, May and Sept. Americanized Mexican food served in cheerful abundance. Inexpensive. &⌀Y

of chicken, steak, and seafood. There is prime rib on weekends and an all-you-can-eat fish fry on Fri. Boat-up service is available to the restaurant's expansive lakeside patio. Moderate/expensive.

EATING OUT ⌀❋ **MinneSoda Fountain** (218-732-3240; facebook.com/TheMinne SodaFountain), 205 S. Main Street, Park Rapids. Open daily for more than 80 years in the heart of this small town, the MinneSoda falls under the category of "don't miss." When you visit this 17-stool confectionary, leave the calorie counter at home. Inexpensive.

&⌀❋Y **Charlie's Up North/Charlie's Boathouse** (218-547-0222; charlies upnorth.com), 6841 NW MN 371, Walker. Charlie's Up North is open daily year-round for all three meals; the Boathouse is open for lunch and dinner during the

summer. Charlie's is a casual, friendly dining spot serving three hearty meals a day, with a special Chinese menu on Tues. and Thurs., and prime rib on Sat.

CHARLIE'S BOATHOUSE

and Sun. The Boathouse is a freestanding outdoor bar with an extensive patio wrapped around an old boat rehabbed into the bar; it's a good spot for enjoying a sunny day. Moderate.

  ✦ ❖ Ⓨ **The Good Life Cafe** (218-237-4212; thegoodlifecafepr.com), 220 Main Avenue S., Park Rapids. Open daily for lunch and dinner. Good Life has contemporary takes on diner classics with an eye to local ingredients, including an updated wild rice hotdish and a lefse falafel. Inexpensive.

  ✦ ❖ **The Great Northern Cafe** (218-732-9565; greatnortherncafe.com), 218 1st Street E., Park Rapids. Open daily for breakfast and lunch. Great Northern follows a more traditional diner path, with basic sandwiches and burgers, along with a full slate of hot sandwiches (meat and gravy on bread with potatoes) and Switchman's Dinners that include chicken fried steak and liver and onions. For a more formal dining option, Necce's Italian Ristorante has pasta, steak, and seafood. Inexpensive.

## ❖ Entertainment

✦ **Long Lake Theater** (218-732-0099; longlaketheater.com), 12183 Beacon Road, Hubbard. Open Wed.–Sat. on selected dates, Jun.–Sept. Summer stock theater offering four to five productions each year, along with holiday productions of *A Christmas Carol*.

  ✦ **Northern Light Opera Company** (1-866-766-7372; northernlightopera.org), 203 Park Avenue S., Park Rapids. Productions on occasion; check website for schedule. The name of this company is a play on words; the light refers to light opera more than northern lights. This grassroots organization has diligently been putting together productions, primarily of Gilbert and Sullivan, since 2001. Their success is demonstrated by their growth and their branching out, including performances of *My Fair Lady* and *South Pacific*.

✦ **Jasper's Jubilee Theater** (218-255-1333; jasperstheater.com), 17339 MN 34, Park Rapids. Open Jul.–Sept. Adults $25; seniors 60 and older $24; children 4–16 $10; children under 4 free if sitting on an adult's lap. Discounts available for groups of 20 or more. A lively family-friendly live show incorporating music, magic, juggling, yodeling, dancing, and comedy skits.

  ✦ **Woodtick Musical Theater** (218-652-4200), 65 Broadway Street E., Akeley. Open mid-Jun.–mid-Sept. Adults $18.50; senior citizens $17.50; children 13–17 $10.50; children 6–12 $8.50; children under 6 free. Billing its show as similar to those in Branson, Missouri, the Woodtick Theater offers a musical variety show each summer that's appropriate for all ages. The music encompasses country, folk, bluegrass, and gospel, and is accompanied by a comedy show.

## ❖ Special Events

*February*: **Eelpout Festival** (eelpoutfestival.com), Walker. Held mid-February each year, the Eelpout Festival, besides having one of the odder names for a state festival, is a good-natured celebration of winter and the joys of ice fishing for one of the state's ugliest fish. Events during the three-day event include, of course, ice fishing, as well as a 5K run, an icehouse decorating contest, on-ice auto and snowmobile races, rugby on ice, and the Polar Plunge, an opportunity to raise money for the local community center by collecting pledges and agreeing to jump in the lake—in February.

*June*: **Moondance Jammin Country Fest** (218-836-1055; jammincountry.com), Walker. Started by the creators of the classic-rock **Moondance Jam** (see *July*, below), Jammin Country Fest is a large outdoor three-day country music fest that allows the option of camping on-site. Ticket rates vary from $125–625 with perks piling up for the latter, including meet-and-greets, free beer, pop, and water, discounted cocktail, and dinners. Recent performers include Kane Brown, the Brothers Osborne, and Neal McCoy. Planning ahead is essential for this festival, especially if you want to camp.

*July*: **Moondance Jam** (218-836-1055; moondancejam.com), Walker. Ticket prices for the three-day festival start at $105 for a one-day pass and $240 for a three-day general admission ticket. Various VIP packages include special seating; a VIP tent with free beer, pop, and water; discounted cocktails; occasional meet-and-greets with some of the bands; dinner and hors d'oeuvres daily; and preferential parking. Tickets go on sale nearly a year in advance, and the closer to festival date, the more they cost. Campsites should be reserved ahead

of time. The classic-rock version of **WE Fest** (see "WE Fest" on page 193), this four-day event held in early July draws thousands of people from across the country to hear live concerts by the likes of Def Leppard, Kansas, Alice Cooper, and REO Speedwagon. Children are not prohibited, but organizers note this is an event intended for adults and may not be appropriate for kids.

*August*: **Leech Lake Regatta** (218-547-1819; shoresofleechlake.com), 6166 Moriss Point Road, Walker. Race participation is $100 for early bird, $135 later; additional fees apply for boat mooring. This early-August event in a multiclass sailboat race for all skill levels. Many sailors opt to spend several days after the race on the water.

# BEMIDJI AREA

Bemidji (pronounced *buh-MIDJ-ee*) is not far from Itasca State Park, home to the Mississippi Headwaters, and Bemidji itself is the first city geographically on the Mississippi River. There are nearly 40 lakes within a 25-mile radius of Bemidji, so water sports are a major draw. But winter is popular, too, with snowmobiling, skiing (cross-country and downhill), ice fishing, and snowshoeing favored activities.

## ✳ To See and Do

MUSEUMS AND COMMUNITY ARTWORK ♿ ✿ ✳ **Bemidji Sculpture Walk** (bemidji sculpture.com). On the lakefront and downtown, Bemidji. Open daily. Stop at the tourist information center to begin your tour of sculptures and murals that appear lakeside and into downtown.

♿ ✿ ✳ **Beltrami County History Center** (218-444-3376; beltramihistory.org), 130 SW Minnesota Avenue, Bemidji. Open Wed.–Sat. Adults $5; senior citizens and students $4; children 12 and under $1; groups of 5 or more $3 per adult; historical society members free. The history center resides in the restored 1912 Great Northern Railway Depot, which was the last depot built by railroad baron James J. Hill. The building's architecture itself is worth a visit, but the collection within is entertaining and enlightening, from Native American artifacts to a restored telegraph office. A separate research area offers historians access to archival materials.

♿ ✿ ✳ **Headwaters Science Center** (218-444-4472; hscbemidji.org), 413 Beltrami Avenue, Bemidji. Open daily in the summer; Wed.–Mon. in the fall and winter. Visitors

BELTRAMI COUNTY HISTORY CENTER

12 and older $9; children under 2–11 $6; seniors 65 and older and military $8; HSC members free. Essentially a children's science museum, the HSC offers a variety of hands-on activities, as well as a collection of live animals (snakes, turtles, salamanders) for kids to learn about and handle.

   &#9830; **Watermark Art Center** (218-444-7570; watermarkartcenter.org), 505 Bemidji Avenue, Bemidji. Open daily in summer; Mon.–Sat. in winter. National and regional artists in a variety of media, as well as ongoing education for all ages. The art center also sponsors a series of First Friday Art Walks, which showcase art and live performances both in the center and around Bemidji.

   &#9830; **Paul Bunyan and Babe the Blue Ox,** Bemidji lakefront, near the tourist information center. Open daily. A visit to Bemidji isn't quite complete without a photo opportunity near the legendary Paul Bunyan statues. Besides, it's a good starting point for visiting the Bemidji Sculpture Walk.

OTHER ATTRACTIONS &#9830; **Concordia Language Villages** (1-800-222-4750; concordialanguagevillages.org), 8607 NE Thorsonveien, Bemidji. This renowned language school, headquartered in Moorhead, holds the majority of its classes and camps at an expansive site just outside Bemidji. The languages (including Arabic, Chinese, Danish, Finnish, French, German, Italian, Japanese, Korean, Norwegian, Portuguese, Russian, Spanish, and Swedish) are taught in villages created to resemble a town in the country of origin. Most of the villages in Bemidji are centered near Turtle Lake, but a few are about 10 miles north. Each village is separate from the other. Programs are offered for kids and adults, but even if you're not planning on learning a foreign language, the lovingly re-created international villages are worth a stop for the beautiful sightseeing alone.

# ✳ Green Space and Outdoor Activities

Not surprisingly, green space is abundant in the northern part of the state.

PARKS AND PARKWAYS **Chippewa National Forest** (218-335-8600; fs.usda.gov/chippewa), 200 NW Ash Avenue, Cass Lake. With more than 666,000 acres, Chippewa National Forest has ample opportunity for outdoor adventures. The forest has 160 miles of hiking trails and cross-country ski trails, 330 miles of snowmobiling trails, 23 developed campgrounds and 380 camping sites, and a sandy swimming beach. Three visitor centers have programs and information: Norway Beach, Cut Foot Sioux, and Edge of the Wilderness Discovery Center. For water fans, the forest holds two of Minnesota's five biggest lakes, and there are nine canoe routes across various rivers and Leech Lake. (Note: Some of these routes are more treacherous than others; when planning a canoe trip, check with the Chippewa National Forest for recommendations based on your skill level.)

   **Edge of the Wilderness Scenic Byway** (edgeofthewilderness.com). East of Bemidji is MN 38, which is the road for the Edge of the Wilderness Byway, a 47-mile roadway that runs from Grand Rapids to Effie. It showcases heavy forests and wetlands, with profusions of wildflowers in the warmer months followed by spectacular foliage colors in the fall. The route is open year-round, with the exception of the occasional snowstorm.

   The byway goes through the Black Spruce/Tamarack Bog Habitat. Lining both sides of the road, this habitat was formed 16,000 years ago when the last of the glaciers still existed. Spruce and tamarack tower over the road, and if you were to wander into the bog, you'd find the ground to be wet and spongy.

# THE LOST 40 SCIENTIFIC AND NATURAL AREA

Near the junction of MN 1 and US 71 is this historical scientific and natural area (SNA). The Lost 40 (dnr.state.mn.us/snas/detail.html?id=sna01063), which is actually 144 acres, is a tract of land that was accidentally misidentified as a lake by a surveyor during the logging boom time. Consequently, it remained untouched when forests around it were decimated. There are pine trees that are more than 300 years old in the Lost 40, and the wildflowers are prolific in the late spring. A 1-mile hiking trail guides you through this special and beautiful untouched wilderness.

For an adventurous detour—and a glimpse into a way of life long gone—turn right on County Route 60 and drive several miles to Blue Water Lake Road, where you'll find a parking lot for the Trout Lake–Joyce Estate Hiking Trail. From the trailhead, the hike to the Joyce Estate is about 6 miles round-trip. The Joyce Estate was built on the shores of Trout Lake between 1917 and 1935 by David Joyce, whose fortunes were made in the logging industry. He built a massive complex out of native stone and lumber, with 40 buildings, a seaplane hangar, nine-hole golf course, and clubhouse. The caretaker's complex itself had 17 buildings. It's a fascinating place to explore how the wealthy lived decades ago in the woods.

Another facet of the area's history is on display at the Camp Rabideau National Historic Landmark, one of the best preserved Civilian Conservation Corps projects in the country. You can take a guided tour, or you can go on your own; interpretive displays with detailed information are present throughout.

**Itasca State Park/Mississippi Headwaters** (218-699-7251; dnr.state.mn.us/state_parks/Itasca/index.html), 36750 Main Park Drive, Park Rapids. Open daily. This is Minnesota's oldest state park, and a large one (although not the largest) at 32,000 acres. It's also well known for being the starting point of the Mississippi River, and the point at which you easily walk across the river. But Itasca State Park has several other spots to visit, including a 500-year-old Native American cemetery and Wegmann's Cabin, a pioneer artifact. Pines inhabit the Wilderness Sanctuary, a 2,000-acre stand of white and red pines, some upward of 300 years old. There are 49 miles of hiking trails and 16 miles of paved biking trails (bike rental is available within the park, as are boat and canoe rentals). Plan ahead if you'd like to stay at **Douglas Lodge** (see *Lodging*), located right within the park.

**Lake Bemidji State Park** (218-308-2300; dnr.state.mn.us/state_parks/lake_bemidji /index.html), 3401 NE State Park Road, Bemidji. Open daily year-round. It may not have the Mississippi Headwaters, but Lake Bemidji State Park is a worthy stop, with acres of forest, access to Lake Bemidji for boating and fishing, a paved bike trail, hiking trails that run along the lake, and scores for birds to watch.

**Big Bog State Recreation Area** (218-647-8592; dnr.state.mn.us/state_parks/big_bog/index.html), 55716 NE MN 72, Waskish. Open daily year-round. Opened in 2005, this recreation area provides a way for visitors to explore the ecology of a bog without overly disturbing it. A mile-long boardwalk was installed through the bog, so visitors can go deep into the natural area without damaging the plant life. Signs posted frequently along the way explain the significance of the bog and point out different aspects of plants and wildlife that can be viewed from the walk.

SKIING AND WINTER SPORTS **Buena Vista Ski Village** (218-243-2231 or 1-800-777-7958; bvskiarea.com), 19600 NW Irvine Avenue, Bemidji. Open for winter sports mid-Nov.–Mar., depending on weather. The mountains may not be the highest, but Buena Vista offers beautiful scenery to enjoy with its 16 runs. Cross-country skiing, tubing, snowboarding, and horse-drawn sleigh rides are all offered while there's snow. In the summer, the ski resort transforms into Buena Vista Ranch, a logging village and visitor center. Activities include covered wagon tours, horsemanship training clinics, and fall foliage rides. Reservations are recommended; call for information.

# ❄ Lodging

**BED-AND-BREAKFASTS** 🌿 ❄ **Lake Bemidji Bed and Breakfast** (218-556-8815; lakebemidjibandb.com), 915 Lake Boulevard NE, Bemidji. This bed-and-breakfast, located near Lake Bemidji, offers three rooms, each with private bath. All rooms have upgraded bed coverings and bathrobes, and full breakfast is included, as is an early-evening glass of wine. A common great room serves as the breakfast point, with lovely views of the lake, and the backyard has a fire pit and double hammock for guest relaxation. The bed-and-breakfast is on the Paul Bunyan Trail, a 17-mile paved trail open for bikes and inline skates. Children 10 and older are welcome. Rates start at $125. Packages are available.

**HOTELS** ♿ 🌿 ((ɢ)) ❄ ⛳ 🍴 ⸙ **Hampton Inn** (218-751-3600; hamptoninn3.hilton.com), 1019 S. Paul Bunyan Drive, Bemidji. The Hampton Inn is right on Lake Bemidji, a short walk from the tourist information center and the beginning of the Bemidji Sculpture Walk. Full breakfast is included in the rates, and there's an indoor pool. The hotel also has a Green Mill pizza restaurant (see *Where to Eat*) for lunch and dinner. Rates start at $126.

♿ 🌿 🐾 ((ɢ)) ❄ ⸙ **AmericInn Motel & Suites** (218-751-3000; wyndhamhotels .com), 1200 NW Paul Bunyan Drive, Bemidji. Near the Paul Bunyan Mall, the AmericInn offers 59 units, 26 of which are suites. The property has an indoor pool, whirlpool, and sauna, and the rates include full breakfast. Rates start at $95.

♿ 🌿 🐾 ((ɢ)) ❄ ⸙ **Holiday Inn Express** (218-751-2487; ichotelsgroup.com), 2422 NW Ridgeway Avenue, Bemidji. A basic but comfortable Holiday Inn, near the Paul Bunyan Mall. Most rooms have two queen beds, while a few upgraded rooms have king beds and Jacuzzi baths. Full breakfast is provided. Expensive.

**LODGES AND RESORTS** ✪ ♿ 🌿 🐾 ((ɢ)) ❄ ⛳ **Ruttger's Birchmont Lodge** (218-444-3463 or 1-888-788-8437; ruttgersbemidji .com), 7598 Bemidji Road NE, Bemidji. A family resort that's something of a tradition on Lake Bemidji, Ruttger's offers both lodge and cabin accommodations. The Cedar Lodge offers the most luxurious suites, with lakefront setting and fireplaces, while the Main Lodge offers the more economical rooms. Cedar Lodge is open year-round, while the Main Lodge is open only in the summer. In addition, there are 22 cottages (mostly open only mid-May–Labor Day) and seven villas (open year-round), which are larger than the cottages. The resort has a restaurant and bar open during the summer months. There is an indoor pool and hot tub, open all year, and boat and bike rental during the summer. A large sandy beach makes for a great summer resting spot, and during the summer Ruttger's offers a supervised kids' program for children ages 4–12. Rates start at $75.

♿ 🌿 ((ɢ)) ❄ **Douglas Lodge** (218-266-2114; stayatmnparks.com), 36750 Main Park Drive, Itasca State Park. This gorgeous lodge was built in 1905 with timber from Itasca State Park and houses five guest rooms, a dining room, and a lounge. There is also a clubhouse with rooms available, as well as several cabins. Common areas center around a large stone fireplace, and rocking chairs rest on the spacious porch. It's an easy walk down to the fishing pier and hiking trails. Campgrounds can be reserved as well. Rates start at $105.

## ❋ Where to Eat

As Bemidji has grown, thanks to the university, county government, and the local health-care system, the restaurant scene has not quite kept pace. There are plenty of chains to choose from—including Applebee's, Ground Round, Perkins, Country Kitchen, Bonanza, McDonald's, Burger King, Pizza Hut, Subway, and Quizno's—but there are also some restaurants without a major chain behind them that offer good dining.

EATING OUT ⟑ ✿ ❋ **Raphael's Bakery Café** (218-444-2867; raphaelsbakery .com), 319 Bemidji Avenue NW, Bemidji. Open Mon.–Sat. for breakfast and lunch. The quintessential small-town bakery and café, Raphael's serves delicious breakfasts and lunches, and sells baked goods to go. The menu may be limited (salads, sandwiches, soups), but the baked goods are pleasingly fresh, and the soups are homemade and worth buying extra for take-out. Inexpensive.

⟑ ✿ ❋ 🍸 **Brigid's Cross** (218-444-0567; facebook.com/brigidscrossirish-pub), 317 Beltrami Avenue NW, Bemidji. Open Mon.–Sat. for lunch and dinner. This cheerful Irish pub offers the usual suspects (fish-and-chips, ploughman's lunch, shepherd's pie) and some not-so-Irish variations (macaroni and cheese bites, mini burger basket). The food is hearty, a full bar is available, and a variety of events is offered, from open mike to trivia contests to live music. Moderate.

⟑ ✿ ❋ 🍸 **Keg n' Cork** (218-444-7600; kegncorkbemidji.com), 310 Beltrami Avenue NW, Bemidji. Open Mon.–Sat. for lunch and dinner. A friendly neighborhood bar and grill with a significant burger and sandwich menu. The locals love it, so you know it's good. Moderate.

✿ ❋ 🍸 **Dave's Pizza** (218-751-3225; davespizza.biz), 422 15th Street NW, Bemidji. Open daily for dinner. It's not much to look at, but Dave's has been meeting pizza lovers' needs for decades. Moderate.

TUTTO BENE

&♿ ✆ ✻ **Minnesota Nice Café** (218-444-6656; minnesotanicecafe.com), 315 Irvine Avenue NW, Bemidji. Open daily for breakfast and lunch. As their sign says, "Homemade meals like Grandma used to make." An enormous breakfast menu with pretty much anything anyone could ever want, along with Uff Dah Burgers and "Nice" lunch sandwiches and baskets. Inexpensive.

&♿ ✆ **Lucky Dogs** (218-444-0288; luckydogsbemidji.com), 201 Beltrami Avenue NW, Bemidji. Open daily for lunch and early dinner, and late nights Fri.–Sat. Apr.–Oct. Lucky Dogs takes the hot dog concept to entirely new levels. Try the Bronco, with peanut butter, BBQ sauce, bacon, pineapple, pepperoncini, onion, and cilantro, or go classic with the Backseat Driver: brown mustard, sauerkraut, and onions. The eatery uses Nathan's Dogs as its usual base, but you can (and should) try the locally made Stittsworth's brat instead, or there are also veggie dogs. A few beers available. Inexpensive.

&♿ ✆ ✻ **Wild Hare Bistro and Coffee House** (218-444-5282; wildharebistro .com), 523 Minnesota Avenue NW, Bemidji. Open daily for breakfast and lunch. A coffee shop with a much better than average food menu that includes creative items like the Wild Rice Salad Platter or the Burrito Francais with Swiss, sautéed mushrooms, and scallions. Inexpensive/moderate.

&♿ ✆ ✻ ✵ **Green Mill Restaurant** (218-444-1875; greenmill.com), 1025 Paul Bunyan Drive NW, Bemidji. Open daily for lunch and dinner. Yes, it's a chain, but it's also got a prime location at the **Hampton Inn** (see *Lodging*), with great views of Lake Bemidji. Plus the pizza is excellent. Moderate.

&♿ ✆ ✻ ✵ **Bemidji Brewing** (218-444-7011; bemidjibeer.com), 211 America Avenue NW, Bemidji. Open daily for lunch and dinner. A craft brewery with taproom offering several varieties, including IPAs, porters, pilsners, sours, and pale ales, among others. The brewery also has a kitchen on-site with lots of beer-friendly foods: Pizza, burgers, gyros, and appetizers, and a kids' menu

LUCKY DOGS

## ✳ Entertainment

**Paul Bunyan Playhouse** (218-751-7270; thechieftheater.com), 314 Beltrami Avenue, Bemidji. With more than 55 years of productions, this is one of the country's longest continuously operating summer stock theaters and is currently located in the historic former Chief Movie Theater. The Paul Bunyan Playhouse uses both national professional actors as well as locals for its summer season. Veterans of the playhouse have gone on to professional theater careers in the Twin Cities.

## ✳ Selective Shopping

& ✳ **Paul Bunyan Mall** (218-751-3195; paulbunyanmall.com), 1401 Paul Bunyan Drive NW, Bemidji. Open daily. The Paul Bunyan Mall is anchored by JC Penney; other stores include Foot Locker, Claire's, Bath & Body Works, and General Nutrition Center.

& ✳ **Bemidji Woolen Mills** (1-888-751-5166; bemidjiwoolen mills.com), 301 Irvine Avenue NW, Bemidji. Open daily. Manufacturer and retailer of woolen apparel, Woolen Mills's products are high in quality; the store also carries Hudson's Bay, Woolrich, and Dale of Norway wool clothing.

& ✳ **Stittsworth Meats** (218-751-1320; stittsworthmeats.com), 722 Paul Bunyan Drive NW, Bemidji. Open daily. Local meat shop with high-quality products made on-site, including blueberry wild rice brats and sausages made with Bemidji Brewing.

## ✳ Special Events

The northern lakes region isn't short of festivals and events. Note: This list does not include an extensive, ongoing list of events that take place at **Concordia Language Villages** (see *To See and Do*). Check Concordia's website for detailed information on their festivals and weekend events.

*June*: **Chippewa Triathlon** (chippewa triathlon.com), Cass Lake. The traditional triathlon elements of a run (5 miles) and bike ride (29 miles) are combined with a 14-mile canoe ride. Held annually in June.

*July*: **Art in the Park** (218-444-7570; watermarkartcenter.org), Lake Bemidji. This annual event, which has taken place for 40 years, showcases local and national artists, and offers food and live entertainment. Dates are scheduled for mid-July.

**Woodcarver's Festival** (218-835-4949; blackduckmn.com), Blackduck. This annual festival has grown from its beginnings in 1983 to include woodcarvers from across the United States and Canada. Held the last Saturday in July, the outdoor festival (rain or shine) brings visitors from all over the region. Carvers exhibit their wares for purchase, and food is available for sale. Look for the Uffda Taco.

# BAUDETTE/ROSEAU/ WARROAD

The northwestern border of Minnesota is all about the outdoors and year-round outdoor activities: fishing, hiking, snowmobiling, skating, cross-country skiing. There are some attractions and historical sites, but the emphasis here is outside, not inside.

## ❋ To See and Do

Attractions are open year-round unless otherwise noted.

MUSEUMS AND HISTORIC SITES ♿ ✐ **Lake of the Woods County Museum** (218-634-1200; lakeofthewoodshistoricalsociety.com), 206 8th Avenue SE, Baudette. Open Mon.–Sat. mid-May–mid-Oct.; off-season by appointment. No admission fee. This small but well-stocked museum has exhibits on various aspects of northern Minnesota's history and development, including a re-created homestead kitchen, school, country store, and tavern, as well as information on the geology of the area.

THE PIONEER VILLAGE IN ROSEAU

♿ ✐ ❋ **The Polaris Experience Center** (218-463-4999; polaris.com/en-us/polaris -experience-center), 205 5th Avenue SW, Suite 2, Roseau. Open Mon.–Sat. No admission fee. One of the leading manufacturers of snowmobiles, Polaris built this visitor center adjacent to its plant to showcase the company's history. The exhibits range from the earliest snowmobile prototypes to today's sleeker machines, as well as history and trivia from the age of snowmobiles. Free tours of the Polaris Plant itself are scheduled daily at 2 p.m.; call ahead or stop by the office to sign up.

♿ ✐ **Roseau Pioneer Farm & Village** (218-463-1045 or 218-463-1118; roseau pioneerfarm.com), MN 11, Roseau. Open daily Apr.–Aug.; other times by appointment. Admission is free. This lovingly preserved village is a testament to the pioneer days of northwestern Minnesota's agricultural history. Most of the 16 buildings are restored artifacts, done primarily by volunteer labor (volunteer opportunities are available on Tues.; call

THE MARVIN WINDOWS VISITOR CENTER

the village for more information). Visitors are welcome to explore on their own or take a guided tour through the post office, parish hall, church, barn, blacksmith shop, and log cabin. Bathroom facilities are, fittingly, of an outhouse nature, in a vintage porta-potty.

 𝒫 **Fort St. Charles** (218-223-4611), The Point, Lake Street NE, Warroad. Open daily 10–4, Memorial Day–Sept., weather permitting. Admission is free. In the early 1700s a French explorer and trader by the name of Pierre Gaultier de Varennes, Sieur de la Verendrye, established this fort as a base for trading and for launching expeditions. However, lack of food and hostility from local Sioux made the fort difficult to maintain, and it was abandoned after 1760. The buildings were discovered and reconstructed as a historical site in the mid-1900s.

 & 𝒫 ❋ **Wm. S. Marvin Training and Visitor Center** (218-386-4334; marvin .com), 704 MN 313, Warroad. Open daily. Admission is free. The Marvin Visitor Center is a historic and industrial exhibition featuring the growth and technology behind Marvin Windows and Doors. Theatrical highlights include a recounting of the fire that destroyed the Marvin plant in 1961 and how the Marvin company rebuilt and expanded. Tours of the Marvin plant itself are available by appointment Mon.–Fri. by calling 218-386-4333.

OTHER ATTRACTIONS & 𝒫 ❋ **Willie Walleye**, Main Street and 1st Avenue NE, Baudette. No visit to the northern lakes

WILLIE WALLEYE

would be complete without a photo op at the walleye equivalent of the **Paul Bunyan statues in Bemidji** (see page 176). Forty feet long and weighing 2 tons, Willie represents Baudette's claim of being the Walleye Capital of the World.

## ❋ Green Space and Outdoor Activities

The northwestern stretch of the state is geared primarily toward visitors who want to enjoy outdoor activities, including fishing (both summer and winter), boating, hiking, hunting, snowmobiling, snowshoeing, and cross-country skiing. Consequently, many resorts in this area are open year-round to cater to clients who favor activities in the different seasons. Note: Because winter can be unpredictable, don't head out to this part of the state in the middle of January without a snow emergency kit in your vehicle, as well as a charged-up cell phone. Pay close attention to the weather, as snowstorms (complete with dangerous winds and wind chills) can arise quickly.

CANOEING **Lake of the Woods**, north through the Northwest Angle, makes for excellent canoeing, as does the meandering **Rainy River**.

FISHING **Lake of the Woods** is one of the nation's largest lakes (after the Great Lakes and Salt Lake), and it's become a favored place of anglers from all over the country and Canada. The region is proud of its walleye population (although its claim as Walleye Capital of the World is disputed by other walleye lakes), but there are many kinds of fish for the catching: Lake sturgeon, northern pike, smallmouth and largemouth bass, perch, and muskie are just some of the plentiful fish. You can bring your own boat and manage your fishing yourself, or you can hire a guide through one of the many guide services (and through many of the dozens of resorts throughout the area) available to assist you.

There is a separate summer and winter fishing season. Winter's ice fishing has gained considerable ground as more resorts offer ice houses for rent, many of which are outfitted with propane heaters and cooktops. The popularity of "sleeper" fish houses, outfitted like rustic cabins, also continues to grow. Fish spearing is another activity that is increasing in interest.

Official seasons and regulations can be found through the **Minnesota Department of Natural Resources** (651-296-6157 or 1-888-646-6367; dnr.state.mn.us/regulations/fishing/index.html).

HUNTING Deer hunting in Minnesota begins in late October for bow hunters and early November for firearms. Besides deer, duck, grouse, and goose hunting are all popular activities. Because there is so much open land near Lake of the Woods, it's easy to mistake private property for public hunting grounds. Check with the local tourist offices or with your resort owners, who can provide necessary information to help you avoid trespassing. **Minnesota DNR** (651-296-6157 or 1-888-646-6367; dnr.state.mn.us/regulations/hunting/index.html) has specific licensing and regulation information.

PARKS **Zippel Bay State Park** (218-783-6252; dnr.state.mn.us/state_parks/zippel_bay/index.html), County Route 8, Williams. Fishing, swimming, camping, bird-watching—Zippel Bay State Park offers these and more in its 3,000-plus acres along Lake of the Woods. Six miles of hiking trails available during the summer are expanded to 11 miles in the winter for cross-country skiers.

# GOLF

Golf's charm is felt this far north, and there are several courses available to the public across the region.

**Oak Harbor Golf Course** (218-634-9939), 2805 24th Street NW, Baudette. Open May 1–Oct. 15, weather permitting. Nine-hole course.

**Oakcrest Golf Club** (218-463-3016; oakcrestgolfcourse.com), 310 5th Street SE, Roseau. Open mid-May–mid-Oct., weather permitting. An 18-hole championship course that winds along the river and through the woods.

**Warroad Estates Golf Course** (218-386-2025; warroadestates.com), 37293 Elm Drive, Warroad. Open Apr. 15–Oct. 15, weather permitting. An 18-hole course that straddles the US–Canadian border.

**Northwest Angle Country Club** (218-223-8001; pasturegolf.com), Angle Inlet. Open May–Sept., weather permitting. When a golf course's location is described as "north of northern Minnesota," you know you're truly going "up north." This nine-hole course may not be the most pristinely groomed course you've ever played, but you may never be able to see quite so much wildlife while golfing, either.

SNOWMOBILING There are more than 400 miles of snowmobile trails in the Lake of the Woods area, most groomed and maintained by a local snowmobiling organization, the **Lake of the Woods Drifters Snowmobile Club** (lakeofthewoodsdrifters.org), in Baudette. The Drifters can provide maps and trail conditions during the winter season. If you're going to be using the trails extensively, it's worth considering a Drifters membership (annual individual fee is $25, family rate is $35) in order to participate in one of the many events they sponsor during the snowmobiling season.

## ❄ Lodging

BED-AND-BREAKFAST **Wildwood Inn Bed & Breakfast** (218-634-1631; wildwood innbb.com), 3361 Cottonwood Road NW, Baudette. Five guest rooms, each with private bath in a historic former summer club house with easy access to lakes and woods. Rates start at $75.

HOTELS ♿ ✏ 🐾 ((ŋ)) ❄ ✂ **AmericInn Baudette** (218-634-3200; wyndhamhotels .com), 1179 W. Main Street, Baudette. The nicest hotel in Baudette is the Americ-Inn, which offers rooms and suites, an indoor pool, cold-weather hookups, a fish-cleaning area, and free high-speed Internet access. Upgraded rooms include a fireplace. Full breakfast is included. Rates start at $101.

♿ ✏ 🐾 ❄ ((ŋ)) ✂ **AmericInn Roseau** (218-463-1045; wyndhamhotels.com), 1110 3rd Street NW, Roseau. Like the AmericInn in Baudette, this is one of the nicest hotels in Roseau, offering rooms and suites, an indoor pool, and cold-weather hookups. Full breakfast is included. Rates start at $97.

♿ ✏ ((ŋ)) ❄ ✂ **North Country Inn and Suites** (1-888-300-2196; northcountry innandsuites.com), 902 3rd Street NW, Roseau. This motel offers 48 rooms and suites, all with refrigerators and microwaves, and daily continental breakfast. There is an indoor pool and hot tub as well. Rates start at $109.

❄ **St. Mary's Motel Room** (612-910-3678), 202 Roberts Avenue NE, Warroad. The most distinctive lodging in this part of the state is a room in a local historical church, in the former balcony area, with 22-foot-high ceilings and a kitchenette. Rates start at $79.

RESORTS ✏ ❄ ((ŋ)) ▽ ¶ **Border View Lodge** (218-634-1631 or 1-800-776-3474; borderviewlodge.com), 3409 MN 172

NW, Baudette. This year-round resort north of Baudette, located where the Rainy River meets Lake of the Woods, has several cabins, all of which are fully equipped and have the option of full daily maid service (i.e., bed making, dish washing). Border View also offers ice houses, both for daily use and for accommodation for that all-night ice fishing getaway. There's a bar and restaurant in the lodge. Rates start at $106. Packages are available.

& ✿ 🐾 ❄ ♈ ⑪ **Wigwam Resort** (218-634-2168 or 1-800-448-9260; wigwam resortlow.com), 3502 Four Mile Bay Drive NW, Baudette. The Wigwam offers both hotel rooms in the lodge and cabins for rental. Guests can book accommodations only, or they can reserve packages that include meals at the resort's restaurant and charter fishing with a guide. Breakfast and dinner are served year-round in the resort's restaurant, with lunch available in summer. Rates start at $95.

& ✿ ❄ **Zippel Bay Resort** (1-800-222-2537; zippelbay.com), 6080 39th Street NW, Williams. Zippel Bay has both budget cabins and deluxe log cabins complete with fireplace and Jacuzzi; the log cabins are attractive and spacious, located on the water's edge. There's also an Out Post cabin, adjacent to Beltrami State Forest, which is an ideal location for hunters. The resort has an outdoor pool for the summer months and a restaurant. Packages are available with or without meals; during the winter, sleeper ice houses can be rented. (Not to mention the Zippel Igloo, an on-ice "igloo" offering catered food and drinks, and even a satellite TV.) Rates start at $65. Packages are available.

ZIPPEL BAY STATE PARK

## ✳ Where to Eat

Because so many of the fishing and outdoor-activity resorts are located well out of city limits, many of the resorts offer restaurants or cafés themselves. Within the cities of Baudette, Roseau, and Warroad, there are several fast-food options, plus these selections.

EATING OUT ⚬ ❁ ✳ **Alice's Family Restaurant** (218-634-1165), 203 Main Street, Baudette. Open daily for breakfast and lunch. Extensive breakfast entrées and soups, salads, and sandwiches. Inexpensive.

⚬ ❁ ✳ **Northlake Café** (218-634-9807), 813 2nd Street NW, Baudette. Open Tues.–Sat. for breakfast, lunch, and early dinner, Sun. for breakfast and lunch. Abundant breakfast plates and massive burgers and sandwiches. Inexpensive.

⚬ ❁ ✳ ❦ **Rosalie's Restaurant and Lounge** (218-634-9422; wiktel.com/menus/rosalies/menu.htm), 1229 W. Main Street, Baudette. Open daily for dinner, Mon.–Fri. for lunch. Chicken sandwiches, burgers, steaks, and ribs, with several lighter options. Inexpensive/moderate.

⚬ ❁ ✳ **Williams Bar and Grill** (218-783-6195; facebook.com/WilliamsBarGrill), 170 MN 11 NW, Williams. Open daily for lunch and dinner.Williams Bar and Grill has offers solid bar food, especially burgers. Inexpensive.

⚬ ❁ ✳ ❦ **Brickhouse Restaurant** (218-463-0993; mnbrickhouse.com), 205 5th Avenue SE, Roseau. Open daily for lunch and dinner. A full restaurant and bar located near the **Polaris Experience Center** (see *To See and Do*), Brickhouse has burgers, sandwiches, steaks, and ribs. Moderate.

⚬ ❁ ✳ ❦ **Izzy's Lounge and Grill** (218-386-2723; patchmotel.com/lounge-grill), 801 N. State Avenue, Warroad. Open daily for lunch and dinner. At this local bar and grill, the bar is fully stocked, and the grill provides enormous meals in the form of burgers and chicken. Service is friendly, and the casual environment, with a large stone fireplace, is downright cozy. Inexpensive.

## ✳ Special Events

*June*: **Willie Walleye Day**, Baudette. Held in early June, Willie Walleye Day celebrates Baudette's claim that it's the Walleye Capital of the World with a day of fun and frolic, including a 5K run/walk, lumberjack show, chainsaw carving, and, of course, food.

**Scandinavian Festival**, Roseau. Held each year in mid-June, the two-day Scandinavian Festival celebrates the region's roots with events in the town of Roseau and at the **Pioneer Village** (see *To See and Do*).

*August*: **Pioneer Village Festival** (218-463-1045; roseaupioneerfarm.com), MN 11, Roseau. This event, held each year the last weekend of August before Labor Day weekend, re-creates pioneer entertainment by having a pancake breakfast, children's games and activities, demonstrations of pioneer skills, and a parade.

**Angle Days** (218-395-0648; facebook.com/minnesotaangledays), Northwest Angle. An annual August event celebrating the fruit of the season—blueberries—with a pie-baking contest, fun run and walk, fish fry, clay pigeon tournament, and other events.

# THIEF RIVER FALLS/RED RIVER VALLEY/DETROIT LAKES

In this region, the topography of Minnesota changes dramatically within a short distance, from flat agricultural areas to rolling wooded countryside dotted with lakes. Along the state's edge, you'll see miles of sunflowers, soybeans, and beets; veer east, and the views are pastoral. There's history and nature in abundance.

## ❋ To See and Do

GAMING ♿ ✒ ❋ ⍦ 𝗻 **Shooting Star Casino** (starcasino.com), 777 Casino Road, Mahnomen. Open 24/7. North of Detroit Lakes is this casino, run by the White Earth Band of Ojibwe Indians. Large and well run, the casino has slots, blackjack, bingo, and poker, as well as childcare and a kids' arcade. Live concerts are offered regularly in the casino's main stage, and there is dining in four venues. A hotel is attached to the casino (see *Lodging*).

MUSEUMS AND HISTORIC SITES ♿ ✒ **Peder Engelstad Pioneer Village** (218-681-5767; visittrf.com/location/peder-engelstad-pioneer-village), 825 Oakland Park Road, Thief River Falls. Open daily Memorial Day–Labor Day. Adults $5; children under 12 free with paid adult. Like the Pioneer Village in Roseau (see *To See and Do* in the "Baudette/Roseau/Warroad" chapter), this is a collection of 19 historical buildings, each housing several artifacts from the early settler days of northwestern Minnesota. Buildings include a church, a school, log cabins, and a two-story Victorian house.

    ♿ ✒ ⚙ **Heritage Village** (218-791-5313; egfheritage.com), 219 20th Street NE, East Grand Forks. Open by appointment. Festivals and events open to the public are held frequently; call or check the website for details. A preserved historic village re-creating life in pioneer days, including a variety of farm implements.

    ♿ ✒ ❋ **Rourke Art Museum** (218-236-8861; therourke.org), 521 Main Avenue, Moorhead. Open Fri.–Sun. Admission is free. A small but thoughtful collection of permanent and traveling exhibits focused on contemporary American, Hispanic, African, and Native American art.

    ✒ **Comstock House** (218-291-4211; mnhs.org/comstock), 506 8th Street S., Moorhead. Open Sat. and Sun. Memorial Day–Labor Day. Adults $7; seniors 65 and older, veterans, active military, and college students $6; children 5–17 $5; children under 5 and Minnesota Historical Society members free. The 1882 home of Solomon Comstock, who founded Moorhead State University. The home has been restored and includes original furnishings.

TOURS ♿ ✒ ❋ **Arctic Cat** (218-681-8558; visittrf.com/location/arctic-cat-inc), 600 Brooks Avenue, Thief River Falls. Open Mon.–Fri. A large manufacturer of snowmobiles and ATVs, Arctic Cat offers tours of its plant at 1 p.m. Call ahead for reservations.

THE STAVE CHURCH AT THE HJEMKOMST CENTER

✦ ✳ **Digi-Key** (218-681-6674; digikey.com), 701 Brooks Avenue S., Thief River Falls. Open Mon.–Fri. This manufacturer of electrical components offers tours by appointment.

WINERIES ⚲ **Two Fools Vineyard** (218-465-4655), 12501 240th Avenue SE, Plummer. Open Sat. and Sun. 12–3, Jun.–Oct. Thumbing their noses at those who say grapes can't be grown in northern climates, Carol and LeRoy Stumpf grow grapes (among other fruits) and make wines such as pinot noir, chardonnay, and orange muscat.

## ✳ Green Space and Outdoor Activities

**Historical Riverwalk,** Thief River Falls. More than 7 miles of trails wind through Thief River Falls along the Thief and Red Lake rivers. The trail is open for walking, biking,

# A MAN, A DREAM, AND A BOAT

The Hjemkomst Center is named after the replica Viking ship built by a local man who wanted to sail it to Norway. He completed the ship and took it on Lake Superior, but before he could journey farther, he died; family and friends rallied and sailed the ship to Norway in 1982. The ship is on display as a permanent exhibit, along with a Norwegian stave church replica and a historical Red River Valley exhibit. Don't miss the center's introductory film; although a bit on the sappy side, the actual footage taken during the ship's voyage to Norway is amazing. Temporary exhibits are brought in on rotation, and the center sponsors several special events each year. Call or check the website for specific events.

Hjemkomst Center (218-299-5515; hjemkomstcenter.com), 202 1st Avenue N., Moorhead. Open daily. Adults 18–54 $10; seniors 55 and older and college students $9; youth 5–17 $8; children under 5 and museum members free. Admission is free every third Tues. 5–8. ♿ ✿ ❄ ☀

THE HJEMKOMST CENTER

and cross-country skiing, and it passes through several city parks, some historical sites, and near the dam.

**Agassiz National Wildlife Refuge** (218-449-4115; fws.gov/refuge/agassiz), 22996 220th Street NE, Middle River. Open daily during daylight hours, May–Oct. The headquarters is open for questions and visitor assistance Mon.–Fri. 7:30–4, excluding federal holidays. Admission is free. This refuge has more than 60,000 acres encompassing a wide variety of environments—wetland, forest, and prairie—and is home to a diverse assortment of wildlife; bald eagles, ducks, geese, wolves, herons, moose, and deer are just a few of the animals residing here. There is a 4-mile self-guided habitat drive as well as a 0.5-mile hiking trail; a 100-foot observation tower with a 14-foot observation deck is available during non-snow times. Check in at headquarters to obtain the key for the tower.

❄ **Red River State Recreation Area** (218-773-4950; dnr.state.mn.us/state_parks /red_river/index.html), 515 2nd Street NW, East Grand Forks. Open daily 8 a.m.– 10 p.m. A state park permit is required for admission; a day pass is $7 per vehicle. One of the state's newer recreation areas was created after the disastrous 1997 floods, which destroyed homes and farms along the river. More than 500 homes and buildings were removed from the area after the floodplain was reconfigured, and a 1,200-acre recreation area was created instead. Hiking and biking trails, fishing and boating access, and campsites are now available within easy access of both East Grand Forks and Grand Forks, North Dakota.

❄ **Tamarac National Wildlife Refuge** (218-847-2641; fws.gov/midwest/tamarac), 35704 170th Street, Rochert. Open daily. No admission fee. Tamarac has 43,000 acres set aside for wildlife preservation. The visitor center, open weekdays 7:30–4 and weekends 10–5, has exhibits and a video presentation explaining what the refuge contains. Self-guided driving and hiking tours can lend views of bald eagle, deer, porcupine, and even the occasional black bear. In the winter, ice fishing, cross-country skiing, and snowshoeing are all available.

## ❄ Lodging

&. ♂ (ⁱ) ❄ ℱ **AmericInn Lodge and Suites Thief River Falls** (218-681-4411; wyndhamhotels.com), 1920 US 59 SE, Thief River Falls. This property has rooms and suites, some of the latter with fireplaces and whirlpools. There's an indoor pool and a complimentary daily breakfast; for winter enthusiasts, the hotel offers cold-weather vehicle hookups. Rates start at $101.

&. ♂ ❄ ℱ **C'mon Inn** (218-681-3000 or 1-800-950-8111; cmoninn.com), 1586 US 59 SE, Thief River Falls. A small but comfortable hotel with 44 rooms, an indoor pool and hot tub, and daily continental breakfast. Rates start at $101.

&. ♂ (ⁱ) ♂ ❄ ♈ ❙❙ ℱ **Courtyard Moorhead** (218-284-1000; marriott.com), 1080 28th Avenue S., Moorhead. The

Courtyard, a Marriott property, was designed primarily for business travelers, so the rooms are well equipped with two phone lines, and higher-end desks and desk chairs. The hotel also has an indoor pool, and a restaurant on-site that is open for breakfast and dinner. Rates start at $123.

&. ♂ (ⁱ) ❄ ℱ **AmericInn Lodge and Suites Detroit Lakes** (218-847-8795; americinn.com), 777 US 10 E., Detroit Lakes. This AmericInn has rooms and suites, the latter of which have fireplaces and Jacuzzis), and all rooms have HDTVs. The hotel has an indoor pool and includes a full breakfast daily. Cold-weather hookups are available, and there is access from the hotel to local snowmobile trails. Rates start at $101.

&. ♂ ♂ ♈ ❄ ℱ **Best Western Premier: The Lodge on Lake Detroit** (218-847-8439 or 1-800-780-7234;

thelodgeonlakedetroit.com), 1200 E. Shore Drive, Detroit Lakes. This lakefront hotel, opened in 2006, boasts rooms that all face the lake; first-floor rooms have walkout patios, and most second- and third-floor rooms have private balconies. The rooms are nicely appointed, all coming with HDTV and free Internet access, and are the most luxurious in the area. Suites have additional features, such as gas fireplaces, full kitchens, or aromatherapy whirlpool tubs. There's a sandy beach outside for the summer, and an indoor pool and hot tub for inclement weather. A full-service spa is on-site. Full breakfast is served daily, and the lounge offers drinks and appetizers in the evening, but other meals are not provided. Rates start at $110. Packages are available.

&. ♨ ☂ (ᵖ) ❋ ♈ ⑂ ⌇ **Holiday Inn Lakeside** (218-847-2121 or 1-877-251-9348; dlinn.com), 1155 US 10 E., Detroit Lakes. A lakeside property, the Holiday Inn has a sandy beach, as well as an indoor pool, whirlpool, and sauna. The rooms are standard Holiday Inn issue, but there is a full-service restaurant on-site serving three meals daily. Rates start at $112.

&. ♨ (ᵖ) ❋ ♈ ⑂ ⌇ **Shooting Star Casino Hotel and RV Park** (218-935-2711 or 1-800-453-7827; starcasino.com), 777 Casino Road, Mahnomen. Attached to the casino (see *To See and Do*) is a hotel with a range of accommodation options, from standard rooms to deluxe suites. An on-site spa offers massage, body wraps, facials, and mani/pedis. There's an indoor pool and hot tub, and room service from the casino's restaurants is available. Behind the hotel is an RV park with water, sewer, and electricity hookups. Rates start at $79.

## ❋ Where to Eat

DINING OUT &. ♨ ❋ ♈ **The Blue Moose Bar and Grill** (218-773-6516; thebluemoose.net), 507 2nd Street NW, East Grand Forks. Open daily for lunch and dinner, Sun. for breakfast. Perhaps one of the few restaurants in history to have crossed a river, the Blue Moose did so following the Red River flooding in 1999. Now housed on the river in a comfortable lodge setting, this restaurant serves hearty steaks and sandwiches in huge portions. Expensive.

&. ❋ ♈ **The Fireside** (218-847-8192; firesidedl.com), 1462 East Shore Drive, Detroit Lakes. Open daily for dinner, Memorial Day–Sept.; Mon.–Sat. for dinner, Oct.–May. Call for details. One of the best choices for an upscale dining experience, the Fireside serves old-fashioned supper-club foods with a contemporary flair. Steaks are available in all sizes, and walleye comes in multiple iterations. The grilled duck breast is a good bet if you're not in a steak or seafood mood. Expensive.

EATING OUT ♨ ❋ **Johnnie's Café** (218-681-0436), 304 N. Main Avenue, Thief River Falls. Open Mon.–Fri. for breakfast and lunch. A classic small-town café popular with the locals, Johnnie's breakfasts are primarily eggs and pancakes, but they're plentiful and good (be sure to get the hash browns). Lunch is classic sandwiches (Reuben, grilled cheese) and burgers. Nothing fancy, but done well. Inexpensive.

&. ♨ ❋ ♈ **Black Cat Sports Bar and Grill** (218-681-8910; facebook.com /Black-Cat-Sports-Bar-and-Grill -113099832060025), 1080 MN 32 S., Thief River Falls. Open daily for lunch and dinner. This is a sports bar with a snowmobiling theme, thanks to the memorabilia on display from local manufacturer Arctic Cat. Burgers, sandwiches, pizzas, and a handful of bigger dinners, including walleye and sirloin plates. Inexpensive.

&. ♨ ❋ ♈ **Spitfire Bar and Grill** (218-844-3473; spitfirebarandgrill.com), 1100 N. Shore Drive, Detroit Lakes. Open daily for lunch and dinner, Sat.–Sun. for brunch. A cheerful bar and grill with wood-fired steaks, smoked meats, and

# WE FEST

WE Fest (1-844-227-8075; wefest.com), 25526 County Route 22, Detroit Lakes. A three-day celebration of country music held annually since 1983, the festival is outdoors, rain or shine, in early August and attracts more than 50,000 people from around the country. The festival is sited at the Soo Pass Ranch on US 59, southeast of Detroit Lakes. Tickets are sold at varying levels, from general admission and reserved lawn seats to reserved box seats to a VIP experience, with prices for the three days ranging from $110 to $1,050. Many attendees return year after year, and an entire culture has built up at this festival, with some visitors setting up stores or "cafes" where they sell grilled foods and beverages off-limits to drinkers under 21. Campsites are available, but reserve well in advance—this is a very popular option for WE Fest attendees. Recent performers include Keith Urban, Brooks & Dunn, LeAnn Rimes, and Chris Stapleton.

Note: While children are not prohibited, WE Fest tends to be an adult event; campers frequently bring in large quantities of alcohol to enjoy, and not all of the entertainment is family-friendly.

spit-roasted chicken, as well as burgers and pasta. Moderate.

  Ⴠ ✿ ❋ ♉ **Zorbaz on the Lake** (218-847-5305; zorbaz.com), 402 W. Lake Drive, Detroit Lakes. Open daily for lunch and dinner. A beach bar with Mexican food, pizza, pasta, and plenty of beer. A dock is provided for diners arriving by boat. Moderate.

  Ⴠ ✿ ❋ ♉ **Shooting Star Casino** (218-935-2711 or 1-800-453-7827; starcasino.com), 777 Casino Road, Mahnomen. This casino, north of Detroit Lakes, offers four restaurants from sit-down to casual quick food, including a buffet that's plentiful. Moderate.

## ❋ Special Events

*May*: **Festival of Birds** (218-847-9202 or 1-800-542-3992; visitdetroitlakes.com), Detroit Lakes. A basic event fee of $20 for the full festival or $12 per day is required, plus fees ranging from $5 to $55 for the individual events. This annual event, held in May, is for serious birders. The Detroit Lakes area is home to more than 200 kinds of birds, and the festival provides birdwatchers with three days of guided tours, presentations by experts, early-morning and evening field trips, workshops, and a dinner in the forest.

*June*: **Scandinavian Hjemkomst & Midwest Viking Festival** (218-299-5452; hjemkomstcenter.com), Hjemkomst Center, 202 1st Avenue N., Moorhead. Adult pass is $15; teens and senior citizens $10; and free for children. Held each year in late June, the festival is all things Scandinavian—children's story hours, a midsummer's fest picnic, Nordic marketplace, Viking village, a banquet, dance and music performances and lessons, art exhibits, and food and craft sales.

*August*: **Barnesville Potato Days** (218-354-2888; potatodays.com), Barnesville. As you might expect from the theme of this festival, Barnesville is a major potato producer, and this annual festival, held the last weekend in August, reflects that heritage. This festival draws more than 14,000 people each year due to its good-natured view of potato activities, including mashed potato wrestling, mashed potato sculpting, potato peeling and mashed potato eating contests, and potato car races. There's also a Miss Tater Tot Pageant, a 5K/10K race, softball, and a demolition derby. Mashed potatoes, lefse (a Scandinavian potato-based pastry), and

French fries are readily available, as is—oddly—chocolate.

**Heritage Days Festival** (egfheritage .com), N. MN 220 and 20th Street NE, East Grand Forks. Admission $5; free for active duty and reserve military members and families, and children under 12 with a paid adult. An annual festival held in late August at the Heritage Village, Heritage Days takes visitors back in time to the beginning of the last century with blacksmith demonstrations, threshing, broom making, and a tractor pull. A parade and bountiful food round out the celebration.

*September*: **Rollag Western Minnesota Steam Threshers Reunion** (218-238-5407; rollag.com), 27512 102nd Avenue, Rawley. Labor Day weekend. Daily tickets are $14 for ages 15 and older, 14 and under free. Season pass available for $20. This popular event is spread out over 200 acres and includes demonstrations of various generations of farm power, including horse-, gas-, and steam-powered equipment. Food and craft demonstrations are held daily, as are train (full-sized and miniature) rides, merry-go-round rides, and a parade.

# CENTRAL LAKE DISTRICT

ST. CLOUD AND ENVIRONS

MILLE LACS

WILLMAR

ALEXANDRIA LAKES

BRAINERD

# CENTRAL LAKE DISTRICT

I f lakes are what people think of when they think about Minnesota, it's likely that they're thinking about the Central Lake District, particularly the Brainerd area. Slightly more than two hours north of the Twin Cities, this area has long been a popular weekend getaway spot in the summer, where a community of mom-and-pop resorts and upscale enclaves serve all types of interests. Brainerd and its twin city of Baxter are the most prominent communities, but they are not the only cities to consider when looking at a lake vacation; many of the small towns surrounding Brainerd, including Nisswa, Pequot Lakes, and Crosslake, are all good bets. These are towns that grew up during the railroad and logging boom, and when that died back, they turned to the abundant lakes to develop tourism.

But even beyond the Brainerd region are good options for water enthusiasts. Going west to the area around Willmar, visitors can find beautiful rolling countryside and lakes created by glaciers 10,000 years ago, although those seeking higher-end accommodations may be disappointed. Northwest of Brainerd is the Alexandria Lakes area, a growing and highly scenic multiple-lake community. Minnesota's second-largest lake,

BEACHSIDE AT MADDEN'S RESORT

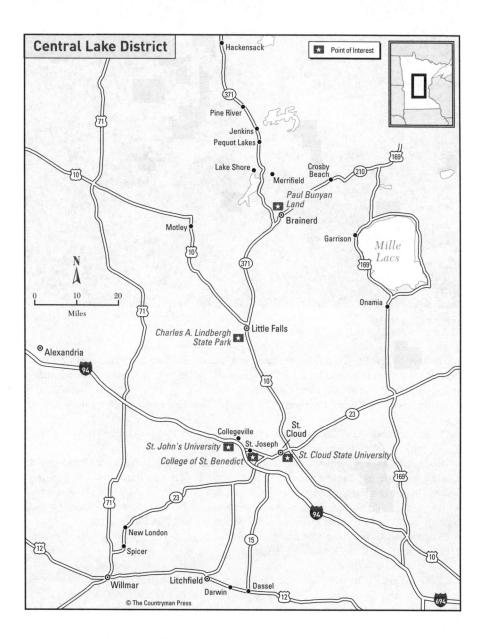

**Central Lake District**

★ Point of Interest

Hackensack

371

Pine River

Jenkins
Pequot Lakes

Lake Shore

169

210

Crosby
Beach

Merrifield

Paul Bunyan
★ Land

Brainerd

Motley

Garrison

Mille
Lacs

71

N

0    10    20
Miles

10

371

169

Onamia

Little Falls

71

Charles A. Lindbergh ★
State Park

10

Alexandria

94

23

St.
Cloud

Collegeville

St. John's University ★

St. Joseph

College of St. Benedict

St. Cloud State University

169

71

23

94

New London

15

Spicer

12

10

Willmar

Litchfield

Darwin

Dassel

12

694

© The Countryman Press

Lake Mille Lacs, rests east of Brainerd and is also an idyllic area for visitors, especially avid fishermen, summer and winter. Along the way, whether en route to Brainerd/Mille Lacs or Willmar, are a number of historical and cultural sites of interest, particularly through the St. Cloud area.

Because these popular lake regions are relatively close to the Twin Cities, traffic can be heavy, especially on weekends. The route to Brainerd has been improved by the addition of traffic lanes on MN 371, but Brainerd and Baxter are not towns designed for heavy traffic flow; be prepared for slow going at times.

TURTLE RACES IN NISSWA

**GUIDANCE The St. Cloud Convention and Visitor Bureau** (320-251-4170 or 1-800-264-2940; visitstcloud.com), 1411 W. St. Germain, Suite 104, St. Cloud. Provides information for St. Cloud lodging and tourism.

**Mille Lacs Lake Area Tourism** (320-676-9972 or 1-888-350-2692; millelacs.com), 630 W. Main Street, Isle.

**Willmar Lakes Area Chamber of Commerce** (320-235-0300; willmarareachamber .com), 2104 E. US 12, Willmar.

**Brainerd Lakes Chamber and Convention and Visitor Bureau** (218-829-2838 or 1-800-450-2838; explorebrainerdlakes.com), 7393 S. MN 371, Brainerd. The Brainerd Lakes Chamber offers extensive lodging and activity information for the Brainerd/Baxter region and surrounding areas. The visitor center on MN 371 is large and well equipped with information and brochures about the Brainerd Lakes area.

**Alexandria Lakes Area Chamber of Commerce** (320-763-3161 or 1-800-235-9441; alexandriamn.org), 206 Broadway, Alexandria.

**GETTING THERE By air:** Delta Air Lines and its SkyWest subsidiary serve the cities of Brainerd and St. Cloud. Willmar has a municipal airport that can handle small corporate planes. Taxis and rental cars are available from the airports: **Brainerd Lakes Regional Airport** (218-825-2166; brainerdairport.com), 16384 Airport Road, in Brainerd, and **St. Cloud Regional Airport** (320-255-7292; stcloudairport.com), 1550 SE 45th Avenue, in St. Cloud.

**By car:** I-94 and US 10 both traverse St. Cloud. From St. Cloud, US 10 meets MN 371, which continues north to Brainerd. Willmar is servedfrom the east and west by US 12, and from the north and south by US 71. The Mille Lacs area is ringed by US 169 and MN 18, MN 27, and MN 47.

**GETTING AROUND** Having a vehicle is a necessity when traveling around the Central Lakes region, unless you plan to stay solely at your resort.

WHEN TO COME  The summer months see an influx of tourists who come to enjoy the multitude of lakes and beaches, but summer isn't the only popular time, especially for fishing enthusiasts who cast their poles in open water in summer and through holes in the ice in winter. Hunters and winter-sports aficionados appreciate the fall and winter seasons as well.

MEDICAL EMERGENCY  Call 911.

**CentraCare St. Cloud Hospital** (320-251-2700; centracare.com), 1406 N. 6th Avenue, St. Cloud.

**Mille Lacs Health System** (320-532-3154; mlhealth.org), 200 N. Elm Street, Onamia.

**Long Prairie Memorial Hospital** (320-732-2131; centracare.com), 50 Centra Care Drive, Long Prairie.

**Melrose Area Hospital** (320-256-4231; centracare.com), 525 W. Main Street, Melrose.

**Carris Health—Rice Memorial Hospital** (320-235-4543; carrishealth.com), 301 SW Becker Avenue, Willmar.

**Essentia Health—St. Joseph's Medical Center** (218-829-2861; essentiahealth.org), 523 N. 3rd Street, Brainerd.

**Alomere Health—Douglas County Hospital** (320-762-1511; alomerehealth.com), 111 E. 17th Avenue, Alexandria.

# ST. CLOUD AND ENVIRONS

**S**t. Cloud is home to four colleges and universities, giving it a youthful population and a wide variety of activities, both historical and cultural. Its history is reflected in its nickname, Granite City, and granite is still produced and carved in the area. It's somewhat of a gateway to the north, as most travelers heading to the Brainerd area or Lake of the Woods will pass through here. Consequently, traffic through the city can be quite congested, especially on summer weekends.

## ✳ To See and Do

Attractions are open year-round unless otherwise noted.

MUSEUMS AND HISTORIC SITES ♿ ✎ ✳ **Stearns History Museum** (320-253-8424 or 1-866-253-8424; stearns-museum.org), 235 33rd Avenue S., St. Cloud. Open Tues.–Sat. Adults $7; children $3; families (two adults and all children under 18 living at the same address) $17; museum members free. This county historical museum walks the fine line between education and entertainment, and succeeds on both counts. A clothing exhibit reflects the changing attitudes toward clothes and employment over the years; the area's agricultural history is documented, and there is a life-sized replica of a granite quarry. Documents from pioneers traveling to and settling in this region are displayed, and there is a young children's learn-and-play area.

✎ **Charles A. Lindbergh Historic Site** (320-616-5421; mnhs.org/lindbergh), 1620 Lindbergh Drive S., Little Falls. Open Thurs.–Sun. 12–5, Memorial Day–Labor Day. Adults $8; seniors ages 65 and older, active military and veterans, and college students $6; children 5–17 $6; children under 5 and Minnesota Historical Society members free. Charles Lindbergh's childhood home, complete with original furnishings and belongings, is on display. Next door is a visitor center with exhibits and films about Lindbergh's life and time, and a gift shop. An interpretive trail leads visitors along the river.

✎ ✳ **Grasshopper Chapel** (320-685-3653; visitstcloud.com/things/grasshopper -chapel), 22912 Chapel Hill Road, Cold Spring. Open daily. No admission fee, although donations are welcome. A few miles west of St. Cloud is this little chapel, built originally in 1877 in response to a grasshopper plague that was decimating crops. The governor declared a day of prayer, and local townsfolk promised to build a chapel if the grasshoppers were removed. The grasshoppers disappeared the next day due to an unusual sleet storm, and the chapel was built as promised. The original wood building was destroyed by a tornado in 1894, but it was rebuilt in the 1950s with donated granite. Today the tiny chapel is in a wooded, peaceful area, a beautiful spot to visit.

♿ ✳ **Saint Benedict's Monastery Haehn Museum** (320-363-7113; sbm.osb.org), 104 Chapel Lane, St. Joseph. Open Tues.–Sun. 1–3:30. The 150-year history of the Sisters of Saint Benedict in on display, with items dating back to the monastery's founding. Rotating exhibitions have included explorations of sustainability, liturgical vestments and needlework, Native American cultures where the sisters lived and worked, and the important role of music. The collection is comprised of more than 7,000 artifacts dating back more than 150 years.

THE CHARLES LINDBERGH HOME IN THE CHARLES A. LINDBERGH STATE PARK

&#9855; &#10031; **St. Cloud State University** (320-308-0121; stcloudstate.edu), 720 4th Avenue S., St. Cloud. The university has two art exhibits that are of note. The first is the Atwood Collection, in the Atwood Memorial Center (hours vary by season; no admission fee), which is an ever-growing collection of contemporary American art. The second is the Kiehle Gallery (hours vary by season; no admission fee), a frequently changing collection bringing in guest artists on a national level as well as promoting local and student artists.

WINERIES &#10031; **Millner Heritage Vineyard & Winery** (320-398-2081; millnerheritage .com), 32025 MN 15, Kimball. Open Wed.–Sun. Apr.–Dec.; Fri.–Sun. Jan.–Mar. Millner gives trolley tours of its vineyard, which grows 12 weather-hardy varietals. Wine and hard cider tastings are offered as well, and catered dinners are available.

## &#10031; Green Space and Outdoor Activities

HIKING AND BIKING **Lake Wobegon Trail** (320-255-6172; lakewobegontrail.com). A 62-mile paved hiking and biking trail (with a 13-mile extension trail) that stretches from St. Joseph to Sauk Centre. Snowmobilers have access to it in the winter. The trail is highly scenic, winding through woods, near lakes, and through several small towns. Near Osakis, it intersects with the **Central Lakes Trail** (see page 213).

PARKS AND GARDENS **Munsinger and Clemens Gardens** (320-257-5959; munsinger clemens.com), 1515 Riverside Drive SE, St. Cloud. Open daily, spring–fall. No admission fee, although donations are requested. Two beautiful gardens along the banks of the Mississippi, the Munsinger and Clemens Gardens offer both historic and contemporary gardening highlights. Munsinger Gardens was developed in the 1930s and named after the superintendent of parks; it's an informal garden space, with winding paths lined with wildflowers and pine trees. Clemens Gardens was constructed in the

# THE SAINT JOHN'S BIBLE AND SAINT JOHN'S UNIVERSITY

Visiting the campus of Saint John's University in Collegeville is worthwhile for several reasons, including the beauty of the lakeside campus itself, the 2,700-acre arboretum, and Saint John's Pottery, a working studio that not only examines the artistry, but the ethics, behind the potter's work. Tour the abbey, an impressive piece of unique religious architecture with the world's largest stained-glass window. The campus's spiritual center offers accommodations (see *Lodging*).

In addition to these other highlights, the Saint John's Bible project should be included in any visit to the campus. A deeply felt homage to the days when monasteries kept literature alive by hand-transcribing texts in elaborate calligraphy, the Saint John's Bible is a newly written bible complete with extravagant illustrations and exquisite handwritten text. The project was completed in September 2011 after 15 years in the making. Parts will remain on display at Saint John's, with other sections to be loaned out to other museums.

**Saint John's Bible** (320-363-3351; saintjohnsbible.org), Hill Museum and Manuscript Library, Saint John's University, Collegeville. Open Mon.–Sat. year-round, but closed for several holidays; see the website for updated information. No admission fee. ♿ ✎ ❄

1990s and is a more formal set of gardens, complete with rose gardens and the tallest fountain in Minnesota, the 24-foot Renaissance Fountain.

✎ ❀ ❄ **Quarry Park and Nature Preserve** (320-255-6172; co.stearns.mn.us), 1802 County Route 137, Waite Park. Open daily. A park permit is required for entrance; a one-day permit is $5, an annual permit is $20. Quarry Park is comprised of land that has gradually grown back to a natural state after years of granite quarrying. More than 600 acres of parkland provide a wide array of experiences for visitors: open prairie, wetlands, wooded areas, a 116-foot-deep swimming hole, granite reflecting pools, and 30 granite quarries. Certified scuba divers traveling with scuba buddies can dive in one of four swimmingholes, and with the proper permit, visitors can tackle some rock climbing. Mountain bikers can ride across terrain made up of billion-year-old bedrock, while hikers can explore woodlands and open prairie. Winter brings ample cross-country skiing or snowshoeing opportunities.

## ❄ Lodging

All accommodations are open year-round unless otherwise noted.

BED-AND-BREAKFASTS (ᵖ) ❄ **The Estates Bed and Breakfast** (320-557-0300; estatesbedandbreakfast.com), 29 E. Minnesota Street, St. Joseph. This home was built in 1909 and was a former rental to Saint Benedict and St. John's University students. The home has been modernized and has three suites, all with private bath, two of which have steam showers, while the third unit has a private deck. A self-serve continental breakfast is provided daily. Rates start at $89.

HOTELS ♿ ✎ (ᵖ) ❄ Y ¶ ⚲ **Courtyard by Marriott St. Cloud** (320-654-1661 or 1-888-201-1718; lestgermainsuitehotel .com), 404 W. St. Germain Street, St. Cloud. The prime choice in St. Cloud, the Courtyard, connected by skyway to the St. Cloud Civic Center along the shores of the Mississippi River, is an all-suite property with larger accommodations including sitting areas and river views. The hotel has an indoor pool, whirlpool, and sauna, as well as a sit-down restaurant, **The Bistro** (see *Where* *to Eat*). Rates start at $136. Packages are available.

     &#9855; &#128694; &#9737; **Holiday Inn and Suites** (320-253-9000 or 1-877-666-3243; holidayinn.com/stcloudmn), 75 37th Avenue S., St. Cloud. The Holiday Inn offers an indoor pool, whirlpool, basketball court, sauna, and fitness center. Two restaurants are on-site, one a family-oriented café (kids eat free with paying adults) and one a bar and grill. Rates start at $107.

UNIQUE LODGINGS &#9855; &#9737; **St. Benedict's Monastery** (320-363-7112; sbm.osb.org), 104 Chapel Lane, St. Joseph. This 150-year-old monastery has a spiritual center that welcomes guests for day- or week-long visits known as hermitages. Private retreats can be customized with spiritual counseling, or visitors can simply relax in the quiet grounds and facilities, complete with a garden labyrinth, and visit the **Haehn Museum** (see *To See and Do*). Rates start at $75.

## &#10033; Where to Eat

DINING OUT &#9855; &#9737; **The Bistro** (320-258-2580; facebook.com/thebistrof saintcloud), 404 W. St. Germain Street, St. Cloud. Open daily for all three meals. The Bistro, located in the **Courtyard St. Cloud Hotel** (see *Lodging*) is an upscale American eatery with a focus on healthy and accessible. Expensive.

     &#9855; &#9737; **Anton's** (320-253-3611; antonsrestaurant.com), 2001 Frontage Road N., Waite Park. Open Mon.–Sat. for lunch, daily for dinner. Originally a speakeasy during the Prohibition years, Anton's is now a laid-back log cabin restaurant specializing in grilled meats and sandwiches. If that's not enough to make someone happy, the bar's impressive Scotch list should take care of it. Expensive.

EATING OUT &#9855; &#9737; **The Pickled Loon** (320-281-3581; thepickledloon.com), 715

W. St. Germain Street, St. Cloud. Open daily for lunch and dinner. Creative bar and grill food, including items like blue gill fish and chips and roasted turkey poutine. Try the sriracha BBQ meatloaf. Moderate.

     &#9855; &#9737; **Jules' Bistro** (320-252-7125; julesbistrostcloud.com), 921 W. St. Germain Street, St. Cloud. Open Mon.–Sat. for all three meals. A charming coffee shop and wine bar, Jules' also has homemade pizzas, paninis, and salads. Moderate.

     &#9855; &#9737; **Food Ecstasy** (320-259-5613; foodecstasy.com), 619 W. St. Germain Street, St. Cloud. Open daily for breakfast and lunch. A playful menu focuses on foods crafted with care. Try one of the omelets, or any of the Rapturous Delights Stuffed Potatoes. Inexpensive.

     &#9855; &#9737; **RJ's American Grill & Bar** (320-257-7757; rjsamericangrill.com), 4221 Clearwater Road, St. Cloud. Open daily for lunch and dinner. Its location in a strip mall doesn't appear promising, but the interior is much nicer than the outside. Besides several steak options, there's Grown Up Mac and Cheese (made with shallots, smoked bacon, and broccoli) as well as a walleye BLT. Moderate.

HISTORIC LOG VILLAGE IN CROSSLAKE

&#x267F; &#x1F4CD; &#x274B; &#x1F377; **Mexican Village** (320-252-7134; mexicanvillagestcloud.com), 509 W. St. Germain Street, St. Cloud. Open daily for lunch and dinner. Don't go looking for authentic Mexican; instead, plan on enjoying reasonably priced Americanized Mexican served in a cheerfully (and unrepentantly) kitschy atmosphere. Inexpensive/moderate.

&#x1F37D; &#x1F4CD; &#x274B; **Val's Rapid Serv** (320-251-5775), 628 E. St. Germain Street, St. Cloud. Open daily for lunch and dinner. This local landmark, in business for decades, has changed very little; from its A-frame building on the corner to its inexpensive but tasty burgers and heaping orders of fries, it's still the same. The only nod to modern times is several touchscreen order devices. There's no sitting area—this is grab-and-go food. Inexpensive.

VAL'S RAPID SERV

## &#x274B; Entertainment

Probably because it's a college town, St. Cloud has a large number of live-performance venues for a city its size.

&#x267F; &#x1F4CD; &#x274B; **Paramount Center for the Arts** (320-259-5463; paramountarts.org), 913 W. St. Germain Street, St. Cloud. A vintage 1920s movie theater, the Paramount has gone through its era of neglect and has emerged as a classy setting for a variety of live performances, as well as an art exhibition area. Offerings vary greatly and include comedians, Broadway shows and local and regional theater groups, musicians, and orchestras.

&#x267F; &#x1F4CD; &#x274B; **Fine Arts Series** (320-363-5777; csbsju.edu/fine-arts), 37 S. College Avenue, Benedicta Arts Center, College of Saint Benedict/Saint John's University, St. Joseph. The College of Saint Benedict has an active schedule of fine arts performers. Recent performers include Chris Thile, Kevin Kling, Ana Gasteyer, and Jeremy Messersmith.

&#x274B; &#x1F377; **Bo Diddley's Pub & Deli** (320-252-9475; bodiddleysdeli.com), 129 25th Avenue S., St. Cloud (second location in St. Joseph). Open daily for lunch and dinner. A mellower-than-expected venue with live music on Wed. and most weekends.

## &#x274B; Selective Shopping

DOWNTOWN SHOPS  Unlike some small towns, St. Cloud has managed to keep an active downtown area in spite of the growth of shopping centers and strip malls. Here are a few of the independent retailers worth visiting.

&#x1F4CD; &#x274B; **Books Revisited** (320-259-7959; booksrevisited.com), 607 W. St. Germain, St. Cloud. Open Mon.–Sat. While there's also a location at Crossroads Center, the downtown branch is the original store, and it's packed floor-to-ceiling with new and used books, including some rare items.

&#x274B; **Arts Co-Op** (320-252-3242), 619 W. St. Germain, St. Cloud. Open Mon.–Sat. Represents local and national artists in varying media.

&#x274B; **Rush Boutique** (320-381-5277), 805 W. St. Germain, St. Cloud. Open Mon.–Sat. Call for special Sunday hours. Women's resale fashion with designer and name-brand clothing, shoes, and accessories.

❄ **Copper Pony** (320-774-3210; copper pony.com), 710 W St. Germain, St. Cloud. Open Tues.–Sat. High-quality home décor, accessories, and gifts.

🚲 ❄ **Green Thumb Etc.** (320-493-2955; greenthumbetc.com), 912 W. St. Germain Street, St. Cloud. Call for hours. Individually made custom accent furniture.

MALLS ♿ 🚲 ❄ ⁋ **Crossroads Center** (320-252-2856; crossroadscenter.com), 4101 W. Division Street, St. Cloud. Open daily. This large mall has many of the classic national retailers, including Scheel's, Victoria's Secret, Macy's, and Foot Locker. The mall itself is surrounded by smaller strip malls. Note: The retail area here is very popular, and the roads that surround and run through it (primarily County Route 15) struggle with the traffic loads during busy times. Be prepared to spend a considerable amount of time inching along through stoplights en route to your shopping.

## ❋ Special Events

*June*: **The Caramel Roll** (320-356-7191; lakewobegon trails.com), St. Joseph. An annual bike-and-eat event with your choice of 8-, 15-, or 25-mile routes, with pit stops for caramel rolls. As the Lake Wobegon Trails Association people say, "A sweet roll on a sweet trail."

**Granite City Days** (granitecitydays .com), St. Cloud. This four-day festival in June includes a golf tournament, historic homes and downtown St. Cloud tours, a parade, a blockparty, and a fly-in pancake breakfast, among other events.

*July*: **Tour of Saints** (320-363-1311 or 1-800-651-8687; tourofsaints.com), College of Saint Benedict, St. Joseph. Early bird registration is $32 for adults; $20 for students 18–22; $10 for youth 5–17; free for 4 and under. This is not a religious event, but one for serious bikers. The tour starts and ends at the college, and riders choose either a 35- or 50-mile route through the rolling countryside and small towns in the St. Cloud area.

The state's second-largest lake is Lake Mille Lacs, and as such, it draws thousands of fishing and water-sports lovers each year. Located on the Mille Lacs Reservation, Mille Lacs is just about as popular in winter as it is in summer, thanks to continued growing interest in ice fishing. The region has responded by adding more options for ice house rental, including some very deluxe buildings with electricity and heat.

## ✳ To See and Do

GAMING ♿ ✎ ❋ ❢ **Grand Casino Mille Lacs** (1-800-626-5825; grandcasinomn.com), 777 Grand Avenue, Onamia. Open 24/7. A full-scale gambling complex with slots, blackjack, and bingo, it also has several restaurants (see *Where to Eat*), a hotel, a theater with frequent live performances, a Kids Cove child-care area, and an extensive video arcade.

MUSEUMS AND HISTORIC SITES ♿ ✎ **Mille Lacs Indian Museum** (320-532-3632; mnhs.org/millelacs), 43411 Oodena Drive, Onamia. Open Tues.–Sat. Memorial Day–Labor Day; Wed.–Sat. Sept.–Oct. Adults $10; seniors 65 and older, active military

MILLE LACS INDIAN MUSEUM

members and veterans, and college students $8; children5–17 $6; children under 5 and Minnesota Historical Society members free. This museum is a joint venture between the Mille Lacs Indians and the Minnesota Historical Society, and it's a thoughtful, detailed collection of exhibits showing how Native Americans of the region lived and worked centuries ago. The crafts room has an especially lovely collection of beadwork and birch bark basketry. Check the website for event information, as they often have interesting classes and demonstrations. An adjacent trading post, a re-creation of a 1930s-era trading post, sells Native American gift items.

## ✳ Green Space and Outdoor Activities

The Lake Mille Lacs area is all about the outdoor activities, many of which are centered around the massive lake (the second largest lake in Minnesota). Fishing, hunting, boating, biking, hiking, cross-country skiing, snowshoeing, snowmobiling—it's all here.

**Kathio State Park** (320-532-3523; dnr.state.mn.us/state_parks/mille_lacs_kathio/index.html), 15066 Kathio State Park Road, Onamia. Open daily. Near the **Mille Lacs Indian Museum** (see *To See and Do*) is the entrance to this park, which has year-round opportunities for recreation. The Rum River flows through the park from its source in Lake Mille Lacs, and visitors can use canoes or rowboats to explore. A swimming beach is open during the summer, as is a 100-foot observation tower and a wide variety of campsites and cabins (some of which are available year-round). Winter enthusiasts can cross-country ski, snowshoe, or snowmobile on groomed trails.

**Mille Lacs Wildlife Management Area** (651-296-5484; dnr.state.mn.us/wmas/index.html), 29172 100th Avenue, Onamia. Open daily. This small wildlife management area (61 acres) is a carefully preserved area of forests and wetlands. During hunting season, camping is allowed, and hunters with permits can hunt deer, bear, and small game.

## ✳ Lodging

♿ ✒ ((φ)) ♂ ❋ ‖ ⵠ ⸙ **Izatys Resort** (320-532-4574; izatys.com), 40005 85th Avenue, Onamia. On the shores of Lake Mille Lacs, this luxury complex includes townhomes and villas (ranging from two to four bedrooms), as well as a lodge offering hotel rooms. Boat rental, two 18-hole golf courses, fishing and hunting guides, tennis courts, spa, seasonal kids program, and indoor and outdoor pools are all available on-site. There is also a fine-dining restaurant (see *Where to Eat*). Rates start at $129.

♿ ✒ ((φ)) ❋ ‖ ⵠ **Grand Casino Mille Lacs** (1-800-468-3517; grandcasinomn.com), 777 Grand Avenue, Onamia. This huge hotel has several room types, including a number of luxurious suites with four-person Jacuzzis and separate living areas. The large indoor swimming pool and whirlpool are in a nicely decorated wing. Rates start at $89.

✒ ((φ)) ❋ **Mille Lacs Lodge** (320-532-3384; millelacslodge.com), 8659 340th Street, Onamia. This rustic, cozy lodge has just six rooms, which are available for rent only as a group. All rooms have private baths. The lodge has a full kitchen, satellite TV, two-story fieldstone fireplace, deck, pool table, and large dining area. Rate is $650 per night.

♿ ✒ 🐾 ❋ ‖ ⵠ **Eddy's Resort** (320-532-3657 or 1-800-657-4704; eddysresort.com), 41334 Shakopee Lake Road, Onamia. A hotel with two- and three-bedroom cabins as well. The hotel is more upscale than what's usually found in this area, with walkout balconies and patios and large flat-screen TVs. Guests have access to the Grand Casino Mille Lacs pool and arcade. Rates start at $89.

  ♿ ✍ 🐾 ❄ 🍴 ♈ **Twin Pines Resort** (320-692-4413; twinpinesmillelacs.com), 7827 US 169, Garrison. A family-friendly resort with cabins and motel rooms on Lake Mille Lacs, the property is a good value, with summer and winter fishing guides available (as well as ice house rental in the winter). A restaurant/bar is on-site. Rates start at $69.

## ✳ Where to Eat

DINING OUT ♿ ✍ ❄ ♈ **Izatys** (1-800-533-1728; izatys.com), 40005 85th Avenue, Onamia. Open daily for dinner year-round, seasonally for lunch (check their website). One of the few fine-dining restaurants in the area, Izatys has an upscale dinner menu that includes traditional steakhouse foods, including grilled steak panzanella, as well as stuffed peppers and shrimp and smoked tomato pasta. Moderate/expensive.

EATING OUT ♿ ✍ ❄ ♈ **Grand Casino Mille Lacs** (1-800-626-5825; grand casinomn.com), 777 Grand Avenue, Onamia. The casino has five restaurants on-site, one of which (Plums, a quick-service burger-and-pizza café) is open 24 hours. There's also a buffet restaurant (open Wed.–Sun.), a burger bar, coffee shop, and the 1991 Kitchen, a casual grill restaurant with supper club entrées including prime rib and chicken-fried steak. Inexpensive/expensive.

  ♿ ✍ ❄ ♈ **Eddy's** (320-532-8590; eddysresort.com/eat), 41334 Shakopee Lake Road, Onamia. Open daily for all three meals. Located at Eddy's Resort, this eatery has a limited but thoughtful menu, with Jars (house-made jams and spreads served with grilled flatbread and crostini, including a Thai chili hummus), smoked walleye salad, and beef brisket sandwiches. Moderate.

  ♿ ✍ ❄ **Svoboda's Spotlite** (320-692-4692), 9653 Madison Street, Garrison. Open daily for breakfast and lunch, Fri.–Sun. for dinner. Breakfast is served all day at this friendly café, a local institution. The home-cooked foods are simple but delicious, and prices are reasonable. Kids' and senior citizens' menus available. Inexpensive.

# WILLMAR

The Willmar area has not seen the same kind of tourism growth experienced by the Brainerd area, which is not necessarily a bad thing; the rolling, forested countryside and quiet lakes can provide the utmost in tranquility. The downside is that there is less to do for visitors who don't want to spend their entire vacation on the lake. But for those who appreciate a restful, beautiful retreat, the Willmar area has plenty to offer.

## ❋ To See and Do

FOR FAMILIES ✎ **Big Kahuna Fun Park** (320-796-2445; spicerfunpark.com), 190 Progress Way, Spicer. Open daily 11–9, Memorial Day–Labor Day, and a few weekends into the fall depending on weather. Rates for individual activities vary from $4.50 to $6.75. This outdoor amusement park has mini golf, junior mini golf, bumper boats, two go-cart tracks, and a kids' Power Wheels course.

MUSEUMS AND HISTORIC SITES ♿ ✎ **Schwanke's Museum** (320-235-4341 or 800-537-5582; schwanketractor.com/museum), 3310 S. US 71, Willmar. Open daily mid-May–Sept. Gift shop open year-round. Adults $6; children 5–12 $3; free for under 5. The vehicular counterpart to the Mikkelson Collection, this museum has more than 300 antique tractors, cars, and trucks.

   ♿ ✎ ❋ **Cokato Museum** (320-286-2427; cokatomuseum.org), 175 SW 4th Street, Cokato. Open Tues.–Sat. Admission is free (but donations are appreciated). The region's Finnish and Swedish heritage is celebrated and documented in this museum, which includes a log home and sauna, as well as a rather intimidating early dentist's office.

OTHER ATTRACTIONS ♿ ✎ ❋ **Darwin Twine Ball Museum** (320-693-7544; darwin twineball.com), US 12, Darwin. Museum open daily Apr.–Sept., by appointment the rest of the year. Admission free. Memorialized in song by Weird Al Yankovic, the centerpiece of the little town of Darwin (east of Willmar) is the giant ball of twine, the largest to be rolled by one person. It took Francis Johnson (son of US senator Magnus Johnson) nearly 30 years to roll this ball, which now stands 11 feet tall. The accompanying museum has interesting exhibits about the accomplishment. The twine ball itself is on display outdoors and can be seen year-round.

## ❋ Green Space and Outdoor Activities

The Willmar lakes area is really about the outdoor activities. There are more than 100 lakes scattered throughout the rolling land, punctuated by farmland and forest, and ringed with small resorts. Fishing, boating, biking, hiking, snowmobiling, cross-country skiing—it's a playground for the outdoors lover.

# GOLF

While lake-related activities are extremely popular, golf is also a big draw in this area.

**Eagle Creek Golf Course** (320-235-1166; willmargolf.com), 1000 NE 26th Avenue, Willmar. A nearly 90-year-old course situated right between two lakes, Eagle Creek offers 18 holes and an upscale restaurant (see *Dining Out*).

**Little Crow Golf Resort** (320-347-1500 or 1-877-659-5023; littlecrowresort.com), 15980 MN 23, Spicer. Little Crow has three nine-hole courses and a tavern and grille (see *Where to Eat*).

**Island Pine Golf Club** (320-974-8600; islandpinegolf.com), 1601 W. Wyoming Avenue, Atwater. Island Pine has an 18-hole championship course and some of the largest greens in the area.

**Hawk Creek Country Club** (320-967-4653; hawkcreekcc.com), 100 NE Spicer Avenue, Raymond. Hawk Creek offers a nine-hole course, driving range, and putting green.

HIKING AND BIKING **Glacial Lakes State Trail** (dnr.state.mn.us/state_trails/glacial_lakes/index.html). A great way to get a feel for the glacier-created topography of the area is to explore the Glacial Lakes Trail, a 22-mile paved trail that travels from Stearns County on the east into Willmar, Spicer, New London, and Hawick. There are large segments of the trail that have horseback trails adjacent, and the trail (a former Burlington Northern Railroad grade) has become very popular with hikers, bikers, and inline skaters. Parts of the trail are groomed for winter activities, but studded tracks are prohibited.

PARKS **Sibley State Park** (320-354-2055; dnr.state.mn.us/state_parks/sibley/index.html), 800 NE Sibley Park Road, New London. Open daily. A state park permit is required; a day pass is $7 per vehicle ($35 for an annual pass). Sibley State Park has a wide variety of activities, including hiking to the top of Mount Tom, the tallest hill for miles, and swimming, fishing, boating, and canoeing on one of the many lakes. Camping is allowed, including one camping area specifically for horse riding campers.

## ✱ Lodging

HOTELS ♿ ⌂ (ᵖ) ❄ ⋔ **Holiday Inn Express & Suites** (320-231-2601 or 877-666-3243; ihg.com), 250 23rd Street SE, Willmar. Several accommodation types in a newer hotel with a fitness center and indoor pool. Buffet breakfast included. Rates start at $140.

♿ ⌂ (ᵖ) ❄ ⋔ **Country Inn & Suites** (320-214-0300 or 1-800-830-5222; countryinns.com), 201 28th Avenue SE, Willmar. This recently renovated hotel offers both standard rooms along with whirlpool and extended-stay suites. There's an indoor pool with a weekend water slide. Full breakfast included. Rates start at $119.

♿ ⌂ 🏠 (ᵖ) ❄ ⋔ **AmericInn** (320-231-1962; wyndhamhotels.com), 2404 E. US 12, Willmar. An all-suite hotel with flat-screen HDTVs, refrigerators, and microwaves. Rates start at $90.

CABINS ⌂ ❄ **Diamond Lake Resort** (320-444-5440; diamondlakeresortmn.com), 14800 49th Avenue NE, Atwater. Six recently remodeled cabins along Diamond Lake, all with air conditioning, flat-screen TVs, and fire pits. The resort also has a good sandy beach, and guests have free use of kayaks, canoes, paddleboats, paddleboards, and fun bugs. Rates start at $215.

    ✆ ✿ **Island View Resort** (320-796-2775 or 1-800-421-9708; islandviewresort.ws), 5910 132nd Avenue NE, Spicer. Open May–Sept. Island View is located on quiet Nest Lake, and the resort has a decent sandy beach. The resort offers several small but comfortable cabins, all with private fire rings. There are plenty of beach toys, and boat and motor rental areavailable. Rates start at $170.

## ✳ Where to Eat

EATING OUT ✆ ✳ ▽ **The Oaks at Eagle Creek** (320-235-4448; oaksateaglecreek.com), 1000 26th Avenue NE, Willmar. Open daily for lunch and dinner in summer, call for winter hours. Located at the Eagle Creek Golf Course, this casual but upscale restaurant offers burgers, sandwiches, steaks, and prime rib on weekends. Try the Peppercorn Pork Tenderloin or the Topless Martini Burger (bleu cheese, gin BBQ, green olive relish, and no bun). Moderate/expensive.

    ✆ ▽ **Little Crow Tavern & Grille** (320-347-1500; littlecrowresort.com/restaurant), 15980 MN 23, Spicer. Open Mon.–Sat. for lunch and dinner, Sun. for brunch, Memorial Day–Labor Day; open Tues.–Sat. for lunch and dinner, Sun. for brunch, mid-May–Memorial Day. Steak burgers, walleye, BBQ ribs, and other sandwiches and salads. Try the maple-pepper bacon burger with Havarti cheese, maple pepper bacon, aioli, and arugula, or the wild rice stuffed chicken breast. Moderate/expensive.

    ✆ ✳ **LuLu Beans** (320-214-9633; lulubeans.net), 1020 1st Street S., Willmar. Open daily for all three meals. This cozy coffee shop and café is popular with locals and visitors alike, no doubt due in no small part to the scrumptious pastries and lunch paninis. Inexpensive.

    ✆ ✳ **Westwood Café** (320-796-5355; westwoodcafe.com), 142 Lake Avenue N., Spicer. Open daily for breakfast and lunch. Solid diner food with lots of flavor. Try the Lake Avenue breakfast (wild rice sausage, green peppers, onion, and Swiss cheese) or the German burger (caramelized onions, grilled sauerkraut, and Swiss cheese). Inexpensive.

## ✳ Special Events

*June*: **Lakes Area Studio Hop** (studiohop.wordpress.com), Willmar. Taking place in mid-June, the Hop allows guests to visit numerous artists in and around the Willmar area, either in their private studios or in local art galleries.

# ALEXANDRIA LAKES

"**E**asy to get to, hard to leave" is the Alexandria Lakes–area motto, and it's an apt one. Alexandria itself has been around for more than 150 years and was named after the town's first postmaster. The abundance of lakes makes it a valued tourist attraction. One of Alexandria's claims to fame is the story of its being the birthplace of windsurfing back in 1960, when Al Seltz and Lewis Whinnery experimented with the then-new technology of fiberboard to see how it would work with pleasure boats and surfboards. Another claim to fame, although one hotly disputed, is that it's the home of the infamous **Kensington Runestone** (see below).

## ✳ To See and Do

MUSEUMS AND HISTORIC SITES ⅙ ✐ ✳ **Runestone Museum** (320-763-3160; runestonemuseum.org), 206 Broadway Street, Alexandria. Open daily in summer; Mon.–Sat. in winter. Adults $8; seniors 65 and older $7; and students $5; a family rate is capped at $20. The highlight of this museum is the highly controversial Kensington Runestone, discovered in 1898 but thought to date back to 1362. The 200-pound stone is carved with runes and, if authentic, would indicate that Scandinavian explorers had arrived in the Midwest far earlier than previously supposed. However, that point is hotly disputed by a variety of experts. Nevertheless, the Runestone Museum is an interesting place to visit, not just for the Runestone itself, but also for an extensive collection of other historical artifacts and a pioneer village.

⅙ ✐ **Minnesota Lakes Maritime Museum** (320-759-1114; legacyofthelakes.org), 205 W. 3rd Avenue, Alexandria. Open daily late May–Oct. Closed holidays. Adults $10; seniors 65 and older $8; active military members, veterans, and students 5–17 $5; and children under 5 free; a family rate is capped at $25. You don't need an ocean to have a maritime museum. This set of exhibits includes numerous rare wooden boats, vintage yachts, and toy boats, and fishing and fishing club memorabilia. There's also an exhibit focused on the history of Minnesota-made boats, as well as one about the extensive resort history of the area. The museum offers many events, including classes and live music, during the summer.

✐ ✳ **Historic Knute and Nicolina Nelson Museum** (320-762-0382; dchsmn.org), 1219 Nokomis Street, Alexandria. Open Mon.–Fri. for guided tours. Admission is $5 for adults; $3 for ages 11 and under. Housed in the former home of statesman Knute Nelson, the DCHS has extensive collection of photos and slides about the communities in the Alexandria Lakes area.

✐ **Sinclair Lewis Boyhood Home** (320-352-5201), 810 Sinclair Lewis Avenue, Sauk Centre. Open Tues.–Sun. Memorial Day–Labor Day. Adults $5; students 6–17 $3.50; children under 6 free. Talk about making lemonade out of lemons. Sinclair Lewis, the Nobel Prize–winning American novelist who skewered Sauk Centre in his novel Main Street, spent his formative years in the home that is now a museum. In spite of—or perhaps because of—the attention, Sauk Centre has guarded Lewis's legacy in this carefully preserved home (a National Historic Landmark), as well as in the Sinclair Lewis Interpretive Center on I-94 coming into town. To cap things off is the annual **Sinclair**

**Lewis Days** (see *Special Events*). Today Lewis's boyhood home is a beautiful piece of nostalgia, whether or not you're a fan of his work. Kids who haven't read his works will enjoy the old-time ambience of the home, including some dangerous (by today's standards) heating methods.

WINERIES ᕙ ❋ **Carlos Creek Winery** (320-846-5443; carloscreekwinery.com), 6693 County Route 34 NW, Alexandria. Open daily. Winery tours, tastings, and, during the summer, plenty of special events. Carlos Creek was Minnesota's first federally designated Viticulture Area.

## ❋ Green Space and Outdoor Activities

GOLF **Geneva Golf Club** (320-762-7089; genevagolfclub.com), 4181 Geneva Golf Club Drive, Alexandria. Geneva Golf Club has a 27-hole championship course designed by Joel Goldstrand, as well as a well-regarded dining room (see *Where to Eat*).

HIKING AND BIKING **Central Lakes Trail** (centrallakestrail.com). This 55-mile paved trail winds from Fergus Falls to Osakis and is open to nonmotorized vehicles in the summer, although snowmobiles are allowed in the winter. There are few road crossings, making this a particularly safe trail for families. The Central Lakes Trail connects in Osakis to the **Lake Wobegone Trail** (see page 201).

PARKS **Rune Stone Park** (320-762-2999; co.douglas.mn.us/Kensington-runestone -park), 8965 County Route 103, Kensington. In conjunction with the **Runestone Museum** (see *To See and Do*) is this park, the former farm of Olaf Ohman, the man who discovered the Kensington Runestone. A memorial marks the spot where he discovered the controversial slab, and other historical buildings have been moved onto the farm for visitors as well. There are picnic shelters, a playground, indoor toilets, and nearly 8 miles of multiuse trails.

## ❋ Lodging

The Alexandria Lakes area has a nice mix of bed-and-breakfasts and resorts of all sizes and amenities.

BED-AND-BREAKFASTS ❋ **Cedar Rose Inn** (320-760-7694; cedarroseinn.com), 422 7th Avenue W., Alexandria. This 1903 beauty is listed on the National Register of Historic Places and resides in what was known as the Silk Stocking District and offers four spacious rooms with private baths, some of which have whirlpool claw-foot tubs. Located near shops and antiquing opportunities. Rates start at $120.

❋ **Lake Le Homme Dieu Bed and Breakfast** (320-846-5875 or 1-800-943-5875; llbedandbreakfast.com), 441 S. Le Homme Dieu Drive NE, Alexandria. On the shores of Lake Le Homme Dieu, this bed-and-breakfast offers easy access to the Central Lakes Trail. There are four rooms with private bath; amenities include an outdoor hot tub and access to the lakeview living room. Children 12 and over are welcome. Rates start at $145.

CABINS ✿ ❀ **Shady Lawn Resort** (320-763-3559; shadylawnresort.net), 1321 S. Darling Drive NW, Alexandria. Open Memorial Day–Labor Day. Eight cabins along Lake Darling, with plenty of children's amenities and fishing options. Rates start at $120.

✐ ((ɪ)) ❋ **Canary Beach Resort** (320-554-2471; canarybeachresort.com), 17405 County Route 28, Villard. Canary Beach has been welcoming visitors since 1920 and offers eight cabins and two larger "dens" along an 800-foot groomed sandy beach. Rates start at $119.

✐ ❋ ⌂ **Brophy Lake Resort** (320-762-8386; brophylakeresort.com), 1532 Brophy Park Road NW, Alexandria. There are 13 cabins here, and they are far more deluxe than usually expected from a small resort. Most of the cabins are on Lake Brophy, but a few are on Mina Creek, which connects to the lake. Rates start at $130.

✐ ❋ **Westridge Shores Resort** (320-886-5434; westridgeshores.com), 6907 MN 114 SW, Alexandria. Eleven cabins on Lake Mary, and ice fishing houses available for rental during the winter. Guests can make appointments (kids, too) to try their hand in the on-site pottery studio. Two-night minimum stay. Rates start at $125.

## ❋ Where to Eat

DINING OUT ✐ ♈ **Geneva Grill** (320-762-7092; genevagolfclub.com), 4181 Geneva Golf Club Drive, Alexandria. Open Mon.–Sat. for lunch and dinner, Sun. for brunch and early dinner during golf season. Located at the **Geneva Golf Club** (see *Green Space and Outdoor Activities*), the grill offers steak, prime rib, walleye, and pasta. Expensive.

♈ ❋ **The Garden Bar on Sixth** (320-759-2277; thegardenbaronsixth.com), 115 6th Avenue E., Alexandria. Open Mon.–Sat. for lunch and dinner. This cozy bar and bistro has dozens of wines by the glass and a solid beer list as well, plus a menu of foods easy to pair with either. Steaks, chicken, seafood, several veggie sautés and salads, and a list of starters

that could be used to create a meal on its own. Moderate/expensive.

♿ ✐ ❋ ♈ **La Ferme** (320-846-0777; lafermemn.net), 613 Broadway Street, Alexandria. Open Tues.–Sat. for lunch, Thurs.–Sat. for dinner. This is a chef-owned farm-to-table restaurant focused on local ingredients whenever possible, which means the menu changes regularly. Items might include grilled chicken, duck breast, pastured beef, and sizable sandwiches. Moderate/expensive.

EATING OUT ✐ ❋ **Jan's Place** (320-763-3877), 612 3rd Avenue W., Alexandria. Open daily for breakfast and lunch. Hearty plated breakfasts; soups and sandwiches at lunchtime. Inexpensive.

♿ ✐ ❋ **Northwoods Café** (320-763-3700; facebook.com/Northwoods-Cafe/100196716711411), 903 3rd Avenue E. Open daily for breakfast and lunch. Classic diner food with enormous, delicious portions, and a friendly staff. Inexpensive.

♿ ✐ ❋ ♈ **Pike & Pint Grill** (320-763-7468; pikeandpint.com), 110 30th Avenue W. Open daily Handcrafted food and regional craft beer, with a gluten-free menu available. Try the hand-pressed burgers or any of the meat options, but don't ignore the extensive seafood menu. Moderate.

♿ ✐ ❋ **The Brass Lantern** (320-763-4818; facebook.com/TheBrassLantern AlexandriaMN), 3015 MN 29. Open daily for breakfast and lunch. Full breakfast menu and a large lunch selection of sandwiches, salads, burgers, home-made soups and chili, and a salad bar. Inexpensive.

♿ ✐ ❋ ♈ **Mi Mexico** (320-759-5686; mimexicoalex.com), 401 N. Nokomis Sreet. Open daily for lunch and dinner. A good mix of authentic and American-ized Mexican dishes to choose from, along with a robust cocktail menu. Inexpensive/moderate.

## ✳ Entertainment

 & ✎ **Theatre L'Homme Dieu** (320-846-3150; tlhd.org), 1875 County Route 120 NE, Alexandria. Open summers only. Tickets start at $25. A local theater that also hosts touring shows, Theatre L'Homme Dieu has been keeping summer visitors and residents alike entertained for 50 years. A mix of comedies, dramas, and musicals make up each season, including such productions as The Church Basement Ladies and a tribute to Glen Campbell. Fridays are Food Truck Fridays, where local food trucks sell food.

## ✳ Special Events

*July*: **Sinclair Lewis Days** (320-352-5201), Sauk Centre. This annual celebration of the life of Sauk Centre's most famous and possibly most contentious former resident occurs in late July. A week of events includes a 5K run, horseshoe and softball tournaments, street dance, live music, and the crowning of Miss Sauk Centre.

# BRAINERD

rguably one of the most popular lake areas in the state, the Brainerd lakes area has undergone a shift over the last several years. The small-town community with a few large resorts and dozens of small mom-and-pop resorts is evolving into a larger-scale resort community, complete with more lodging, restaurant, and off-the-lake entertainment activities. The increased efforts to bring in more traffic year-round have succeeded, and that means the area is perhaps not as restful as some of the other resort areas, particularly around Willmar and Spicer. That said, for visitors wanting a wider variety of options for their vacations, the Brainerd area is hard to beat.

## ✳ To See and Do

FOR FAMILIES ✐ **Pirate's Cove Mini-Golf and Billy Bones Raceway** (218-828-9002; piratescove.net), 17992 MN 371 N., Brainerd. Open daily Memorial Day–Labor Day; weekends (call for hours) from the last weekend in Apr. to the third weekend of Oct. Rates start at $8.95 for adults and $7.95 for children. At this very fun pirate-themed mini golf course, you can play one of the two 18-hole courses, or play both at a discount. Next door is the Billy Bones Raceway, which has three go-cart tracks.

&. ✐ **Paul Bunyan Land and Pioneer Village** (218-764-2524; paulbunyanland .com), 17553 MN 18, Brainerd. Open daily Memorial Day–Labor Day; selected weekends in Oct. and Dec. (for Halloween and Christmas). Ages 3–64 $21.95; seniors 65 and older $18.95; children under 2 free. Part history village, part amusement park, Paul Bunyan Land's attractions include a 26-foot-tall talking Paul Bunyan, amusement rides, and the Pioneer Village, which includes an original log cabin, dentist's office, schoolhouse, and post office.

MUSEUMS AND HISTORIC SITES &. ✐ ✳ **Crow Wing County Historical Museum** (218-829-3268; crowwinghistory.org), 320 Laurel Street, Brainerd. Open Tues.–Sat. Adults $3, children under 12 free. This lively museum used to be the sheriff's office and county jail. Now it houses a wide-ranging collection of historical items detailing the region's lumber, railroad, and mining history, as well as Native American artifacts.

PIRATE'S COVE MINI-GOLF

&#x267F; &#x2133; **Nisswa Pioneer Village** (218-963-3570), Nisswa. Open Wed.–Sat. mid-Jun.–Aug.; weekends May–mid-Jun. Admission is $2. Nisswa Pioneer Village is comprised of nine buildings, including log homes and a schoolhouse, while the old caboose and train depot hold railroad relics. An annual Scandinavian festival attracts large crowds (see *Special Events*).

OTHER ATTRACTIONS &#x267F; &#x2133; **Brainerd International Raceway** (218-824-7223 or 1-866-444-4455; brainerdraceway.com), 5523 Birchdale Road, Brainerd. Races usually start in early May and run until early October. Drag racing and road racing at its finest. Paul Newman was among the racing participants.

&#x267F; &#x2133; **Nisswa Turtle Races**, Nisswa Trailside Information Center, Main Street, Nisswa. No worries about breakneck speeds in these races, held every Wednesday at 2 p.m., rain or shine, in the summer months. They're immensely popular with kids, and participation can rise into the hundreds. If you don't have your own turtle, it's possible to rent one.

NISSWA'S PIONEER VILLAGE

## &#x273B; Green Space and Outdoor Activities

HIKING AND BIKING **Pequot Lakes Fire Tower**, County Route 11, Pequot Lakes. Admission is free. It's definitely not for the faint of heart or weak of knees, but if you'd like a spectacular view of the surrounding forestland, climb this 100-foot tower. The tower itself is not the only climb; the walk from the parking lot is straight uphill as well.

**Paul Bunyan State Trail** (paulbunyantrail.com). Starting at **Paul Bunyan Land** (see *To See and Do*) and ending in **Crow Wing State Park** (see *Parks*), this is the longest bike trail in Minnesota, with 120 paved miles. The Paul Bunyan Trail connects several other state trails and currently ends at **Lake Bemidji State Park** (see page 177). The trail isn't just for bikes, but also for hiking and inline skating. The trail runs parallel to several swimmable lakes, and bike-in campsites are available.

PARKS &#x267F; &#x2740; &#x273B; **Northland Arboretum** (218-829-8770; northlandarb.org), 14250 Conservation Drive, Brainerd. Open daily year-round. Admission $5 adults; $1 per child 12 and under; free for members. Rather incongruously located behind the Westgate Mall in Brainerd, this nature preserve covers 500 acres of forest and prairie that has evolved on the site of a former landfill. The Nature Conservancy owns about 40 percent of the arboretum. There are several miles of hiking and cross-country ski trails.

&#x273B; **Crow Wing State Park** (218-829-8022; dnr.state.mn.us/state_parks/crow_wing /index.html), 3124 State Park Road, Brainerd. Open daily. $7 for a day pass ($35 for

CROW WING STATE PARK

an annual parks pass). Not only a pristine state forest, Crow Wing State Park is also a remnant of the area's past as a fur trading hotbed. The town of Crow Wing flourished during the heyday, but when the railroad decided to pass through Brainerd rather than Crow Wing, the town's fate was sealed. Today the nearly 2,100-acre park has several miles of hiking trails (some of which are groomed for cross-country skiing in the winter) and excellent canoeing opportunities, including a canoe-in campsite. Within the park is the Beaulieu House, the last remaining building from the fur trading days.

# ✳ Lodging

BED-AND-BREAKFASTS ♿ ✎ 🐾 ❄ ♈
**House of Steinarr Nordic Inn Medieval Brew and Bed** (218-839-2900; steinarr .com), 210 1st Avenue NW, Crosby. This bed-and-breakfast works only with groups of 10–12 people. Get truly into the spirit of ancient Minnesota history with a stay at this bed-and-breakfast. Housed in a former Methodist church, the Nordic Inn has five rooms with disparate themes, including Odin's Loft, decorated with armor and weapons, and the Locker Room, decorated with Minnesota Vikings football fans in mind. Breakfast is included in the room rates. The whole-house rate is $2,000 for two nights, including two breakfasts and one dinner.

RESORTS ♿ ✎ 🛜 ✎ ❄ ♈ ❚❙ ⚲ **Cragun's Resort** (1-866-988-0562; craguns.com), 11000 Craguns Drive, Brainerd. This is one of Minnesota's biggest resorts, and it's also one of the nicest. Besides the well-appointed rooms, cabins, and reunion houses, the resort has a 22,000-square-foot indoor sports complex with tennis and basketball courts, a running track, and fitness center. The hotel itself has an indoor pool. A full-service spa is on-site. There are three restaurants that are open year-round, plus two more open in the summer.

# A TRADITIONAL FAMILY ESCAPE

**M**adden's, one of the state's largest and nicest resorts, comes with a nice bit of history. The resort's roots rest in the need of early 20th-century residents of St. Louis and Kansas City to seek refuge from terribly hot summers (there being no air-conditioning then) by escaping north. The early days were a bit rough-and-tumble, with the resort's then-remote location offering perfect hideaways from 1920s gangsters and Prohibition scofflaws. But Madden's survived to become a highly respected resort of the Dirty Dancing variety, with families spending weeks of their summers there. Today, the sophisticated complex has everything from rustic hotel rooms to cabins, deluxe golf villas, and reunion houses. Three 18-hole golf courses are on the property, along with one nine-hole social course. Fishing, boating, hiking, swimming, croquet, and tennis are all offered, as are trapshooting (with one week's notice) and sea plane certification. A full-service spa is on-site, and a kids' program, Adventure Cove, is offered from June to mid-August for kids 4–12. There are eight restaurants, three fine dining and five casual. The amenities are attractive enough to keep some of those Kansas City and St. Louis guests, some of which are fourth generation, returning year after year.

Madden's (218-829-2811 or 1-800-642-5363; maddens.com), 11266 Pine Beach Peninsula, Brainerd. Open late Apr.–late Oct. Rates start at $141. Packages are available. ✪ ♿ ✒ ⚭ ((•)) ☕ 🍴

GOLFING AT MADDEN'S

Fifty-four holes of golf will keep golfers happy, while boaters and anglers have direct access to Gull Lake. (Note: Cragun's does not allow personal watercraft, or Jet Skis, to be stored or launched from their property.) Bikes can be rented, and snowmobiles can be hired during the winter. Rates start at $139. Packages and off-season discounts are available.

✪ ♿ ✿ ☛ (ᵖ) ❋ ☂ ¶ ℱ **Grand View Lodge** (218-963-2234 or 1-866-801-2951; grandviewlodge.com), 23521 Nokomis Avenue, Nisswa. Grand View hearkens back to the grand old days of lake resorts. Built in 1919, this venerable resort has maintained its historic elegance while modernizing with the amenities today's resort travelers want. The resort offers lodge rooms, cabins, and suites, and villas on the property's golf course. An indoor pool and water slide share a building with a fitness center, but in good weather swimming is done at the sandy beach. Boats can be rented,

as can bikes and horses for riding. There are three 18-hole golf courses and one nine-hole course. The full-service spa is open year-round, as are the resort's restaurants. A Kids' Club for ages 3–11 gives parents a break. Rates start at $130. Packages and off-season discounts are available.

♿ ☛ ❋ (ᵖ) ☛ ☂ ¶ ℱ **Breezy Point Resort** (1-800-432-3777; breezypointresort.com), 9252 Breezy Point Drive, Breezy Point. Located on Pelican Lake, this resort has a huge variety of accommodations to choose from—lodge rooms, one- and two-bedroom apartments, and a series of lodgings called Unique Retreats (log cabins, A-frame cabins, and full houses). The largest has 10 bedrooms and can accommodate 18 people. For recreation, there are three 18-hole golf courses, an indoor pool, and an extensive sandy beach with boat rentals. The summer months bring live musical performances. Winter brings a new round of activity,

GRAND VIEW LODGE

including a nine-hole golf course set up directly on the frozen lake, skating rinks, cross-country skiing (equipment available for rental), and a snow tubing hill adjacent to the resort. The Serenity Spa offers full-service spa services. The resort has two full-service dining areas, the most attractive of which is the Antlers Dining Room, which was built with post-and-beam construction and features two large antler chandeliers. The resort also has a coffee shop and a restaurant exclusively for large groups. Rates start at $149. Packages and specials are available.

    &#9855; &#9998; (&#8226;) &#89; &#127869; **Lost Lake Lodge** (218-963-2681; lostlake.site), 7965 Lost Lake Road, Lakeshore. Open mid-May–early Oct. This small but lovely resort has beautifully outfitted cabins in a quiet, tucked-away location on Lost Lake. Rates are all-inclusive, meaning daily full breakfast and four-course dinner are included in the rates, and the food is well worth it. (Dinner is available to the public; see *Where to Eat*.) The use of canoes, fishing boats, and bikes are also included in the rates, and fishing guides as well as massage therapists can be hired at an additional fee. Rates start at $250. Packages and specials are available.

    &#9855; &#9998; &#10052; **Train Bell Resort** (218-829-4841 or 1-800-252-2102; trainbellresort .com), 21489 Train Bell Road, Merrifield. North of Brainerd on North Long Lake, Train Bell Resort is owned and operated by Mike and Connie Bruesch, who left corporate life to run this family-friendly resort. There are several well-maintained lakeside cabins as well as a condo complex and a lake house, but the resort still keeps its cozy feeling, assisted by weekly activities such as a pancake breakfasts, minnow races, and Friday night dances. Fishing boats are available for rental, and use of the kayaks and paddleboats at the sandy beach are included in the rates. Rates start at $235. Packages and specials are available.

    &#9855; &#9998; (&#8226;) &#10052; **Campfire Bay Resort** (218-575-2432; campfirebayresort.com),

31504 Azure Road, Cushing. Located on beautiful Fish Trap Lake, Campfire Bay Resort has 16 one- to four-bedroom cabins, all fully equipped with household items. During summer weekends there are special family activities such as Nature Day, woodworking, and ice cream socials. Rates start at $182. Packages and specials are available.

    &#9998; (&#8226;) **Pine Terrace Resort** (218-543-4606; pineterrace.com), 35101 Pine Terrace Road, Crosslake. Open May–Oct. Pine Terrace is the only resort on Star Lake, and it offers 13 cabins with lake views and 34 acres of grounds, including nature trails. Most of the cabins have one or two bedrooms, with one larger building housing seven bedrooms. Rates start at $145. Packages are available.

    &#9998; &#10052; (&#8226;) **Black Pine Beach Resort** (218-543-4714; blackpinebeach.com), 10732 County Route 16, Pequot Lakes. The resort, with 13 lake cottages, all with kitchens and fireplaces, also has its very own Secret Garden, complete with an elfin mailbox young visitors can deliver letters to. Rates start at $200.

## &#10051; Where to Eat

DINING OUT &#9855; &#9998; &#10052; &#89; **Prairie Bay Grill** (218-824-6444; prairiebay.3cheersmn .com), 15115 Edgewood Drive N., Baxter. Open daily for lunch and dinner. Wood-fired pizza, sandwiches, and entrées including rib eye and lobster ravioli, served in a casual yet upscale environment. Kids are welcome, as are vegetarians, who have several options on the menu. Expensive.

    &#9855; &#9998; &#10052; &#89; **Black Bear Lodge and Saloon** (218-828-8400; blackbearlodgemn .com), 14819 Edgewood Drive N., Baxter. Open daily for lunch and dinner, Sun. for brunch. Standard bar and grill fare, including sandwiches and burgers, steaks, and seafood. Expensive.

    &#89; &#10052; **The Classic Grill** (1-800-642-5363; maddens.com), 11266 Pine Beach Peninsula, Brainerd. Even though

**Madden's Resort** (see "A Traditional Family Escape" on page 219) is only open part of the year, this stand-alone restaurant is open daily year-round for lunch and dinner. The dining room overlooks one of the resort's golf courses, and large stone patios with patio heaters stretch the outdoor season as long as possible. The food is upscale and gourmet, with seasonal touches on the menu. Offerings may include steak, lamb, walleye, Sicilian Corvina, and a daily risotto. Expensive/very expensive.

    ♿ ✎ ⓨ **Lost Lake Lodge** (218-963-2681 or 1-800-450-2681; lostlake.com), 7965 Lost Lake Road, Lakeshore. Open daily for dinner, Memorial Day–Labor Day; weekends for dinner the rest of the year. One of the best fine-dining options in the Brainerd lakes area, Lost Lake Lodge takes food staples such as walleye and chicken and turns them into unexpected and delicious offerings. Expensive.

EATING OUT ♿ ✎ ✳ **371 Diner** (218-829-3356), 14901 Edgewood Drive N., Brainerd. Open daily for all three meals. Located on US 371 through Brainerd, the 371 is a replica of a 1950s diner and has a respectable (if high-calorie) menu of burgers, sandwiches, and ice cream treats. Kids get their meals served in a cardboard race car. Inexpensive.

THE 371 DINER

♿ ✎ ✳ **Sawmill Inn** (218-829-5444; sawmillinnbrainerd.com), 601 Washington Street, Brainerd. Open Mon.–Sat. for all three meals, Sun. for breakfast and lunch. It doesn't look like much on the outside, but the Sawmill is the classic small-town café, complete with huge breakfasts and hearty sandwiches. Inexpensive.

    ♿ ✎ ✳ ⓨ **Zorbaz on the Lake** (218-963-4790; zorbaz.com), 8105 Lost Lake Road, Lake Shore. Open daily for lunch and dinner in the summer; daily for dinner, weekends for lunch the rest of the year. This is a beach bar with Mexican food, pizza, pasta, and plenty of beer, not to mention a groaningly silly menu. Take the kids for the arcade. A dock is provided for diners arriving by boat. Moderate.

## ✳ Selective Shopping

ANTIQUES  Just north of Brainerd on MN 371, Pequot Lakes has some browseworthy antiques shops. If you'd like to explore a little more in the antiques realm, you might want to detour slightly here and go a few miles north on MN 371 to Jenkins, a very small town, but with a crowded antiques store right on the highway.

    ✳ **The Flour Sack Antiques Shop** (218-568-5658), 4464 County Road 168. Hours change seasonally, so call to confirm.

    ✳ **Castoffs** (218-568-6155; facebook.com/vintagefunstore), 4242 Jokela Drive. Open daily.

    ✳ **Treasures 'n' Tiques** (218-820-7931), 34008 MN 371, Jenkins. Open Wed.–Mon.

    ✳ **Finders Keepers Depot** (218-851-3602), 3285 Veterans Street, Jenkins. Open Wed.–Sun.

    ✳ **Annie's Attic** (218-568-5225; facebook.com/anniesattic371), 34010 2nd Avenue, Jenkins. Open Wed.–Sun.

BOOKS ✎ ✳ **Cat Tale's Books and Gifts** (218-825-8611; cattalesbooks.com), 609

# NISSWA SQUARE SHOPPING

The little town of Nisswa, just north of Brainerd on MN 371, has become a central shopping spot with several small but fun shops, especially in the Nisswa Square complex along the highway.

**Turtle Town Books & Gifts** (218-963-4891; turtletownnisswa.com), 25491 Main Street. Open daily. This is a bookseller for book lovers, with a wide range of reading material for grown-ups and for kids. ✎ ❋

**Rebecca's Dolls and Miniatures** (218-963-0165; rebeccasnisswa.com), 25458 Main Street. Open daily May–Oct. Dolls and dollhouses and accessories, movie memorabilia, miniatures, and shadow boxes. ✎

**Fun Sisters** (218-961-0071; funsisters.com/Nisswa), 5380 Merril Avenue. Open daily May–Dec.; Fri.–Sun. from Jan.–Apr. Fun, reasonably prices women's clothing and accessories. ✎ ❋

**Lundrigan's Clothing** (218-963-2647; lundrigansclothing.com), 25521 Main Street. Open daily mid-May–Dec.; Mon.–Sat. Jan.–mid-May. High-quality, durable men's and women's clothing, with an outdoor focus. ✎ ❋

**Simpler Thymes of Nisswa** (218-963-9463), 25410 Main Street. Open daily Memorial Day–Labor Day; limited hours Apr., May, Sept., and Oct. Gift shop focused on personal luxuries, including lotions and soaps, candles, gourmet foods (many locally produced), robes, and women's accessories.

**The Chocolate Ox** (218-963-4443; chocolateox.com), 25425 Main Street. Open daily Apr.–Jan. Gourmet truffles, an extensive collection of licorice and saltwater taffies, and a huge variety of vintage candies—it's a place kids and adults can enjoy together. Don't forget to visit the ice cream parlor in the back. ✎

THE CHOCOLATE OX

Laurel Street, Brainerd. Open Mon.–Sat. A browser-friendly shop full of new and used books as well as cards, jewelry, and other gifts.

WOMEN'S CLOTHING ❄ **Among the Pines** (218-828-6364; amongthepines .com), 15670 Edgewood Drive N., Baxter. Open Mon.–Sat. Gifts and women's and children's clothing.

# ❄ Special Events

*January*: **Brainerd Jaycees Ice Fishing Extravaganza** (icefishing.org), Brainerd. This annual fishing tournament takes place in late January. Significant prizes, including ATVs and underwater cameras, are offered; competitors must purchase tickets, with the proceeds going to charity.

*June*: **Granite City Days** (stcloud granitecitydays.com). Each year in late June, St. Cloud celebrates its quarrying history with a multiday festival featuring an art fair, 5K, talent show, canoe rides, fishing derby, and plenty of live music and food.

**Nisswa-Stämman Festival** (nisswa stamman.org), Nisswa. This popular annual festival takes place in early June

and features Scandinavian folk music, including traditional Scandinavian musical instruments. There are several live performances, dances, kids' activities, and classes and workshops.

**Tour of Lakes Bicycle Ride** (218-833-8122; paulbunyancyclists.com), Brainerd. This annual ride, held in early June, is not a race, but a way to use a bicycle to take in the spectacular scenery around the Central Lakes area. There are two routes each year, although the routes change every year to maximize scenery possibilities. Preregistration is recommended.

*July*: **Bean Hole Days** (218-568-8911), Trailside Park, Pequot Lakes. This two-day event draws on the traditional cooking of baked beans by burying them in large kettles for 24 hours, then raising them back up for the impatient consumers. A craft fair and Bean Hole Days coronation ceremony help make the waiting easier.

*November*: **Fish House Parade, Aitkin**. The day after Thanksgiving marks not only the official start of the holiday retail season, but to this annual rite of passage into winter. Participants parade their fish houses, usually decorated to the hilt in what appears to be a one-upmanship show of hilarity.

# ST. CROIX VALLEY

UPPER ST. CROIX

LOWER ST. CROIX

# ST. CROIX VALLEY

This small but highly scenic region derives its beauty from the St. Croix River and the surrounding landscapes, as well as the wealthy New England families who settled here more than a century ago, re-creating their home villages along the riverside, small towns that remain intact and as charming and historic as they were when they were first built. Along with the New Englanders came the Scandinavians, building tight agricultural and cultural enclaves, and today there is still a close-knit community known informally as Little Sweden. Going up the river can provide insight into some of Minnesota's Scandinavian heritage. Logging and the fur trade drove the growth of the area during the 19th century, and today's visitors can still find remnants of those trades, primarily in placenames, but also in the quaint, wonderful small towns. Artists have not been immune to the area's beauty, and there is a strong and growing arts community throughout the valley.

GUIDANCE **Falls Chamber of Commerce** (715-483-3580; fallschamber.org), St. Croix Falls, WI. Open Mon.–Thurs. Provides visitor info for Taylors Falls in Minnesota and St. Croix Falls in Wisconsin.

THE STILLWATER LIFT BRIDGE

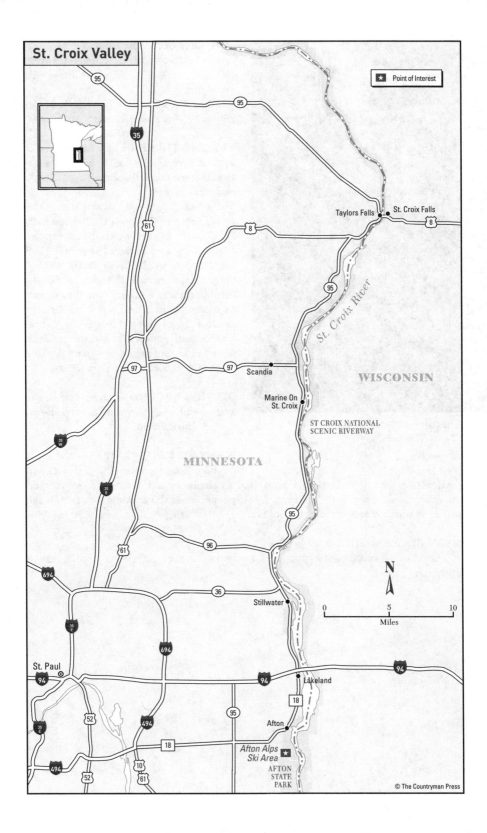

St. Croix Valley

Point of Interest

Taylors Falls · St. Croix Falls

St. Croix River

WISCONSIN

Scandia

Marine On
St. Croix

ST CROIX NATIONAL
SCENIC RIVERWAY

MINNESOTA

N

0          5          10
Miles

Stillwater

St. Paul

Lakeland

Afton

Afton Alps
Ski Area ★

AFTON
STATE
PARK

© The Countryman Press

INTERSTATE STATE PARK

**Greater Stillwater Chamber of Commerce** (651-439-4001; greaterstillwater chamber.com), 200 Chestnut Street E., Stillwater.

**Afton Area Business Association** (701-269-4639; exploreafton.com), Afton.

GETTING THERE **By air:** Air service is available through the **Minneapolis–St. Paul International Airport** (612-726-5555; mspairport.com).

**By car:** From the Twin Cities, take I-35W north to US 8 east to Chisago City. Follow US 8 east through Lindstrom, Center City, and Taylors Falls. Take US 8 south to MN 95 (St. Croix Trail) to reach Franconia. Continue on MN 95 to MN 97, turning right to arrive in Scandia. Return to MN 95 and travel south to County Route 4 (Maple Street) to stop in Marine on St. Croix. Follow MN 95 south to Stillwater. From Stillwater, you can take MN 96 or MN 36 back to the Twin Cities.

GETTING AROUND Having a vehicle is a necessity when traveling around the St. Croix Valley region.

WHEN TO COME Summer is the most popular time to visit, and Stillwater in particular can be quite busy and congested as shoppers and boaters converge upon the quaint little town. Fall is busy with leaf-peepers, but the area quiets down in the winter as traffic involves mostly shoppers.

MEDICAL EMERGENCY Call 911.

Lakeview Hospital (651-439-5330; lakeviewhealth.org), 927 W. Churchill Street, Stillwater.

# UPPER ST. CROIX

The upper St. Croix Valley, from Marine on St. Croix up toward Hinckley, is full of natural beauty, from rivers to woodlands to prairies to glacial trails, and is a park lover's dream region. Some of Minnesota's most beautiful state parks are in this area, running along the river and offering nearly every kind of recreational opportunity, including swimming, canoeing, hiking, camping, horseback riding, cross-country skiing, and snowshoeing. The little village of Marine on St. Croix is peaceful and picturesque, and the river town of Taylors Falls has an area (the Angel Hill District) that could have been lifted right out of a New England portrait. Scandinavian culture is alive and well in Scandia and in the series of little towns known as Little Sweden, and the region's popularity with artists is demonstrated in Franconia.

## ✳ To See and Do

Inland from the river, in an area heavily populated with lakes and farmland, is a part of the state known as America's Little Sweden. A series of small towns—including Chisago City, Lindstrom, and Center City—settled by Swedish (and other Scandinavian) immigrants, Little Sweden is a place you can still hear faint traces of Swedish accents

THE FOLSOM HOUSE

## VILHELM MOBERG

Vilhelm Moberg, a Swedish author and historian, was best known for The Emigrant novels, fictional accounts of a Swedish family's journey to Chisago County to build a new life against harsh odds. Moberg spent time in this true-life Swedish American community in 1948 to research his series, and they have not forgotten him. Chisago City has Vilhelm Moberg Park, which includes a statue of Moberg and his bicycle, which he was famous for riding about the town. Lindstrom has a statue of Karl Oskar and Kristina, a fictional couple featured in The Emigrant series (in fact, they're also represented on Lindstrom's city logo), and south of Lindstrom is Kichi-Saga Park, the site of Nya Duvemåla, the house Moberg used as a model for Karl Oskar and Kristina's fictional home. A boulder in front of the house was donated by Volvo from Åseda, Sweden. Today, Karl Oskar Days are celebrated every summer (see *Special Events*).

THE KARL OSKAR HOUSE

in the residents and are likely to see store and street signs in both English and Swedish. Most of these communities have active relationships with sister cities in Sweden, and the food and culture still strongly reflect that ancestry.

MUSEUMS AND HISTORIC SITES **Chisago County History Center** (651-257-9585; chisagocountyhistory.org), 12795 Lake Boulevard, Lindstrom. This county historical society is caretaker to several historical properties, and visits can be arranged by contacting the center. The society itself recently opened its own museum in Chisago City, which is open Mon., Tues., and Thurs.–Sat. in the summer and Mon., Tues., Fri., and Sat. in the winter. The Moody Round Barn, Gustaf Anderson House, and the Delmore-Fransen Log House are part of the collection, as well as the Polish Shtetl House, a replica built and used during the filming of the Coen brothers' film *A Serious Man*.

✳ **Chisago Lake Evangelical Lutheran Church** (651-257-6300; facebook.com/chisagolakelutheran), 1 Summit Avenue, Center City. This is the oldest continuously operating church in the area. It opened in 1854 and has been in its current building since 1889.

❋ **Center City Historic District**, Summit Avenue, Center City. Original homes of the Swedish pioneers can be seen along Summit Avenue, which has numerous homes of first- and second-generation families, built in period style.

🖉 **Folsom House** (651-465-3125; mnhs.org/folsomhouse), 272 W. Government Street, Taylors Falls. Open Fri.–Sun., Memorial Day weekend–mid-Oct. Adults $6; seniors 65 and older, active military members and veterans, and college students $5; children 5–17 $4; children under 5 and Minnesota Historical Society members free. This charming home looks like it was plucked out of a New England landscape, along with several of its neighbors, and replanted in the Angel Hill District of Taylors Falls. Home of a lumber baron and state senator, the Folsom House gives a view of Minnesota's early days—and of the St. Croix River. Check the website for events; the house has hosted traveling theater groups performing Chekhov dramas on-site.

🖉 ❋ **Angel Hill District**, Taylors Falls. Just up the hill from the Folsom House is a historic residential district known as Angel Hill. Many of Taylors Falls's early wealthy settlers built here, and the homes have been beautifully maintained. A stroll before or after a Folsom House tour will give visitors a strong sense of the historical roots of the area.

**Stone House Museum** (651-433-3636; facebook.com/Stone-House-Museum), 241 5th Street, Marine on St. Croix. Open Sat. and Sun. Memorial Day–Labor Day. Admission is free, but donations are requested. This historic Scandinavian site is tucked into the small, picturesque town of Marine on St. Croix. The Stone House, aptly named for its Scandinavian stone architecture, was originally the town meetinghouse. Today it's

THE GROUNDS AT GAMMELGÅRDEN

a repository for artifacts and photographs documenting the Scandinavian settlers who arrived in the early 19th century.

✔ **Gammelgården** (651-433-5053; gammelgardenmuseum.org), 20880 Olinda Trail N., Scandia. The historic log buildings are open Fri–Sun. from May 1–mid-Oct.; the main exhibit space and gift shop are open daily May–Dec. Special events are offered throughout the year. Adults $7; children under 12 free. Gammelgården is a living-history museum paying tribute to the Scandinavian roots of the region. Several original immigrant homes and other buildings, including a church, have been restored on 11 acres of farmland. The site is open for public tours during the summer, but year-round the museum offers a vast array of special events and classes (see website for details), including music festivals, sausage-making classes, and an annual **Midsommar Dag (Midsummer Day) celebration** (see *Special Events*). On a sunny summer day, it's worth a visit just to stroll the beautiful grounds.

✔ **Hay Lake School and Erickson Log Home** (651-433-4014; wchsmn.org/museums/hay-lake), 14020 195th Street N., Marine on St. Croix. Open Fri.–Sun. Jun.–Aug.; Sat. and Sun. May, Sept., and Oct. Adults $5; children 17 and under $1; Washington County Historical Society members free. If Gammelgården isn't enough history for you, check out the nearby Hay Lake School Museum. Listed on the National Register of Historic Places, this museum is made up of a former schoolhouse and a log home built in the late 1800s.

WINERIES ❄ **Winehaven Winery and Vineyard** (651-257-1017; winehaven.com), 10020 Deer Garden Lane, Chisago City. Open daily. At this award-winning vineyard, take a tour, learn about viticulture, and sample the specialty: Stinger Honeywine (mead).

OTHER ATTRACTIONS ❄ **Lindstrom Water Tower**, 12849 N. 1st Avenue, Lindstrom. It's not just a water tower—it's a coffeepot-shaped water tower with rosemaling designs welcoming visitors.

## ❄ Green Space and Outdoor Activities

There are lakes in this area, but the primary source of outdoor recreation in the St. Croix Valley rests along the riverbanks.

CANOEING **St. Croix National Scenic Riverway** (715-483-2274; nps.gov/sacn). This is what the region is all about—252 miles of lush river scenery, starting in Wisconsin and including both the St. Croix River and the Namekagon River. The headquarters for information is the St. Croix Visitor Center in St. Croix Falls,

ANTIQUE SCANDINAVIAN CUPBOARD AT GAMMELGÅRDEN

Wisconsin, which is just across the river from Taylors Falls. Where the St. Croix ambles south along the Minnesota border, canoeing and camping are popular activities, but check with the visitor center before making plans—there are restrictions regarding use of campsites and boats to protect the river itself and the land on either side of it. In times of low rainfall, fire restrictions are strictly enforced.

THE HISTORIC LINDSTROM WATER TOWER

PARKS **Franconia Sculpture Park** (651-257-6668; franconia.org), US 8 and MN 95, Franconia. Open daily. Admission is free. The Franconia Sculpture Park is, intentionally, a work in progress. There are more than 120 exhibits in this rural exhibition area, and each year somewhere between 15 and 25 artists are invited to work and contribute art on a rotating basis. There are concerts in the summer, as well as hands-on classes for kids. The artworks are spread across a field with flat mowed paths; self-guided tours and guided tours are offered.

TAYLORS FALLS' ANGEL HILL DISTRICT

VILHELM MOBERG STATUE

**Wild River State Park** (651-583-2125; dnr.state.mn.us/state_parks/wild_river/index.html), 39797 Park Trail, Center City. Open daily. $7 for a day pass ($35 for an annual parks pass). Thirty-five miles of hiking and cross-country ski trails, guesthouse and camping within the park, and 18 miles of riverside beauty make this park a gem. There are also campsites for visitors with horses. Spring provides some of the most beautiful wildflower displays in the state. For those with GPS units and an itch to explore, the afore-mentioned Minnesota DNR site provides coordinates for historical searches within the park.

**William O'Brien State Park** (651-539-4980; dnr.state.mn.us/state_parks/william_obrien/index.html), 16821 N. O'Brien Trail, Marine on St. Croix. Open daily. $7 for a day pass ($35 for an annual parks pass). This small but lovely park is just north of Marine on St. Croix. Named after a lumber baron who had originally cleared the land of trees, the park is now (more than a century later) reforested and full of wildlife and river access. It's open year-round

WILLIAM O'BRIEN STATE PARK

# ST. CROIX STATE PARK

S t. Croix State Park (320-384-6591; dnr.state.mn.us/state_parks/st_croix/index.html), 30065 St. Croix Park Road, Hinckley. Open daily. The state's largest state park was built as a Civilian Conservation Corps (CCC) project during the Depression years. More than 34,000 acres of former farmland has been redeveloped into open parkland, and the buildings built by the CCC helped lead to the park's designation as a National Historic Landmark.

But besides the history, recreational opportunities abound. In addition to the St. Croix River, the park also has the Kettle River, the first State Wild and Scenic River. There are 100 miles of trails for hiking, some of which are open to horseback riders and mountain bikers, and during the summer visitors can rent bikes at the Adventure St. Croix Store by the campground. A swimming beach is available, and canoers and kayakers can launch on the river of their choice. Splendid views are available by climbing the park's 100-foot fire tower, or spend some time in the company of your fishing pole. A six-bedroom guesthouse, cabins, and rustic campsites can be reserved in advance (the guesthouse is open year-round). During the winter, trails are groomed for cross-country skiers and snowmobilers.

and offers trails for cross-country skiing and snowshoeing, as well as campsites with electricity for winter camping. There's a swimming beach in the summer with a large picnic area adjacent, and canoeing on the river is made possible by rentals in the park. Canoe shuttle service is offered during summer. Birdwatchers can spot hundreds of different birds. The visitor center has a seasonal checklist of what might be seen, from the more commonly found Canada goose and northern flicker to the uncommon (but still possible!) great blue heron, ruffed grouse, and scarlet tanager.

SKIING **Wild Mountain & Taylors Falls Recreation** (651-465-6315; wildmountain .com), 37200 Wild Mountain Road, Taylors Falls. Wild Mountain takes advantage of the rolling terrain in the river area to run 25 ski and boarding runs during the winter, along with a snow-tubing course. During the summer, the "recreation" part of the company offers a water park with alpine slide and go-cart tracks, as well as public and private charter river cruises, canoe and kayak rental, and an RV park and campground.

## ✳ Lodging

The upper St. Croix Valley has been compared to quaint New England villages, so it's fitting that there are some charming, historic bed-and-breakfasts in the area.

✳ (((•))) **The Old Jail** (651-900-1694; oldjail .com), 349 Government Street W., Taylors Falls. Two suites are offered, one in a former jail cell, the other in part of a cave originally used to store beer for a saloon. Despite its gruesome history, the suites are lovely, all including private bath, some including old-fashioned record players, one including a bathroom in a cave, and one not recommended for people over 6 feet tall. Rates include breakfast at a nearby restaurant. Rates start at $150.

✳ **Women's Environmental Institute at Amador Hill** (651-583-0705; w-e-i.org), 15715 River Road, North Branch. Located in an organic apple orchard on the edge of Wild River State Park, the WEI offers four rooms for guests or groups. Two of the rooms share a bath, and the largest room has a fireplace. The rooms are simple but attractive; it's the location that makes this a worthwhile getaway. Rates start at $75.

## ✳ Where to Eat

DINING OUT ♿ ✎ ✳ ⊻ **Tangled Up in Blue** (651-465-1000; tangledupinblue

# GLACIAL POTHOLES?

Interstate State Park is located on US 8 just at the entrance of Taylors Falls. The park's name reflects its cross-river location, with the park stretching from Minnesota to Wisconsin. River access makes kayaking and canoeing popular, and interesting geological formations, including exposed lava flows and glacial deposits, make this an intriguing area for exploration. Of particular interest are the glacial potholes, immense holes (the deepest one is 60 feet) made in the bedrock when the Glacial St. Croix River forced its way through. Interstate State Park has more of these glacial potholes in one area than any other place in the world. Rock climbing is popular, and during the fall, the autumn colors provide a major draw. Interstate State Park (651-465-5711; dnr.state.mn.us/state_parks/interstate/index.html), 307 Milltown Road, Taylors Falls. Open daily. $7 for a day pass ($35 for an annual parks pass).

restaurant.net), 425 Bench Street, Taylors Falls. Open Fri. and Sat. for dinner, Thurs. and Sun. on occasion (call for specifics). A French fusion restaurant with upscale fare and a good wine list. Try the Coubulliac of salmon, and don't forget the Bananas Foster for dessert. Expensive.

EATING OUT ✐ ❄ **Swedish Inn** (651-257-2571; facebook.com/Swedish-Inn-115562678470817), 12678 Lake Boulevard, Lindstrom. Open daily for breakfast and lunch, Tues.–Fri. for dinner. Get your Swedish on here, especially with the breakfast foods—Swedish pancakes, anyone? Inexpensive.

TRADITIONAL PAINTED FLOWERBOX IN LINDSTROM

❄ **Lindstrom Bakery** (651-257-1374; facebook.com/Lindstrom-Bakery-Inc-120703007945281), 12830 Lake Boulevard, Lindstrom. Open Mon.–Sat. All the baked goods are worthwhile (and some are organic), but what you really want is a Scandinavian doughnut, crunchy on the outside, soft on the inside. Inexpensive.

& ✆ ❄ ⛾ **Eichten's Market** (651-257-1566; eichtensmarket.com), 16440 Lake Boulevard, Center City. Open daily. Eichten's, a purveyor of locally farmed meats and locally produced cheese, serves salads, sandwiches, and home-baked pies. Inexpensive/moderate.

& ✆ **The Drive In** (651-465-7831; taylorsfallsdrivein.com), 572 Bench Street, Taylors Falls. Open daily for lunch and dinner, mid-Apr.–mid-Oct. It's retro, it's got a giant rotating root-beer cup on a stick, and its burgers and malts are served to your vehicle by carhops. Oh, and there's mini golf. Inexpensive.

EICHTEN'S MARKET

## ❋ Special Events

*June*: **Midsommar Dag** (651-433-5053; gammelgardenmuseum.org/events), Scandia. Held each year in late June at the **Gammelgården Museum** (see *To See and Do*), Midsommar Dag is a celebration of the community's Scandinavian heritage. The traditional raising of the maypole is accompanied by food, music, and dancing in traditional costumes.

*July*: **Karl Oskar Days** (651-257-7648; cityoflindstrom.us/parks-KOD.htm), Lindstrom. The annual celebration of Vilhelm Moberg's fictional Swedish immigrant couple is the county's largest festival and includes a Taste of Sweden, arts and crafts, a parade, live entertainment, and a street dance.

*August*: **Spelmansstamma Music Festival** (651-433-5053; gammelgarden museum.org/events), Scandia. Held each year at the **Gammelgården Museum** (see *To See and Do*), the Spelmansstamma Music Festival provides a variety of traditional Scandinavian folk music, with a Swedish smorgasbord, craft fair, and children's activities.

THE DRIVE IN

# LOWER ST. CROIX

Stillwater is the central attraction on the lower part of the St. Croix Valley. Calling itself the Birthplace of Minnesota, it's one of the oldest cities in the state, built by lumber barons and transplanted New Englanders. Like any town that suffers the loss of its primary industry, Stillwater went through its slump in the early 20th century. But the natural beauty surrounding the area combined with the charm of the downtown streets and buildings drove a renaissance that has created thriving shops and galleries and a busy tourist trade, particularly on summer weekends, when driving down Main Street can require patience and time.

But the payoff is in the ability to stop, shop, wander along the river and watch the Stillwater Lift Bridge operate, see the sailboats and yachts dotting the water, and have almost more choices of places to dine than seems reasonable. Whether wandering on your own for a private retreat, as part of a couple's romantic getaway, or with a family, Stillwater is a lovely place to spend a day or two. Add in the recreation and dining options south of Stillwater, and the stay could be longer.

HISTORIC STILLWATER

## ✤ To See and Do

⚓ **Warden's House Museum** (651-439-5956; wchsmn.org/museums/wardens-house-museum), 602 Main Street N., Stillwater. Open Thurs.–Sun. from May–Oct. Adults $5; children 17 and younger $1; Washington County Historical Society members free. The Warden's House was built in 1853 and used as a residence for prison wardens and superintendents until 1941, when the building was sold to the Washington County Historical Society. Several of the rooms are furnished as they would have been in the late 19th century, while a few rooms are reserved for displays relevant to the region's overall history, including the lumber industry and children's items.

## ✤ Green Space and Outdoor Activities

ST. CROIX RIVER AT INTERSTATE STATE PARK

PARKS **Afton State Park** (651-436-5391; dnr.state.mn.us/state_parks/afton/index .html), Afton. Open daily. $7 day pass ($35 for an annual parks pass). A beautiful nature preserve that provides a strenuous workout for visitors. There are 20 miles of hiking trails, most of which have some sharply steep inclines. However, the views of the St. Croix River make it worth the effort. One area allows horseback riders, and several miles of trail are open for cross-country skiers in the winter. Year-round camping is available.

SKIING **Afton Alps** (651-436-1320; aftonalps.com), 6600 Peller Avenue S., Hastings. This is one of the biggest Minnesota ski resorts, with 40 trails and 18 lifts, a snowboard park, and a tubing hill. During the summer, the resort is open for mountain bikers, and an 18-hole course is available for golfers.

TOURS **St. Croix Boat & Packet Company** (651-430-1234; stillwaterriverboats.com), 525 Main Street S., Stillwater. Open May–mid-Oct. Cruise the St. Croix River on your choice of a lunch, dinner, brunch, or live-music cruise. Boats are also available for private charter. Reservations are recommended.

**Stillwater Trolley Co.** (651-430-0352; stillwatertrolley.com), 400 Nelson Street E., Stillwater. The historic Stillwater trolleys take visitors on tours through the beautiful river city Jun.–Oct. The base historic tour is $13.50 for adults; $12.50 for military members and seniors over 62; and $7.50 for children 4–17. Note that the tours are not recommended for ages 3 and under. There's also a weekly storytime trolley running from The Valley Bookseller, and the company also books kayak tours.

# HOT-AIR BALLOONING

Given the beautiful scenery and the charming small towns, it's only logical that hot-air balloon rides would be a popular pastime in the lower St. Croix Valley. The following companies all offer hot-air balloon service daily May to October, weather permitting. Contact the individual companies for off-season possibilities.

**Stillwater Balloons** (651-439-1800; stillwaterballoons.com), 135 N. St. Croix Trail, Lakeland. Morning or late-afternoon departures are offered during the summer, but balloon rides (dependent on weather) can be done all year long, and all flights conclude with a champagne celebration. Private rides can be arranged. Rides start at $245 per person.

**Wiederkehr Balloons** (651-436-8172; angelfire.com/nm/flyballoons/main.html), 130 N. St. Croix Trail, Lakeland. Morning and afternoon departures are available, with a maximum of eight passengers at a time. Champagne is served at the conclusion of the ride. Rates start at $250 for the first person and $200 for subsequent guests in the same party. Private balloon rides are available.

**Aamodt's Hot Air Balloon Rides** (651-351-0101; aamodtsballoons.com), 6428 N. Manning Avenue, Stillwater. Aamodt's offers hot-air balloon rides with departures from their apple orchard in Stillwater. Rides are reserved for eight people only and include a champagne toast. Private rides can be arranged. Rates start at $500 per couple, $800 for a private excursion.

**Gondola Romantica** (651-439-1783; gondolaromantica.com), 425 Nelson Street E., Stillwater. Open daily May–Oct., weather permitting. Who needs Venice? This entrepreneurial effort brings romantic gondola rides to the St. Croix River. Options include everything from 20-minute sightseeing cruises to a five-course dinner cruise. The company offers customized cruises as well. Gondolas hold six people, but if you'd like a private excursion, reserve ahead.

**St. Croix Valley Segway Tours** (651-508-1448; stcroixvalleysegway.com), 8312 Neal Avenue N., Stillwater. This tour provider has numerous Segway tours around Stillwater, several of which include stops at eateries and breweries. Training and helmets are provided. Tours frequently sell out in advance, so reserving ahead is strongly recommended. Note that all riders must be 14 or older (14–17 must be accompanied by an adult), and there are weight restrictions; riders must be at least 90 pounds, but not more than 300 pounds. Custom and private tours can be arranged. Rates start at $40, with discounts available for military members.

WINERIES/BREWERIES ❋ **Saint Croix Vineyards** (651-430-3310; scvwines.com), 6428 Manning Avenue N., Stillwater. Open daily. This vineyard has won more than 100 national and international awards with their wines, which include Frontenac, Marquette, and fruit wines. On beautiful weather days, bring a picnic to enjoy on the vineyard's deck or on a blanket out in the vineyard.

❋ **Lift Bridge Brewery** (1-888-430-2337; liftbridgebrewer.com), 1900 Tower Drive W., Stillwater. Open daily with brewery tours offered Sat.–Sun. The taproom has a full line of Lift Bridge beers and ales, including the popular Farm Girl Saison, and hard seltzers.

❋ **Maple Island Brewing** (651-430-0044; mapleislandbrewing.com), 225 Main Street N., Stillwater. Open daily. Maple Island brews a wide variety of beers, including kolsch, IPA, bock, lager, hefeweizen, and imperial stout, along with root beer (including a maple-flavored root beer).

# ✳ Lodging

Stillwater is blessed with a number of historic—and romantic—inns for visitors, as well as bed-and-breakfasts.

BED-AND-BREAKFASTS ✳ (ɴ) **The Ann Bean Mansion** (651-430-0355; annbeanmansion.com), 319 Pine Street W., Stillwater. This whimsical home has a colorful history, complete with riches and scandal, and today it has five lovely rooms, all with fireplaces and private baths. The Tower Room is a particularly cozy choice. Rooms come with plush robes, and rates include an afternoon glass of wine and full breakfast daily. Children 10 and older are welcome. Rates start at $175.

✳ (ɴ) **Rivertown Inn** (651-430-2955; rivertowninn.com), 306 Olive Street W., Stillwater. Sitting on a hillside above Stillwater, the Rivertown provides beautiful views along with four rooms and five suites, all elaborately decorated and named after literary heavyweights (Lord Byron, Longfellow). The inn is open year-round, but summer visitors will enjoy the use of the private gardens and screened gazebo. All accommodations have luxurious bedding, Bose sound systems, plush robes, full breakfast, and evening social hour with wine and hors d'oeuvres. Rates start at $325. Packages are available.

✳ 🪶 **Lady Goodwood** (651-439-3771; ladygoodwood.com), 704 1st Street S., Stillwater. This lovingly restored 1895 Queen Anne home has several original details, including a parlor fireplace. The three guest rooms are all lavishly decorated in Victorian style and have private baths; the St. Croix Suite comes with a round king-sized bed. Rates start at $109. Packages are available.

✳ **Aurora Staples Inn** (651-351-1187 or 1-800-580-3092; aurorastaplesinn.com), 303 4th Street N., Stillwater. This Victorian home has rooms and suites in period décor, all with private baths. Some rooms have gas fireplaces and whirlpool tubs.

The Carriage House suites has a private covered parking spot. Rates start at $169.

INNS AND HOTELS ✿ ♿ 🪶 ✳ (ɴ) 🐾 ♀ ⅋ **Lowell Inn** (651-439-1100; lowellinn.com), 102 2nd Street N., Stillwater. The Lowell Inn is the granddaddy of historic hotels in Stillwater. Built in 1927 on the site of a former lumberjack hotel, this stately building has 23 impeccably decorated rooms, some with stained-glass windows, antique furnishings, and fireplaces, but all with modern conveniences. Several rooms have Jacuzzis. The romance factor here is high. The hotel also has two highly regarded restaurants on-site (see *Where to Eat*). Rates start at $155. Packages and specials are available.

♿ 🪶 ✳ (ɴ) ♀ ⅋ **Water Street Inn** (651-439-6000; waterstreetinn.us), 101 Water Street S., Stillwater. A small luxury inn right on the river with rooms and suites, most with gas fireplaces. The rooms are decorated as befitting the upscale visitors of the lumber boom days. A well-regarded restaurant and pub round out the amenities. Rates start at $189. Packages and specials are available.

♿ 🪶 ✳ (ɴ) 🐾 ♀ ⅋ **Afton House Inn** (651-436-8883; aftonhouseinn.com), 3291 St. Croix Trail S., Afton. Afton House has 46 rooms, most with canopy or four-poster beds, and deluxe rooms have balconies overlooking the St. Croix River. The location near **Afton Alps** (see *Green Space and Outdoor Activities*) makes this a good choice for a ski weekend, with a warm, romantic hideaway to return to at the end of the day. The inn has a restaurant and bar on-site. Rates start at $185. Packages are available.

♿ 🪶 🐾 ✳ (ɴ) ♀ ⅋ **Lora Hotel** (651-571-3500 or 1-833-287-8155; lorahotel.com), 402 S. Main Street, Stillwater. Stillwater's newest lodging is this upscale boutique hotel, with sleekly sophisticated rooms and suites (some of which do not have windows). Several rooms have exposed stone walls, showing the hotel's historic origins. Bicycles and helmets are available for guests. The hotel is inclusive to the point where it has not only Bibles for guests, but the Book of Mormon, the Bhagavad Gita, and the Torah, among others. The hotel's restaurant, **Feller**, is a destination on its own (see *Dining Out*). Rates start at $221.

## ❋ Where to Eat

The lower St. Croix Valley enjoys an affluent resident population and close proximity to the Twin Cities, giving it an abundance of notable dining options, even off-season.

DINING OUT ♿ ✿ ❋ ⍋ **Feller** (651-571-3501; lorahotel.com), 402 S. Main Street, Stillwater. Open daily for all three meals. Located inside Stillwater's newest lodging option, the **Lora Hotel** (see *Where to Stay*), Feller has become a destination on its own. The restaurant describes itself as a modern-day homage to hunters and gatherers, by which they mean they're proud to serve as many locally grown and harvest ingredients as possible. For dinner, look at the Tatanka (bison hanger steak with beurre noisette and parsley root puree) or the Rooster in the Grain (brined pheasant breast with barley and gooseberry lacquer). Vegetarians have not been ignored, and there's an extensive wine list. Expensive/very expensive.

♿ ✿ ❋ ⍋ **Lowell Inn** (651-439-1100; lowellinn.com), 102 N. 2nd Street, Stillwater. Open daily for lunch and dinner. Within the historic **Lowell Inn** (see *Lodging*) are two restaurants worth noting. The formal restaurant, in the elegant George Washington Room, serves classic dinner entrées such as duck à l'orange and beef Wellington, while the Matterhorn Room serves a four-course Swiss dinner fondue each evening. Expensive.

♿ ✿ ❋ ⍋ **Lake Elmo Inn** (651-777-8495; lakeelmoinn.com), 3442 Lake Elmo Avenue N., Lake Elmo. Open daily for lunch and dinner. Housed in a former stagecoach stop, the Lake Elmo Inn serves upscale fare in a "come as you are"

ambience. Seafood (local and saltwater), pork, and pasta are the specialties, but be sure to save room for the Sin of the Inn dessert (if it's still on the periodically changing menu). Kids are welcome to check out the "young adult" menu. Expensive/very expensive.

♿ ✿ ❋ ⍋ **Patriot's Tavern** (651-342-1472; patriots-tavern.com), 145 New England Place, Stillwater. Open daily for lunch and dinner. An American-themed tavern right down to its architecture, Patriot's offers up an upscale take on bar and grill food, including wood-fired pizzas, lobster mac and cheese, and ale-cooked pot roast. Moderate/expensive.

♿ ✿ ❋ ⍋ **Phil's Tara Hideaway** (651-439-9850; tarahideaway.com), 15021 N. 60th Street, Oak Park Heights. Open Tues.–Fri. for lunch and dinner, Sat.–Sun. for dinner. This highly regarded restaurant offers a combination of Mediterranean and American cuisine in a log-cabin-themed building. The food tastes high-end, but prices are reasonable given the quality. Look for the various sous vide options, or the pan-roasted stuffed trout or seared duck and potato gnocchi. Moderate/expensive.

♿ ✿ ❋ ⍋ **Domaćin Restaurant and Wine Bar** (651-439-1352; domacinwinebar.com), 102 S. 2nd Street, Stillwater. Open daily for dinner. Fine dining with a limited, seasonally changing menu. The restaurant also has an extensive wine list, and staff is very knowledgeable about the list and pairing with menu items. Entrées could include braised pork with white cheddar grits, spicy tomato confit and chimichurri, or braised rabbit pappardelle. Expensive.

EATING OUT ⍋ ❋ **Dock Café** (651-430-3770; dockcafe.com), 425 E. Nelson Street, Stillwater. Open daily for lunch and dinner. It's open year-round, but this is the place to be during the warm weather months. Situated right on the banks of the St. Croix, the Dock Café has outdoor seating that gives diners full views of river life. Not surprisingly, the outdoor patio is popular—plan to arrive early, or wait. However, the indoor ambience is attractive as well, with a fireplace and wide windows. Menu items run heavily to meats and seafood. Moderate.

♿ ✎ ❋ **Chilkoot Café & Cyclery** (651-342-0429; chilkootcc.com), 826 4th Street S., Stillwater. Open daily for breakfast and lunch, Tues.–Sat. for dinner. This cozy eatery and bike shop has more upscale food than might be expected by the name. Try the seafood cioppino or bacon-wrapped meatloaf. Moderate.

♿ ✎ ❋ ☍ **LoLo American Kitchen** (651-342-2461; loloamericankitchen.com), 233 Main Street S., Stillwater. Open daily for lunch and dinner. This cozy bistro plays with American foods in unexpected ways, with great results. There are duck or falafel tacos, pork Cubano tacos, and smoked salt and rosemary fries. Moderate.

♿ ✎ ❋ ☍ **Brick & Bourbon** (651-342-0777; brickandbourbon.com), 215 Main Street S., Stillwater. Open daily for lunch and dinner, Sat.–Sun. for brunch. Neighborhood bar and grill with cast-iron-grilled burgers, short rib ravioli, and several variations on mac and cheese. Moderate.

♿ ✎ ❋ **Leo's Grill & Malt Shop** (651-351-3943; leosgrill.com), 131 Main Street S., Stillwater. Open daily for lunch and dinner. Everything you'd want a '50s throwback diner to be: full of burgers, Reubens, tuna melts, and pulled pork sandwiches, and all things ice cream. Inexpensive.

♿ ✎ ❋ ☍ **The Tilted Tiki Tropical Bar & Restaurant** (651-342-2545; thetiltedtiki.com), 324 Main Street S., Stillwater. Open daily for lunch and dinner. The tropical theme carries over into the menu, giving its bar and grill options an unusual twist. Look for the tropical pineapple cheeseburger and coconut shrimp and steak kabobs. Inexpensive/moderate.

♿ ✎ ❋ ☍ **Ziggy's** (651-342-1773; ziggysmn.com), 132 Main Street S., Stillwater. Open daily for lunch and dinner. Ziggy's is a major provider of live music in Stillwater, and it has a street food menu format (and sometimes brings in food trucks). Hot dogs, tacos, and Tennessee hot chicken sandwiches. Inexpensive.

# ❋ Selective Shopping

Stillwater's main city center, along the riverfront, has developed into a visitor's shopping haven full of small, charming shops, with hardly any chain stores to be seen. Antiques enthusiasts flock to this community for its large concentration of antiques stores and dealers, but there are plenty of other kinds of retail as well.

ANTIQUES ❋ **Staples Mill Antiques** (651-430-1816; staplesmillantiques.com), 410 Main Street N., Stillwater. Open daily. Located in a historic mill, Staples Mill Antiques is comprised of nearly 80 antiques and collectibles dealers spread over 10,000 square feet and three floors. A great spot for serious antiquing or window shopping.

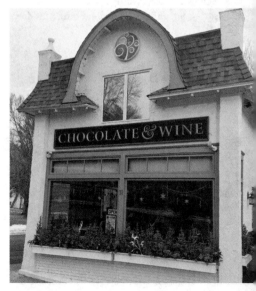

ST. CROIX CHOCOLATE CO.

❄ **Midtown Antique Mall** (651-430-0808; midtownantiques.com), 301 Main Street S., Stillwater. Open daily. A good source for antiques enthusiasts, the Midtown Antique Mall has more than 100 dealers, including several furniture dealers.

ARTS AND CRAFTS ❄ **North Main Studio** (651-351-1379), 402 Main Street N., Stillwater. Open only by appointment. Local resident and artist Carl Erickson displays and sells the pottery he creates here. Visitors are welcome to watch him at work.

❄ **Art 'n' Soul/Stillwater Beads** (651-275-0255; facebook.com/ArtNSoul .StillwaterBeads), 202 Main Street S., Stillwater. Open daily. There are upscale and humorous gifts at Art 'n' Soul, while Stillwater Beads sells a wide variety of beads, including some unusual and hard-to-find items.

✎ ❄ **Darn Knit Anyway** (651-342-1386; darnknitanyway.com), 423 Main Street S., Stillwater. Darn Knit Anyway offers a vast and wide-ranging selection of knitting and crochet items, as well as fabric for the sewing enthusiast.

BOOKS ♿ ✎ ❄ **Valley Bookseller** (651-430-3385; valleybookseller.com), 217 Main Street S., Stillwater. Open daily. A full-service bookseller, along with gift items.

GIFTS ♿ ✎ ❄ **Cooks of Crocus Hill** (651-351-1144; thechefs gallery.com), 324 Main Street S., Stillwater (other locations in Minneapolis and St. Paul). Open daily. The store for all things cookery, Chef's Gallery has a wide selection of cooking tools and gadgets. The shop also offers an extensive list of cooking classes.

TREATS ✎ ❄ 🍸 **St. Croix Chocolate Co.** (651-433-1400; stcroixchocolateco.com), 11 Judd Street, Marine on St. Croix. Open Wed.–Sun. Handcrafted, beautiful, decadent chocolates, made with chocolate from Belgium, Switzerland, and Venezuela, in combination with locally sourced cream and honey from the store owner's own honeybees. On weekends, housemade pizzas are offered along with a selection of Minnesota wines, and a monthly chef dinner is available. Check for added hours around major holidays—and decreased hours right after those same holidays.

## ❄ Special Events

*July*: **Lumberjack Days** (lumberjackdays .com), Stillwater. A summer tradition, Lumberjack Days is held in Lowell Park on the St. Croix in mid-July and offers three days of historically themed fun and frolic. Among the events is the Lumberjack Sports Camp (see *Green Space and Outdoor Activities*), a chess tournament, massive parade, an 1860 vintage "base ball" exhibition, treasure hunt, 5K and 10K races, and lumberjack skills championships.

*September*: **Rivertown Fall Art Festival** (651-439-4001), Stillwater. Held each year in early September, the Rivertown Art Festival takes place on the banks of the St. Croix River and brings dozens of artists in various mediums, some local and some national, to display their work. Food and kids' activities are available.

COOKS OF CROCUS HILL

# MISSISSIPPI RIVER BLUFF COUNTRY

■

HASTINGS

RED WING

WABASHA

WINONA

LANESBORO

AUSTIN

ROCHESTER

NORTHFIELD

# MISSISSIPPI RIVER BLUFF COUNTRY

The southeastern corner of the state, bordered by the mighty Mississippi to the east, has some of the loveliest terrain in Minnesota: river valleys, rolling hills, woods, and wildflowers in season, and one charming small town after the other, including some of the oldest towns in the state, most with many intact historic buildings and landmarks. Unlike more northern reaches, which were leveled and redesigned during the last ice age, the bluff country mostly escaped the glacial ravages and kept instead a variable terrain that includes 500-foot limestone bluffs and deep valleys. The climate here is slightly different, too, warmer and with more rainfall, leading to vegetation not seen elsewhere in the state, including black walnut trees. The region is also home to Minnesota's only poisonous snakes, the timber rattlesnake and the massasauga, which reside mostly in the bluffs themselves or in the swampy areas close to the river. But these snakes are as timid of humans as we are of them and are slow to strike.

Bike trails abound, many of which are paved and can be used for cross-country skiing in the winter months. As you travel westward from the river, clusters of tight-knit Amish communities stand in contrast to the sophistication of cities like Rochester and the tasteful attraction of SPAM in Austin.

**GUIDANCE Hastings Area Chamber of Commerce** (651-437-6775; hastingsmn.org), 314 Vermillion Street, Hastings.

**Red Wing Convention and Visitor Bureau** (651-385-5934; redwing.org), 420 Levee Street, Red Wing.

**Wabasha/Kellogg Chamber of Commerce and Convention and Visitor Bureau** (651-565-4158 or 1-800-565-4158; wabashamn.org), 122 Main Street W., Wabasha.

**Visit Winona** (507-452-2278; visitwinona.com), 924 Huff Street, Winona. Offers extensive lodging and activity information for the Winona area.

**Rochester Convention and Visitor Bureau** (507-288-4331; experiencerochestermn .org), 30 Civic Center Drive SE, Suite 200, Rochester.

**Northfield Convention and Visitor Bureau** (1-800-658-2548; visitingnorthfield .com), 19 Bridge Square, Northfield.

**Lanesboro Chamber of Commerce** (507-467-2696; lanesboro.com), 100 Milwaukee Road, Lanesboro.

**GETTING THERE By air:** Regional commercial airlines, primarily Delta Air Lines and its SkyWest subsidiary, serve the city of Rochester. Taxis and rental cars are available from **Rochester International Airport** (507-282-2328; flyrst.com), at 7600 Helgerson Drive SW in Rochester.

**By car:** US 52 leads south from the Twin Cities into Rochester and connects south of Rochester with I-90, which heads west to Austin or east to Wisconsin. Visitors to Northfield can use MN 19 from US 52. To visit the towns closest to the Mississippi River area, US 61 travels south along the river until it merges with I-90.

**By rail: AMTRAK** (1-800-872-7245; amtrak.com) has stops in Red Wing and Winona, crossing through from either Minneapolis–St. Paul or Chicago. Local stations

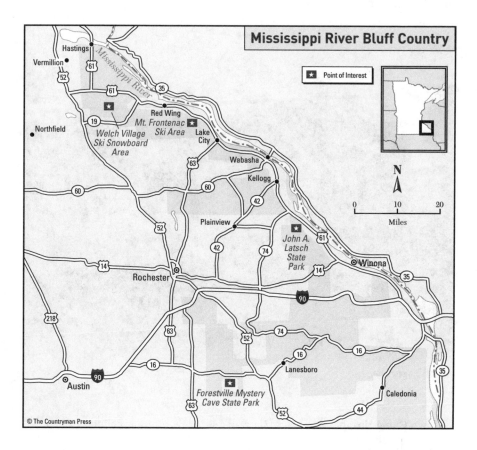

Mississippi River Bluff Country

include the Red Wing Station, 420 Levee Street, Red Wing, and the Winona Station, 65 E. Mark Street, Winona.

**GETTING AROUND** Having a vehicle is a necessity when traveling around the Mississippi River bluffs region.

**WHEN TO COME** The summer months are the most popular time to visit the river bluffs area, although fall foliage continues to draw larger numbers as well. Rochester benefits from the Mayo Clinic's presence to bring in people year-round.

**MEDICAL EMERGENCY** Call 911.

**Regina Medical Center** (651-404-1000; allinahealth.org/regina-hospital), 1175 Nininger Road, Hastings.

**Mayo Clinic Red Wing** (651-267-5000; mayoclinichealthsystem.org), 701 Hewitt Boulevard, Red Wing.

**St. Elizabeth's Medical Center** (651-565-4531; healthcare.ascension.org), 1200 5th Grant Boulevard W., Wabasha.

**Winona Health** (507-454-3650; winonahealth.org), 855 Mankato Avenue, Winona.

**Northfield Hospital** (507-646-1000; northfieldhospital.org), 2000 North Avenue, Northfield.

THE SCANDINAVIAN INN

**Mayo Clinic Hospital, Methodist Campus** (507-266-7067; mayoclinic.org), 201 W. Center Street, Rochester.

**Mayo Clinic Hospital, Saint Mary's Campus** (507-255-5123; mayoclinic.org), 1216 2nd Street SW, Rochester. The second of two Mayo Clinic hospitals.

# HASTINGS

astings is truly a river town, with the Mississippi, St. Croix, and Vermilion rivers all part of the city. It was initially created in 1820 by a military detachment sent to guard blocked shipments of supplies to Fort Snelling. Later it was expected to be a major Midwestern city, given its river access, but the financial downturn of 1857 stalled its growth. Today, it's a charming city with plenty of reminders of its historic river past for visitors to enjoy.

## ✳ To See and Do

GAMING ❧ ✳ ✙ **Treasure Island Resort and Casino** (1-800-222-7077; ticasino.com), 5734 Sturgeon Lake Road, Welch. Open 24/7. Slots, blackjack, poker, and bingo are all available in this massive complex southeast of Hastings. Four restaurants and several cocktail bars provide sustenance, and an attached hotel (see *Lodging*) and marina provide options besides gambling.

MUSEUMS AND HISTORIC SITES ✐ **The LeDuc House** (651-438-8480; dakotahistory.org/leduc-historic-estate), 1629 Vermillion Street. Open Thurs.–Sun. mid-May–late Oct.; also for special holiday events (see website). Adults $7; seniors 60 and older $6; children 6–17 $5; children 5 and under and Dakota County Historical Society members free. This beautiful piece of history and architecture, built in 1866, was designed by Andrew Jackson Downing and is rare in that it is virtually untouched. The former home of William LeDuc, a commissioner of agriculture under President Rutherford Hayes, the building itself is a delight to visit, but the 4.5-acre grounds are lovely as well, encompassing an apple orchard and forests.

HASTINGS

WINERIES ❧ ✙ **Alexis Bailly Vineyard** (651-437-1413; abvwines.com), 18200 Kirby Avenue S. Open Fri.–Sun. from Mar.–Christmas. Minnesota's first and arguably foremost vineyard, Alexis Bailly first produced a vintage in 1978. The winery works with classic and new-breed grapes that have been found to withstand extreme cold.

# ❄ Green Space and Outdoor Activities

BIKING **Hastings Trail System** (651-480-6175; hastingsmn.gov). Thirty miles of paved bike trails wind through Hastings and along the Mississippi River.

PARKS ♿ **Carpenter St. Croix Valley Nature Center** (651-437-4359; carpenternature center.org), 12805 St. Croix Trail S. Open daily. Admission is free. This small (425 acres) but lavish nature preserve was once a private estate and apple orchard. Today it is a well-maintained natural area, the release site for the University of Minnesota's Raptor release program, and offers 10 miles of trails, some of which have been adapted for visitors with limited mobility.

**Vermillion Falls Park**, 215 21st Street E. This park, right in the heart of Hastings, has both beautiful waterfalls and trails for hiking and biking. An oasis in the city.

# ❄ Lodging

HOTELS ♿ ✎ (((•))) ❄ ⊺ ‖ ⸍ **Treasure Island Resort and Casino** (1-888-867-7829; treasureislandcasino.com), 5734 Sturgeon Lake Road, Welch. With more than 200 rooms and suites, an elaborate indoor water park, fitness center, three restaurants, and child-care center, Treasure Island caters to the gambling crowd but offers additional amenities to bring in nongambling spouses and family members. Rates start at $89. Packages are available.

# ❄ Where to Eat

DINING OUT ♿ ✎ ❄ ⊺ **Tado Steakhouse** (1-888-867-7829; ticasino.com), 5734 Sturgeon Lake Road, Welch. Open Wed.–Sun. for dinner. The steakhouse at **Treasure Island Casino** (see *Where to Stay*) has a large list of steak entrées, but it also offers walleye en papillote and seafood. Expensive/very expensive.

♿ ✎ ❄ ⊺ **Wiederholt's Supper Club** (651-437-3528 or 507-263-2263; wiederholtssupperclub.com), 14535 E. 240th Street. Open daily for dinner, Sun. for brunch. This fourth-generation family-owned supper club is keeping the supper club tradition alive and well in this building with wood wainscoting

and a large stone fireplace. Several cuts of steak are on the menu, along with prime rib on weekends, and it also has ham steak and beefburger steak, along with ribs and chicken items. Moderate/expensive.

EATING OUT ♿ ✎ ❄ ⊺ **The Busted Nut** (651-438-6887; thebustednut.com), 118 2nd Street E. Open daily for lunch and dinner. Solid tavern menu in a charming building in historic downtown Hastings. Inexpensive/moderate.

♿ ✎ ❄ ⊺ **Bierstube** (651-437-8259; thebierstube.com), 109 11th Street W. Open daily for lunch and dinner, Sun. for breakfast. There are plenty of German classics on the menu, including wiener schnitzel and sauerbraten, but there are also steaks, seafood, ribs, and burgers and sandwiches. Moderate.

♿ ✎ ❄ ⊺ **The Onion Grille** (651-437-7577; theoniongrille.com), 100 Sibley Street. Open Tues.–Sun. for lunch and dinner. Steak, seafood pasta, creatively done with quality ingredients. Moderate.

♿ ✎ ❄ ⊺ **Lock and Dam Eatery** (651-319-0906; lockanddameatery.com), 101 2nd Street E. Open Tues.–Sun. for lunch and dinner. A Mexican/Italian hybrid menu, with Tuscan Salmon, lobster sauce fettuccine, chipotle camarones, and fajitas. There's a mega burrito on the menu too, and anyone who finishes it within 30 minutes gets it for free, along with a T-shirt. For those who like American foods, there are also several sandwiches, salads, and burgers. Moderate.

       ⌖ ✐ ❋ **Emily's Bakery and Deli** (651-437-2491; emilysbakerydeli.com), 1212 Vermillion Street. Open daily for breakfast and lunch, Mon.–Fri. for early dinner. This bakery, part of Hastings for more than 100 years, has excellent baked goods as well as an extensive deli menu that incorporates the bakery's bread and rolls. Sandwiches, soups, chili and stew, and breakfast burritos. Inexpensive.

## ❋ Selective Shopping

ANTIQUES ❋ **Antiques on Main** (651-480-8129), 205 2nd Street E. Open daily. Twenty dealers, many of whom buy entire estates.

    ❋ **Second Street Antique Mall** (651-480-0513), 204 2nd Street E. Open daily.

More than 30 dealers with a wide variety of antiques.

    ❋ **The Briar Patch** (651-437-4400), 103 2nd Street E. Open Tues.–Sat. Vintage clothing, jewelry, and accessories.

    ❋ **Vintage Inspirations** (651-437-4377; vintageinsp.com), 203 2nd Street E. Open daily. Antiques, collectibles, vintage and painted furniture, and accessories.

ARTS AND CRAFTS ⌖ ❋ **Mississippi Clayworks** (651-437-5901; mississippi clayworks.com), 214 2nd Street E. Open Mon., Tues., Thurs.–Sat. Locally made pottery, including custom orders.

## ❋ Special Events

*Memorial Day Weekend–September:* ✐ **Hastings Saturday Night Cruise-In** (hastingsmn.org), Hastings. Summer

HISTORIC DOWNTOWN HASTINGS

Saturday nights in Hastings draw thousands of visitors for this annual tradition. Cars that are at least 30 years old are given cruising rights down the main drag, with prizes and special weekly events.

*July*: ⚓ ♿ **Little Log House Pioneer Village and Antique Power Show** (651-437-2693; littleloghouseshow.com), 13746 E. 220th Street, Hastings. Held the last weekend in July. This pioneer village is larger than most, with 45 buildings, a replica bridge, extensive gardens, and even a dirt racetrack for vintage auto races. The only downside to the village is that it's not open to the general public except during this annual event, which displays antique vehicles and machines, and offers demonstrations, live music, Old West reenactments, tractor and truck pulls, and a parade. Campsites and RV sites available for rental.

# RED WING

Proximity to the Mississippi River and lush farmlands gave Red Wing its start in the wheat and milling business, until the railroads gave Minneapolis access to southern Minnesota crops. But Red Wing became a favorite place to visit, especially for day-trippers from the Twin Cities, due to its spectacular surrounding river-bluff views and the shopping available from local manufacturers of Red Wing Shoes and Red Wing Pottery.

## ✳ To See and Do

  ✦ **Goodhue County Historical Society** (651-388-6024; good huecountyhistory.org), 1166 Oak Street. Open Tues.–Sun. during the summer. Adults $5; ages 13–18 $2; 12 and under and historical society members free. This sizable regional museum has extensive collections on numerous aspects of the area's history, including archaeology, business, geology, immigration, and agriculture. A clothing exhibit has samples for kids to try out, and there's a tepee to play in. Note: The historical society is in the process of placing signage throughout the county, noting the prior existence of what are now known as ghost towns.

  ✦ ✳ **Red Wing Shoe Museum** (651-385-1811), 315 Main Street. Open daily. Admission is free. Red Wing Shoes are indeed manufactured in Red Wing, and this small but lively museum in the Riverfront Centre has hands-on and historical exhibits showing how the shoes are made and sold, including the opportunity to try to build your own shoe as well as view the world's largest boot.

  ✦ ✳ **Pottery Museum of Red Wing** (potterymuseumredwing.org), Historic Pottery Place Mall, 240 Harrison Street. Open Tues.–Sun. Admission is free. Just like Red Wing Shoes, Red Wing Pottery is made in Red Wing, and it has a museum. Located within a former pottery factory (see *Selective Shopping*), this museum has displays illustrating the pottery process and history, and has an impressive collection of finished objects and historical pieces.

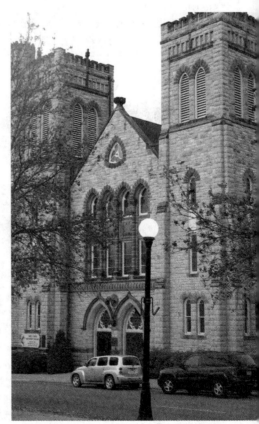

FIRST UNITED METHODIST CHURCH

# ✳ Green Space and Outdoor Activities

BIKING **Cannon Valley Trail** (507-263-0508; cannonvalleytrail.com). A 20-mile paved trail that runs on an old railroad track from Red Wing to Cannon Falls along the Cannon River. A Wheel Pass (adults $5 per day, or $25 for the season) is required. Cannon Falls Canoe and Bike Rental (507-407-4111; cannonfallscanoeandbike.com) in Cannon Falls offers kayak, canoe, and bike rentals as well as shuttle services. Bike offerings include tandem and regular bikes.

PARKS AND PARKWAYS **Great River Road National Scenic Byway** (651-341-4196), US 61. This section of the scenic byway that runs from Canada to the Gulf of Mexico departs Red Wing and travels to La Crescent, running along the Mississippi River. The 107-mile byway encompasses river views, forests, small and historic river towns and villages, and countless opportunities for natural and wildlife exploration.

**Frontenac State Park** (651-345-3401; dnr.state.mn.us/state_parks/frontenac/index .html), 29223 County Route 28 Boulevard, Frontenac. $7 day pass ($35 for an annual pass). This state park is especially valuable for birdwatchers, with more than 250 species of birds recorded here. Camping, hiking, and a winter sliding hill are among the amenities spread across the park's prairie, forest, and river bluff settings.

SKIING **Welch Village** (651-258-4567; welchvillage.com), 26685 County Route 7 Boulevard, Welch. Fifty runs of varying difficulty for skiers and snowboarders, as well as a terrain park. The village also offers slope-side bunkhouses for rental, which are rustic with shared baths but offer the utmost in convenient access for devoted skiers and boarders.

RED WING CITY PARK

FRONTENAC STATE PARK

## ✳ Lodging

Red Wing is a community full of historic inns and bed-and-breakfasts. As many of these inns are small and Red Wing is a popular destination, be sure to book ahead.

✿ ♿ ☎ ❄ ♂ (ᵢ) ♈ **St. James Hotel** (651-388-2846 or 1-800-252-1875; st-james-hotel.com), 406 Main Street. Built in 1875, the St. James is the hotel in Red Wing. All rooms are decorated in handsome Victorian style; larger rooms have whirlpools, and two deluxe rooms include spacious seating areas. Two full-service restaurants stand on their own (the Veranda being a popular restaurant that draws many Twin Cities diners; see *Where to Eat*), and there's a pub and coffee shop as well. Rates start at $129. Packages are available.

✳ **Moondance Inn** (651-388-8145 or 1-866-388-8145; moondanceinn.com),

1105 W. 4th Street. This beautiful stone inn has five spacious guest rooms, all with private bath and fireplace, and featuring antique furniture and sumptuous décor. Rates include daily breakfast. Rates start at $125. Packages are available.

✳ ♂ **Round Barn Farm** (651-385-9250 or 1-866-763-2276; roundbarnfarm.com), 28650 Wildwood Lane. Round Barn Farm, built in 1861 just 4 miles outside of Red Wing, offers five spacious suites beautifully decorated in vintage country style, complete with antique furniture, private baths, and fireplaces or Franklin stoves. Breakfast is provided daily in the dining room, which features a massive limestone fireplace. The property is located on 35 acres complete with walking trails and a gazebo. Children 12 and older are welcome. Rates start at $159. Packages are available.

✿ ✳ (ᵢ) **Candlelight Inn** (651-388-8034 or 1-800-254-9194; candlelight inn-redwing.com), 818 W. 3rd Street. A striking Victorian home built more than 140 years ago offering five rooms and suites, all with private baths and fireplaces. While all the rooms are beautifully decorated, the Butternut Suite in particular is a lesson in opulence and luxury. Full breakfast and evening appetizers, wine, and sparkling cider provided for guests daily. Children 12 and older are welcome. Rates start at $149. Packages are available.

❄ ♂ ⟨⟨ᵧ⟩⟩ **Golden Lantern Inn** (651-388-3315 or 1-888-288-3315; goldenlantern .com), 721 East Avenue. Built in 1923 by the former president of the Red Wing Shoe Company, this English Tudor has five lush rooms and suites, and several public rooms available to guests. Bedrooms all have private baths, and some have fireplaces, sitting rooms, and private balconies. Full breakfast is included daily and is available in the dining room, bedroom, or (during warmer months) on the stone patio. During the summer

THE ST. JAMES HOTEL

months, guests have access to the lavish gardens behind the inn. Children 12 and older are welcome. Rates start at $124. Packages are available.

## ❋ Where to Eat

EATING OUT ♿ ♂ ❄ ♟ **The Veranda** (651-388-2846 or 1-800-252-1875; st -james-hotel.com/the-veranda), 406 Main Street. Open daily for all three meals. A more casual full-service restaurant in the **St. James Hotel** (see *Lodging*), the Veranda overlooks the Mississippi and has outdoor dining in season. Traditional breakfast and lunch fare is served, while dinner has flatbreads, a hummus platter, sandwiches, and salmon and pork tenderloin. Moderate.

♿ ♂ ❄ ♟ **Staghead Gastropub** (651-212-6494; thestaghead.com), 219 Bush Street. Open daily for lunch and dinner. Staghead has a frequently changing menu, but within its menu groupings is a cheese and meat section with a wide variety of charcuterie and cheese plates; burgers, which might include a salmon burger; and entrées such as bouillabaisse or braised beef and pasta. The pub has an impressive list of tap beers, as well as cocktails and wine. Moderate.

♿ ♂ ❄ ♟ **Liberty's** (651-388-8877; libertysrestaurant.com), 303 W. 3rd Street. Open daily for all three meals. There can be no complaints about access to this restaurant—not only do they deliver throughout Red Wing, they also provide free shuttle service to and from boats and hotels. The menu aims to please with Italian, Mexican, burgers, and steaks; breakfast includes pancakes, omelets, and steak and eggs. Moderate.

♿ ♂ ❄ **Bev's Café** (651-388-5227; bevscafe.com), 221 Bush Street. Open daily for breakfast and lunch. Classic small-town café menu, with burgers, fries, pie, and ice cream. Inexpensive.

♿ ♂ ❄ ♟ **The Smokin' Oak Rotisserie and Grill** (651-388-9866; thesmokinoak .com), 4243 MN 61. Open daily for lunch and dinner. Upon entering this eatery, you'll immediately see an impressive wood-fired rotisserie with all kinds of meat being roasted. That's the clear menu theme, and you won't go wrong with the ribs or roasted chicken. Moderate.

## ❋ Entertainment

♿ ✎ ❋ **Sheldon Theatre** (651-388-8700 or 1-800-899-5759; sheldontheatre.org), 443 W. 3rd Street. This lovely turn-of-the-20th-century gem is a venue for a wide range of performances, including all genres of music, silent films, and stage productions.

## ❋ Selective Shopping

♿ ❋ **Pottery Place Red Wing** (651-388-7765; facebook.com/potteryplacered wing), 2000 Old W. Main Street. Open daily. Not all shopping malls are bland boxes. The Pottery Place Mall, in a reno-vated pottery factory and houses, has the **Red Wing Pottery Museum** (see *To See and Do*), antiques shops, art galleries, home furnishings stores, gift shops, and purveyors of fine chocolates.

♿ ✎ ❋ **Red Wing Stoneware & Pottery** (651-388-4610 or 1-800-352-4877;

redwingstoneware.com), 1920 W. Main Street. Open daily late Apr.–Dec., Mon.–Sat. from Jan.–late Apr. In addition to a huge retail selection of Red Wing Pottery items, the Red Wing Pottery facility has several smaller but no less charming shops, including a Minnesota gift store, a candy shop, and a home and garden gift shop.

♿ ✎ ❋ **Red Wing Shoe Store** (651-388-6233; redwingshoe.com), Riverfront Centre, 315 Main Street. Open daily. Not surprisingly, the flagship store of the Red Wing Shoe company sells a wide variety of their high-quality work and athletic shoes.

♿ ✎ ❋ **Uffda Shop** (651-388-8436 or 1-800-488-3332; uffdashoponline.com), 202 Bush Street. Open daily. Uffda, which is a Norwegian exclamation, is the tongue-in-cheek name for this deeply Scandinavian store, filled with specialty baking needs (krumkake irons, lefse grills), fine porcelain tableware, and other gift items.

## ❋ Special Events

*October*: **Red Wing Fall Festival of Arts** (redwingarts.org), Red Wing. This event, taking place annually for more than 50 years, offers two days of art exhibitions, sales, and related activities.

# WABASHA

Wabasha is the oldest continuously occupied city on the Mississippi River, having been founded in 1830 (but with residents documented in 1826). Besides its lovely riverside location, Wabasha is also known for being the site of the movies *Grumpy Old Men* and *Grumpier Old Men*. A large population of nesting eagles gave rise to the National Eagle Center, a popular attraction that houses live bald eagles and a golden eagle.

## ✳ To See and Do

& ♂ ✳ **National Eagle Center** (651-565-4989 or 1-877-332-4537; nationaleaglecenter .org), 50 Pembroke Avenue. Open daily. Adults $10; veterans $9; children 4–17 $7; children 3 and under and members free. Group discounts are available; call ahead for

WATERFRONT PARK IN WABASHA

THE NATIONAL EAGLE CENTER

reservation. Located on the Mississippi River banks, the NEC has a 14,000-square-foot interpretive center with resident eagles, a viewing deck, housing for injured or sick eagles, exhibits with preserved animals and other artifacts, and demonstration and classroom areas. Note that the resident eagles were rescued when injured or ill in the wild, but are not able to survive in the wild on their own again. Every autumn the NEC holds a special "deck opening" event to mark the arrival of bald eagles for the winter; this area of the Mississippi has one of the largest concentrations of bald eagles in the contiguous United States.

✒ **Wabasha County Historical Museum** (651-753-2893; wabashacountyhistory.org), US 61, Reads Landing. Open Sat. and Sun. mid-May–mid-Oct., or by appointment. Adults $5; students $3; free for society members. This small museum on the second floor of a former schoolhouse is not necessarily the most comprehensive historical museum in the state, but it does have some items of interest to fans of Laura Ingalls Wilder.

## ✳ Green Space and Outdoor Activities

♿ ✒ ♟ **Lake Pepin Paddleboat** (651-345-5188; pearlofthelake.com), 100 Central Point Road, Lake City. Public cruises offered Wed.–Sun., mid-May–Oct. Private charters available. A replica of the grand old paddleboats that once dotted the local lakes and rivers, Pearl of the Lake offers public tours and dinner cruises, with snacks and full bar available on all sailings. Cruises start at $17.

HISTORIC DOWNTOWN WABASHA

## ✳ Lodging

BED-AND-BREAKFASTS ♿ ✳ (♔) ⊷ **The River Nest Bed and Breakfast** (651-560-4077; therivernest.com), 20073 County Route 77, Reads Landing. A newer-construction building right on the Mississippi, River Nest's two private suites each have a Jacuzzi tub and fireplace. The proprietors use geothermal heating and cooling. Rates start at $175.

✳ (♔) **Turning Waters Bed, Breakfast, and Brewery** (651-564-1568; turning watersbandb.com), 136 Bridge Avenue. This bed-and-breakfast has two rooms and three suites, all with private bath (some with claw foots), and suites come with whirlpools and robes. Guests receive five-course breakfasts each morning and a complimentary beer or wine each evening. Also on the property is Back Alley Brewing with a small taproom. Rates start at $139.

UNIQUE LODGINGS ✐ ✳ **Eagles on the River & Anderson House Hotel** (651-565-3509 or 1-800-482-8188; eaglesontheriver .com), 152 Main Street W. A historic building on the river now features suites and lofts, some of which are family friendly. Rates start at $99.

## ✳ Where to Eat

EATING OUT ♿ ✐ ✳ ⅄ **The Olde Triangle Pub** (651-565-0256; theoldetriangle pub.com), 219 Main Street W. Open daily for lunch and dinner. A casual, friendly neighborhood spot with good pub grub, including bangers and mash, and Irish stew. Moderate.

♿ ✐ ✳ ⅄ **Slippery's** (651-565-4748; slipperys.com), 10 Church Avenue. Open daily for lunch and dinner. Slippery's greatest claim to fame was being mentioned in the Grumpy Old Men movies, which were filmed in the Wabasha area. The restaurant also has a boat-in feature and great views of the river. Burgers, steaks, and Mexican items are served in hearty portions. You can also buy a Green Hornet Ice Fishing Pole here. Moderate.

✐ ✳ **Stacy's Kitchen** (651-565-4408; facebook.com/Stacys-Kitchen-30611 2585053), 116 Main Street E. Open Wed.–Mon. for breakfast and lunch. Inventive takes on breakfast and lunch stapes, including bruschetta omelets, strawberry cheesecake stuffed French toast, and a wide variety of soups. Inexpensive.

## ✳ Selective Shopping

✐ ✳ **LARK Toys** (507-767-3387; larktoys .com), 63604 170th Avenue, Kellogg. Open daily Mar.–Dec., Fri.–Sun. Jan. and Feb. This massive toy complex (more than 30,000 square feet) is more than just a store, it's a playground. A working carousel offers rides, and a mini golf course is available during the warmer months. LARK stands for Lost Art Revival by Kreofsky, and vintage toys, many made out of wood, are produced and sold here, along with children's books. A café is on-site.

# WINONA

The town of Winona was founded by a steamboat captain who saw the potential of having a river town set on an island in the Mississippi. During the lumber boom years, Winona was a thriving shipping town. Today it's a destination for tourists who enjoy the historical sites and the gorgeous bluffs—not to mention the quirky houseboats along the river.

## ❋ To See and Do

& ✇ ❋ **Historic Downtown Winona**. Winona has more than 100 buildings listed on the National Register of Historic Places, most built between 1857 and 1916 in Italianate or Queen Anne style. The best way to take in this large collection of Victorian commercial buildings (the largest concentration in Minnesota) is by foot. Free walking-tour brochures of the district are available from the **convention and visitor bureau** (507-452-0735 or 1-800-657-4972; visitwinona.com; 160 Johnson Street), the **visitor center** (924 Huff Street), or the **Winona County Historical Society** (507-454-2723; 160 Johnson Street).

& ✇ ❋ **Winona County Historical Museum** (507-454-2723; winonahistory.org), 160 Johnson Street. Open daily. Adults $5; students $3; children under 7, students doing research, and Winona County Historical Society members free. The museum showcases a large and fascinating collection of local and regional historic exhibits, covering the usual (geologic history, river trade) as well as the less so (Cold War parking plans in the event of nuclear war). It's kid-friendly, with lots of hands-on activities, including a climb-through cave and river steamboat.

✇ **Bunnell House** (507-452-7575; winonahistory.org), MN 61 and County Route 14, Homer. Open Thurs.–Sun. from Jun.–Aug.; or by appointment. Adults $5; students $3; children under 7, students doing research, and Winona County Historical Society members free. Built in the mid-1800s by a fur trader named Willard Bunnell, the wood-framed Bunnell House was built in the Rural Gothic style. Tours take visitors through all three floors, which are furnished with many pieces original to the time period.

& ✇ ❋ **Minnesota Marine Art Museum** (507-474-6626 or 1-866-940-6626; mmam .org), 800 Riverview Drive. Open Tues.–Sun. Adults $7; students $3; immediate families $20; children 4 and under museum members free. Every Tuesday is free for students. This attractive museum, with a scenic location along the Mississippi, has an extensive collection of marine art, folk art, photography, maps, and historical displays. The lively and varied artworks include pieces by Monet, O'Keeffe, Van Gogh, and Picasso.

& ✇ **Polish Cultural Institute** (507-454-3431; polishmuseumwinona.org), 102 Liberty Street. Open Mon.–Sat. from May–Oct. Call for hours Nov.–Apr. (closed Good Friday). Admission $2. Group discounts are available. At one time, Winona had the largest concentration of Polish immigrants in the United States, and this museum reflects that heritage with antiques, folk art, religious items, and displays detailing the immigrant experience.

✎ **Pickwick Mill** (507-457-0499; pickwick mill.org), 26421 County Route 7, Pickwick. Open Tues.–Sun. May–Oct.; by appointment Nov.–Apr. Adults $3; teens $2; children 12 and younger $1. A Civil War–era water-powered gristmill, the Pickwick operated continuously until 1978, and many of its original components and machines are on display today. The views from the upper floors of the mill are lovely. Note that the site cannot accept credit or debit cards, so bring cash.

## ❊ Green Space and Outdoor Activities

CITY PARKS  Winona has several city parks, three of which are of special interest.

Windom Park, Huff and W. Broadway Street. Small, only a city block in size, it's surrounded by several Victorian homes (some of which are listed on the National Register of Historic Places), and it has a gazebo and a fountain with a sculpture of Princess Wenonah.

**Lake Park**, 900 Huff Street. On the shores of Lake Winona, Lake is a popular city park with an attractive rose garden (C.A. Rohrer Rose Garden), fishing piers, and a bandshell with weekly live concerts during the summer.

**Gavin Heights City Park**, Gavin Heights Road. Nearly 600 feet above the city, this overlook is spectacular, especially on a clear day.

STATE PARKS **John A. Latsch State Park** (507-643-6849; dnr.state.mn.us/state_parks/john_latsch/index.html), 43605 Kipp Drive. Open daily. $7 day pass (or $35 for

THE MINNESOTA MARINE ART MUSEUM

an annual pass). One of the lesser-visited state parks, this is worth a trip if you're ready for some exercise; there's a 0.5-mile stairway hike up to the top of bluffs, which leads to outstanding views of the Mississippi and surrounding bluffs.

## ✳ Lodging

BED-AND-BREAKFASTS ✳ ((ŋ)) **Alexander Mansion Bed and Breakfast** (507-474-4224; alexandermansionbb.com), 274 E. Broadway Street. Four elaborately detailed Victorian rooms, all with private bath; five-course breakfast and evening wine social and turndown service are included. The 1886 mansion also has an extensive screened porch for guests to enjoy. Rates start at $97.

✳ ((ŋ)) **Carriage House Bed and Breakfast** (507-452-8256; chbb.com), 420 Main Street. Built by lumber baron Conrad Bohn, the Carriage House was literally that—it originally housed six carriages and several horses. Today the renovated carriage house has four rooms and suites, along with access to a four-season porch, all with private baths and some with gas fireplaces, decorated in a cozy Victorian style. There are two additional rooms in the main family home. Breakfast is included daily, as is the use of single and tandem bicycles and, by prearrangement, a Model A Ford for local touring. Rates start at $119. Specials are available.

HOTELS ♿ ✐ 🐾 ((ŋ)) ✳ ⛌ ∱ **Holiday Inn Express & Suites** (507-474-1700; ihg.com), 1128 Homer Road. Of the more conventional hotels in Winona, the Holiday Inn is one of the nicest, with an indoor pool, sauna, and a daily hot breakfast bar. Rates start at $110.

♿ ✐ 🐾 ((ŋ)) ✳ ⛌ ∱ **AmericInn** (1-877-946-6622; wyndhamhotels.com), 303 Pelzer Street. The AmericInn, located on the Mississippi River, has an indoor pool and whirlpool, and includes breakfast bar daily. Less typical of the usual

WATER-POWERED GRISTMILL AT THE PICKWICK MILL

AmericInn, this one has an on-site bar. Rates start at $118.

## ✳ Where to Eat

DINING OUT ♿ ✐ ✳ ⛌ **Signatures** (507-454-3767; signatureswinona.com), 22852 County Route 17. Open daily for lunch and dinner. Don't let the somewhat blah interior fool you; the food here is excellent, and you can feast on the outdoor views through the generous windows. Signatures works closely with local food producers, and this has resulted in some of the region's best and most innovative foods on a frequently changing menu. Try the pork porterhouse or the house-made pastas. Expensive.

♿ ✐ ✳ ⛌ **The Boat House** (507-474-6550; boathousewinona.com), 2 Johnson Street. Open Tues.–Sun. for lunch and

THE ALEXANDER MANSION BED AND BREAKFAST

dinner. The Boathouse took an old ice cream parlor and rehabbed it into a small but lovely restaurant along the river (get there early if you want a table by the windows overlooking the water). Steaks, walleye, salmon, sandwiches, and appetizers. Moderate/expensive.

EATING OUT ⛄ 🗝 ❋ **Blue Heron Coffeehouse** (507-452-7020; blueheroncoffeehouse.com), 162 W. 2nd Street. Open daily for breakfast and lunch. Great home-cooked food with an emphasis on local, seasonal, and organic when possible. The menu of soups and sandwiches offers plenty of choices for vegetarians and vegans. Check out the list of local microbrews. Inexpensive.

⛄ 🗝 ❋ **Acoustic Café** (507-453-0394; acousticcafewinona.com), 77 Lafayette Street. Open daily for all three meals. Hot hoagies, pita sandwiches, salads, and soups, along with a full coffee bar. Inexpensive.

⛄ 🗝 **Lakeview Drive Inn** (507-454-3723; lakeviewdriveinn.com), 610 E. Sarnia Street. In business for more than 80 years, serving up quintessential drive-in food: burgers and sandwiches, hot dogs

and sausages, and home-brewed root beer and ice cream. Inexpensive.

## ❋ Special Events

*June–August*: **Great River Shakespeare Festival** (507-474-7900; grsf.org), 450 Johnson Street, Winona. Held late June to early August. When Great River opened its premier season in 2003, there were plenty of skeptics: Who would

BUNNELL HOUSE IN HOMER

THE BOAT HOUSE RESTAURANT

drive to Winona to watch professional Shakespearian theater? Turns out plenty of people are happy to do just that, especially when it takes them into the heart of the river bluff country. Great River performs several plays each year, always including multiple Shakespeare pieces but along with a few modern shows as well, and the festival has quickly gained national stature. Tickets are $25 for adults, $10 for students. Note that there are "pay as you can" tickets for preview performances on a standby basis.

# LANESBORO

T he little town of Lanesboro is worth seeing in and of itself; the entire business district is on the National Register of Historic Places. This is arguably one of the most beautiful towns in the state. Take some time to wander at your leisure.

## ✳ To See and Do

Along the Minnesota-Iowa border is a small but thriving Amish community, and there are tour companies that offer rides through the beautiful area as well as stops at selected farms and shops. (For other more active tours, see *Green Space and Outdoor Activities*.)

    ⅃ ✎ **Amish Tours of Harmony** (507-886-2303 or 1-800-752-6474; amish-tours.com), 94 2nd Street, Harmony. Tours are given Mon.–Sat., Apr.–Nov. Adults $25; teens $20; children 4–12 $8; children 3 and under free. Discounts given if you use your own vehicle.

    ⅃ ✎ **Bluffscape Amish Tours** (507-467-3070 or 1-800-944-0099; bluffscape.com), 102 E. Beacon Street. Tours are given Mon.–Sat., early Apr.–early Nov. Adults $25; children $8; children 3 and under free.

HISTORIC DOWNTOWN LANESBORO

# ✻ Green Space and Outdoor Activities

BIKING AND BOATING **Root River and Harmony-Preston Valley Trails** (rootriver trail.org). This 60-mile paved trail system wanders along the Root River and through Lanesboro, offering both level trails (along a former railroad grade) and more challenging inclines that lead to gorgeous vistas. Those adventurous enough to bike the entire trail will be rewarded with changing scenery that includes wooded areas, rivers and bluffs, and an attractive array of wildlife. The trails are open for cross-country skiers in the winter (seasonal fees apply). If the riverways are what you want, local outfitters will rent canoes, kayaks, and inner tubes. Contact **Root River Outfitters** (507-467-3400; rootriveroutfitters.net), which offers shuttle service for one-way journeys, or **Little River General Store** (507-467-2943; LRGeneralStore.net), which rents boating equipment. Both outfitters also rent bikes and offer shuttle service with them.

PARKS **Forestville/Mystery Cave State Park** (507-352-5111 or 507-935-3251; dnr.state .mn.us/state_parks/forestville_mystery_cave/index.html), 21071 County Route 118, Preston. Open daily. $7 day pass ($35 for an annual pass). Cave and Forestville tours offered daily Memorial Day–Labor Day, weekends mid-Apr.–Memorial Day and Labor Day–Oct. Various tours are offered at different prices, and advance reservations are recommended. This state park has something for everyone. Mystery Cave takes visitors to underground pools and geological cave formations; aboveground, hikers and horse riders have 15 miles of trails that wind through the bluff areas and through wildflowers (in the spring), and skiers and snowmobilers are welcome in winter. Forestville is a trip back in time to a once-functioning town that declined after the railroad bypassed it. Today visitors cross the Carnegie Steel Bridge to visit the general store, where costumed guides lead tours and demonstrate activities from the store's late-1800s roots, and give tourists the chance to work with the farm laborers in the garden.

 ✑ ✑ **Eagle Bluff Environmental Learning Center** (507-467-2437; eagle-bluff.org), 28097 Goodview Drive. This environmental learning center, with 80 acres nestled into 1,000 acres of state forest, welcomes thousands of school children each year for environmental education. However, Eagle Bluff also welcomes families, retreats, and even weddings. Of special interest is the ropes course, in which participants (using safety gear, of course) cross a wire 30 feet high in the sky, along the treetops.

TOURS ✑ ✑ **Cyclin-Inn's Bluff Country Jeep Tours** (507-467-2415), 439 Half Street, Whalan. Tours offered daily Apr.–Oct. (weather permitting). $30 per person for a one-hour tour. For an adventurous ride, try this tour, which goes over rough terrain and up into the hills and bluffs overlooking the river. Tours last one hour; think hard about doing this if you get carsick easily.

ROOT RIVER OUTFITTERS

THE EAGLE BLUFF ENVIRONMENTAL LEARNING CENTER

OTHER ATTRACTIONS **Old Gribben Mill**, County Route 23, Whalan. Just off a dirt road in the Richard J. Dorer Memorial Hardwood State Forest is the remnants of an old mill, now a stone shell of itself, but beautiful to look at. Hiking back behind the mill will bring you to a seeping waterfall.

## ❋ Lodging

Not surprisingly, this historic area has more than its fair share of historic bed-and-breakfasts.

❋ (ᵗᵖ⁾ **Andor Wenneson Historic Inn** (507-875-2587; andorwennesoninn.com), 425 Prospect Street, Peterson. Nine rooms, all with private bath, are offered between the main house and the carriage house. Rooms are named for their color schemes, and all have period furniture and décor. The inn is a short walk from the Root River Trail. Continental breakfast served on weekends. Rates start at $89.

❋ **Historic Scanlan House B&B** (507-467-2158 or 1-800-944-2158; scanlanhouse.com), 708 Parkway Avenue S. This 1889 Queen Anne mansion is a striking piece of architecture, and the seven rooms and suites, all with private baths, are elaborately finished and very romantic. The home itself is packed with

VIEW FROM EAGLE BLUFF ENVIRONMENTAL LEARNING CENTER

THE OLD GRIBBEN MILL

antiques, and beds and windows are dressed in linens and lace. Full breakfast is included (and if you've reserved the Safari Suite, you can have it served in your room). Rates start at $110. Packages are available.

❋ **JailHouse Inn** (507-765-2181; jailhouseinn.com), 109 Houston Street NW, Preston. This building began its history as a county jail in 1870 and now has 12 rooms and suites, all with private baths, some with dainty names like the Sun Room and other with more pointed titles like Drunk Tank and Court Room. The Cell Block room gives visitors the chance to sleep behind bars. The rooms are beautifully decorated in Victorian style. Breakfast is included. Rates start at $89 (but note that their rate sheet cheekily stipulates this price range is for "friendly people").

❋ (ᵖ) **Mrs. B's Historic Lanesboro Inn** (507-467-2154; mrsbsinn.com), 101 Parkway Avenue N. A large and lovely limestone building on the Root River and right in downtown Lanesboro, Mrs. B's has nine rooms with private baths and are warmly decorated with color and quilts. Full breakfast is included on

Sat.–Sun. from mid-May–Oct. Rates start at $125.

✎ ❋ (ᵖ) **Stone Mill Hotel and Suites** (507-467-8663 or 1-866-897-8663; stonemillsuites.com), 100 Beacon Street E. This limestone mill has served as both an egg and poultry processing plant and as a grain company since it was built in 1885. In 1999, the current owners bought it and created a bed-and-breakfast. Each of the 10 rooms and suites is named and decorated after an aspect of the region, including the Amish Room, Grain Room, and the Egg Jacuzzi Suite. All rooms have private baths, and some suites have fireplaces. On-site massage can be arranged. Continental breakfast is served daily. Kids are welcome. Rates start at $100. Packages are available.

✎ ❋ (ᵖ) **Art Loft Lodging** (507-467-2446; lanesboroarts.org/art-lofts-lodging), 103 N. Parkway Avenue. Located above the **Lanesboro Arts Center** (see *Selective Shopping*) are two simple but attractive loft rooms designed for guests who wish to enjoy artistic endeavors of their own; the rooms both have good access to daylight. Exposed brick walls and original artwork highlight the

STONE MILL HOTEL & SUITES

space's arts-center neighbor. Rates start at $100. Discounts for weeklong stays are offered.

✳ ♻ **Berwood Hill Inn** (612-867-3614; berwood.com), 22139 Hickory Road. Just outside town is this gorgeous inn, located on a hill overlooking the valley. The historic home has been beautifully renovated and is surrounded by lush gardens.

BERWOOD HILL BED & BREAKFAST

Adirondack chairs perch atop the hill, giving guests the option of winding down while enjoying the view of the valley below. Two-night minimum stay required. Rates start at $160.

## ✳ Where to Eat

DINING OUT ♿ ♈ ✳ **Old Village Hall Restaurant & Pub** (507-467-2962; old villagehall.com), 111 Coffee Street E. Open Thurs.–Tues. for dinner and Sat.–Sun. for lunch. The former village hall and jail, on the National Register of Historic Places, houses Lanesboro's nicest restaurant. The stone building has been beautifully renovated, and the outdoor patio is a delight in summer. Changing seasonally and taking advantage of local foods, including herbs from the restaurant's own herb garden, the creative menu might include items like lamb chops with couscous or salmon in curry sauce. Moderate/expensive.

EATING OUT ♿ ♨ ✳ **The Bite** (507-467-2200; facebook.com/TheBiteofLanesboro), 111 Parkway Avenue N. Open Thurs.–Tues. for lunch and dinner. Pizza, sandwiches, and desserts. Inexpensive.

♿ ♨ ✳ ♈ **Pedal Pushers Cafe** (507-467-1050; pedalpusherscafe.com), 121 Parkway Avenue N. Open Mon.–Sat. for lunch and dinner, Sun. for lunch. A 1950s-style restaurant with sandwiches and burgers for lunch, and comfort food like chicken potpie, Norwegian meatballs, and homemade meat loaf for dinner. Fountain treats and homemade pie round out the menu, which also has daily blue plate specials. Moderate.

♿ ♨ **Aroma Pie Shoppe** (507-467-2623; facebook.com/aromapieshoppe), 618 Main Street, Whalan. Open Thurs.–Sun. May–Oct. This little diner, close to the Root River Trail, serves up lunch staples like sandwiches and soups, ice cream and frozen yogurt, and—best of all—homemade pie. Inexpensive.

THE OLD VILLAGE HALL RESTAURANT & PUB

students; or $115 for a season ticket. Discounts offered for seniors 62 and older, 30 and younger, and military members.

## ✳ Selective Shopping

& ✐ **Lanesboro Art Center** (507-467-2446; lanesboroarts.org), 103 N. Parkway Avenue. Open Tues.–Sat. Jan.–Apr., Tues.–Sun. in May, Nov.–Dec., daily Memorial Day–Oct.; Mon. by appointment. An art gallery exhibiting and selling artwork by local and national artists, it also has lofts for rent (see *Lodging*).

## ✳ Special Events

*April*: **Bluff Country Studio Art Tour** (bluffcountrystudioarttour.org), Lanesboro. Held in late April, this art tour spans several communities in the bluff country region, opening private studios and artist workspaces to visitors and potential art buyers.

## ✳ Entertainment

& ✐ **Commonweal Theatre** (1-800-657-7025; commonwealtheatre.org), 208 N. Parkway Avenue. The Commonweal produces at least four other plays each year, sponsors readings of new works, and produces a live radio show every summer. The theater has an unusual employee arrangement that has the resident artists not only perform onstage, but also handle the behind-the-scenes marketing and administrative work. The building is a recent renovation and includes an art gallery on the first floor made up of whimsical local antiques and artifacts. Tickets are $35 for adults; $15 for

THE AROMA PIE SHOPPE

# AUSTIN

**H**ome of Hormel Foods, Austin proudly refers to itself as SPAM Town, USA.

## ❋ To See and Do

     ❋ **SPAM Museum** (507-437-5100; spam.com/museum), 101 NE 3rd Avenue. Open daily. Admission is free. Sure beats an art museum—at least, that's what the SPAM Museum's website says. This homage to canned meat manages to be both informative and irreverent. (You can't fault the museum for including showings of the Monty Python SPAM skit.) But besides the kitsch and humor, the museum has lively exhibits detailing the history of the Hormel Foods company, as well as films such as *SPAM: A Love Story*, that give insight into SPAM's role in history, especially during World War II.

     ❋ **Hormel Historic Home** (507-433-4243; hormelhistorichome.org), 208 NW 4th Avenue. Open Mon.–Fri. Admission $5. The Greek Revival home was built in 1871 for then-mayor John Cook, but it was the residence of the Hormel family in the early 1900s. Self-guided tours showcase this impressive building, and during the warmer months a visit to the Peace Gardens is included.

## ❋ Where to Eat

EATING OUT ❋ **Tendermaid Sandwich Shop** (507-437-7907; facebook.com/The Tendermaid), 217 4th Avenue NE. Open Mon.–Fri. for lunch and early dinner, Sat. for lunch. This speedy diner serves up classic loose-meat burgers with a variety of seasonings, and generously portioned malts. Inexpensive.

# ROCHESTER

H istoric Rochester, home to the internationally renowned Mayo Clinic, also has a wide variety of dining options, driven by the diversity of foreign visitors.

## ✳ To See and Do

MUSEUMS AND HISTORIC SITES ∅ **Historic Mayowood Mansion** (507-282-9447; olmstedhistory.com), 3720 Mayowood Road SW. Open Wed., Sat.–Sun. late Mar.–late Oct.; call for additional days during the year. Adults $17; children 2–12 $5; under 2 free. The 38-room mansion was home to Mayo Clinic founders and family members, and much of the architecture was designed by Dr. Charles H. Mayo himself. The home is filled with antiques from all over Europe and remains decorated as it was when occupied by the Mayos. The surrounding gardens are breathtaking, overlooking the Zumbro River with a complex plan of paths, ponds, sculptures, a pergola, teahouse, and limestone walls.

    &. ∅ ✳ **Olmsted County History Center** (507-282-9447; olmstedhistory.com), 1195 W. Circle Drive SW. Open Tues.–Sat. Adults $5; children $2; center members free. More information about the Mayo family and the Mayo Clinic can be found at this small historical site, as well as information about another prominent Rochester community member, IBM. A hands-on pioneer cabin exhibit for kids and a display of artifacts from the 1883 tornado that ravaged the city are the must-sees here.

    ∅ ✳ **Plummer House of the Arts** (507-328-2525; rochestermn.gov), 1091 Plummer Lane SW. Tours offered on Wed., Jun.–Aug. Private group tours can be arranged. Admission is $10 for adults; $5 for youth. Henry Plummer, a Mayo physician and engineer, poured his design talents and money into this 49-room Tudor mansion surrounded by 11 acres of gardens and forests. House tours focus on the history and spotlight the all-original furniture. The grounds are open daily and can be visited for free if no special events are in progress.

    ∅ **Heritage House** (507-286-9208; heritagehousevictorianmuseum.com), 225 1st Avenue NW. Open Tues.–Thurs. and Sun. Jun.–Aug. Admission is $5 for adults; $3 for students. Built in 1875, this home is one of the few that survived the devastating 1883 tornado, and today it provides insight into what life was like for residents who were not blessed with the wealth of the Mayos and the Plummers. Much of the furniture and decorations on display is original.

TOURS &. ∅ ✳ **Mayo Clinic** (507-538-0440; mayoclinic.org/becomingpat-rst/tours .html), 200 1st Street SW. Tours are free. Mayo Clinic is Rochester's biggest claim to fame, with medical experts in nearly every category drawing patients from all over the world. Several different tours are offered for visitors, some self-guided: the General Tour (Mon.–Fri. at 10 a.m.) presents a short film about the history of the clinic, which is followed by a 90-minute guided tour of the campus. Art and Architecture (Mon.–Fri. at 1:30 p.m.) is a 60-minute guided tour examining the priceless art owned by the Mayo.

Heritage Hall (open Mon.–Fri.) is a self-guided tour of displays that detail the Mayo Clinic's history and future. The Patients and Guests Self-Guided Tour is an audio-enabled tour that visits the artwork, St. Mary's Hospital, or the Mayo Historical Suites (used by the Mayo family). Finally, the High School/College Career Tour (by request by calling 507-284-1496) is for students; it is designed to give them more insight into a career in medicine.

## ✳ Green Space and Outdoor Activities

**Quarry Hill Park and Nature Center** (507-328-3950; qhnc.org), 701 NE Silver Creek Road. Open daily. An urban park with extensive grounds and an active nature center offering year-round programs. Fishing ponds, paved biking trails, sandstone caves, and classes at the nature center are among the many amenities.

**Silver Lake Park** (507-328-2525; experiencerochestermn.com), 840 NE 7th Street. A haven for Canada geese, this lake and park just outside of downtown has ample recreational opportunities in the form of bike trails, and canoeing, kayaking, and paddleboating on the lake. **Silver Lake Rentals** (507-261-9049; silverlakefun.com) rents bikes and boats during the warmer months.

## ✳ Lodging

♻ ♿ ✎ ❄ (ꙮ) ♂ 𝖸 ❙❙ ✔ **Kahler Grand Hotel** (507-280-6200 or 1-800-533-1655; thekahlerhotel.com), 20 2nd Avenue SW. Across the street from the Mayo Clinic, to which it's connected by skyway, the grand dame of Rochester hotels has nearly 700 rooms and suites ranging from basic economy rooms to lavishly appointed suites. The hotel's recreation center, with pool and whirlpool, is domed to allow sky views. On-site there are several sit-down dining options, room service, a martini bar, and Starbucks coffee shop. Rates start at $125. Packages are available.

♿ ✎ ❦ ❄ (ꙮ) ❙❙ **Kahler Inn & Suites** (507-285-9200 or 1-800-533-1655; kahlerinnsuites.com), 9 3rd Avenue NW. The Kahler Grand's sister hotel is just down the street. It's smaller and less opulent, but still a good choice. The inn is connected to the Mayo Clinic via a pedestrian subway. An indoor pool and whirlpool are available for guests. Lodging includes free parking and daily continental breakfast. Onsite dining includes a casual pub. Rates start at $110. Packages are available.

♿ ✎ ❦ ❄ ♂ (ꙮ) 𝖸 ❙❙ ✔ **Rochester Marriott Mayo Clinic Area** (507-280-6000; marriott.com), 101 1st Avenue SW. Also connected to the Mayo Clinic via skyway, the Marriott has bright, up-to-date rooms with upgraded technology. There's an indoor pool and whirlpool, and a restaurant and bar. Rates start at $264. Packages are available.

♿ ✎ ❄ (ꙮ) 𝖸 ❙❙ ✔ **Hilton Garden Inn** (507-285-1234; hilton.com), 225 S. Broadway. The Hilton has an indoor pool and on-site restaurant, and all rooms have either one king or two double beds. Full breakfast is included. Rates start at $200. Packages are available.

♿ ✎ ❦ ❄ (ꙮ) **Aspen Select Hotel** (507-288-2671; fiksdalhotel.com), 1215 2nd Street SW. This modest hotel has spacious rooms, recently renovated, and offers free shuttles to Mayo. Rates start at $135.

♿ ✎ ❄ (ꙮ) ✔ **Hampton Inn** (507-287-9050; hamptoninn3.hilton.com), 1755 S. Broadway. This attractive chain hotel offers comfortable, spacious rooms and suites, as well as full breakfast daily. There is an indoor swimming pool and whirlpool, and complimentary shuttle service to Mayo Clinic and downtown Rochester. Rates start at $103. Packages are available.

## ✳ Where to Eat

**DINING OUT** ♿ ✑ ❄ ⌣ **Lord Essex the Steakhouse** (507-285-2722; cccrmg.com/broadstreet.htm), 20 2nd Avenue SW. Open daily for dinner. Located in the **Kahler Grand Hotel** (see *Where to Stay*), this restaurant has an extensive steak menu and also features lamb, duck, ribs, salmon, and lobster. Preparations tend to the classic versions. Expensive/very expensive.

♿ ✑ ❄ ⌣ **Pescara** (507-280-6900; pescarafresh.com), 150 S. Broadway. Open daily for all three meals. A seafood-focused restaurant, this restaurant has an extensive set of seafood choices (oysters, shrimp, lobster, ahi tuna, Arctic char, striped bass, swordfish, among others) and a variety of preparations, including pan-seared, blackened, and baked. For the non-seafood eater, meats including steak, pork, lamb, and duck are available. Expensive/very expensive.

♿ ✑ ❄ ⌣ **Bleu Duck Kitchen** (507-258-4663; bleuduckkitchen.com), 14 4th Street SW. Open Mon.–Sat. for dinner, Sat. for brunch. Thought be many to be Rochester's best restaurant, Bleu Duck has a straightforward menu of starters, seconds, and mains. Features include steak tartare, scallops with cheesy grits and Andouille gravy, and duck with Dan Dan noodles. Expensive.

♿ ✑ ❄ ⌣ **Cameo at the Castle** (507-361-2070; cameoatthecastle.com), 121 N. Broadway. Open daily for lunch and dinner, Sun. for brunch. Fusion flavors with carefully curated ingredients. Try the chicken schnitzel with white truffle spaetzliand Jaegar sauce, bouillabaisse with mussels, blue crab, salmon, shrimp, and scallops, or—if you're in the mood for spendy—the long bone rib eye (portioned for two). Expensive/very expensive.

♿ ✑ ❄ ⌣ **300 First** (507-281-2451; live2dine.com/300-first), 300 1st Avenue NW. Open daily for dinner. Steak, seafood, and specialties including Cordon Bleu Wellington, Maple Roasted Airline chicken, and house-made Butternut Squash Ravioli. Expensive.

**EATING OUT** ♿ ✑ ❄ ⌣ **Marrow** (507-292-8936; facebook.com/marrowmn), 4 3rd Street SW. Open Mon.–Wed. for dinner. A chef-driven restaurant with a changing menu. Recently featured dishes were smoked pork jowl, celery root schnitzel, chicken liver terrine, and grilled lamb saddle. Moderate/expensive.

♿ ✑ ❄ ⌣ **Jenpachi Japanese Steak House** (507-292-1688; jenpachi.com), 3160 Wellner Drive NE. Open daily for lunch and dinner. Sushi or the drama of tabletop hibachi cooking. Moderate/expensive.

♿ ✑ ❄ ⌣ **Victoria's Ristorante** (507-280-6232; victoriasmn.com), 7 1st Avenue SW. Open daily for lunch and dinner. Victoria's prides itself, rightfully so, on making quality Italian foods from fresh ingredients (local when possible). The menu is extensive and reasonably priced, and there are a number of gluten-free offerings. Moderate.

♿ ✑ ❄ **True Smoke BBQ** (507-258-1088; truesmokebbq.net), 2040 Viking Drive NW. Open Tues.–Sun. for lunch and dinner. All things barbecue, whether

FORT RIDGELY STATE PARK

# ANTIQUES

Rochester is an antiques shopper's paradise, with numerous shops and dealers.
Old Rooster Antique Mall (507-287-6228; facebook.com/Old-Rooster
-Antiques-139053279493340), 106 N. Broadway Avenue. Open daily.

Peterson's Antiques & Stripping (507-282-9100; petersonantiquesandstripping.com), 111 NE 11th Avenue. Open Mon.–Fri. and by appointment.

John Kruesel's General Merchandise (507-289-8049; kruesel.com), 22 SW 3rd Street. Open Tues.–Sat.

in individual plates or in large batches to share. Try the spicy sausage and the baby back ribs. Inexpensive/moderate.

&. ✆ ❄ ☗ **Fiesta Café Bar** (507-288-1116; fiestacafebar.com), 1645 N. Broadway Avenue. Open daily for lunch and dinner. Mexican food in both Americanized and authentic incarnations. Staff is very friendly. Moderate.

&. ✆ ❄ **Lettuce Unite** (507-206-4560; lettuce-unite.com), 100 1st Avenue SW. Open Mon.–Fri. for breakfast and lunch. Taking salads to new highs, this café has several already-created salads, such as the United in Vegetables with kale and broccoli, beets, sweet potato, cucumber, jalapeno, and many other veggies in a spicy orange vinaigrette. But diners have several options to create their own salads as well. Soups available. Inexpensive.

## ✳ Selective Shopping

&. ✆ ❄ ⊪ ☗ **Grand Shops of Kahler** (507-280-6200; thegrandshopsofkahler .com), 20 SW 2nd Avenue. Adjacent to the **Kahler Grand Hotel** (see *Lodging*) is

this retail complex with several shops, including art galleries (Gallery on First), Hanny's Couture, Baby Baby Inc., Rhea's Scarves and More, Peacock's Books, and Mayo Clinic retailers.

&. ✆ ❄ ⊪ ☗ **Apache Mall** (507-288-8056; apachemall.com), 52 US 14. The area's largest shopping mall has 100 shops, including most of the usual chain stores: Barnes & Noble, J.Jill, American Eagle Outfitters, Champs Sports, Victoria's Secret, JC Penney, and Macy's.

## ✳ Special Events

*June*: **Rochesterfest** (507-285-8769; rochesterfest.com), Rochester. Rochesterfest, held for a week in late June, is devoted to celebrating Rochester past and present. The festival packs a lot into a week: disc dog Frisbee championships, block party, hot-air balloon race, Drum and Bugle Corps show, vintage baseball, Dachshund dash, and a fishing tournament, among many other events.

# NORTHFIELD

**N**ot far from the Twin Cities is this quintessential 19th-century European village, home to Carleton and St. Olaf colleges, the mill that produces Malt-O-Meal cereal, and a history involving the infamous Jesse James bank robbery.

## ✳ To See and Do

MUSEUMS AND HISTORIC SITES ✐ ✳ **Northfield Historical Society Museum** (507-645-9268; northfieldhistory.org), 408 Division Street. Open daily; guided tours offered mid-Jun.–Labor Day. Adults $5; seniors 65 and older $4; students with ID $3; children 6–12 $2; children under 6 free. The First National Bank, famous for its Jesse James connection, is part of this museum. Many of the bank's fixtures are original, and other exhibits highlight the infamous bank robbery as well as non–Jesse James parts of Northfield's history. The museum's gift shop hearkens back to the general store days of the late 1800s while carrying a wide variety of local books.

    &#9855; ✐ ✳ **Northfield Arts Guild Gallery** (507-645-8877; northfieldartsguild.org), 304 Division Street. Open Tues.–Sat. Free admission. The Northfield Arts Guild is part visual arts and part theater, with art classes and exhibits in the gallery. Local and national artists are displayed in a wide variety of mediums.

THE ARCHER HOUSE RIVER INN

⏦ ❀ ✳ **Flaten Art Museum** (507-786-3556; wp.stolaf.edu/flaten), Dittmann Center, 1520 St. Olaf Avenue, St. Olaf College. Open daily when the college is open (closed school breaks and summer). Free admission. St. Olaf's art collection encompasses both US and European artists, with an emphasis on textiles, ceramics, and sculpture.

TOURS ⏦ ❀ ✳ **Outlaw Trail Tour** (northfield.org/content/outlaw-trail). Take a self-guided tour of the route the James-Younger gang took on that fateful day in 1876. Brochures and maps are available from the Northfield Chamber of Commerce. Large groups and tour buses can request a tour guide from the chamber.

THE NORTHFIELD HISTORICAL SOCIETY MUSEUM

⏦ ❀ ✳ **Historic Sites and Points of Interest Tour** (1-800-658-2548; visitingnorthfield.com). It's not the most exciting name for a tour, but this self-guided venture takes visitors through the beauty and charm of Northfield, with its century-old buildings and architecture. Brochures and maps are available from the Northfield Chamber of Commerce. Large groups and tour buses can request a tour guide from the chamber.

OTHER ATTRACTIONS ⏦ ❀ ✳ **Goodsell Observatory** (507-646-4000; carleton.edu), Cassat Hall, 139 Olin Drive, Carleton College. Open the first Friday evening of each month (hours vary by season), weather permitting. Free admission. The sky through the telescope is almost as beautiful as the stately architecture of the observatory building itself. Hope for clear skies—on cloudy nights the observatory is closed.

## ✳ Green Space and Outdoor Activities

ST. OLAF COLLEGE

**Cowling Arboretum** (507-646-5413; apps .carleton.edu/campus/arb), MN 19, Carleton College. Open daily. Carleton's Cowling Arboretum has 800 acres of wooded trails along the Cannon River valley. The trails are open to hikers and bikers, and in the winter to cross-country skiers, but be sure to stay on the trails; protected flora and fauna are being studied by Carleton students and are off-limits to visitors.

## ✳ Lodging

 &#x2659; ✳ 🐾 ((•)) ⧖ ⅋ **Archer House River Inn** (507-645-5661 or 1-800-247-2235; archerhouse.com), 212 Division Street S. This is the place to stay when in Northfield. The grand old inn, with its cheerful red exterior with white trim, has 35 impeccably decorated and maintained rooms and suites filled with antique furniture, many with river views. Room sizes range from "cozy" (small) to two-room suites. Three restaurants are on-site (**Chapati Cuisine of India, Smoqehouse**, and **Tavern of Northfield**; see *Where to Eat*), although breakfast is not included in the surprisingly reasonable rates. Rates start at $80.

✳ ((•)) **Magic Door Bed & Breakfast** (507-581-0445; magicdoorbb.com), 818 Division Street S. This bed-and-breakfast's location, just out of the hubbub of downtown, gives it a quiet ambience, while its romantic décor makes it a wonderful getaway. The three guest rooms all have private baths and are beautifully decorated with vibrant but tasteful colors. The Summer Suite has a gas fireplace and whirlpool tub. Rooms come with robes, flat-screen LED TVs, and afternoon fruit and cheese trays and complimentary water, beer, wine, and sherry. Not only is a full breakfast included, but so is a glass of wine or beer in the afternoon; a "bottomless" cookie jar is left out for guests. Rates start at $90.

## ✳ Where to Eat

DINING OUT  ♿ &#x2659; ✳ ⅋ **Reunion** (507-366-1337; reunioneatdrinkgather.com), 501 Division Street S. Open daily for dinner, Fri.–Sun. for lunch. This chic bistro offers wood-fired meats, including several beef options, Duroc pork chop, chicken, and walleye, along with pasta, avocado toast, fried pepper rings, and a meat and cheese plate, among other great choices. Live music happens frequently, and the craft cocktail menu is fun. Moderate/expensive.

EATING OUT  ♿ &#x2659; ✳ ⅋ **Chapati Cuisine of India** (507-645-2462; chapati.us), 214 Division Street S. Open Tues.–Sat. for lunch and dinner. In the **Archer House River Inn** (see *Lodging*), this restaurant's huge menu has choices for both novice and experienced Indian-food enthusiasts. Servers will consult with you as to your preferred level of spiciness. Moderate.

♿ &#x2659; ✳ ⅋ **Tavern of Northfield** (507-663-0342; tavernofnorthfield.com), 212 Division Street S. Open daily for all three meals. Located at the **Archer House River Inn** (see *Lodging*), the tavern has a wide-ranging menu including pasta, steaks, flatbreads, and sandwiches. Moderate.

♿ &#x2659; ✳ **Kahlo** (507-321-1884), 306 Division Street S. Open Mon.–Fri. for lunch and dinner, Sat. for brunch. A changing menu of Mexican specialties with some serious authenticity. Inexpensive.

♿ &#x2659; ✳ **The Contented Cow** (507-663-1351; facebook.com/TheContentedCow), 302 Division Street S. Open daily for happy hour and dinner. A British pub with an extensive beer list. The meat and cheese plate plays well with beer, or try the pork and sage stew. Inexpensive.

♿ &#x2659; ✳ ⅋ **Smoqehouse** (507-664-1008; smoqehouse.com), 212 Division Street S. Open Mon.–Sat. for lunch and dinner. Located at the **Archer House** (see *Where to Stay*), Smoqehouse has an extensive barbecue menu, and a beer list to match. Moderate.

## ✳ Entertainment

♿ ✳ **Northfield Arts Guild Theater** (507-645-8877; northfieldartsguild.org), 304 S. Division Street. The theatrical arm of the **Northfield Arts Guild** (see *To See and*

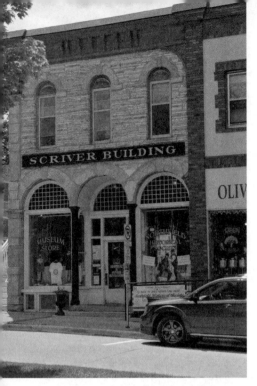

THE NORTHFIELD HISTORICAL SOCIETY MUSEUM

*Do*), this group produces several plays each year, staged in a former church down the street from the guild's art gallery. The company also auditions new plays and conducts staged readings.

## ✳ Special Events

*September*: **Defeat of Jesse James Days** (djjd.org), Northfield. Held annually the first weekend after Labor Day. When your town has something as exciting as this in its history, it's best to have a festival, complete with dramatic reenactments. This popular event is built around the Jesse James shootout, and there's also a parade, golf tournament, antique tractor pull, vintage base ball, a rodeo, square dance, steak fry, 5K and 10K races, and a bike tour. Plan ahead and reserve hotel rooms early if you'd like to stay in the area.

*November–December*: **St. Olaf Christmas Festival** (507-786-2222; Christmas .stolaf.edu), 1520 St. Olaf Avenue, St. Olaf College, Northfield. Held in late November or early December, this annual tradition beganin 1912 and has become a premier event for the state. Several college choral ensembles and the college orchestra put together a magnificent program of Christmas carols and hymns, which are performed live (as well as broadcast on public radio and TV). Purchase tickets well in advance, as they usually sell out quickly.

# SOUTHERN MINNESOTA

■

MINNESOTA RIVER VALLEY

SOUTH THROUGH THE PRAIRIE

THE I-35 CORRIDOR

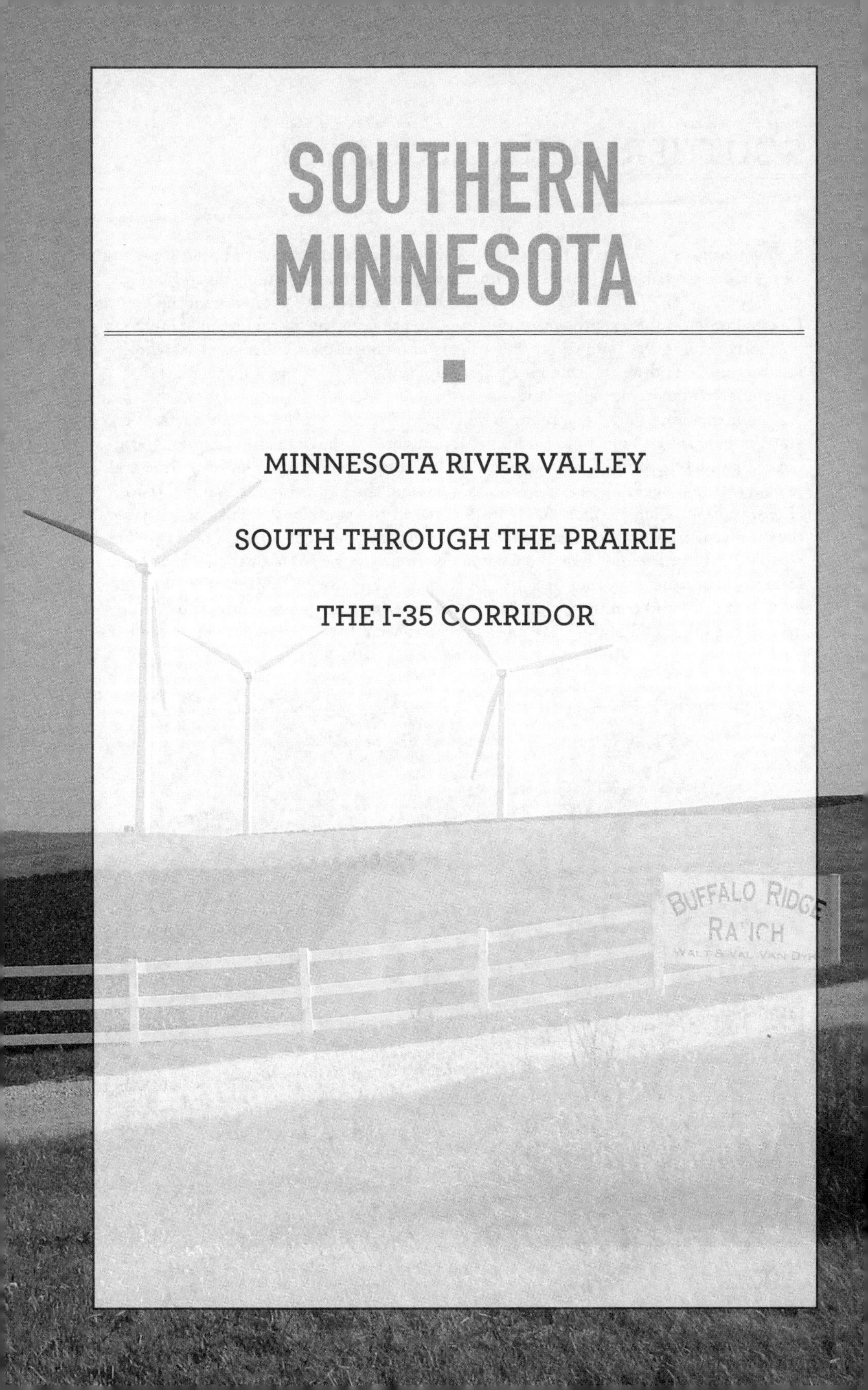

BUFFALO RIDGE
RANCH
WALT & VAL VAN DYK

# SOUTHERN MINNESOTA

The southwest quadrant of the state is primarily agricultural, with miles of prairie land dotted with small towns and intriguing and even occasionally mysterious historic sites. The Minnesota River, which has its source in Ortonville on the South Dakota border, ambles southeast, until Mankato provides the literal turning point for a northerly twist to the Twin Cities. It's an area of pioneers, Native Americans, wildlife, and history, including the Dakota Conflict of 1862, a time of great losses that is still remembered and memorialized today.

The attractions may be spread farther apart than they are in other parts of the state, but stops like Pipestone National Monument and the Jeffers Petroglyphs, state parks like Blue Mounds, towns entrenched in European heritage like New Ulm, and, of course, the pioneer appeal of Walnut Grove and the Laura Ingalls Wilder Historic Highway have much to offer. As visitors come to the southwest corner of the state, they'll discover more wide-open spaces than in other parts of Minnesota, as well as a geological feature known as the Coteau des Prairie, a ridge that runs from western Iowa to the northeast corner of South Dakota that is made up from the debris of glaciers that retreated centuries ago. The wide-open land is a stark contrast to the forests on the other end of the state and is home to what little native prairie remains in

HISTORIC DOWNTOWN NEW ULM

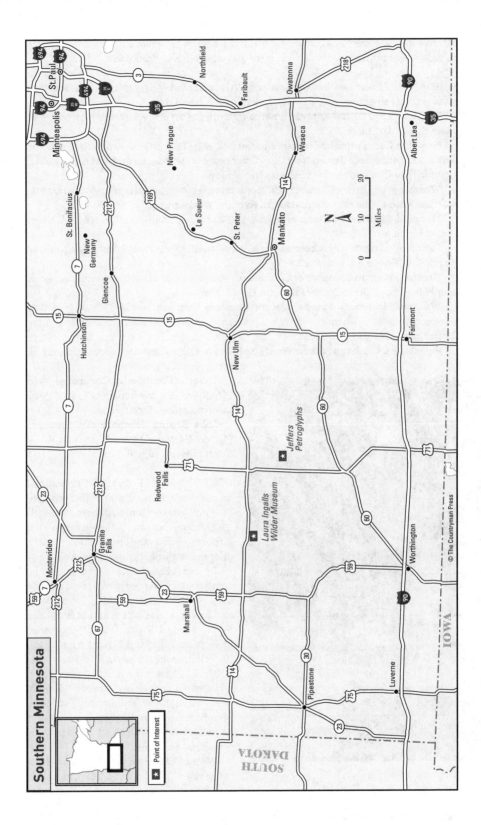

Southern Minnesota

Point of Interest ★

© The Countryman Press

Minnesota. However, local communities in the southwest quadrant are starting to try to rebuild the prairie grasses and flowers that were once so dominant.

GUIDANCE **Albert Lea Convention and Visitor Bureau** (507-373-2316 or 1-800-345-8414; explorealbertlea.org), 102 W. Clark Street, Albert Lea.

**Le Sueur Area Chamber of Commerce** (507-665-2501; lesueurchamber.org), 500 N. Main Street, Le Sueur.

**New Ulm Convention and Visitor Bureau** (507-233-4300 or 1-888-463-9856; newulm .com), 1 N. Minnesota Street, New Ulm. Offers extensive lodging and activity information for New Ulm and the Minnesota River Valley.

**Worthington Area Chamber of Commerce** (507-372-2919 or 1-800-279-2919; worthingtonmnchamber.com), 1121 3rd Avenue, Worthington.

**Marshall Chamber of Commerce** (507-532-4484; marshall-mn.org), 118 W. College Drive, Marshall.

**Faribault Chamber of Commerce** (507-334-4481 or 1-800-658-2354; faribaultmn .com), 530 Wilson Avenue, Faribault.

**Greater Mankato Chamber of Commerce** (507-385-6640 or 1-800-697-0652; greater mankato.com), 3 Civic Center Plaza, Suite 100, Mankato.

**Western Minnesota Prairie Waters Regional Tourism** (1-866-866-5432; prairie waters.com), 323 Schlieman Avenue, Appleton. A good source for information in the Madison and Montevideo areas.

**Pipestone Chamber of Commerce** (507-825-3316; pipestoneminnesota.com), 117 SE 8th Avenue, Pipestone.

**Luverne Chamber of Commerce** (507-283-4061; luvernechamber.com), 213 E. Luverne Street, Luverne.

**Lake Benton Chamber of Commerce** (507-368-9577; lakebenton.us), 106 S. Center Street, Lake Benton.

GETTING THERE **By air:** Commercial air service is available into **Minneapolis–St. Paul International Airport** (612-726-5555; mspairport.com); there are regional airports, such as the one in Mankato, that offer private or corporate service.

**By car:** The primary routes in the southwestern part of the state, connecting Montevideo, Marshall, Pipestone, and Luverne, are MN 7 and MN 29 into Montevideo, US 212 from Montevideo to Granite Falls, and MN 23 from Granite Falls through Marshall to Pipestone, where US 75 travels south to Luverne.

From Luverne, I-90 travels directly east through Worthington, Fairmont, Blue Earth, and into Albert Lea, where it connects with I-35 heading north to Owatonna and Faribault.

West of Owatonna is Mankato, which is accessed by US 14 and US 169, as well as

BLUE MOUNDS STATE PARK

MN 22, MN 68, and MN 66. MN 68 travels west to New Ulm, while US 169 and MN 22 travel north to St. Peter. US 169 continues north to Belle Plaine. Before it reaches Belle Plaine, MN 19 travels east to New Prague. MN 13 travels south from New Prague to Montgomery.

GETTING AROUND Having a vehicle is a necessity when traveling around the southern prairie region.

WHEN TO COME The summer months see an influx of tourists who come to enjoy not only the wide-open prairies and vast state parks, but also the multitude of lakes and beaches. Summer isn't the only popular time, however, especially for fishing enthusiasts who cast their poles in open water in summer and through holes in the ice in winter. Hunters and winter sports aficionados appreciate the fall and winter seasons as well.

MINNEOPA STATE PARK

MEDICAL EMERGENCY Call 911.

**Chippewa County-Montevideo Hospital** (320-269-8877; montevideomedical .com), 824 N. 11th Street, Montevideo.

**Pipestone County Medical Center** (507-825-5811; avera.org), 916 4th Avenue SW, Pipestone.

**Mayo Clinic Health System Albert Lea** (507-373-2384 or 1-888-999-2386; mayo healthsystem.org), 404 W. Fountain Street, Albert Lea.

**New Ulm Medical Center** (507-217-5000; allinahealth.org/new-ulm-medical-center), 1324 N. 5th Street, New Ulm.

**Mayo Clinic Health System Mankato** (507-625-4031 or 1-800-327-3721; mayohealth system.org), 1025 Marsh Street, Mankato.

**River's Edge Hospital** (507-931-2200; riversedgehealth.org), 1900 N. Sunrise Drive, St. Peter.

# MINNESOTA RIVER VALLEY

L eaving the Twin Cities to explore the Minnesota River Valley is a lovely way to spend an afternoon. The Minnesota River was formed by glaciers during the last North American ice age, roughly 10,000 years ago. Today it flows southeast from Big Stone Lake in the western edge of the state, near the North and South Dakota borders, until it reaches Mankato, when it redirects northeast until it meets the Mississippi near the Twin Cities. It's an area full of changes, from closely wooded stretches along rolling riverbanks to wide-open prairie spaces.

It's also full of history, perhaps most notably the **Dakota Conflict of 1862** (see page 288). New Ulm served as a refuge for those trying to escape the conflict, and in the 1920s the town developed another type of infamy, as resident Whoopee John Wilfahrt and his musical magic gave New Ulm the moniker of the Polka Capital of the Nation. In addition to New Ulm's German heritage—apparent today in the architecture, landmarks, shops, restaurants, and festivals and celebrations that take place each year—the area is known for its numerous Native American sites, an unexpected partnership between a central Minnesota town and its counterpart in Uruguay, and the homes and hometowns of some iconic Minnesota people and companies, including the founder of the Mayo Clinic and the Jolly Green Giant.

## ✻ To See and Do

### MUSEUMS AND HISTORIC SITES

#### BELLE PLAINE

**Hooper-Bowler-Hillstrom House** (952-873-6109; belleplainemn.com/hooper-bowler -hillstrom-house), 405 N. Chestnut Street. Open the second Sun. of the month May–Sept.; other days by appointment. Admission is $5. The former home of State Bank founder Samuel Bowler, this house was built in 1871, but its primary claim to fame, besides being an attractive version of a 19th-century home, is the addition Mr. Bowler added to accommodate his rather large family: a two-story outhouse. A skyway connects the second floor of the "five-holer" to the house; the upstairs facilities are situated farther back, so the waste landed behind the wall of the first floor. Souvenirs are available for sale.

#### LE SUEUR

✐ **W. W. Mayo House** (507-665-3250; mnhs.org/mayohouse), 118 N. Main Street. Open Sat.–Sun. May–Sept. Adults $6; seniors 65 and older, veterans, active military members, and college students $5; children 5–17 $4; children under 5 free. This little Gothic-style home was hand built in 1859 by Dr. Mayo himself, who then set up shop on the second floor. The Civil War interrupted his practice; he traveled to New Ulm to help with wounded veterans while his wife, Louise, remained in the house to shelter 11 refugee families. By 1864 the Mayo family was reunited and moved to Rochester, where they founded the Mayo Clinic. The home's story doesn't end there; in the 1870s, the

THE HOOPER-BOWLER-HILLSTROM HOUSE

Carson Nesbit Cosgrove family moved into the home. Cosgrove founded the Minnesota Valley Canning Company, which later became Green Giant.

## MANKATO

✍ **The Betsy-Tacy Society** (507-345-9777; betsy-tacysociety.org), 333 Center Street. Open Sat. early Apr.–mid-Dec. or by appointment. Adults $5; children 6–16 $2; children under 6 and society members free. Fans of the children's classic Betsy-Tacy series by Maud Hart Lovelace can visit the sites of the fictional Deep Valley in Lovelace's home city of Mankato. Tacy's home is open for tours; Betsy's house is around the corner. The society also has a brochure detailing 55 important stops in Mankato for Betsy-Tacy fans; the map was created in part by Lovelace herself.

♿ ✍ **Hubbard House** (507-345-5566; blueearthcountyhistory.com/hubbard-house), 606 S. Broad Street. Open Fri.–Sun. from Jun.–Aug., Sat.–Sun. during May and Sept. Adults $7; children 5–17 $3; children under 5 and historical society members free. This Victorian gem was occupied only by the Hubbard family before the Blue Earth County Historical Society acquired it, and the lack of turnover allowed the building to retain its turn-of-the-20th-century charm. Elaborate woodwork, stained glass, fabric wall coverings, and an adjacent carriage house with a collection of antique vehicles give visitors a true glimpse of the era.

♿ ✍ ❋ **Blue Earth History Center** (507-345-5566; blueearthcountyhistory.com), 424 Warren Street. Open Tues.–Sat. year-round. Adults $7; children 5–17 $3; children under 5 and society members free. The museum of the Blue Earth County Historical Society has wide-ranging exhibits covering local historic events, including a Maud Hart Lovelace exhibit, displays featuring Native American artifacts, remnants from the region's early days of farming and milling, and a diorama of old Mankato.

# THE DAKOTA CONFLICT OF 1862

T he year 1862 was a dark time in Minnesota history. The state was young, and immigrants and pioneers shared land with the Native American population, a situation that made both sides uneasy. In the years leading up to the conflict, the US government and its agents repeatedly broke promises and violated treaties previously agreed to with the Dakota, who were becoming perilously hungry and angry. Tensions broke out in August 1862 when a small Dakota hunting party killed five settlers who were also out hunting. A Dakota council decided at that point to attack white settlers throughout the region to drive them away permanently. It's not clear how many settlers died during the conflict, but the number is thought to be in the hundreds. By December, the US Army stepped in and captured more than a thousand Dakota, who were jailed. The day after Christmas, 38 Dakota were hanged, the largest single-day execution in US history. The remaining Dakota were sent to North and South Dakota, and their Minnesota reservations were abolished.

## MONTEVIDEO TO ORTONVILLE

✎ & ❊ **José Artigas Statue**, Artigas Plaza, 100 N. 1st Street, Montevideo. This statue of the national hero of Uruguay might seem out of place in a central Minnesota town, until you realize that this town has been a sister city to its namesake in Uruguay for more than a century. The statue was a gift from the South American country in 1949, cementing the two communities' relationship, and every year visitors from South America travel to Minnesota to see their gift. The **Minnesota Montevideo** has an annual event to commemorate the friendship (see *Special Events*).

✎ **Swensson Farm Museum** (320-269-7636), 115 County Route 15 SE, Granite Falls. Open Sun. Memorial Day–Labor Day. Adults $5; students 6–17 $2; children 5 and under free. Olof Swensson was a Norwegian immigrant who settled in this area in 1872. He was a highly active resident, a builder who worked on his 22-room farmhouse and timber-framed barn, a Lutheran minister, and a political activist. The farm has been restored, including a gristmill with hand-cut granite grist stones. The buildings were used during the filming of the movie *The Sweet Land*.

& ✎ **Historic Chippewa City** (320-269-7636; chippewacohistory.org), 151 Arnie Anderson Drive, Montevideo. Open daily Memorial Day–Labor Day; Mon.–Fri. 9–5 the rest of Sept. Adults $5; children 6–18 $2; children under 6 free. Chippewa City was originally the county seat, but as a town it declined after Montevideo took over the governmental role. Today 24 restored buildings have been preserved as a living-history museum, including a buggy shop (containing a horse-drawn hearse), the village hall, and a log cabin. Parts of the movie *The Sweet Land* were filmed in the town.

✎ **Lac Qui Parle Mission** (320-269-7636; mnhs.org/lacquiparle), junction of County Route 13 and County Route 32, Montevideo. Open daily May–Oct. Free admission. The mission, dating back to before Minnesota actually became a state, holds some "firsts" within the state, including the first church bell to toll and the first organized Dakota church, complete with the first Dakota Bible.

## NEW ULM

& ✎ ❊ **Glockenspiel**, 327 N. Minnesota Street. New Ulm is home to one of the world's few freestanding carillons. The 45-foot glockenspiel puts on its show three times a day (at noon, 3, and 5 p.m.), more often during festivals; when the bells chime, 3-foot-tall polka figures dance out, except at Christmas, when a nativity scene appears instead.

 &#9855; &#128736; &#10052; **August Schell's Brewery** (507-354-5528 or 1-800-770-5020; schells brewery.com). 1860 Schell's Road. Museum open daily Memorial Day–Labor Day. Afternoon tours are offered daily Memorial Day–Labor Day, Fri.–Sun. the rest of the year. Tour admission: visitors 13 and older $5; children 12 and under free. The museum does not charge an admission fee. The surrounding gardens and deer park are open daily, no admission. Schell's is the second-oldest family brewing company in the United States, having opened in 1860. As the brewery offered hospitality to visiting Dakota, it was largely left alone during the Dakota Conflict. It also remained operational by producing "near beer" and root beer during Prohibition (it still produces root beer, called 1919 after the year the 18th Amendment was passed). Today the brewery is open for tours (kids are

THE NEW ULM GLOCKENSPIEL

welcome—while the adults enjoy a beer tasting at the end, minors and nondrinkers can sample the 1919 Root Beer), and there's a small museum and gift shop. What's also very much worth a visit are the brewery grounds and gardens. Stop in the spring for

THE GARDENS AT SCHELLS BREWERY

the arrival of the bulbs, or midsummer to see the rest of the garden in full bloom. You might even see some wildlife in the adjacent deer park.

✎ **Hermann Monument** (hermannmonument.com), Center Street and Monument Street. Open daily Memorial Day–Labor Day; weekends from the day after Labor Day–Oct. Visitors six and older $3; children five and under free. This towering monument was built in 1897 in honor of Hermann of Cherusci, who is recognized for freeing Germany from Rome in AD 9 and is considered the liberator of the German people. The memorial stands 102 feet tall and, for those willing to climb the stairs, provides an excellent view of greater New Ulm. Bring a picnic lunch to enjoy in the park grounds.

✎ **Wanda Gág House** (507-359-2632; wandagaghouse.org), 226 N. Washington Street. Open Sat.–Sun. from mid-May–mid-Oct.; by appointment year-round. Admission $5. Children's author Wanda Gág, author and illustrator of such classics as *Millions of Cats*, was born and raised in this home in New Ulm. The compact house with turrets and skylights makes for an interesting afternoon's exploration.

& ✎ ❄ **Brown County Historical Museum** (507-233-2616; browncountyhistorymn .org), 2 N. Broadway Street. Open Tues.–Sat. Adults $7; seniors and active military $5; students and children free. Housed in a 1910 post office, the museum is a surprisingly diverse and comprehensive repository of historic and cultural artifacts and displays. German heritage, Native American presence, and the economic mainstays of the area (known as "beer, brats, and bricks") are all detailed in various exhibits. The Dakota Conflict is especially well covered.

✎ **John Lind House** (507-354-8802; lindhouse.org), 622 Center Street. Open Wed.–Sun. from Jun.–Aug.; Fri.–Sun. from Sept.–mid-Oct.; by appointment the rest of the year.

Admission $3, free for ages 12 and under. Built in 1887, this Victorian beauty served as the home of Governor John Lind, as well as the site of state functions he hosted. The house had fallen into serious disrepair before being listed on the National Register of Historic Places and purchased by the newly formed Lind House Association, which restored it and operates it today. While tours are available, this is still a working building, home to the local United Way.

✎ **Harkin Store** (507-354-8666; mnhs .org/harkinstore), 66250 County Route 21. Open Fri.–Sun. early May–Labor Day; Sat.–Sun. Labor Day–mid-Oct. Adults $6; seniors 65 and older, active military members and veterans, and college students $5; children 5–17 $4; and children under 5 and society members free. Eight miles northwest of New Ulm is this classic store, a piece of history still vibrant today. The Harkin Store was a community general store until the day the railroad decided to bypass it, and it was forced to close. Today, much of the merchandise seen on the shelves has been there since the closing. Costumed guides provide

THE WANDA GAG HOUSE

THE BROWN COUNTY HISTORICAL SOCIETY

historical background and explain what some of the products, common in their day but unknown today, were for.

## ST. PETER

✎ **E. St. Julien Cox House** (507-934-2160; nchsmn.org), 500 N. Washington Avenue. Open hours vary; usually one day per month in summer. Call for details. Adults $6; seniors 65 and older $5; children 5–17 $4; children under 6 and society members free. E. St. Julien Cox was a Civil War officer, attorney, and eventually state senator, and he built this Gothic/Italianate home in 1871. Filled with furnishings from the 1880s, the home is open for display; during the summer costumed guides explain the significance of both the home and the family.

&. ✎ ❄ **Treaty Site History Center** (507-934-2160; nchsmn.org), 1851 N. Minnesota Avenue. Open Tues.–Sat. Adults $6; seniors 65 and older $5; children 5–17 $4; children under 5 free. The history center has permanent and seasonal exhibitions detailing the creation of what is now southern Minnesota, along with Iowa and South Dakota, in the signing of the Traverse des Sioux Treaty in 1851. History aficionados will note that the terms of the treaty were not upheld, leading to the Dakota Conflict several years later. The center doesn't shy away from the uglier side of the history, but if you need something more peaceful and soothing, take some time to explore the restored prairie that surrounds the center.

WINERIES ⚜ **Morgan Creek Vineyards** (507-947-3547; morgancreekvineyards.com), 23707 478th Avenue, New Ulm. Open Sat. and Sun. in Apr.; Thurs.–Sun. from May–Oct.; Fri.–Sun. from Nov.–Dec. Morgan Creek is still the only Minnesota vineyard with an underground winery. Stop by during their regular business hours for tours and tastings, or check their website for one of the numerous special events.

# ❋ Green Space and Outdoor Activities

HIKING AND BIKING **Sakatah Singing Hills State Trail** (dnr.state.mn.us/state _trails/sakatah/index.html), Lime Valley Road, Mankato. A 39-mile paved trail utilizing a former railroad bed, the Sakatah winds from Mankato to Faribault through farmland and woods. The trail is multiuse, open to all forms of recreation (with the exception of snowmobiles with studded tracks—regular snowmobiles are welcome). A secondary trail is available for horseback riders only.

PARKS

MANKATO

**Minneopa State Park** (507-386-3910; dnr.state.mn.us/state_parks/minneopa/index .html), 54497 Gadwall Road. Open daily. $7 day pass ($35 annual parks pass). In the Dakota language, *minneopa* means "water falling twice," a perfect name for this park, home to Minnesota's largest waterfall. A winding trail leads to and around the falls, with a limestone stairway descending into the valley. Seppmann Mill, a wind-driven gristmill made of stone and wood, is no longer functional but continues to draw admirers. At one time there was a town here as well, but three consecutive years of grasshopper plagues in the 1870s drove the residents away. Tourists, however, continue to flock to this popular park, for the waterfalls and for the hiking/cross-country skiing trails and bird-watching. Campsites and one cabin are available for rental.

MONTEVIDEO TO ORTONVILLE

**Big Stone National Wildlife Refuge** (320-273-2191; fws.gov/midwest/bigstone), 44843 County Route 19, Odessa. Open daily. An 11,500-acre wildlife refuge southeast of Ortonville, Big Stone counts more than 260 bird species, including bald eagles, and bison can be seen wandering in the 1,700 acres of prairie grasses. A 9-mile paved auto trail is open in summer, and hiking trails and canoe routes provide more intimate access.

    **Big Stone Lake State Park** (320-839-3663; dnr.state.mn.us/state_parks/big_stone _lake/index.html), 35889 Meadowbrook State Park Road, Ortonville. Open daily. $7 day pass ($35 annual parks pass). Big Stone Lake is the source of the Minnesota River. The southern part of the park is known as the Meadowbrook Area, which is the most user friendly in terms of amenities: campground, beach, canoe rental, good fishing, and hiking trails (noted for views of wildflowers in spring). The northern area is the Bonanza Area, designated as a Scientific & Natural Area for its 80 acres of native oak savanna and glacial till prairie habitat. There is a hiking trail here also, but be sure not to disturb the protected habitat.

NEW ULM

**Flandrau State Park** (507-233-9800; dnr.state.mn.us/state_parks/flandrau/index.html), 1300 Summit Avenue. Open daily. $7 day pass ($35 annual parks pass). At only 800 acres, this is a smaller park, but popular nonetheless due in no small part to the fact that it's within walking distance from downtown New Ulm. The sand-bottomed swimming pond

# LAC QUI PARLE STATE PARK

Lac Qui Parle State Park (320-734-4450; dnr.state.mn.us/state_parks/lac_qui_parle/index.html), 14047 NW 20th Street, Watson. Open daily. $7 day pass ($35 annual parks pass). Lac Qui Parle, which translates into "lake that speaks," was also the name of the band of Wahpeton Dakota who built a small village here centuries ago. In 1826, a trading post was built by explorer Joseph Renville, and a mission soon followed, which saw the translation of the bible into Dakota. Today all that remains of the trading post is an interpretive sign, but the mission is marked by a chapel that was rebuilt by the WPA in the 1940s.

Besides Native American and trade history, Lac Qui Parle has 6 miles of trails for hiking and horseback riding, and the trails are groomed in winter for cross-country skiing. Canoers can watch for wildlife while canoeing on the Lac Qui Parle and Minnesota rivers. There are several campsites and a small sandy beach. The park is adjacent to the 27,000-acre Lac Qui Parle Wildlife Management Area, which is home to geese, deer, and bald eagles. The lake itself is a migratory stopping point for thousands of Canada geese each spring and fall.

and extensive campgrounds are a big draw here, as are the hiking trails. The trails are groomed for cross-country skiing in the winter, and ski and snowshoe rentals are available.

## ✳ Lodging

### BED-AND-BREAKFASTS

#### NEW ULM

✳ **Bingham Hall Bed & Breakfast** (507-276-5070; bingham-hall.com), 500 S. German Street. This luxurious bed-and-breakfast has four rooms, all with private baths and queen-sized beds with down comforters. Most of the rooms have fireplaces or whirlpool baths, and one room (Elijah) has an air massage chair. Rates start at $119.

### HOTELS

#### MANKATO

&. ✆ ✳ (ⁿ) ⨍ **AmericInn** (507-413-7360; wyndhamhotels.com), 240 Stadium Road. With 95 rooms and suites, some of which have fireplaces and whirlpools, the hotel also has an indoor pool and whirlpool. Daily breakfast is provided. Rates start at $85.

&. ✆ ✳ (ⁿ) ✆ ⵀ ⨍ **Country Inn and Suites** (507-388-8555 or 1-800-830-5222; countryinns.com/mankatomn), 1900 Premier Drive. All rooms include microwaves, refrigerators, and full daily breakfast. Suites have whirlpools and wet bars. An indoor pool is available for guests, and Bonfire Wood Fire Cooking is attached to the hotel for lunch and dinner. Rates start at $128.

&. ✆ ✳ (ⁿ) ⵀ ⨍ **Hilton Garden Inn** (507-344-1111; hiltongardeninn3.hilton.com), 20 Civic Center Plaza. One of the nicest hotels in Mankato. Rooms and suites include flat panel HDTVs and overstuffed chairs and ottomans. There's an indoor pool and a full-service restaurant on-site as well. Rates start at $124. Packages are available.

#### MONTEVIDEO TO ORTONVILLE

&. ✆ 🐾 (ⁿ) ✳ ⨍ **GrandStay Hotel and Suites** (320-269-8000; grandstay hospitality.com), 1805 E. County Route 7, Montevideo. Rooms and suites, as well as an indoor pool and whirlpool. Full breakfast included. Rates start at $99.

#### NEW ULM

&. ✆ 🐾 ✳ (ⁿ) ⵀ ✳ ⵙ ⨍ **Best Western Plus New Ulm** (507-359-2941 or 1-800-780-7234; bestwestern.com), 2101 S. Broadway. Even Best Western gets into the spirit of things with its old-world Germany exterior. Otherwise it's a standard Best Western, with an indoor pool and complimentary hot breakfast. Rates start at $110.

UNIQUE LODGINGS ❄ ⟨•⟩ ↝ **The Broodio at Moonstone Farm** (320-269-8971; moonstonefarm.net/farmstay.html), 9060 SW 40th Street, Montevideo. A one-room cottage that used to be a chicken brooding house, the Broodio is a charming and idyllic getaway for the visitor looking for peace and quiet. Moonstone Farm is an organic, sustainable agriculture farm, and guests have access to a canoe, beach, and sauna. The owners are committed to permaculture design, solar technology, and organic, local foods when possible. Continental breakfast is delivered to the cottage. Rates start at $90.

## ❄ Where to Eat

### DINING OUT

#### MANKATO

♿ ✎ ❄ ⟨ **Number 4 American Bar & Kitchen** (507-344-1444; number 4mankato.com), 124 E. Walnut Street. Open daily for lunch and dinner. A gastropub, Number 4 offers both traditional pub foods and updated versions, black-and-bleu penne Quattro, chicken pot pie, and Duroc pork chops. Moderate/expensive.

♿ ✎ ❄ ⟨ **Pappageorge Restaurant & Bar** (507-387-8974; pappageorge.net), 1028 N. Riverfront Drive. Open Mon.–Sat. for lunch and dinner. The interior is fairly casual, but the menu is pure Minnesota supper club. Enjoy a 1-pound rib eye, steak and shrimp, walleye, or pasta. Moderate/expensive.

♿ ✎ ❄ ⟨ **Olive's Mediterranean** (507-386-1001; olivesmankato.com), 20 Civic Center Plaza. Open daily for all three meals. This restaurant is fairly casual during the day, befitting its hotel location, but at dinner a more extensive

menu comes out. Try the Chilean Steelhead Trout or the Herb Stuffed Flank Steak, along with some of the Mediterranean starters. Moderate/expensive.

#### MONTEVIDEO TO ORTONVILLE

♿ ✎ ❄ ⟨ **The Crossings at Montevideo** (320-269-8600; montegolf.com), 4490 W. MN 212, Montevideo. Open Tues.–Sun. for lunch and dinner, Mon. for dinner. The clubhouse at the Crossings Golf Course, also known as Johnny's on the Tee, offers plenty of steak, pork chop, and chicken dishes, as well as a long list of sandwiches and wraps. Expensive.

#### NEW ULM

♿ ✎ ❄ ⟨ **George's Fine Steaks and Spirits** (507-354-7440; georgessteaks.biz), 301 N. Minnesota Street. Open Mon.–Sat. for dinner. A congenial steakhouse in a pretty bistro building, George's has steaks, ribs, walleye, lamb, duck, chicken, and some pasta options. The respectable beer and wine list includes items from New Ulm's Morgan Creek Vineyards and Schell's Brewery. Moderate/expensive.

### EATING OUT

#### MANKATO

♿ ✎ ❄ ⟨ **Wine Café** (507-345-1516; wine cafebar.com), 301 N. Riverfront Drive. Open daily for lunch and dinner. A charming bistro and wine shop with more than just wine. A limited bar menu is available for lunch and dinner, but there's a full bar, including 70 wines by the glass and a comparable number of beers. Live music on weekends, when the bar remains open until 2 a.m. Moderate.

♿ ✎ ❄ ⟨ **Tav on the Ave** (507-345-3308; thetavontheave), 1120 E. Madison Avenue. Open daily for lunch and dinner. Tav has solid bar food, especially the buffalo wings and burgers. Moderate.

♿ ✎ ❄ ⟨ **Dino's Pizzeria** (507-385-3466; dinospizzeria.com), 239 Belgrade

Avenue. Open daily for lunch and dinner. This New York-style pizzeria uses fresh ingredients for its pizzas, pastas, and sandwiches. Moderate.

  ♿ ✇ ❄ ⍦ **La Terraza Mexican Grill and Bar** (507-344-0607; laterrazamankato .com), 1404 Madison Avenue. Open daily for lunch and dinner. There are Americanized options here, but also plenty of more authentic Mexican options. Everything is made from scratch, including the tortillas. Inexpensive/moderate.

  ♿ ✇ ❄ ⍦ **Pagliai's Pizza** (507-345-6080 or 507-387-7274; pagliaismankato.com), 524 S. Front Street. Open daily for lunch and dinner. Mankato's oldest pizzeria has developed staunch fans over the decades. You can build your own pizza, or choose from the lengthy list of special pizzas. Pasta and sandwiches, including a pizza po'boy, are also available. Inexpensive.

## MONTEVIDEO TO ORTONVILLE

♿ ✇ ❄ **Valentino's** (320-269-5106), 110 S. 1st Street, Montevideo. Open Mon.–Thurs. for all three meals, Fri. and Sat. for breakfast and lunch. A surprisingly elegant yet casual restaurant, Valentino's has tasteful wood décor and artwork, and a simple but delectable menu of soups, sandwiches, and daily specials. Moderate.

  ✇ ♿ ❄ ♿ **Java River Café** (320-269-7106), 210 S. 1st Street, Montevideo. Open Sun.–Fri. for breakfast and lunch. Although its coffee is top-notch, Java offers much more than just coffee drinks: well-made sandwiches, soups, and pastries, frequently incorporating locally grown and raised food sources. Live music and book discussions are regularly scheduled. Moderate.

## NEW ULM

♿ ✇ ❄ ⍦ **Veigel's Kaiserhoff** (507-359-2071; kaiserhoff.org), 221 N. Minnesota Street. Open daily for lunch and dinner.

New Ulm's oldest German restaurant, this place is a local institution, serving up heaping portions of German and American foods. The ribs are their specialty, but make sure to try the sauerkraut balls. Moderate.

  ♿ ✇ ❄ **Ulmer Café** (507-354-8122; facebook.com/ulmercafe), 115 N. Minnesota Street. Open daily for breakfast and lunch. The local diner with plentiful breakfasts and lunches. Inexpensive.

  ♿ ✇ ❄ **Backerei and Coffee Shop** (507-354-6011; backereinewulm.com), 27 S. Minnesota Street. Open Mon.–Sat. for breakfast and lunch. This fourth-generation family-owned local bakery still knows how to produce the pastries, and the prices are very reasonable. Inexpensive.

  ♿ ✇ ❄ ⍦ **Lola: An American Bistro** (507-359-2500; lolaamericanbistro .com), 16 N. Minnesota Street. Open Mon.–Sun. for breakfast and lunch, Fri.–Sat. for all three meals. Offering sumptuous baked goods and a changing daily menu of lunch specials, the café is located within a gift shop full of kitchen and gourmet food products as well as bath and body gifts. Meals include a nice mix of Italian and home cooking. Moderate.

  ♿ ✇ ❄ ⍦ **Lamplighter Family Sports Bar & Grill** (507-324-2185; lamplighter barandgrill.com), 214 N. Minnesota Street. Open daily for lunch and dinner. Extensive burger and sandwich menu (including a country fried steak sandwich), as well as pasta, shrimp, and steak. Friday nights means a choice between prime rib and the all-you-can-eat fish fry. Inexpensive/moderate.

  ♿ ✇ ❄ ⍦ **Plaza Garibaldi** (507-359-7073; plazagaribaldinewulm.com), 1707 N. Broadway. Open daily for lunch and dinner. A good mix of both authentic and Americanized Mexican options, with many components (tortillas, sauces, etc.) made from scratch in-house. Inexpensive/moderate.

## ☀ Entertainment

LIVE PERFORMANCES **Highland Summer Theatre** (507-389-6661; Mankato
.mnsu.edu), 210 Performing Arts Center,
Minnesota State University, Mankato. A
professional summer stock theater for
more than 50 years, Highland presents
four productions each season (June and
July), two of which are musicals.

## ☀ Selective Shopping

❊ **Domeier's German Store** (507-354-
4231), 1020 S. Minnesota Street, New
Ulm. Open Thurs.–Sat. Domeier's is
packed full of German imports, from
kitschy to classic to collector's items.

❊ **Guten Tag Haus** (507-233-4287;
gutentaghaus.com), 127 N. Minnesota
Street, New Ulm. Open Mon.–Sat.
Importer of German gifts, including a
large array of Christmas items.

❊ **The Sausage Shop** (507-354-3300;
facebook.com/The-Sausage-Shop-174987
029220871), 301 N. Broadway Street,
New Ulm. Open Mon.–Sat. All kinds of
meats—especially sausage—and baked
goods, too.

## ☀ Special Events

*June*: & ✐ **Fiesta Days** (prairiewaters
.com), Montevideo. An annual event

for more than 60 years, Fiesta Days is
celebrated Father's Day weekend and
pays homage to the town's century-long
partnership with Montevideo, Uruguay,
complete with a parade, fireworks, and,
of course, plenty of food.

**Sauerkraut Days** (kraut.hendersonmn
.com), Henderson. Held in late June.
Parades, tournaments, food, music, and a
kraut-eating contest.

*July*: **Kolacky Days Czech Festival**
(montgomerymn.org), Montgomery.
Held in late July, this three-day festival
has occurred every year since 1929,
focusing on the town's Czech heritage.
Kolacky is a Czech fruit-filled bun, and
that's just one of the many native dishes
that can be found during the festival.
Events include softball, volleyball, and
horseshoe tournaments; the Bun Run
footrace; Tour de Bun bike race; contemporary and classic Czech music; and
dancing.

*September*: **Mahkato Traditional Pow
Wow** (mahkatowacipi.org), Mankato.
Held in September. The Land of Memories Park in Mankato is home to this
annual event, where thousands of Native
Americans of many different tribes
gather to reenact ceremonial dance
in traditional garb. Displays of Native
American costumes, traditional foods,
and crafts are offered.

*October*: **Oktoberfest** (newulm.com),
New Ulm. Held the first two weekends
in October. German food and beer, live
music, trolley tours, and children's games.

# SOUTH THROUGH THE PRAIRIE

Along the border between Minnesota and South Dakota, from the Iowa border north, is an area known as the Coteau des Prairie. It's the remnant of many glacial movements and retreats. The highest part of the coteau in Minnesota is known as Buffalo Ridge, an area around Lake Benson and Pipestone with a bedrock of shale, sandstone, and clay that has settled over Sioux quartzite before being covered by layers of glacial drift. As opposed to other parts of Minnesota, which have dramatic hills and valleys covered with trees, the Coteau des Prairie has long, sloping hills that were once covered with tall grass prairie. Today most of that natural prairie growth has given way to agricultural endeavors, with long stretches of soybean and cornfields. However, in the farthest southwest corner, there are still some natural prairie areas remaining or are in the process of being cultivated again. It's a unique kind of beauty. As Minnesota poet and essayist Bill Holm said in his essay "Horizontal Grandeur": "A woods man looks at twenty miles of prairie and sees nothing but grass, but a prairie man looks at a square foot and sees a universe; ten or twenty flowers and grasses, heights, heads, colors, shades, configurations, bearded, rough, smooth, simple, elegant. When a cloud passes over the sun, colors shift, like a child's kaleidoscope." Taking the time to explore this part of the state, less traveled than other areas, is a richly rewarding experience full of natural beauty, wide-open skies, wildlife, rivers, Native American sites, and the slowly returning prairie.

There are also several worthwhile communities to visit. **Luverne**, a town of about 4,600 people, is the county seat for Rock County. From a tourist's perspective, though, it's representative of what most people dream of when they envision small-town America: a walkable downtown with historic buildings, quiet residential streets with charming Victorian homes and cottages, and a pride of place and history. Perhaps its biggest claim to fame is being one of the four towns profiled in Ken Burns' landmark documentary, *The War*. The documentary interviewed several residents of Luverne, all World War II veterans, including fighter pilot Quentin Aanenson, for whom the local airport is named.

**Pipestone**, a town rich in Native American and quarrying history, is named after the red stone called pipestone, or catlinite, after the artist and writer George Catlin, who visited the area first in 1836, sketching it and recording the local legends. The community was further memorialized by poet Henry Wadsworth Longfellow's "Song of Hiawatha," although Longfellow never actually

THE INGALLS' FAMILY DUGOUT SITE AT PLUM CREEK

traveled to Pipestone. The pipestone was, and still is, central to Native American ceremonial rites. They quarried it to create pipes and have been recorded doing so by Lewis and Clark in the early 1800s. (See "Pipestone National Monument" on page 302 for more details.)

A few miles north on US 75 is **Lake Benton**, located on the shores of Lake Benton and in the valley of the Buffalo Ridge. Around Lake Benton you'll see a number of wind turbines. These turbines take advantage of the rolling prairie land, relatively unobstructed by forest, to collect wind power. There are more than 600 of these turbines in operation, generating enough power to provide electricity to hundreds, even thousands, of homes.

THE SANBORN SOD HOUSE

One of the biggest draws in southwestern Minnesota is the **Laura Ingalls Wilder Historic Highway** and the connection to Laura Ingalls Wilder and her pioneer family and friends. A trip along this road (which primarily remains on US 14 in Minnesota but occasionally traverses county routes) and through Walnut Grove, Tracy, and Sanborn will take you back in time to the days of the Ingalls and the life they made here in the 1870s.

THE LAKE BENTON HOUSE BED & BREAKFAST

## ✳ To See and Do

MUSEUMS AND HISTORIC SITES ⚓ 🐾
**Heritage Center and Wind Power Learning Center** (507-368-9577), 108 S. Center Street, Lake Benton. Open Mon.–Fri. Admission free. The center offers changing exhibits that illustrate how the wind power is collected and how it's used, along with displays examining the history of the Lake Benton area.

### LAURA INGALLS WILDER HISTORIC HIGHWAY

⚓ 🐾 **Laura Ingalls Wilder Museum** (507-528-7280 or 507-859-2358; walnutgrove .org), 330 8th Street, Walnut Grove. Open daily Apr.–Oct. Admission ages 13 and older $10; ages 5–12 $4; under 4 free. The museum covers two different eras: that of Wilder's family's stay in the region back in the 1800s, and that of the popular 1970s TV series based on her life. The displays are fun and informative for visitors who are either general history buffs or fans of the Little House books. There are some items (including photos and a quilt sewn by Laura and her daughter, Rose) that either belonged to Laura herself or to friends and family (although serious Wilder buffs will note that most of the displays are replicas or photos from the Missouri Wilder museum), several exhibits related to the time period itself, and artifacts from the TV series.

INSIDE THE LAURA INGALLS WILDER MUSEUM

✎ **Ingalls Dugout Site** (507-528-7280 or 507-859-2358; walnutgrove.org), 13501 County Route 5, Walnut Grove. Open daylight hours May–Oct., weather permitting. Admission $5 per car or $30 per bus. Along the banks of Plum Creek is this dugout home, where the Ingalls family lived from 1874 to 1876 before selling it after several crop failures and moving to Iowa. The Ingalls's ownership was discovered by the books' illustrator, Garth Williams, who informed the owners of the historic nature of their property. There's not necessarily a lot to see here; the original sod house disintegrated decades ago, leaving behind a depression in the ground, yet for Ingalls fans, it's as worthy a stop as the museum. The site is scenic, picnic tables are available, and visitors can wade into Plum Creek and look for minnows, just like Laura and Mary did.

✎ **Sod House on the Prairie** (507-723-5138; sodhouse.org), 12598 Magnolia Avenue, Sanborn. Open sunrise to sunset, spring–fall. Admission $4; ages 6 and under free. No credit or debit cards accepted, so bring cash. Laura Ingalls Wilder may not have lived here, but this is the perfect pairing with the dugout site. This replica home site includes a sod home, dugout, and log cabin; the "soddie" was built in the style of Laura's day with 2-foot-thick walls and lumber roof and floor, as opposed to the dugout, which has a dirt floor and roof.

THE INTERIOR OF THE SANBORN SOD HOUSE

✎ **Wheels Across the Prairie Museum** (507-626-1949; wheelsacrosstheprairie .org), 3297 US 14, Tracy. Open weekends mid-May–Jun., Oct., and Nov.; Wed.–Sun. from Jun.–Sept. Admission $6 for 13 and over; $2 for 12 and under. Essentially a pioneer museum, Wheels Across the Prairie includes several vintage buildings, such as a one-room schoolhouse, Episcopal church, log cabin, and train depot. Tracy is the small-town Laura Ingalls Wilder visited on her first train trip, so the railway exhibit is of particular interest.

## LUVERNE

 &#9855; ❀ **Rock County Courthouse/Veterans Memorial** (507-283-5020), 204 E. Brown Street. Open Mon.–Fri. The community's respect for its veterans is evident in the Rock County Veterans Memorial, on the grounds of the beautiful Rock County Courthouse. The courthouse, built in 1888 of Sioux quartzite, is on the National Register of Historic Places.

 &#9855; ❀ **Rock County History Center** (507-283-2122; rockcountyhistorical.com), 312 Main Street. Open Tues.–Sat. No admission fee, but donations welcome. A fairly new museum built to showcase and maintain artifacts from the area's pioneer days and more recent history.

&#9855; **Hinkly House** (507-283-4061; rockcountyhistorical.com), 217 N. Freeman Avenue. Open Thurs. Jun.–Aug. No admission fee. Originally built by the town's mayor, the Hinkly House is a lovely Sioux quartzite building from 1892 and is on the National Register of Historic Places.

 &#9855; ❀ **Brandenburg Gallery** (507-283-1884 or 1-888-283-4061; jimbrandenburg .com), 213 E. Luverne Street. Open Mon.–Sat. Internationally renowned nature photographer Jim Brandenburg, a Luverne native and *National Geographer* photographer, has a gallery of his works for viewing and for sale here, with a focus on the prairie lands around Luverne. He is also one of the founders of the Brandenburg Prairie Foundation and the Touch the Sky Prairie Project (see *Green Space and Outdoor Activities*).

## PIPESTONE

 &#9855; ❀ **Pipestone Commercial Historic District** (507-825-3316; pipestoneminnesota .com). This stretch in the downtown area of Pipestone contains 30 buildings and is

THE HINKLY HOUSE

HISTORIC DOWNTOWN PIPESTONE

listed in its entirety on the National Register of Historic Places. An easy walk of about 12 blocks, mostly along Main Street and N. Hiawatha Avenue, will take you past the towering stone buildings, each with its year of construction at the top, and sometimes the name of the original owner. The buildings are striking not just for their days-gone-by architecture, but also because of the distinctive red stone used to build them. Most of the building took place in the 1890s after railroad service was established. Of particular note is the use of Sioux quartzite in 17 of the buildings.

    &#9832; &#10070; &#10043; **Pipestone County Museum** (507-825-2563; pipestonecountymuseum.com), 113 S. Hiawatha Avenue. Open Mon.–Sat. Admission $3 for non-museum members. This lovely, elaborate building was once the imposing city hall and now houses the historical museum. Check with the museum for its special events.

    &#9832; &#10070; &#10043; **Syndicate Block** (507-825-3316; pipestoneminnesota.com), 201–205 W. Main Street. This block holds the oldest and largest of the Sioux quartzite buildings. Originally containing a post office and meat market, the block is now mostly filled with retail and offices.

    &#9832; &#10070; &#10043; **Moore Block** (507-825-3316; pipestoneminnesota.com), 102 E. Main Street. This smaller Sioux quartzite building is distinguished by the work of Leon Moore, an amateur sculptor who created the gargoyles and biblical scenes on the building's exterior.

## WORTHINGTON

    &#9832; &#10070; **Pioneer Village** (507-376-4431; noblescountyhistory.org), 1600 Stower Drive. Open Tues.–Sun. Memorial Day–Labor Day. Admission $6 adults; $1 ages 6–15; free for under 6 and 90 and over. Located on the county fairgrounds, this village is one of the largest collections of pioneer buildings in the state and a fascinating place to visit. There are nearly 50 items of interest, including an early hospital, millinery shop, gas station, farmhouse, and sod house (the last constructed in the 1970s as a replica).

# PIPESTONE NATIONAL MONUMENT

Pipestone National Monument is a significant historic and cultural site. The red pipestone, so called because its primary use is to be carved into ceremonial pipe bowls, has been quarried by Native Americans since at least the 17th century, and the quarry is viewed as a sacred site. The pipes from this quarry were highly acclaimed across the United States, and the land that produced it was, for the most part, neutral territory for different tribes because of the symbolic power of the site. Today the only quarrying allowed is by Native Americans, a right they retained when they sold the land to the US government in 1937. A comprehensive visitor center details the significance and history of the area, and there are locally made pipestone products in the gift shop. During the summer months, visitors can watch as quarrying takes place. Hiking the Circle Trail, a 0.75-mile walk from the visitor center, provides beautiful views of quartzite, as well as native prairie grasses. Other points of interest include Winnewissa Falls and the Oracle, a naturally occurring stone face that Native Americans believe to be a sentient being.

Pipestone National Monument (507-825-5464; nps.gov/pipe), US 75, Pipestone. Open daily. Admission free at the time of this writing; the National Parks Service had suspended admission fees while studying the fee structure. Check with the NPS to see if fees have been reinstated. ♿ ✎ ❄

PIPESTONE NATIONAL MONUMENT

Guided tours can be arranged, but brochures allow easy self-guiding. Picnic tables are available.

## ❋ Green Space and Outdoor Activities

**Touch the Sky Prairie** (507-283-4061; facebook.com/touchtheskyprairie), 171st Street, Luverne. Nature photographer **Jim Brandenburg** (see **Brandenburg Gallery** in *To See and Do*) started the Brandenburg Prairie Foundation in 1999 to purchase, along with the US Fish and Wildlife Service, more than 800 acres of land northwest of Luverne and developed a long-term plan to return the prairie lands to their original state. Visitors to the site will get a glimpse of what real prairies looked like when the pioneers arrived so many years ago and experience just how beautiful a native prairie can be.

BLUE MOUNDS STATE PARK

**Blue Mounds State Park** (507-283-6050; dnr.state.mn.us/state_parks/blue_mounds), 1410 161st Street, Luverne. Open daily. $7 day pass ($35 for annual state parks pass). This 1,800-acre park sits above surrounding farmland by virtue of a natural pedestal of Sioux quartzite. The Blue Mounds, named after its blue appearance to westward-moving settlers, is a 1,250-foot-long stretch of rock that runs in an east–west direction and is thought to have been placed by early Dakota. Interesting fact about the rock: Each year on the spring and autumn equinoxes, the sunrise happens right on the east end and the sunset on the west end. Deer, coyote, and numerous birds reside here and can be seen by visitors.

The park is an excellent place to immerse yourself in the loveliness of the prairie, especially midsummer, when the wildflowers are in full bloom. Thirteen miles of hiking trails wander deep into the prairie, and in some of the lower stretches hikers will find themselves threading a narrow path surrounded by wildflowers nearly 6 feet tall on either side. Bikers have access to 2 miles of paved trails as well. Rock climbing is available, as are swimming and camping. Don't miss the bison viewing stand—the park is home to a herd of bison that peacefully roams a large, fenced space.

## ✳ Lodging

### BED-AND-BREAKFASTS

#### LAKE BENTON

✳ **Benton House Bed & Breakfast** (507-368-9484), 211 W. Benton Street. If you're looking for a cozy, romantic escape, this Italianate Victorian charmer on the edge of town has three rooms, each with private bath. A full breakfast is included. Rates start at $79.

✳ **Wooden Diamond Bed & Breakfast** (507-368-4305; facebook.com/BandJ Vollmer), 1593 Shady Shore Drive. Just outside the city is the Wooden Diamond, which doesn't have any Victorian charm—but its location on the shores of Lake Benton more than makes up for it. There's just one suite, with private entrance. Full breakfast included. Rates start at $79.

#### WORTHINGTON

♻ ♿ (ᵖ) ♂ ✳ **Historic Dayton House Bed & Breakfast** (507-727-1311; daytonhouse .org), 1311 4th Avenue. This grand home in Worthington was owned by three prominent families in succession, including the Dayton family (eventually of department store fame, with the Dayton's chain later sold to Marshall Fields, and then to Macy's; the family also founded Target stores). A local historic group took over the restoration of the building with excellent results, and there are now two plush suites available. Both have private baths, sitting areas, antique furnishings, and flat-screen TVs. A better-than-average continental breakfast is served daily. Rates start at $145.

## HOTELS

### LAURA INGALLS WILDER HISTORIC HIGHWAY

 &#9855; &#9986; &#10052; **Wilder Inn** (507-629-3350), 1000 Craig Avenue, Tracy. Bare-bones motel that serves its basic purpose just fine. Rates start at $59.

## INNS

### PIPESTONE

&#9855; &#9986; (((•))) &#10052; &#9786; ¶¶ **Historic Calumet Inn** (507-825-5871; calumetinn.com), 104 W. Main Street. Built in direct response to the needs of travelers arriving with the new railroad, the Calumet has suffered its share of tragedies (fire on more than one occasion) over the decades. At one point, the hotel was in such disrepair that it was closed, but in 1979 it was purchased and renovated. Today it offers 36 guest rooms furnished with period antiques, and some rooms have amenities like whirlpools. There's also a lounge and pub (see *Where to Eat*). Rates start at $45.

# &#10052; Where to Eat

## DINING OUT

### LAKE BENTON

&#9855; &#9986; &#10052; &#9786; **Knotty Pine Supper Club** (507-548-3781; theknottypinesupperclub.com), 1014 County Route 10, Elkton, SD. Open Wed.–Sun. for dinner. Old-fashioned American supper club menu

with rib eye, prime rib (on weekends), walleye, shrimp, chicken, and ribs. Moderate.

&#9855; &#9986; &#10052; &#9786; **The Country House Supper Club** (507-368-4223; facebook.com/Country-House-Supper-Club-59185 8510905189), 405 E. Benton Street. Open Thurs.–Sun. for dinner. Steaks, walleye, shrimp, broasted chicken, and combo platters. Inexpensive/moderate.

### PIPESTONE

&#9855; &#9986; &#10052; &#9786; **Stonehouse Supper Club** (507-562-2580; stonehousepipestone.com), 123 W. Main Street. Open daily for lunch and dinner. A bit more upscale than the other local supper clubs, Stonehouse has a full range of steaks along with walleye and shrimp, but it also has a charcuterie board, flatbreads, sandwiches, and a local specialty known as *chislic*— barbecued beef bites. Inexpensive/moderate.

## EATING OUT

### LAURA INGALLS WILDER HISTORIC HIGHWAY

&#9855; &#9986; &#10052; **Nellie's Café** (507-859-2384; facebook.com/Nellies-Cafe), 550 US 14, Walnut Grove. Open daily for breakfast and lunch. Hearty breakfasts, soups, and sandwiches. Inexpensive.

### PIPESTONE

&#9855; &#9986; &#10052; &#9786; **Calumet Inn** (507-825-5871; calumetinn1888.com), 104 W. Main Street. Open Mon.–Sat. for all three meals, Sun. for breakfast and lunch. Located in the **Historic Calumet Inn** (see *Lodging*). This restaurant has a few steaks on the menu, but is more focused on sandwiches and salads. Inexpensive/moderate.

&#9855; &#9986; &#10052; **Lange's Café** (507-825-4488; facebook.com/Langes-Cafe -1485911208345597), 110 SE 8th Avenue. Open 24/7. Serves homecooked meals, including the usual sandwiches and soups, but also some supper club

# JEFFERS PETROGLYPHS

The petroglyphs are southwest of the Laura Ingalls Wilder Historic Highway, but they're well worth the slight detour. Thought to date from 3000 BC to possibly as recently as the mid-1700s, there are more than 2,000 Native American carvings found across the islands of rock that appear throughout the prairie grasses. Two separate trails visit the glyphs, both starting at the visitor center, one only 0.5 mile round-trip, the other slightly over a mile. Interpreters are available to explain the significance of the glyphs, which have a wide range of subject matter and meaning; humans, arrows, elk, buffalo, deer, and turtles are just some of the identifiable figures. The glyphs detail the history of the region and the people, identifying important events and sacred ceremonies. Native Americans still come today for religious visits. Note: For best viewing, visit early or late in the day—the midday sunlight can make it harder to see the glyphs.

It's not the just historic or spiritual aspects that make this a worthy visit. The landscape is striking: pink quartzite, prairie grasses, prickly pear cactus, and dozens of wildflowers surround the site. In the northern reaches, areas of buffalo rubs can be seen where migrating bison would stop to rub their coats against the rocks, eventually leaving a glossy surface. Take some time after visiting the glyphs to admire the rest of the scenery.

Jeffers Petroglyphs (507-628-5991; mnhs.org/jefferspetroglyphs), 27160 County Route 60, Comfrey. Open Wed.–Mon. from Memorial Day–Labor Day; Sat. the rest of Sept.; groups by appointment through the end of Dec., weather permitting. Admission $8 adult; $6 seniors 65 and older; active military members and veterans, college students and children age 5–17; free for ages 4 and younger and historical society members.

THE JEFFERS PETROGLYPHS

offerings, including steak and broasted chicken, as well as pasta. Be sure to save room for pie; it's what Lange's is famous for. Inexpensive/moderate.

  ♿ ✏ ❋ **Dari King** (507-825-2755), 605 W. 7th Street. Open daily for lunch and dinner. Cute café with quick-service sandwiches and ice cream delights. Inexpensive.

# ❋ Entertainment

## CINEMA AND LIVE PERFORMANCES

### LAKE BENTON

♿ ✏ ❋ **Lake Benton Opera House** (507-368-4620; lakebentonoperahouse.org), 118 E. Benton Street. The Lake Benton Opera House was first opened in 1896 but fell into disuse and disrepair in the late 1950s. In 1970, a group of local residents launched a campaign to save and restore the building, a process that took nearly 30 years because of the efforts to restore rather than replace. Now it offers several Broadway shows and family-friendly performances each year.

### LUVERNE

✏ ❋ **Historic Palace Theatre** (507-283-4339; palacetheatre.us), 104 Main Street. Luverne's downtown area along Main Street is dotted with century-old buildings, many constructed of Sioux quartzite. Of particular note is the Historic Palace Theatre, which has been showing movies since 1915. Along the way, it has modernized its operations, but still has its large pipe organ, and it's the oldest working theater organ of its kind in the United States. The theater hosts both movies and live events, and it was also the site of the premiere of Ken Burns' *The War*.

### PIPESTONE

♿ ✏ ❋ **Pipestone Performing Arts Center** (507-825-2020; pipestoneperforming

artscenter.com), 104 E. Main Street. Housed in a Sioux quartzite building that dates back to 1897, the center offers live performances year-round, with a variety of family-friendly concerts and shows.

# ❋ Special Events

*June*: **Worthington Windsurfing Regatta & Music Festival** (worthington windsurfing.net), Worthington. Held in June. Windsurfing championships and an indie music festival make for a great combination of interests. Beachfront waveboarding, an art fair, and possibly even fire eaters round up the entertainment.

*July*: **Laura Ingalls Wilder Pageant** (1-888-528-7298; walnutgrove.org), Walnut Grove. Held the last three weekends in July. This annual homage to Laura Ingalls Wilder is held on the banks of Plum Creek and covers some of the significant points of the Little House books. Note: This is a very popular event, and tickets can sell out in advance. Local lodging options are limited, so book ahead (see **Wilder Inn** under *Lodging*).

*August*: **Pipestone Civil War Days** (pipestoneminnesota.com/cwd), Pipestone. Held mid-August in even-numbered years. Civil War life is brought alive in various ways: battle reenactments, church services, children's games, dancing and etiquette lessons, a grand ball, and camp tours.

*September*: **King Turkey Day** (507-372-2919; kingturkeyday.net), Worthington. Held mid-September. At this tongue-in-cheek festival, held annually since 1939, people have raced turkeys in an attempt to win the coveted title of King Turkey. Other highlights include pancake breakfasts, volleyball tournaments, and a parade. But the crowning event is the Great Gobbler Gallop, in which teams of wild turkeys take to the streets.

# THE I-35 CORRIDOR

T he I-35 corridor, leading to Iowa, includes the communities of Albert Lea, Owa-tonna, and Faribault, areas that were once the domain of Native Americans. This area has seen considerable agricultural growth and, in the case of Faribault, had a happier experience than that of the **Dakota Conflict** (see "The Dakota Conflict of 1862" on page 288); founder Alexander Faribault learned the Dakota language and helped the tribe resettle in an effort to protect the trading fort Faribault established with them.

## ✳ To See and Do

MUSEUMS AND HISTORIC SITES

ALBERT LEA

& ✎ ✳ **Freeborn County Historical Museum, Library & Village** (507-373-8003; freeborncountyhistory.org), 1031 Bridge Avenue. Open Wed.–Fri. each week and the second Sat. of each month; village open daily May–Sept. Admission $7.50 adults; $3 ages 12–18; under 12 free. An extensive and eclectic collection of memorabilia and his-torical exhibits make this a worthwhile visit. Pop culture icons Eddie Cochran (early rock 'n' roll singer) and Marion Ross (of TV's *Happy Days*) both spent part of their childhoods here, and accordingly earned exhibits. But beyond celebrities, the museum has artifacts and displays from the Civil War and World Wars I and II; stagecoaches and railroads; farm implements; formal clothing; and antique appliances, to name a few. The adjacent village has several buildings, including a furnished parsonage, bar-ber shop, and general store.

FARIBAULT

✎ ✳ **Alexander Faribault House** (507-332-2121; rchistory.org/alexander-faribault -house), 1814 NW 2nd Avenue. Open Mon.–Fri., weekends by appointment. Admission $3 adults; $2 seniors; $1 ages 12 and under. Built in 1853 by town founding father Alex-ander Faribault, this Greek Revival home is one of Minnesota's oldest surviving build-ings. The Rice County Historical Society took over the daunting task of restoration in 1945, with the end result a beautifully preserved piece of Minnesota history. Furnish-ings aren't original, but they accurately reflect the period.

OWATONNA

& ✎ **Village of Yesteryear** (507-451-1420; schsmn.org/village-of-yesteryear), 1700 Aus-tin Road. Tours available Tues.–Sun. from May–Sept. Admission $5 adults; $3 ages 7–6; free 6 and under. Group rates are available. A collection of 20 pioneer buildings, many with original or period-appropriate furnishings.

✎ **State School Orphanage Museum** (507-774-7369; orphanagemuseum.com), 540 W. Hills Circle. Open Tues.–Sun. from Mar.–Dec. Admission free, but $2 donation requested. The former home of more than 10,000 Minnesota orphans between 1886 and 1945, State School's large main building is impressive, but it must have been imposing for the children being sent here. There's video footage of the orphans from the 1930s, and visitors are welcome to explore the building and grounds, right down to the underground root cellar. Most poignant is the Children's Cemetery.

## ❋ Green Space and Outdoor Activities

**Myre-Big Island State Park** (507-668-7060; dnr.state.mn.us/state_parks), 19499 780th Avenue, Albert Lea. Open daily. $7 day pass ($35 for an annual state parks pass). Migrating waterfowl, evidence of possibly permanent Native American settlements that date back 9,000 years, 16 miles of hiking trails through oak savanna and prairie (several of which are groomed for winter sports), and campsites make this park a favorite of locals and visitors alike.

**Rice Lake State Park** (507-414-6190; dnr.state.mn.us/state_parks), 8485 Rose Street, Owatonna. Open daily. $7 day pass ($35 for an annual state parks pass). Native Americans used this area long ago to harvest wild rice. Today it's a rich tapestry of habitats, from wetlands to hardwoods, that makes a home for a wide variety of birds, including black terns, whistling swans, diving ducks, and pied-billed grebes. There are 5 miles of easy hiking trails; in winter, there are ungroomed cross country ski and snowshoe trails, as well as snowmobile trails.

## ❋ Lodging

### BED-AND-BREAKFASTS

### ALBERT LEA

✎ ❋ **1858 Log Cabin Bed & Breakfast** (507-448-0089), 11859 755th Avenue, Glenville. South of Albert Lea, this pre-Civil War log cabin has been retrofitted for today's travelers (electricity and indoor plumbing) but still offers a glimpse into living quarters of days past. Kids are welcome. Antique furniture with hand-painted Norwegian rosemaling and patchwork quilts enhance the pioneer experience. Daily breakfast included. Rates start at $89.

❋ ((ᵧ)) **Czech Inn Bed & Breakfast and Retreat** (507-373-2477; czechinnand retreat.com), 19158 800th Avenue, Hayward. Not far from Albert Lea is this bed-and-breakfast, simple but attractive. Five rooms, all with private bath, and there's also a retreat room available for groups. Rates start at $110.

### FARIBAULT

❋ ((ᵧ)) **Historic Hutchinson House** (507-384-3291; historichutchhouse.com), 305 NW 2nd Street. This colorful 1892 Queen Anne Victorian home has five lovingly restored rooms, all with private bath, that have been decorated with period furnishings as well as modern amenities. Rates start at $129.

### OWATONNA

❋ ((ᵧ)) **Northrop Oftedahl House Bed & Breakfast** (507-451-4040; northrophouse .com), 358 E. Main Street. This 1898 Victorian mansion has four rooms on the second floor, furnished with family heirlooms, including chandeliers and a fireplace in one room. Rates start at $86.

### CABINS

### FARIBAULT

✎ 🐾 ❋ ((ᵧ)) ⴹ ‖ **Winjum's Shady Acres Resort** (507-334-6661; winjumsshady acres.com), 17759 W. 177th Street, Faribault. Winjum's has several lakeside cabins, as well as a two-bedroom lake house on a private lot with a private dock. There's also a restaurant and bar on-site. Weekly rates start at $590.

♂ 🏕 (ᵒ) **Roberds Lake Resort & Campground** (507-332-8978; roberdslakeresort .com), 18197 Roberds Lake Boulevard. This lakeside resort is fourth-generation family-owned and has several cabins and campsites. There's a nice sandy beach and large playground as well. Open May–Sept. Rates start at $75.

HOTELS

ALBERT LEA

♿ ♂ 🏕 (ᵒ) ❄ ⸮ **AmericInn** (507-373-4324; wyndhamhotels.com), 811 E. Plaza Street. Rooms and suites with breakfast included, and an indoor pool on-site. Rates start at $110.

FARIBAULT

♿ ♂ (ᵒ) ♂ ❄ **The Inn at Shattuck–St. Mary's** (507-333-1900; theinnatssm.org), 1000 Shumway Avenue. Located on the Shattuck–St. Mary's college campus, this newer lodging in a restored historic building has 12 rooms with conference and kitchen space for meetings. Rates start at $120.

♿ ♂ 🏕 (ᵒ) ❄ ⸮ **Boarders Inn & Suites** (507-334-9464; staycobblestone.com), 1801 Lavender Drive. This simple hotel is pleasantly furnished and offers a daily breakfast buffet. Rooms have microwaves, flat panel TVs, and refrigerators. Rates start at $95.

OWATONNA

♿ ♂ 🏕 (ᵒ) ❄ Y ⏹ ⸮ **Baymont by Wyndham** (507-455-1142; baymontowatonna.com), 245 Florence Avenue. Several rooms and suites with flat-screen TVs, some with whirlpools, fireplaces, microwaves,

and refrigerators. The hotel also has an indoor pool, as well as a pub with beer, wine, and pizza. Full breakfast is included. Rates start at $102.

## ✳ Where to Eat

DINING OUT

ALBERT LEA

♿ ♂ ❄ Y **Crescendo** (507-377-2425; crescendodining.com), 118 S. Broadway Avenue. Open Thurs.–Sat. for dinner. The frequently changing menu at Crescendo may offer sweet corn fritters, seared scallops with Mexican street corn, or filet mignon with brandy and shallot reduction. Chef/owner Robert Tewes may also supply dinner music on the house piano. Reservations recommended. Moderate/ expensive.

OWATONNA

♿ ♂ ❄ Y **Torey's Restaurant & Bar** (507-455-9260; toreys.net), 208 N. Cedar Avenue. Open Mon.–Sat. for lunch and dinner. A supper club with an extensive steak menu, but also several pasta dishes and fish. Note that along with the steaks, there are several options for steak toppers, including jumbo shrimp. Moderate/ expensive.

EATING OUT

ALBERT LEA

♿ ♂ ❄ Y **The Interchange Wine & Coffee Bistro** (507-383-4070; theinterchangebistro.com), 211 S. Broadway. Open Mon.–Sat. for breakfast, lunch, and early dinner. An attractive bistro in Albert Lea's historic district, Interchange offers sandwiches and flatbreads earlier in the day, and tapas in the evening. Try the bleu cheese bacon bread or smoked salmon and dill flatbread. Inexpensive.

Albert Lea's downtown area along Broadway and Main is a cozy stretch of lovely historic buildings, many of which hold shops and boutiques. Here's a sampling of what to explore.

Between Friends Boutique (507-473-2111; facebook.com/Betweenfriends2.boutique), 144 S. Broadway Avenue. Open Mon.–Sat. Chic and casual women's clothing and accessories. ♿ ✳

Midwest Antiques (507-210-5104; facebook.com/MidwestAntiquesofAlbertLea), 302 S. Broadway Avenue. Open Mon.–Sat. Vintage furniture, accessories, tools, farm equipment, kitchen items, and glassware. ♿ ✿ ✳

Adam's Originals (507-369-0205), 238 S. Broadway Avenue. Open daily. Original pottery, vintage dolls, and flowers. ♿ ✳

BG Brick Girls (507-373-2514; facebook.com/bgbrickgirls), 225 S. Broadway Avenue. Open Mon.–Sat. Fun, fashionable women's clothing and accessories. ♿ ✳

The Color Wheel Gifts & Décor (507-402-5650), 122 W. Main Street. Open Mon.–Sat. Repainted and repurposed furniture, new gifts, décor, and items from local artists. ♿ ✿ ✳

## FARIBAULT

♿ ✿ ✳ ⛾ **Depot Bar & Grill** (507-332-2825; depotbarandgrillfaribault.com), 311 Heritage Place. Open daily for lunch and dinner. Hearty burgers and sandwiches, flatbreads, steak and walleye. Inexpensive/moderate.

♿ ✿ ✳ ⛾ **El Colibri Restaurante** (507-384-3773; facebook.com/El-Colibri-Restaurante-1293733657371690), 508 N. Central Avenue. Open daily for lunch and dinner. Authentic Mexican food, served in large portions. Inexpensive.

♿ ✿ ✳ ⛾ **Cheese Cave** (507-334-3988; cheesecave.net), 318 N. Central Avenue. Open Tues.–Sat. for lunch and dinner. Besides retailing cheese from acclaimed Caves of Faribault and Prairie Farms cheesemakers, this eatery uses those high-quality products as stars of its menu, including pizzas, cheese plates, and, of course, grilled cheese sandwiches. Save room for the cheesecake. Inexpensive.

## OWATONNA

♿ ✿ ✳ **Costas Candies & Restaurant** (507-451-9050; costas-candies.com), 112 N. Cedar Avenue. Open Mon.–Sat. for breakfast and lunch. Does it get any better than having a good café combined with a candy store? Probably not. Start your meal with one of the grilled sandwiches (especially George's Gyro), and end with some handmade candies and truffles. Or a malt. Or both. Inexpensive.

♿ ✿ ✳ ⛾ **Lava Burgers and Wings** (507-413-8444; lavaburgers.com), 369 SE 18th Street. Open Tues.–Sun. for lunch and dinner. You can build your own burger here, but the specialty burgers on the menu already give you plenty of choices: Mac Cheese Burger, Spinach and Artichoke Burger, or Peanut Butter and Havarti Burger, to name a few. There's also a street taco menu (including a vegan option) and a long wing list. Inexpensive.

## ✳ Selective Shopping

♿ ✿ ✳ ⛾ **Cabela's** (507-451-4545; cabelas.com), 3900 Cabela Drive NW, Owatonna. Open daily. The 150,000-square-foot hunting and fishing giant has been elevated to a major tourist attraction, including the frequent appearance of tour buses. Hundreds of animal mounts are posted around the story, and not just of the Minnesota variety; African animals, including elephant and baboon, are represented. A 60,000-gallon freshwater aquarium has examples of Minnesota fish. You can shop, or you can sightsee, or you can do both. There's also a restaurant.

    &#9855; &#9998; &#10052; **Faribault Woolen Mill** (507-412-5510; faribaultmill.com), 1500 NW 2nd Avenue, Faribault. Open Mon.–Sat. In business since 1865, Faribault Woolen Mill is the maker of heirloom-quality woolen blankets, throws, scarves, and accessories in one of the last vertical woolen mills still operating in the United States. Mill tours are also available.

## &#10055; Special Events

*June*: **Heritage Days** (faribaultheritage days.com), Faribault. Held in June. Food, music, carnival rides, dances, and a parade celebrating Faribault's rich history.

    *October*: **South Central Minnesota Studio Art Tour** (studioartour.com), Faribault, Northfield, and Owatonna. Held in late October. These three communities join forces to sponsor this art tour, in which local artists open their galleries and studios to the public.

# INDEX